# Lecture Notes in Computer Science    16109

Founding Editors

Gerhard Goos
Juris Hartmanis

Editorial Board Members

Elisa Bertino, *Purdue University, West Lafayette, IN, USA*
Wen Gao, *Peking University, Beijing, China*
Bernhard Steffen , *TU Dortmund University, Dortmund, Germany*
Moti Yung , *Columbia University, New York, NY, USA*

The series Lecture Notes in Computer Science (LNCS), including its subseries Lecture Notes in Artificial Intelligence (LNAI) and Lecture Notes in Bioinformatics (LNBI), has established itself as a medium for the publication of new developments in computer science and information technology research, teaching, and education.

LNCS enjoys close cooperation with the computer science R & D community, the series counts many renowned academics among its volume editors and paper authors, and collaborates with prestigious societies. Its mission is to serve this international community by providing an invaluable service, mainly focused on the publication of conference and workshop proceedings and postproceedings. LNCS commenced publication in 1973.

Carmelo Ardito ·
Simone Diniz Junqueira Barbosa · Tayana Conte ·
André Freire · Isabela Gasparini ·
Philippe Palanque · Raquel Prates
Editors

# Human-Computer Interaction – INTERACT 2025

20th IFIP TC 13 International Conference
Belo Horizonte, Brazil, September 8–12, 2025
Proceedings, Part II

*Editors*
Carmelo Ardito
Polytechnic University of Bari
Bari, Italy

Tayana Conte
Universidade Federal do Amazonas
Manaus, Brazil

Isabela Gasparini
Universidade do Estado de Santa Catarina
Florianópolis, Brazil

Raquel Prates
Universidade Federal de Minas Gerais
Belo Horizonte, Brazil

Simone Diniz Junqueira Barbosa
Pontifical Catholic University of Rio de Janeiro – PUC-Rio
Rio de Janeiro, Brazil

André Freire
Universidade Federal de Lavras
Lavras, Brazil

Philippe Palanque
Université de Toulouse
Toulouse, France

ISSN 0302-9743   ISSN 1611-3349 (electronic)
Lecture Notes in Computer Science
ISBN 978-3-032-05001-4   ISBN 978-3-032-05002-1 (eBook)
https://doi.org/10.1007/978-3-032-05002-1

© IFIP International Federation for Information Processing 2026, corrected publication 2026
Chapters "An Exploration to Enhance Response Rate and Sampling Density During ESM Experiments by Online Supervised Learning and Edge Computing on Smartwatches" and " Framing the Risk: A Large-Scale Field Experiment on Risk Communication in Responsible Gambling" are licensed under the terms of the Creative Commons Attribution 4.0 International License (http://creativecommons.org/licenses/by/4.0/). For further details see license information in the chapters.

This work is subject to copyright. All rights are solely and exclusively licensed by the Publisher, whether the whole or part of the material is concerned, specifically the rights of translation, reprinting, reuse of illustrations, recitation, broadcasting, reproduction on microfilms or in any other physical way, and transmission or information storage and retrieval, electronic adaptation, computer software, or by similar or dissimilar methodology now known or hereafter developed.
The use of general descriptive names, registered names, trademarks, service marks, etc. in this publication does not imply, even in the absence of a specific statement, that such names are exempt from the relevant protective laws and regulations and therefore free for general use.
The publisher, the authors and the editors are safe to assume that the advice and information in this book are believed to be true and accurate at the date of publication. Neither the publisher nor the authors or the editors give a warranty, expressed or implied, with respect to the material contained herein or for any errors or omissions that may have been made. The publisher remains neutral with regard to jurisdictional claims in published maps and institutional affiliations.

This Springer imprint is published by the registered company Springer Nature Switzerland AG
The registered company address is: Gewerbestrasse 11, 6330 Cham, Switzerland

If disposing of this product, please recycle the paper.

# Foreword

INTERACT 2025 was the 20th International Conference on Human-Computer Interaction organized by Technical Committee 13 (Human-Computer Interaction) of the International Federation for Information Processing (IFIP). IFIP was created in 1960 under the auspices of UNESCO. The IFIP Technical Committee 13 (TC13) aims to develop the science and technology of human-computer interaction (HCI). TC13 started the series of INTERACT conferences in 1984, making it one of the longest-running conferences on HCI. At first running triennially, becoming a biennial event in 1993, this INTERACT series of conferences is an important showcase for researchers and practitioners in the field of HCI. As a multidisciplinary field, HCI requires interaction and discussion among diverse people with different interests and backgrounds. Situated under the open, inclusive umbrella of the IFIP, INTERACT is truly international in its spirit and has attracted researchers from several countries and cultures. The venues of the INTERACT conferences over the years bear testimony to this inclusiveness.

INTERACT 2025 was held from September 8 to 12 September 2025 at the Universidade Federal de Minas Gerais, in the city of Belo Horizonte, the capital city of the state of Minas Gerais in Brazil. INTERACT 2025 was held in-person and was co-located with the XXIV Brazilian Symposium on Human Factors in Computing Systems (IHC), the main scientific forum in the area of HCI in Brazil.

The theme of INTERACT 2025, "Blending Experiences in Interaction Design", reflects on the increasing challenges faced by the field of HCI in the design of interactive experiences in several different contexts. The expansion of artificial intelligence (AI), for example, has brought numerous opportunities and challenges to HCI researchers across the globe. The growing use of virtual and augmented reality technologies, combined with more affordable technologies, also poses challenges to designing technologies with blended realities. The blending of people and cultures provides a further significant scenario for opportunities and challenges in designing systems for a broad audience of people.

The state of Minas Gerais has a rich diversity, encompassing a mélange of experiences, cultures, and ancestries from around the world, mixing heritage and modern, hand-made traditional artefacts and high-tech industry. This context provided inspiration for the research challenges of designing experiences blending the virtual and the physical, different cultures, and a growing blending of human-created and artefacts generated by AI.

Finally, great research is the heart of a good conference. Like its predecessors, INTERACT 2025 aimed to bring together high-quality research. We thank all the authors who chose INTERACT 2025 as the venue to publish their research.

We received a total of 470 submissions distributed in 3 peer-reviewed tracks, 4 curated tracks, and 2 juried tracks. Of these, the following contributions were accepted:

- 69 Full Papers (peer reviewed)
- 34 Short Papers (peer reviewed)

- 33 Posters (reviewed)
- 10 Courses (curated)
- 7 Industrial Experience papers (curated)
- 11 Interactive Demonstrations (curated)
- 2 Panels (curated)
- 13 Workshops (juried)
- 8 Doctoral Consortium (juried).

The acceptance rate for contributions received on the peer-reviewed tracks was 31% for full papers and 31% for short papers. In addition to full papers and short papers, the present proceedings feature contributions accepted in the form of industrial experiences, courses, interactive demonstrations, posters, panels, invited keynote papers, and descriptions of accepted workshops. The contributions submitted to workshops were published as independent post-proceedings.

The reviewing process was primary carried out by a panel of international experts organized in subcommittees. Each subcommittee had a chair and a set of associated chairs who were in charge of coordinating a double-blind reviewing process. Each paper received at least 2 reviews by associated chairs and two reviews from external experts in the HCI field. Hereafter we enlist the thirteen subcommittees of INTERACT 2025:

- Accessibility, Assistive Technologies, and Aging
- Collaborative, Social and Ubiquitous Interaction
- Design for Safe, Secure and Resilient Interactive Systems and Human Work Interaction Design
- Design of Interactive Entertainment Systems
- HCI and Emergent Technologies and Needs
- HCI for Education and Education for HCI
- HCI Methods, Processes and Methodologies
- Human-Centred Intelligent Interactive Systems
- Interaction Design and Children
- Interaction Design for Culture, Diversity, Sustainability and International Development
- Interactive Systems Technologies and Engineering
- Understanding Users and Human Behaviour
- Visualization and Visual Analytics

The final decision on acceptance or rejection of full papers was taken in a Program Committee meeting organized in a hybrid mode in Paris, France in March 2025. The full-papers chairs and the subcommittee chairs attended the meeting. The meeting discussed a consistent set of criteria to deal with inevitable differences among the large number of reviewers and between subcommittees. The final decisions on other tracks were made by the corresponding track chairs and reviewers, often after electronic meetings and discussions.

INTERACT 2025 was made possible by the persistent efforts across several months by 26 subcommittee chairs, 116 associated chairs, and more globally by 29 track chairs and 392 reviewers. We thank them all.

September 2025

Carmelo Ardito
Simone Diniz Junqueira Barbosa
Tayana Conte
André Freire
Isabela Gasparini
Philippe Palanque
Raquel Prates

# IFIP TC13 – The International Federation for Information Processing Technical Committee on Human–Computer Interaction

Established in 1989, the International Federation for Information Processing Technical Committee on Human–Computer Interaction (IFIP TC13) focuses on the field of human-computer interaction (HCI), an interdisciplinary area of study and research that focuses on the design, development, implementation and validation of human-centred interactive computational systems and devices. The field revolves around the interaction between living beings (users) and computational devices and the use thereof, or such devices as facilitators for social human-human interaction. Focusing primarily on knowing, understanding and comprehending how humans interact with computational systems and devices, the goal is societal improvements that serve people and communities by making computational systems and devices enabling, effective, inclusive, accessible, efficient, safe, secure, emotionally satisfying and enjoyable to use, while ensuring ethical use and promoting equal opportunities, diversity, digital equity and sustainable use of non-renewable resources.

The IFIP TC13 Committee currently consists of 55 Members from 39 IFIP Member National Societies and 11 Working Groups, representing specialists from various sub-domains in HCI, and has members from across the world who seek to expand knowledge and find solutions to HCI issues and concerns within their domains. The TC13 WGs and their areas of interest are:

- WG 13.1 (HCI Education) aims to advance global HCI education by integrating emerging technologies, embedding HCI into diverse curricula, supporting pedagogical research and championing social responsibility in HCI teaching and learning.
- WG 13.2 (Methodologies for User-Centered Systems Design) aims to foster research, dissemination of information and good practice in the methodical application of HCI to software engineering. WG 13.2 encourages research into and development of HCI principles, methods and techniques applied to system design and integrated with principles, methods and tools, and the integration thereof into software engineering design methods.
- WG 13.3 (Human Computer Interaction, Disability and Aging) aims to make HCI designers aware of the needs of people with disabilities and older people and encourage the development of information and communication technologies and complementary tools which permit their adaptation to each specific user.
- WG 13.4/WG 2.7 (User Interface Engineering) aims at advancing the state of the art in all aspects of designing, building and evaluating interactive computing systems, with a particular focus on principled, methodological engineering approaches, including methods (human-, model- or AI-based approaches) and tools for modelling,

prototyping, developing and evaluating interactive computing systems, quality models for interactive systems, and new interface technologies suitable to improve user interaction.
- WG 13.5 (Resilience, Reliability, Safety and Human Error in System Development) seeks a framework for studying human factors relating to systems failure, develops leading-edge techniques in hazard analysis and safety engineering of computer-based systems, and guides international accreditation activities for safety-critical systems.
- WG 13.6 (Human-Work Interaction Design) aims at establishing relationships between extensive empirical work-domain studies and HCI design. It promotes the use of knowledge, concepts, methods and techniques that enable user studies to procure a better apprehension of the complex interplay between individual, social and organizational contexts and thereby a better understanding of how and why people work in the ways that they do.
- WG 13.7 (Human–Computer Interaction and Visualization) aims to establish a study and research program that will combine both scientific work and practical applications in the fields of HCI and visualization by integrating aspects such as scientific visualization, data mining, information design, computer graphics, cognition sciences, perception theory or psychology.
- WG 13.8 (Interaction Design and International Development) aims to support and develop the research, practice and education capabilities of HCI in institutions and organizations based around the world considering their diverse local needs and cultural perspectives, to promote interaction design practice in cross-cultural settings, with a special focus to address the needs, desires and aspirations of people across the developing world and in emerging economies.
- WG 13.9 (Interaction Design and Children) aims to support practitioners, regulators and researchers to develop the study of interaction design and children across international contexts.
- WG 13.10 (Human-Centred Technology for Sustainability) aims to promote research, design, development, evaluation and deployment of human-centred technology to encourage sustainable use of resources in various domains.
- WG 13.11/12.1 (Human-Centred Intelligent Interactive Systems), established under the auspices of both TC13 (HCI) and TC12 (AI), aims to focus on how AI can empower humans and support their endeavours, as well as to find ways for humans to understand AI-based systems and the means to allow human control and oversight. By developing scientific foundations for human-centred intelligent interactive systems, it emphasises the human side of the interaction between people and AI.

The IFIP TC13 International Conference on Human-Computer Interaction, INTERACT, is the flagship conference of TC13, staged biennially in different countries around the world. The first INTERACT conference was held in 1984, at first running triennially and becoming a biennial event in 1993. INTERACT 2025 was the 20th Conference in the series. In 2015, IFIP TC13 setup a steering committee for the INTERACT conference series. The Steering Committee, currently chaired by Marco Winckler (France), is responsible for, among other things, promoting and maintaining the INTERACT conference as the premiere venue for researchers and practitioners interested in the topics of the conference and ensuring the highest quality for the contents of the event.

IFIP TC13 also stimulates working events and activities through its Working Groups, including, but not limited to, the Human-Centered Software Engineering Conference (HCSE) organised by WG 13.2, the Human Work Interaction Design Conference (HWID) organised by WG 13.6, and the Interaction Design and International Development Conference (IDID) organised by WG 13.8. A total of eight Workshops by the Working Groups were organised alongside INTERACT 2025.

Furthermore, IFIP TC13 recognises contributions to HCI through both its Pioneer in HCI Award and various paper awards associated with each INTERACT conference. Since the processes to decide the various awards take place after papers are sent to the publisher for publication, the recipients of the awards are not identified in the Proceedings.

- The IFIP TC13 Pioneer in Human-Computer Interaction Award recognises the contributions and achievements of pioneers in HCI. An IFIP TC13 Pioneer is one who, through active participation in IFIP Technical Committees or related IFIP groups, has made outstanding contributions to the educational, theoretical, technical, commercial or professional aspects of analysis, design, construction, evaluation and use of interactive systems. The IFIP TC13 Pioneer Awards are presented during an awards ceremony at each INTERACT conference.
- In 1999, TC13 initiated a special IFIP Award, the Brian Shackel Award, for the most outstanding contribution in the form of a refereed paper submitted to and delivered at each INTERACT Conference, which draws attention to the need for a comprehensive human-centred approach in the design and use of information technology in which the human and social implications have been considered.
- The IFIP TC13 Accessibility Award, launched in 2007 by IFIP WG 13.3, recognises the most outstanding contribution with international impact in the field of ageing, disability and inclusive design in the form of a refereed paper submitted to and delivered at the INTERACT Conference.
- The IFIP TC13 Interaction Design for International Development Award, launched in 2013 by IFIP WG 13.8, recognises the most outstanding contribution to the application of interactive systems for social and economic development of people around the world considering their diverse local needs and cultural perspectives.
- The IFIP TC13 Pioneers' Award for Best Doctoral Student Paper at INTERACT, first awarded in 2019, is selected by the past recipients of the IFIP TC13 Pioneer title. The award is made to the best research paper accepted to the INTERACT Conference, which is based on the doctoral research of the student and authored and presented by the student.

Further information on IFIP TC13 and its activities is available on the IFIP TC13 website: https://ifip-tc13.org/.

# IFIP TC13 Members

## Officers

**Chair**

Paula Kotzé, South Africa

**Vice-chair for Conferences**

Marco Winckler, France

**Vice-chair for Media and Communications**

Helen Petrie, UK

**Vice-chair for Membership and Collaboration**

Philippe Palanque, France

**Vice-chair for Working Groups**

Simone D. J. Barbosa, Brazil

**Vice-chair for Finance (Treasurer)**

Regina Bernhaupt, The Netherlands

**Vice-chair for Awards**

Barbara Rita Barricelli, Italy

**Secretary**

Janet Wesson, South Africa

## Websites Manager

Antonio Piccinno, Italy

## INTERACT Steering Committee Chair

Marco Winckler, France

# Country Representatives

### Australia

Aaron Quigley
Australian Computer Society

### Austria

Paweł W. Woźniak
Österreichische Computer Gesellschaft (OCG)

### Belgium

Bruno Dumas
IMEC – Interuniversity Micro-Electronics Centre

### Brazil

André Freire
Simone D. J. Barbosa (Member Recommended by TC)
Sociedade Brasileira de Computação (SBC)

### Bulgaria

Petia Koprinkova-Hristova
Bulgarian Academy of Sciences

### Canada

Regan Mandryk
Canadian Computer Society

## China

Yue Li
Zhengjie Liu (Member Recommended by TC)
Chinese Institute of Electronics – CIE

## Croatia

Andrina Granić
Croatian Information Technology Association (CITA)

## Cyprus

Panayiotis Zaphiris
Cyprus Computer Society

## Czech Republic

Zdeněk Míkovec
Czech Society for Cybernetics and Informatics

## Denmark

Jan Stage
Danish Federation for Information Processing (DANFIP)

## Finland

Virpi Roto
Finnish Information Processing Association (TIVIA)

## France

Philippe Palanque
Marco Winckler (Member Recommended by TC)
Société Informatique de France (SIF)

## Germany

Tom Gross
Gesellschaft fur Informatik e.V.

## Ireland

Gavin Doherty (Member Recommended by TC)
Irish Computer Society

## Italy

Fabio Paternò
Carmelo Ardito (Member Recommended by TC)
Barbara Rita Barricelli (Member Recommended by TC)
Associazione Italiana per l' Informatica ed il Calcolo Automatico (AICA)

## Japan

Yoshifumi Kitamura
Information Processing Society of Japan

## Netherlands

Regina Bernhaupt
Koninklijke Nederlandse Vereniging van Informatieprofessionals (KNVI)

## New Zealand

Mark Apperley
Judy Bowen (Member Recommended by TC)
Institute of IT Professionals New Zealand

## Norway

Frode Eika Sandnes
Den Norske Dataforening (DND)

## Poland

Marcin Sikorski
Komitetu Informatyki Polska Akademia Nauk (PAN)

## Portugal

José Creissac Campos
Ordem dos Engenheiros Portugal

## Serbia

Aleksandar Jevremovic
Informatics Association of Serbia (IAS)

## Slovenia

Matjaž Kljun
Slovensko Društvo INFORMATIKA

## South Africa

Janet L. Wesson
Paula Kotzé (Member Recommended by TC)
Institute of Information Technology Professionals South Africa (IITPSA)

## Sri Lanka

Thilina Halloluwa
Computer Society of Sri Lanka (CSSL)

## Sweden

Jan Gulliksen
Dataföreningen i Sverige
Swedish Computer Society

## Switzerland

Denis Lalanne
Schweizer Informatik Gesellschaft (SI)

## United Kingdom

José Luis Abdelnour Nocera
Helen Petrie (Member Recommended by TC)
British Computer Society (BCS), Chartered Institute for IT

## International Members at Large Representatives

### ACM

Gerrit van der Veer
Association for Computing Machinery

### CLEI

César Collazos
Centro Latinoamericano de Estudios en Informatica

## Expert Members

Ahmed Seffah, UAE
Anirudha Joshi, India
Antonio Piccinno, Italy
Constantinos Coursaris, Canada
Christos Fidas, Greece
Daniel Orwa Ochieng, Kenya
David Lamas, Estonia
Dorian Gorgan, Romania
Fernando Loizides, UK/Cyprus
Ivan Burmistrov, Russia
Kaveh Bazargan, Iran
Lourdes Moreno, Spain
Marta Kristin Lárusdóttir, Iceland
Nikolaos Avouris, Greece
Peter Forbrig, Germany
Torkil Clemmensen, Denmark

## Working Group Chairpersons

### WG 13.1 (HCI Education)

Lara Piccolo, Germany

### WG 13.2 (Methodologies for User-Centered System Design)

Stefan Sauer, Germany

**WG 13.3 (HCI, Disability and Aging)**

Anna Bramwell-Dicks, UK

**WG 13.4/2.7 (User Interface Engineering)**

Davide Spano, Italy

**WG 13.5 (Human Error, Resilience, Reliability, Safety and System Development)**

Tilo Mentler, Germany

**WG13.6 (Human-Work Interaction Design)**

Élodie Bouzekri, France

**WG13.7 (HCI and Visualization)**

Gerrit van der Veer, Netherlands

**WG 13.8 (Interaction Design and International Development)**

José Adbelnour Nocera, UK

**WG 13.9 (Interaction Design and Children)**

Gavin Sim, UK

**WG 13.10 (Human-Centred Technology for Sustainability)**

Masood Masoodian, Finland

**WG 13.11/12.14 (Human-Centered Intelligent Systems)**

Albrecht Schmidt, Germany

# Organization

## General Chairs

Raquel Prates — Universidade Federal de Minas Gerais, Brazil
André Freire — Universidade Federal de Lavras, Brazil

## Technical Program Chairs

Carmelo Ardito — Polytechnic University of Bari, Italy
Tayana Conte — Universidade Federal do Amazonas, Brazil
Isabela Gasparini — Universidade do Estado de Santa Catarina, Brazil

## Full Papers Chairs

Philippe Palanque — Université de Toulouse, France
Simone Barbosa — Pontifical Catholic University of Rio de Janeiro, Brazil

## Short Papers Chairs

Luciana Nedel — Universidade Federal do Rio Grande do Sul, Brazil
Barbara Rita Barricelli — Università degli Studi di Brescia, Italy

## Courses Chairs

Roberto Pereira — Universidade Federal do Paraná, Brazil
Christos A. Fidas — University of Patras, Greece

## Doctoral Consortium Chairs

Fábio Paternò          CNR-ISTI, Italy
Luciana Zaina          Universidade Federal de São Carlos, Brazil
Marco Winckler         Université Côte d'Azur, France

## Industrial Experiences Chairs

Juliana Jansen         IBM Research, Brazil
Regina Bernhaupt       Eindhoven University of Technology, Netherlands

## Interactive Demonstrations Chairs

Saul Delabrida         Universidade Federal de Ouro Preto, Brazil
James Eagan            Télécom Paris, France

## Panels Chairs

Carla Freitas          Universidade Federal do Rio Grande do Sul, Brazil
Tom Gross              University of Bamberg, Germany

## Poster Chairs

Luciana Salgado        Universidade Federal Fluminense, Brazil
Lilian Motti Ader      University of Limerick, Ireland

## Workshops Chairs

Cristiano Maciel       Universidade Federal de Mato Grosso, Brazil
Davide Spano           Università di Cagliari, Italy

## Student Volunteers Chairs

| | |
|---|---|
| Marcelle Mota | Universidade Federal do Pará, Brazil |
| Ticianne de Gois Ribeiro Darin | Universidade Federal do Ceará, Brazil |

## Advisor

Marco Winckler        Université Côte d'Azur, France

## Webmasters

| | |
|---|---|
| Davi Pedro da Silva | Universidade Federal de Lavras, Brazil |
| Marcos Firmino Diniz | Universidade Federal de Lavras, Brazil |
| Rodrigo Oliveira | Universidade Federal Fluminense, Brazil |
| Vinicius Ferreira Oliveira | Universidade Federal de Lavras, Brazil |

## INTERACT Subcommittee Chairs

| | |
|---|---|
| Albrecht Schmidt | LMU Munich, Germany |
| Anirudha Joshi | IIT Bombay, India |
| Barbara Rita Barricelli | Università degli Studi di Brescia, Italy |
| Carla Dal Sasso Freitas | Federal University of Rio Grande do Sul, Brazil |
| Célia Martinie | Université de Toulouse, France |
| Christos Fidas | University of Patras, Greece |
| David Lamas | Tallinn University, Estonia |
| Gavin Sim | University of Central Lancashire, UK |
| Gerhard Weber | TU Dresden, Germany |
| Giuliana Vitiello | Università di Salerno, Italy |
| Günter Wallner | Johannes Kepler University Linz, Austria |
| Helen Petrie | University of York, UK |
| Jean Vanderdonckt | Université Catholique de Louvain, Belgium |
| Jessica Korte | Queensland University of Technology, Australia |
| José Campos | University of Minho, Portugal |
| Kamila Rodrigues | Universidade de São Paulo, Brazil |
| Lara Piccolo | CODE University of Applied Sciences, Germany |
| Lucio Davide Spano | ISTI-CNR, Italy |
| Marta Lárusdóttir | Reykjavik University, Iceland |
| Paolo Buono | University of Bari Aldo Moro, Italy |
| Paula Kotzé | University of Pretoria, South Africa |

Rainer Malaka              University of Bremen, Germany
Simone Stumpf              University of Glasgow, UK
Stefan Sauer               Paderborn University, Germany
Torkil Clemmensen          Copenhagen Business School, Denmark
Virpi Roto                 Aalto University, Finland

## INTERACT Steering Committee

André Freire               Universidade Federal de Lavras, Brazil
Anirudha Joshi             IIT Bombay, India
Antonio Piccinno           University of Bari Aldo Moro, Italy
Carmelo Ardito             Polytechnic University of Bari, Italy
Fernando Loizides          University of Cardiff, UK
Frode Sandnes              Oslo Metropolitan University, Norway
Helen Petrie               University of York, UK
Marco Winckler (Chair)     Université Côte d'Azur, France
Paula Kotzé                University of Pretoria, South Africa
Philippe Palanque          Université de Toulouse, France
Raquel Oliveira Prates     Universidade Federal de Minas Gerais, Brazil
Simone D. J. Barbosa       Pontifical Catholic University of Rio de Janeiro, Brazil
Tom Gross                  University of Bamberg, Germany

## Program Committee

Abdullah Al Mahmud         Swinburne University of Technology, Australia
Alessandra Alaniz Macedo   University of São Paulo, Brazil
Amanda Swearngin           Apple, USA
Ana Paula Afonso           Universidade de Lisboa, Portugal
Andrea Esposito            University of Bari Aldo Moro, Italy
Andrea Marrella            Sapienza University of Rome, Italy
Andrés Lucero              Aalto University, Finland
Anna Sigríður Islind       Reykjavik University, Iceland
Antonio Piccinno           University of Bari Aldo Moro, Italy
Antony William Joseph      Aalto University, Finland
Ashley Colley              University of Lapland, Finland
Barbara Rita Barricelli    Università degli Studi di Brescia, Italy
Bilal Naqvi                LUT University, Finland
Bruna Rodrigues da Cunha   Federal Institute of São Paulo, Brazil
Bruno Dumas                University of Namur, Belgium

| | |
|---|---|
| Carmen Santoro | CNR-ISTI, Italy |
| Célia Martinie | Université de Toulouse, France |
| César Collazos | Universidad del Cauca, Colombia |
| Changkun Ou | LMU Munich, Germany |
| Charlotte Magnusson | Lund University, Sweden |
| Chi Thanh Vi | VNU-HCM International University, Vietnam |
| Christian Sturm | Technical University of Ingolstadt, Germany |
| Christina Vasiliou | University of York, UK |
| Christopher Power | University of Prince Edward Island, Canada |
| Costin Pribeanu | AOSR, Romania |
| Daniel Fitton | Lancaster University, UK |
| Daniela Fogli | University of Brescia, Italy |
| Daniela Trevisan | Universidade Federal Fluminense, Brazil |
| David Lamas | Tallinn University, Estonia |
| Deborah Fels | University of Toronto, Canada |
| Denis Lalanne | University of Fribourg, Switzerland |
| Ebba Hvannberg | University of Iceland, Iceland |
| Effie Law | Durham University, UK |
| Eleftherios Papachristos | Norwegian University of Science and Technology, Norway |
| Elizabeth Furtado | Universidade de Fortaleza, Brazil |
| Elodie Bouzekri | Université de Bretagne Occidentale, France |
| Enes Yigitbas | Paderborn University, Germany |
| Esteban Clua | Universidade Federal Fluminense, Brazil |
| Fernando Loizides | Cardiff University, UK |
| Fiona Draxler | University of Mannheim, Germany |
| Florence Kirstin | FernUniversität in Hagen, Germany |
| Francesco Greco | University of Bari Aldo Moro, Italy |
| Frode Eika Sandnes | Oslo Metropolitan University, Norway |
| Gerhard Weber | TU Dresden, Germany |
| Graziano Blasilli | Sapienza University of Rome, Italy |
| Haishuai Wang | Zhejiang University, Cina |
| Helen Petrie | University of York, UK |
| Hideki Koike | Tokyo Institute of Technology, Japan |
| Himanshu Verma | TU Delft, Netherlands |
| Ignacio Aedo | Universidad Carlos III de Madrid, Spain |
| Isabelle Pecci | Université de Lorraine, France |
| Jaakko Peltonen | Tampere University, Finland |
| Jan Gulliksen | KTH Royal Institute of Technology, Sweden |
| Jan Van den Bergh | UHasselt - tUL - Flanders Make, Belgium |
| Jean Vanderdonckt | Université Catholique de Louvain, Belgium |
| Jens Gerken | TU Dortmund University, Germany |

| | |
|---|---|
| Jil Klünder | FHDW Hannover, Germany |
| Johannes Pfau | Utrecht University, Netherlands |
| John Alexis Guerra-Gomez | Northeastern University, USA |
| José Abdelnour Nocera | University of West London, UK |
| Judy Bowen | University of Waikato, New Zealand |
| Kai Kunze | Keio University, Japan |
| Kris Luyten | Hasselt University - tUL - Flanders Make, Belgium |
| Kshitij Sharma | Norwegian University of Science and Technology, Norway |
| Laurent Grisoni | University of Lille 1, France |
| Leonardo Pereira | Universidade Estadual Paulista, Brazil |
| Licinio Roque | University of Coimbra, Portugal |
| Luciana Berretta | Federal University of Goiás, Brazil |
| Luciana Nedel | Federal University of Rio Grande do Sul, Brazil |
| Lucio Davide Spano | ISTI-CNR, Italy |
| Luis Leiva | University of Luxembourg, Luxembourg |
| Manjiri Joshi | Swansea University, UK |
| Marcelo Eler | University of São Paulo, Brazil |
| Marco Angelini | Sapienza University of Rome, Italy |
| Marco Manca | CNR-ISTI, Italy |
| Marco Romano | Università degli Studi Internazionali di Roma, Italy |
| Marco Winckler | Université Côte d'Azur, France |
| Marios Constantinides | CYENS Centre of Excellence, Cyprus |
| Maristella Matera | Politecnico di Milano, Italy |
| Mark Apperley | University of Waikato, New Zealand |
| Mark Colley | University College London, UK |
| Mark Sujan | Health Services Safety Investigations Body, UK |
| Matja Kljun | University of Primorska, Slovenia |
| Miroslav Bachinski | University of Bergen, Norway |
| Monica Sebillo | Università di Salerno, Italy |
| Nikolaos Avouris | University of Patras, Greece |
| Nita Mennega | University of Pretoria, South Africa |
| Nuno N. Correia | Tallinn University, Estonia |
| Paloma Diaz | University Carlos III of Madrid, Spain |
| Paolo Buono | University of Bari Aldo Moro, Italy |
| Passant ElAgroudy | German Research Centre for Artificial Intelligence (DFKI), Germany |
| Paula Alexandra Silva | Universidade de Coimbra, Portugal |
| Per Ola Kristensson | University of Cambridge, UK |
| Peter Forbrig | University of Rostock, Germany |

| | |
|---|---|
| Rachid Gherbi | Paris Saclay University, France |
| Renan Guarese | University of Bari Aldo Moro, Italy |
| Rosa Lanzilotti | University of Bari Aldo Moro, Italy |
| Rui José | University of Minho, Portugal |
| Sandra Gama | Instituto Superior Técnico - Universidade de Lisboa, Portugal |
| Sayan Sarcar | Birmingham City University, UK |
| Shrikant Salve | Indian Institute of Information Technology, Pune, India |
| Sofia Ouhbi | Uppsala University, Sweden |
| Sophie Dupuy-Chessa | Université Grenoble Alpes, France |
| Sumita Sharma | University of Oulu, Finland |
| Sven Mayer | TU Dortmund University, Germany |
| Tariq Zaman | University of Technology Sarawak, Malaysia |
| Teija Vainio | Tampere University, Finland |
| Theodoros Georgiou | Heriot-Watt University, UK |
| Thiago Malheiros Porcino | National Laboratory for Scientific Computing, Brazil |
| Ticianne Darin | Federal University of Ceará, Brazil |
| Tilman Dingler | Delft University of Technology, Netherlands |
| Valentin Schwind | Frankfurt University of Applied Sciences, Germany |
| Vania Neris | Federal University of São Carlos, Brazil |
| Vivian Genaro Motti | George Mason University, USA |
| Yoram Chisik | Goldsmiths, University of London, UK |
| Zdeněk Míkovec | Czech Technical University in Prague, Czech Republic |

## Additional Reviewers

Adamu Adamu Habu
Adson Damasceno
Ahmed Seffah
Aimée Sousa Calepso
Aisha Jaddoh
Ajay Krishnan Prabhakaran
Alberto Monge Roffarello
Alberto Oliveira
Alessandra Alaniz Macedo
Alessandro Pagano
Alessandro Palma
Alessia Romani

Ali Mohamed
Aline Menin
Alistair Sutcliffe
Amira Ghenai
Anabela Marto
Anand Patel
Anant Bhaskar Garg
Anders Lundström
Andre Salgado
André Freire
André Salgado
André da Silva

Andrea Esposito
Andrea Mattioli
Andrea Antonio Cantone
Andreas Wübbeke
Andrew Manches
Andrii Matviienko
Angela Locoro
Angelo Casciani
Angelo Rega
Anil Ufuk Batmaz
Anindya Das Antar
Anke Brock
Anmol Srivastava
Anna Bramwell-Dicks
Anna Marques
Anqi Wang
Antonio Curci
Antonio Esposito
Antonio Piccinno
António Ramires Fernandes
Antony William Joseph
Anusha Yella
Arthur Theil
Avinab Singh
Awais Ahmad
B. L. William Wong
Barbara Rita Barricelli
Benedetta Catricalà
Benoit Bossavit
Bineeth Kuriakose
Botao Zhang
Bruce Wilson
Caetano Ranieri
Camille Fayollas
Camino Fernández-Llamas
Carl Bettosi
Carla Dal Sasso Freitas
Carla Silva
Carlos Duarte
Carlos Souza
Carlos Toxtli
Carmen Santoro
Cat Kutay
César Collazos
Cesare Tucci

Chang Yu
Charu Monga
Chengtian Li
Chiara Natali
Chirag Chheda
Chizoba Agwaonye
Chra Abdoulqadir
Christian Maertin
Christianna Petrichou
Christophe Kolski
C. M. Nadeem Faisal
Corentin Conan
Damianos Dumi Sigalas
Daniel Cabezas Lopez
Daniel Gonçalves
Daniela Fogli
Daniela Trevisan
Danielle Szafir
David Gollasch
David Robb
Debjani Roy
Debora Muchaluat-Saade
Deepika Tripathee
Demetrios Lambropoulos
Denise Lengyel
Deogenes Silva
Diego Bruno
Diego Morra
Diogo Cabral
Domenico Bloisi
Dominic Muriungi
Dorian Gorgan
Dorina Rajanen
Duarte Sousa
Eder Oliveira
Edna Dias Canedo
Eduardo Palmeira
Edyta Bogucka
Elen Sargsyan
Eleonora Zedda
Eliott Dutronc
Elise Hallaert
Elmira Yadollahi
Elodie Bouzekri
Emanuel Felipe Duarte

Emilie Tortel
Emma Pretty
Emma Reay
Eric Cariou
Erica Mourão
Erica Mourao
Esteban Clua
Fabio Pittarello
Farkhandah Aziz
Felipe Besoain
Filip Škola
Florence Kirstin
Florent Robert
Florian Kuhlmeier
Francesca Perillo
Francesco Greco
Francisco Maria Calisto
Frode Volden
Funmi Adebesin
Ganesh Bhutkar
Gavin Sim
George Valença
Gerd Berget
Gerhard Weber
Gilles Coppin
Giovanna Calogiuri
Giuseppe Desolda
Giuseppe Fasano
Gosia Kwiatkowska
Grazia Ragone
Graziano Blasilli
Guillaume Rivière
Guillaume Petit
Günter Wallner
Gustavo Constain
Hannah Deters
Haodong Chen
Harini Shankar
Heidi Hartikainen
Helen Petrie
Himanshu Sharma
Horácio Henriques
Hrishikesh Rao
Ingrid Monteiro
Ioana Visescu

Irene Zanardi
Iuliia Paramonova
Ivo Malý
Jake Kaner
Jakob Droste
Janet Read
Jari Kangas
Jean Cheiran
Jean-Philippe Rivière
Jed Brubaker
Jennifer Gross
Jeroen Ceyssens
Jeroen Put
Jessica Turner
Jessica Maria Echterhoff
Jo Herstad
Joakim Kavrestad
João Moreira
Jochen Meyer
John Dempsey
Jonas Borell
Jonas Moll
Jonathan Cullen
Joongi Shin
Jordan Aiko Deja
Jorge Cardoso
Jorge Wagner
José Campos
José A. García-Berná
Judy Bowen
Julia Anken
Juliana Feitosa
Julie Henry
Jussi Holopainen
Jutta Treviranus
Kamila Rodrigues
Kate Preston
Kaveh Bazargan
Kelly Caine
Ken Pfeuffer
Kin Chung Kwan
Klaus Miesenberger
Konstantin Lackner
Krist Wongsuphasawat
Kunal Lanjewar

Ladislav Čmolík
Larbi Abdenebaoui
Laura Stojko
Laxman Doddipatla
Leena Ventä-Olkkonen
Leo Paschoal
Leonel Morgado
Leticia Machado
Lilian Motti Ader
Liliana Vale Costa
Lou Grimal
Lourdes Moreno
Luca Marconi
Luciana Berretta
Luciana Nedel
Luciana Zaina
Luciana Cardoso de Castro Salgado
Lucie Kruse
Lucio Davide Spano
Luigi Gargioni
Lukas Koehler
Machdel Matthee
Maitreyi Chatterjee
Marc Herrmann
Marc Hesenius
Marcelle Pereira Mota
Marcelo Pimenta
Marcelo Walter
Marco Manca
Marco Winckler
Marcos Alexandre Rose Silva
Margi Engineer
Margot Whitfield
Maria Kasinidou
Maria Luigia Natalia De Bonis
Mariana Kolberg
Marie-Ange Stefanos
Marie-Monique Schaper
Marina Buzzi
Mark Apperley
Mark Marshall
Marta Larusdottir
Martin Rumpler
Mateus Monteiro
Matheus Negrao
Mathieu Raynal
Matteo Filosa
Matthew Horton
Matthew McGinity
Max Rädler
Maximiliano Jeanneret Medina
Mehdi Rizvi
Michelle Tizuka
Micol Spitale
Mika Nieminen
Milene Silveira
Milka Trajkova
Min Zhang
Mireia Yurrita
Miriana Calvano
Mirko De Vincentiis
Miroslav Macík
Miroslav Bachinski
Miruna Vasiliu
Mohammad Hajarian
Monique Janneck
Nadine Flegel
Nadine Vigouroux
Najmuddin Aamer
Nathan Hughes
Navya Krishna Alapati
Neeranjan Chitare
Nic Vanderschantz
Nikhil Wani
Niklas Grabbe
Nixalkumar Patel
Noemi Mauro
Orkun Yildiz
Paolo Buono
Parisa Daeijavad
Patrick Ebel
Patrick Harms
Paula Toledo Palomino
Pavel Okopnyi
Pavel Slavik
Pedro Albuquerque Santos
Philippe Doyon-Poulin
Pia Brandt
Pietro Murano
Pooja Rao

Pradeesh Ashokan
Pragya Verma
Prithviraj Kumar Dasari
Priyanka Sebastian
Rabail Tahir
Radu-Daniel Vatavu
Rafael Vrečar
Raju Shrestha
Rakhi Jain
Ramesh Komperla
Renan Guarese
Renan Aranha
Richard Govada Joshua
Roberto Pereira
Ronan Querrec
Rosa Lanzilotti
Rufat Rzayev
Sabrina Knappe
Sabrina Panëels
Sahil Miglani
Sameera Pisupati
Sandra Gama
Sanjit Samaddar
Sanzida Mojib Luna
Sara Bouzit
Sarah Krings
Saul Delabrida
Sebastian Rings
Sergio Carvalho
Shazra Asmy
Sheethal Tom
Shreya Gupta
Shuowei Li
Shweta Premanandan
Siddharth Gulati
Sidney Fels
Siiri Paananen
Simone Gallo
Simone Kriglstein
Somang Nam
Sophia Ppali
Sophie Dupuy-Chessa
Srikrishna Jayaram
Stefan Resch
Stefan Sauer
Stefano Valtolina
Stephen Azeez
Stig Nyman
Sumit Sinha
Susmita Sharma
Suzane Santos
Talita Pagani Britto Pichiliani
Tania Prinsloo
Tânia Rocha
Taqwa Saeed
Telmo Zarraonandia
Teodor Stefanut
Teresa Colombi
Test Reviewer
Theodoros Georgiou
Thiago Coleti
Thiago Malheiros Porcino
Thiago Porcino
Thiago Rocha Silva
Thierry Coye De Brunelis
Thomas Kosch
Thomas Neumayr
Thorsten Schwarz
Ticianne Darin
Tilman Dingler
Timothy Merritt
Tom Gross
Vaishnavi Sanjay Gadve
Valentino Artizzu
Vania Neris
Velvet Spors
Vickie Nguyen
Victor Vieira
Vinicius Carvalho Pereira
Vishal Jain
Vishnu Kakaraparthi
Vivek Lakshman Bhargav Sunkara
Way Kiat Bong
Wei Wang
Weiwei Jiang
Wilko Heuten
Xiang Pan
Xiaopo Cheng
Xinqi Zhang
Xinyue Han

Yang Bong
Yavuz Inal
Yize Wei
Yogesh Deshpande

Yosra Rekik
Yvon Ruitenburg
Zhijun Guo

## Organisers, Sponsors and Partners

# Sponsors

**In-cooperation Partners**

# Contents – Part II

**Computer-Supported Cooperative Work**

Collaborative Knowledge Management in the Digitized Train Maintenance
Workplace: A Case Study at the Dutch Railways .......................... 3
  *Hannah Visser, Anouk van Kasteren, and Judith Masthoff*

Support for Building Relationships in Speed Dating Through Observation
of Pre-dialogue Simulations Using Digital Twins ......................... 25
  *Yoko Ishii, Ryo Ishii, Lidwina Andarini, Kazuya Matsuo,
  and Atsushi Otsuka*

When Design Collaboration Goes Remote: Intermediate-Level Knowledge
for Empowering Remote Co-exploration .................................. 45
  *Xinhui Ye, Joep Frens, and Jun Hu*

**Context-Dependent Systems**

An Exploration to Enhance Response Rate and Sampling Density During
ESM Experiments by Online Supervised Learning and Edge Computing
on Smartwatches ...................................................... 71
  *Alireza Khanshan, Pieter Van Gorp, and Panos Markopoulos*

From Explaining to Engaging: The Effect of Interactive AI Explanations
on Citizens' Fairness and Adoption Perceptions .......................... 87
  *Saja Aljuneidi, Wilko Heuten, Maria Wolters, and Susanne Boll*

Mitigating Interruptions in Digital Reading: Strategic Pauses
and Note-Taking for Enhanced Cognitive Performance ..................... 109
  *Naile Hacioglu, Maria Chiara Leva, Nakyung Kim, and Hyowon Lee*

**Design and Evaluation in Smart and Ubiquitous Contexts**

Behind Customer Satisfaction Metrics: Exploring User Perceptions of Net
Promoter Score (NPS) as a Measure of Satisfaction ...................... 135
  *Jade Logan, Daniele Doneddu, Kevin McLafferty, Muneeb I. Ahmad,
  and Nicholas Micallef*

Moving Toward Natural Gesture Interaction: Understanding User
Preferences in Smart Homes ............................................. 157
  Mauro Filho, Ana Patrícia Rocha, Tiago Silvestre,
  Gonçalo Lourenço Silva, Diogo Matos, Inês Santos, Nuno Vidal,
  António Teixeira, and Samuel Silva

The Rhetoric of Smartness ............................................. 167
  Girish Dalvi and Malay Dhamelia

Ubiquity on the Road: Co-designing an Itinerant Ubiquitous Computing
Laboratory ............................................................ 177
  Josiane Rosa de Oliveira Gaia Pimenta, Deógenes P. Junior da Silva,
  and M. Cecilia C. Baranauskas

**Designing for Identity, Safety, and Cultural Values**

Dancing with Data: Privacy Compromises of Egyptian Women
Reconciling Westernized Social Media Sharing with Local Cultural Values .... 203
  Mennatallah Saleh, Shaun Macdonald, and Christian Sturm

Towards Design Guidelines for Safety Experience in Mobile Applications
for Tourism ........................................................... 226
  Minna Virkkula, Siiri Paananen, and Jonna Häkkilä

Who We Are and What We Mean: a Scoping Review of Concepts
and Terminology on Digital Legacy ..................................... 243
  Cristiano Maciel, Vinícius Carvalho Pereira,
  Francisco Wesley Gomes Bezerra, and Tânia Saraiva de Melo Pinheiro

**Emotionally-Informed Design**

Applying the Laws of Simplicity to Redesign an Educational Social
Network ............................................................... 269
  Jonas Lopes Guerra, Deógenes P. Junior da Silva,
  Krissia M. L. Menezes, and Roberto Pereira

Designing for *Einfühlung:* Strategies for Embodied Sensitivity
in Interactive Spaces ................................................. 289
  Maja Fagerberg Ranten, Mads Hobye, Troels Andreasen,
  Karen Eide Bøen, and Lise Aagaard Knudsen

Framing the Risk: A Large-Scale Field Experiment on Risk
Communication in Responsible Gambling ................................. 300
  Carly Grace Allen, Tanja Sveen, Frode Volden, and Yavuz Inal

Towards Smart Workplaces: Understanding Mood-Influencing Factors
of the Physical Workspace in Collaborative Group Settings .................. 309
  *Tzu-Hui Wu, Sebastian Cmentowski, Yunyin Lou, Jun Hu,
  and Regina Bernhaupt*

When Motivation Can Be More Than a Message: Designing Agents
to Boost Physical Activity ............................................. 332
  *Alessandro Silacci, Maurizio Caon, and Mauro Cherubini*

**HCD for Mission-Critical Systems**

Before It Falls: Supporting Drone Fleet Management Through Battery
Visualizations ...................................................... 347
  *Maria-Theresa Bahodi, Nathan Lau, Niels van Berkel,
  Kasper Andreas Rømer Grøntved, Mikael B. Skov, and Timothy Merritt*

Multi-Variant UCD - A Process for the Design of Interactive System
Variants: Application to Launch Vehicles Flight Safety Operations ............ 371
  *Daniel Rodriguez-Hernando, Célia Martinie, Philippe Palanque,
  and Sandra Steere*

**HCI in Formal and Inclusive Learning Contexts**

Designing from Within: HCI4D and PD4D in Sahrawi Refugee Camps ........ 399
  *Daniel Cabezas, Enric Mor, José Luis Abdelnour-Nocera,
  and Clara Amorim*

From Design to Evaluation: A Case Study on Learner Experience ............ 410
  *Deivid Silva, Tayna Conte, Guilherme Guerino,
  and Natasha M. C. Valentim*

From Prototype to the Classroom: Iterative Development of Conditionals
in Early Childhood Robotics ......................................... 430
  *Ewelina Bakala, Gonzalo Tejera, and Juan Pablo Hourcade*

Serious Games Development by Educators: Opportunities and Challenges ..... 452
  *Joana Gabriela Ribeiro de Souza, Letícia da Silva Macedo Alves,
  Marcos Vinícius Caldeira Pacheco, Lucas Xavier Veneroso,
  and Raquel O. Prates*

## HCI in Healthcare and Wellbeing

Design of Temporal Interfaces of Digital Twins in Domestic Energy
Consumption .................................................... 477
    *Yaxin Zheng, Harm van Essen, Scott Mitchell, Liam Fennessy,*
    *Laurene Vaughan, and Regina Bernhaupt*

Exploring the Potential of Interacting with a Virtual Dog in a Virtual Forest
for Well-Being: A Study with Informal Caregivers of People with Dementia ... 499
    *Beatriz Peres, Lilian Motti, Genesis Nobrega, Jana Janković,*
    *Diogo Manuel Gouveia, and Pedro Campos*

Human-Centered Design of Digital Twins: The Case of Green Smart Homes ... 509
    *Barbara Rita Barricelli, Daniela Fogli, and Davide Guizzardi*

Making Predictions Tangible: Using Data Physicalization to Explore
Expectations Around Health Predictions .................................. 521
    *Yinchu Li, Carine Lallemand, and Regina Bernhaupt*

Nail pHolish: Sensing Hand-Fluid Interactions Through Biocosmetic
Interfaces ........................................................ 540
    *Shuyi Sun, Dana Mayfield, Yuan-Hao Ku, Jinho Yon, and Katia Vega*

## Human-AI Interaction

A Feature Mapping on GenAI Tools from the Perspective of HCI ............. 565
    *Rafael A. Pereira and Natasha M. C. Valentim*

Eliciting Multimodal Approaches for Machine Learning–Assisted
Photobook Creation ................................................ 576
    *Sara-Jane Bittner, Michael Barz, and Daniel Sonntag*

Interaction Trace Analysis to Identify AI Competencies: Preliminary
Results from a Pilot Project .......................................... 602
    *Daniela Marques and Marcelo Morandini*

The Challenge of Understanding Explanations for User Trust in AI:
Insights From an Online Experiment About Job Matching .................. 612
    *Glenda Hannibal and Christine Bauer*

Correction to: Before It Falls: Supporting Drone Fleet Management
Through Battery Visualizations ........................................ C1
   *Maria-Theresa Bahodi, Nathan Lau, Niels van Berkel,*
   *Kasper Andreas Rømer Grøntved, Mikael B. Skov, and Timothy Merritt*

**Author Index** ....................................................... 637

# Computer-Supported Cooperative Work

# Collaborative Knowledge Management in the Digitized Train Maintenance Workplace: A Case Study at the Dutch Railways

Hannah Visser, Anouk van Kasteren(✉) [ID], and Judith Masthoff [ID]

Utrecht University, Utrecht, The Netherlands
a.vankasteren@uu.nl

**Abstract.** Dutch train maintenance faces challenges due to workforce losses and skill gaps driven by rapid technological advancements. Effective knowledge management (KM) is vital to prevent knowledge loss and optimise total productive maintenance (TPM). Maintenance workers' processes and knowledge-sharing behaviours are currently underexplored. Human-Computer Interaction (HCI) methods can reveal key challenges and opportunities for improvement. This study illustrates the use of contextual inquiry combined with affinity and ideation workshops, which led to valuable insights and concepts. Eight opportunities were identified and grouped into three clusters: Communication, information accessibility, and administration adequacy. Further ideation produced four concepts. Research in a complex, safety-critical environment like maintenance requires thorough preparation and expectation management. Despite these challenges, involving maintenance workers in the innovation process has proven highly valuable.

**Keywords:** Train maintenance · Contextual Inquiry · Knowledge Management · Collaboration

## 1 Introduction

In the years ahead, an increase in train travel in the Netherlands is expected due to population growth and urban expansion [26]. Consequently, the Dutch train maintenance industry faces increasing demand. However, the expected retirement wave of baby boomers in the sector [19,26], as well as the job-hopping behaviour of millennials [62], affects the maintenance operations. The loss of both manpower and valuable knowledge and skills developed over time can significantly reduce efficiency [49]. Moreover, the labour market is expected to remain tight, resulting in staff shortages, especially in sectors such as transportation [14]. Another challenge is the introduction of the fourth industrial revolution (I4.0) in the workplace. This has greatly impacted work in modern industrial factories, including train maintenance [29]. Workers must acquire new skills to work with digital systems and perform more complex tasks [43], hindering efficiency.

The widely used Total Productive Maintenance (TPM) strategy, which focuses on preventive rather than reactive maintenance, involves all employees to enhance productivity and efficiency [45]. Smart Maintenance (SM) extends TPM with new, innovative digital capabilities. To adapt to the changing maintenance workplace, Knowledge Management (KM) has become more important [41]. The effectiveness and efficiency of train maintenance strongly depend on how workers manage information [49]. Sustainable KM ensures that knowledge is retained and transferred into systems to prevent knowledge loss and assist workers in acquiring new knowledge [25]. I4.0 has also created new possibilities for collaboration, both human-human and human-machine, that can transform maintenance practices. Sharmin et al. [66] highlight the importance of community in maintenance work. They state how new technologies could improve collaboration through easier knowledge sharing. These collaborative KM tools, when introduced with proper instruction, can be utilised to boost the efficiency of TPM [57].

Currently, the added value of using I4.0 technologies in the train maintenance industry is understudied, despite its proven benefits in other sectors [32]. Research into how maintenance workers are affected by the digitised work environment is limited for several reasons [23]. First, informal learning through various information sources is common. Second, organising empirical studies in event-driven work environments faces obstacles such as obtaining workplace access and constraints on time and resources [13]. This results in a notable gap in user research in train maintenance management. However, there are opportunities for innovations to reduce errors, decrease cognitive load, and enhance performance [39]. Oftentimes, issues are reported incidentally. HCI methods, such as contextual inquiry, journey mapping, and ideation workshops, are valuable in uncovering these issues and corresponding opportunities systematically. This paper demonstrates how to leverage HCI methods to understand collaborative knowledge management practices at the Dutch railways (NS). To answer the following research question: *"How can technologies improve the collaboration of train maintenance workers within NS to enhance TPM?"*.

This paper is organised as follows: Sect. 2 reviews the relevant literature, Sect. 3 outlines the methodology for the contextual inquiry and ideation workshop, Sect. 4 presents the results, and Sect. 5 offers conclusions, lessons learned, limitations, and future considerations.

## 2 Background

### 2.1 Total Productive Maintenance

Due to the high costs of downtime, labour, and material transport [24], the maintenance industry has shifted from a reactive model [2], where machines were repaired only after breakdowns, to a more proactive approach centred around (TPM). This approach emphasises preventive and predictive maintenance to minimise operational disruptions [45,57]. TPM aims for zero maintenance errors by involving all employees in equipment upkeep and ensuring timely interventions that enhance safety, product quality, and work efficiency [65]. TPM is now widely used in Dutch train maintenance to address industry challenges.

Industry 4.0 (I4.0) technologies have given rise to SM, which extends TPM principles with new digital capabilities. Technologies such as Artificial Intelligence (AI), Internet of Things (IoT), Augmented Reality (AR) and cloud computing transformed TPM by enabling automation, real-time monitoring, remote diagnostics and enhanced collaboration or data-flows [9,40,68]. In this sense, SM builds on TPM by introducing system-wide intelligence and connectivity that reshape maintenance coordination and decision-making. However, successful implementation depends on contextual factors such as company resources, workforce digital literacy, and organisational structure and culture [34,58].

This paper positions SM as an extension of TPM, requiring not only technological integration but also new forms of collaboration. In this context, KM and collaborative tool design become essential to support effective adaptation.

**Maintenance Work at NS.** Maintenance at the Dutch Railways is divided over Service Facilities (SF) and Maintenance Facilities (MF). Activities as SFs involve outdoor inspections and minor repairs with high mobility and safety risks. whereas MFs are indoor workshops for extensive, scheduled, and complex unforeseen repairs. Work being done at MFs often requires specialised skills. Tasks at both facilities are organised through work orders assigned to individual mechanics. Each day begins with a day-start meeting to discuss planned tasks, which may include mechanical or electrical inspections and repairs on trains. Mechanics gather materials, complete their assignments, and report the results.

## 2.2 Knowledge Management

Collaborative KM is key to supporting workflows in digitalised maintenance environments. KM supports efficient workflows by collecting, sharing, and transforming information into actionable knowledge [38]. Workplace learning, a key KM component, involves developing skills and adapting mental models through digital resources and peer learning [23]. Especially in the fast-paced context of maintenance work, knowledge sharing among seniors and newcomers is a vital part of workplace learning [55]. Organisational learning strategies, such as codification (e.g., manuals, databases) and personalisation (e.g., mentoring), further drive performance improvements and innovation [21,42]. Additionally, Smart KM leverages Industry 4.0 technologies to enhance learning and collaboration by delivering high-quality, timely information tailored to diverse learning styles [13,37]. Together, KM tailors knowledge delivery to the needs of different users, supports collaboration, improves learning outcomes, and promotes timely access to information. These practices are particularly relevant in high-pressure environments like train maintenance, where effective knowledge sharing directly impacts safety and efficiency. This highlights the importance of empirical research on KM in understanding digitalising SM environments. Therefore, this study builds on existing work by exploring how collaborative KM can be improved in digitalised maintenance contexts and how tools and practices can be designed to address real-world challenges.

## 2.3 Collaborative Maintenance Tools

Collaboration tools support coordination and KM in complex workplaces. Platforms like intranets, wikis, and shared drives enable asynchronous knowledge sharing and collaboration. They promote engagement and reduce information gaps [35,44]. Collaborative AI facilitates human-machine collaboration. For instance, conversational agents support real-time information access, while extended reality (XR) technologies enable immersive training and remote collaboration [5,11]. IoT systems enhance real-time monitoring and decision-making by integrating sensors and operational technologies [40].

However, poorly implemented technologies can lead to collaboration overload and underuse. Designing them with a human-centred approach is crucial, balancing technology integration with user needs, workflows and capacities [47,50]. Additionally, digital tools for maintenance work can have significant implications for human roles, responsibilities, and workplace dynamics. Prior research has shown that technologies such as AR can enhance collaboration by bridging expertise gaps and overcoming spatial constraints [3]. Similarly, studies in highly controlled environments like clean rooms have shown how portable digital tools support task documentation and coordination among maintenance workers [55]. These technologies are often associated with increased efficiency and productivity [27,61].

Nevertheless, the adoption of digital tools is not without challenges. Concerns have been raised about job insecurity, reduced social interaction, and increased cognitive demands [23,36]. For example, [8] found that digital workplaces lacking transparency can lead to polarisation, exclusion, and hindered conflict resolution. To mitigate such risks, researchers advocate for human-centred design (HCD) approaches that emphasise co-creation and iterative feedback from employees to improve usability and acceptance [29]. Additionally, clear communication and proper training are essential to foster trust and engagement [16,59]. Balancing workload and task complexity is also necessary. Overly complex tasks can overwhelm workers, while overly simple ones may reduce engagement [4,39].

Despite these insights, there remains a need for practical guidance on how to design collaborative, human-centred digital tools that support maintenance workers in knowledge-intensive and safety-critical domains. This study addresses this gap by studying collaborative behaviour among train maintenance workers and investigating how tools can better support collaborative knowledge management in these contexts. By focusing on employee needs and workplace dynamics, we aim to contribute solutions that promote both productivity and worker well-being in the digitised workplace.

# 3 Methodology

## 3.1 Contextual Inquiry

A contextual inquiry study was carried out to understand better the information behaviour of train maintenance workers and the challenges they face with collaborative knowledge management. This study, conducted in the natural environment, highlights the efficacy of contextual inquiries to uncover more profound insights into the complexity of the maintenance work process and workers' perceptions, motivations, and mental models [7,12]. Moreover, due to the practical nature and the context sensitivity of the logistics, work culture and time pressure of the job, contextual inquiries are of great value in understanding subtle behaviours such as tool usage, informal communications, and workarounds.

In this study, fifteen (15) contextual inquiry interviews documented the work process, pain points and improvement opportunities. These were conducted during eight visits to maintenance facilities across the Netherlands, covering both early and late shifts, enhancing findings' generalizability across diverse contexts [31]. Participants were shadowed and interviewed individually. Each session lasted on average 3 h, depending on the schedule and tasks of each worker. The study was approved by the Ethics and Privacy Quick Scan of the Utrecht University Research Institute of Information and Computing Sciences.

**Participants.** The sample for this study consisted of train maintenance workers recruited from SFs and MFs across various locations (Rotterdam, Nijmegen, Utrecht, Zwolle for SF; Leidschendam, Maastricht, Onnen, Watergraafsmeer for MF) to gather diverse perspectives. A purposive sampling method was used to ensure participants had a mix of experience and expertise levels. Participants with over three months of job experience were eligible, given they provided informed consent. In total, fifteen (15) workers participated. The sample consisted of all males due to the male dominance in the train maintenance field. Participants were aged 21-61 (mean = 35), with varying years of experience: 0-1 (n = 1), 1-2 (n = 2), 2-5 (n = 4), 5-10 (n = 2), and 10+ years (n = 6).

**Procedure.** Each session consisted of four parts as described by [53]. The sessions included: *(1) The primer:* Introduction of the research, obtaining consent, and asking standard interview questions to understand the participant and their work. *(2) The Transition:* A clear transition between the end of the introduction interview and the start of observations. In the context of train maintenance, suitable timing was discussed beforehand to avoid disrupting focus-critical tasks during the observations. *(3) The Contextual Interview:* Observation of the employee at work, coupled with questions to clarify actions and mental models, balancing work periods and discussions. A set of topics and potential questions was prepared to assist the researcher during the contextual inquiries. This was to ensure enough insights were gathered. Figure 1 shows one of the visits to a maintenance facility. *(4) The debrief:* The observations and interpretations were summarised, allowing participants to provide feedback. Here, unresolved questions were addressed as well. During the contextual inquiries, notes were written down. This structure ensured comprehensive data collection, respecting the participants' workflow and safety considerations. The complete protocol can be found in the Supplementary Materials.

**Fig. 1.** Illustration of a visit to a maintenance facility to conduct a contextual inquiry interview. Joining the worker on top of the train to observe the work process.

**Analysis.** The contextual inquiry results were first analysed through a thematic analysis. The notes were imported to Nvivo(14.23) [48]. The data was coded with a top-down approach to describe the "environment", "events", "actions", and "experiences" through the words of the participants [1]. Moreover, classifications were created based on location, job title, work experience, age, and type of shift. This method revealed patterns and discrepancies within the data, leading to the discovery of more themes, ideas, and concepts. These findings were subsequently defined as secondary codes to the top-level codes.

The results were used to create two employee journey maps, one for SFs and one for MFs, representing different phases of executing work orders. The journey's columns represent different phases of executing work orders. These originate from the secondary codes from the top-level code 'Work order process phases': Start of workday, Work preparation, Work execution, Planned maintenance (MF) or quality checks (SF), Repair work, Work completion, and End of workday. The journeys consist of 8 rows: actions, information required, information gathered, tools, collaboration, quotes, emotions and pain points. First, a crosstab query was run in NVivo [48] to discover child codes relevant for OB and SB workers separately. Next, the tasks in the work order process of MFs and SFs were identified through a hierarchical task analysis. Tasks were broken down into subtasks, and through the data from the 'Work order process phases', the frequency of each task mentioned could be determined to define the actions. One MB and SF worker evaluated the journey maps, and their feedback was incorporated to improve the representations.

After the work order process and collaborative aspects were visualised, issues and challenges could be further analysed. Grounded theory was employed to develop theoretical frameworks addressing problems revealed through axial and selective coding [20]. Analysis was jump-started through a 2-hour affinity workshop with 4 UX designers experienced in the train maintenance domain to cluster the data. The workshop involved axial coding of the data. Common themes were identified through code categorisation and group decision-making. For this analysis, only the child codes from the top-level codes 'collaboration' and 'comments and observations on work execution' were considered relevant to use in the workshop. Previously established top-level and secondary codes were excluded to avoid biasing the participants in their decision-making. During the workshop, 77 yellow post-its were used for SF and 76 orange for MF, containing the relevant child codes. After the workshop, the themes, related child codes and problem categories were digitised in an online whiteboard tool. The workshop data on the two separate facility types were integrated into a single visualisation. From the identified themes, eight were selected as the most important by the UX experts and the researchers, as they aligned best with the research scope and possess the potential for UX design solutions.

From there, three distinct clusters were identified to encompass the problem categories that had emerged during axial coding. Subsequently, specific issues were allocated to these clusters through selective coding. After the workshop, detailed attributes were incorporated from the contextual inquiry data to enrich the theories. These attributes addressed the following questions: (1) When does the problem occur? (2) Where does the problem occur? (3) What devices are involved in the problem? (4) What tools are involved in the problem? (5) Who does the problem relate to? (6) What causes the problem? (7) What are the consequences of the problem? These findings form the basis of problem theories.

## 3.2 Ideation Workshop

The identified problem theories are opportunities for improvement. A two-hour ideation workshop involving different stakeholders was organised to generate possible solutions. In this workshop, multiple methods were used to generate ideas through individual and group ideation. The "How might we" (HMW) question technique was used to frame the right design challenges based on the problem theories [51]. The Crazy 8 method encouraged divergent thinking by having participants generate eight ideas in eight minutes individually, ensuring equal participation [28]. The impact-effort matrix guided decision-making by categorising ideas into four types: money pits (low-impact, high-effort), fill-ins (low-impact, low-effort), big bets (high-impact, high-effort), and quick wins (high-impact, low-effort), prioritising the latter two for their value [17]. Dot voting and the concept canvas supported convergent thinking by selecting and refining top ideas through group reflection, preventing tunnel vision [18]. A subset of the resulting concepts was selected for further exploration and form design recommendations.

**Participants.** The participant selection was designed to balance input from a diverse group, engaging key stakeholders in the design process and consolidating knowledge from varied backgrounds, while maintaining a manageable group size to foster productive discussions. The workshop participants included:

two UX designers, selected for their expertise in design and ideation within the domain and relevant applications; one product owner, two tactical business consultants, and two strategic business consultants, contributing insights into ongoing innovations, organisational strategies, and resource management; one enterprise architect, to support early identification of technical risks and limitations; and one maintenance worker and one maintenance team coordinator, to provide direct user input and help build trust to reduce barriers for future implementations. This diversity was intended to promote more realistic and impactful solutions. Although we aimed to include additional maintenance workers, recruitment proved challenging due to their high workload and limited availability at the time of the workshop. All participants provided informed consent.

**Procedure.** Three HMW-questions were formed to guide the workshop, one for each problem theory cluster. For communication, this was: "How might we improve communication around work orders and relevant information?". The question "How might we make information more accessible within the tools?" was made for the category of information accessibility. Lastly, for administrative adequacy, the following question was formulated: "How can we better align administrative requirements with the work of maintenance workers?".

The participants were split into three groups, each assigned a "How-might-we" question to tackle. They were informed about the associated problem theories before starting ideation. The workshop was facilitated by one researcher supported by one UX designer from the Dutch Railways to make sure the participants remained engaged and refrained from falling into limitations. The workshop was structured as follows:

(1) *Introduction:* The workshop started with introducing the workshop and problem context through a PowerPoint presentation. Additionally, informed consent forms were signed by the participants.
(2) *Individual brain writing:* Here, the Crazy 8 method was used. Every participant created eight ideas for their assigned HMW question.
(3) *Selecting ideas:* Each group member was told to choose their 3 best ideas and take these to the group discussion by shortly pitching them. Subsequently, ideas were put on the impact-effort matrix for prioritisation to determine which were best to develop further.
(4) *Break.*
(5) *Concept development:* Participants received three dots to vote for their preferred ideas on the impact-effort matrix. The two highest-voted ideas from each group were selected for further development using concept canvases. On these canvases, participants provided a description and visualisation of the idea (Fig. 2), explained its value to maintenance workers, indicated its placement on the impact-effort matrix, and outlined the needs it meets, problems it addresses, and key factors to consider.
(6) *Pitches and feedback:* The ideas were pitched to the group. Because stakeholders had different background knowledge, fruitful discussion arose, which provided a clear picture of an idea's potential and possible obstacles.

**Analysis.** All generated ideas were evaluated through the weighted objectives method [60]. This included estimations about the expected impact on productivity (weight = 35), relatedness to UX design (weight = 20), impact on task satisfaction (weight = 20), costs (weight = 10), and implementation effort (weight = 15), including labour intensity and technological complexity. Together with designers, the ideas were scored on a scale from 1–10 on these criteria to calculate overall scores. After, the ranking was discussed with a UX designer who provided information about planned implementations and limitations within the existing application. Consequently, several ideas were further developed.

## 4 Results

### 4.1 Contextual Inquiry

The coding scheme resulting from the thematic analysis is shown in Table 1. From all the collected data, 309 distinct child codes were created with 885 references.

In composing the employee journey maps, a total of 184 codes were used to determine actions in the work order process at MFs and 155 for SFs. This resulted in 56 actions for MF maintenance workers and 49 for workers at SFs. Next, associations for these actions were added on information required, information gathered, tools, collaboration, quotes, emotions, and pain points. Examples of actions include logging in, reviewing assigned work orders, starting the work order, and travelling to the work location. Information required and gathered involves passwords, work priorities, work locations, and work descriptions. Tools include documentation, real-time information and administration applications, and equipment for carrying out work. Further, collaboration happens between colleague maintenance workers, team coordinators, specialists, and warehouse

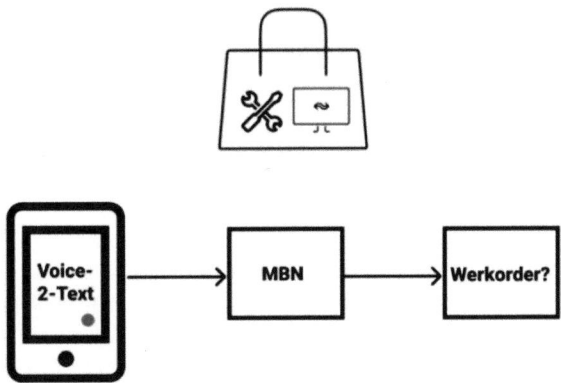

**Fig. 2.** Examples of the participants' concept drawings during the ideation workshop. Illustrated is the "mobile work station", a bag for each worker with all the tools they may need during their job. Additionally, a drawing of a "voice-to-text module", where workers can document work orders through speech is shown.

**Table 1.** Thematic coding scheme including the top-level and secondary codes, example child codes and the number of child codes.

| Top-level code | Secondary codes | Example child code | child codes |
|---|---|---|---|
| Work-order process phases | Start of workday, work preparation, work execution, work completion, end of workday | I start a work order in Maximo | 125 |
| Tools | Documentation, administration, real-time information | I use Triplo for refreshing my knowledge | 37 |
| Information | – | I need information on the work location | 20 |
| Collaboration | – | I ask help from an expert | 24 |
| Comments and observation on work execution | General comments, negative comments, positive comments, comments on tools, solutions and wishes | The tablets are quite slow, making them unpleasant to use | 103 |

**Table 2.** An example from the journey for the action "On-site diagnosis" as part of the work execution phase of repair work.

|  | On-site diagnosis |
|---|---|
| Required information | Work order description and the location of the problem |
| Information gathered | Information on faults, materials needed and their quantity |
| Tools | Digital or paper notebook, and the real-time monitoring system |
| Collaboration | Does not happen |
| Emotions | Frustration |
| Pain points | Time-consuming, incomplete work descriptions, inaccessible information |

employees. Lastly, pain points include logging in often, needing two different applications to book materials, and repetitive tasks that need to be completed multiple times. Table 2 shows an example column from the employee journeys.

Subsequently, the grounded theory analysis of the contextual inquiry findings resulted in recurring data patterns across locations. However, due to the exploratory nature of the study, full data saturation was not achieved. The data also revealed location-specific issues. For example, unclear work descriptions for new trains were reported only at the Amsterdam location, while concerns regarding the administrative load of checklists and communication with work planners were raised solely in Maastricht. Challenges related to accessing information were noted primarily in Zwolle, whereas reliance on support from experienced colleagues was highlighted only in Utrecht, and issues in communication between mechanics and team coordinators was merely mentioned in Onnen. These findings may reflect specific ways of working at individual locations; however, it is also possible that certain issues remain unobserved in other, unstudied locations.

Based on the grounded theory analysis, 14 themes and 13 problem categories were established. These results can be seen in Table 3. From these findings, eight

**Table 3.** Axial coding results from the contextual inquiries. Not all child codes within these problem categories represent challenges, as they encompass various experiences. As a result, not every category necessarily reveals a problem and some multiple.

| Theme | Description | Example child code | Related problem categories |
|---|---|---|---|
| Entering administration | Recording behaviour of administrative tasks | 'Performing a series of tasks consecutively without reporting them in real-time' | Administration is not properly carried out, Resistance to create work orders |
| Administration frustrations | Challenges encountered in administrative tasks | 'Accurate hours are expected, but this is very time-consuming' | Administration is too much work |
| Communication in general | Overall communication practices and challenges | 'Information transfer from the previous shift is sometimes unclear' | Communication insufficient |
| Information needs | Information utilisation and challenges for work execution | 'Capturing a picture of the screen or making a note to refer to later' | Work description does not match reality, Information not available in desired way |
| Information quality | Accuracy and reliability of available information | 'Colleagues are not corrected when information is not properly filled out' | Information quality insufficient |
| Knowledge | Exchanging, acquiring, and organising information | 'Fear of knowledge loss when experienced maintenance workers retire' | Knowledge loss |
| Direct collaboration | Team interactions and joint efforts for task execution | 'Working together to carry out tasks' | – |
| Support | Indirect collaboration and assistance from colleagues | 'Contacting MBN (help desk) to report an issue' | Ineffective communication |
| Work method | Approaches of task execution | 'I never call for help but always ask in person' | Reduced efficient work method |
| New implementations | Introduction and integration of systems for maintenance work | 'New systems that are not functioning well are rushed into implementation' | Insufficient guidance of implementations |
| Digital tools | Utilisation and effectiveness of technologies | 'Dino and Triplo function more effectively on the computer' | Poor alignment of digital tools and work process |
| Monteursapp | Utilisation and effectiveness of Monteursapp | 'Monteursapp is suitable for inspections but less for handling repairs' | Insufficient information provision in Monteursapp |
| Satisfaction | Experiences of contentment in the workplace | 'Effective communication within the team' | – |
| Personal preferences | Favored work methods and desired capabilities | 'I prefer working on the computer' | – |

KM problem theories were established, each being an opportunity for improvement. These were then grouped, which resulted in three clusters.

**1. Communication.** This cluster consists of two KM problem theories and corresponding improvement opportunities.

*1a. Informing maintenance workers about changing arrival and departure times.* Information about schedule changes is important to avoid delays of work because the train may be absent or need relocation. Information about arrival and departure times is available through various tools but is not always up-to-date. Additionally, there is a lack of communication with maintenance workers, as they do not receive phone calls or notifications about updates. Occasionally, a train with a maintenance worker inside might accidentally be moved while the worker is still on it. Better communication towards maintenance workers would allow work to progress more effectively.

*1b. Informing maintenance workers and team coordinators promptly about new work orders.* Maintenance workers often delay reporting new work orders due to preference for certain communication methods, time constraints, or lack of tools. Workers could make more use of verbal or phone communication to report new work. Moreover, information about new work orders in the system should be easily accessible. Currently, MF workers need to log in on a computer to access updates. While SF workers have phone access, they do not receive notifications. Increasing the awareness about tasks and quickly assigning them could decrease the number of tasks left unfinished.

**2. Information Accessibility.** This cluster consists of three KM problem theories and corresponding improvement opportunities.

*2a. Information accessibility and convenience across multiple tools.* Currently, information needs to be retrieved from multiple tools. Each application requires opening, logging in, and navigating through multiple menu layers to access work descriptions and material details. Combining the information frhe different sources saves workers substantial tiwhen me consulting these systems or colleagues.

*2b. Work information accessibility at the work site.* Portable devices like tablets and phones can improve information access inside and outside the train. Currently, not all workers have access to these. While SF workers use work phones, small screens, and poor network coverage pose challenges. As a result, maintenance workers often have to walk or travel to computers or consult colleagues for information, which is especially critical for complex repairs.

*2c. The availability of desired information in the systems.* Maintenance workers occasionally lack the necessary information and must find alternative, time-consuming methods to obtain it. Work descriptions for routine inspections and repairs are available in one of the applications. This should be extended for more uncommon or complex problems as well. Additionally, limitations in searching, filtering, and visualising information in the various tools should be overcome.

**3. Administration Adequacy.** This cluster also consists of three problem theories and corresponding improvement opportunities.

*3a. Reporting of new and executed work.* For efficient task execution, workers must diagnose, solve issues and source materials and information. Currently, workers do this all themselves instead of finding the appropriate information in the system. Maintenance workers lack the time or don't recognise the importance of proper administration. They learn reporting from colleagues a lack of formal training, and the absence of reporting guidelines results in incomplete work orders. Proper communication and access to historical data are crucial to resolving current issues, especially recurring ones.

*3b. Real-time reporting and assignment of work.* Delays in updating the system prevent the team coordinator from promptly delegating new tasks and can lead to pending tasks being duplicated. Workers should be trained to complete admin tasks immediately rather than memorising information and completing tasks sequentially. Workers favour reporting defects on larger screens for ease of use. These should be available at the work site. Further, it should be avoided that working hours are adjusted retrospectively, hindering data-driven analysis on work duration and impairing predictive maintenance improvements.

*3c. Reporting of defects by first-line staff working on the train.* First-line staff have limited time for reporting defects. As a result, maintenance workers must spend a lot of time identifying and documenting defects during the quality checks, which decreases repair time. Availability of time, resources, and proper training for first-line staff would enhance maintenance efficiency.

## 4.2 Ideation Workshop

The workshop resulted in several ideas for the problem theories and related HMW questions. These were further developed on the concept canvases, taking into account persuasive system design [46] and findings from Woods et al. [66], who emphasise the importance of considering work identity, agency and community when designing for maintenance work. The ideas were evaluated using the weighted objectives method (Results in Table 4). One idea was excluded as its implementation was already being considered by the application developers. Additionally, one was excluded due to its complexity and effort to implement. The others were developed in more detail.

**AI-Powered Search Engine.** This idea was proposed by several workshop participants. It involves developing a unified interface that consolidates information from multiple sources, addressing problem 2a (information accessibility across tools). Leveraging current generative AI capabilities, the solution could take the form of a natural language-based search engine, allowing maintenance workers to quickly retrieve information such as materials, work descriptions, diagrams, fault trees, and maintenance histories. By eliminating the need to navigate multiple systems, this approach is expected to reduce frustration, save time, and allow workers to focus more on core maintenance tasks [6,22,23,66]. It is suitable for both SF and MF staff using shared technologies.

**Table 4.** Results of the weighted objectives evaluation of the selected ideas.

| Criteria (weight) | Work order alarm | Voice-to-text entry | Quick entries | Mobile workstation | Intelligent search engine |
|---|---|---|---|---|---|
| Productivity (35) | 8 | 7 | 7 | 8 | 7 |
| UX design (20) | 6 | 6 | 9 | 1 | 9 |
| Task satisfaction (20) | 7 | 6 | 9 | 7 | 10 |
| Effort (15) | 8 | 6 | 7 | 9 | 4 |
| Cost (10) | 8 | 6 | 7 | 8 | 5 |
| Total | **740** | **635** | **760** | **795** | **765** |

Implementation would require compiling a centralised database and using indexing to support efficient information retrieval. A Retrieval-Augmented Generation (RAG) model could be applied to enable accurate, natural language search functionality. While this system has the potential to enhance human-machine collaboration and promote standardisation, it comes with notable challenges. Technical infrastructure must be established, and ongoing resources allocated for development, maintenance, and updates. A common limitation of current generative language models is faulty information or "hallucinations". Therefore, information quality assurance is essential in these high-risk maintenance environments. Additionally, successful adoption depends on training staff in both technological literacy and effective information-seeking behaviours [23]. Further research is recommended to assess such a tool's feasibility and real-world integration, particularly in dynamic and time-pressured environments.

**Mobile Workstation.** Problem 2b concerns the lack of accessible information at the work site. The "small screen" devices currently in use do not sufficiently support workers' needs. A proposed solution is to equip mechanics with a bag containing a laptop, enabling on-site access to larger screens and better supporting their physiological capabilities [23]. This also addresses Problem 3b (real-time reporting difficulties caused by limited screen size) by facilitating easier information retrieval and reporting in the field. As MF workers typically follow routine tasks, this solution is particularly relevant for SF workers.

The concept is straightforward and would require an investment in laptops and bags, which could be shared among SF workers. Implementation would be relatively simple but may face monetary and logistical constraints, particularly regarding device management and maintenance. Nonetheless, the mobile workstation was highly valued by the maintenance worker during the workshop. While not a high-tech solution, it offers a practical, immediately actionable improvement that could enhance usability, save time, and increase productivity. Not all problems require complex solutions; sometimes, well-targeted and straightforward tools can have a meaningful impact on day-to-day operations.

**Improved Reporting Tool.** Several ideas were proposed to improve the reporting tool. To address problem 1a (informing maintenance workers about changing arrival and departure times), a real-time work order alarm was suggested. This feature would automatically notify team coordinators and mechanics of schedule changes and new tasks via push notifications, enabling quicker response and task delegation. As workers often feel not up to date, adoption of this feature is expected to be high. It can reduce overlooked tasks and lower cognitive load [56] by eliminating the need for (mental) tracking of updates. Given its relatively simple technical implementation, this solution appears feasible. However, successful adoption may still depend on ensuring notifications are timely but not disruptive, and that alert fatigue and a loss of agency are avoided [66].

To further streamline reporting (Problems 3a and 3c), additional functionalities were proposed. A voice-to-text feature would allow mechanics to document issues hands-free while performing tasks, making reporting more efficient and reducing the likelihood of forgetting details. This functionality could also support first-line staff in defect reporting. However, actual usability and effectiveness would depend on robust voice recognition in noisy environments. Developing and implementing voice-to-text features would require significant effort. Field testing would be needed to assess whether these tools truly reduce complexity and improve knowledge sharing across teams. This will help to establish their value and justify the effort needed for their implementation.

**Persuasive System Design.** Current administrative inconsistencies stem from a lack of standardised procedures and understanding of proper administration. This leads maintenance workers to mimic poor practices due to descriptive norms bias and prioritise immediate rewards over long-term benefits due to present bias [63]. Consequently, completing maintenance tasks is valued more than administrative duties. Persuasive technology can facilitate behavioural change by influencing users' attitudes [15], although deep-rooted habits make this a challenge. The maintenance workplace is complex, with diverse backgrounds, skills, beliefs, needs and with essential safety protocols.

A study by Selassie, Oyibo, and Vassileva [54] on healthcare employees found that Cialdini's [10] persuasive principles, commitment, reciprocity, and authority significantly influenced behaviour. Applying these principles in system design can enhance data entry quality and improve the administrative habits of maintenance workers. Consequently, several ideas have been developed further based on persuasive design principles by Oinas-Kukkonen and Harjumaa [46].

*Primary Task Support.* According to the reduction principle, decreasing task complexity can motivate employees to engage in desired behaviours. The contextual inquiry identified incomplete and delayed administration as a recurring issue (Problem 3b), negatively affecting both productivity and employee satisfaction. To address this, we suggest integrating predefined input options, photo uploads, multiple data entry formats, and guided choice menus into the administrative process. These features simplify and standardise reporting, which may improve data consistency, completeness, and overall user experience. Additionally, such improvements can support more effective knowledge sharing and coordination among workers [23, 35]. Workers expressed a clear desire to reduce their administrative workload, suggesting that such solutions may be well-received. These ideas are also in line with suggestions made by [66]. Reducing administrative workload leaves more time to be out in the field where workers feel their strongest "work identity". However, successful adoption depends on intuitive menu design and overall usability. If not well-designed, these systems could become cumbersome or be bypassed. Therefore, iterative testing with end users is essential to ensure the interface truly reduces complexity and meets workers' needs.

In addition, the system could employ goal setting to enhance autonomy and agency for maintenance workers by allowing them to choose personal and recommended goals [66]. In turn, this increases intrinsic motivation [52]. Goals like completing tasks within two hours and submitting detailed work descriptions can help structure traceable progress. The self-monitoring principle could be applied through visual feedback mechanisms, such as progress bars or graphs, which help sustain engagement. However, it is crucial to prevent surveillance bias. If workers perceive the system as overly controlling, it may undermine trust and acceptance. To mitigate this risk, transparency about how data is used and a focus on supportive, rather than punitive, feedback will be crucial [64].

*Dialogue Support.* To influence maintenance worker behaviour through reciprocity, we propose deploying praise and reward principles. Positive incentives like feedback, compliments, and rewards reinforce desired actions [10,46]. Connecting these incentives to administrative goals could enhance motivation. Allowing both to receive and provide feedback could increase agency experienced by workers [66]. Agency is important for work to be experienced as meaningful. It prevents workers from unquestioningly following procedures and helps them stay sharp.

For example, the system could award virtual badges, certificates, or points for accurate and timely task completion, visible on a public scoreboard. Research shows that workplace behaviour is positively influenced by external rewards [64], and gamification can make routine tasks more enjoyable, thereby supporting intrinsic motivation [33]. However, these mechanisms must be implemented thoughtfully. Ensuring fairness, transparency, and voluntary participation is essential, as gamification is not a one-size-fits-all solution [30,46], [?]. To avoid cognitive overload or unintended competition, the system must be tested thoroughly. Without careful design and evaluation, such features risk being perceived as intrusive or demotivating, potentially undermining their intended effect. Moreover, incorporating these mechanisms in current ecosystems might pose technical feasibility constraints.

*System Credibility Support.* The expertise design principle could be used to increase credibility by using expert-validated information [10,46]. Workers are more likely to follow expert recommendations embedded in content creation and guidelines. Moreover, a lack of guidance is a barrier to desired behaviour adoption [67]. Expert-backed messages and explanations of administrative needs can serve as effective persuasive elements [54].

For new employees, mobile apps could provide instructional videos and interactive guides for data entry, developed by experienced workers or domain experts. This supports the development of accurate and consistent administrative practices. Additionally, professional tips could be integrated directly into the interface through context-sensitive icons or pop-ups, making support accessible at the point of use. Prior research shows that interactivity in workplace technologies enhances user experience, and timely persuasive prompts can encourage ongoing engagement with desired behaviours [64]. Providing instructions in different formats enables workers to develop a greater understanding of the work, enhancing their work identity [66]. Moreover, feelings of community can also be enhanced by knowledge being shared by (experienced) colleagues. However, to be effective, these features must be intuitively accessible and non-intrusive. Usability testing is essential to ensure that the guidance provided is helpful without becoming disruptive or ignored. Additionally, experienced employees must be willing to or given the opportunity to dedicate time to creating this supportive content. This may pose motivational as well as organisational challenges.

Persuasive system design can enhance knowledge sharing and collaboration by simplifying administration and promoting consistent record-keeping. This fosters better teamwork, decision-making, and a more efficient workflow.

## 5 Discussion and Conclusion

This case study investigated train maintenance work from an HCI perspective. It revealed work processes, KM practices, worker perceptions, collaborative practices, and technology integration, all of which affect TPM. It emphasises the importance of a human-centric approach for optimising work efficiency and increasing job satisfaction. This in-depth analysis was achieved through a contextual inquiry study. Most identified issues were previously unknown, as indicated by the business stakeholders. If issues were raised, this was mostly incidental, accentuating the importance of a systematic approach including maintenance workers to accelerate issue identification in a comprehensive way.

Based on the findings, three clusters of problem theories were identified: communication, information accessibility, and administrative adequacy. These findings are in line with [55] and can steer future research on collaborative technology integration in maintenance work for smart KM [13]. Following a stakeholder ideation workshop, feasible and impactful ideas were generated. These insights can aid in designing information systems, enhancing usability, KM, determining requirements, and improving UX in maintenance settings [38].

From a societal perspective, human resources can be more effectively deployed through optimised information access, reliable communication, and streamlined administration, as identified in the problem analysis. This is particularly important given the increasing pressure on and scarcity of public transportation resources. A human-centric design approach supports employee well-being, fosters collaboration, and improves operational efficiency, ultimately reducing costs by enabling more work to be completed in less time [27,36]. Efficient maintenance reduces service disruptions and enhances system reliability

[57], contributing to safer and more convenient travel for nearly one million daily NS passengers.

Although this research focused on train maintenance, its insights may apply to other domains facing similar challenges, such as aviation, intralogistics, or the semiconductor industry. For instance, aircraft maintenance involves complex scheduling and depends on accurate documentation, while warehouse operations may face issues with remote access to critical information. However, the specific nature and impact of these challenges, should be studied independently.

### 5.1 Lessons from HCI Research in the Maintenance Workplace

Extra precautions are crucial when conducting research in complex environments like maintenance workshops. Not only to account for safety hazards but also to avoid disrupting time-sensitive work. Each visit requires proper preparation, including securing clearance and aligning with participants to minimise workflow disruptions and manage expectations. This study highlights the value of involving maintenance workers in the innovation process. Their inclusion helps bridge the gap with corporate stakeholders, fostering a sense of involvement and being heard. During ideation, they can clarify practical constraints, contribute valuable ideas, and assess the feasibility of proposed solutions based on their on-the-ground experience.

### 5.2 Limitations and Future Considerations

This study faced several limitations. Observational data collection was occasionally hindered during periods of worker inactivity, and nighttime shifts were excluded due to logistical and safety constraints, possibly omitting relevant insights. As the research was exploratory, full data saturation was not reached; some behaviours and issues appeared to be location-specific. Further research is needed to confirm whether these are unique to certain sites or remain undetected in others. While the study's naturalistic setting across multiple locations supports ecological validity, external validity limitations must be acknowledged.

All mechanic participants were male, reflecting both the gender imbalance in the workforce and the difficulty of recruiting under high workload and time constraints. Although we aimed for a more diverse sample, this was not feasible within the study's time frame. This limits the diversity of perspectives, particularly regarding collaboration challenges faced by underrepresented groups. Future studies should include a broader participant base to capture a wider range of experiences and needs.

The ideation phase involved diverse stakeholders, but in-depth evaluation of the concepts by maintenance workers was beyond the study's scope. Future work should further develop and test these concepts for feasibility and effectiveness. Large-scale usability and survey studies could help quantify their impact on workplace satisfaction. Additionally, exploring these technologies in varied domains may inform a generalised framework for workplace collaboration.

Mixed-methods approaches may provide deeper insights and quantifiable outcomes, further strengthening the implementation of collaborative technologies.

**Acknowledgments.** We would like to thank the participants for their time and effort. We want to thank the Dutch Railways for the resources made available to conduct this study, with special thanks to Joëlle van Schaaik for her supervision.

# References

1. Adu, P.: A Step-by-Step Guide to Qualitative Data Coding. Routledge (2019)
2. Agustiady, T.K., Cudney, E.A.: Total productive maintenance. Total Quality Management & Business Excellence, pp. 1–8 (2018)
3. Allen, E.S., de Carvalho, A.F.P., Hoffmann, S., Schweitzer, M., Schaumann, K.: Workplace aspects of knowledge and expertise sharing practices supported by augmented reality systems: findings from a design case study. Comput. Support. Coop. Work (CSCW) **34**(1), 155–205 (2025)
4. Alsuraykh, N.H., Wilson, M.L., Tennent, P., Sharples, S.: How stress and mental workload are connected. In: Proceedings of the 13th EAI International Conference on Pervasive Computing Technologies for Healthcare, pp. 371–376 (2019)
5. Aromaa, S., Aaltonen, I., Kaasinen, E., Elo, J., Parkkinen, I.: Use of wearable and augmented reality technologies in industrial maintenance work. In: Proceedings of the 20th International Academic Mindtrek Conference, pp. 235–242 (2016)
6. Bates, M.: Information behavior (2010)
7. Beyer, H., Holtzblatt, K.: Contextual design. Interactions **6**(1), 32–42 (1999)
8. Pinatti de Carvalho, A.F., Reichel, S., Sanchez Martin, M.M., Allen, E.S., Schweitzer, M.: Group effect aspects in digitalisation production contexts: articulation spaces for emerging cooperation challenges. Proc. ACM Hum. Comput. Interact. **7**(GROUP), 1–28 (2023)
9. Chiarini, A., Belvedere, V., Grando, A.: Industry 4.0 strategies and technological developments. An exploratory research from Italian manufacturing companies. Prod. Plann. Control **31**(16), 1385–1398 (2020)
10. Cialdini, R.B.: Pre-suasion. First (2017)
11. Dale, R.: The return of the chatbots. Nat. Lang. Eng. **22**(5), 811–817 (2016)
12. Davis, M., Beidas, R.S.: Refining contextual inquiry to maximize generalizability and accelerate the implementation process. Implementation Res. Pract. **2**, 2633489521994941 (2021)
13. De Bem Machado, A., Secinaro, S., Calandra, D., Lanzalonga, F.: Knowledge management and digital transformation for industry 4.0: a structured literature review. Knowl. Manag. Res. Pract. **20**(2), 320–338 (2022)
14. van Financiën., M.: 1.1.3 krapte op de arbeidsmarkt (2022). https://www.rijksfinancien.nl/miljoenennota/2023/1468731
15. Fogg, B.J.: Persuasive technology: using computers to change what we think and do. Ubiquity **2002**(December), 2 (2002)
16. Gertler, M.S.: Manufacturing culture: The institutional geography of industrial practice. Oxford University Press (2004)
17. Gibbons, S.: Using prioritization matrices to inform UX decisions. Nielsen Norman Group, Archived at the Internet Archive (2018)

18. Gibbons, S., et al.: Dot voting: A simple decision-making and prioritizing technique in ux. WP Nielsen Norman Group. https://www.nngroup.com/articles/dot-voting/. Accessed 30 July 2022 (2019)
19. Giffi, C., Wellener, P., Dollar, B., Manolian, H.A., Monck, L., Moutray, C.: 2018 deloitte skills gap and future of work in manufacturing study (2018)
20. Glaser, B., Strauss, A.: Discovery of grounded theory: Strategies for qualitative research. Routledge (2017)
21. Hansen, M.T., Nohria, N., Tierney, T.: What's Your Strategy for Managing Knowledge? In: The Knowledge Management Yearbook 2000–2001, pp. 55–69. Routledge (2005)
22. Harbo, O., Ingwersen, P., Timmermann, P.: Cognitive processes in information storage and retrieval. In: International Workshop on the Cognitive Viewpoint. Ghent: University of Ghent, pp. 214–218 (1977)
23. Harteis, C., Goller, M., Caruso, C.: Conceptual change in the face of digitalization: challenges for workplaces and workplace learning. In: Frontiers in Education. vol. 5, p. 1. Frontiers Media SA (2020)
24. Hooi, L.W., Leong, T.Y.: Total productive maintenance and manufacturing performance improvement. J. Qual. Maint. Eng. **23**(1), 2–21 (2017)
25. Jasiulewicz-Kaczmarek, M., Legutko, S., Kluk, P.: Maintenance 4.0 technologies–new opportunities for sustainability driven maintenance. Manag. Prod. Eng. Rev. **11** (2020)
26. de Jong, A.: PBL/CBS regionale bevolkings- en huishoudensprognose 2022 (2022). https://themasites.pbl.nl/o/regionale-bevolkingsprognose/
27. Kaasinen, E., et al.: Empowering and engaging industrial workers with operator 4.0 solutions. Comput. Ind. Eng. **139**, 105678 (2020)
28. Kaplan, K.: Facilitating an effective design studio workshop. Nielsen Norman Group **2**, 2017 (2017)
29. Khamaisi, R.K., Brunzini, A., Grandi, F., Peruzzini, M., Pellicciari, M.: UX assessment strategy to identify potential stressful conditions for workers. Robot. Comput. Integr. Manufact. **78**, 102403 (2022)
30. Klimmt, C., Rizzo, A., Vorderer, P., Koch, J., Fischer, T.: Experimental evidence for suspense as determinant of video game enjoyment. Cyberpsychology Behav. **12**(1), 29–31 (2009)
31. Kochanowska, M., Gagliardi, W.R.: The double diamond model: In pursuit of simplicity and flexibility. Perspectives on Design II: Research, Education and Practice, pp. 19–32 (2022)
32. Kour, R., Castaño, M., Karim, R., Patwardhan, A., Kumar, M., Granström, R.: A human-centric model for sustainable asset management in railway: a case study. Sustainability **14**(2), 936 (2022)
33. Kumar, J., Herger, M., Deterding, S., Schnaars, S., Landes, M., Webb, E.: Gamification@ work. In: CHI'13 Extended Abstracts on Human Factors in Computing Systems, pp. 2427–2432 (2013)
34. Lasi, H., Fettke, P., Kemper, H.G., Feld, T., Hoffmann, M.: Industry 4.0. Bus. Inf. Syst. Eng. **6**, 239–242 (2014)
35. Lee, I.: Overview of emerging web 2.0-based business models and web 2.0 applications in businesses: an ecological perspective. Int. J. E-Bus. Res. (IJEBR) **7**(4), 1–16 (2011)
36. Leesakul, N., Oostveen, A.M., Eimontaite, I., Wilson, M.L., Hyde, R.: Workplace 4.0: exploring the implications of technology adoption in digital manufacturing on a sustainable workforce. Sustainability **14**(6), 3311 (2022)

37. Lenart-Gansiniec, R.: Organizational learning in industry 4.0. Problemy Zarzadzania **17**(2 (82)), 96–108 (2019)
38. Li, J., Herd, A.M.: Shifting practices in digital workplace learning: An integrated approach to learning, knowledge management, and knowledge sharing (2017)
39. Lindblom, J., Laaksoharju, M.: A roadmap for UX in rail: changing tracks in train traffic research. In: 51st NES Conference: Work Well-Ergonomics in an unpredictable world, Uppsala, 23-25 October 2022, pp. 51–58. Nordic Ergonomic Society (NES) & Uppsala University (2022)
40. Madakam, S., Ramaswamy, R., Tripathi, S.: Internet of things (IoT): a literature review. J. Comput. Commun. **3**(5), 164–173 (2015)
41. Manesh, M.F., Pellegrini, M.M., Marzi, G., Dabic, M.: Knowledge management in the fourth industrial revolution: mapping the literature and scoping future avenues. IEEE Trans. Eng. Manage. **68**(1), 289–300 (2020)
42. Marsick, V.J., Watkins, K.E.: Demonstrating the value of an organization's learning culture: the dimensions of the learning organization questionnaire. Adv. Dev. Hum. Resour. **5**(2), 132–151 (2003)
43. Matt, D.T., Orzes, G., Rauch, E., Dallasega, P.: Urban production-a socially sustainable factory concept to overcome shortcomings of qualified workers in smart smes. Comput. Ind. Eng. **139**, 105384 (2020)
44. Mishra, K., Mishra, A.K., Walker, K.: Using innovative internal communication to enhance employee engagement. In: Handbook of Research on Strategic Communication, Leadership, and Conflict Management in Modern Organizations, pp. 445–468. IGI Global (2019)
45. Nakajima, S.: Introduction to TPM: total productive maintenance.(translation). Productivity Press, Inc., 1988, p. 129 (1988)
46. Oinas-Kukkonen, H., Harjumaa, M.: Persuasive systems design: key issues, process model, and system features. Commun. Assoc. Inf. Syst. **24**(1), 28 (2009)
47. Pacaux-Lemoine, M.P., Trentesaux, D., Rey, G.Z., Millot, P.: Designing intelligent manufacturing systems through human-machine cooperation principles: a human-centered approach. Comput. Ind. Eng. **111**, 581–595 (2017)
48. QSR International Pty.: Nvivo 20. https://www.qsrinternational.com/nvivo-qualitative-data-analysis-software/home (2022)
49. Ribeiro, V.B., Nakano, D., Muniz Jr, J., Oliveira, R.B.d.: Knowledge management and industry 4.0: a critical analysis and future agenda. Gestão & Produção **29**, e5222 (2022)
50. Romero, D., Stahre, J., Taisch, M.: The operator 4.0: Towards socially sustainable factories of the future (2020)
51. Rosala, M.: Using "how might we" questions to ideate on the right problems. Nielsen Norman Group (2021)
52. Ryan, R.M., Deci, E.L.: Self-determination theory and the facilitation of intrinsic motivation, social development, and well-being. Am. Psychol. **55**(1), 68 (2000)
53. Salazar, K.: Contextual inquiry: inspire design by observing and interviewing users in their context. Nielsen Norman Group **6** (2020)
54. Selassie, H.H., Oyibo, K., Vassileva, J.: Responsiveness to persuasive strategies at the workplace: a case study. In: E-Technologies: Embracing the Internet of Things: 7th International Conference, MCETECH 2017, Ottawa, ON, Canada, May 17-19, 2017, Proceedings 7, pp. 273–284. Springer (2017)
55. Silva, I., Silva, I., Barros, A.C.: Digitalisation of maintenance work in cleanrooms: user research insights for interaction design. In: International Conference on Design and Digital Communication, pp. 42–54. Springer (2024)

56. Sweller, J.: Cognitive load during problem solving: effects on learning. Cogn. Sci. **12**(2), 257–285 (1988)
57. Tortorella, G.L., et al.: Digitalization of maintenance: exploratory study on the adoption of industry 4.0 technologies and total productive maintenance practices. Prod. Plann. Control **35**(4), 352–372 (2024)
58. Tortorella, G.L., Silva, E., Vargas, D.: An empirical analysis of total quality management and total productive maintenance in industry 4.0. In: Proceedings of the International Conference on Industrial Engineering and Operations Management (IEOM), pp. 742–753 (2018)
59. Treviño-Elizondo, B.L., García-Reyes, H.: An employee competency development maturity model for industry 4.0 adoption. Sustainability **15**(14), 11371 (2023)
60. Van Boeijen, A., Daalhuizen, J., Zijlstra, J., Van Der Schoor, R.: Delft design guide (rev.). Delft University of Technology, Faculty of Industrial Design Engineering NL: NBN International. Recuperado de http://replace-me/ebraryid **11221437** (2013)
61. Villani, V., Pini, F., Leali, F., Secchi, C.: Survey on human-robot collaboration in industrial settings: safety, intuitive interfaces and applications. Mechatronics **55**, 248–266 (2018)
62. Waikar, A., Sweet, T., Morgan, Y.C.: Millennials and job hopping–myth or reality? Implications for organizational management. Leadersh. Organ. Manag. J. **2016**(1) (2016)
63. Wendel, S.: Designing for behavior change: Applying psychology and behavioral economics. O'Reilly Media (2020)
64. Wenker, K.: A systematic literature review on persuasive technology at the workplace. Patterns **3**(8) (2022)
65. Wickramasinghe, G., Perera, A.: Effect of total productive maintenance practices on manufacturing performance: investigation of textile and apparel manufacturing firms. J. Manuf. Technol. Manag. **27**(5), 713–729 (2016)
66. Woods, C., Griffin, M.A., French, T., Hodkiewicz, M.: Using job characteristics to inform interface design for industrial maintenance procedures. In: Proceedings of the 2021 CHI Conference on Human Factors in Computing Systems, pp. 1–10 (2021)
67. Yun, R., Scupelli, P., Aziz, A., Loftness, V.: Sustainability in the workplace: nine intervention techniques for behavior change. In: Persuasive Technology: 8th International Conference, PERSUASIVE 2013, Sydney, NSW, Australia, April 3-5, 2013. Proceedings 8, pp. 253–265. Springer (2013)
68. Zheng, T., Ardolino, M., Bacchetti, A., Perona, M.: The applications of industry 4.0 technologies in manufacturing context: a systematic literature review. Int. J. Prod. Res. **59**(6), 1922–1954 (2021)

# Support for Building Relationships in Speed Dating Through Observation of Pre-dialogue Simulations Using Digital Twins

Yoko Ishii[✉], Ryo Ishii, Lidwina Andarini, Kazuya Matsuo, and Atsushi Otsuka

NTT Human Informatics Laboratories, 1-1-1 Hikarinooka, Yokosuka-shi, Kanagawa, Japan
{yoko.ishii,ryoct.ishii,lidwina.andarini,kazuya.matsuo, atsushi.otsuka}@ntt.com

**Abstract.** Advancements in science and technology have enabled communication beyond the constraints of time, distance, and physical limitations. In particular, the metaverse has facilitated interactions through avatars, and increasing attention is being given to "digital twins," which are nearly identical digital replicas of real-world entities. Digital twins allow for simulations, future predictions, and iterative analyses that would otherwise be costly in the real world. Among these, "human digital twins" are particularly promising, with potential applications in personalized treatments based on individual characteristics, medical history, and real-time physiological data, as well as behavioral simulations. This study examines the potential application of human digital twin technology in interpersonal relationship-building. Establishing positive human relationships is crucial for well-being, contributing to reduced feelings of isolation and an improved quality of life. In first-time interactions, mutual self-disclosure is typically a key process in deepening relationships. Human digital twins, which can communicate through both verbal and non-verbal cues, may help reduce psychological barriers in initial conversations. In this research, we investigated whether watching a conversation between digital twins before an initial meeting influences relationship formation, using a Speed Dating scenario. The experimental results suggest that viewing digital twin interactions promotes psychological readiness before face-to-face meetings and helps establish a foundation for familiarity with the other person. This study demonstrates the potential of digital twin technology in facilitating interpersonal relationship-building and opens new possibilities for digital communication.

**Keywords:** Digital Twin · Building Relationships · Speed Dating

## 1 Introduction

Advancements in science and technology have revolutionized communication, allowing individuals to connect beyond physical constraints, time, and distance. One of the most recent developments in this area is the metaverse, a virtual digital space where people interact through avatars. Within such environments, a near-identical digital representation of the real world is referred to as a Digital Twin [6]. Digital twins enable simulations of real-world scenarios, predictive analyses, and cost-effective testing that would otherwise be expensive or impractical in the physical world [4]. Recently, Human Digital Twin has been gathering attentions [10,24]. These digital representations of individuals can provide personalized healthcare recommendations based on medical history, physiological data, and behavioral patterns [20]. Additionally, they can simulate psychological and physical responses, offering valuable insights into decision-making and behavioral tendencies. This study explores how human digital twin technology can support interpersonal relationship building. Positive social connections are essential for well-being, as they help reduce feelings of loneliness and enhance overall quality of life [2]. Since human digital twins can engage in both verbal and non-verbal interactions, they may offer a new approach to facilitating relationship formation, particularly among strangers. This research experimentally examines the impact of providing individuals with feedback based on simulated conversations between their digital twins. Specifically, we investigate whether watching an interaction between digital twins prior to a face-to-face meeting enhances relationship-building in real-life conversations. A key scenario explored in this study is Speed Dating, where individuals meet potential partners in a structured setting. We assess whether observing digital twin interactions beforehand improves rapport and engagement during real-life encounters.

To achieve our research objectives, we focus on the following one research question:

**RQ: How Do Participants Perceive the Interaction Between Digital Twins?**

This research question explores how participants perceive their own and their partner's Human Digital Twin, as well as how they evaluate the pre-recorded digital twin conversation video. Additionally, it examines the impact of watching the digital twin interaction on relationship-building during subsequent face-to-face conversations. Through this analysis, we aim to clarify:

- How participants perceive their own and their partner's digital twin after watching the conversation video.
- How participants evaluate the digital twin interaction in terms of engagement, naturalness, and overall impression.
- Whether exposure to a digital twin interaction before an actual conversation influences relationship-building, including reducing anxiety, increasing familiarity, and improving interpersonal impressions.

By addressing these aspects, we can assess the effectiveness of digital twin-based social interaction models and their potential role in enhancing communication and interpersonal connections in real-world applications.

## 2 Related Work

### 2.1 Supporting Communication Between Strangers

Various approaches have been proposed to support communication between individuals meeting for the first time. For instance, some studies utilize pre-collected personal information to facilitate conversation and relationship building through the use of conversational agents.

Although not specifically focused on dyadic interactions like Speed Dating, research has explored the inclusion of robots in multi-party conversations to introduce topics and promote smoother discussions [19]. In this study, a robot collects and organizes participants' experiences, identifies semantic similarities, and forms shared narratives linked to personal photographs, thereby enhancing conversational engagement and fostering group cohesion. Additionally, Zhang's research demonstrated that humanoid robots can successfully act as facilitators to elicit deeper conversations [23]. While these studies effectively promote information exchange among users, some concerns have been raised that the presence of conversational agents might hinder natural human-to-human interactions, potentially suppressing direct communication. In contrast, the method proposed in this study ensures conversational freedom by allowing participants to observe an interaction between their respective digital twins (avatars) before engaging in a real-life dialogue. This approach minimizes the risk of suppressing direct human interaction, as the digital twin simulation occurs prior to the actual conversation.

In initial interactions between strangers, it has been reported that individuals tend to experience state anxiety, a temporary emotional state, more frequently than in conversations with friends [16]. This occurs because, in first-time encounters, individuals lack sufficient information about their conversation partners, leading to concerns such as "needing to pay extra attention to topics and speaking styles" or "struggling to find suitable conversation topics," which in turn makes the conversation feel more challenging. If these conversational difficulties can be alleviated, it may be possible to facilitate smooth interactions without the need for active intervention by robots or other agents. This study explores an approach that reduces conversational anxiety and enhances the natural flow of dialogue without direct external facilitation.

### 2.2 Digital Twin

Digital twin technology has been increasingly utilized in fields such as healthcare and sports as a method for real-time monitoring and simulation.

In the medical field, digital models are constructed based on individual patient data to monitor health conditions and simulate treatment effects [5,14].

In sports, digital twins are used for motion analysis and optimization of training programs, helping to enhance athletic performance [1]. Currently, the primary applications of digital twin technology focus on individual health and performance enhancement. However, there have been no direct applications aimed at facilitating interpersonal relationship building. This study introduces a novel application of digital twins by utilizing them to support human-to-human interactions, marking a unique contribution in this research area.

## 2.3 Human Digital Twin Reproduction

This study aims to develop a digital twin that replicates both the external and internal aspects of an individual. This section reviews related research on technologies for reproducing internal and external characteristics and identifies the requirements necessary for relationship-building digital twins based on existing studies.

**Reproducing Internal Aspects.** The internal aspect of a person refers to their experiences, memories, and preferences, which can be modeled to maintain a consistent personality and enable autonomous speech, allowing for natural conversations with dialogue partners [18]. Since internal characteristics are not directly visible, the reproduction process involves predicting, understanding, and accurately representing these attributes. Human internal states are shaped by complex interactions of values, thoughts, and sensitivities, which are deeply linked to brain functions. While there has been some success in measuring and reproducing specific aspects of these functions, achieving a fully comprehensive digital reproduction remains a significant challenge. Given this complexity, current mainstream approaches focus on using large-scale dialogue data to develop conversational systems capable of generating speech that closely resembles an individual's own speaking style [22].

This study follows this approach by utilizing personal dialogue data to construct a conversational system that accurately represents a person's speech characteristics, thus striving to replicate their internal attributes.

**Reproducing External Aspects.** A wide variety of methods utilizing generative AI have emerged for replicating a person's appearance and voice [12]. These technologies have enabled the creation of photorealistic avatars, making it possible to reproduce an individual's external features with high fidelity [8]. Research has also shown that when individuals control their own avatars (Virtual Doppelgnger), they experience an increased sense of connection and engagement with the avatar [11]. However, concerns have been raised regarding the privacy risks associated with the use of photorealistic avatars [9]. Since our research focuses on supporting relationship building between strangers, deploying photorealistic avatars without practical privacy safeguards could pose potential risks. To address these concerns, this study opts to reproduce avatars in a stylized anime-like deformed form rather than using fully photorealistic representations.

The external reproduction of a person is not limited to visual appearance but also includes gestures, body movements, and voice replication. For example, Yamaha has developed an AI system that learns and replicates the piano performances of the renowned pianist Glenn Gould, even allowing it to play pieces that he never performed himself [21]. Similarly, this study aims to reproduce gestures and voice characteristics as accurately as possible to enhance the realism of the digital twin's interactions.

## 3 System Structure

This section describes the system configuration designed to simulate conversations between individuals meeting for the first time. The overall data flow is illustrated in Fig. 1.

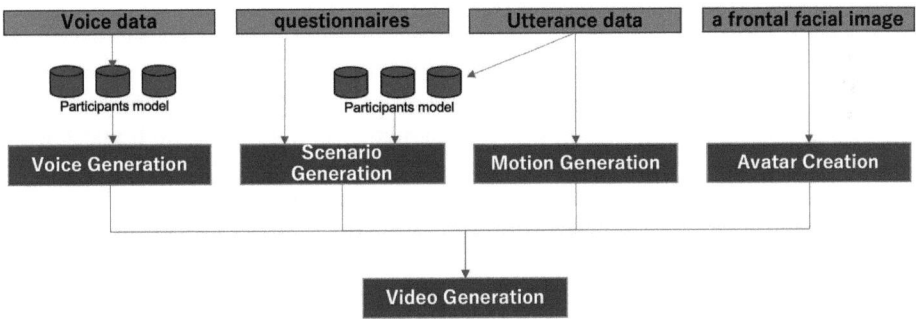

**Fig. 1.** The system architecture.

### 3.1 Reproducing Internal Aspects: Scenario Generation

This subsection explains the method for generating conversation scenarios between participants' digital twins as a means of reproducing their internal characteristics. For pretraining, we first developed a Persona Pair Prompt Dialogue Model [25], which is capable of generating contextually appropriate utterances based on participants ' profile information. This model was pretrained using a Transformer Encoder-Decoder architecture with 222M parameters [18], leveraging a dataset consisting of "Dialogue logs composed of multiple reply pairs from Twitter" and "Profile information inferred from reply content." To further personalize the model, we fine-tuned the pretrained model using transcriptions of past Speed Dating conversations conducted by each participant. This allowed us to adapt the model to each individual's unique conversational style, creating a separate fine-tuned model for each participant.

Since the model is trained to generate the next utterance based on an input prompt, it is essential to prepare the initial utterance that sets the topic for conversation. The topic of conversation varies depending on the first utterance, so we selected seven topics that are commonly discussed during profile exchanges in Speed Dating scenarios. These topics are listed in Table 2, under "Profile Information" (1: About Personal). Before the experiment, each participant's responses to these seven topics were collected. For each topic, an initial utterance was manually created. Using this initial utterance, the model simulates Speaker A's response, which is then input into Speaker B's model to generate a reply. This iterative process continues, producing a sequence of ten utterances per topic. Finally, the generated dialogues from all seven topics are concatenated to form a complete conversation scenario. Since some generated dialogue contained incoherent or meaningless segments, these were manually reviewed and removed. Additionally, grammatical errors (e.g., incorrect use of particles) were manually corrected. Table 1 presents an example of an output scenario. In this example, the A1 utterance was manually created to confirm B's preference for driving and theme park dates, as indicated in B's pre-experiment responses. Although the scenarios were originally generated in Japanese, they were translated into English for use in the study. Three different conversation scenarios were generated each pair of participants, and after manual refinement, the one with the highest word count was selected for video generation.

To encourage relationship-building, two random topics from the conversation were selected, and a next-meeting proposal was added at the end of the dialogue. For instance, in Table 1, after the final utterance by A, the following dialogue was appended:

B: "Would you like to visit Yasaka Shrine together sometime?" (Proposal)
A: "Sounds great! I'll check my schedule for the weekend." (Acceptance)

Both A-to-B and B-to-A proposal-acceptance patterns were incorporated into different conversation scenarios to ensure variation.

Each utterance in the revised scenario was annotated with an emotional label: Happy, Surprised, Sad, Angry, or Neutral. This was done using ChatGPT-3.5, which assigned emotions to each utterance.

**Table 1.** Example of scenario output.

| |
|---|
| A1: By the way, you want to go on a drive or a theme park date, right? |
| B: Yeah, that's right. I like going on drives too. |
| A: I like driving as well. Is there anywhere you want to go? |
| B: Hmm, lately, I've been thinking about going to Kyoto. |
| A: That sounds nice. Kyoto has a stylish vibe. |
| B: Yeah, exactly. I'd love to visit some temples there too. |
| A: Temples are great. Also, the area around Kiyomizu-dera is nice. |
| B: Kiyomizu-dera has such a great atmosphere, doesn't it? |
| A: Yeah, it really does. And Yasaka Shrine in Kyoto is also nice. |
| B: Yasaka Shrine? I'd love to go there too. |
| A: Yeah, Yasaka Shrine in Kyoto is really great. |

## 3.2 Reproducing External Aspects: Avatar Creation, Voice Synthesis, and Motion Generation

Avatars were generated in VRM format based on a frontal image of the participant. The system extracted facial features, hairstyle, hair color, and skin tone to create an avatar resembling the participant. Movements were generated using motion synthesis technology based on speech text and video data. A model was trained on facial expressions and gestures, allowing it to generate corresponding movements from text inputs. This study adopts the approach of generating movements from text-based information [7]. This method is implemented using a machine learning approach trained on paired data consisting of speech text and full-body motion labels collected from several dozen hours of real human conversations. The trained model generates full-body motion labels for each word in the input utterance text. Based on these motion labels, natural and human-like avatar movements are achieved. Facial expressions were adjusted to match the emotion labels assigned to each utterance. Although personalized motion synthesis would ideally be based on each participant's actual movement data, collecting such data would require a large dataset. Therefore, as an initial implementation, a sample individual's motion data was used, and model customization for each participant was not conducted in this study.

## 3.3 Video Generation

For video generation, the emotion-annotated conversation scenario was processed as follows: The speaking speed and interval between utterances were manually adjusted for each utterance. The avatar's voice and movements were generated according to the annotated dialogue. All settings were pre-recorded in a YAML file for processing. Using Unreal Engine, two avatars were placed in a virtual space, and the YAML file was loaded to synchronize speech, motion, and gestures for each utterance. When an avatar spoke, the dialogue was also displayed in a speech bubble. A separate video was generated for each participant pair, with an average length of 34 min. An example of the final output is shown in Fig. 2.

**Fig. 2.** Examples of the video capture.

## 4 Experiment

### 4.1 Target Conversations and Participants

This study focuses on speed-dating conversations between men and women meeting for the first time. Participants were seeking connections through speed dating, and were recruited from the general public, targeting those in their 20s to 40s, which is the typical age range for speed-dating events. After each conversation, participants were asked whether they wished to exchange contact information with their conversation partner. A match was considered successful only if both participants mutually agreed to exchange their contact details. For this experiment, participants engaged in two conditions:

Video Condition: Participants watched a pre-recorded video of a conversation between their respective digital twins before engaging in real-life dialogue.

No-Video Condition: Participants did not watch the digital twin conversation before their interaction.

Participants were selected from those who had previously contributed data for training the personalized conversation models used in this study.

A total of 16 male and 16 female participants (native Japanese speakers) were recruited. The mean age of the female participants was 35.4 years (SD = 6.5), and the mean age of the male participants was 35.2 years (SD = 5.9). Each participant was paired with a completely new partner whom they had not interacted with before. During the experiment, each participant engaged in four conversations with different partners, with two conversations conducted under the Video Condition and two under the No-Video Condition. In total, 32 trials were conducted for each condition. To minimize order effects, the sequence of Video Condition and No-Video Condition trials was randomized as much as possible for each participant.

### 4.2 Experimental Procedure

The experimental procedure is illustrated in Fig. 3. The questionnaires labeled 18 in Fig. 3 are explained in the next section. In both the Video Condition and No-Video Condition, participants first created and verified their avatars. The avatar was generated based on facial features, hairstyle, hair color, and skin tone extracted from a frontal facial image. Participants were also allowed to manually select or modify these features as they preferred. Thirteen types of clothing were provided, and participants could select their preferred outfit. Additionally, if a participant requested a color change for their clothing, it was accommodated. After creating their avatars, participants engaged in a 10-minute avatar interaction session, where their avatars mirrored their movements and facial expressions in real-time via a PC camera. This allowed participants to verify the behavior and appearance of their avatars. WebcamMotionCapture[1] was used for this step.

---

[1] https://webcammotioncapture.info/.

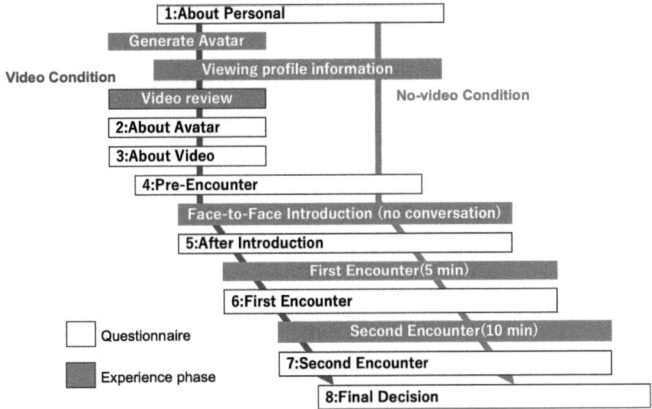

**Fig. 3.** Flow of the Experiment.

Participants reviewed their conversation partner's profile information before the dialogue session. The 21 profile attributes displayed were based on the questionnaire categories listed in Table 2, specifically under "Profile Information" in 1: About Personal Questionnaire.

Participants in the Video Condition watched a pre-recorded video of a conversation between their own digital twin and their partner's digital twin before meeting in person. Both participants in a pair viewed the same video featuring their respective avatars. After watching the video (for the Video Condition) or after profile viewing (for the No-Video Condition), participants met their conversation partner in person for the first time. At this stage, no conversation was allowed between them yet.

Subsequently, participants engaged in two face-to-face conversation sessions: the first session lasted 5 min, and the second session lasted 10 min. The conversation topics were not restricted, allowing participants to talk freely.

The questionnaire items used in this experiment are summarized in Tables 2, 3. Each questionnaire was administered at specific stages of the experiment, as shown in Fig. 3. "2: About Avatar" and "3: About Video" were conducted only for the Video Condition. After all four conversation sessions were completed (8: Final Decision), participants ranked their conversation partners in order of preference (14) based on their impressions. Additionally, participants indicated whether they wished to exchange contact information with each conversation partner (Table 3).

Most survey items were rated on a 6-point Likert scale, with responses ranging from: 6-Strongly Agree, 5-Agree, 4-Slightly Agree, 3-Slightly Disagree, 2-Disagree, 1-Strongly Disagree. To assess participants' emotional responses toward their conversation partners, this study employed the Love-Liking Scale [15], which distinguishes affection (love) from attraction (liking) when evaluating interpersonal impressions.

**Table 2.** List of questionnaires (Before Introduction).

| Type | Content<br>Bold indicates category, numbers in () indicate the number of questions | Response Format |
|---|---|---|
| 1: About Personal | **Topic Generation (7)**: Hobbies, special skills, favorite visual works, favorite music, how to spend holidays, recent personal trends, preferred date locations. | Free response |
| | **Profile Information (21)**: Age, residential area, place of birth, height, blood type, highest educational attainment, occupation, workplace, holidays, annual income, family, presence of pets, cohabitation status, marital history, presence of children, smoking habits, drinking habits, desired marriage timing, preferred partner type, top 3 favorite things, topics they would like to talk about. | Mainly free response (presence/absence questions use selection options) |
| | **Motivation (2)**: Excitement about getting to know others, I want to exchange contact information. | 6-point scale |
| 2: About Avatar | **About Self-Avatar (15)**: human-like appearance/movement/speech/tone/voice, feel unnatural about appearance/movement/speech/tone/voice, resemble yourself about appearance/movement/speech/tone/voice | 6-point scale |
| | **About Partner's Avatar (10)**: human-like appearance/movement/speech/tone/voice, feel unnatural about appearance/movement/speech/tone/voice | 6-point scale |
| | **Expectations for Partner (5)**: Do you expect the partner's [A] to be close to yours? (A refers to appearance, movement, speech content, tone, voice.) | 6-point scale |
| 3: About Video | **Content Comprehension (3)**: Was the conversation atmosphere good? Was the conversation engaging? Was the content understandable? | 6-point scale |
| 4: Pre-Encounter | **About the Conversation (14)**: Expected enjoyment, seriousness, relaxation, satisfaction, good atmosphere, motivation, concentration, interest, friendliness, engagement, nervousness, anxiety, expectations, confidence in good conversation. | 6-point scale |
| | **About the Partner (6)**: Likelihood of getting along, desire to know more, nervousness about meeting, anxiety about meeting, expectations, excitement about meeting. | 6-point scale |
| | **About Shared Topics (4)**: Found a common topic, ease of imagining conversation reduced anxiety/nervousness. | 6-point scale |
| | **Feeling of Being Understood (4)**: Felt understood, feeling of reassurance increased/decreased anxiety/nervousness. | 6-point scale |
| | **Information About the Partner (6)**: Understood well, could predict appearance/movement/speech/tone/voice. | 6-point scale |
| | **Expectations for Dialogue (3)**: ability to expand topics, ability to develop conversation, expectation of mutual self-disclosure. | 6-point scale |

**Table 3.** List of questionnaires (After Introduction).

| Type | Content  Bold indicates category, numbers in () indicate the number of questions | Response Format |
|---|---|---|
| 5: After Introduction | **Same items as 4: Pre-Encounter Questionnaires** | 6-point scale |
| 6: First Encounter | **Same items as 4: Pre-Encounter Questionnaires** | 6-point scale |
| | **Love-Liking Scale (26)** | 6-point scale |
| 7: Second Encounter | **Same items as 4: Pre-Encounter Questionnaires** | 6-point scale |
| | **Love-Liking Scale (26)** | 6-point scale |
| 8: Final decision | **Ranking of Conversation Partners (1)**: Rank the conversation partners. | 1–4 |
| | **Exchange of Contact Information (1)**: Would you exchange contact details? | yes/no |

## 5 Result

This paper presents the analysis results based on the following perspectives:

- How participants perceive their own and their partner's digital twin after watching the video.
- How participants evaluate the digital twin interaction in terms of engagement, naturalness, and overall impression.
- Whether exposure to a digital twin interaction before an actual conversation influences relationship-building, including reducing anxiety, increasing familiarity, and improving interpersonal impressions.

By addressing these aspects, we can assess the effectiveness of digital twin-based social interaction models and their potential role in enhancing communication and interpersonal connections in real-world applications.

### 5.1 Responses from Participants

To generate digital twin conversation models, we re-invited participants who had previously taken part in Speed Dating experiments. Some of these participants had high motivation to exchange contact information in the past but might have had lower motivation in the current experiment.

To exclude participants with low motivation, we removed those who answered 3 or below on the motivation category question "I want to exchange contact information." from "Motivation" in 1: About Personal Questionnaire (Table 2). As a result, 14 male and 15 female participants provided valid responses, leading to a total of 116 trials (58 trials in the Video Condition/58 trials in the No-Video Condition).

Among the valid responses, 47 trials included at least one participant who wanted to exchange contact information, and 6 pairs mutually agreed to exchange contact details.

All analysis results shown in the following figures represent mean rating scores, with error bars indicating standard error.

## 5.2 How Did Participants Perceive Their Own Digital Twin and Their Partner's Digital Twin? (2:About Avatar)

To examine how participants perceived their own avatar and their partner's avatar, we analyzed 2: About Avatar results. As shown in Table 4, the human-likeness of both self and partner avatars was rated neutral across all attributes (appearance, movement, speech, tone, and voice). There was no significant difference in perceived unnaturalness, though self-avatars showed a slight tendency toward higher discomfort compared to partner avatars. Similarly, no significant difference was found in how much the self-avatar resembled the participant, but movement ratings were slightly lower than other attributes, with overall evaluations remaining neutral (Table 5).

**Table 4.** Result of 2: About Avatar Questionnaires(human-like, feel unnatural.

| Questionnaires | About self avatar M(SD) | About partner's Avatar M(SD) |
|---|---|---|
| Human-like appearance | 3.89(1.11) | 3.86(1.02) |
| Human-like movement | 3.45(1.21) | 3.51(1.11) |
| Human-like speech | 3.85(1.25) | 3.91(1.12) |
| Human-like tone | 3.74(1.23) | 3.81(1.10) |
| Human-like voice | 3.65(1.25) | 3.80(1.10) |
| Feel unnatural about appearance | 3.73(1.18) | 3.25(1.16) |
| Feel unnatural about movement | 3.86(1.22) | 3.45(1.05) |
| Feel unnatural about speech | 3.90(1.45) | 3.09(1.23) |
| Feel unnatural about tone | 3.48(1.35) | 3.08(1.14) |
| Feel unnatural about voice | 3.23(1.34) | 2.95(1.15) |

## 5.3 How Did Participants Perceive the Video?3: About Video Questionnaires

This section reports how participants in the Video Condition perceived the pre-recorded digital twin conversation videos (Table 6). These results indicate a slightly positive perception of the conversation atmosphere and engagement level between the avatars. The high rating for the question "Was the content understandable?" suggests that participants found the conversation content easy to understand.

**Table 5.** Result of 2: About Avatar Questionnaires(resemble themselves).

| Questionnaires | M(SD) |
|---|---|
| Resemble yourself about appearance | 3.16(1.25) |
| Resemble yourself about movement | 2.70(1.04) |
| Resemble yourself about speech | 3.24(1.35) |
| Resemble yourself about tone | 3.25(1.43) |
| Resemble yourself about voice | 3.46(1.63) |

**Table 6.** Result of 3: About Video Questionnaires.

| Questionnaires | M(SD) |
|---|---|
| Was the conversation atmosphere good? | 3.83(1.26) |
| Was the conversation engaging? | 3.58(1.31) |
| Was the content understandable? | 4.75(1.08) |

### 5.4 Differences in Pre-conversation Feelings4: Pre-encounter, 5: After Introduction

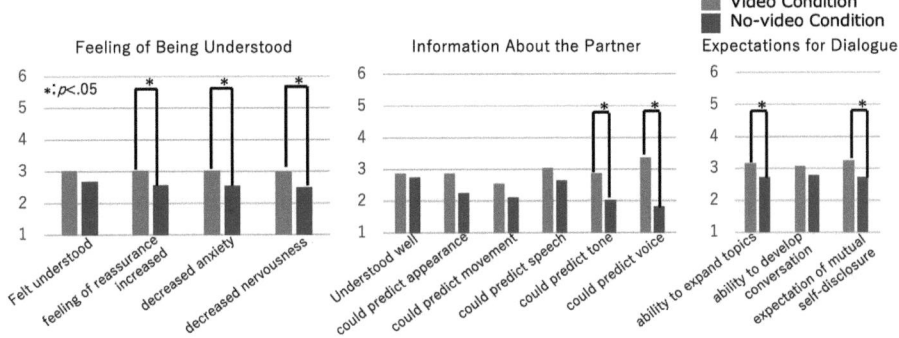

**Fig. 4.** Result of 4: Pre-Encounter Questionnaires.

To examine differences in pre-conversation feelings between the Video Condition and No-Video Condition, we analyzed their responses to 4: Pre-Encounter and 5: After Introduction.

A t-test comparing the Video Condition and No-Video Condition showed significant differences.

4: Pre-Encounter Questionnaires:
- "Feeling of Being Understood"
  In "feeling of reassurance increased, t(114) = −2.36, p = .02", "decreased anxiety, t(114) = −2.45, p = .01", "decreased nervousness, t(114) = −2.46, p = .016", the Video Condition had significantly higher ratings (Left of Fig. 4).

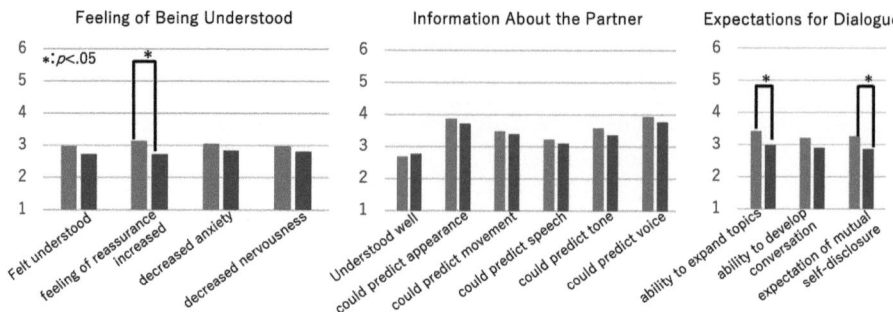

**Fig. 5.** Result of 5: After Introduction Questionnaires.

- "Information About the Partner"
  In "could predict appearance, t(114) = −2.56, p = .012", "could predict tone, t(114) = −3.66, p = .00", "could predict voice, t(114) = −7.69, p = .00", the Video Condition had significantly higher ratings (Middle of Fig. 4).
- "Expectations for Dialogue"
  "ability to expand topics, t(114) = −2.42, p = .017", "expectation of mutual self-disclosure, t(114) = −3.2, p = .00", the Video Condition had significantly higher ratings (Right of Fig. 4).

5: After Introduction Questionnaires:
- "feeling of Being understood" and "Expectations for Dialogue":
  Higher expectations that "feeling of reassurance increased, t(114) = −2.02, p = .046", "The partner will expand the conversation well, t(114) = −2.1, p = .038" and "The partner will match my level of self-disclosure, t(114) = −2.06, p = .041" (Fig. 5).

### 5.5 Effect on Impression of Conversation Partner 6: First Encounter, 7: Second Encounter: Love-Liking Scale

To examine differences in impressions of conversation partners, we analyzed responses from the Past-Conversation Questionnaires using the Love-Liking Scale. Specifically, we examined the following two sessions:

6: First Encounter Questionnaires:
- "Love Scale"
  No significant difference (t(114) = −0.46, p> .05).
- "Liking Scale"
  Significantly higher in the Video Condition (t(114) = −2.00, p = .04).

7: Second Encounter Questionnaires:
- "Love Scale"
  No significant difference (t(114) = −0.36, p> .05).
- "Liking Scale"
  significant difference (t(114) = −1.46, p> .05).

These results indicate that the Video Condition had significantly higher "liking" scores after the first conversation, but the difference disappeared after the second conversation.

## 5.6  8: Final Decision

Participants interacted with four conversation partners in totaltwo under the Video Condition and two under the No Video Condition. After completing all interactions, they ranked the four partners from 1 to 4 based on their overall impressions, with 1 indicating the most favorable impression. The number of participants assigned to each rank is shown in the Fig. 6. The Wilcoxon signed-rank test was conducted to compare the mean ranks. A significant difference was found between the video condition (Mean = 2.2, SD = 0.7) and the no-video condition (Mean = 2.8, SD = 0.7), $Z = -2.4$, $p = .016$. These results suggest that the average rank of impressions toward the conversational partner was significantly higher in the video condition than in the no-video condition.

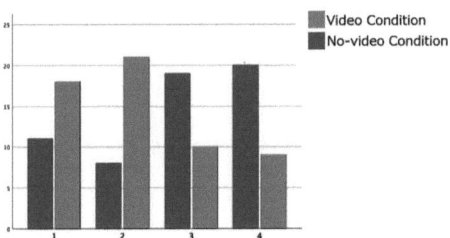

**Fig. 6.** Result of Rank the conversation partners.

Next, regarding contact information exchange, among the valid responses, 47 trials included at least one participant who wanted to exchange contact information, and 6 pairs mutually agreed to exchange details.

## 6  Discussion

### 6.1  RQ:How Do Participants Perceive the Interaction Between Digital Twins?

In this study, we constructed digital twins that replicate both internal and external aspects of participants. This section discusses how accurately the digital twins reflected the actual individuals and how participants perceived these interactions.

According to the analysis results from 2: About Avatar Questionnaires, participants did not strongly perceive their avatars as unnatural or dissimilar to themselves. However, they also did not feel a strong resemblance, suggesting a neutral perception of similarity. Additionally, participants' evaluation of the conversation atmosphere and engagement in the digital twin interaction video was neutral. The conversation content was well understood, indicating that the dialogue was coherent and comprehensible. Furthermore, participants who watched the digital twin interaction video did not express any negative opinions about it. Instead, their responses reflected a generally positive perception, suggesting that they accepted the digital twin interaction without resistance.

In the Video Condition, higher expectations that "I can predict the partner's tone", "I can predict the partner's voice", "The partner will expand the conversation well", and "The partner will match my level of self-disclosure". Furthermore, "feeling of reassurance increased", "decreased anxiety", "decreased nervousness" were significantly higher compared to the No-Video Condition. These findings suggest that viewing the digital twin conversation before the interaction helped participants gather information about their conversation partner, thereby reducing pre-conversation anxiety. Consequently, participants in the Video Condition felt more at ease, experienced lower nervousness and anxiety, and were less likely to feel situational anxiety compared to those in the No-Video Condition. Additionally, the expectations for the conversation were also higher in the Video Condition, as participants expected that their partner would expand the conversation effectively and self-disclose appropriately. This indicates that watching the digital twin interaction may have helped facilitate psychological preparation before the actual conversation. Moreover, in the Liking Scale, the Video Condition showed significantly higher ratings after the first conversation session, suggesting that watching the digital twin conversation video was effective in establishing a foundation for mutual familiarity and rapport.

However, this significant difference decreased or disappeared after the second conversation session. This is likely because as participants engaged in repeated conversations, their understanding of their conversation partner naturally increased. This does not indicate that the effect of the Video Condition's pre-exposure to the conversation was lost, but rather that the No-Video Condition eventually caught up in terms of familiarity and reduced anxiety.

Since the average impression rank toward the conversational partner was significantly lower in the video condition, it can be inferred that participants formed more positive impressions compared to the no-video condition. This can likely be attributed to at least two key factors:

**Reduced Psychological Burden.** As discussed earlier, participants in the Video Condition likely experienced lower state anxiety, which may have alleviated the psychological burden of engaging in conversation. This may have allowed them to communicate in a more relaxed manner, leading to a more positive impression of their partner. The relationship between mood and judgment consistency has been widely studied in social psychology [3]. Based on these studies, it is plausible that participants who experienced lower anxiety and a more positive mood were also more likely to form positive impressions of their conversation partners.

**Influence of the Conversation Scenario.** Another possible factor influencing the results is the content of the pre-recorded conversation scenario shown to the Video Condition.

In the Video Condition's digital twin conversation, a "next meeting proposal" was intentionally included at the end of the interaction. This type of dialogue explicitly conveys the intention to advance the relationship, potentially fostering a sense of mutual acceptance between the participants. Additionally, the scenario topics were generated based on "Profile Information" (1: About Personal questionnaires), leading to a structure in which both participants engaged in self-disclosure throughout the conversation. Watching this self-disclosure process may have had a positive impact on their impression of their conversation partner. Previous research on initial conversations has shown that mutual self-disclosure leads to higher levels of liking and intimacy between individuals [17]. A similar mechanism may have been at play in this study, where observing their partner's positive and open attitude in the video contributed to a more favorable impression during the actual conversation.

Although this study demonstrated that viewing a pre-recorded digital twin conversation influences impressions, it remains unclear which specific factors contributed the most to the positive perception of conversation partners. Further research is needed to isolate and analyze the precise factors that drive this effect.

## 6.2 Ethical Implications

Potential negative impacts such as the ethical implications of voice cloning and discomfort caused by AI-replicated identities must be taken into account. Recent studies have reported that current speech generation technologies can exhibit performance disparities across accents, inadvertently reinforcing linguistic privilege and posing risks of digital exclusion [29]. Hutiri et al. conducted a comprehensive study that systematically categorizes the ethical and safety concerns associated with such technologies [28]. Complementing this work, ongoing research is also exploring technical safeguards aimed at preventing the misuse of voice cloning technology [30,31]. In our own experiment, as described in Sect. 5.2, participants did not report negative reactions toward their AI-generated avatars. The evaluations were largely neutral, and no explicit signs of discomfort or psychological distress were observed. However, such responses are likely to be context-dependent, influenced by the content of the speech and the situational environment. This highlights the importance of careful design and contextual sensitivity in future applications. Especially when deploying these technologies in real-world systems or commercial services, particular attention must be paid to issues of user consent and the explainability of replicated personas. Therefore, this study also emphasizes the need to further strengthen ethical risk assessments and to establish a more robust framework for ensuring informed consent.

## 6.3 Limitation

This study has several limitations. First, the participant sample16 Japanese men and 16 Japanese womenwas relatively small and culturally specific. Caution is therefore warranted when attempting to generalize the findings to broader cultural contexts. Notably, the study is grounded in the Japanese cultural context. Previous research suggests that participants' cognition and interpersonal evaluations may be shaped by culture-specific biases [26,27]. According to Markus et al., East Asian cultures are typically characterized by an interdependent self-construal, whereas Western cultures tend to emphasize an independent self-construal [26]. These cultural differences imply that the findings of this study may not be directly applicable to Western societies. Consequently, future research should aim to verify the replicability of these effects in other cultural contexts and explore the underlying psychological mechanisms. Second, it remains unclear whether the effects observed in this study persist in real-life relationship building following first encounters, or in long-term interpersonal evaluations. To address this issue, further research should involve larger sample sizes and employ evaluation tasks conducted over an extended period.

# 7 Conclusion

This study explored the application of digital twin technology to support initial face-to-face interactions, particularly in Speed Dating scenarios. By constructing digital twins that replicate both internal (personality, dialogue style) and external (appearance, voice, and movement) characteristics, we examined their impact on pre-conversation emotions, partner impressions, and interpersonal relationship building. This study suggests that digital twin interactions can enhance relationship-building processes by reducing pre-conversation anxiety and facilitating psychological preparation. Additionally, by observing their partner's digital twin engage in a friendly and engaging conversation, participants may develop a more positive first impression before meeting in person. However, while the Video Condition showed initial advantages, these effects diminished over time, indicating that natural human interaction eventually bridges the gap. Future research should investigate which specific factors in digital twin interactions contribute most to positive partner impressions, as well as explore the long-term effects of digital twin-based interactions in various social settings. This study demonstrates the potential of avatar-based dialogue simulations in enhancing interpersonal relationships and reducing the difficulties of first-time interactions. Moving forward, integrating more dynamic self-expression and real-time adaptation in digital twins could further improve their effectiveness in real-world applications, such as social networking, online matchmaking, and professional networking scenarios.

# References

1. Barricelli, B.R., Casiraghi, E., Gliozzo, J., Petrini, A., Valtolina, S.: Human digital twin for fitness management. IEEE Access **8**, 26637–26664 (2020)
2. Diener, E., Seligman, M.E.P.: Very happy people. Psychol. Sci. **13**(1), 81–84 (2002)
3. Forgas, J.P.: Mood and judgment: the affect infusion model (AIM). Psychol. Bull. **117**(1), 39–66 (1995)
4. Fuller, A., Fan, Z., Day, C., Barlow, C.: Digital twin: enabling technologies, challenges and open research. IEEE Access **8**, 108952–108971 (2020). https://doi.org/10.1109/ACCESS.2020.2998358
5. Gabrielli, S., Piras, E.M., Ibarra, O.: Digital twins in the future design of digital therapeutics. In: Adjunct Proceedings of the 2023 ACM International Joint Conference on Pervasive and Ubiquitous Computing and the 2023 ACM International Symposium on Wearable Computing (UbiComp/ISWC '23 Adjunct), pp. 602–605 (2023)
6. Grieves, M., Vickers, J.: Digital twin: mitigating unpredictable, undesirable emergent behavior in complex systems. In: Kahlen, J., Flumerfelt, S., Alves, A. (eds.) Transdisciplinary Perspectives on Complex Systems, pp. 85–113. Springer, Cham (2017)
7. Ishii, R., Higashinaka, R., et al.: Methods of efficiently constructing text-dialogue-agent system using existing anime character. J. Inf. Process. **29**, 30–44 (2021)
8. Li, Z., Zheng, Z., Wang, L., Liu, Y.: Animatable gaussians: learning Pose-dependent Gaussian Maps for High-fidelity Human Avatar Modeling, Proceedings of the IEEE/CVF Conference on Computer Vision and Pattern Recognition (CVPR), pp. 19711–19722,(2024)
9. Lin, J., Latoschik, M.E.: Digital body, identity and privacy in social virtual reality: a systematic review; Virtual Reality, vol. 3 (2022)
10. Lin, Y., Chen, L., Ali, A., et al.: Human digital twin: a survey. J. Cloud Comp. **13**, 131 (2024)
11. Lucas, G., Szablowski, E., et al.: The effect of operating a virtual doppleganger in a 3D simulation; MIG '16, pp. 167–174 (2016)
12. Mirsky, Y., Lee, W.: The creation and detection of deepfakes: a survey. ACM Comput. Surv. **54**(1), 7 (2022)
13. Otsuchi, S., Ishii, Y., et al.: Prediction of interlocutors' subjective impressions based on functional head-movement features in group meetings. In: ICMI2021, pp. 352–360 (2021)
14. Papachristou, K., Katsakiori, P.F., Papadimitroulas, P., Strigari, L., Kagadis, G.C.: Digital twins' advancements and applications in healthcare, towards precision medicine. J. Personalized Med. **14**(11), 1101 (2024). https://doi.org/10.3390/jpm14111101
15. Rubin, Z.: Measurement of romantic love. J. Pers. Soc. Psychol. **16**, 265–273 (1970)
16. Sasaki, Y.: Study on the relationship between state-anxiety and Agari of Japanese college students and their living-abroad experiences and self-construals in dyadic conversations with strangers and friends. Jpn. J. Commun. Stud. **52**(1), 41–64 (2023)
17. Sprecher, S., Treger, S.: The benefits of turn-taking reciprocal self-disclosure in get-acquainted interactions. Personal Relat. **22**(3), 460–475 (2015)
18. Sugiyama, H., Mizukami, M., et al.: Empirical analysis of training strategies of transformer-based Japanese chit-chat systems. In: SLT2022, pp. 685–691 (2023)

19. Uchida, T., Ishiguro, H., Dominey, P.F.: Improving quality of life with a narrative robot companion: II – creating group cohesion via shared narrative experience. In: 2020 29th IEEE International Conference on Robot and Human Interactive Communication (RO-MAN), pp. 906–913 (2020)
20. Vallée, A.: Digital twin for healthcare systems. Front. Digit. Health **5**, 1253050 (2023). https://doi.org/10.3389/fdgth.2023.1253050
21. Yamaha.: Yamaha Dear Glenn Project AI System Gives Concert in Style of Legendary Pianist Glenn Gould at Ars Electronica Festival; Retrieved from (2019)
22. Saizheng Zhang, S., Dinan, E., Urbanek, J., Szlam, A., Kiela, D., Weston, J.: Personalizing Dialogue agents: i have a dog, do you have pets too?. In: Proceedings of the 56th Annual Meeting of the Association for Computational Linguistics (Volume 1: Long Papers), pp. 2204–2213 (2018)
23. Zhang, A.W., Lin, T.-H., Zhao, X., Sebo, S.: IceBreaking technology: robots and computers can foster meaningful connections between strangers through in-person conversations. In: Proceedings of the 2023 CHI Conference on Human Factors in Computing Systems, pp. 1–14 (2023)
24. Lauer-Schmaltz, M., Cash, P., Hansen, J., Maier, A.: Towards the Human Digital Twin: Definition and Design - A survey, pp. 1–30. Ithaca, NY (2024)
25. Otsuka, A., Matsuo, K., Ishii, R., Nomoto, N., Augiyama, H.: User-Specific Dialogue Generation with User Profile-Aware Pre-Training Model and Parameter-Efficient Fine-Tuning. arXiv preprint arXiv:2409.00887 (2024)
26. Markus, H.R., Kitayama, S.: Culture and the self: implications for cognition, emotion, and motivation. Psychol. Rev. **98**, 224–253 (1991)
27. Varnum, M.E., Grossmann, I., Kitayama, S., Nisbett R.E.: The origin of cultural differences in cognition: evidence for the social orientation hypothesis. Curr. Dir. Psychol. Sci. **19**(1), 9–13 (2019)
28. Hutiri, W., Papakyriakopoulos, O., Xiang, A.: Not my voice! A taxonomy of ethical and safety harms of speech generators. In: Proceedings of the 2024 ACM Conference on Fairness, Accountability, and Transparency (FAccT '24). Association for Computing Machinery, New York, NY, USA, pp. 359–376 (2024)
29. Michel, S., Kaur, S., Gillespie, S.E., Gleason, J., Wilson, C., Ghosh, A.: It's not a representation of me: Examining Accent Bias and Digital Exclusion in Synthetic AI Voice Services (2025). arXiv:2504.09346
30. Bird, J.J., Lotfi, A.: Real-time Detection of AI-Generated Speech for DeepFake Voice Conversion, (2025). arXiv:2308.12734
31. Sakka, S., Liagkou, V., Stylios, C.: Preserving Voice Message Integrity: Strategies Against AI Cloning, Reliability and Statistics in Transportation and Communication: Human Sustainability and Resilience in the Digital Age. RelStat 2024. Lecture Notes in Networks and Systems, vol. 1337, pp. 443–452 (2025)

# When Design Collaboration Goes Remote: Intermediate-Level Knowledge for Empowering Remote Co-exploration

Xinhui Ye[✉], Joep Frens, and Jun Hu

Eindhoven University of Technology, Eindhoven, The Netherlands
{x.ye, j.w.frens, j.hu}@tue.nl

**Abstract.** The rise of remote work has reshaped how design teams collaborate, introducing challenges in replicating the benefits of in-person collaboration. As remote collaboration normalized, accelerated by the COVID-19 pandemic, new challenges emerged that had previously gone unnoticed. Among these, designers report the loss of co-exploration, the experience of iteratively exploring prototypes, ideas, and concepts together. Prior research has identified five patterns of co-exploration, demonstrating its functional and social value in collaborative design. However, because that research was conducted in educational settings, it remains unclear whether the five co-exploration patterns also reflect the experiences of professional designers, and how such co-exploration should be supported in remote design activities based on expert perspectives. To explore these questions, we interviewed design experts to examine how the five co-exploration patterns apply in both co-located and remote settings. While they described a variety of challenges in remote collaboration, our analysis showed how remote collaboration affects both the execution and quality of co-exploration. These findings informed a speculative ideation process, in which experts used Inspiration Cards to propose solutions grounded in practice. Their insights revealed the importance of shaping conditions that support co-exploration through the coordinated use of people, materials, and interactions. These findings led to the development of the Designing Tools for Co-exploration (DTC) guideline, which provides intermediate-level design knowledge to guide tool creation and help design teams strengthen their collaborative practices.

**Keywords:** Remote design collaboration · Co-exploration · Designerly activity · Expert interview · Design guidelines

## 1 Introduction

In the post-COVID-19 era, remote work has become increasingly common, offering the opportunity to collaborate with talented individuals worldwide while saving on travel time (and cost) and reducing our carbon footprint [24]. However, the effectiveness of remote collaboration, particularly in creative industries, remains a point of debate. Industries that thrive on collective creativity and physical interaction struggle to replicate the dynamics of co-located collaboration. In design, remote collaboration presents challenges; researchers such as Ostergaard and Summers emphasized that distributed design teams require targeted and specialized support compared to collocated teams [46].

Comparative studies on remote and co-located design collaboration highlight these challenges. Remote collaboration tends to reduce engagement, limits ideation, and complicates communication between team members. For example, designers working remotely may produce fewer design alternatives [20] and use fewer gestures [13]. To mitigate these challenges, researchers in Human-Computer Interaction (HCI) and Computer-Supported Cooperative Work (CSCW) have developed various tools that bring back qualities of in-person collaboration benefits. These tools support a variety of activities such as remote co-sketching [54], physical interactions with design materials [23,53], sharing work-in-progress in online communities [30], and enabling informal communication before and after formal meetings [26]. While these tools are valuable, such task-specific solutions often fall short of addressing the full complexity of remote design collaboration. More specifically, Idi and Khaidzir emphasized that design collaboration involves multidisciplinary aspects, which encompasses not only communication, technology, and social interaction, but also design theories, processes, and methods [28].

Fifteen years after Gary and Judith Olson's foundational work "Distance Matters" [45], Bjørn et al. revisited the question of whether distance still matters in light of technological advances and evolving work practices [4]. As remote work has become even more prevalent, particularly post-COVID-19, this question is more relevant than ever. Following this work, we focused on the design field to investigate emerging challenges that had previously gone unnoticed. Recent research by Ye et al. highlighted a loss of co-exploration in remote design teams, the experience of iteratively exploring prototypes, ideas, and concepts together [56]. They called for attention to co-exploration when designing tools for remote collaboration. Our study responds to this call, seeking to understand how co-exploration can be effectively supported.

This paper presents a follow-up study that builds on prior research aimed at understanding co-exploration, where five recurring patterns were identified through a longitudinal study of 16 student design teams. Extending this work to the professional design context, we gathered insights from experienced designers to explore how co-exploration manifests in remote collaboration. Experts reflected on the five patterns, shared practical challenges, and engaged in speculative ideation using Inspiration Cards to envision new tool concepts. By analyzing their ideas and rationales, we identified recurring themes and mapped their interconnections. These insights are synthesized into the Designing Tools for Co-exploration (DTC) guideline, which offers intermediate-level knowledge [25] to support tool development for remote co-exploration. The guideline serves as both a starting point for design focus and a reflective resource for evaluating design decisions and outcomes.

Together, this work expands the understanding of co-exploration in professional design collaboration, offers actionable insights through the DTC guideline, and addresses remote design collaboration as a complex topic. By considering social interactions, materials, and collaborative dynamics, it provides a more holistic and applicable foundation for improving the remote design experience.

## 2 Background and Related Work

The design process is inherently iterative and exploratory, evolving through a dynamic interaction between problem and solution spaces [11] – a process characterized as 'design as exploration' [22]. This process embraces uncertainty and creativity, allowing teams to explore 'what' to create without a predetermined 'how' [10]. Within collaborative settings, this exploratory spirit becomes deeply social, as team members contribute diverse perspectives to build common ground when collaborators engage in communication and express confirmation of comprehension through words or bodily movements - an aspect central to effective remote collaboration, as emphasized in research on why distance matters during remote collaboration [4,45].

However, remote collaboration introduces challenges to these collaborative dynamics. Studies have shown that remote collaboration tends to reduce engagement, limit ideation, and complicate communication between team members. Hammond et al. [20] found that, although designers spent more time collaborating in a distributed collaborative design process, they experience higher workloads and discuss fewer topics. Rice et al. [47] reported that distributed teams show lower effectiveness in understanding and negotiating concepts. Eris et al. [13] added that distributed collaborators use fewer gestures, with graphical communication appearing to increase as a compensatory mechanism. The remote settings, according to Kvan [35] and Cross [9], can lead to compromised design decisions, restricting the ability to explore the best solutions.

These challenges have prompted a wave of tool development aimed at recreating the affordances of in-person collaboration. For instance, DigitalDesk [54] supports remote co-sketching, while DigiTable [7] and ClearBoard [29] integrate gestures and eye contact for richer interactions. For activities such as brainstorming, the Distributed Designers' Outpost [31] incorporates physical elements like post-its as interaction primitives. Beyond sketching, design processes often involve collaborating around 3D objects. Tools such as Syco3D [44] enable real-time 3D CAD modeling, and the Immersive Discussion Tool (IDT) [8] facilitates reasoning and annotating 3D models during discussion. More comprehensive platforms like CollaboVR [23] and BeHere [53] allow remote teams to manipulate, point at, and edit 3D objects remotely, combining multiple functions to support different actions during the design process.

The COVID-19 pandemic drastically accelerated the adoption of remote collaboration, further amplifying the urgency of understanding how to support it effectively. Alongside new practices, new challenges also emerged. For example, Ye et al. [56] reported a loss of co-exploration during remote prototyping, where designers experienced reduced collaborative engagement. Activities such as jointly editing, manipulating, and interacting with prototypes while building on each other's ideas became less frequent. They called for tools that better support these co-explorative activities.

Yet this raises a deeper question: what exactly are co-exploration activities? Although the term may sound self-explanatory, its meaning remains unclear in the literature. In some contexts, it has been used interchangeably with collaborative design exploration, such as when using cultural probes to support shared interpretation and new understanding in early design stages [40]. In other cases, it is described as a continuous team activity spanning the design process – from brainstorming and concept development to prototyping and evaluation [52]. This inconsistency is not unique to co-exploration; as Mattelmäki and Visser [41] noted, the widespread use of "co-" terms in design research often leads to conceptual ambiguity, with many terms lacking clearly defined boundaries or distinct contributions.

Recognizing this ambiguity, we argued that it is necessary to first understand what co-exploration is before proposing how to support it. We conducted a five-month longitudinal study following the full design processes of 16 student teams. Across 1562 documented activities, we identified 161 instances as co-exploration activities for further examination. As shown in Fig. 1, we developed a four-dimensional analytical framework that divides co-exploration into two stages: before and during the activity. Each stage includes two dimensions. The framework is read vertically. The first two columns represent the *Pre-co-exploration* phase: (1) how information is shared in advance (e.g., synchronously or asynchronously), and (2) how diverse insights are introduced (e.g., individually prepared or generated through group methods). The next two columns correspond to the *During co-exploration* phase: (3) the type of communication that occurs (e.g., diverging to generate more ideas or converging to refine existing thoughts), and (4) how participants are physically or virtually distributed (e.g., all co-located, hybrid, or fully remote). Each co-exploration activity is described by selecting one value from each of the four dimensions, allowing for the visualization and comparison of different types of collaborative engagement across teams. From 161 documented co-exploration activities, we identified five recurring patterns:

1. Merging Different Insights: Co-exploration happens when teams synthesize different perspectives to unify varied ideas into a coherent design direction.
2. Reflecting on Existing Materials: Co-exploration occurs as teams revisit earlier work to regain shared understanding and clarify assumptions.
3. Refining Initial Concepts: Teams experience co-exploration by jointly refining already aligned ideas, adjusting and enriching them to develop more focused design concepts.

4. Generating More Ideas: Co-exploration emerges when teams engage in idea-generation sessions, using creative techniques to build on each other's insights and uncover unexpected design directions.
5. Seeking Cooperation: Co-exploration occurs when people from different teams spontaneously look for ways to connect their designs, exploring how to avoid conflicts, share data or resources, or ensure that separate design outcomes can work together effectively.

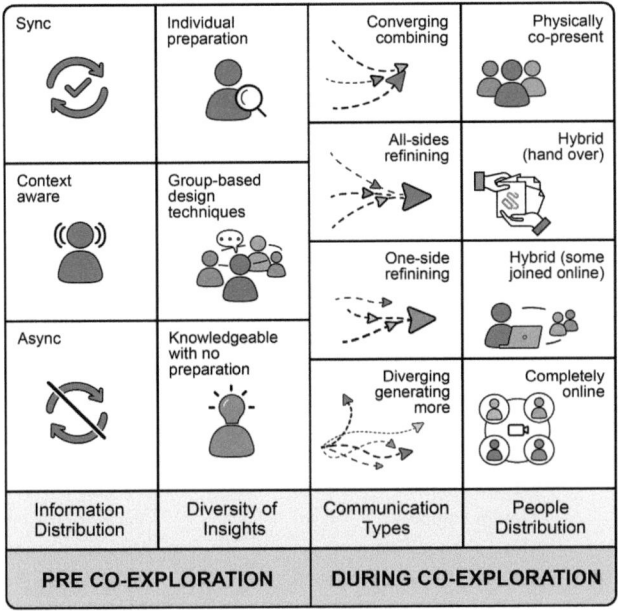

**Fig. 1.** The analytical framework for examining co-exploration activities.

Although participants engaged in many collaborative design activities, only a small portion were described as co-exploration. Activities that appeared similar in form differed in how they were experienced–what mattered was not the type of activity, but the way people engaged with it. Factors such as attitudes, communication dynamics, shared goals, and interpersonal relationships shaped whether a moment became co-explorative or remained task-driven. These findings highlight that co-exploration is not a fixed activity but an emergent experience shaped by context. As Hassenzahl [21] noted, while experiences cannot be replicated exactly, we can shape the conditions so that the desired experience is more likely to occur. Supporting co-exploration, therefore, means creating the right conditions for it to emerge

## 3 Method

This study received ethical approval from the university's Ethical Review Board, and informed consent was obtained from all experts before the study commenced.

### 3.1 Professional Design Experts

In this study, we aimed to involve experts from various roles within the design industry to ensure a broad spectrum of knowledge and experience. We recruited eight professionals holding different positions across multiple design companies, each with extensive experience ranging from years to decades. An overview of recruited experts and their respective background information can be found in Table 1. We asked them about the typical scale of their collaborative teams, focusing on how many people they closely collaborate with and the types of occupations these collaborators have. The team sizes reported varied but generally consisted of small groups. Since we are especially interested in remote collaboration, we gathered information on their experience with remote design collaboration. The responses revealed varying levels of remote collaboration, including working with colleagues in different cities, neighboring countries, and various parts of the world.

**Table 1.** Overview of recruited experts and their respective background information

| Expert | Experience (years) | Position | Team scale (people) | Location of remote collaborators |
|---|---|---|---|---|
| P1 | 6–10 | Design engineer | 6–10 | Various parts of the world |
| P2 | >35 | Design engineer | 6–10 | Various cities in same country |
| P3 | 26–30 | Design consultant | 1–5 | Various cities in same country |
| P4 | 6–10 | Industrial designer | 6–10 | Neighboring countries |
| P5 | >35 | CEO of design studio | 1–5 | Neighboring countries |
| P6 | 16–20 | Product designer | 1–5 | Various cities in same country |
| P7 | 6–10 | Head of product | 1–5 | Various parts of the world |
| P8 | 6–10 | COO of design studio | 6–10 | Neighboring countries |

### 3.2 Procedure

The study consisted of a series of one-on-one semi-structured interviews, divided into two phases: Experience-mapping exercise and an ideation practice. The study materials used in each part are explained in detail in Sect. 3.3. With the expert's consent, we audio-recorded the study for later analysis.

In the experience-mapping exercise, we introduced the five patterns of co-exploration and explained the double-diamond model. To ensure participants had a clear understanding of the concept, we first walked through each of the five patterns in detail, providing concrete examples from previous studies to illustrate what each pattern looked like in practice. After this introduction, Experts were provided with color-coded tokens representing each pattern and asked to map their co-exploration experiences on a double-diamond model - first for co-located and then for remote experiences. This exercise aimed to 1) gain insights into experts' experiences with co-exploration in both co-located and remote settings. and 2) ensure that experts had a clear understanding of co-exploration before proceeding to the ideation practice. While we acknowledge ongoing critiques of the Double Diamond model for oversimplifying real-world design practices, we align with Kochanowska and Gagliardi's perspective that it serves as a useful point of reference rather than a prescriptive framework [33]. Our intention was not to enforce a strict process but to use the model as a tangible prompt to encourage experts to reflect on, discuss, and articulate their co-exploration experiences through storytelling and dialogue.

In the ideation practice, we used Inspiration Cards to prompt experts to envision tools and solutions for supporting remote co-exploration. To help participants get familiar with the method, the first author introduced the cards one by one, explaining the meaning of each card and how it related to challenges in remote collaboration. When participants asked for further clarification, we provided examples of existing tools or research to illustrate how such challenges had been addressed in other contexts. Experts could start with either the Domain Cards, if they had specific co-exploration experiences in mind, or the Technology Cards if they were inspired by a particular technology and wanted to explore its potential applications. Our goal in this phase was to have experts draw from their own experiences to speculate on how remote co-exploration could be better supported. By analyzing the envisioned solutions and underlying rationale, we aimed to extract design knowledge to inform guidelines for developing tools that support remote co-exploration. Throughout the interviews, the first author positioned themselves as a listener and learner, encouraging experts to point out any missing aspects of co-exploration or suggest additional patterns that better reflected their experiences.

### 3.3 Study Materials: Maps, Tokens, and Inspiration Cards

The study involved several materials to support both the experience-mapping exercise and the ideation practice. To help participants grasp the five co-exploration patterns, we first provided illustrated sketch cards (70×140 mm) as visual references, making the abstract concepts more tangible. For the mapping activity itself, experts used an A3 Double Diamond map along with a set of color-coded circular tokens (25 mm), each corresponding to one of the five patterns. These tokens enabled participants to annotate and reflect on their past co-located and remote co-exploration experiences directly on the map. This reflective activity helped ground their thinking and prepared them for the ideation phase.

In the ideation practice, we followed the Inspiration Cards approach [19] to develop the *Domain Cards* and *Technology Cards*. The *Domain Cards* represented the five co-exploration patterns, providing experts with a goal of the types of activities their tools could support. The *Technology Cards* were designed to cover a range of tools and technologies, encouraging experts to think about how these could support remote co-exploration activities. These technology cards were first informed by including key elements from a comprehensive review of the current state of remote assistance technologies, devices, visual display technologies, and communication cues [12]. This was then finetuned through the lens of a second literature review that addressed the specific needs of designers during remote collaboration [57]. These two reviews ensured that our selection of technologies addressed practical demands in remote collaborative design. When determining the number of cards to include, we were guided by Lucero et al. [38], whose work showed how the number of cards affects experts' engagement with the design process. Following their insights, we included 33 Technology Cards and 5 Domain Cards (Appendix A), ensuring experts were inspired without becoming overwhelmed by too many choices.

**Fig. 2.** Study setup showing an expert engaging with sketching and Inspiration Cards during the ideation session, with mapping materials and pattern tokens visible in the background.

A pilot study led to card refinements: reducing images to one for clarity and resizing to post-it size ($75 \times 75$mm) for better A3 poster integration. Blank cards were also provided so that experts could add specific terms during their ideation sessions. As depicted in Fig. 2, an expert used the materials to sketch ideas on a poster, with the full card set laid out nearby, including a newly created card labeled "facial expression."

## 3.4 Data Collection and Analysis

To gain firsthand insights into their everyday working environment, we conducted interviews at their design studios, allowing them to reference specific projects, tools, and materials. This provided a more contextual understanding of their design processes. With their consent, interviews were audio-recorded, and photos were taken of study materials, including double-diamond maps and idea posters. In total, we collected 15 h of audio data and 24 posters – 22 containing fully formed ideas with implementation thoughts and two depicting past co-exploration scenarios that aided recall but did not generate new tool ideas.

For the first part of the analysis, we employed an inductive/deductive hybrid thematic approach [14] in MAXQDA [17]. Given that our study was grounded in the co-exploration framework and existing literature, our goal was not to introduce new terms but to provide actionable insights. This hybrid method allowed us to use predefined concepts while remaining open to emerging themes through iterative review. By analyzing how experts mapped the five co-exploration patterns and described their experiences in both co-located and remote settings, we identified the specific impacts of remote collaboration on co-exploration in professional practice.

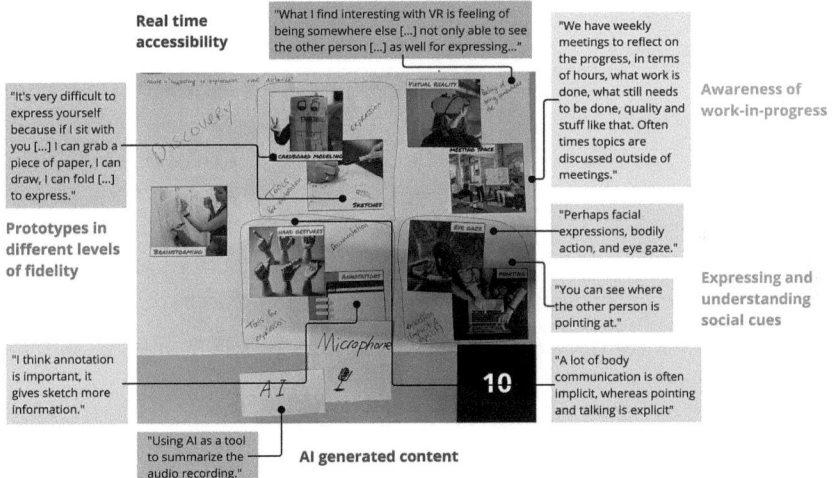

**Fig. 3.** An excerpt from our analysis, illustrating idea no. 10 is annotated with quotes (in rectangular boxes) and categorized into themes (in bold fonts) with distinct colors.

In the second part of the analysis, we sought to visually connect the experts' ideas with their underpinning theories, as shown in Fig. 3. Drawing inspiration from Sauerwein et al.'s work [48], where they adapted the original concept of annotated portfolios as an instrument for analyzing interviews, we applied this approach to our study. We followed a five-step process to conduct our analysis: We (1) highlighted 244 relevant quotes (between 18 and 39 per interview) by reading through the transcriptions multiple times and marking all relevant passages. (2) We summarized these quotes and connected them to specific parts of the ideas. (3) We categorized the quotes into themes, assigning different colors to represent each theme. (4) We organized the themes into hierarchies to determine relationships and overall structure. (5) We examined connections between ideas across the annotated posters and conducted a map of the themes and key aspects (Appendix B).

## 4 Results

This section presents expert insights on co-exploration and ideas for supporting it remotely. We analyzed challenges and proposed solutions, identifying key themes and relationships (Appendix B). While these themes reflected the participants' input, the lines between them were not explicit. To clearly communicate these insights, we sought a structured approach that provides a clearer and more comprehensive representation.

**Fig. 4.** A map illustrates three conceptual spaces, with people, materials, and interactions that occur in these spaces marked.

Drawing from co-located collaboration, we structured our findings around three distinct but interconnected spaces: working space, meeting space, and project-specific space (Fig. 4). These spaces reflect how people, materials, and interactions intertwine in co-exploration. We then use narratives to explore how each space supports different co-exploration activities.

### 4.1 Iterative Exploring vs. Linear Searching

Participants noted that co-exploration patterns still occur in remote settings, but less frequently and with different qualities (P1, P2, P4, P7, P8). In co-located environments, design teams often engage in an iterative process. P7 described it as *"trying to discover what is the actual problem and solve it on the go."* In contrast, remote co-exploration tends to be more linear and task-driven (P7). They noted, *"It's much more functional and focused on the problem at hand."* This shift toward linearity was also reflected in their hesitation when mapping the five patterns on the remote map, stating, *"Maybe it is [co-exploring], but then it's like you propose a solution and the other one will say those solutions do or don't work. Instead of saying 'OK, but we could also do this.'"* P8 shared similar concerns, explaining that *"There's much less of what people would call a creative atmosphere, where you have the freedom to think around and build on the ideas of someone else."* Additionally, remote collaboration often requires more time, yet stakeholders may not understand this added effort. As a result, P8 said that they *"definitely do less iteration"* in remote settings.

## 4.2 The Impact of Lost Informal Social Interaction

Experts identified the loss of social interaction as a critical issue in remote settings. While co-located teams benefit from spontaneous conversations, such as at the coffee machine, in the corridor, or at someone's desk, remote collaboration often confines communication to formal meetings (P1, P2, P5). These informal moments are crucial for surfacing concerns and maintaining team alignment. As P2 noted, *"They know it [the design outcome] is not good, but the interaction between them is so poor. If you are with people in one place. In the social interaction, you can say, OK, what are we gonna do? Are we gonna leave it like that?"* The absence of such informal moments can delay discussions of key issues, compromising outcomes or allowing crucial problems to go unaddressed until it's too late. P7 reflected, *"At some point, you say maybe this is good enough. If there wasn't such a pain in communication, we would do something more."* Across all interviews, experts expressed trying different approaches to adapt, but progress and team morale still slow down, as P1 put it: *"It slows down the progress and can really slow down the mood.'*

## 4.3 The Burden of Preparation for Remote Co-exploration

In co-located settings, co-exploration occurs naturally and is spread more evenly across the design process. In contrast, remote collaboration often compresses multiple co-exploration activities into a single meeting. P1 attributed this to the accumulation of deferred issues, requiring them to be addressed all at once. With limited information sharing between meetings, participants arrive with prepared questions and insights, leading to an overloaded and often exhausting experience. P3 emphasized the huge preparation effort remote co-exploration demands. While sketches or mood boards (P6) can be shared in real-time, other materials, such as 3D print files with assembly instructions (P1), or prototypes (P5), must often be sent in advance to allow participants to review. P8 added that maintaining engagement requires making meetings more interactive. P2 and P4 expressed frustration that the time invested in preparation does not necessarily improve design quality. As P4 remarked, *"Preparing presentations is time-consuming, and it doesn't really help you with the design process."*

### 4.4 Specific Challenges and Participants' Ideas for Tackling Them

**Meeting Space.** The meeting space was frequently described as the primary setting for co-exploration. This is also how experts began their ideation. As Fig. 3 shows, P1 structures a meeting scenario in the discovery phase. Their ideas clustered around three elements: people, materials, and interactions.

People: As outlined in Sect. 2, insights emerge through individual preparation, group-based techniques, or spontaneous contributions from knowledgeable participants. Experts noted that in remote settings, the absence of proximity-based awareness makes individual preparation more important (P3, P4, P5). P3 shared experiences of constantly sending pictures of their work to the group chat to ensure alignment. P5 described this as *"preparing them as members of the process,"* highlighting the need to keep everyone aligned.

Materials: Synchronizing and accessing shared materials proved challenging. 14 of 22 tool ideas involved design artifacts. P8 suggested using identical kits inspired by the Apollo 13 mission, where NASA engineers on Earth had to quickly build and test solutions using identical materials to those available to astronauts in space [2]. Other suggestions included robotic arms for remote clay modeling (P1) and using auditory cues to convey physical properties like shape, color, and texture (P6). P2 emphasized continuity by proposing a portable kit to preserve the state of whiteboards or post-its between sessions: *"Then everyone enters the room, and you say let's start from where we were last time."*

Interactions: Interactions in the meeting space revolve around the dynamic between people-material interactions and people-people interactions. Experts described the difficulty of balancing the visibility of people and materials in video calls (P1, P3, P7). Co-located collaboration enables richer non-verbal cues (P2) and sustained engagement (P1, P3, P5, P8), which are difficult to replicate online. P2 lamented the lack of such subtleties in remote settings: *"You cannot see whether they are bored, or starting to yawn, or still listening, or they're on their phone while you're presenting. It's terrible."* To address these challenges, P3 and P5 suggested incorporating regular breaks into remote co-exploration sessions to mitigate *Zoom fatigue* [3]. P1 and P7 imagined AI-enhanced whiteboards that could generate quick concept suggestions, as P7 explained, *"You put your post-its there, and then it immediately generates for you an example of what it could look like"'* Another key aspect that participants missed was spontaneous side conversations. P8 suggested using eye gaze to trigger brief sidebar conversations, supporting the kind of informal interaction that often leads to new insights.

**Working Space.** Co-located working spaces facilitate spontaneous interactions that foster social connections and design awareness. Six experts (P1, P2, P3, P5, P6, P7) emphasized the value of this shared space, and three experts (P2, P5, P7) proposed tools to address the lack of such spaces in remote collaboration.

People: The absence of informal social remote environments made it harder to maintain awareness of colleagues' work (P1, P3, P5, P7), often leading to "cold starts" in meetings (P2). P3 used WhatsApp to share updates asynchronously. P7, missing overheard conversations that sparked co-exploration, envisioned a gaze-based tool to signal interest in spontaneous discussion.

Materials: The physical working space not only provides a place for people to gather but also holds the tangible materials that inspire co-exploration. P6 criticized the sterility of digital environments: *"Designers need catalysts, as a designer, your environment is the catalyst, online environment is too clean!"* P5 proposed setting up a dedicated room with visual stimuli. Referencing their office, they advised the author to print and hang materials: *"It's different than having it on the screen."*

Interactions: P1 noted that many activities in co-located collaboration happen outside formal meetings. P5 envisioned a shared virtual space where team members could meet regularly, just like real-life office routines: *"If we are not in the same location, I create a same location, everyone is in the same virtual space."* Such informal meetups, they explained, might make collaborators feel more comfortable sharing concerns or discussing mistakes – topics harder to address in formal settings. P2 shared how casual encounters in offices allowed for easier discussions of mistakes: *"Massive amounts of these design engineers like me make something that they know is not good. But the interaction between them and the higher management and everybody is so poor [...] If they are all together, then they can bring a piece of cake, like 'Hey, I have a big cake for us, and I have bad news: I made a little mistake [...] You don't do it with people on Teams."* During the ideation practice, P2 emphasized the need to design remote experiences that feel *"more human, more communicative."*

**Project-Specific Space.** Project-specific spaces serve as repositories for ongoing work, often found within both working and meeting areas. These spaces–filled with uncleaned whiteboards, mind maps, reference images, and prototypes–help teams revisit, refine, and continue their design work. Five experts (P2, P3, P4, P6, P7) emphasized the value of this space, with four experts (P2, P3, P6, P7) offering specific ideas.

People: Unlike the working space, which centers on individual tasks, the project-specific space emphasizes team progress. P3 described their textile lab as a project-specific space where team members could explore machinery, leading to new insights and a shared understanding that advanced co-exploration.

Materials: P6 stressed the need to be physically surrounded by materials and proposed a shared digital table to synchronize drawings and annotations across locations. P7 similarly envisioned a *"shared remote desk"* projecting 2D and 3D artifacts across collaborators' spaces to ensure accessibility and continuity.

Interactions: P2 missed the large table in their previous workspace, which had encouraged spontaneous discussions when people passed by. They envisioned a shared virtual meeting room that would display project-related information, such as to-do lists and references, creating a persistent project-specific context for all collaborators. P4 shared their positive experience of setting up such a virtual space using Gravity Sketch, where they integrated research images and pinboards for references, helping their team maintain focus and revisit key project information.

## 5 Discussion

Through in-depth interviews with eight experts in design who are experienced in both co-located and remote co-exploration, we gained valuable insights into the dynamics of co-exploration across different settings. Our evaluation confirmed that co-exploration still occurs in remote settings, although the execution and quality of co-exploration were negatively impacted. These challenges prompted experts to propose concepts aimed at overcoming the challenges of remote environments. We documented their ideas and rationales in tables to provide a clear understanding of how to support remote co-exploration. In the following discussion, we explore the evolving dynamics of co-exploration, operationalize the design knowledge gathered, and reflect on the experts' critiques and visions for new technologies. Finally, we present an updated version of the co-exploration framework, incorporating these insights.

### 5.1 Persistent Patterns and Changing Dynamics

Recent research during the COVID-19 pandemic highlighted that design teams felt co-exploration was missing in remote collaborations due to inadequate tools for conveying ideas [56]. While our study appears to contrast with these findings, as the experts we interviewed recognized all five patterns of co-exploration in remote processes, our analysis offers three explanations that build upon and extend prior research.

First, advancements in technology and shifting mindsets post-pandemic play an important role. Online meeting platforms like Teams and Zoom, along with online design collaboration tools such as Miro [43] and Gravity Sketch [50], have strengthened the infrastructure for remote design collaboration. Moreover, as remote work became widespread, design teams adapted to these tools and workflows [36]. Thus, what was perceived as heavily missing has potentially rebounded or transformed due to these advancements.

Second, social bonding remains a critical factor. Previous studies indicated that teams without prior in-person interaction struggled with misunderstandings and dehumanization during remote work. In contrast, the experts in our study had histories of in-person collaboration or were able to meet regularly, building trust and understanding of each other's work styles. These pre-existing bonds likely enabled smoother remote co-exploration, as the foundation of rapport had already been established.

Third, there may be a shift in the nature or quality of co-exploration. P7 noted that remote settings have reduced the creative atmosphere typical in co-located collaboration. This concern underpins a shift from 'design as exploration'

– an iterative exploratory process where both the problem and solution are still taking shape [22]- to 'design as search,' a linear search process where design teams focus on solving well-defined problems [22]. This observation aligns with Brucks and Levav [6], who found that virtual interaction narrows the cognitive scope and reduces creative idea generation. Similarly, Lin et al. [37] found that remote collaboration is more often associated with late-stage technical execution, while co-located teams are more likely to engage in conceptual tasks such as idea generation and framing research questions. These results suggest that remote collaboration may inherently limit the conditions needed for rich, iterative co-exploration. While experts have adapted co-exploration to remote contexts, the reduction of informal communication has compressed spontaneous, iterative discussions into fewer, agenda-driven meetings. This shift can constrain the exploratory nature of design. As for the quality of co-exploration, although the five patterns continue to occur, the depth and breadth of design exploration [15], described as vertical and lateral transformations in Goel's theory [18], have diminished. This means that although the design process has not entirely shifted to a linear problem-solving approach, teams seem to engage in less expansive exploration compared to co-located collaboration. As a result, the richness of design outcomes has decreased, contributing to the perception that co-exploration is lacking in remote settings.

Our findings do not contradict the prior findings from Ye et al. [56] but rather provide deeper insights into why design teams felt a loss in co-exploration during the pandemic. The five patterns of co-exploration persist, but the experience and execution have transformed, highlighting the need for continued adaptation and enhancement of design tools to support the co-exploration.

## 5.2 Operationalizing the Design Knowledge

Drawing on insights from our participants, we developed the "Designing Tools for Co-exploration" (DTC) guideline, a structured table that organizes design knowledge into spaces, themes, key aspects, considerations, and examples. The considerations are intentionally phrased as questions rather than instructions, reflecting the fact that each remote collaboration unfolds in its own context and addresses specific needs. For example, the considerations for the key aspect of individual preparation include: "What information should be prepared in advance?" and "How can this information be effectively shared?" This approach aligns with how designers typically work, as they continuously reflect on what the design challenge is and how it might be addressed [11]. To support practical use, the guideline includes examples drawn from both existing methods and expert-generated ideas. These are not intended to prescribe solutions, but to stimulate thinking and offer inspiration. Table 2 presents the first three columns of the guideline. A complete version, detailing all considerations and corresponding examples, is provided in a separate companion publication [55].

The DTC guideline can be applied in two distinct ways. It serves both as a resource for those designing tools to support remote co-exploration and as a reflective tool for teams looking to improve their ongoing collaborative practices.

Designers creating collaboration tools, for instance, may want to reintroduce the kinds of spontaneous interactions that typically spark cooperation across projects (Pattern 5: seeking cooperation). In remote settings, informal encounters like hallway chats are often missing. The DTC can help identify ways to support such interactions virtually, by pointing to aspects such as "Working space → People → Informal encounters" and "Interactions → Informal social interactions." These entries can inspire features that enable lightweight, impromptu exchanges between colleagues.

Teams already working together remotely can also use the DTC to assess and improve how they collaborate. When a team feels stuck and chooses to revisit earlier design materials (Pattern 2: reflecting on existing materials), the DTC can help them evaluate whether everyone is aware of the need for reflection, referencing "People → Contextual awareness of the project's status." They might

**Table 2.** The first three columns of the DTC guideline

| Spaces | Theme | Key Aspects |
|---|---|---|
| Meeting space | People | - Contextual awareness of individual's work-in-progress |
| | | - Contextual awareness of project's status |
| | | - Individual preparation |
| | Materials | - Multi-fidelity prototypes |
| | | - Accessibility and synchronization |
| | | - Meeting continuity |
| | Interactions | - Group-based techniques |
| | | - Maintaining enthusiasm and engagement |
| | | - Expressing and understanding communication cues |
| | | - Facilitating side conversation |
| | | - AI-generated content |
| Working space | People | - Informal encounters |
| | | - Contextual awareness of individual's work-in-progress |
| | | - Contextual awareness of project's status |
| | Materials | - Ambient creative stimulus |
| | Interactions | - Informal social interactions |
| | | - Maintaining togetherness |
| | | - Pre-meeting huddle |
| | | - Expressing and understanding communication cues |
| Project-specific space | People | - Contextual awareness of project's status |
| | Materials | - Material archives for future reference |
| | | - Encouraging knowledge sharing |
| | | - Accessibility and synchronization |
| | Interactions | - Traces of interactions with materials |

begin with a brief "Pre-meeting huddle" to align expectations. To facilitate the session, they would ensure easy access to relevant resources, ensure materials are accessible by consulting "Materials → Material archives for future reference," and use guidance from "Interactions → Expressing and understanding communication cues" to sustain a productive conversation.

### 5.3 Views on Recently Prominent Technologies

**AR, VR, and MR** offer new possibilities for remote collaboration, particularly in training, social activities, and virtual environments such as the Metaverse [42]. While experts explored these technologies through inspiration cards, half (P2, P3, P6, P8) were skeptical about their current value for remote co-exploration.

Prior research suggests VR adoption evolves over time rather than being determined by initial impressions [1]. However, P3, an experienced AR/VR user and researcher, remained doubtful: *"It's a great area of research. For now, it doesn't really solve anything."* Younger designers, such as P8, echoed concerns, noting the distractions caused by the novelty of VR, which often takes focus away from the design task. P2 further criticized avatar-based communication for lacking natural expressions, emphasizing that physical presence fosters trust and collaboration. These concerns highlight a key limitation of virtual environments: the disconnect between digital representations and essential human social cues [34].

Despite these concerns, we don't dismiss the potential of AR, VR, and MR technologies. Developments like Apple Vision Pro or Meta Quest 3 demonstrate that these tools are evolving. As these technologies mature, they can become more intuitive and better suited for co-exploration, especially when designed with a deeper understanding of designerly activities and designers' needs. Our study provides intermediate-level design knowledge [25] that can guide the development of such tools.

**AI-Generated Content (AIGC).** Generative AI, combined with large language models, is reshaping computer-aided design. AIGC enables designers to quickly transform rough ideas into detailed visuals, which may speed up feedback loops and lower the barrier to design ideation [27]. Studies also show how tools like DALL-E and Midjourney help expand ideas and improve communication in design workflows [5,32].

Experts in our study expressed optimism about AIGC's role in remote co-exploration, envisioning AI-generated content that enables designers to iterate more swiftly. However, introducing highly detailed visuals early in the process raises concerns about ambiguity – a critical factor for creativity [16]. Ambiguity, particularly during the early stages of divergent thinking, helps generate a wide range of ideas before narrowing down options through convergent thinking [51].

While AI-generated images can facilitate ideation, excessive detail may constrain creativity by limiting open-ended interpretations [39]. The challenge, then, is balancing AIGC's efficiency with the need for ambiguity to foster innovation.

Despite these challenges, AIGC offers promising opportunities for human-AI collaboration and certainly warrants further investigation and exploration. Based on its potential and the insights from our study, we propose adding AIGC as an additional value to the "diversity of insights" dimension in our analytical framework, providing new ways to enhance and expand idea generation.

### 5.4 Difference Between Educational and Professional Design Practices

While we did not find noticeable differences between young and senior professional designers in terms of the five co-exploration patterns, we did observe clear distinctions between professional designers and student teams from our earlier study. We received valuable feedback regarding the "people distribution" dimension. In our previous study within an educational context, we observed student teams handing over ongoing tasks due to differing academic schedules. Despite these transitions, students continued working on the same design challenge and perceived this process as co-exploration. However, none of the experts in our current study reported experiencing co-exploration in this manner. P7 explicitly disagreed, arguing that such processes should be categorized as "iterative design" rather than co-exploration. We align with P7's perspective and offer the following explanation. In educational settings, co-exploration appeared to persist because of an 'information carrier' – a team member responsible for transferring key insights to others and partially re-experiencing past discussions to maintain continuity. In professional design practice, however, this workflow does not exist; once a co-exploration has passed, it remains in the past. Co-exploration requires active, simultaneous participation, and team members who miss prior discussions must independently catch up before rejoining the process. The absence of this workflow in expert interviews suggests it is unique to educational contexts.

## 6 Conclusion

This study offers new insights and practical guidance for supporting co-exploration in remote design collaboration, articulated through three key contributions.

First, the study advances the understanding of co-exploration by examining how five previously identified patterns, originally observed in educational settings, manifest in professional practice. Interviews with eight experienced designers show that while these patterns persist, their dynamics shift in remote settings. Iterative practices are perceived as more linear and goal-driven, with teams facing reduced spontaneity and depth in co-exploration.

Second, it introduces the Designing Tools for Co-exploration (DTC) guideline, which translates expert insights into intermediate-level design knowledge. Organized into themes, aspects, considerations, and examples, the DTC offers actionable guidance for tool developers and serves as a reflective aid for design teams.

Third, it takes a holistic view of remote co-exploration by integrating social interaction, material engagement, and collaborative dynamics. This comprehensive perspective emphasizes the need to support the full complexity of remote design collaboration.

Together, these three contributions provide both conceptual depth and practical direction for improving remote design collaboration.

## A  Study Materials: Inspiration Cards

| Cards | Categories | Name of the cards |
|---|---|---|
| Technology Cards | Multi-fidelity prototypes | Sketches, Cardboard modeling, 3D view, 3D printing, Laser cutting, Digital prototyping, Physical prototyping, Material testing, Evaluating |
| | Social cues | Hand gestures, Pointing, Eye gaze, Annotations, Robotic devices |
| | Providing different use of spaces | Meeting space, Working space, Project-specific space, Display, Projector, Smart devices, 2D video stream, Video camera, Virtual reality, Augmented reality, Mixed reality, 360 panoramas |
| | Encouraging creative social practices | Brainstorming, Role playing, Co-reflection |
| Domain Cards | Five patterns of co-exploration | Merging different insights, Reflecting on existing materials, Refining initial concepts, Generating more ideas, Seeking cooperation |

## B Results: Maps of Identified Themes, Key Aspects, and Their Relations Between Them

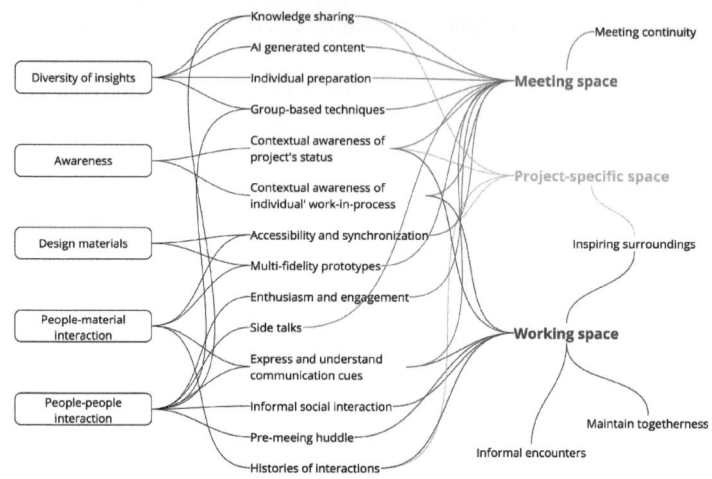

## References

1. Abramczuk, K., Bohdanowicz, Z., Muczyński, B., Skorupska, K.H., Cnotkowski, D.: Meet me in VR! can VR space help remote teams connect: a seven-week study with horizon workrooms. Int. J. Hum. Comput. Stud. **179**, 103104 (2023)
2. Aeronautics, N., Administration, S.: Apollo 13: Mission details (2009). https://www.nasa.gov/missions/apollo/apollo-13-mission-details/. Accessed 26 Oct 2024
3. Bennett, A.A., Campion, E.D., Keeler, K.R., Keener, S.K.: Videoconference fatigue? Exploring changes in fatigue after videoconference meetings during COVID-19. J. Appl. Psychol. **106**(3), 330 (2021)
4. Bjørn, P., Esbensen, M., Jensen, R.E., Matthiesen, S.: Does distance still matter? Revisiting the CSCW fundamentals on distributed collaboration. ACM Trans. Comput. Hum. Interact. (TOCHI) **21**(5), 1–26 (2014)
5. Brade, S., Wang, B., Sousa, M., Oore, S., Grossman, T.: Promptify: text-to-image generation through interactive prompt exploration with large language models. In: Proceedings of the 36th Annual ACM Symposium on User Interface Software and Technology, pp. 1–14 (2023)
6. Brucks, M.S., Levav, J.: Virtual communication curbs creative idea generation. Nature **605**(7908), 108–112 (2022)
7. Coldefy, F., Louis-dit Picard, S.: DigiTable: an interactive multiuser table for collocated and remote collaboration enabling remote gesture visualization. In: 2007 IEEE Conference on Computer Vision and Pattern Recognition, pp. 1–8. IEEE (2007)
8. Craig, D.L., Zimring, C.: Support for collaborative design reasoning in shared virtual spaces. Autom. Constr. **11**(2), 249–259 (2002)
9. Cross, N., Cross, A.C.: Observations of teamwork and social processes in design. Des. Stud. **16**(2), 143–170 (1995)
10. Dorst, K.: The core of "design thinking" and its application. Des. Stud. **32**(6), 521–532 (2011)

11. Dorst, K., Cross, N.: Creativity in the design process: co-evolution of problem-solution. Des. Stud. **22**(5), 425–437 (2001)
12. Druta, R., Druta, C., Negirla, P., Silea, I.: A review on methods and systems for remote collaboration. Appl. Sci. **11**(21), 10035 (2021)
13. Eris, O., Martelaro, N., Badke-Schaub, P.: A comparative analysis of multimodal communication during design sketching in co-located and distributed environments. Des. Stud. **35**(6), 559–592 (2014)
14. Fereday, J., Muir-Cochrane, E.: Demonstrating rigor using thematic analysis: a hybrid approach of inductive and deductive coding and theme development. Int. J. Qual. Methods **5**(1), 80–92 (2006)
15. Frens, J.: Cardboard modeling: exploring, experiencing and communicating. In: Collaboration in Creative Design: Methods and Tools, pp. 149–177. Springer (2016)
16. Gaver, W.W., Beaver, J., Benford, S.: Ambiguity as a resource for design. In: Proceedings of the SIGCHI Conference on Human Factors in Computing Systems, pp. 233–240 (2003)
17. GmbH, V.: MAXQDA (2024). https://www.maxqda.com/. Accessed 26 Oct 2024
18. Goel, V.: Cognitive processes involved in design problem solving. Sketches of Thought, pp. 95–126 (1995)
19. Halskov, K., Dalsgård, P.: Inspiration card workshops. In: Proceedings of the 6th Conference on Designing Interactive Systems, pp. 2–11 (2006)
20. Hammond, J.M., Harvey, C.M., Koubek, R.J., Compton, W.D., Darisipudi, A.: Distributed collaborative design teams: media effects on design processes. Int. J. Hum. Comput. Interact. **18**(2), 145–165 (2005)
21. Hassenzahl, M.: Experience design: Technology for all the right reasons, vol. 8. Morgan & Claypool Publishers (2010)
22. Hay, L., Duffy, A.H., McTeague, C., Pidgeon, L.M., Vuletic, T., Grealy, M.: A systematic review of protocol studies on conceptual design cognition: design as search and exploration. Design Sci. **3**, e10 (2017)
23. He, Z., Du, R., Perlin, K.: CollaboVR: a reconfigurable framework for creative collaboration in virtual reality. In: 2020 IEEE International Symposium on Mixed and Augmented Reality (ISMAR), pp. 542–554. IEEE (2020)
24. Hensher, D.A., Wei, E., Beck, M., Balbontin, C.: The impact of COVID-19 on cost outlays for car and public transport commuting-the case of the greater Sydney metropolitan area after three months of restrictions. Transp. Policy **101**, 71–80 (2021)
25. Höök, K., Löwgren, J.: Strong concepts: intermediate-level knowledge in interaction design research. ACM Trans. Comput. Hum. Interact. (TOCHI) **19**(3), 1–18 (2012)
26. Hu, E., Azim, M.A.R., Heo, S.: FluidMeet: enabling frictionless transitions between in-group, between-group, and private conversations during virtual breakout meetings. In: Proceedings of the 2022 CHI Conference on Human Factors in Computing Systems, pp. 1–17 (2022)
27. Huang, K.L., Liu, Y.c., Dong, M.Q.: Incorporating AIGC into design ideation: a study on self-efficacy and learning experience acceptance under higher-order thinking. Thinking Skills Creativity **52**, 101508 (2024)
28. Idi, D.B., Khaidzir, K.A.M.: Critical perspective of design collaboration: a review. Front. Architectural Res. **7**(4), 544–560 (2018)
29. Ishii, H., Kobayashi, M.: ClearBoard: a seamless medium for shared drawing and conversation with eye contact. In: Proceedings of the SIGCHI Conference on Human Factors in Computing Systems, pp. 525–532 (1992)

30. Kim, J., Agrawala, M., Bernstein, M.S.: Mosaic: designing online creative communities for sharing works-in-progress. In: Proceedings of the 2017 ACM Conference on Computer Supported Cooperative Work and Social Computing, pp. 246–258 (2017)
31. Klemmer, S.R., Newman, M.W., Farrell, R., Bilezikjian, M., Landay, J.A.: The designers' outpost: a tangible interface for collaborative web site. In: Proceedings of the 14th Annual ACM Symposium on User Interface Software and Technology, pp. 1–10 (2001)
32. Ko, H.K., Park, G., Jeon, H., Jo, J., Kim, J., Seo, J.: Large-scale text-to-image generation models for visual artists' creative works. In: Proceedings of the 28th International Conference on Intelligent User Interfaces, pp. 919–933 (2023)
33. Kochanowska, M., Gagliardi, W.R.: The double diamond model: In pursuit of simplicity and flexibility. Perspect. Design II: Res. Educ. Pract. 19–32 (2022)
34. Kraut, R.E., Fussell, S.R., Brennan, S.E., Siegel, J.: Understanding effects of proximity on collaboration: implications for technologies to support remote collaborative work. In: Distributed Work, pp. 137–162. The MIT Press (2002)
35. Kvan, T.: Collaborative design: what is it? Autom. Constr. **9**(4), 409–415 (2000)
36. Lee, J.H., Ostwald, M.J.: The impacts of digital design platforms on design cognition during remote collaboration: a systematic review of protocol studies. Heliyon **8**(11) (2022)
37. Lin, Y., Frey, C.B., Wu, L.: Remote collaboration fuses fewer breakthrough ideas. Nature **623**(7989), 987–991 (2023)
38. Lucero, A., Dalsgaard, P., Halskov, K., Buur, J.: Designing with cards. Collaboration in creative design: Methods and tools, pp. 75–95 (2016)
39. Ma, S.Y.: Exploring ambiguity in generative AI images and its impact on collaborative design ideation
40. Mattelmäki, T.: Probing for co-exploring. Co-design **4**(1), 65–78 (2008)
41. Mattelmäki, T., Visser, F.S.: Lost in CO-X. In: Proceedings of the IASDR2011 (2011)
42. Meta: The metaverse is the future of digital connection (2024). https://about.meta.com/metaverse/. Accessed 26 Oct 2024
43. Miro: Miro—workspace for innovation (2024). https://www.miro.com/. Accessed 26 Oct 2024
44. Nam, T.J., Wright, D.: The development and evaluation of Syco3D: a real-time collaborative 3D cad system. Des. Stud. **22**(6), 557–582 (2001)
45. Olson, G.M., Olson, J.S.: Distance matters. Hum. Comput. Interact. **15**(2–3), 139–178 (2000)
46. Ostergaard, K.J., Summers, J.D.: Development of a systematic classification and taxonomy of collaborative design activities. J. Eng. Des. **20**(1), 57–81 (2009)
47. Rice, D.J., Davidson, B.D., Dannenhoffer, J.F., Gay, G.K.: Improving the effectiveness of virtual teams by adapting team processes. Comput. Support. Coop. Work (CSCW) **16**, 567–594 (2007)
48. Sauerwein, M., Bakker, C., Balkenende, R.: Annotated portfolios as a method to analyse interviews. DRS International Conference 2018 (2018)
49. Sawyer, R.K., DeZutter, S.: Distributed creativity: how collective creations emerge from collaboration. Psychol. Aesthet. Creat. Arts **3**(2), 81 (2009)
50. Sketch, G.: Gravity sketch (2024). https://gravitysketch.com/. Accessed 26 Oct 2024
51. Tan, L., Kvan, T.: Finding and using ambiguity to search for innovation opportunities. Design Manag. J. **13**(1), 17–29 (2018)

52. Vyas, D., Van der Veer, G., Nijholt, A.: Creative practices in the design studio culture: collaboration and communication. Cogn. Technol. Work **15**, 415–443 (2013)
53. Wang, P., Wang, Y., Billinghurst, M., Yang, H., Xu, P., Li, Y.: BeHere: a VR/SAR remote collaboration system based on virtual replicas sharing gesture and avatar in a procedural task. Virtual Reality **27**(2), 1409–1430 (2023)
54. Wellner, P.: Interacting with paper on the digitaldesk. Commun. ACM **36**(7), 87–96 (1993)
55. Ye, X.: Designing tools for co-exploration: A guideline to support remote design collaboration. https://github.com/kkkrisy/Designing-Tools-for-Co-exploration.git (2025)
56. Ye, X., Frens, J., Hu, J.: Adjusting to a distributed collaborative design process during the COVID-19 pandemic. IEEE Pervasive Comput. **20**(4), 9–17 (2021)
57. Ye, X., Frens, J., Hu, J.: Design tools for supporting the remote collaborative design process: a systematic review. In: Proceedings of the Tenth International Symposium of Chinese CHI, pp. 83–95 (2022)

**Context-Dependent Systems**

Context-Dependent Memory

# An Exploration to Enhance Response Rate and Sampling Density During ESM Experiments by Online Supervised Learning and Edge Computing on Smartwatches

Alireza Khanshan[1,3](✉), Pieter Van Gorp[2,3], and Panos Markopoulos[1,3]

[1] Industrial Design Department, Eindhoven University of Technology, Eindhoven, The Netherlands
[2] Industrial Engineering Department, Eindhoven University of Technology, Eindhoven, The Netherlands
[3] Eindhoven Artificial Intelligence Systems Institute, Eindhoven, The Netherlands
{a.khanshan,p.m.e.v.gorp,p.markopoulos}@tue.nl

**Abstract.** Powered by smartphones and wearable devices, the Experience Sampling Method (ESM) has increased in popularity for studying behaviors, thoughts, and experiences over time and in situ. Participants in ESM studies receive several notifications a day to self-report but often disengage due to intrusive and poorly timed notifications. Consequently, the response rate drops over time, hampering data collection and degrading ecological validity. Researchers have experimented with various strategies to optimize notification scheduling, including personalization, context sensing, and machine learning (ML). Edge computing can facilitate the training of ML models without the need for server communications, which is especially convenient for in-the-wild studies with unreliable network connectivity. Complementary logical evaluations on edge devices can minimize participant burden by accounting for sampling density, i.e., ensuring a minimum number of well-distributed daily notifications. However, these efforts raise engineering and scientific challenges related to avoiding cold start and training models on smartwatches. To overcome these challenges, we propose an open-source architecture and software that facilitates online learning to optimize notification delivery. Our feasibility study with $N = 37$ participants resulted in a response rate of 10.2% higher and a reaction time of 9.6% lower on average compared to the classical interval-based sampling.

**Keywords:** Experience Sampling Method · Response Rate · Smartwatches · Online Supervised Learning · Edge Computing · Human-Computer Interaction

## 1 Introduction

The Experience Sampling Method (ESM) is a popular approach for studying behaviors, thoughts, and feelings in real-world settings, offering higher ecological validity compared to traditional retrospective self-report methods [8,17]. ESM involves collecting self-report data multiple times throughout the day via notifications sent to participants' devices, typically smartphones or smartwatches. The effectiveness of ESM studies is hindered by response rates that decrease over time, leading to the dropout of participants [11,39]. This decline is often attributed to notifications that are intrusive and poorly timed [11].

Adapting the timing of ESM notifications to participant response behavior has been shown to mitigate these issues and increase response rates [4,29]. Intelligent sensor-driven machine learning (ML) models can further improve the timeliness of notifications by leveraging contextual information from wearable devices such as smartwatches [13,32]. Wearable ESM (wESM) systems, which utilize sensors in smartwatches to enhance context awareness of the ESM sampling strategy, can potentially improve the ecological validity of ESM studies [22].

Using sensor data to trigger notifications may not be sufficient, as it does not capture nuanced aspects of participants' context [24,25]. Personalizing the timing of notifications based on user preferences [9] and predictive modeling has shown promise in addressing this limitation [1,21,24,41]. Unfortunately, such personalization could incur sampling bias, as responses may cluster around specific events or times of day that are convenient to the user [25]. This phenomenon is detrimental to the ecological validity of the ESM, which aims to sample a variety of contexts and situations (not necessarily the times most convenient to the respondent) so that self-reporting is done close to the occurrence of events of interest as they unfold in natural situations of daily life [16].

To address these challenges and optimize the timing of the notification, we investigated using supervised online learning [15] on smartwatches. Our approach involves training a general model of the response behavior of the ESM participant (whether and how they respond to the prompts) on population-level data and transferring it to edge devices used for the ESM upon initialization. Subsequently, the model is personalized locally based on user interactions with notifications and moments of self-reporting. To improve ecological validity, our aim is to ensure *sampling density*, i.e., a minimum number of well-spread notifications per day. ML-based personalization occurs within predefined time windows, and if a window closes without a notification, one is sent to the participant regardless. This ensures that a minimum number of notifications are issued, respecting a designated inter-notification interval. This constraint is specifically important in the context of ESM, where researchers require a minimum number of notifications spread throughout the day, increasing the ecological validity of data collection.

In this paper, we present an architecture and an algorithm of our open-source software implementation to facilitate online learning with complementary windowing logic to optimize notification scheduling in ESM studies. We present the preliminary findings of a pilot ESM study, which demonstrated higher response rates and shorter reaction times compared to traditional interval-based sampling methods. In addition, we provide guidelines for employing reinforcement learning techniques that prioritize both ecological validity and timely notification delivery.

The remainder of this paper is organized as follows. Section 2 reviews related work on ESM and wearable technology. Section 3 outlines the methods used in our study. Section 4 presents the results of our pilot ESM study. In Sect. 5, we discuss the implications of our findings and future research directions. Finally, Sect. 6 concludes the paper.

## 2 Related Work

Mobile notifications are crucial in engaging users with timely and relevant information, influencing their response rates and overall engagement. Following advances in ML techniques, researchers have explored personalized notification delivery strategies to optimize response rates and enhance user engagement in ESM studies. This section reviews earlier work on the effectiveness of ML-based personalization, the impact of notification timing on response rates and engagement, and the use of ML to optimize notification delivery.

Research suggests that ML-based personalization improves the effectiveness of notification delivery by tailoring it to individual user preferences and contexts. Iqbal et al. demonstrated that scheduling notifications at break points based on content relevance can reduce frustration and reaction time [19]. Muralidharan et al. showcased successful ML implementations on LinkedIn, optimizing notification timing, frequency, and channel selection to encourage long-term user engagement [33]. These findings collectively support the idea that the application of ML in personalization enhances user experiences and responses to notifications.

The timing of mobile notifications influences response rates and user engagement. Avraham Bahir et al. observed that visually enhanced notifications and those sent during specific times of the day yield higher response rates [1]. Morrison et al. found that frequent notifications tailored to the user context increase exposure to intervention content without deterring engagement [32]. Balebako et al. emphasized that timing nuances, such as displaying privacy notices during app use, can impact recall rates [3]. However, Bidargaddi et al. [6] and Pham et al. [35] report mixed results, suggesting the need for further exploration of effective timing and frequency strategies.

Personalizing the timing of notifications has shown promise in enhancing user engagement, although results are mixed. Avraham Bahir et al. highlighted the effectiveness of contextually tailored messages, especially on weekends and at mid-day [1]. Okoshi et al. demonstrated that a delay in delivering notifications until the user may be interrupted can increase engagement [34]. Khanshan et al. found a significant difference in the response rate between study groups that received notifications during different levels of physical activity, indicating the importance of context sensitivity [24]. However, Morrison et al. cautioned that adaptive tailoring of timing does not consistently enhance response rates [32]. These works underscore the importance of considering individual preferences and contexts to optimize engagement.

Recent studies have explored how ML can help personalize notification timing, providing information on effective strategies. Gonul et al. proposed a reinforcement learning-based algorithm considering momentary context data for optimized notification delivery [10]. Poppinga et al. developed a model predicting opportune notification moments based on mobile context data [36]. Li et al. demonstrated that personalized ML models using user actions significantly improve prediction performance [27]. A range of ML features, including reinforcement learning (e.g., [42]), preference learning (e.g., [30,31]), and time-aware recommendation models (e.g., [43]), contribute to the personalization of mobile notification timing.

In the smartwatch domain, reinforcement learning and deep learning techniques have been used to optimize notification delivery. Ho et al. utilized reinforcement learning to identify optimal notification timing, enhancing response rates using smartphones and wristbands [14]. Bhattacharya et al. applied deep learning to activity recognition on smartwatches, achieving superior performance with acceptable resource consumption [5]. Lee et al. proposed an intelligent notification delivery system leveraging deep learning to predict important notifications, reducing user distraction [26]. Lutze et al. focused on reinforcement learning for dialogue design and control in health-oriented smartwatch apps, determining appropriate intervention times [28]. These studies underscore the potential of ML techniques in improving user experiences and functionality in smartwatches.

The Context-Aware Experience Sampling was first introduced by Intille et al. with a tool that allowed researchers to acquire information by focusing on moments and activities of interest based on sensor-based triggers [18,37]. Bachmann et al. demonstrated how to mitigate compliance challenges by sending event-based notifications only in situations of relevance and skipping ESM questions where assessment was possible by sensor reading [2]. Seo et al. developed an experience sampling system for context-aware mobile application development [38]. Context-Aware Experience Sampling leverages sensor technologies to increase data quality and mitigate the challenges regarding participant engagement, calling for the use of ML for optimizing the sampling strategy and exploiting emerging wearables such as smartwatches for pervasive sensor recording [2,37].

The related work outlined above shows the potential of ML-based personalization, the impact of notification timing on response rates and engagement, the utilization of ML techniques to optimize notification delivery across mobile devices and smartwatches, and Context-Aware Experience Sampling. However, in the context of ESM, context-awareness and personalization need to account for sampling bias and preserve ecological validity while balancing intrusiveness. This is a challenge that has not been sufficiently addressed in prior work and is therefore the focus of this paper.

## 3 Method

Based on the premise that personalized notification delivery can produce greater engagement (i.e., higher response rate, shorter reaction time, and longer participation), we explore the design, implementation, and evaluation of a personalized ESM notification system, following edge computing practices. The process begins with an ESM study design. Then we propose a notification delivery process that satisfies a researcher-specified minimum number of notifications spread over the study days to conduct an ecologically valid ESM experiment. Subsequently, detailed data collection procedures capture user interactions and preferences, forming the foundation for ML model development. The training process employs carefully selected algorithms and metrics to refine the ability of the model to predict opportune moments of prompting. For transparency and replicability, the general trained model is open access. We then detail the personalization process, where contextual and user-specific data are leveraged to tailor notification timing for individuals. Finally, a model evaluation assesses the efficacy of the system in enhancing user engagement, utilizing quantitative measures. Through this approach, we strive to contribute to the advancement of personalized notification in ESM by ensuring data validity, fostering transparency, and evaluating both general and individual performance.

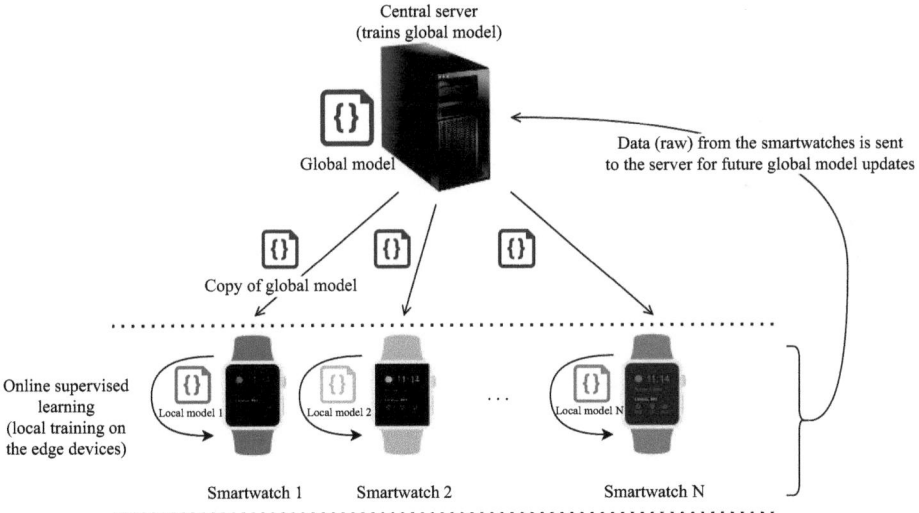

**Fig. 1.** Communication flow diagram illustrating the transfer of the model from the server to the smartwatches. A global model is trained centrally, and a copy of it is sent to the smartwatches, where they are trained further locally (different colors/local model numbers indicate that training on a device is independent of other models on other devices).

## 3.1 Study Design

To test our hypothesis we conducted a quasi-experiment in a field context, following a between-subjects design. We recruited $N = 53$ participants through convenience sampling for a 2-month experiment among students and staff of the Eindhoven University of Technology. However, only $N = 37$ participated and the rest dropped out. The study received ethical approval from the Ethics Review Board of Eindhoven University of Technology with reference number ERB2023ID457.

## 3.2 Procedure

We sent notifications to two groups: **a)** ALL: participants who received notifications in *all* contexts and based on the inter-notification time; and **b)** ML: the participants who received notifications based on the inference of the *ML* model. The participants were not told in which group they were in; therefore, they were not aware whether they received notifications based on intervals or based on ML inference. This was done to minimize potential biases related to their awareness of the experimental condition. The inter-notification time was set to 1 hour and 45 minutes, and the participants were asked to self-report upon receiving each notification. The questionnaire included questions related to understanding the user's context and state of being (e.g., How happy are you right now?, and Are you currently physically active?). The analysis of the recorded responses lies outside the scope of this paper, as we solely focus on the interaction with the notification and the act of responding rather than the responses themselves.

## 3.3 Machine Learning

**Data Collection.** The system (Fig. 1) uses data extracted from our previous ESM studies for training. The dataset contains fine-grained user interaction and sensor data, including user notification response behavior and physical activity. The inclusion of these features is based on the findings of previous research that suggest that the level of physical activity and the time of day can significantly influence the response rate with a high effect size [24]. The features related to the delivery of notifications and the response times are incorporated based on psychological theories related to memory accessibility and motivation [23]. Our feature set includes: (1) the number of received notifications in 15-minute intervals; (2) movement speed in km/h, as measured by the smartwatch accelerometer; (3) the previous reaction to a notification (0 for inopportune, 1 for opportune); (4) current physical activity type (not moving, walking, running, or unknown, as detected by the smartwatch pedometer); (5) day type (working day or weekend); and (6) time of day (morning, afternoon, evening, or night). Categorical variables are encoded as one-hot vectors.

**Training Process.** The input of the ML model comprises a 2-dimensional tensor[1] with input features as described in 3.3. The model output represents a binary classification, where 0 indicates inopportune moments for delivering notifications, and 1 indicates opportune moments. As illustrated in Fig. 1 we trained a general model with data from our previous ESM studies that predicts opportune moments (global model trained centrally). The model is then transferred to the smartwatches. Each model is updated as the user interacts with the device and the notifications (the local model trained on edge is separately trained for each individual). Fig. 1 provides an overview of the communication flow of our proposed architecture. Furthermore, the details of the training process are as follows:

> **Data Processing:** Features are formed by combining and analyzing the user response behavior data from our previous ESM studies. The data is split into training and testing sets (90% and 10% respectively) and is stratified to ensure a balanced class distribution in both sets.
> 
> **Model Architecture:** The model is a sequential neural network with three hidden layers having 128, 64, and 32 neurons, each using Rectified Linear Unit (ReLU) activation. The output layer has one neuron with a sigmoid activation, typical for binary classifications. We chose a neural network based on its ability to model complex, non-linear relationships in data [7], which we believed was crucial for personalized notification timing based on user behavior data.
> 
> **Class Weights:** Class weights are calculated to address class imbalance [12]. The weights are based on the ratio of total samples to the number of samples for each class, giving more weight (importance) to the minority class during training.
> 
> **Model Compilation:** The model is compiled using the Adam optimizer with a learning rate of 0.001, binary cross-entropy loss (suitable for binary classification), and Area Under the Curve (AUC) as the evaluation metric.
> 
> **Model Training:** The model is trained for 20 epochs with a batch size of 8. Class weights are used during training to handle unbalanced data. Validation data are used to assess the performance of the model on unseen data during training.

**Model Evaluation.** Response rate, reaction time, and participation are calculated to assess the effectiveness of personalized notifications. The response rate is the ratio of the number of responses to the notifications sent. The reaction time is defined as the time between receiving a notification and starting self-reporting. Participation is calculated as the total number of daily active participants during the experiment period. These metrics are compared between a control group receiving classic ESM notifications with fixed intervals (ALL group) and a treatment group receiving personalized ML-based notifications (ML group).

---

[1] We used the tensorflow.js library for our implementation (https://www.tensorflow.org/js).

**Algorithm 1:** Notification delivery and model update

```
 1  local_model ←fetch_global_model();
 2  lnotif_time ← 0 ;                              /* last notification time */
 3  inter_notification_time ←get_config().inter_notification_time;
 4  while smartwatch is worn do
 5      t ←get_current_time();
 6      features_matrix[t] ← get_features(t);
 7      ΔT ← t − lnotif_time;
 8      if ΔT > inter_notification_time then
 9          if local_model.infer(features_matrix[t]) > 0.5 or
             ΔT ≥ 2 × inter_notification_time then
10              if not last_notification_responded() then
11                  label_{lnotif_time} ← 0 ;         /* inopportune */
12                  local_model.update(features_matrix[lnotif_time], label_{lnotif_time});

13              send_notification();
14              lnotif_time ← t;

15      if last_notification_responded() then
16          ΔT ← lnotif_time − time_of_response ;     /* time between
                                                        notification and self-report */
17          if ΔT < 1 minute then
18              label_{lnotif_time} ← 1 ;             /* opportune */
19          else
20              label_t ← 1 ;                         /* opportune now */
21              label_{lnotif_time} ← 0 ;             /* inopportune before */
22              local_model.update(features_matrix[t], label_t);
23          local_model.update(features_matrix[lnotif_time], label_{lnotif_time});
```

**A Sampling-Density-Aware Notification Delivery Process.** Instead of delivering notifications immediately when the inter-notification time has passed (interval-based), randomly (signal-based), or upon occurrence of an event such as a change in location (event-based), our proposed system consults an ML model (see Fig. 1, and Algorithm 1). This model, informed by a feature vector that represents the current context, decides whether the moment is opportune for notification delivery. If not, the model is consulted every minute until an opportune moment is predicted. In case the model fails to predict an opportune moment within another inter-notification period, to reduce the bias introduced by favoring opportune moments and to guarantee sampling density (a spread of the notifications over the day in predefined time windows), a notification is sent regardless.

When a notification receives a response within a minute after delivery, the corresponding context is labeled 'opportune' and used for retraining the model (online feedback, one instance). If a participant responds later, the moment of delivering the notification is considered 'inopportune', while the response moment itself is labeled as 'opportune' (two instances). See Algorithm 1 for the pseudocode. These labeled vectors are used for incremental model fitting, explained in detail in the following subsections. Our implementation extends the Experiencer software [22] and is available on GitHub[2].

## 4 Results

We collected data during a period of 2 months. The distribution between the two groups was monitored during recruitment, however, several participants in both, but mostly in the ML group, did not begin participation, which resulted in data imbalance; ML group with 10 and ALL with 27 participants.

This imbalance affects the validity of the results, and readers should interpret the findings with caution. However, we observed patterns that suggest potential insights, which we believe are valuable to share despite the possibility of confounding factors. The descriptive statistics in Table 1 summarize the response behavior of the participants.

**Table 1.** Descriptive statistics

| Group | N | Read Count | | | Received Count | | |
|---|---|---|---|---|---|---|---|
| | | Total | $M$ | $SD$ | Total | $M$ | $SD$ |
| ALL | 27 | 982 | 36.37 | 27.52 | 1631 | 60.40 | 39.82 |
| ML | 10 | 474 | 47.40 | 30.70 | 697 | 69.70 | 42.10 |

In our study, the number of participants varied daily, making it essential to assess the response rate in a way that accounts for both engagement levels and the number of active participants. With a more balanced dataset and a larger, more stable participant pool, such a consideration would not be necessary. However, given the fluctuations in participation, a daily response rate calculation could misrepresent engagement, especially on days with few participants, where even a small number of responses could lead to an inflated response rate value for that day.

To address this limitation and provide a more reliable measure, we calculated the daily response rate (responses divided by notifications received), then weighted it by the number of active participants, and finally normalized it by the expected number of participants (i.e., the total number of individuals who opted in to participate and used the smartwatch at least once during the study; $N$ in Table 1). This approach ensures that days with a larger number of active participants have a proportionally greater influence on the overall engagement measure.

---

[2] https://github.com/khnshn/Experiencer.

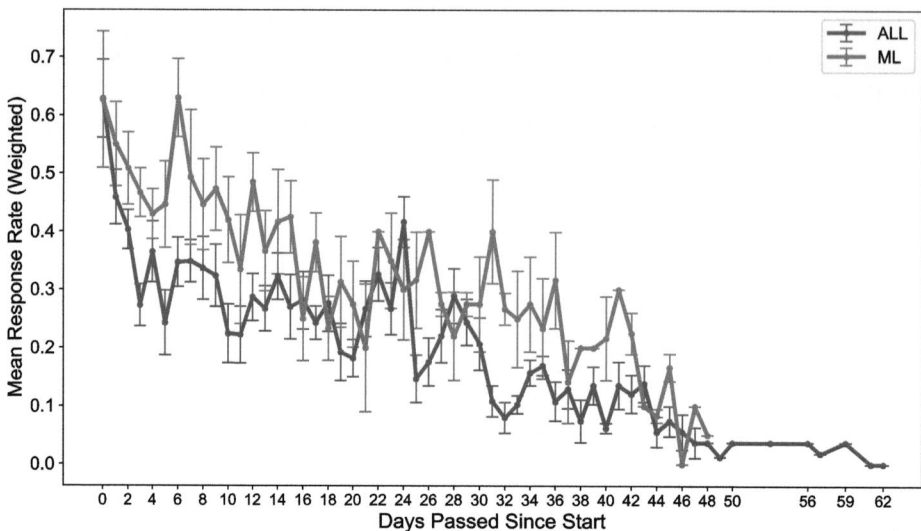

**Fig. 2.** Day-by-day mean response rate comparison between the groups.

$$\text{Weighted Daily Response Rate}_d = \frac{\left(\frac{\sum_{i=1}^{n_d} \text{responses}_{i,d}}{\sum_{i=1}^{n_d} \text{notifications received}_{i,d}}\right) \times n_d}{N}$$

where $d$ is the current day, $n_d$ is the number of active participants on day $d$, responses$_{i,d}$ is the number of responses by participant $i$ on day $d$, notifications received$_{i,d}$ is the number of notifications received by participant $i$ on day $d$, and $N$ is the expected number of participants.

By applying this weighted method, we mitigate the distortions caused by daily fluctuations in participation. This provides a more accurate assessment of participant engagement and ensures that trends reflect actual patterns rather than being skewed by days with particularly low or high participation.

A Welch's t-test was conducted to compare the mean response rates between the two groups. This test was chosen due to the class imbalance and the different sample sizes between the groups.

The mean response rate of the ML group was found 10.2% higher than that of the ALL group, indicating a better response rate when personalization is applied. But there were no statistically significant differences in the mean response rates between the ALL group ($M = 0.57$, $SD = 0.17$, $n = 27$) and the ML group ($M = 0.67$, $SD = 0.11$, $n = 10$), $t(19.87) = -1.98$, $p = .057$. The effect size, calculated using Cohen's d, was $d = -0.62$. The descriptive means indicate promising trends that suggest potential improvements with our ML-based approach.

The mean reaction time for each group was also calculated (see Fig. 3). The mean reaction time of the ML group to notification was found 9.6% faster than

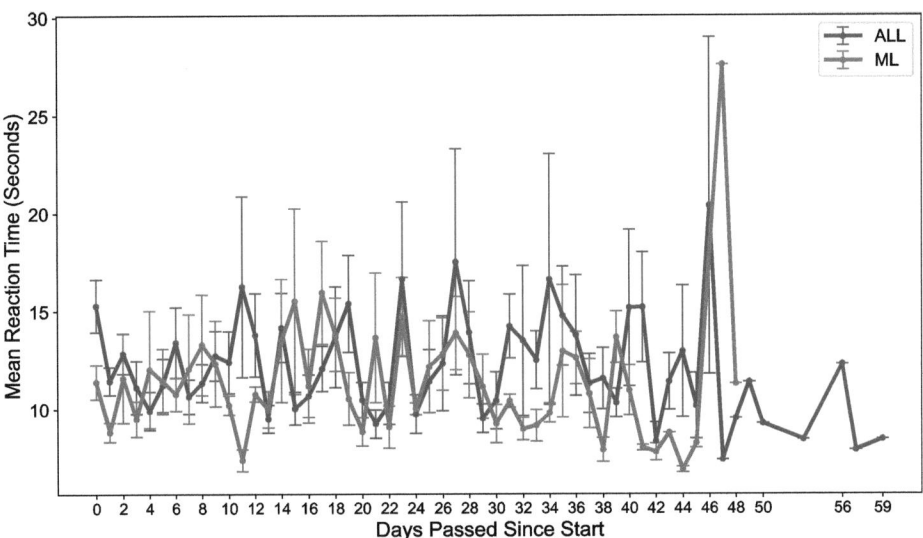

**Fig. 3.** Day-by-day mean reaction time comparison between the groups.

that of the ALL group, which could indicate the positive impact of personalization.

To compare the mean reaction times between the two groups, a Welch's t-test was conducted. The results indicated that there were no statistically significant differences in the mean reaction times between the ALL group ($M = 12382.07$, $SD = 1529.86$, $n = 27$) and the ML group ($M = 11246.22$, $SD = 1441.77$, $n = 10$), $t(19.64) = 1.98$, $p = .062$. The effect size, calculated using Cohen's d, was $d = 0.73$ (see Fig. 2).

Although our initial statistical tests did not reveal significant differences at the conventional $\alpha = 0.05$ threshold, the descriptive statistics suggested that the ML-based approach had potential, with trends indicating higher response rates and faster reaction times. However, the imbalance between groups reduced the statistical power of our tests, increasing the likelihood of a Type II error, i.e., failing to detect an effect that may exist.

These findings suggest that with a larger, more balanced sample, stronger statistical evidence may emerge. While our results should be interpreted with caution, they provide preliminary insights that warrant further investigation. To support future research, we have shared our source code, encouraging replication and studies with increased participation.

## 5 Discussion and Future Work

The class imbalance in our dataset, with negative labels outnumbering positive ones approximately fivefold, presents a challenge that must be carefully considered in model training. To mitigate the impact of this imbalance, we employed techniques such as oversampling the minority class and incorporating class weights during training. While these methods help improve model robustness, they do not fully eliminate potential biases. Future research would benefit from larger, more balanced datasets to further validate these findings. Additionally, academic research should prioritize open data-sharing practices, particularly for interaction-related datasets, to facilitate the creation of larger, more diverse datasets that collectively improve model training and generalizability.

We utilized a server-edge architecture for our online supervised learning, which provides flexibility for real-time adaptation. While our approach shows promise, privacy considerations remain crucial. Federated learning offers a potential alternative that could enhance data privacy while still enabling centralized model training [20]. Although not yet widely adopted in ESM tools, transmitting anonymized model parameters instead of raw data could support collaborative model training across distributed edge devices. Future research should explore the feasibility and trade-offs of this approach in real-world ESM applications.

Although our current method involves online supervised learning on smartwatches, the flexibility of our system allows for continuous or interval-based model updates. This adaptability could help capture evolving user behavior patterns and improve the responsiveness of notification delivery strategies. However, the effectiveness of such updates depends on the stability of behavior patterns over time, and further investigation is needed to determine optimal update intervals and mechanisms.

Future work could also explore meta-analysis techniques by clustering local models from different devices and aggregating them based on participant characteristics. Linking these clusters to traits collected through intake surveys could enable more personalized notification strategies while mitigating the cold start problem. For instance, new study participants could receive a model aligned with their characteristics rather than a generic global model. While this approach holds potential, its effectiveness in real-world scenarios remains to be fully evaluated.

A lightweight neural network was trained as a general model and deployed on smartwatches for online training. While this model was selected for its ability to capture potential non-linearities in individual user behavior, exploring more interpretable and explainable models, such as random forests, remains a valuable direction for future research in this domain.

The choice of online supervised learning in our study was motivated by the availability of labeled data from previous ESM studies, enabling deterministic labeling of feature vectors based on user interactions. However, as we consider expanding the feature set in future work to incorporate additional sensors and complex feature interactions, Reinforcement Learning (RL) presents an alternative that may be better suited for decision-making in uncertain environments. RL could allow models to learn optimal notification strategies through interaction rather than relying on predetermined labels [40]. However, its application in ESM settings would require careful design, particularly in defining reward functions that align with research objectives.

In this study, we incorporated logic to explicitly enforce inter-notification time constraints, ensuring appropriate sampling density. If reinforcement learning were to be applied, these constraints should be embedded in the reward function. Rather than optimizing for response rates alone, the reward function should also account for the required notification frequency and spacing to maintain the ecological validity of the ESM approach. Specifically, the model should be incentivized to send notifications in alignment with predefined intervals while discouraging excessive clustering or overly sparse sampling. Implementing such an approach would require further experimentation to balance exploration, exploitation, and compliance with study requirements.

While our findings and methodological choices are subject to limitations, they provide valuable insights into optimizing notification delivery in ESM studies. The software and techniques introduced here demonstrate the potential for more adaptive, data-driven approaches. We encourage future research to build upon these findings, particularly through larger-scale studies that address the current constraints and further explore the integration of reinforcement learning and privacy-preserving techniques.

## 6 Conclusion

This paper addresses the pressing issue of notification timing in Experience Sampling Method (ESM) studies, where participant engagement often wanes due to frequent and poorly timed notifications. By leveraging machine learning (ML) methods, particularly through server-edge architecture, we demonstrated the potential to enhance notification delivery strategies. Our findings highlighted the effectiveness of online supervised learning on smartwatches, enforced with additional windowing logic to attain ecological validity. While our data was too small to demonstrate the gains convincingly, the results show promising trends and call for more extensive validation studies. We discussed the importance of addressing dataset imbalance and the potential of federated learning for preserving user privacy while still enabling collaborative model training. Future research should explore meta-analysis techniques for personalized notification strategies, simulating participant behavior for improved model training, and leveraging reinforcement learning to optimize notification timing in dynamic environments. Our study underscored the promise of ML-driven approaches in enhancing the quality and relevance of context-aware ESM data collection, ultimately advancing our understanding of human behavior in real-world contexts.

**Acknowledgment.** This project was financed by the Dutch Research Council (NWO), grant number 628.011.214.

# References

1. Avraham Bahir, R., Parmet, Y., Tractinsky, N.: Effects of visual enhancements and delivery time on receptivity of mobile push notifications. In: Extended Abstracts of the 2019 CHI Conference on Human Factors in Computing Systems, pp. 1–6 (2019)
2. Bachmann, A., et al.: ESMAC: a web-based configurator for context-aware experience sampling apps in ambulatory assessment. In: Proceedings of the 5th EAI International Conference on Wireless Mobile Communication and Healthcare, pp. 15–18 (2015)
3. Balebako, R., Schaub, F., Adjerid, I., Acquisti, A., Cranor, L.: The impact of timing on the salience of smartphone app privacy notices. In: Proceedings of the 5th Annual ACM CCS Workshop on Security and Privacy in Smartphones and Mobile Devices, pp. 63–74 (2015)
4. van Berkel, N., Goncalves, J., Lovén, L., Ferreira, D., Hosio, S., Kostakos, V.: Effect of experience sampling schedules on response rate and recall accuracy of objective self-reports. Int. J. Hum. Comput. Stud. **125**, 118–128 (2019)
5. Bhattacharya, S., Lane, N.D.: From smart to deep: robust activity recognition on smartwatches using deep learning. In: 2016 IEEE International Conference on Pervasive Computing and Communication Workshops (PerCom Workshops), pp. 1–6. IEEE (2016)
6. Bidargaddi, N., et al.: To prompt or not to prompt? A microrandomized trial of time-varying push notifications to increase proximal engagement with a mobile health app. JMIR Mhealth Uhealth **6**(11), e10123 (2018)
7. Bishop, C.M.: Neural networks for pattern recognition. Oxford University Press (1995)
8. Csikszentmihalyi, M., Larson, R., et al.: Flow and the foundations of positive psychology, vol. 10. Springer (2014)
9. De Russis, L., Monge Roffarello, A.: On the benefit of adding user preferences to notification delivery. In: Proceedings of the 2017 CHI Conference Extended Abstracts on Human Factors in Computing Systems, pp. 1561–1568 (2017)
10. Gonul, S., Namli, T., Baskaya, M., Sinaci, A.A., Cosar, A., Toroslu, I.H.: Optimization of just-in-time adaptive interventions using reinforcement learning. In: Recent Trends and Future Technology in Applied Intelligence: 31st International Conference on Industrial Engineering and Other Applications of Applied Intelligent Systems, IEA/AIE 2018, Montreal, QC, Canada, June 25-28, 2018, Proceedings 31, pp. 334–341. Springer (2018)
11. Gouveia, R., Karapanos, E.: Footprint tracker: supporting diary studies with lifelogging. In: Proceedings of the SIGCHI Conference on Human Factors in Computing Systems, pp. 2921–2930 (2013)
12. He, H., Garcia, E.A.: Learning from imbalanced data. IEEE Trans. Knowl. Data Eng. **21**(9), 1263–1284 (2009)
13. Hernandez, J., McDuff, D., Infante, C., Maes, P., Quigley, K., Picard, R.: Wearable ESM: differences in the experience sampling method across wearable devices. In: Proceedings of the 18th International Conference on Human-Computer Interaction with Mobile Devices and Services, pp. 195–205 (2016)
14. Ho, B.J., Balaji, B., Koseoglu, M., Srivastava, M.: Nurture: notifying users at the right time using reinforcement learning. In: Proceedings of the 2018 ACM International Joint Conference and 2018 International Symposium on Pervasive and Ubiquitous Computing and Wearable Computers, pp. 1194–1201 (2018)

15. Hoi, S.C., Sahoo, D., Lu, J., Zhao, P.: Online learning: a comprehensive survey. Neurocomputing **459**, 249–289 (2021)
16. Hormuth, S.E.: The sampling of experiences in situ. J. Pers. **54**(1), 262–293 (1986)
17. Iida, M., Shrout, P.E., Laurenceau, J.P., Bolger, N.: Using diary methods in psychological research (2012)
18. Intille, S.S., Rondoni, J., Kukla, C., Ancona, I., Bao, L.: A context-aware experience sampling tool. In: CHI'03 Extended Abstracts on Human Factors in Computing Systems, pp. 972–973 (2003)
19. Iqbal, S.T., Bailey, B.P.: Effects of intelligent notification management on users and their tasks. In: Proceedings of the SIGCHI Conference on Human Factors in Computing Systems, pp. 93–102 (2008)
20. Kairouz, P., et al.: Advances and open problems in federated learning. Found. Trends® Mach. Learn. **14**(1–2), 1–210 (2021)
21. Kapoor, A., Horvitz, E.: Experience sampling for building predictive user models: a comparative study. In: Proceedings of the SIGCHI Conference on Human Factors in Computing Systems, pp. 657–666 (2008)
22. Khanshan, A., Van Gorp, P., Markopoulos, P.: Experiencer: an open-source context-sensitive wearable experience sampling tool. In: International Conference on Pervasive Computing Technologies for Healthcare, pp. 315–331. Springer (2022)
23. Khanshan, A., Van Gorp, P., Markopoulos, P.: Simulating participant behavior in experience sampling method research. In: Extended Abstracts of the 2023 CHI Conference on Human Factors in Computing Systems, pp. 1–7 (2023)
24. Khanshan, A., Van Gorp, P., Nuijten, R., Markopoulos, P.: Assessing the influence of physical activity upon the experience sampling response rate on wrist-worn devices. Int. J. Environ. Res. Public Health **18**(20), 10593 (2021)
25. Lathia, N., Rachuri, K.K., Mascolo, C., Rentfrow, P.J.: Contextual dissonance: design bias in sensor-based experience sampling methods. In: Proceedings of the 2013 ACM International Joint Conference on Pervasive and Ubiquitous Computing, pp. 183–192 (2013)
26. Lee, J., Kwon, J., Kim, H.: Reducing distraction of smartwatch users with deep learning. In: Proceedings of the 18th International Conference on Human-Computer Interaction with Mobile Devices and Services Adjunct, pp. 948–953 (2016)
27. Li, T., Haines, J.K., De Eguino, M.F.R., Hong, J.I., Nichols, J.: Alert now or never: understanding and predicting notification preferences of smartphone users. ACM Trans. Comput. Hum. Interact. **29**(5), 1–33 (2023)
28. Lutze, R., Waldhör, K.: Improving dialogue design and control for smartwatches by reinforcement learning based behavioral acceptance patterns. In: Human-Computer Interaction. Human Values and Quality of Life: Thematic Area, HCI 2020, Held as Part of the 22nd International Conference, HCII 2020, Copenhagen, Denmark, July 19–24, 2020, Proceedings, Part III 22, pp. 75–85. Springer (2020)
29. Markopoulos, P., Batalas, N., Timmermans, A.: On the use of personalization to enhance compliance in experience sampling. In: Proceedings of the European Conference on Cognitive Ergonomics 2015, pp. 1–4 (2015)
30. Mehrotra, A., Hendley, R., Musolesi, M.: Prefminer: Mining user's preferences for intelligent mobile notification management. In: Proceedings of the 2016 ACM International Joint Conference on Pervasive and Ubiquitous Computing, pp. 1223–1234 (2016)
31. Mehrotra, A., Hendley, R., Musolesi, M.: Interpretable machine learning for mobile notification management: an overview of prefminer. GetMobile: Mobile Comput. Commun. **21**(2), 35–38 (2017)

32. Morrison, L.G., et al.: The effect of timing and frequency of push notifications on usage of a smartphone-based stress management intervention: an exploratory trial. PLoS ONE **12**(1), e0169162 (2017)
33. Muralidharan, A.: Near real time AI personalization for notifications at LinkedIn. In: Proceedings of the Fifteenth ACM International Conference on Web Search and Data Mining, pp. 1648–1648 (2022)
34. Okoshi, T., Tsubouchi, K., Taji, M., Ichikawa, T., Tokuda, H.: Attention and engagement-awareness in the wild: a large-scale study with adaptive notifications. In: 2017 IEEE International Conference on Pervasive Computing and Communications (PerCom), pp. 100–110. IEEE (2017)
35. Pham, X.L., Nguyen, T.H., Hwang, W.Y., Chen, G.D.: Effects of push notifications on learner engagement in a mobile learning app. In: 2016 IEEE 16th International Conference on Advanced Learning Technologies (ICALT), pp. 90–94. IEEE (2016)
36. Poppinga, B., Heuten, W., Boll, S.: Sensor-based identification of opportune moments for triggering notifications. IEEE Pervasive Comput. **13**(1), 22–29 (2014)
37. Rondoni, J.C.: Context-aware experience sampling for the design and study of ubiquitous technologies. Ph.D. thesis, Massachusetts Institute of Technology (2003)
38. Seo, J., Lee, S., Lee, G.: An experience sampling system for context-aware mobile application development. In: Design, User Experience, and Usability. Theory, Methods, Tools and Practice: First International Conference, DUXU 2011, Held as Part of HCI International 2011, Orlando, FL, USA, July 9-14, 2011, Proceedings, Part I 1, pp. 648–657. Springer (2011)
39. Stone, A.A., Kessler, R.C., Haythomthwatte, J.A.: Measuring daily events and experiences: decisions for the researcher. J. Pers. **59**(3), 575–607 (1991)
40. Sutton, R.S., Barto, A.G.: Reinforcement Learning: An Introduction. MIT Press (2018)
41. Wang, S., Zhang, C., Kröse, B., van Hoof, H.: Optimizing adaptive notifications in mobile health interventions systems: reinforcement learning from a data-driven behavioral simulator. J. Med. Syst. **45**, 1–8 (2021)
42. Yuan, Y., Muralidharan, A., Nandy, P., Cheng, M., Prabhakar, P.: Offline reinforcement learning for mobile notifications. In: Proceedings of the 31st ACM International Conference on Information & Knowledge Management, pp. 3614–3623 (2022)
43. Zeng, C., Cui, L., Wang, Z.: An exponential time-aware recommendation model for mobile notification services. In: Pacific-Asia Conference on Knowledge Discovery and Data Mining, pp. 592–603. Springer (2017)

**Open Access** This chapter is licensed under the terms of the Creative Commons Attribution 4.0 International License (http://creativecommons.org/licenses/by/4.0/), which permits use, sharing, adaptation, distribution and reproduction in any medium or format, as long as you give appropriate credit to the original author(s) and the source, provide a link to the Creative Commons license and indicate if changes were made.

The images or other third party material in this chapter are included in the chapter's Creative Commons license, unless indicated otherwise in a credit line to the material. If material is not included in the chapter's Creative Commons license and your intended use is not permitted by statutory regulation or exceeds the permitted use, you will need to obtain permission directly from the copyright holder.

# From Explaining to Engaging: The Effect of Interactive AI Explanations on Citizens' Fairness and Adoption Perceptions

Saja Aljuneidi[1]($^{\boxtimes}$), Wilko Heuten[1], Maria Wolters[1], and Susanne Boll[2]

[1] OFFIS - Institute for Information Technology, Oldenburg, Germany
{saja.aljuneidi,wilko.heuten,maria.wolters}@offis.de
[2] University of Oldenburg, Oldenburg, Germany
susanne.boll@uni-oldenburg.de

**Abstract.** Integrating Artificial Intelligence (AI) into public administration decision-making requires clear explanations to ensure citizens maintain positive perceptions, particularly when AI systems make decisions that require discretion without human intervention. While existing research focuses on explanation *content*, the role of explanation *interactivity* in shaping citizens' perceptions remains underexplored. This gap is especially critical in high-stakes contexts like child welfare, where there are several plausible legal decisions. Interactive explanations can help citizens better understand, question, and engage directly with the AI systems. This study investigates how interactive explanations influence citizens' fairness perceptions and willingness to adopt AI systems in the high-stakes child welfare scenario. Through an online vignette survey (N = 562), we compared three levels of explanation interactivity: none (static), moderate (allowing citizens to reorder decision factors), and enhanced (allowing for a Q&A session). Surprisingly, interactivity *does not* significantly affect citizens' perception of fairness or willingness to adopt the AI system. Instead, explanation content and citizens' prior attitudes toward AI play a more decisive role. This work contributes to understanding how interactive explanations influence public perceptions. It further underscores the role of pre-existing biases, individual differences, and attitudes in shaping how citizens perceive AI-based decisions in high-stakes public administration contexts.

**Keywords:** Interactive Explanation · AI-based Decision-Making · Public Administration · Child Welfare · Fairness · Intention to Adopt

## 1 Introduction

The integration of AI into public administration decision-making processes is increasing, with applications ranging from the automation of routine tasks (e.g., license renewals [22]), to fully making autonomous decisions (e.g., student loan repayment [42]). These systems often operate with minimal human oversight and are capable of directly providing decisions and explanations to citizens. This evolution is due to the AI's potential to enhance operational efficiency [19,26], availability, service quality [24,26], and its ability to bridge global staffing deficits in public administrations [28].

Although AI-based decision-making offers significant benefits in public administrations, its complex nature raises concerns about fairness, transparency, and citizen engagement, especially in decisions requiring leeway or discretion[1]. Providing explanations for such decisions is essential to address these concerns, mitigate the risks of autonomous decision-making, and help citizens understand how the AI systems work [4,23]. Explanations are even more vital when decisions directly impact citizens' lives, which is the case in public administration.

Research on eXplainable AI (XAI) often emphasizes explanation content [49], focusing on describing models, data, or decision logic to foster understanding of AI outputs. This approach, while informative, results in static, one-directional explanations that limit user engagement [2,49]. However, in high-stakes scenarios such as child welfare or housing allocation, static explanations are insufficient [2,41]. Interactive explanations prioritize engagement and provide a more dynamic experience, empowering citizens to inspect decisions, ask questions, or adjust decision parameters [6,9]. This reduces perceptions of arbitrariness, enhances user agency, and encourages long-term adoption [27,41]. Despite that, the potential of interactive explanations from citizens' perspectives remains under-explored [53]. Thus, our research question addresses this gap:

***RQ****: How do interactive explanations of AI-based decisions influence citizens' fairness perceptions and intention to adopt autonomous AI systems in high-stakes public administration context?*

We conducted a preliminary workshop to explore the design space for interactive explanations in public administration. Building on its findings, we conducted an online vignette survey (N = 562) to examine citizens' perception of fairness and willingness to adopt AI in child welfare decisions. Based on a scenario of a family navigating their divorce, we tested three levels of explanation interactivity: (1) static explanations, (2) moderate interactivity, where citizens could reorder the importance of factors that affected the AI's decision, and (3) enhanced interactivity, which included a Q&A session to address concerns about the decision. Contrary to expectations, our results *did not* demonstrate any significant differences between interactivity levels. Instead, we found that pre-existing individual differences between citizens, such as AI literacy and attitude towards AI, strongly influence perception of fairness and adoption intention.

Our findings contribute citizen-centric insights into how interactive explanations impact fairness perceptions and AI adoption. We highlight the interplay between explanations' interactivity and content, as well as how citizens' prior biases and expectations impact their perceptions. Fundamentally, we contributes to the broader discussion on AI-based decision-making in public administration.

---

[1] Administrative discretion is the autonomy of civil servants to use their own judgment when making decisions, within the boundaries of the law.

## 2 Related Work and Hypotheses

Research on interactive explanations in public administration is still emerging; existing studies highlight the benefits of interactive explanations for civil servants in high-stake areas such as child welfare [29] and unemployment services [53]. The perspective of citizens, who are directly impacted and often have no alternatives, remains underexplored. Moreover, the introduction of AI-based decision-making in public services may alter power dynamics [32], making it critical to address citizen perspectives to avoid public backlash.

### 2.1 Explanation of AI-Based Decisions

Humans inherently seek explanations to understand the world, a need that extends to AI systems. Explanations are essential for demystifying the "black box" by providing insights into AI logic, methods, and reasoning [10], which improves fairness perceptions [4,20,47,48], and supports transparency in public administration. To achieve these benefits, it is essential to consider not only the content of the explanations but also their level of interactivity to inform and engage users effectively.

**Explanation Types.** AI and HCI researchers have identified various types of explanation (also called explanation styles), with the most prominent being feature or factor relevance explanations. These explanations highlight how factors contribute to the model's decision (e.g., LIME [43]). Other explanation types extend that and provide insights into feature importance in decision-making (e.g., [48]). Counterfactual explanations, inspired by human reasoning, illustrate how changes in input alter output (e.g., [25,39]). Some explanations focus on clarifying datasets, their structure, and the influence of training cases on decisions [20,21]. All these types emphasize explanation *content* but leave a gap in exploring the interactive nature of explanations and their effects on user perceptions.

**Interactive Explanations.** Interactivity in XAI refers to allowing users to engage, interpret, or discover information about the model or decision-making process [9,55]. Bertrand et al. [9] categorize nine interactive explanation techniques into three cognitive support types: selective, mutable, and dialogic. Selective features allow users to clarify information, arrange parameters and visual representation, and filter content to highlight specific metrics (e.g., [16,36]). Mutable features enable dataset or models reconfiguration, simulating changes in inputs and outputs, and comparisons (e.g., [36]). Dialogic features support iterative explanation sequences, feedback, and follow-up questions (e.g., [45,51]).

Many studies emphasize the benefits of interactivity, particularly in enhancing user comprehension of complex algorithms, despite the added time required for interaction [16,41]. Research in the education context (e.g., [16,37]) underscores the positive role of interactivity in fostering cognitive engagement, suggesting that users can gain a more nuanced understanding of AI decisions. However, findings from other contexts, like healthcare, suggest no significant differences in user satisfaction or comprehension between mutable interactive and static explanations [36]. These mixed results highlight that the effectiveness of interactivity is highly context-dependent. Notably, there is limited research examining the impact of interactive XAI in public service settings, let alone in high-stakes decisions, underscoring a critical gap in the literature.

## 2.2 Citizens' Perceptions of the Fairness of AI-Based Decisions

Understanding how citizens perceive AI-based decisions in public administration is essential for fostering successful implementation of AI systems. Fairness has long been a central criterion for evaluating public institutions, as citizens expect decisions that affect them to be just and impartial [15,52]. Defined as discrimination-free treatment for all [34], fairness encompasses multiple interrelated dimensions: informational (transparency and clarity of information), procedural (fairness in decision-making processes), distributive (equity in outcomes), and interpersonal (respectful treatment) [17]. While AI explanations positively influence fairness perception [31], this area remains understudied compared to areas like trustworthiness or accountability of AI [31]. Prior research in public administration suggests that the amount and density of explanation positively impact fairness [4,52], however, few studies explore the impact of interactive explanations on fairness perception in public services.

## 2.3 Hypotheses

Building on the reviewed literature, we hypothesize that interactive explanations influence both procedural and distributive fairness perceptions (H1a, H1b), as interactive explanations can enhance procedural fairness [33], which in turn shapes distributive fairness [10]. In contrast, informational fairness is typically shaped by explanation detail [48], and thus is not expected to vary due to consistent content depth across interactivity styles (H1d). Finally, hypothesis (H1c) suggests that interactivity may positively impact citizens' willingness to adopt AI systems. By fostering a sense of control and engagement potentially boosting citizens' willingness to adopt the technology [23].

*H1*: *Higher interactive explanation leads to higher perceived (a) procedural fairness, (b) distributive fairness, (c) adoption, but (d) does not affect perceived informational fairness*

**Individual Differences: AI Literacy.** The literature suggests that AI literacy may influence perceptions of fairness and adoption intentions. Wang et al. [52] found that computer literacy has a positive influence on users' fairness perception of algorithmic decisions. Moreover, higher AI literacy positively influences both informational and distributive fairness in public services [4], and in loan approval in banking [48,56]. We hypothesize that AI literacy will continue to influence fairness perceptions and adoption.

*H2*: *The level of AI literacy positively correlates with citizens' perceptions of (a) procedural, (b) distributive, (c) informational fairness, as well as (d) adoption intentions.*

## 3 Approach and Studies

To address our research question, we selected child welfare as our high-stakes administrative scenario. This choice was driven by the body of existing research on AI as a decision-support tool in this field (e.g., [13,29,50]), as well as its significant societal impact. Drawing on our interdisciplinary expertise and prior research with municipalities, we designed the scenario to align with key challenges in German child welfare agencies (Sect. 3.1). Then, we explored the design space of interactive explanations through the perspectives of AI and HCI experts (Sect. 3.2). Insights from this workshop informed the design of our citizen-centric online vignette survey (Sect. 3.3). We used a vignette-based approach to simulate a real-world scenario and assess explanation design, bypassing the need for a functional system at this stage.

### 3.1 Scenario: Wagner Family in Child Welfare

The story centers on the Wagner family, consisting of a hardworking lawyer, a creative artist, and their beloved daughter, facing the challenges of divorce after 12 years of marriage. Seeking guidance on custody, visitation rights, and financial contributions, they approach their local child welfare agency, only to find that the earliest available appointment is 15 weeks away. Alternatively, they are offered the option to address their concerns sooner with an AI-based Intelligent Self-Service Kiosk (ISSK). The Wagners approach the ISSK with their wishes for a smooth divorce and minimal disruption for their child (see detailed wishes in Table 1). The ISSK allows the parents to explain their issues and then collects detailed information about their lives, incomes, parenting styles, and relationships with their daughter. Based on this data, the ISSK makes binding decisions regarding the three concerns and delivers them directly to the parents (see decisions in Table 1). In this scenario, decisions are fully autonomous, with no human intervention, but subject to human oversight through periodic reviews. The full illustrated vignette is included in the supplementary material.

### 3.2 Preliminary Workshop with Experts

The workshop with AI and HCI experts aimed to define the design space and constraints for interactive explanations in the high-stakes child welfare service, ensuring that the subsequent citizen study evaluates refined and relevant designs.

**Workshop Design and Methods:** We recruited seven participants: three AI experts (1F, 2M) and four HCI experts (2F, 2M). All participants had a minimum of two years of professional or academic experience. Recruitment was conducted through advertisements within the research institute and the university community, and supplemented by convenience sampling to ensure diverse participation.

**Table 1.** Wagner parents' wishes and ISSK decisions on custody, visitation rights, and financial contributions.

| Category | Custody | Visitation Rights | Financial Contribution |
|---|---|---|---|
| Parents' Wishes | Joint custody. | Minimize disruptions to the daughter's routine (e.g., school, activities). | One parent argues contributions should match income, while the other believes the primary caregiver should contribute less. |
| ISSK's Decision | Joint custody. | Weekdays with father, weekends with mother, holidays split equally. | Both parents contribute equally. |
| Decision Rationale | Ensures active involvement of both parents. | Minimizes disruption to daily routine by considering school location and parents' work schedules. | Considering parent's income and household costs, equal contributions ensure shared responsibility in upbringing. |

The three-hour workshop was piloted once to refine structure and timing. It began with a brainstorming session on AI decision-making and explanation methods, followed by clustering of key strategies. Then, participants received a 6-page illustrated handout detailing the Wagner family case, their wishes, the AI decisions, and a list of possible explanations (see supplementary material). In two mixed groups, they then designed how the ISSK should communicate decisions and provide interactive explanations to enhance perceived fairness. Each group analyzed the scenario, selected design strategies from the brainstorming cluster, and developed concepts, concluding with presentations and a final discussion.

The first author facilitated the workshop and collected qualitative data through observation and taking notes during group tasks and presentations. To deepen our insights, a 15-min post-workshop reflection was conducted with one participant per group, clarifying design concepts and capturing views on ideation.

**Results and Insights:** A descriptive analysis of collected notes and visual materials identified key characteristics of the design of explanation interactivity. Follow-up discussions with coauthors yield the following interactivity highlights:

*(1) Decision Framing and Clarity:* Decision framing was seen as crucial for fostering acceptance and adoption. Group 2 emphasized clear yet empathetic framing by highlighting the factors behind the AI's decisions, focusing on the positive impacts of these decisions on the daughter's life, even when the outcomes appeared negative. They also emphasized the need to reference parents' initial wishes to enhance a clear narrative and reduce conflict.

*(2) Interaction Interface:* The groups favored minimalistic, abstract interfaces. Group 1 proposed a voice-based ISSK with a touch screen and visualizations to communicate decision factors (e.g., mapping school-to-parent distances).

Group 2 designed a "talking circle" as an abstract, non-human entity, deliberately avoiding avatars to maintain professionalism in high-stakes scenarios.

*(3) Explanation on Demand*: Participants emphasized layered, modular, and context-sensitive explanations. Both groups designed the ISSK to provide an initial, concise explanation overview of each decision, with deeper explanation layers available for on-demand exploration. Group 1 proposed a "Discuss with AI" button for interactive questions and customized responses.

Participants' engagement with explanation formats underscored the need for varying interactivity levels, ranging from minimal to fully interactive, on-demand explanations. These insights informed the vignette survey conditions (see Study Conditions: Explanation Interactivity levels), and guided refinements to the vignette itself, including shortening its length and clarifying contextual details such as the child's current living situation.

### 3.3 Online Vignette Survey with Citizens

To evaluate the impact of interactive explanations on citizens' perceptions of procedural, informational, and distributive fairness, as well as adoption intentions, we conducted a between-subjects online survey using illustrated vignettes. The survey used the Wagner family scenario to provide a realistic context for assessing ISSK decisions on custody, visitation schedules, and financial responsibilities. This allowed the survey participants to assess the AI system's decisions from a third-person perspective, promoting objectivity and reducing bias caused by personal interests [5,52]. To balance realism and clarity in the vignette, some variables (e.g., parents' salaries and working hours) were made concrete, while others (e.g., travel duration) remained abstract. Based on the workshop recommendation, the survey vignettes indicated a voice-based interaction between the parents and the ISSK. The full survey and scales can be found in the supplementary material.

**Study Conditions: Explanation Interactivity Levels.** We designed three levels of interactive explanations, each presented in a separate vignette. Informed by the workshop results and existing literature, especially Miller's constructs of selective, contrastive, and social explanations [38]. These conditions are outlined below, and illustrated in Fig. 1.

1. *Baseline – Static Explanation:* The workshop emphasized the importance of clear, sufficient initial explanations that align with parents' needs and their prior wishes and interactions with the ISSK before decisions are made. Accordingly, the static condition presents the factors considered by the ISSK (e.g., relationship with the child, income, etc.), ordered by importance, alongside a reference to the parents' expressed wishes. This approach resonates with prior research [4,5,29], and with Miller's concept of selective explanations [38], which emphasize providing only the essential information for understanding a decision. This condition serves as a baseline to evaluate the impact of interactivity in subsequent conditions.

2. **Moderate Interactivity:** This design builds on the static explanation and introduces an interactive component, aligning with the workshop recommendation for layered explanations. It allows citizens (the parents in the vignettes) to reorder the decision factors, including reordering the importance of their original wishes. For example, parents can explore how the ISSK decision changes if the commute duration to school is weighed less than the commute to extracurricular activities. This condition is also informed by the concept of contrastive (or counterfactual) explanations [38], illustrating how decisions might differ under alternative scenarios [53,56].
3. **Enhanced Interactivity:** Aligning with the workshop's third recommendation, this condition builds on the previous ones by adding a Q&A feature, allowing citizens to engage in a post-decision interactive dialogue with the ISSK. This human-like interaction mimics Miller's concept of social explanations, which stresses the importance of conversational exchanges [31,38]. Prior studies indicate that Q&A capabilities help users better understand predictions and risk scores, providing a sense of control and agency over decision-making processes [29].

**Fig. 1.** Vignette excerpts for the three conditions: (1) Baseline (yellow) shows static explanations with key factors ordered by importance; (2) Moderate Interactivity (green) adds reordering of factors, possibly changing the decision; (3) Enhanced Interactivity (orange) allows parents to ask follow-up questions. (Color figure online)

**Participants.** Power analysis using the pwr package in R [14] determined that 515 participants were needed for three conditions, assuming small effect size ($f = 0.1$) to achieve 95% power at $\alpha = 0.05$. To ensure quality control and meaningful engagement, we ran pilots, implemented attention checks, and response time thresholds. A pilot test with five colleagues refined the survey's wording and structure, followed by a soft launch with 52 participants to assess technical issues and completion time ($\bar{x} = 10.85$ min, $\sigma = 8.11$). A total of 664 responses were collected, 34 failed the attention check, and 68 completed the survey in less than 5.5 min, leaving **562** valid responses.

**Procedure.** Following ethics approval, we recruited a German adult sample via the crowdsourcing platform Bilendi[2], representative in terms of age and gender. Participants were randomly assigned to one of the vignette conditions. At the survey's outset, they were informed that the ISSK was intended to address staff shortages and increase efficiency in child welfare, while periodic human oversight ensured accuracy. Informed consent was obtained, and participants were compensated at a rate equivalent to EUR 10 per hour.

**Data Collection.** This study used a Convergent Mixed Methods Design [18], collecting both qualitative and quantitative data in the same survey to provide complementary insights and contextual understanding of the research problem.

Before viewing the vignette, participants provided demographic details (age, gender, education, social status, number of children, and experience with child welfare). They then completed a six-item version, following [4], of the General Attitudes Towards Artificial Intelligence Scale (GAAIS) [46] to measure positive and negative attitudes in a unified scale. AI literacy was assessed using a four-item scale measuring knowledge, confidence, and professional use of AI, following [4,48,56]. After viewing the vignette, participants responded to items measuring the four primary dependent variables:

- *Perceived Procedural Fairness*: Average of six items focusing on parents' ability to express their views, influence the outcome, consistency, impartiality of procedures, appeal opportunities, bias-free processes, and adherence to ethical standards, following scale used in [17,56].
- *Perceived Informational Fairness*: Average of five items, focusing on clarity, depth, and adequacy of explanations, following scale used in [4,48,56].
- *Perceived Distributive Fairness*: Average of two items covering the fairness of the decision outcome and perceived deservingness, following [10].
- *Willingness to Adopt*: Average of three items measuring satisfaction with the service and likelihood to use it if implemented in local municipalities, following scale used in [4].

To deepen our understanding of participant perspectives, we incorporated qualitative data collection through voluntary open-ended questions at the survey's conclusion. These questions were: "Do you consider the decision-making process fair? Why or why not?" and "Do you have any suggestions to improve the clarity of the decision-making process?". Additional feedback was provided through the final open-ended question: "Do you have further comments?". All scales used in the survey are provided in the supplementary material.

**Statistical Analysis.** All scales used a 5-point Likert format (1 = strongly disagree, 5 = strongly agree). Using the psych package in R [54], we calculated Cronbach's alpha for each scale, results demonstrated strong internal consistency, with all values exceeding 0.85. We used linear mixed models (LMMs) to test our hypotheses on informational, procedural, and distributive fairness, as well as adoption. LMMs were appropriate for accounting for both fixed and random

---

[2] Bilendi (https://www.bilendi.de/).

effects, particularly individual attitudes and literacy levels nested within experimental conditions. Using the restricted maximum likelihood (REML) estimation method in the lme4 package [8], we developed models tailored to each outcome variable. To that end, we tested for interactions between both individual-level predictors and the group-level predictor using ANOVAs. Positive AI attitude emerged as a key predictor across all outcome variables and thus was included as a random effect in all models. Other influential predictors included negative AI attitude, AI literacy, social status, age, gender, and position of children, with their specific inclusion varying by outcome. Significance was assessed through nested model comparisons through ANOVA, and model fit was evaluated using Akaike Information Criterion (AIC) scores. Final model specifications are:

$$outcome(Info.fair.) \sim 1 + condition + (1|pos.ai.att) \tag{1}$$

$$outcome(Dist.fair.) \sim 1 + condition + (1|pos.ai.att) + (1|age) \tag{2}$$

$$outcome(Proc.fair.) \sim 1 + condition + (1|pos.ai.att) + (1|neg.ai.att) \tag{3}$$

$$outcome(Adop.) \sim 1 + condition + (1|pos.ai.att) + (1|neg.ai.att) \tag{4}$$

**Qualitative Analysis.** We performed a reflective thematic analysis [11] on the open-ended survey responses. In the first coding cycle, the first author inductively segmented and coded the data, developing a preliminary thematic framework in discussion with co-authors. In the second cycle, the first author deepened the analysis by applying emotional, values, and versus coding [44]. *Emotional codes* capture the contextual nuances of parental emotions during divorce and custody hearings, especially in the context of AI involvement. *Values codes* revealed underlying beliefs, values, and attitudes expressed by participants, while *Versus Codes* identified conflicting perspectives. In iterative discussions, the resulting set of codes was refined into three main themes.

## 4 Results

In this section, we present the results of our survey analysis, starting with quantitative findings, followed by qualitative findings.

### 4.1 Descriptive Statistics

The 562 participants were fairly evenly distributed by gender (53.4% female) and age: 15.5% were 18–30, 28% were 31–45, 28% were 46–60, and 28.5% were over 60 years old. Most participants had vocational training (57%), 32% held a Bachelor's degree or higher, and 11% had a high school education or lower. Regarding social status, 33% were married, 22% single, 15% divorced, 18% in a stable relationship, and the remainder were widowed, separated, or preferred not to say. Most participants had one child or more (67%). Finally, only 30% had prior experience with the child welfare agency.

## 4.2 Modeling and Hypothesis Tests

To statistically assess the effect of explanation interactivity level on citizens' perception of information, procedural and distributive fairness, as well as adoption intention, we fit the linear mixed models described in Sect. 3.3.

**H1: Explanation Interactivity Effect on Outcome Variables.** H1 predicted that higher interactive explanations would lead to higher perceived (a) procedural fairness, (b) distributive fairness, and (c) adoption, but (d) not affect informational fairness. The models, presented in Table 2, show that the interactivity level has no significant effect on either dependent variable. The violin plots in Fig. 2 provide a visualization of that relationship. We therefore conclude that Hypotheses H1a, H1b, H1c, could not be confirmed. As expected (c.f. H1d), we did not see evidence that interactivity level significantly affects perceived informational fairness.

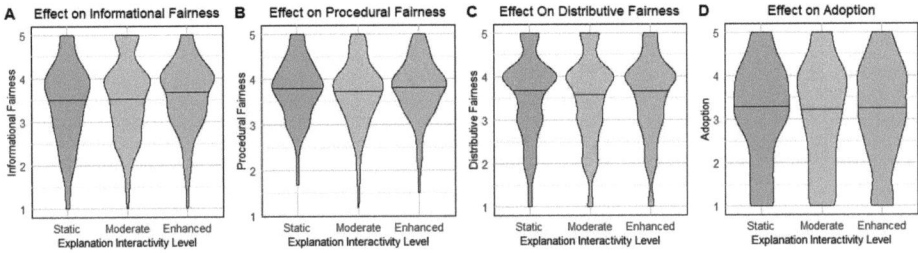

**Fig. 2.** Violin plots showing the effects of explanation interactivity levels on citizens' perceptions of informational, procedural, and distributive fairness, as well as adoption intention. Means are represented by horizontal lines, and the plot width reflects the proportion of ratings.

**H2: AI Literacy Effect on Outcome Variables.** We further investigated the impact of AI literacy on citizens' perceptions. AI literacy affected all outcome variables. Pearson correlation coefficients ranged from $r = 0.15$ to $r = 0.28$ ($p < 0.001$). The strongest correlation was observed between AI literacy and adoption intentions, suggesting that higher levels of AI literacy are associated with greater willingness to adopt the ISSK in child welfare. These results collectively support our hypotheses H2a, H2b, H2c, and H2d and are visualized in a combined scatter plot in Fig. 3-A.

**Post-Hoc Analysis:** Pearson correlations among individual difference measures indicated a moderate positive relationship between AI literacy and positive AI attitude ($r = 0.45$) and a weak negative correlation with negative AI attitude ($r = -0.19$), suggesting that higher literacy is associated with more favorable and slightly fewer unfavorable views of AI. Positive and negative AI attitudes were moderately inversely related ($r = -0.45$).

**Table 2.** Models showing the impact of Explanation Interactivity Level on citizens' ratings of informational fairness, procedural fairness, distributive fairness, and adoption, based on all 562 observations.

|  | Informational | Procedural | Distributive | Adoption |
|---|---|---|---|---|
| Enhanced | 0.090 | −0.065 | −0.064 | −0.078 |
|  | (−0.076, 0.255) | (−0.191, 0.061) | (−0.251, 0.123) | (−0.285, 0.130) |
| Moderate | 0.141 | 0.007 | −0.060 | −0.050 |
|  | (−0.028, 0.310) | (−0.122, 0.135) | (−0.252, 0.131) | (−0.261, 0.161) |
| Baseline | 3.320*** | 3.770*** | 3.484*** | 2.937*** |
|  | (2.861, 3.779) | (3.368, 4.172) | (3.084, 3.884) | (2.017, 3.858) |
| Log Likelihood | −696.189 | −542.783 | −765.436 | −821.720 |
| Akaike Inf. Crit. | 1,402.379 | 1,097.567 | 1,542.872 | 1,655.440 |
| Bayesian Inf. Crit. | 1,424.036 | 1,123.556 | 1,568.861 | 1,681.429 |

Note: *p<0.1; **p<0.05; ***p<0.01

Next, we examined the relationships between the individual difference measures of positive AI attitude and negative AI attitude and our four outcome variables using correlation analysis. Figure 3-B, C shows the interplay between citizens' attitudes toward AI and the outcome variables. We see strong positive relationships between positive AI attitude and all outcomes ($r = 0.28$ to $0.53$, $p < 0.001$), particularly for willingness to adopt. Conversely, negative AI attitude displayed inverse relationships, with the steepest negative slope observed for willingness to adopt ($r = -0.18$ to $-0.35$, $p < 0.001$). Lastly, positive AI attitude had a stronger effect on citizens' judgments across all outcomes compared to AI literacy and negative AI attitudes.

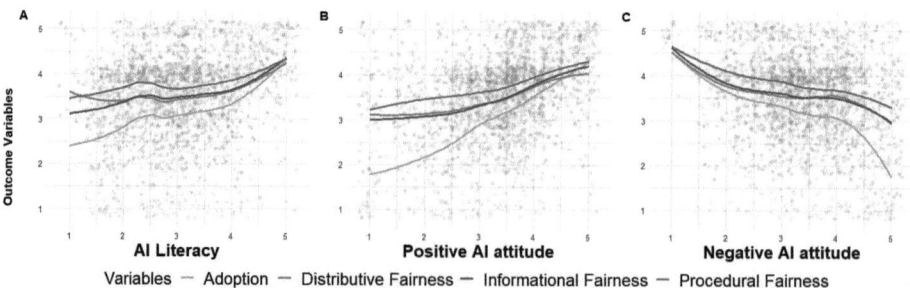

**Fig. 3.** Relationships of AI Literacy, Positive and Negative AI Attitudes with Informational, Distributive, Procedural Fairness, and Adoption.

## 4.3 Qualitative Analysis

A total of 1,140 textual contributions were received from 480 participants. Of these, 356 entries were deemed irrelevant (e.g., "no," "no comment," "no opinion"), resulting in 784 statements available for analysis. Following the approach outlined in Qualitative Analysis, three themes emerged:

**Theme 1: When Explanation Content Outweighs Interactivity:** This theme explores the relative importance of content quality versus interactivity of AI-driven child welfare explanations. Many participants judged decision fairness based on the *explanation content* rather than the level of interactivity, particularly when disagreed with the decision (i.e., the decision of equal financial support, see Table 1). Several respondents argued that equal payments were unfair, given income disparities: *"Due to the wage gap, it is not reasonable for parents to pay the same amount of maintenance" (P186)*. Concerns about visitation arrangements also arose, with some believing that weekend custody inequitably divides parental responsibilities, *"I also think that the weekends should be shared. Otherwise, [one parent] only has all the good times" (P1571)*. Given these disagreements, the level of explanation interactivity had minimal impact on citizens' perceptions, implying that interactivity only influences perceptions when explanation content is deemed sufficient. In contrast, participants who were generally satisfied with the decisions valued interactivity as a way to affirm fairness. These individuals appreciated the ability to engage in the process, noting: *"Good that the parents also had the opportunity to ask questions" (P774)* and *"Objections could be raised, which made a fair decision possible" (P2309)*. Furthermore, some participants who encountered static explanations expressed a need for interactive options, particularly to address objections: *"[...] it should be possible to describe your objection to the system, and the system will optimize the proposed solution" (P2400)*.

Overall, interactivity was appreciated by those satisfied with the decision outcomes and sought by those who wished to refine decisions, but decision outcome and content quality remained the primary determinant of fairness.

**Theme 2: The Tension Between Objectivity and Empathy.** Participants highlighted friction between AI's objective, data-driven approach and its lack of human empathy. Roughly half of the participants frequently praised AI for its impartiality and capacity to deliver unbiased decisions, viewing it as an advantage over human decision-makers swayed by biases and emotions. One participant noted, *"The decision-making process by AI is neutral. People [...] can be influenced by [...] whether the official likes or dislikes someone. Therefore, the decision-making process by AI is probably fair" (P738)*. Another emphasized, *"The AI is unbiased, unlike humans who may be guided by prejudices" (P699)*. For these participants, AI's factuality fostered trust in its fairness, with many favoring either full acceptance of AI or limited human oversight (see Theme 3). However, for the other half of the participants, this objectivity was perceived as

AI's greatest limitation in sensitive, human-centered matters. Its lack of empathy and inability to account for psychological or emotional nuances were seen as significant drawbacks. One participant remarked, *"AI cannot make decisions based on emotions. But people have feelings that need to be taken into account" (P667)*. Another shared, *"In a face-to-face conversation, needs can be discussed more personally [...] this is a very emotional matter, [...] a contact person can respond to this better than an AI" (P821)*.

Overall, there is tension between two types of participants, those who consider there to be an optimal solution that the AI can find, and those who argue that we need human values, intuitions, and lived experience. As one participant concluded, *"An AI only acts on information and data, but in such a case you also need humanity and empathy" (P311)*.

**Theme 3: In Search for Collaboration: Human vs. AI Roles.** This theme captures participants' diverse perspectives on the role of AI as a decision-maker in child welfare decision-making, ranging from full acceptance to absolute rejection. Many respondents fully accepted AI's involvement, finding its decisions fair and raising no objections. One stated, *"I think it's fair [...] a "human" employee would have made the same or similar decision" (P878)*. While acknowledging the benefits of AI-based decision-making, many participants valued *human oversight* after the decision is made to prevent errors and ensure accountability, particularly in the early stages of AI implementation in child welfare. They appreciated knowing autonomous decisions could be reviewed or appealed by civil servants, with one suggesting, *"I consider the decisions to be fair and believe that they will be reviewed by employees of the youth welfare office" (P1334)*. The largest group supported a collaborative approach, expressing cautious optimism, valuing AI's ability to analyze, prepare, and expedite decisions while insisting that humans retain final *authority and control* of binding decisions in emotionally charged, high-stakes cases. Some acknowledged AI's accuracy but felt uneasy entrusting such decisions solely to a machine, stating, *"[the decision] was fair. However, it somehow has a strange aftertaste if an AI decides this alone" (P2697)*, especially given previous negative encounters, *"The decision was fair. However, this does not remove my reservations about AI. My experiences [...with AI..] are rather negative. I am always delighted when a real person takes care of my concerns." (P939)*. Lastly, some citizens rejected the use of AI entirely, citing distrust, fear of AI, manipulation or bias, and the belief that only humans can adequately handle such ethical and emotionally complex decisions (see Theme 2). They stressed the irreplaceable value of human empathy and connection in decisions affecting lives, stating *"Decisions regarding children must always be made by people, preferably by several people! (P205)"*.

Taken together, there is a strong sentiment that decisions affecting children's welfare should not rely solely on AI but require meaningful human participation to ensure procedural fairness. Human involvement is seen as essential for oversight, control, and incorporating the child's perspective, which AI cannot fully capture due to its lack of empathy and contextual sensitivity.

## 5 Discussion

This section discusses the implications of our findings, focusing on enhancing citizen satisfaction.

### 5.1 If Not Interactivity, What Shapes Citizens' Perceptions?

Our findings indicate that explanation interactivity had no significant effect on fairness perceptions or adoption intentions, contradicting prior research that associates interactivity with increased engagement and more favorable perceptions of AI systems [38]. These results suggest that the effectiveness of interactivity may be strongly influenced by contextual factors such as domain, task complexity, or user expectations [9], highlighting the importance of identifying additional determinants of public perception. Our hypothesis testing revealed that higher levels of *AI literacy and more positive attitudes toward AI* were associated with increased perceptions of fairness and adoption, particularly in sensitive decision-making scenarios. This aligns with existing findings from public administration (i.e., ID renewal [4]), and banking domain (i.e., loan approval [48,56]).

Our thematic analysis (Theme 1) shows that participants' perceptions were shaped by both the *content of the explanation* and the extent to which the ISSK *decision aligned with their preferred outcome*. This supports findings by Sokol et al. [49], who argue that users bring specific expectations to high-stakes decisions and assess initial explanations based on how well they justify the outcome. When these expectations are unmet, users' perceptions of the system can diminish. Furthermore, users tend to inspect explanations more critically when they disagree with a decision outcome, leading to more negative perceptions if the explanation content is insufficient [32].

Furthermore, our findings highlight how broader *societal perceptions of AI*, particularly in high-stakes decisions, influence how citizens perceive AI systems. As seen in Theme 3, some participants rejected AI involvement in child welfare altogether, arguing that such cases inherently require human judgment. This aligns with previous work by Lee [32], who found that tasks perceived as fundamentally human may generate lower fairness perceptions, regardless of the explanation quality or decision outcome. Our results extend this by demonstrating that increased explanation interactivity cannot mitigate those tendencies when a task is perceived as inherently human. This resistance against AI is often rooted in deeper *expectation bias* regarding *AI's role* in decision-making, meaning that citizens' pre-existing beliefs and prior experiences with AI strongly shape their perceptions of what AI should or should not do [30]. As seen in Theme 3, many participants expressed clear discomfort with AI making autonomous high-stakes decisions, even when they acknowledged that the decisions made seemed faire.

In summary, citizens' attitudes and biases, decision outcomes, explanation content, and task nature (e.g., human tasks) play a more significant role than interactivity in shaping perceptions of AI in high-stake decisions.

## 5.2 Objectivity vs. Empathy Dilemma: Balancing Human-AI Roles

The tension between objectivity and empathy reflects a core contradiction in human nature. As social beings, we value fairness and impartiality, yet demand compassion and context-sensitive understanding, even when these ideals conflict. This duality has long been present in public administration, as citizens expect frontline workers to balance neutrality and responsiveness to their circumstances [35]. Leaning too heavily on one side can lead to distrust and dissatisfaction [32]. AI amplifies this dilemma, tasked with balancing what humans struggle to master, particularly in high-stakes, emotionally charged contexts like child welfare. Theme 2 illustrates this dilemma, revealing a divide between citizens who desire an ISSK that is impartial and another that is emotionally engaged.

This dilemma is not limited to citizens. Even civil servants perceive fully automated processes as less fair, particularly when decisions involve discretion and human judgment. For example, [3] found that police officers viewed AI-driven bodycam review policies as less fair than human-supervised ones. Interestingly, this negative perception was mitigated when supervisors conducted reviews at random, suggesting that the mere presence of human oversight can improve perceived fairness. This reinforces that human involvement plays a critical role in how legitimacy is socially constructed.

A promising approach to tackle this dilemma is a collaborative human-AI system. AI can provide data-driven insights, while humans contribute emotional and contextual understanding and ethical judgment (see Theme 3). Current research on collaborative human-AI decision-making in high-stakes administrative contexts explores the design of AI systems that support social workers in considering AI-generated predictions and recommendations, particularly in child maltreatment screening [29] and unemployment consultation [53]. These studies reveal that social workers value tools that provide accurate risk assessments while also allowing them to integrate their contextual human knowledge. Both studies report positive feedback on the effectiveness of some interactive explanation techniques in supporting civil servants' decision-making.

## 5.3 AI in High-Stake Administrative Scenarios

While some citizens in our study accept AI as an autonomous decision-maker, the majority remain skeptical of fully autonomous AI in the high-stakes scenario of child welfare, with many insisting on final human control. A reaction likely caused by two factors: ethical concerns about AI-bias and decision accountability, and the stakes of the decision, as we see similar concerns in prior research exploring AI's role in child welfare [13,50]. In contrast, findings from Aljuneidi et al. [5] suggest that in lower-stakes administrative contexts (i.e., ID renewal), citizens are more receptive to AI exercising discretion, provided they are actively engaged in the decision-making process. This distinction underscores the heightened sensitivity surrounding AI's role in high-risk areas like child welfare.

Our participants appeared receptive to AI as an assistive tool in child welfare. For example, it can identify at-risk children through predictive analytics, help civil servants prioritize cases to manage workloads, and offer confidential reporting mechanisms, such as chatbots, enabling individuals to safely report abuse or neglect in sensitive situations. An example of assistive use of AI in public administration appears in BUKI [1], where a generative chatbot helps citizens navigate complex applications like housing allocation, without taking part in decision-making.

Finally, human oversight is also mandated in relevant legal frameworks. For example, the German General Administrative Procedure Act restricts full automation to predefined, non-discretionary tasks [12]. The European AI Act mandates civil servants to disclose AI use in high-risk scenarios and limits AI to an assistive role [40]. These regulations may have influenced participant expectations, potentially reinforcing the belief that AI should support rather than replace human judgment.

## 5.4 Limitations and Future Work

While our study provides valuable insights into citizens' perceptions of AI-based decision-making in high-stakes administrative scenarios, several limitations must be considered. First, conducting the study in an online environment limited our ability to probe participants' reasoning beyond open-ended inputs. Although the scale used to measure AI attitudes has been used in previous work, it has not been fully validated in this form. While vignettes offer a practical way to test scenarios, especially in this early explorative phase, they simplify the complexities of real-life decision-making in emotionally charged contexts [7] and limit the participants to an observe-role, those directly impacted by child welfare decisions might exhibit a stronger need for interactive explanations. Finally, our study did not account for citizens' broader attitudes toward public administration, which may have subtly influenced participants' perceptions of AI in child welfare.

Future research should address these gaps by involving directly impacted individuals, potentially using Wizard-of-Oz methods, to better understand interactivity needs and fairness perceptions. Also, following initial insights from [30], future work can investigate methods of tuning explanation designs to align or even alter citizens' biases and expectations. This can be achieved through exploring how citizens perceive collaborative Human-AI decision-making, focusing on factors such as the perceived quality of AI reasoning, human compassion, and the level of effect of citizens' prior biases, expectations, and attitudes on their perceptions. It would also be valuable to examine whether joint human-AI decisions are viewed as fairer than decisions made solely by AI or humans, and to determine the optimal level of human oversight. Additionally, AI could be used to help citizens reflect on their expectations, fostering more informed interactions with AI-driven governance. Finally, future research should investigate how trust in public administration interacts with citizens' acceptance of AI in decision-making processes.

## 6 Conclusion and Recommendations

As public administrations worldwide face growing workloads and staffing shortages [28], AI presents a potential solution. Prioritizing citizen-centered insights, this paper investigated the effect of interactive explanations on citizens' perception of fairness and willingness to adopt AI in high-stakes public administration decisions with legal leeway. It highlights the complexity of public responses to AI in high-stakes contexts and emphasizes the need for effective explanations to account for citizens' biases and expectations, and their AI literacy and attitudes.

Based on our findings, we propose the following recommendations for researchers and policy makers: First, generalizing our results to other countries and contexts requires caution; we expect similar patterns in European public administrations or other regions with comparable legal frameworks, as well as in emotionally charged, high-stakes scenarios like immigrants' naturalization. Second, meaningful human oversight remains essential, particularly in emotionally sensitive high-stakes decisions. However, legal frameworks should be supported by clear guidelines that specify what counts as adequate human involvement. Third, the transition to AI-supported decision-making must be gradual and context-sensitive. Abrupt shifts from traditional human-led systems to fully automated ones risk provoking resistance. An incremental approach, starting with AI in assistive roles before moving to more autonomous tasks, can foster familiarity and acceptance among citizens. Finally, enhancing AI literacy is vital. Our findings indicate that greater familiarity with AI improves perceptions of fairness and increases willingness to reuse AI-supported systems. Policymakers should therefore prioritize educational initiatives that empower both citizens and civil servants to engage knowledgeably with AI technologies.

## References

1. Abdenebaoui, L., Aljuneidi, S., Horstmannshoff, F., Meyer, J., Boll, S.: Value-driven design for public administration: insights from a generative chatbot in a housing application case study. In: Proceedings of the 2025 ACM Conference on Fairness, Accountability, and Transparency, FAccT 2025, p. 11. ACM, Athens, Greece (2025). https://doi.org/10.1145/3715275.3732103
2. Abdul, A., Vermeulen, J., Wang, D., Lim, B.Y., Kankanhalli, M.: Trends and trajectories for explainable, accountable and intelligible systems: an HCI research agenda. In: Proceedings of the 2018 CHI Conference on Human Factors in Computing Systems, CHI 2018, pp. 1–18. Association for Computing Machinery, New York, NY, USA (2018). https://doi.org/10.1145/3173574.3174156
3. Adams, I.T.: Automation and artificial intelligence in police body-worn cameras: experimental evidence of impact on perceptions of fairness among officers. J. Crim. Justice **97** (2025). https://doi.org/10.1016/j.jcrimjus.2025.102373
4. Aljuneidi, S., Heuten, W., Abdenebaoui, L., Wolters, M.K., Boll, S.: Why the fine, AI? The effect of explanation level on citizens' fairness perception of AI-based discretion in public administrations. In: Proceedings of the 2024 CHI Conference

on Human Factors in Computing Systems, CHI 2024. Association for Computing Machinery, New York, NY, USA (2024). https://doi.org/10.1145/3613904.3642535
5. Aljuneidi, S., Heuten, W., Tepe, M., Boll, S.: Did that AI just charge me a fine? Citizens' perceptions of AI-based discretion in public administration. In: Proceedings of the 2023 ACM Conference on Information Technology for Social Good, GoodIT 2023, pp. 57–67. Association for Computing Machinery, New York, NY, USA (2023). https://doi.org/10.1145/3582515.3609518
6. Arya, V., et al.: One explanation does not fit all: a toolkit and taxonomy of AI explainability techniques. arXiv preprint arXiv:1909.03012 (2019)
7. Bahmani, N.D., Mohsen: A narrative on using vignettes: its advantages and drawbacks. J. Midwifery Reprod. Health **8** (2020)
8. Bates, D., Mächler, M., Bolker, B., Walker, S.: Fitting linear mixed-effects models using lme4. J. Stat. Softw. **67**(1), 1–48 (2015). https://doi.org/10.18637/jss.v067.i01
9. Bertrand, A., Viard, T., Belloum, R., Eagan, J.R., Maxwell, W.: On selective, mutable and dialogic XAI: a review of what users say about different types of interactive explanations. In: Proceedings of the 2023 CHI Conference on Human Factors in Computing Systems, CHI 2023. Association for Computing Machinery, New York, NY, USA (2023). https://doi.org/10.1145/3544548.3581314
10. Binns, R., Van Kleek, M., Veale, M., Lyngs, U., Zhao, J., Shadbolt, N.: 'It's reducing a human being to a percentage': perceptions of justice in algorithmic decisions. In: Proceedings of the 2018 CHI Conference on Human Factors in Computing Systems, CHI 2018, pp. 1–14. Association for Computing Machinery, New York, NY, USA (2018). https://doi.org/10.1145/3173574.3173951
11. Braun, V., Clarke, V.: Thematic Analysis. American Psychological Association (2012)
12. Braun Binder, N.: Weg frei für vollautomatisierte Verwaltungsverfahren in deutschland (German) (2016)
13. Brown, A., Chouldechova, A., Putnam-Hornstein, E., Tobin, A., Vaithianathan, R.: Toward algorithmic accountability in public services: a qualitative study of affected community perspectives on algorithmic decision-making in child welfare services. In: Proceedings of the 2019 CHI Conference on Human Factors in Computing Systems, CHI 2019, pp. 1–12. Association for Computing Machinery, New York, NY, USA (2019). https://doi.org/10.1145/3290605.3300271
14. Champely, S.: pwr: basic functions for power analysis (2020). r package version 1.3-0. https://CRAN.R-project.org/package=pwr
15. Chan, D.: Perceptions of fairness (2011). https://www.csc.gov.sg/articles/perceptions-of-fairness
16. Cheng, H.F., et al.: Explaining decision-making algorithms through UI: strategies to help non-expert stakeholders, CHI 2019, pp. 1–12. Association for Computing Machinery, New York, NY, USA (2019). https://doi.org/10.1145/3290605.3300789
17. Colquitt, J.A.: On the dimensionality of organizational justice: a construct validation of a measure. J. Appl. Psychol. **86**(3), 386 (2001)
18. Creswell, J.W., Clark, V.L.P.: Designing and Conducting Mixed Methods Research. Sage Publications (2007)
19. Denk, T., Hedström, K., Karlsson, F.: Citizens' attitudes towards automated decisionmaking. Inf. Polity, 1–18 (2022)

20. Dodge, J., Liao, Q.V., Zhang, Y., Bellamy, R.K.E., Dugan, C.: Explaining models: an empirical study of how explanations impact fairness judgment. In: Proceedings of the 24th International Conference on Intelligent User Interfaces, IUI 2019, pp. 275–285. Association for Computing Machinery, New York, NY, USA (2019). https://doi.org/10.1145/3301275.3302310
21. Doyle, D., Tsymbal, A., Cunningham, P.: A review of explanation and explanation in case-based reasoning (2003)
22. Emirates 24/7: Lost your Dubai driving licence? This machine will print a new one (2013). https://bit.ly/3ZGXiV1
23. Fine Licht, K.D., Fine Licht, J.: Artificial intelligence, transparency, and public decision-making: why explanations are key when trying to produce perceived legitimacy. AI Soc. **35**(4), 917–926 (2020)
24. Global Government Gorum: Global citizen experience survey: How public services are standing up to unprecedented pressure (2023). https://www.globalgovernmentforum.com/wp-content/uploads/Global_Government_Forum_Appian_Citizen_experience_report_2023.pdf. Accessed 07 Dec 2023
25. Hancox-Li, L.: Robustness in machine learning explanations: does it matter? In: Proceedings of the 2020 Conference on Fairness, Accountability, and Transparency, FAT* 2020, pp. 640–647. Association for Computing Machinery, New York, NY, USA (2020). https://doi.org/10.1145/3351095.3372836
26. Henman, P.: Improving public services using artificial intelligence: possibilities, pitfalls, governance. Asia Pac. J. Public Adm. **42**(4), 209–221 (2020). https://doi.org/10.1080/23276665.2020.1816188
27. Kamar, E.: Directions in hybrid intelligence: complementing AI systems with human intelligence. In: Proceedings of IJCAI 2016. AAAI Press (2016)
28. Kantar for Initiative D21 and the Technical University of Munich (TUM): egovernment monitor 2023: Use and acceptance of digital administrative services from the citizens' perspective. A comparison of the German federal states, Germany, Austria, and Switzerland. In: eGovernment MONITOR. Initiative D21 (2023). https://initiatived21.de/publikationen/egovernment-monitor
29. Kawakami, A., et al.: "Why do I care what's similar?" Probing challenges in AI-assisted child welfare decision-making through worker-AI interface design concepts. In: Proceedings of the 2022 ACM Designing Interactive Systems Conference, DIS 2022, pp. 454–470. Association for Computing Machinery, New York, NY, USA (2022). https://doi.org/10.1145/3532106.3533556
30. Kocielnik, R., Amershi, S., Bennett, P.N.: Will you accept an imperfect AI? Exploring designs for adjusting end-user expectations of AI systems. In: Proceedings of the 2019 CHI Conference on Human Factors in Computing Systems, CHI 2019, pp. 1–14. Association for Computing Machinery, New York, NY, USA (2019). https://doi.org/10.1145/3290605.3300641
31. Laato, S., Tiainen, M., Najmul Islam, A., Mäntymäki, M.: How to explain AI systems to end users: a systematic literature review and research agenda. Internet Res. **32**(7), 1–31 (2022)
32. Lee, M.K.: Understanding perception of algorithmic decisions: fairness, trust, and emotion in response to algorithmic management. Big Data Soc. **5**(1) (2018). https://doi.org/10.1177/2053951718756684
33. Lee, M.K., Jain, A., Cha, H.J., Ojha, S., Kusbit, D.: Procedural justice in algorithmic fairness: leveraging transparency and outcome control for fair algorithmic mediation. Proc. ACM Hum.-Comput. Interact. **3**(CSCW) (2019). https://doi.org/10.1145/3359284

34. Leventhal, G.S.: What should be done with equity theory? In: Gergen, K.J., Greenberg, M.S., Willis, R.H. (eds.) Social Exchange, pp. 27–55. Springer, Boston (1980). https://doi.org/10.1007/978-1-4613-3087-5_2
35. Lipsky, M.: Street-Level Bureaucracy: Dilemmas of the Individual in Public Service. Russell Sage Foundation (2010)
36. Liu, H., Lai, V., Tan, C.: Understanding the effect of out-of-distribution examples and interactive explanations on human-AI decision making. Proc. ACM Hum.-Comput. Interact. **5**(CSCW2) (2021). https://doi.org/10.1145/3479552
37. Melsión, G.I., Torre, I., Vidal, E., Leite, I.: Using explainability to help children understandgender bias in AI. In: Proceedings of the 20th Annual ACM Interaction Design and Children Conference, IDC 2021, pp. 87–99. Association for Computing Machinery, New York, NY, USA (2021). https://doi.org/10.1145/3459990.3460719
38. Miller, T.: Explanation in artificial intelligence: insights from the social sciences. Artif. Intell. **267** (2019). https://doi.org/10.1016/j.artint.2018.07.007
39. Mothilal, R.K., Sharma, A., Tan, C.: Explaining machine learning classifiers through diverse counterfactual explanations. In: Proceedings of the 2020 Conference on Fairness, Accountability, and Transparency, pp. 607–617 (2020)
40. Official Journal of the European Union: Artificial intelligence act (regulation (EU) 2024/1689) (2024). https://artificialintelligenceact.eu/. Accessed Jan 2025
41. Raees, M., Meijerink, I., Lykourentzou, I., Khan, V.J., Papangelis, K.: From explainable to interactive AI: a literature review on current trends in human-AI interaction. Int. J. Hum Comput Stud. **189**, 103301 (2024). https://doi.org/10.1016/j.ijhcs.2024.103301
42. Ranerup, A., Henriksen, H.Z.: Digital discretion: unpacking human and technological agency in automated decision making in Sweden's social services. Soc. Sci. Comput. Rev. **40**(2), 445–461 (2022). https://doi.org/10.1177/0894439320980434
43. Ribeiro, M., Singh, S., Guestrin, C.: "Why should I trust you?": explaining the predictions of any classifier. In: Proceedings of the 2016 Conference of the North American Chapter of the Association for Computational Linguistics: Demonstrations, pp. 97–101. Association for Computational Linguistics, San Diego, California, June 2016. https://doi.org/10.18653/v1/N16-3020
44. Saldaña, J.: The coding manual for qualitative researchers (2021)
45. Sarra, C.: Put dialectics into the machine: protection against automatic-decision-making through a deeper understanding of contestability by design. Global Jurist **20**(3) (2020). https://doi.org/10.1515/gj-2020-0003
46. Schepman, A., Rodway, P.: The general attitudes towards artificial intelligence scale (GAAIS): confirmatory validation and associations with personality, corporate distrust, and general trust. Int. J. Hum.-Comput. Interact. **39**(13), 2724–2741 (2023). https://doi.org/10.1080/10447318.2022.2085400
47. Schoeffer, J., De-Arteaga, M., Kühl, N.: Explanations, fairness, and appropriate reliance in human-AI decision-making. In: Proceedings of the 2024 CHI Conference on Human Factors in Computing Systems, CHI 2024. Association for Computing Machinery, New York, NY, USA (2024). https://doi.org/10.1145/3613904.3642621
48. Schoeffer, J., Kuehl, N., Machowski, Y.: "There is not enough information": on the effects of explanations on perceptions of informational fairness and trustworthiness in automated decision-making. In: 2022 ACM Conference on Fairness, Accountability, and Transparency, FAccT 2022, pp. 1616–1628. Association for Computing Machinery, New York, NY, USA (2022). https://doi.org/10.1145/3531146.3533218
49. Sokol, K., Flach, P.: One explanation does not fit all. KI - Künstliche Intelligenz **34**(2), 235–250 (2020). https://doi.org/10.1007/s13218-020-00637-y

50. Stapleton, L., et al.: Imagining new futures beyond predictive systems in child welfare: a qualitative study with impacted stakeholders. In: 2022 ACM Conference on Fairness, Accountability, and Transparency, FAccT 2022, pp. 1162–1177. Association for Computing Machinery, New York, NY, USA (2022). https://doi.org/10.1145/3531146.3533177
51. Sun, Y., Sundar, S.S.: Exploring the effects of interactive dialogue in improving user control for explainable online symptom checkers. In: Extended Abstracts of the 2022 CHI Conference on Human Factors in Computing Systems, CHI EA 2022. Association for Computing Machinery, New York, NY, USA (2022). https://doi.org/10.1145/3491101.3519668
52. Wang, R., Harper, F.M., Zhu, H.: Factors influencing perceived fairness in algorithmic decision-making: algorithm outcomes, development procedures, and individual differences. In: Proceedings of the 2020 CHI Conference on Human Factors in Computing Systems, CHI 2020, pp. 1–14. Association for Computing Machinery, New York, NY, USA (2020). https://doi.org/10.1145/3313831.3376813
53. Weitz, K., Schlagowski, R., André, E., Männiste, M., George, C.: Explaining it Your way - findings from a co-creative design workshop on designing XAI applications with AI end-users from the public sector. In: Proceedings of the 2024 CHI Conference on Human Factors in Computing Systems, CHI 2024. Association for Computing Machinery, New York, NY, USA (2024). https://doi.org/10.1145/3613904.3642563
54. Revelle, W.: psych: Procedures for Psychological, Psychometric, and Personality Research. Northwestern University, Evanston, Illinois (2024). r package version 2.3.6. https://CRAN.R-project.org/package=psych
55. Yi, J.S., Kang, Y.A., Stasko, J., Jacko, J.: Toward a deeper understanding of the role of interaction in information visualization. IEEE Trans. Vis. Comput. Graph. **13**(6), 1224–1231 (2007). https://doi.org/10.1109/TVCG.2007.70515
56. Yurrita, M., Draws, T., Balayn, A., Murray-Rust, D., Tintarev, N., Bozzon, A.: Disentangling fairness perceptions in algorithmic decision-making: the effects of explanations, human oversight, and contestability. In: Proceedings of the 2023 CHI Conference on Human Factors in Computing Systems, CHI 2023. Association for Computing Machinery, New York, NY, USA (2023). https://doi.org/10.1145/3544548.3581161

# Mitigating Interruptions in Digital Reading: Strategic Pauses and Note-Taking for Enhanced Cognitive Performance

Naile Hacioglu[1(✉)], Maria Chiara Leva[2], Nakyung Kim[3], and Hyowon Lee[1,3]

[1] School of Computing, Dublin City University, Glasnevin, Dublin 9, Ireland
naile.hacioglu2@mail.dcu.ie
[2] School of Food Science and Environmental Health, Technological University Dublin, Grangegorman, Dublin, Ireland
[3] Insight Centre for Data Analytics, Dublin City University, Glasnevin, Dublin 9, Ireland

**Abstract.** This study investigates how structured interventions—specifically pausing at natural breakpoints and guided note-taking—affect cognitive performance, memory retention, and task continuity in digital reading. We introduce *SmartPause*, a context-aware bookmarking system that nudges users to pause at meaningful points and externalise insights through lightweight notes. In a controlled experiment (N = 51), participants were assigned to one of three conditions: (1) interruption at an arbitrary point, (2) guided pause at a natural breakpoint, or (3) guided pause with note-taking. Results reveal that guided pauses, particularly when combined with note-taking, significantly enhance long-term memory retention while having no measurable impact on perceived cognitive load or selective attention. These findings highlight the potential of digital tools to support cognitive load management and task continuity by structuring interruptions in alignment with natural cognitive rhythms. The high usability rating of SmartPause underscores its practical applicability across e-reading platforms. This study contributes to human-computer interaction (HCI) by integrating principles from cognitive science into design solutions that enhance comprehension and information retention. Future research should explore personalised interventions, extended retention intervals, and real-world deployment to further optimise cognitive load in digital reading contexts.

**Keywords:** Human-Computer Interaction · Digital Reading · Cognitive Load Management · Memory Retention · Interruption Design · Strategic Pausing · Note-taking

## 1 Introduction

Interruptions during task execution significantly impact cognitive performance, with their disruptive effects varying depending on when they occur. Prior research demonstrates that interruptions at natural breakpoints—moments when fewer cognitive resources are engaged—are less disruptive than interruptions during active task execution, which is characterised by high memory load and intense cognitive demand [1, 2]. This insight highlights the potential of strategically timed interruptions to minimise cognitive disruption and improve task transitions. However, while studies have explored this concept in contexts such as web searching and media consumption, its application to reading tasks—where unique cognitive processes like language comprehension and memory consolidation come into play—remains underexplored.

Reading tasks involve unique cognitive processes, such as mental workload management and long-term memory retention, making them an important but understudied context for examining interruption management strategies [3–6]. This study addresses this gap by investigating the impact of guided pauses at natural breakpoints and note-taking within a digital reading task. Unlike prior research, which focused on short-term memory or immediate task performance, our study examines long-term memory retention, task continuity, and user experience in the context of reading.

Our study contributes to the field by being the first to explore interruption management strategies in reading tasks using natural breakpoints and note-taking. A controlled experiment with 51 participants tested three conditions: (1) interrupted reading with artificial breakpoints, (2) guided pausing at natural breakpoints, and (3) guided pausing combined with note-taking. The results showed that guided pausing and note-taking enhanced memory retention but had no significant impact on selective attention or mental workload. These findings highlight the potential of strategic design interventions to optimise cognitive performance in reading tasks, particularly by aligning task transitions with natural cognitive rhythms.

By bridging prior research on interruption management with the unique cognitive demands of reading tasks, this study provides actionable insights for designing digital applications that promote cognitive health, efficient task transitions, and user satisfaction, as demonstrated through an e-book reading application incorporating guided pausing and note-taking interventions. This work advances HCI knowledge by empirically studying the impact of interruptions on cognitive performance in reading tasks and offering a novel approach to managing interruptions in digital environments.

## 2 Background and Related Work

### 2.1 Interruptions and Task Continuity

Interruptions disrupt task execution by imposing cognitive and memory demands, interfering with neural mechanisms needed to sustain focus and resume tasks efficiently [7]. Natural breakpoints, such as subtask completion, are identified as optimal moments for interruptions, as they minimise disruption to the user's mental model [2]. Additionally, well-timed interruptions reduce stress and enhance task performance across domains [1]. However, their impact on reading tasks, particularly comprehension and memory retention, remains understudied.

### 2.2 Memory Retention and the Zeigarnik Effect

The Zeigarnik Effect, first described in 1927, highlights the psychological tension associated with incomplete tasks, which linger in memory more than completed ones [8, 9].

While this tension can aid task resumption, it also increases cognitive load and impedes focus. Strategies such as note-taking externalise this tension, improving mental clarity and enabling more efficient task resumption, particularly in digital contexts where they also enhance memory retention [10, 11]. Building on these insights, our study combines natural breakpoints with note-taking to manage cognitive load and enhance long-term memory retention during reading. This dual approach addresses the disruptive impact of interruptions while fostering task continuity.

### 2.3 Strategic Pausing and Guided Interventions

Strategic pausing at natural breakpoints offers a promising approach for managing interruptions in cognitively demanding tasks. Such pauses align with cognitive rhythms, facilitating smoother transitions and reducing mental strain [2, 6]. While this concept has been applied in various experiments for diverse task contexts, their impact on reading tasks has not been sufficiently studied. Combining strategic pausing with interventions such as note-taking can further support memory retention by externalising information, thus reducing cognitive effort [11–13]. This approach holds potential to enhance memory retention but also to maintain task continuity in reading tasks that require complex linguistic integration over time.

### 2.4 Self-interruption and Attention Management

Interruptions are not always external; internal factors, such as curiosity or habitual task-switching, often lead to self-interruptions. González and Mark [2004] found that individuals self-interrupt to seek information or alleviate boredom, disrupting focus and prolonging task completion [14]. These behaviours were categorised as discretionary task-switching, which impedes attention and diminishes productivity, and it was further demonstrated that external interruptions often trigger self-interruptions, creating a feedback loop of fragmented attention [15, 16]. In reading, structured interventions, such as guided pauses at logical stopping points, may help manage both external and internal interruptions, fostering sustained focus and cognitive continuity. Given the significance of attention in reading, this approach could improve the user's ability to stay focused and retain information.

### 2.5 Managing Cognitive Resources During Reading

Reading is a cognitively intensive activity that demands sustained attention, linguistic processing, and memory integration. Interruptions during reading disrupt these processes, requiring additional cognitive resources to reorient the mental model of the text [3]. Strategically timed pauses at natural breakpoints, such as at the end of a section or chapter, combined with note-taking, can reduce memory demands and improve task resumption efficiency.

Previous systems have explored ways to support users during interruptions. For example, Pan et al. [17] developed a bookmarking tool that uses galvanic skin response (GSR) to detect orienting responses and place markers during unplanned disruptions.

While effective, such systems are reactive and depend on biometric sensing. In contrast, SmartPause proactively guides users to pause at meaningful points based on content structure and includes lightweight note-taking prompts to externalise memory. This user-driven design presents a lightweight alternative to sensor-based approaches focused primarily on task resumption.

These interventions have yet to be tested in digital reading contexts, especially as end-user features in digital applications. Therefore, investigating their impact on cognitive resources in this domain presents an important research opportunity, particularly for digital reading applications aimed at mitigating cognitive disruption.

### 2.6 Research Aims and Questions

While previous research has advanced our understanding of interruption management and cognitive load in general task contexts, there remains a significant gap in applying these strategies and collecting evidence on actual human performance effects in digital reading tasks. This study aims to address this gap by investigating how strategic pausing at natural breakpoints, combined with note-taking, can improve cognitive performance, memory retention, and task continuity during digital reading. By exploring this, we contribute to the broader discourse on HCI design and interruption management, offering insights into how these strategies can be optimised for digital reading environments.

## 3 SmartPause: A Cognitive Bookmarking System

### 3.1 Design Overview

SmartPause is a high-fidelity design concept aimed at optimising digital reading experiences by guiding users to pause at strategic moments and externalise their thoughts. Grounded in cognitive psychology and HCI principles, the design reduces cognitive load, enhances memory retention (both long-term and for subsequent tasks), improves selective attention, and supports smoother transitions between reading and subsequent tasks. Leveraging research on task continuity, memory externalisation, and behavioural nudges, SmartPause addresses cognitive challenges faced by readers, improving engagement with reading material and cognitive performance [1, 9]. The prototype simulates the interaction logic through conceptual interfaces and structured prompts but is not a fully interactive system. Rather, it provides a high-fidelity representation of core features for evaluating user perception and cognitive outcomes.

### 3.2 Key Features and Interaction Flow

The SmartPause prototype was developed as a high-fidelity conceptual system designed to support cognitive continuity in digital reading. Rather than implementing a fully functional application, the prototype simulates a lightweight system architecture that models the user's disengagement intent and delivers structured interventions. Specifically, the interaction flow is organised into five cognitively aligned stages: (1) detecting user disengagement or task exit, (2) prompting continuation to a nearby natural breakpoint, (3) inviting note-taking upon reaching the breakpoint, (4) saving the note and line-level reading position, and (5) restoring both contextual cues when the user returns. While no real-time sensors or adaptive tracking mechanisms were used, the system assumes intent through user-initiated pause or exit actions. The prototype was evaluated through structured interaction scenarios and a narrated video walkthrough that demonstrated the core features to participants during the study. The prototype's interaction flow is illustrated in Figs. 1 and 2, which visualise the sequential user experience—from initial bookmarking and pause detection to note-taking and context restoration.

**Precise Bookmarking with Line-Level Precision.** Our design improves traditional eBook bookmarks by allowing users to bookmark specific lines within a page. A slidable widget helps users mark the exact line where they stopped reading, ensuring precise resumption of the task. This feature reduces cognitive load, aiding users in re-engaging with the text without needing to recall where they stopped, thereby improving attention and task continuity. This interaction also reduces task resumption latency by providing exact visual and semantic continuity.

**Encouragement to Pause at Natural Breakpoints.** A nudge system encourages users pausing at natural breakpoints, like section or chapter endings. If users pause mid-section, a prompt raises awareness of the cognitive benefits of completing the section first [18]. This system aims to reduce cognitive fragmentation and enhance task transitions [2]. Its rationale is grounded in event segmentation theory, which suggests that interruptions occurring at natural boundaries facilitate smoother reorientation and better memory encoding, as they align with shifts in mental models and perceived event structure [19].

**Externalising Memories with Note-Taking Integration.** Upon placing the bookmark pointer at a natural breakpoint, SmartPause prompts users to summarise their reading before exiting the task. They can type or dictate their thoughts using speech-to-text functionality. This externalises cognitive load and prepares users to resume reading with greater clarity. Mueller and Oppenheimer's work [20] provides empirical support for this design rationale, showing that generative note-taking—particularly when summarising or paraphrasing—leads to deeper processing and better conceptual retention than verbatim transcription. This feature is informed by memory externalisation literature, suggesting that lightweight elaboration improves encoding and later retrieval. It also helps close the memory loop created by unfinished cognitive tasks, consistent with the Zeigarnik Effect.

**Visual Continuity for Resumption.** When users return, the exact line bookmarked along with the user's notes is displayed. This ensures visual continuity, reducing the cognitive effort needed to recall the context of the previous session. The seamless transition facilitates smoother reading sessions and reduces cognitive interruptions.

This continuity mechanism reinforces the reader's mental model and improves task resumption by bridging the gap between sessions with both location and content cues, consistent with theories of goal resumption which emphasize the importance of contextual retrieval cues for suspended tasks [3].

These features were selected based on an extensive review of literature in cognitive psychology, interruption design, and task scaffolding, ensuring theoretical alignment rather than arbitrary inclusion. The design was conveyed to participants through a narrated video walkthrough, allowing them to experience the intended interaction flow during the usability assessment.

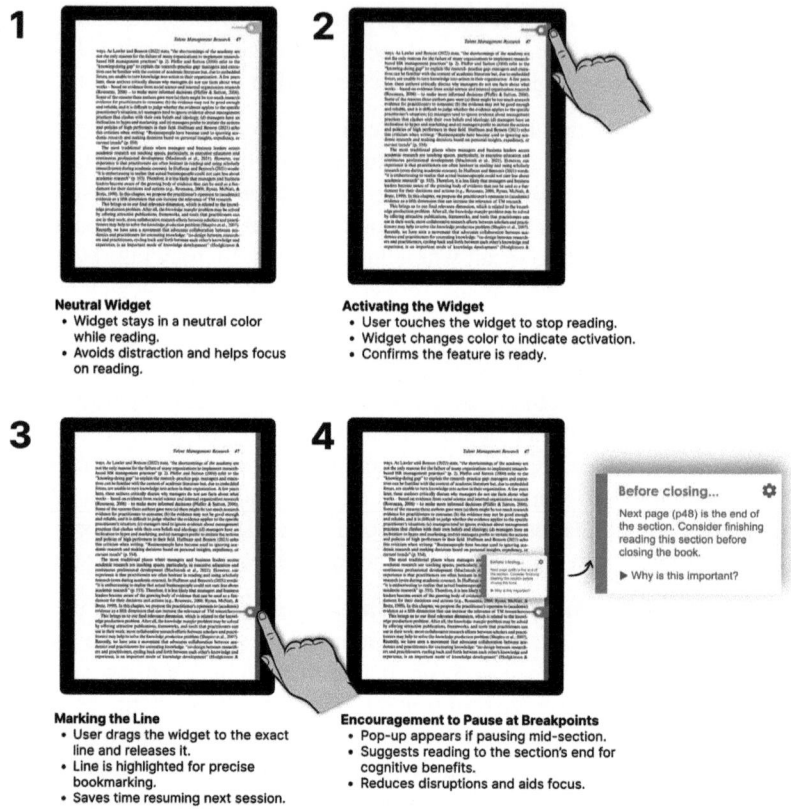

Fig. 1. **SmartPause: Prototype interaction flow (1/2).** This diagram illustrates the early phase of SmartPause, featuring a bookmarking interface with line-level precision and system-driven detection of disengagement. A visual nudge encourages continued reading toward a nearby natural breakpoint, supporting cognitively aligned transitions and minimizing disruption.

## 3.3 Hypotheses and Experimental Evaluation

To evaluate the effectiveness of the proposed design, we conducted a controlled experiment using a high-fidelity conceptual prototype of SmartPause. Although the system was not fully interactive, the prototype conveyed a realistic simulation of its core features—including strategically timed pauses, note-taking prompts, and visual continuity—which enabled empirical assessment of its cognitive and usability impacts.

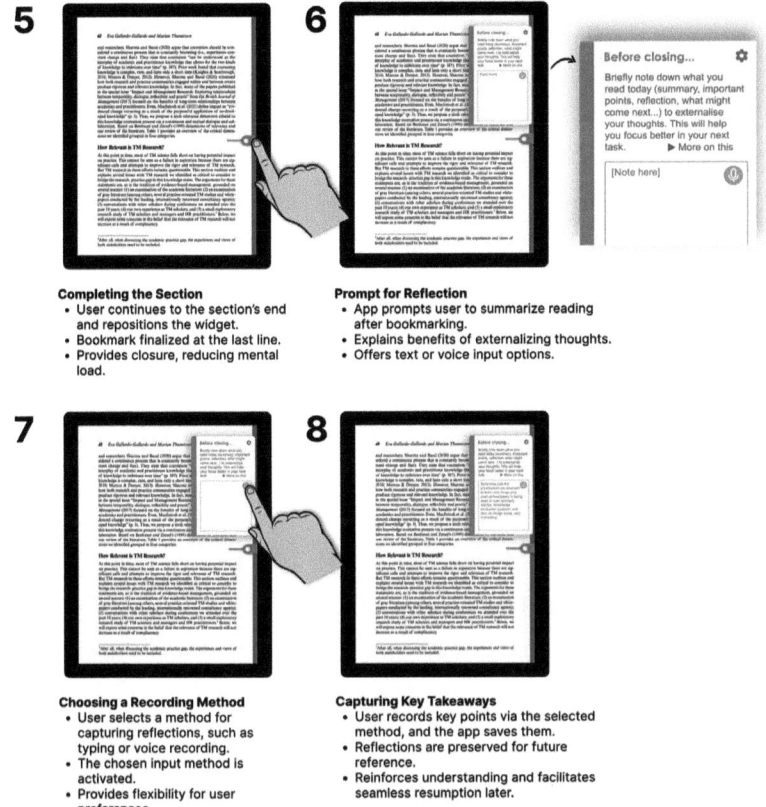

**Fig. 2. SmartPause: Prototype interaction flow (2/2).** This phase shows post-breakpoint features: an optional note-taking prompt and a return interface restoring the bookmarked line and notes. These support task resumption, lower cognitive load, and aid memory retention.

- H1: Selective attention and processing speed performance will be significantly better when users pause their reading at a natural breakpoint, in at least one of the natural breakpoint conditions (with or without note-taking).
- H2: Cognitive workload will be significantly lower—both in terms of perceived mental load and task engagement duration—when users pause their reading at a natural breakpoint, in at least one of the natural breakpoint conditions (with or without note-taking).
- H3: Long-term memory retention will be significantly improved when users pause their reading at a natural breakpoint, in at least one of the natural breakpoint conditions (with or without note-taking).
- H4: Participants will report high usability and positive engagement with the SmartPause prototype, as measured by the System Usability Scale (SUS) and qualitative feedback.

These hypotheses aim to test whether SmartPause can optimise cognitive resources, enhance user experience, and demonstrate high usability during digital reading by aligning task interruptions with natural cognitive rhythms.

## 4 Method

### 4.1 Participants

A total of 51 participants (aged 18–36, M = 25, 25 females, 26 males) were recruited for the study. Among them, 32 were native English speakers. Participants represented a diverse range of ethnic backgrounds, including EU citizens, as well as participants from Asia, Africa, and the Americas. All participants were at least high school graduates and were currently enrolled in or had completed undergraduate education. Inclusion criteria required participants to have normal or corrected-to-normal vision, no history of attention or memory-related disorders, and fluency in English (native or advanced proficiency). The study received ethical approval from the university's Research Ethics Committee.

### 4.2 Experimental Design and Procedure

This study employed a between-subjects design, with participants randomly assigned conditions: Control Group (Control, n = 17), Intervention Group 1 (IG1, n = 16) and Intervention Group 2 (IG2, n = 16). The experiment aimed to investigate the effects of pausing at natural breakpoints and note-taking on cognitive performance and memory retention during a digital reading task.

1. Control Group: Participants read a 3-page passage, with the latter portion of the text blurred, stopping at a predefined point before the section's conclusion.
2. Intervention Group 1 (IG1): Participants read the same 3-page passage, but they were instructed to pause at the natural breakpoint (i.e., the end of a section), without any additional tasks.
3. Intervention Group 2 (IG2): Participants followed the same procedure as IG1, but with the additional task of note-taking. After reaching the natural breakpoint, they were prompted to take notes on their reading by typing on the laptop.

Participants were first provided with a Participant Information Sheet and an Informed Consent Form. Following consent, participants completed a pre-reading Stroop task to measure baseline selective attention and processing speed. They were then asked to read the assigned passage (and take notes) under their group's condition. After the reading task, participants completed a post-reading Stroop task, the NASA-TLX questionnaire to assess perceived mental workload, and the Big Five Personality Test to assess individual differences in personality traits [21]. A Demographics Survey was also completed at this stage, followed by a Recall Test to measure memory retention based on the text they had read. Finally, participants watched a short video about the SmartPause design and completed a usability questionnaire to provide their feedback.

After completing the recall test, participants were presented with a narrated video demonstration of the SmartPause prototype. This demonstration provided a structured walkthrough of the system's intended features, including pausing at natural breakpoints, note-taking prompts, and context restoration. The video served as the basis for the subsequent usability evaluation using the System Usability Scale (SUS) (see Fig. 3 for the visual workflow of the experiment).

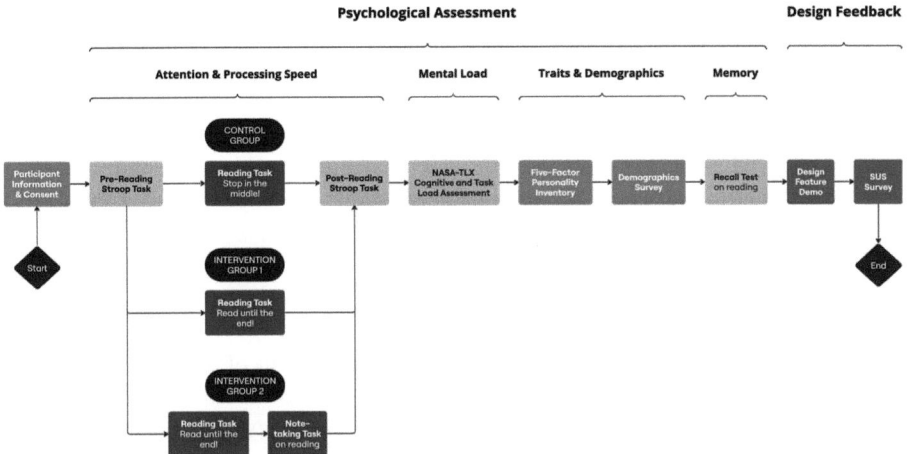

**Fig. 3. Experimental workflow diagram.** This figure outlines the full experimental sequence: baseline and post-task cognitive assessments, the reading task under one of three conditions, and memory and workload evaluations. The SmartPause demo video followed the recall test and served as the basis for the SUS usability evaluation.

All forms and questionnaires were developed using the Qualtrics platform, hosted on an institution-managed account at the university. A consistent setup was used for all tasks, with participants working on a MacBook Air laptop (M2, 2022, 16 GB RAM) in full-screen mode to minimise distractions. The study was conducted in a controlled, quiet environment with only the participant and the two researchers.

### 4.3 Materials

The reading material for the study was a 3-page with a Flesch-Kincaid reading score of 60, indicating moderate difficulty suitable for the participants' reading level [22, 23]. The text met the following criteria: it was a standalone section that could be understood independently, the content was non-controversial and free of sensitive material, and the topic was accessible and of a similar level for all participants. To ensure that participants paused before completing the section, 0.5 pages before the section's end were blurred for all groups.

To assess selective attention and processing speed, a Computerised Colour-Word Stroop task was administered using Inquisit Lab 6 software [24, 25]. This task, which involved keyboard input, was conducted both before and after the reading task, allowing for a comparison of attention and processing speed before and after reading [26]. After completing the reading task, participants filled out the NASA-TLX to gauge the cognitive load they experienced during the reading task [27]. The Big Five Personality Test

(BFI-2) was used to assess participants' personality traits, specifically neuroticism. This assessment was included determine how individual personality traits might influence their task performance.

A Recall Test, consisting of 12 multiple-choice, true/false, fill-in-the-blank, matching, and short-answer questions, was designed based on the first 2.5 pages of the text read by all participants. This test assessed their ability to recall specific details from the passage, serving as a measure of long-term memory retention.

Following the recall test, participants were shown a narrated demonstration video of the SmartPause prototype, which visually presented the system's intended features and interaction flow, including strategic pausing, note-taking, and resumption mechanisms. This video served as the basis for the subsequent usability evaluation, conducted using the System Usability Scale (SUS), a validated instrument for assessing user satisfaction and system usability [28].

### 4.4 Data Analysis Approach

We conducted paired t-tests and ANOVA to compare the effects of reading conditions on the dependent variables. We also examined the main and interaction effects of neuroticism as a personality trait and self-reported English proficiency (native vs. non-native). The dependent variables analysed were Stroop Effect (selective attention and processing speed), NASA-TLX results and time-on-task during reading (both as indicators of mental load), recall test scores (long-term memory), and usability scores. For the Stroop Effect, we calculated three values for both reaction time and accuracy: pre-reading Stroop Effect, post-reading Stroop Effect, and the difference between them. Mental workload was measured using unweighted NASA-TLX scores and time-on-task as a behavioral proxy for cognitive effort. Recall test scores assessed long-term memory, with half credit awarded for inferred short answer responses. Usability scores were analysed based on feedback from the design concept video illustrating features (Sect. 3.2) in the e-book application.

Post hoc t-tests were conducted only when the omnibus ANOVA reached statistical significance, with *p*-values adjusted using the Benjamini-Hochberg (BH) procedure to control for multiple comparisons [29]. Effect sizes were calculated using Cohen's *d* for *t*-tests and partial $\eta^2$ for ANOVA. They were interpreted based on Cohen's [30] benchmarks: 0.2 = small, 0.5 = medium, and 0.8 = large, providing a measure of practical significance alongside statistical outcomes.

**Table 1.** Statistics for Stroop Task Performance, Mental Load, and Recall Metrics

|  | Control Group | | IG1 | | IG2 | | Overall | |
| --- | --- | --- | --- | --- | --- | --- | --- | --- |
|  | M | SD | M | SD | M | SD | M | SD |
| Pre Stroop Effect RT | 189.58 | 191.72 | 311.4 | 328.56 | 311.74 | 235.59 | 269.25 | 258.41 |
| Post Stroop Effect RT | 197.15 | 146.05 | 199.33 | 187.82 | 200.19 | 230.84 | 198.86 | 186.51 |

*(continued)*

**Table 1.** (*continued*)

|  | Control Group | | IG1 | | IG2 | | Overall | |
| --- | --- | --- | --- | --- | --- | --- | --- | --- |
|  | M | SD | M | SD | M | SD | M | SD |
| *Stroop RT Difference* | 7.57 | 168.44 | −112.06 | 205.44 | −111.55 | 322.36 | −70.39 | 241.69 |
| *Pre Stroop Effect Accuracy* | 0.04 | 0.06 | 0.06 | 0.17 | 0.04 | 0.07 | 0.05 | 0.11 |
| *Post Stroop Effect Accuracy* | 0.01 | 0.05 | 0.03 | 0.12 | 0.02 | 0.04 | 0.02 | 0.07 |
| *Stroop Accuracy Difference* | −0.03 | 0.1 | −0.03 | 0.09 | −0.01 | 0.08 | −0.02 | 0.09 |
| *NASA-TLX Score* | 46.57 | 15.50 | 41.30 | 13.96 | 40.10 | 11.48 | 42.74 | 13.80 |
| *Reading Time-on-Task* | 551.35 | 170.00 | 670.13 | 363.68 | 841.38 | 253.14 | 684.84 | 292.47 |
| *Recall Score* | 38.15 | 15.59 | 49.83 | 13.04 | 51.91 | 18.80 | 46.46 | 16.82 |

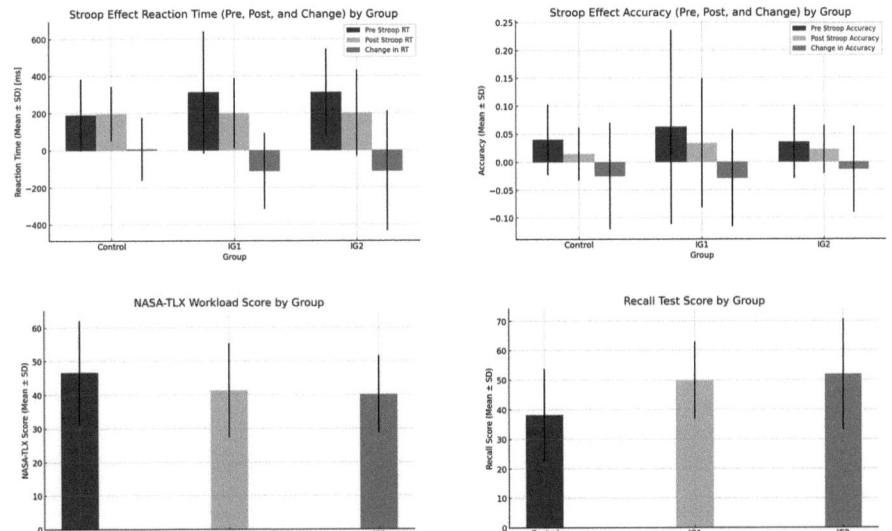

**Fig. 4.** Stroop Effect Reaction Time, Accuracy NASA-TLX and Recall statistics across groups/

# 5 Results

The analysis aimed to investigate the effects of the interventions on Selective Attention, Processing Speed, Mental Load and Long-term Memory. Two of the original 51 participants were excluded from the data analysis: one for not reporting ADHD prior to the study, and another due to missing post-reading Stroop task data from a software issue. Table 1 presents the descriptive statistics for each group and overall Stroop Task performance, mental load, and recall metrics while Fig. 4 provides a comparative visualisation of means with standard deviations across groups.

**Table 2.** Paired Samples t-Test Results for Pre- and Post-Stroop Task Changes

|  |  | t(df) | p | Mean diff | SE diff | Cohen's d | 95% Confidence Interval | |
|---|---|---|---|---|---|---|---|---|
|  |  |  |  |  |  |  | Lower | Upper |
| Reaction Time | Control | 0.19 (16) | 0.855 | 7.58 | 40.90 | 0.045 | −79.04 | 94.18 |
|  | IG1 | −2.18 (15) | **0.045*** | −112.06 | 51.36 | −0.545 | −221.53 | −2.59 |
|  | IG2 | −1.38 (15) | 0.187 | −111.55 | 80.59 | −0.346 | −283.32 | 60.22 |
| Accuracy | Control | −1.09 (16) | 0.291 | −0.03 | 0.02 | −0.265 | −0.07 | 0.02 |
|  | IG1 | −1.34 (15) | 0.201 | −0.03 | 0.02 | −0.335 | −0.08 | 0.02 |
|  | IG2 | −0.70 (15) | 0.497 | −0.01 | 0.02 | −0.174 | −0.05 | 0.03 |

**Table 3.** ANOVA Results for Between-Group Analysis of Pre-Post Stroop Effect Reaction Time, Accuracy Difference, Mental Load, and Recall Test Scores

|  | Sum of Squares | df | Mean Square | F | p | $\eta^2$ |
|---|---|---|---|---|---|---|
| *Stroop Effect RT Difference* | 158211 | 2 | 79105 | 1.38 | 0.263 | 0.056 |
| *Stroop Accuracy Difference* | 0.00213 | 2 | 0.00107 | 0.141 | 0.868 | 0.006 |
| *NASA-TLX Score* | 393 | 2 | 197 | 1.03 | 0.363 | 0.043 |
| *Reading Time-on-Task* | 698435 | 2 | 349218 | 4.71 | **0.014*** | 0.170 |
| *Recall Test Score* | 1830 | 2 | 915 | 3.58 | **0.036*** | 0.135 |

**Table 4.** Main and Interaction Effects of Language Level and Neuroticism on Cognitive Metrics

|  | Language Level (Main Effect) | Language Level (Interaction Effect) | Neuroticism (Main Effect) | Neuroticism (Interaction Effect) |
| --- | --- | --- | --- | --- |
| *Stroop RT Difference* | F = 1.80<br>p = 0.186 | F = 1.05<br>p = 0.360 | F = 0.03<br>p = 0.867 | F = 0.22<br>p = 0.801 |
| *Stroop Accuracy Difference* | F = 0.723<br>p = 0.400 | F = 1.84<br>p = 0.171 | F = 0.50<br>p = 0.484 | F = 0.05<br>p = 0.949 |
| *NASA-TLX Score* | F = 7.64<br>**p = 0.008*** | F = 0.84<br>p = 0.437 | F = 0.56<br>p = 0.458 | F = 0.61<br>p = 0.547 |
| *Recall Test Score* | F = 6.24<br>**p = 0.016*** | F = 0.36<br>p = 0.701 | F = 0.86<br>p = 0.358 | F = 0.85<br>p = 0.436 |

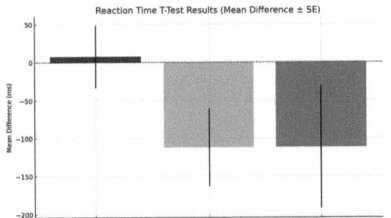 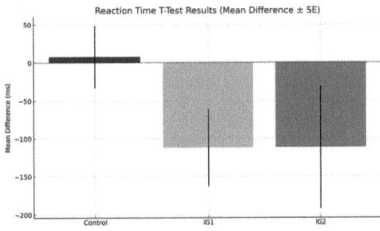

**Fig. 5.** T-Test Results for Pre- and Post-Stroop Effect Changes

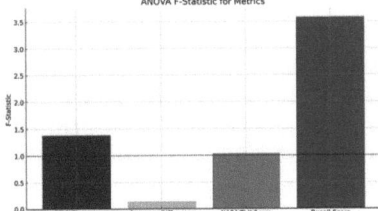 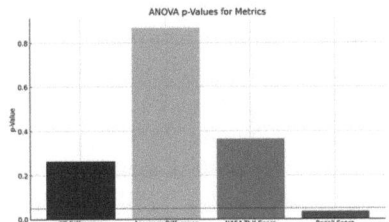

**Fig. 6.** ANOVA Results for Between-Group Comparison of Reaction Time, Accuracy, and Recall Score

## 5.1 Selective Attention and Processing Speed Performance

For reaction time, Intervention Group 1 (IG1) showed a significant reduction (M = −112.06, SD = 205.44; $t(15) = -2.18$, $p = .045$, Cohen's $d = -0.545$), suggesting that pausing at natural breakpoints enhances Selective Attention and Processing Speed. This finding supports Hypothesis 1 (H1), which predicted that pausing would improve reaction time. However, the between-group analysis using ANOVA revealed no significant differences in reaction time or accuracy across the three groups ($F(2, 46) = 1.38$, $p = .263$, $\eta^2 = .056$), indicating that while IG1 demonstrated a significant reduction, the differences between groups were not statistically meaningful as shown in Table 3 and Fig. 6. This suggests that while pausing at a natural breakpoint may improve cognitive processing speed, it does not significantly impact accuracy, nor does it create substantial differences between the groups.

Table 2 further details the paired t-test results for pre- and post-Stroop Effect changes, confirming the significant reaction time improvement within IG1. Figure 5 visualises these changes, illustrating how the pre- and post-reading Stroop Effect differed across conditions.

In terms of accuracy, IG1 showed a slight improvement, but the change was not statistically significant ($t(15) = -1.34$, $p = .201$, Cohen's $d = -0.335$). Similarly, the Control Group and IG2 showed no significant change either ($p > 0.05$). An ANOVA across the groups (Table 3) revealed no significant difference ($F(2, 46) = 0.14$, $p = .868$, $\eta^2 = .006$), suggesting that the interventions did not have a significant effect on accuracy. These results reinforce the idea that pausing at a natural breakpoint may facilitate faster processing but does not necessarily affect the accuracy of task performance.

Language proficiency and neuroticism were also examined for their effect on both reaction times and accuracy but neither showed a significant main effect or interaction ($p > 0.05$), as detailed in Table 4.

## 5.2 Mental Load

The intervention groups, particularly IG2, showed reduced mental load compared to the control group. IG2's mean NASA-TLX score was 40.10 (SD $= 11.48$), while the control group's mean was 46.57 (SD $= 15.5$). An ANOVA revealed no significant difference ($F(2, 46) = 1.03$, $p = .363$, $\eta^2 = .043$), as shown in Table 3, indicating that the interventions had no significant effect on perceived mental load.

To complement these subjective results, we also examined time-on-task during reading as a behavioural proxy for cognitive effort. A one-way ANOVA revealed a significant difference in time-on-task across groups, $F(2, 46) = 4.71$, $p = .014$, $\eta^2 = .170$. Post hoc comparisons using the Benjamini-Hochberg correction showed that IG2 spent significantly more time on-task than the control group ($t(31) = -3.89$, $p < .001$, BH-adjusted $p = .002$, Cohen's $d = -1.35$), while differences between control and IG1 ($p = .234$) and between IG1 and IG2 ($p = .133$) were not statistically significant. These results suggest that the note-taking intervention led to deeper cognitive engagement, even though participants did not report increased mental effort.

We also examined the relationship between subjective and behavioural indicators using Pearson correlation. The correlation between time-on-task and NASA-TLX scores was weak and non-significant, $r(47) = 0.216$, $p = .136$, suggesting that longer task duration did not correspond to higher perceived cognitive load. However, the visual trend differs across groups: IG1 displays a positive relationship between self-reported mental load and reading duration, while the control group shows little to no association as visualised in Fig. 8. Taken together, these findings provide only partial support for H2: while perceived mental load did not differ significantly across groups, behavioural indicators point to increased engagement in the note-taking condition.

### 5.3 Long-Term Memory

The ANOVA results revealed a significant effect of the interventions on memory retention ($F(2, 46) = 3.58$, $p = .036$, $\eta^2 = .135$), supporting H3 and indicating that the interventions meaningfully enhanced recall performance. Specifically, participants in the condition with guided pausing and note-taking had the highest mean recall score 51.91 (SD = 18.8), followed by those who received guided pausing alone 49.83 (SD = 13.04). In contrast, the control condition showed a lower mean score 38.15 (SD = 15.59), suggesting that the interventions contributed to improved memory retention. Interruptions during reading have been shown to disrupt cognitive flow; however, these results indicate that strategically timed pauses and note-taking may serve as effective countermeasures, reinforcing memory retention processes (Table 5).

**Table 5.** Pairwise t-test results for Reading Time-on-Task values with Benjamini-Hochberg correction and Cohen's $d$ effect sizes

| Comparison | t | df | p (raw) | P (BH-adjusted) | Cohen's d |
|---|---|---|---|---|---|
| Control vs IG1 | −1.21 | 31 | 0.234 | 0.234 | −0.423 |
| Control vs IG2 | −3.89 | 31 | <.001 | **0.002*** | −1.35 |
| IG1 vs IG2 | −1.55 | 30 | 0.133 | 0.177 | −0.547 |

**Table 6.** Pairwise t-test results for recall scores with Benjamini-Hochberg correction and Cohen's $d$ effect sizes

| Comparison | t | df | p (raw) | P (BH-adjusted) | Cohen's d |
|---|---|---|---|---|---|
| Control vs IG1 | −2.33 | 31 | 0.027 | **0.0435*** | −0.81 |
| Control vs IG2 | −2.29 | 31 | 0.029 | **0.0435*** | −0.80 |
| IG1 vs IG2 | −0.36 | 30 | 0.718 | 0.718 | −0.13 |

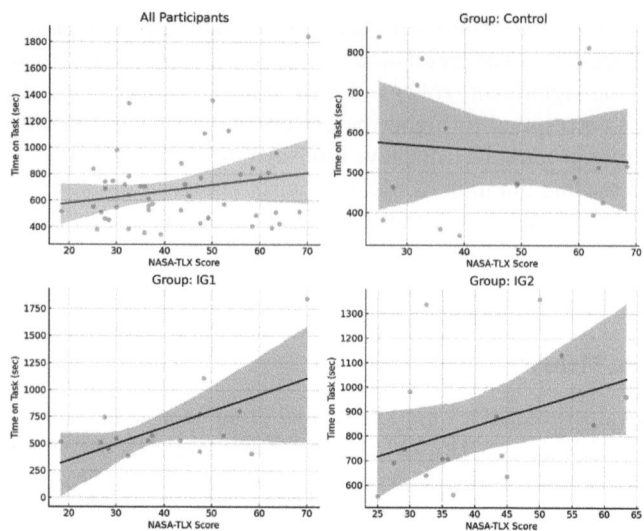

**Fig. 7. Correlation between NASA-TLX Scores and Reading Time-on-Task.** Scatterplots with regression lines and 95% confidence intervals are shown for all participants and separately by group. IG1 shows the strongest positive trend, IG2 a moderate one, and the Control group displays no apparent relationship.

To examine specific group differences, post hoc independent samples t-tests were conducted and adjusted using the Benjamini-Hochberg procedure. The comparisons between the control group and both intervention groups remained statistically significant after correction (Control vs IG1: $p = .027$, BH-adjusted $p = .0435$; Control vs IG2: $p = .029$, BH-adjusted $p = .0435$), while no significant difference was found between IG1 and IG2 ($p = .718$, BH-adjusted $p = .718$), as detailed in Table 6.

Additionally, language proficiency significantly influenced recall performance, with native speakers outperforming non-native speakers. This finding highlights the impact of language proficiency on memory retention, suggesting that individuals with higher language proficiency may have an advantage in recalling details from the reading task (Fig. 7).

### 5.4 Usability

Participants evaluated the usability of the system using the SUS questionnaire. The mean SUS score was 85.46 (SD = 12.18), which is considered excellent usability [31]. This score highlights the system's strong user satisfaction, though some participants suggested enhancing note-taking customisation for greater flexibility.

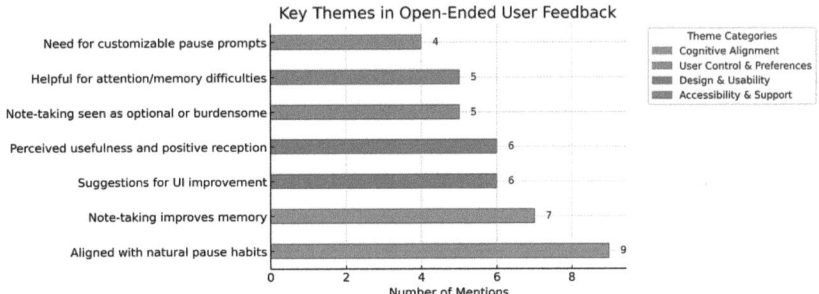

**Fig. 8.** Key themes identified in open-ended usability feedback from participants. Responses were categorised into four groups: Cognitive Alignment, User Control & Preferences, Design & Usability, and Accessibility & Support. Each bar indicates the frequency of mentions per theme across all participants highlighting perceptions of SmartPause's value and usability features.

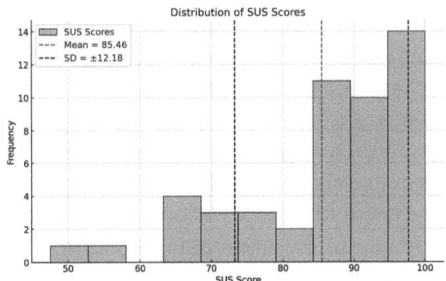

**Fig. 9.** Distribution of SUS Scores Across Participants

To complement the SUS scores, we analysed open-ended responses to gain deeper insight into users' subjective experiences. Participants generally found the system intuitive and easy to use, particularly valuing how the guided pause mechanism aligned with their natural reading rhythms. Thematic analysis of this feedback revealed several key perceptions (see Fig. 8). The most frequently noted benefit was the alignment with existing pause habits. Many users also reported that note-taking supported memory retention, while a smaller group expressed a preference for disabling this feature in certain contexts, such as casual reading.

Additional themes included appreciation for the bookmark's line-level precision, general satisfaction with the feature's usefulness, and perceived benefits for users with attention or memory challenges. Some participants suggested improvements such as greater flexibility in prompting frequency or the ability to disable summarisation prompts. These responses highlight the need to accommodate varying user preferences through more customisable features.

The usability feedback aligns with the results observed in memory retention, suggesting that guided pauses and note-taking not only improve cognitive performance but also enhance user experience in digital reading environments. Figure 9 illustrates the distribution of SUS scores across participants, providing insights into individual variations in perceived usability.

## 6 Discussion

### 6.1 Cognitive Performance Findings and Interpretation

This study explored the impact of strategic pausing and note-taking interventions on Selective Attention, Processing Speed, Mental Load, and Long-term Memory Retention in digital reading tasks. By testing a system that incorporated these interventions, we demonstrated that pausing at natural breakpoints improved reaction time and processing speed for IG1, while the combination of pausing and note-taking significantly enhanced memory retention. Well-placed pauses are known to reduce the cognitive effort required to resume tasks, aligning with these findings [32].

However, the between-group analysis revealed no significant differences in reaction time or accuracy across the three groups, suggesting it did not create meaningful differences between the groups. This partial support for H1 indicates that pausing may facilitate faster cognitive processing, but its impact on accuracy and between-group performance remains inconclusive.

The mental load results offered mixed evidence for H2. While NASA-TLX scores did not differ significantly across groups, suggesting that perceived mental effort remained stable, time-on-task—a behavioural proxy for cognitive workload—revealed a significant group effect. Participants in the note-taking condition (IG2) spent significantly more time on the reading task than those in the control group, a result interpreted as increased engagement rather than cognitive overload. A weak and non-significant correlation between time-on-task and NASA-TLX scores further supports the notion that behavioural and subjective measures capture distinct aspects of cognitive effort. Thus, H2 was only partially supported: the interventions did not reduce perceived mental load, but they did meaningfully alter behavioural engagement.

In contrast, the memory retention results were robust. Participants in the guided pausing and note-taking condition demonstrated significantly higher recall scores compared to the control group. Post hoc analyses, adjusted using the Benjamini-Hochberg procedure, confirmed that both intervention groups outperformed the control group in memory performance. Moreover, the effect sizes for these differences (Cohen's $d \approx 0.8$) indicate large and practically meaningful impacts. However, the difference between IG1 and IG2 was not statistically significant, suggesting that note-taking may not have provided additional measurable benefit to recall performance. Similar findings have been observed in various digital and non-digital contexts like lecture-based learning, where structured pauses and note-taking enhance memory retention, suggesting the potential for broader application of these techniques [20, 33, 34].

Language proficiency was also found to significantly influence memory retention, with native speakers outperforming non-native speakers. This highlights the importance of considering individual differences, such as language proficiency, when evaluating the effectiveness of cognitive interventions in diverse populations.

## 6.2 Implications for Design and Research

This study provides insights for designing digital reading platforms and other cognitive task environments. One promising direction is identifying natural breakpoints—moments of lower mental load—and recommending optimal pausing points, aligning with activity theory's emphasis on tools that support user goals and cognitive workflows [35]. SmartPause was intentionally designed not to interrupt arbitrarily, but to respond when users are already attempting to disengage—such as pausing or preparing to leave the task. By encouraging users to continue to a nearby breakpoint, the system aligns with users' cognitive rhythms and intentions, thereby reducing the risk of disruption.

For example, SmartPause could guide users to pause at these breakpoints, while AI tools could detect these moments in real-time, improving focus, memory retention, and overall performance. The SUS results underscore the high usability of the SmartPause system, showcasing its potential to strengthen user engagement and streamline task transitions through an intuitive interface and guided features [36]. Qualitative feedback revealed opportunities to refine note-taking functionality, such as adding tagging and reorganising notes, to provide a more tailored experience and address diverse preferences. The overall feedback reflects key design components such as efficiency and user satisfaction [37]. By managing mental load, systems can help users stay engaged without cognitive overload, enhancing cognitive performance and long-term retention as well-designed interventions reduce cognitive disruptions and improve performance.

In addition to usability considerations, the open-ended feedback contributes to the ecological validity of the findings. Several participants described SmartPause as a natural extension of their reading routines, noting that the system's prompts aligned well with how they typically take breaks. While the study was conducted in a controlled environment, these reflections suggest that the core interaction model may be transferable to real-world digital reading scenarios.

Subsequent research should investigate how interventions like SmartPause function in naturalistic contexts such as e-learning, digital scholarship, or workplace reading, where patterns of distraction and engagement are more variable. These investigations would offer a more nuanced understanding of how guided pausing and note-taking function in authentic, everyday reading contexts.

While real-world deployments hold promise, they also raise new challenges. Emerging adaptive systems may introduce friction if they misjudge user intent or overstep the boundaries of user control. Automatically suggesting or enforcing pauses could feel intrusive if not properly personalised or explainable. Designing such features will require careful attention to transparency, timing, and user agency to avoid undermining trust or increasing cognitive burden.

The findings highlight the need for updated design guidelines that prioritise cognitive well-being. Incorporating features like strategic pausing and note-taking can improve memory retention and processing speed. Applications in which the user interfaces provide such interventions to prioritise the users' cognitive well-being is very rare today. Design knowledge available today in the field of HCI could more explicitly make this aspect actionable as principles and guidelines so that interaction designers will more readily consider incorporating such features in their designs. Expanding Nielsen's Usability Heuristics to include methods for managing mental load could enhance user experience in a variety of applications [38]. Later work should explore how interventions like SmartPause can be personalised based on cognitive profiles and task complexity, with a focus on integrating them into real-world environments to optimise usability and cognitive wellbeing.

## 7 Limitations and Future Work

Although the study offers valuable insights, several limitations must be addressed. The learning effects from the Stroop task may have influenced reaction times, and individual differences in working memory, attention span, and cognitive resilience were not fully explored [39]. While the cognitive demands of the task were appropriate, the short reading duration limited the ability to assess the full impact of the interventions [40].

The study employed a between-subjects design to avoid learning transfer and reduce participant fatigue, especially given the number of cognitive measures involved. However, this design introduces individual variability, which may reduce sensitivity to condition-level effects. Future studies may benefit from within-subjects designs to better control for such variability and isolate the influence of each intervention.

Moreover, the short retention interval between the reading and recall tests restricts our understanding of the long-term effects. Although the immediate testing allowed for internal consistency, future research should incorporate delayed recall—such as after 24 h or one week—to better assess how guided pausing and note-taking influence long-term memory consolidation. These limitations suggest the need for future work to control for learning effects, account for individual differences through within-group studies, extend reading durations, increase retention intervals, and involve larger, more diverse samples to improve the generalisability of the findings.

While the current study relied on subjective and behavioral measures of mental workload, future research should incorporate physiological indicators such as eye-tracking to better understand attention shifts and cognitive effort in real-time. These methods can provide fine-grained, continuous insights into how users interact with reading interventions, particularly during transition points and pause decisions. Incorporating such objective data would strengthen the triangulation of cognitive engagement and inform the development of adaptive features in SmartPause.

A promising direction for SmartPause is the personalisation of pause timing based on users' engagement patterns. While the current prototype uses static logic, recent advances in explainable AI offer opportunities for adaptive support. For example, Zoppis et al. [41] demonstrate how neural recommendation models can personalise content delivery by weighting user-resource relationships. Although their systems do not address interaction timing, they highlight techniques for tailoring educational technologies to individual needs. SmartPause could extend this line of work by adapting its intervention strategy using lightweight, engagement-sensitive cues.

Building on this, SmartPause could incorporate real-time behavioural and attentional data to dynamically determine whether a pause should be suggested, and if so, how far ahead to nudge the user—e.g., suggesting a section rather than a chapter break if the user typically stops reading within shorter spans. Over time, such a system could learn from individual pause histories, attentional lapses, or task duration to adjust the granularity and frequency of interventions, thereby balancing continuity and cognitive load.

Finally, the use of AI-driven user modelling, particularly in educational and assistive reading platforms, opens pathways for scaling SmartPause to diverse populations, including readers with cognitive or attentional impairments [42]. Future work should explore how human-AI collaboration in cognitive load adaptation can be applied to enhance usability and engagement in real-world digital reading environments. While these mechanisms remain beyond the current scope, acknowledging them helps position this study within the broader research landscape of adaptive learning systems.

## 8 Conclusion

This study demonstrates that cognitive interventions, such as pausing at natural breakpoints and note-taking, can optimise available cognitive resources and improve long-term memory retention in digital reading tasks. By aligning task activities with users' cognitive rhythms, these strategies present a promising approach for enhancing engagement and recall outcomes.

Building on these findings, subsequent research should explore how such interventions can be adapted to accommodate varying levels of language proficiency, attentional profiles, and cognitive differences, including those experienced by readers with learning difficulties. Expanding task durations, increasing retention intervals, and conducting ecologically valid studies will further elucidate their long-term efficacy. Given the platform-agnostic nature of SmartPause, its applicability across desktop, tablet, and mobile environments positions it as a scalable solution for cognitively supportive digital reading. Together, these directions underscore the importance of inclusive and adaptive design in shaping next-generation digital reading systems.

**Acknowledgments.** This work was conducted with the financial support of the Research Ireland Centre for Research Training in Digitally-Enhanced Reality (d-real) under Grant No. 18/CRT/6224 and the Research Ireland Centre Grant No. 12/RC/2289_P2 at Insight Centre for Data Analytics at Dublin City University. For the purpose of Open Access, the author has applied a CC BY public copyright license to any Author Accepted Manuscript version arising from this submission. The authors would like to thank Dr Brendan Rooney, University College Dublin, for his advice in the planning part of the experiment.

## References

1. Adamczyk, P.D., Bailey, B.P.: If not now, when? The effects of interruption at different moments within task execution. In: Proceedings of the SIGCHI Conference on Human Factors in Computing Systems, pp. 271–278. Association for Computing Machinery, New York, NY, USA (2004). https://doi.org/10.1145/985692.985727
2. Bailey, B.P., Iqbal, S.T.: Understanding changes in mental workload during execution of goal-directed tasks and its application for interruption management. ACM Trans. Comput.-Hum. Interact. **14**, 21:1–21:28 (2008). https://doi.org/10.1145/1314683.1314689
3. Altmann, E.M., Trafton, J.G.: Memory for goals: an activation-based model. Cogn. Sci. **26**, 39–83 (2002). https://doi.org/10.1207/s15516709cog2601_2

4. Grundgeiger, T., Sanderson, P., MacDougall, H.G., Venkatesh, B.: Interruption management in the intensive care unit: predicting resumption times and assessing distributed support. J. Exp. Psychol. Appl. **16**, 317–334 (2010). https://doi.org/10.1037/a0021912
5. Khalifa, H., Weir, C.J.: Examining Reading: Research and Practice in Assessing Second Language Reading. Cambridge University Press, New York, NY (2009)
6. Monk, C.A., Trafton, J.G., Boehm-Davis, D.A.: The effect of interruption duration and demand on resuming suspended goals. J. Exp. Psychol. Appl. **14**, 299–313 (2008). https://doi.org/10.1037/a0014402
7. Clapp, W.C., Rubens, M.T., Gazzaley, A.: Mechanisms of working memory disruption by external interference. Cereb. Cortex **20**, 859–872 (2010). https://doi.org/10.1093/cercor/bhp150
8. Zeigarnik, B.: Über das Behalten von erledigten und unerledigten Handlungen [Retention of completed and uncompleted actions.]. Psychologische Forschung **9**, 1–85 (1927)
9. Zeigarnik, B.: On finished and unfinished tasks. In: A Source Book of Gestalt Psychology, pp. 300–314. Kegan Paul, Trench, Trubner & Company, London, England (1938). https://doi.org/10.1037/11496-025
10. Hollender, N., Hofmann, C., Deneke, M., Schmitz, B.: Integrating cognitive load theory and concepts of human–computer interaction. Comput. Hum. Behav. **26**, 1278–1288 (2010). https://doi.org/10.1016/j.chb.2010.05.031
11. Scullin, M.K., Krueger, M.L., Ballard, H.K., Pruett, N., Bliwise, D.L.: The effects of bedtime writing on difficulty falling asleep: a polysomnographic study comparing to-do lists and completed activity lists. J. Exp. Psychol. Gen. **147**, 139–146 (2018). https://doi.org/10.1037/xge0000374
12. Westman, M.: Stress and strain crossover. Hum. Relat. **54**, 717–751 (2001). https://doi.org/10.1177/0018726701546002
13. Bannert, M., Reimann, P.: Supporting self-regulated hypermedia learning through prompts. Instr. Sci. **40**, 193–211 (2012). https://doi.org/10.1007/s11251-011-9167-4
14. González, V.M., Mark, G.: "Constant, constant, multi-tasking craziness": managing multiple working spheres. In: Proceedings of the SIGCHI Conference on Human Factors in Computing Systems, pp. 113–120. Association for Computing Machinery, New York, NY, USA (2004). https://doi.org/10.1145/985692.985707
15. Jin, J., Dabbish, L.A.: Self-interruption on the computer: a typology of discretionary task interleaving. In: Proceedings of the SIGCHI Conference on Human Factors in Computing Systems, pp. 1799–1808. Association for Computing Machinery, New York, NY, USA (2009). https://doi.org/10.1145/1518701.1518979
16. Dabbish, L., Mark, G., González, V.M.: Why do I keep interrupting myself? Environment, habit and self-interruption. In: CHI 2011: Proceedings of the SIGCHI Conference on Human Factors in Computing Systems, pp. 3127–3130. Association for Computing Machinery, New York, NY, USA (2011). https://doi.org/10.1145/1978942.1979405
17. Pan, M.K.X.J., et al.: Now where was I? Physiologically-triggered bookmarking. In: Proceedings of the SIGCHI Conference on Human Factors in Computing Systems, pp. 363–372. Association for Computing Machinery, New York, NY, USA (2011). https://doi.org/10.1145/1978942.1978995
18. Endsley, M.R.: Toward a theory of situation awareness in dynamic systems. Hum. Fact. **37**, 32–64 (1995). https://doi.org/10.1518/001872095779049543
19. Zacks, J.M., Speer, N.K., Swallow, K.M., Braver, T.S., Reynolds, J.R.: Event perception: a mind/brain perspective. Psychol. Bull. **133**, 273–293 (2007). https://doi.org/10.1037/0033-2909.133.2.273
20. Mueller, P.A., Oppenheimer, D.M.: The pen is mightier than the keyboard: advantages of longhand over laptop note taking. Psychol. Sci. **25**, 1159–1168 (2014). https://doi.org/10.1177/0956797614524581

21. Smederevac, S., Mitrović, D., Sadiković, S., Dinić, B.M., John, O.P., Soto, C.J.: The big five inventory (BFI-2): psychometric properties and validation in Serbian language. J. Res. Pers. **110**, 104492 (2024). https://doi.org/10.1016/j.jrp.2024.104492
22. Wohlleben, P.: The Hidden Life of Trees: What They Feel, How They communicate—Discoveries From A Secret World. Greystone Books, Vancouver/Berkeley (2016)
23. Kincaid, J., Fishburne, R., Rogers, R., Chissom, B.: Derivation of New Readability Formulas (Automated Readability Index, Fog Count and Flesch Reading Ease Formula) For Navy Enlisted Personnel. Institute for Simulation and Training (1975)
24. Download Inquisit Lab. https://www.millisecond.com/download. Accessed 11 Jan 2025
25. Stroop Task – Millisecond. https://www.millisecond.com/download/library/stroop. Accessed 11 Jan 2025
26. Stroop, J.R.: Studies of interference in serial verbal reactions. J. Exp. Psychol. **18**, 643–662 (1935). https://doi.org/10.1037/h0054651
27. Hart, S.G., Staveland, L.E.: Development of NASA-TLX (task load index): results of empirical and theoretical research. In: Hancock, P.A., Meshkati, N. (eds.) Advances in Psychology, pp. 139–183. North-Holland (1988). https://doi.org/10.1016/S0166-4115(08)62386-9
28. Brooke, J.: SUS: A "Quick and Dirty" Usability Scale. In: Usability Evaluation in Industry. CRC Press (1996)
29. Benjamini, Y., Hochberg, Y.: Controlling the false discovery rate: a practical and powerful approach to multiple testing. J. Roy. Stat. Soc. Ser. B (Methodol.) **57**, 289–300 (1995). https://doi.org/10.1111/j.2517-6161.1995.tb02031.x
30. Cohen, J.: Statistical Power Analysis for the Behavioral Sciences. Lawrence Erlbaum Associates, Hillsdale, NJ (1988)
31. Bangor, A., Kortum, P.T., Miller, J.T.: Determining what individual SUS scores mean: adding an adjective rating scale. J. Usability Stud. **4**, 114–123 (2009)
32. Trafton, J.G., Altmann, E.M., Brock, D.P., Mintz, F.E.: Preparing to resume an interrupted task: effects of prospective goal encoding and retrospective rehearsal. Int. J. Hum. Comput. Stud. **58**, 583–603 (2003). https://doi.org/10.1016/S1071-5819(03)00023-5
33. Ruhl, K.L., Hughes, C.A., Gajar, A.H.: Efficacy of the pause procedure for enhancing learning disabled and nondisabled college students' long- and short-term recall of facts presented through lecture. Learn. Disabil. Q. **13**, 55–64 (1990). https://doi.org/10.2307/1510392
34. Bohay, M., Blakely, D.P., Tamplin, A.K., Radvansky, G.A.: Note taking, review, memory, and comprehension. Am. J. Psychol. **124**, 63–73 (2011). https://doi.org/10.5406/amerjpsyc.124.1.0063
35. Kaptelinin, V.: The object of activity: making sense of the sense-maker. Mind Cult. Act. **12**, 4–18 (2005). https://doi.org/10.1207/s15327884mca1201_2
36. Bangor, A., Kortum, P.T., Miller, J.T.: An empirical evaluation of the system usability scale. Int. J. Hum.-Comput. Interact. **24**, 574–594 (2008). https://doi.org/10.1080/10447310802205776
37. Nielsen, J.: Usability Engineering. Morgan Kaufmann, San Francisco (1994)
38. Nielsen, J.: Heuristic evaluation. In: Usability Inspection Methods, pp. 25–62. John Wiley & Sons, Inc., USA (1994)
39. Yuan, X., Zhong, L.: Effects of multitasking and task interruptions on task performance and cognitive load: considering the moderating role of individual resilience. Curr. Psychol. **43**, 23892–23902 (2024). https://doi.org/10.1007/s12144-024-06094-2
40. Czerwinski, M., Horvitz, E., Wilhite, S.: A diary study of task switching and interruptions. In: Proceedings of the SIGCHI Conference on Human Factors in Computing Systems, pp. 175–182. Association for Computing Machinery, New York, NY, USA (2004). https://doi.org/10.1145/985692.985715

41. Zoppis, I., Manzoni, S., Mauri, G., Aragon, R.A.M., Marconi, L., Epifania, F.: Attentional neural mechanisms for social recommendations in educational platforms. Presented at the 12th International Conference on Computer Supported Education, May 25 (2025)
42. Alnfiai, M.M., Alsudairy, N.A., Alharbi, A.I., Alotaibi, N.N., Alnefaie, S.M.M.: Cognitive augmentation: AI-enhanced tools for supporting individuals with cognitive disabilities. Cogn. Process. (2025). https://doi.org/10.1007/s10339-025-01258-9

# Design and Evaluation in Smart
# and Ubiquitous Contexts

# Behind Customer Satisfaction Metrics: Exploring User Perceptions of Net Promoter Score (NPS) as a Measure of Satisfaction

Jade Logan[✉], Daniele Doneddu, Kevin McLafferty, Muneeb I. Ahmad, and Nicholas Micallef

Swansea University, Swansea, UK
{850852,d.doneddu,kevin.mclafferty,m.i.ahmad,
nicholas.micallef}@swansea.ac.uk

**Abstract.** Customer satisfaction is a critical component of user experience, shaping brand perception and influencing long-term customer relationships. Net Promoter Score (NPS) is a widely used metric to measure satisfaction, but its rigid classification thresholds and simplistic design often fail to capture the complexity of customer perceptions. While critics advocate for alternative models, NPS remains deeply embedded in industry practices. Rather than seeking to replace it, this study focuses on enhancing its interpretability by examining how customers understand and express satisfaction through NPS.

Adopting an approach that focuses on the users point-of-view, this research explores customer perception of NPS scores within a UK banking context, investigating how individuals classify themselves within the metric and how the tone of their feedback reflects their true sentiment. Findings reveal that while many UK banking customers correctly identify their NPS category, misclassification is common, particularly among those who feel positive about their experience but provide scores that place them in lower categories.

These results could highlight the importance of designing customer satisfaction measures that align with user expectations and communication styles. Furthermore, analysis of feedback tone suggests that sentiment-based models could complement existing metrics, offering a more nuanced understanding of customer experiences. This research underscores the need for a more nuanced interpretation of customer satisfaction, ensuring that feedback mechanisms capture the complexity of user sentiment and drive meaningful service improvements. More broadly, these findings may have implications for the design of customer feedback systems, underscoring the need for interpretive approaches that can capture the complexity of user sentiment and drive meaningful service improvements.

**Keywords:** Customer Satisfaction · Customer Experience · User Study · Net Promoter Score · User Perception

## 1 Introduction

Understanding customer behaviour is essential for measuring and improving user experience, particularly in service industries where perceptions and emotions shape decision-making [29] such as retail banking. Customer satisfaction is a key determinant of long-term engagement, trust, and advocacy, making it critical to develop accurate and meaningful ways to assess how individuals feel about a company. One widely adopted metric for capturing customer sentiment is the Net Promoter Score (NPS). NPS, a simple yet influential measure, classifies customers based on their likelihood of recommending a company [50]. Despite its prevalence, there is growing concern over whether NPS genuinely reflects the complexity of customer sentiment, particularly given the limitations in how users interpret and classify their own experiences [5,28,48].

Academic literature has largely focused on evaluating the accuracy of NPS rather than understanding how customers interact with the metric itself. A key critique is that the categorical boundaries within the NPS scale are rigid and may misrepresent the intent behind a customer's score [17,33]. Customers unfamiliar with the metric could struggle to classify themselves correctly, leading to misalignment between their actual experience and the way their responses are interpreted by businesses. This raises fundamental questions about whether NPS, in its current form, provides a reliable reflection of customer perceptions. To explore this issue, this study investigates. *RQ1: How accurately do individuals perceive the classification criteria for their NPS response?*

Beyond individual perception, broader behavioural shifts also challenge the conventional NPS framework. Since its introduction in 2003, NPS has assumed that recommendations are shared primarily through personal networks [50]. However, customer behaviour has evolved significantly, with digital platforms and online reviews increasingly shaping purchasing decisions [27]. Traditional word-of-mouth has given way to public, visible, and often more influential digital endorsements or criticisms, particularly in sensitive industries such as finance. Customers now seek validation through online rating systems [7], which often use a Likert scale or five-star ratings rather than NPS-style classifications. This shift raises the question of whether NPS remains a valid method for capturing customer sentiment in the digital age. Hence, our second research question. *RQ2: What is the relationship between traditional online rating systems and NPS?*

A deeper issue arises when considering the way customers express their emotions and experiences. Understanding the language customers use in feedback is critical for interpreting their sentiment accurately [22]. While some research has attempted to link NPS ratings to emotion [34,44], few studies have explored whether NPS reflects the natural ways in which customers describe their experiences. Traditional survey methodologies often force structured responses, potentially leading to skewed or incomplete insights. In contrast, online reviews—where customers self-initiate feedback—may offer a more authentic and emotionally-driven representation of sentiment [47]. If there is a mismatch between how customers rate their experiences using NPS and how they naturally describe them in reviews, it may indicate a fundamental gap between structured satisfaction metrics and real-world consumer behaviour, which leads to our third research question. *RQ3: How do the language and tone of customer reviews relate to their corresponding NPS ratings?*

To answer these questions, a mixed-methods approach was used, with the aim to focus on how individuals interact with and interpret NPS rather than evaluating its validity as a business metric. The study was conducted within a retail banking context because its high-frequency customer interactions provided a rich dataset for applying NPS, which is further supported by the availability of publicly accessible industry data. It is important to note that NPS research is inherently context-dependent. Each industry and cultural setting introduces distinct factors that influence how customers interpret and respond to NPS questions [2,25]. As such, findings from this study are not intended to be universally generalisable, but rather specific to the nuances of the UK retail banking sector. While this research focuses specifically on the UK banking sector, studies from other industries also highlight limitations in NPS as a measure of true customer sentiment [3,13]. Although these works do not directly examine misclassification rates, their findings suggest that NPS may fail to capture the nuances of customer experience—supporting the case for a broader, hypothetical generalisation of these issues across sectors.

The study collected 300 customer responses via a Prolific survey, incorporating both structured NPS questions and free-text feedback to examine how individuals classified their own experiences. Additionally, Trustpilot[1] review data and CMA (Competition and Markets Authority)[2]-published NPS scores were analysed to assess the relationship between traditional NPS classifications and naturally occurring customer sentiment in online environments.

Our findings reveal that while many customers align with their NPS categories, a significant number misclassified themselves, often placing their score in a higher category than assigned. Customers rating their experience as a six were most prone to misclassification, suggesting ambiguity in the lower and neutral categories. While NPS and Likert-scale ratings showed a strong correlation, no significant relationship was found between NPS and Trustpilot sentiment, raising concerns about whether NPS effectively captures customer perceptions.

This study makes three key contributions to HCI literature in customer experience (CX) measurement:

- **User Focused Analysis of NPS:** This study addresses a gap in the literature by comparing customer satisfaction perspectives with their NPS scores, aiming to assess the metric's effectiveness in capturing true customer sentiment rather than merely critiquing its limitations.
- **Customer Perception of NPS Categories:** Many customers misunderstand how their responses are categorised, highlighting the need for greater transparency in NPS interpretation.

---

[1] https://www.trustpilot.com/.
[2] a UK non-ministerial government department dedicated to preventing anti-competitive practices and protecting consumer interests in competitive markets.

- **Emotional Expression in Customer Feedback:** By comparing NPS responses with online reviews, this research underscores the importance of behavioural and context-sensitive satisfaction evaluation methods.

The following sections provide a literature review on customer satisfaction measurement, digital recommendation behaviours, and the psychology of sentiment expression. The methodology details the strategies for data collection and analysis, followed by the research findings, a discussion, and conclusions that provide recommendations for enhancing satisfaction metrics so that they more accurately capture user sentiment.

## 2 Background

NPS, introduced by Fred Reichheld in a 2003 Harvard company Review article, was developed following two years of research focused on predicting company growth [50]. Reichheld's research concluded that a single question, centred on the likelihood of customers recommending a company, served as a key indicator of customer loyalty - *"How likely are you to recommend us to a friend or family?"*. His claim was that the propensity to recommend a brand was the ultimate measure of loyalty. External research supports this claim, as 92% of consumers reportedly trust recommendations from friends and family [46]. Reichheld's hypothesis that companies with higher NPS grow faster, due to promoters driving repeat company referrals, is therefore grounded in this broader understanding of consumer behaviour.

Promoters (those answering 9 or 10) are considered highly valuable to the company due to their enthusiasm and likelihood to promote the brand, passives (7 or 8) exhibit a lack of enthusiasm and are more vulnerable to competitive influence and detractors (0 to 6) pose a risk through negative word-of-mouth communication [50]. Despite Reichheld pre-emptively addressing concerns by highlighting the need to avoid grade inflation, where mildly satisfied customers are often counted as loyal [50], there is significant debate in the academic community regarding the robustness of these categories [14,29,33].

The broad categorisation of users into promoters, passives, and detractors does not fully capture the nuances of customer sentiment. Kristensen and Eskildsen's analysis suggests that a more accurate grouping would place detractors between zero and four, passives between five and seven, and promoters between eight and ten [28]. This misclassification limits NPS's ability to accurately measure customer loyalty and satisfaction, as the metric often oversimplifies context and relies heavily on industry-specific factors despite being industry ambiguous, explaining why NPS is better suited for certain industries than others [28]. Furthermore, the grouping of customers is not fully supported by empirical analysis. They propose alternative groupings based on statistical significance, highlighting the need for more sophisticated tools to measure customer satisfaction.

## 3 Related Work

Despite criticisms, NPS remains widely used due to its simplicity and efficiency in tracking customer loyalty [2]. However, its broad classification system and rigid scoring thresholds limit its ability to capture nuanced customer sentiment; this oversimplification misrepresents user experiences and can lead to misaligned business decisions. Additionally, NPS lacks a neutral or unsure option, forcing users into predefined categories that may not accurately reflect their opinions [29]. Studies indicate that when users can provide neutral responses, the distribution of scores shifts, reducing the number of detractors and improving reliability [28]. The absence of such flexibility weakens NPS's ability to serve as a fully representative satisfaction metric.

To address these limitations, various technological solutions have been proposed. Sentiment analysis and natural language processing (NLP) enrich NPS data with qualitative insights from customer feedback [55], allowing businesses to identify common pain points beyond numerical scores. However, requiring written responses increases cognitive effort and reduces survey participation, undermining NPS's key advantage—its speed and ease of use [28].

Another suggested improvement is adaptive survey methodologies, which adjust follow-up questions based on initial responses to clarify intent and sentiment in real time [42]. While this aligns with HCI principles by reducing the cognitive burden of rigid surveys, excessive questioning may deter participation or introduce bias if users feel overwhelmed [9].

Hybrid models combining NPS with alternative satisfaction metrics, such as Customer Effort Score (CES) or the American Customer Satisfaction Index (ACSI), provide a more comprehensive measure of CX [39]. However, while these models enhance insight depth, they risk complicating NPS's appeal as a simple, industry-benchmarked tool [2]. Balancing usability with accuracy remains a key challenge to ensure customer feedback mechanisms remain both actionable and representative. Building on the widespread integration of NPS within banking culture, this study aims to enhance its effectiveness by examining it from the customer's perspective. It seeks to not only explore how customers interpret NPS but also investigate the underlying factors driving their responses, particularly in relation to demographic characteristics. The following sections review existing literature that similarly endeavours to understand these dynamics.

### 3.1 Users Perceptions of Customers Satisfaction Metrics

Customer perceptions of satisfaction metrics are shaped by usability, clarity, and alignment with real-world experiences. Research suggests customers favour intuitive feedback systems that require minimal effort and accurately reflect their experiences [41]. However, many satisfaction metrics, including NPS, often fail to meet these expectations, leading to frustration and disengagement [17]. Customers may struggle to understand how their responses contribute to business decisions, particularly when surveys use ambiguous rating scales or lack meaningful follow-up actions.

The one-dimensional nature of some metrics, such as NPS, can prevent customers from expressing the complexity of their experiences, resulting in disengagement or inaccurate responses [45]. HCI research highlights that feedback systems perform best when they allow users to clarify or contextualise their ratings while maintaining ease of use [8]. Without this balance, satisfaction metrics risk being perceived as corporate formalities rather than meaningful tools for improving CX, ultimately reducing their credibility and effectiveness. While the simplicity of NPS makes it an appealing and near-ideal metric for engaging customers, our research seeks to determine the extent to which its ease of use may compromise the accurate capture of nuanced customer sentiment.

### 3.2 Online Reviews: Their Role in Customer Perception and Decision-Making

The influence of online reviews has grown exponentially, shaping consumer perceptions and decision-making [27]. Studies indicate that over 70% of consumers trust online reviews as much as personal recommendations [1], making them a key factor in purchasing decisions. For industries like banking, where customer trust is critical, satisfaction and loyalty function as both business objectives and powerful marketing tools. The rapid spread of customer opinions via online platforms amplifies word-of-mouth marketing globally [6].

Consumer behaviour research shows that purchase decisions are closely tied to the information available [24]. Online reviews provide this information, helping customers evaluate businesses. Given that 93% of consumers consult online reviews before making decisions [7], their influence on brand perception is significant. Unlike traditional surveys, online reviews offer public, candid feedback at scale, making them an attractive alternative for understanding customer sentiment [12]. Companies increasingly use sentiment analysis to mine these insights for CX improvements [56].

As online reviews gain prominence, companies adjust their strategies to manage public perception. Research suggests that while NPS scores correlate with Likert-style ratings on these platforms [25], their functions differ: NPS is an internal metric for tracking long-term loyalty, whereas online ratings are public and shaped by social proof. Given that nearly half of all consumers avoid businesses rated below four stars [19], online reputation now plays a crucial role in customer engagement. As reliance on online reviews grows, the potential integration of these metrics with NPS presents an opportunity for a more comprehensive CX measure. This research will investigate the relationship between NPS and online reviews to study whether this approach represents a viable method for more comprehensive understanding of customer perceptions.

Generational differences further complicate this evolving relationship. Age significantly impacts NPS scoring patterns [54] and influences how individuals seek recommendations online. Generation Z (Gen Z), for example, conducts more online research before purchasing than previous generations [16], increasing the importance of online reputation management. As Gen Z enters adulthood and makes financial decisions, they become a key demographic for banks and other industries. With 40% of the British population remaining loyal to one bank for life [15], financial institutions must adapt strategies to attract and retain younger consumers. Understanding generational differences in feedback interpretation will be essential in refining NPS strategies and customer engagement efforts. It is for this reason that this research will examine the impact of demographic factors on how customers articulate their opinions, thereby providing deeper insights into the true perceptions underlying all forms of qualitative feedback—not just online reviews.

### 3.3 Sentiment Analysis and Customer Feedback

Sentiment analysis provides valuable insights into customer emotions as expressed in online reviews. Computational models like VADER classify textual feedback as positive, neutral, or negative, offering a more detailed understanding of satisfaction and loyalty trends [22]. Compared to structured survey responses, sentiment analysis enhances NPS by identifying underlying factors influencing promoters, passives, and detractors [55].

However, discrepancies often arise between NPS classifications and underlying customer sentiment. Customers with limited brand exposure may assign NPS scores based on superficial impressions rather than well-formed opinions, raising concerns about the long-term validity of early-stage NPS scores [14]. This misalignment underscores the importance of incorporating sentiment analysis into NPS evaluations to capture customer sentiment more accurately over time.

The rigid NPS structure further complicates sentiment interpretation. The absence of a "no answer" option forces an indifferent user to select a score between zero and five, classifying them as detractors despite lacking dissatisfaction [28]. Similarly, customers who do not typically engage in brand recommendations may provide scores that fail to reflect their actual satisfaction levels [52]. Without sentiment analysis, companies risk misinterpreting these classifications, leading to skewed insights and flawed decision-making. This research investigates whether sentiment analysis can strengthen NPS's predictive value and provide a more holistic view of customer satisfaction.

## 4 Methodology

This study employs a mixed-methods approach to provide a comprehensive examination of customer perceptions related to the NPS in the UK banking landscape. A combination of qualitative and quantitative methods was essential to effectively address the research questions, ensuring both statistical validity and contextual depth in the analysis. By integrating survey data with sentiment analysis and online review metrics, this approach enables a multi-faceted investigation into how accurately customers understand NPS classifications *(RQ1)*, the relationship between NPS and traditional online rating systems *(RQ2)*, and the linguistic and tonal characteristics of customer reviews in relation to their NPS scores *(RQ3)*. The mixed-methods approach allows for triangulation across multiple data sources, enhancing the reliability of findings while providing richer insights into user perceptions. Given the complexity of customer interactions with feedback mechanisms, this approach is particularly well-suited to HCI research, where quantitative patterns must be contextualised within user experiences and perceptions. All study procedures were reviewed and approved by Swansea University's Institutional Review Board (IRB).

## 4.1 Primary Data: Survey

**Survey Design and Pilot Study:** The survey was distributed through Prolific to collect a representative sample of UK adult population. Considering only 2% of UK adults do not have a bank account,[3] this was fairly representative of the UK banking population, further exclusions included those who have had experiences with 16 of the major UK banks. These banks were selected as they are recognised by the CMA and have publicly available NPS results. The banks included in the study were HSBC, Barclays, Virgin Money, NatWest, Lloyds, Santander, Monzo, Co-Operative Banking, Starling Bank, First Direct, Metro Bank, Halifax, Bank of Scotland, TSB, The Royal Bank of Scotland, and Nationwide.

Before the full survey launch, a pilot study was conducted with 20 participants to ensure the clarity of the survey questions and to confirm the estimated completion time. The pilot highlighted several areas that required improvement. A number of users provided brief responses to the open-ended questions, and many encountered difficulties understanding how to classify their NPS ratings. In response to these findings, we revised the questions. Furthermore, the NPS classification question was revised and divided into two distinct questions. The quantitative question remained but was reworded to emphasise the key instructions with bold font, while an additional question specifically asked participants to classify themselves as promoters, detractors, or passives, each accompanied by clear definitions.

**Survey Distribution and Sample:** After revisions based on the pilot study, the survey was distributed to 300 participants. The target sample was carefully constructed to be representative of the UK population, which in turn is representative of the UK banking population with strict inclusion criteria ensuring that participants were aged 18 or older, residing in the UK, and customers of one of the 16 aforementioned banks. These criteria ensured that all responses were directly relevant to our research focus. The representative sample consisted of 152 females and 148 males. In terms of ethnicity, the majority identified as White (256), followed by Asian or Asian British (23), Mixed or Multiple Ethnic Groups (10), and Black (8). Employment status varied across the sample, with 118 participants in full-time employment, 54 in part-time roles, 46 retired, 26 self-employed, and 28 unemployed. The remaining participants categorised their employment status or ethnicity as 'Other'.

---

[3] https://www.fca.org.uk/publications/financial-lives/financial-lives-2023.

The resulting sample was mostly representative of the UK population. After comparing our Prolific-collected sample with national demographic data from the Office for National Statistics (ONS),[4] Chi-square goodness-of-fit tests indicated that there were no significant differences in gender, income or ethnicity distributions. However, significant deviations were observed in age and employment status. Specifically, the dataset skews younger and includes fewer full-time employed individuals, with a slight over representation of retired participants. These differences are likely due to the nature of Prolific's participant pool, which is known to attract younger users and individuals who may seek supplemental income—characteristics less common among those in full-time employment.

To minimise social desirability bias, demographic questions were placed after the primary content of the survey [11]. These demographic variables included gender, ethnicity, employment status, annual income, education level, and geographic location until the age of 18, as these factors were hypothesised to influence participants' understanding of NPS. Participants were offered £1.50 for the completion of a 10 min survey. The monetary incentive provided through Prolific raised concerns about potential response bias, where participants might rush through the survey to obtain the reward. However, Prolific's built-in quality control mechanisms mitigated this risk. Additionally, an attention check question was strategically placed within the demographic section to identify participants who were not responding attentively, further ensuring the integrity and reliability of the collected data.

## 4.2 Secondary Data: Trustpilot Reviews

A Python script was developed to scrape publicly available reviews from each of the banks Trustpilot pages using Selenium, which is a widely used automated browser interaction tool [37,49]. Trustpilot was selected as the primary data source for this research due to its extensive collection of publicly available customer reviews and its established role as a key platform for consumer feedback. Its large-scale dataset ensures sufficient volume for robust sentiment analysis while maintaining accessibility. Moreover, Trustpilot's structured rating system and textual review format allow for a direct comparison between structured numerical feedback and unstructured sentiment analysis, making it particularly well-suited for addressing *RQ2* and *RQ3*. Additionally, Trustpilot has been widely used in prior sentiment analysis research [38,40], enhancing the validity and comparability of this study. Given its influence on consumer decision-making and cross-industry applications, Trustpilot provides an ideal dataset for investigating the relationship between NPS, online ratings, and customer sentiment in retail banking.

---

[4] https://www.ons.gov.uk/peoplepopulationandcommunity.

### 4.3 Data Analysis

**Qualitative Analysis:** For the qualitative analysis of the survey data thematic analysis was used. NVivo software was employed to code and categorise the open-ended responses and was conducted by the first author, having been reviewed by the other authors which agreed with all the generated codes. NVivo enabled the identification of key themes related to customer satisfaction. The identified themes were analysed across different NPS scores, allowing for the comparison of patterns and trends among specific subgroups, particularly when interesting trends were identified within the data.

**Tone Analysis:** Sentiment analysis was conducted using VADER's SentimentIntensityAnalyzer [22], a widely used tool for sentiment classification [53]. In this study, it was adapted to classify Trustpilot reviews as positive, neutral, or negative, with the compound sentiment score serving as the primary metric. This approach aligned with other averaged variables, allowing for trend identification without separately analysing individual sentiment dimensions. 30 randomly selected reviews were manually reviewed and classified as either positive, neutral or negative and compared to the classifications completed by VADER, resulting in an 80% accuracy. This level of agreement reflects reasonable reliability for identifying sentiment trends in naturally expressed feedback.

Politeness analysis was performed using ConvoKit [10], which assigns binary scores to text indicators: polite (1), neutral (0), and negative (-1). These were aggregated to generate a net politeness score per review. Toxicity was assessed using Detoxify [18], quantifying offensive or aggressive language indicative of negative experiences, including insult levels.

A challenge arose from the presence of emojis in customer reviews, as sentiment analysis tools struggled to interpret them accurately. Since emojis contribute to tone and sentiment, simply removing them would risk losing critical context. To address this, we developed the replace_emojis() function, converting emojis into textual descriptions for improved sentiment interpretation [32,51].

Both qualitative survey responses and Trustpilot reviews underwent sentiment, politeness, and toxicity analysis using these Python tools. The Trustpilot data was aggregated into six-month periods and correlated with NPS scores for the corresponding intervals. Statistical correlation tests were performed to assess relationships between review sentiment, tone, and NPS scores. Prior research has explored the impact of politeness strategies on customer satisfaction [21] and examined how toxic content can affect overall product sentiment [43]. Building on these studies, our analysis aims to determine if similar patterns are observable within our dataset.

## 5 Findings

The findings are structured according to the research questions, with each section presenting the most relevant findings. The analysis follows a consistent format:

first, results from primary data collection (the survey) are reported, followed by demographic influences, and finally, secondary data findings from online sources. As *RQ1* pertains solely to survey responses, no secondary data is included in that section.

### 5.1 RQ1: Customer Understanding of NPS Categories

This section reports the findings from the survey before analysing the demographical results which were found to be related to the research question.

**Study Results:** The collected data revealed that 110/300 (37%) individuals misclassified themselves, believing their NPS score placed them in a different category than it actually did. A Cohen's Kappa value of 0.388 was calculated, despite indicating a fair level of agreement between participants' self-classifications and the actual categories, this is still a high number of participants who failed to fully comprehend how their opinions are being measured by the NPS metric.

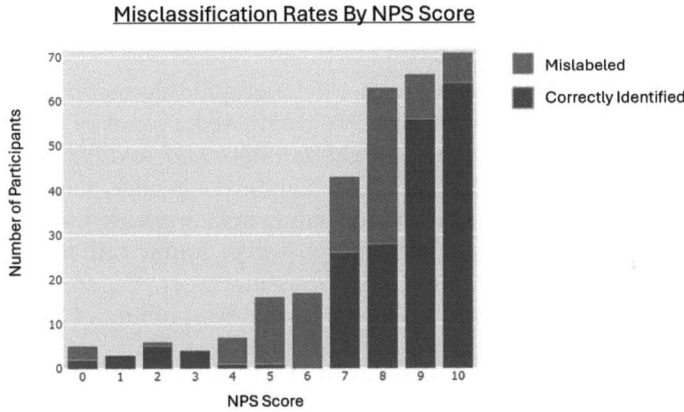

**Fig. 1.** This graph demonstrates the misclassification rates found split by their corresponding NPS scores.

Given that the Kappa value is closer to zero than to one, implying a greater proximity to random chance than to certainty, it is crucial to consider the factors influencing participants' misjudgements. Among the participants who misclassified their NPS category, 92/110 (82%) believed they belonged to a higher category than their score indicated. Further analysis (see Fig. 1), revealed that the NPS score of 8 was the most frequently misinterpreted, with users often believing that this score categorised them as promoters of the brand. Qualitative analysis of these responses uncovered overwhelmingly positive feedback, with frequent references to positive experiences with the bank's app and customer service. A recurring theme was a strong intention to recommend the bank, as 25 of the 34 responses associated with a score of 8 included the word "recommend".

More notably, misclassification was highest within the upper range of the detractor category. None of the participants who provided a score of six were able to accurately identify their corresponding category, and only a small proportion of those who responded with a score of four or five correctly recognised their classification. Furthermore, all users who selected a score of six perceived themselves to belong to a higher NPS category than was actually the case.

An in-depth analysis of these scores revealed that the most frequently cited factor was the willingness to recommend if prompted, combined with a general sense of satisfaction. However, participants didn't perceive the banks as performing exceptionally well. These findings suggest that NPS scores may be artificially deflated and may fail to accurately capture customers' true sentiments, potentially due to a lack of understanding of the metric on the part of the users.

Additionally, it is noteworthy that all of those who misclassified themselves when responding 0 on the NPS scale, which is typically associated with being a detractor, classified themselves as passives. These participants selected 0 because they would not recommend the bank under any circumstances, reflecting a fundamentally different interpretation of the NPS rating system, highlighting a disconnect between their intentions and the NPS metric itself.

**Demographics:** To investigate whether demographic characteristics influenced the likelihood of NPS misclassification, we conducted a series of statistical tests, including chi-squared tests for categorical variables and ANOVA for the continuous variable of age. Across all variables examined—gender, income, education level, employment status, ethnic background, area lived in until age 18, and age—no statistically significant associations were found (all p-values $> .05$). This suggests that misclassification is not systematically related to demographic factors and may instead reflect a broader misunderstanding of NPS categories across the sample. These findings imply that improved clarity and design of NPS feedback systems may be more impactful than targeting demographic-specific interventions.

## 5.2 RQ2: NPS and Likert Rating Relationship

**Survey Results:** To investigate the potential relationship between Likert scale ratings commonly used on online review platforms and NPS, the survey included two questions: one asked participant to rate their bank on a scale of one to five (Likert scale), while the other followed the traditional NPS format, asking participants to rate their likelihood of recommending the bank on a scale of zero to ten. Pearson and Spearman correlation tests were applied to compare each participant's score across both scales. The results yielded a correlation coefficient of 0.761, with a p-value of $<0.001$, indicating a significant positive correlation between the two scoring systems (see Fig. 2). This suggests that as the Likert score increases, so does the corresponding NPS score.

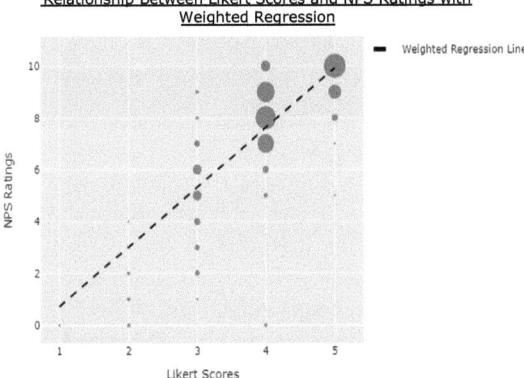

**Fig. 2.** This graph visualises the relationship between Likert Scores and NPS Ratings, with the size of the bubbles representing the frequency of occurrences. A weighted regression line is included to highlight the trend in the data, indicating a positive correlation between the two variables.

**Demographics:** Interestingly, it was only the age demographics that revealed variation. While most age groups showed strong and significant correlations, participants aged 25–29 and 30–34 demonstrated no statistically significant correlations. This contrasts with other age groups, which generally showed significant and strong correlations, particularly those aged 40–44, 45–49, and 50–54. A detailed breakdown of correlations by age is presented in Table 1.

**Table 1.** Correlation and P-Values by Age Group

| Age Group | Correlation (R) | P-Value |
|---|---|---|
| 18–24 | 0.552 | <0.05 |
| 25–29 | 0.614 | 0.079 |
| 30–34 | 0.186 | 0.632 |
| 35–39 | 0.514 | <0.05 |
| 40–44 | 0.957 | <0.001 |
| 45–49 | 0.940 | <0.001 |
| 50–54 | 0.874 | <0.001 |
| 55–59 | 0.800 | <0.001 |
| 60–64 | 0.757 | <0.001 |
| 65–69 | 0.866 | <0.001 |

These results indicate that while there is generally a strong correlation between Likert and NPS scores across various demographics, certain groups—particularly some age ranges—show weaker or no statistically significant correlations, suggesting that factors beyond age may influence how individuals perceive and report their satisfaction across different scoring systems. However, the strength of the correlation especially in the age groups of 40–44 and 45–49 makes this a particularly interesting finding.

**Publicly Available Data:** The Pearson correlation test and Spearman Correlation test both returned no statistically significant correlations suggesting that there is no relationship in this instance. A key consideration is the temporal mismatch between the datasets, which may influence comparability. While CMA NPS scores are collected and published biannually, Trustpilot reviews were aggregated over a six-month period to align with this cycle. This approach, while necessary, could blur specific trends and reflect variations due to shifting sentiment, campaign activity, or isolated events within that time frame. As such, public review data should be interpreted with caution when used alongside formal NPS scores, given the differing contexts and collection methods.

## 5.3 RQ3: NPS Relationship to Language and Tone

**Study Results:** This question will focuses on analysing the qualitative data that was collected during this study. In the study this was the question which asked the individual to describe their Likert rating and the question which asked them to elaborate on their NPS score. In the secondary data we analysed the reviews left online. Every qualitative piece of data was analysed using the same python packages and for the secondary data the scores were combined to create six month averages which were comparable to the NPS scores used.

***Toxicity and Politeness*** – The Spearman correlation analysis revealed a very weak but significant negative relationship between the toxicity of the Likert Explanation and the Likert Rating, with a Spearman coefficient of $-0.169$ ($p = 0.003$). Similarly, a slightly stronger but still low negative correlation was observed between the toxicity of the NPS Explanation and the NPS Rating, with a Spearman coefficient of $-0.250$ ($p < 0.001$). Although these results indicate that as the toxicity in explanations increases, both Likert and NPS ratings tend to decrease, the correlations are low suggesting that toxic language is not a strong indicator of low customer satisfaction on its own. When examining the correlation between politeness in both Likert and NPS explanations and NPS scores, no statistically significant results were found. Therefore similar to toxicity, these findings suggest that politeness does not indicate customer satisfaction.

***Sentiment*** – The correlation between compound sentiment in explanations and NPS scores demonstrated a moderately positive relationship. For NPS explanations, the correlation coefficient was low but present with 0.23 ($p < 0.001$). In contrast, the correlation between Compound Sentiment in Likert explanations and NPS scores was stronger, with a coefficient of 0.44 ($p < 0.001$). These results suggest that more positive sentiment in customer explanations is strongly associated with higher NPS scores, with Likert explanations exhibiting an especially pronounced positive relationship.

**Demographics** – Income levels were more closely related to differences in tone. Participants in the lowest income category exhibited significantly higher levels of toxicity and insult in their Likert explanations. Conversely, participants in the highest income category showed the lowest toxicity and insult levels across both types of explanations, indicating a more neutral or polite tone. Interestingly, participants in the £70,000-£79,999 income bracket had the highest levels of insult in their Likert explanations, suggesting income alone doesn't predict tone consistently. Employment status also influenced the tone of explanations. Participants who were unemployed or students showed higher levels of toxicity in both NPS and Likert explanations compared to those who were employed full-time. In contrast, retired participants demonstrated lower levels of toxicity, particularly in NPS explanations, indicating that life experience may contribute to more polite or neutral language.

Gender differences were also apparent, with female participants generally showing lower levels of toxicity and insult. Age-related differences in tone were also observed. Participants aged 40–44 had the highest overall insult levels in both NPS and Likert explanations whilst participants aged 50–54 had the lowest insult scores, indicating a more polite tone overall. Participants aged 65–69 demonstrated lower insult levels and higher politeness, suggesting that older individuals may be more likely to use neutral or positive language.

**Publicly Available Data:** *Toxicity and Politeness* – The Spearman correlation analysis of the web-scraped data revealed a statistically significant negative correlation between toxicity levels in customer reviews and NPS, with a medium correlation coefficient of -0.31 ($p = 0.001$). This indicates that as toxicity in reviews increases, NPS scores tend to decrease. In contrast, a positive correlation was observed between politeness in reviews and NPS scores, with a stronger Spearman correlation coefficient of 0.43 ($p < 0.001$). This finding suggests that in the online space, more polite reviews are associated with higher NPS scores and more toxic reviews are linked to lower NPS scores.

*Sentiment* – The overall correlation between compound sentiment and NPS scores across all banks revealed a moderate positive relationship. A high Spearman correlation coefficient was found at 0.52, ($p < 0.001$). This suggests that as the sentiment of customer reviews becomes more positive, NPS scores tend to increase. These results suggest compound sentiment to be a strong predictor of NPS.

## 6 Discussion and Implications

Below we discuss the salient insight gained from our findings.

### 6.1 Customer Misclassification in NPS Responses

The overall misclassification rate among participants indicates only a "fair" agreement between perceived and actual NPS categories. While better than random chance, this level of agreement suggests that customers frequently misunderstand the distinctions between promoters, passives, and detractors. Given that NPS scores are highly sensitive to classification errors [28], such misinterpretations can significantly distort the intended measurement of customer sentiment. The most common error involved overestimation, where participants perceived themselves as more loyal or satisfied than their numerical score would indicate. This misalignment was reinforced by qualitative data in which customers who misclassified themselves used positive language and words like "recommend," despite their assigned NPS category suggesting otherwise.

These results highlight the need for a more user-centred approach to NPS data collection, as companies continue to rely on this metric for key performance evaluations [41]. A potential solution is the introduction of visual aids to help users better grasp what each score represents, improving internalisation and reducing misclassification errors [9, 26].

Additionally, users who rated their bank a "0" but self-identified as passives demonstrated a fundamental misunderstanding of the implications of their score. This is particularly relevant in industries like banking, where recommending a provider is not a common behaviour due to the complexity and stakes involved in financial decisions [4]. The assumption that all customers understand or engage with the concept of brand advocacy in the same way seems flawed, reinforcing the argument that NPS should offer a "no response" option [29]. However, this approach may reduce usable data, making an alternative—such as emphasising the hypothetical nature of the recommendation question—a more viable solution.

### 6.2 Correlation Between NPS and Traditional Online Ratings

A strong correlation between NPS and Likert scale ratings echoes prior research indicating that both reflect overall CX [25]. While Likert measures specific satisfaction aspects and NPS assesses brand advocacy, customers use both in similar ways [50]. However, analysis of Trustpilot data did not show a statistically significant correlation. This is likely due to selection bias being inherent in open review platforms like Trustpilot, where contributors are typically self-selected and disproportionately represent those with highly polarised experiences—often the most satisfied or dissatisfied customers [20]. Also, response motivation differs substantially, NPS responses are usually prompted and structured within a specific feedback window, whereas Trustpilot reviews are voluntary, public-facing, and often emotionally charged.

### 6.3 Emotional Tone and Customer Sentiment in NPS Responses

Toxic language strongly correlated with lower NPS scores, reinforcing findings that negative emotional expressions—such as frustration or anger—are linked to lower satisfaction ratings [12]. Since toxicity in both Likert and NPS explanations affected ratings similarly, organisations can use sentiment analysis to monitor customer dissatisfaction and intervene proactively. AI-driven tools can detect trends in negative feedback, allowing businesses to enhance service quality and customer retention.

While toxicity indicated dissatisfaction, politeness showed no significant correlation with NPS, suggesting that courteous language does not necessarily reflect satisfaction or loyalty [31]. In some cases, politeness may even mask criticism. Sarcasm, particularly in British culture, further complicates sentiment analysis, as polite phrasing can disguise negative sentiment [30]. This complicates automated sentiment analysis, as sarcasm can distort conventional politeness metrics, making it harder to extract true customer sentiment from text-based feedback. To further examine the impact of such cultural influences, future work should replicate this work across diverse cultural contexts, thereby elucidating the extent to which British sarcasm contributes as a significant factor. This highlights just one example of how cultural nuances—such as British politeness and sarcasm, can shape NPS responses, demonstrating why understanding NPS through emotinoal tone cannot be reliably generalised beyond the specific cultural context in which it is studied.

### 6.4 Influence of Demographics on Sentiment Expression

Demographics played a key role in how customers expressed sentiment. Lower-income participants exhibited higher toxicity and insult levels, while higher-income users used more neutral or polite language. Socioeconomic background influences communication style, with individuals from lower-income areas more likely to use direct, emotionally charged language [35]. This can lead to misinterpretations in sentiment analysis, as blunt feedback may be mistakenly classified as overly negative.

Generational differences also shaped sentiment expression. Millennials and Gen Z use more unfiltered language, including profanity, without necessarily indicating dissatisfaction [23]. In contrast, older generations view such language as negative [36]. This generational gap suggests that sentiment analysis must be adapted to consider evolving communication styles when assessing feedback.

As AI tools become increasingly prevalent in CX management, there's a risk that critical factors—such as the influence of demographic characteristics on sentiment expression—may be overlooked. Consequently, trends analysed without accounting for these variables may be misinterpreted, leading to poor management decisions that could ultimately prove detrimental to business performance.

### 6.5 Limitations

We addressed dataset-specific constraints by incorporating both primary and secondary data, which was essential for answering our research questions. While NPS effectiveness varies across industries and our findings are specific to the banking sector, they still provide valuable insights into customer satisfaction within this context. Additionally, computational linguistic tools for sentiment analysis face challenges in detecting nuances such as sarcasm and cultural differences, which can lead to misclassification. To mitigate this limitation, we employed multiple sentiment measures—compound sentiment, toxicity, and politeness—offering a more nuanced perspective on perceptions of customer satisfaction to strengthen the reliability of our conclusions. Finally, using Prolific may have introduced some bias regarding the sample leaning to slightly younger participants; however, it was the most practical and efficient method for data collection within the project's limited time frame.

# 7 Conclusion

This study contributes to the literature in three key areas. First, it fills an important gap by comparing customers' perceived satisfaction with their actual NPS classifications, revealing that 37% misclassified themselves, often overestimating their status. This misalignment, highlights the need for greater transparency in NPS interpretation and adaptive survey designs that account for user literacy and provide in-the-moment explanation of scoring consequences.

Second, the study challenges the assumption that NPS is universally understood by those interacting with it in the UK banking sector, reinforcing concerns that many UK banking customers misunderstand how their responses are categorised. For HCI practitioners, this underscores the importance of interface transparency and user-centred explanations in feedback tools—particularly in industries where customer trust and clarity are paramount such as banking but with potential to expand to other similar industries.

Finally, by analysing sentiment in both structured NPS surveys and online reviews, we highlight the role of emotional expression in customer feedback. While NPS correlated well with Likert scales, publicly available Trustpilot data showed a weaker correlation with no statistical significance, indicating contextual differences in customer engagement. Additionally, sentiment analysis revealed higher toxicity linked to lower scores and politeness sometimes masking dissatisfaction, reinforcing the need for context-sensitive satisfaction evaluation methods. These insights suggest that sentiment-aware feedback interfaces—capable of detecting linguistic cues such as politeness or emotional intensity—should offer real-time prompts or clarifications to help users accurately express their experiences, ultimately improving the reliability and interpretability of the feedback collected.

Further studies could investigate the implications identified here, particularly the role of visual cues in improving NPS response accuracy. A key question is whether such prompts help users better align their responses with their true sentiments or risk introducing bias by subtly guiding choices. Controlled experiments could explore how users interact with these elements, assessing whether they enhance comprehension or distort feedback, supported by in-depth interviews and follow-ups to more accurately capture participants' intended meanings and interpretations. Additionally, future research could examine the use of real-time sentiment analysis to proactively address dissatisfaction before it impacts NPS scores, and explore how socio-technical characteristics can be meaningfully integrated into CX measurement. To advance inclusivity and accuracy, future work should also consider how personalised feedback systems can accommodate individual differences in communication styles. Crucially, we advocate for a more human-centred approach to the design of customer satisfaction measures. This includes incorporating qualitative interviews and co-design workshops, enabling stakeholders to collaboratively shape feedback mechanisms that reflect natural user expression while balancing conceptual rigour and practical usability.

**Acknowledgements.** This work was funded by EPSRC grant number EP/S021892/1 and HSBC UK Bank PLC. We thank the study participants for their time and effort. We are grateful to anonymous reviewers who helped us further improve the paper.

# References

1. Anderson, E.: Customer satisfaction and word of mouth. https://journals.sagepub.com/doi/10.1177/109467059800100102 (1998)
2. Baehre, S., O'Dwyer, M., O'Malley, L., Lee, N.: The use of Net Promoter Score (NPS) to predict sales growth: insights from an empirical investigation. J. Acad. Mark. Sci. **50**(1), 67–84 (2021). https://doi.org/10.1007/s11747-021-00790-2
3. Baquero, S.D., Castañeda, J.A., Gómez, M.: Does net promoter score reflect real customer satisfaction? evidence from the hotel industry. Sustainability **14**(4), 2011 (2022). https://doi.org/10.3390/su14042011
4. Bennett, R., Kottasz, R.: Public attitudes towards the UK banking industry following the global financial crisis. Int. J. Bank Market. **30**(2), 128–147 (2012). https://doi.org/10.1108/02652321211210877
5. Brandt, D.R.: For good measure. Market. Manage. **16**(1), 20–25 (2007)
6. Busalim, A., Hollebeek, L.D., Lynn, T.: The effect of social commerce attributes on customer engagement: an empirical investigation. Internet Res. **34**(7), 187–214 (2023). https://doi.org/10.1108/INTR-03-2022-0165
7. Chen, T., Samaranayake, P., Cen, X., Qi, M., Lan, Y.C.: The impact of online reviews on consumers' purchasing decisions: evidence from an eye-tracking study. Front. Psychol. **13** (2022). https://doi.org/10.3389/fpsyg.2022.865702
8. Chevalier, J.A., Mayzlin, D.: The effect of word of mouth on sales: Online book reviews. J. Mark. Res. **43**(3), 345–354 (2006). https://doi.org/10.1509/jmkr.43.3.345
9. Couper, M.P., Traugott, M.W., Lamias, M.J.: Web survey design and administration. Public Opin. Q. **65**(2), 230–253 (2001). https://doi.org/10.1086/322199
10. Danescu-Niculescu-Mizil, C., Sudhof, M., Jurafsky, D., Leskovec, J., Potts, C.: A computational approach to politeness with application to social factors. In: Proceedings of the 51st Annual Meeting of the Association for Computational Linguistics (Volume 1: Long Papers), pp. 250–259 (2013), https://aclanthology.org/P13-1025
11. Dillman, D.A., Smyth, J.D., Christian, L.M.: Internet, Phone, Mail, and Mixed Mode Surveys: The Tailored Design Method, 4th edn. John Wiley & Sons Inc, Hoboken, NJ, US (2014)
12. Fan, W., Liu, Y., Li, H., Tuunainen, V.K., Lin, Y.: Quantifying the effects of online review content structures on hotel review helpfulness. Internet Res. **32**(7), 202–227 (2021). https://doi.org/10.1108/INTR-11-2019-0452

13. Fisher, N.I., Kordupleski, R.E.: Good and bad market research: A critical review of net promoter score. arXiv preprint arXiv:1806.10452 (2018), https://arxiv.org/abs/1806.10452
14. Fisher, N.I., Kordupleski, R.E.: Good and bad market research: a critical review of net promoter score. Appl. Stoch. Model. Bus. Ind. **35**(1), 138–151 (2019). https://doi.org/10.1002/asmb.2417
15. Gordon, J.: 40% of brits stay loyal to one bank for their entire lives (2020). https://www.theinvestmentobserver.co.uk/money/2020/09/25/40-of-brits-stay-loyal-to-one-bank-for-their-entire-lives/
16. Grigoreva, E.A., Garifova, L.F., Polovkina, E.A.: Consumer behavior in the information economy: generation z. Int. J. Fin. Res. **12**(2), 164 (2021). https://doi.org/10.5430/ijfr.v12n2p164
17. Grisaffe, D.B.: Questions about the ultimate question: conceptual considerations in evaluating Reichheld's net promoter score (NPS). J. Consum. Satisfaction, Dissatisfaction Complaining Behav. **20**, 36–53 (2016)
18. Hanu, L., Team, U.: Detoxify (2020). https://doi.org/10.5281/zenodo.7925667
19. Howarth, J.: 81 online review statistics (new 2024 data) (2022). https://explodingtopics.com/blog/online-review-stats. Accessed 28 Sept 2024
20. Hu, N., Pavlou, P.A., Zhang, J.J.: Overcoming the j-shaped distribution of product reviews (2009). https://papers.ssrn.com/abstract=2369332
21. Hu, Y., Huang, D., Kim, H., Koh, R.: Read this, please? the role of politeness in customer service engagement on social media. In: Proceedings of the 52nd Hawaii International Conference on System Sciences, pp. 1–10 (2019)
22. Hutto, C., Gilbert, E.: Vader: A parsimonious rule-based model for sentiment analysis of social media text. In: Proceedings of the International AAAI Conference on Web and Social Media, vol. 8, pp. 216–225 (2014). https://doi.org/10.1609/icwsm.v8i1.14550
23. Jay, T., Janschewitz, K.: The pragmatics of swearing. J. Politeness Res. Lang., Behav., Cult. **4**(2) (2008). https://doi.org/10.1515/JPLR.2008.013
24. Karimi, S., Holland, C.P., Papamichail, K.N.: The impact of consumer archetypes on online purchase decision-making processes and outcomes: a behavioural process perspective. J. Bus. Res. **91**, 71–82 (2018). https://doi.org/10.1016/j.jbusres.2018.05.038
25. Keiningham, T.L., Cooil, B., Andreassen, T.W., Aksoy, L.: A longitudinal examination of net promoter and firm revenue growth. J. Mark. **71**(3), 39–51 (2007). https://doi.org/10.1509/jmkg.71.3.039
26. Khandelwal, M.: Expert advice on the impact of color coding the NPS scale (2023). https://www.surveysensum.com/blog/color-coding-nps-scale. Accessed 28 Sept 2024
27. Kim, W.G., Park, S.A.: Social media review rating versus traditional customer satisfaction: which one has more incremental predictive power in explaining hotel performance? Int. J. Contemp. Hosp. Manag. **29**(2), 784–802 (2017). https://doi.org/10.1108/IJCHM-11-2015-0627
28. Kristensen, K., Eskildsen, J.: Is the net promoter score a reliable performance measure? In: 2011 IEEE International Conference on Quality and Reliability, pp. 249–253 (2011). https://doi.org/10.1109/ICQR.2011.6031719
29. Kristensen, K., Eskildsen, J.: Is the NPS a trustworthy performance measure? The TQM J. **26**(2), 202–214 (2014). https://doi.org/10.1108/TQM-03-2011-0021
30. Kádár, D.Z.: Politeness, impoliteness and ritual: maintaining the moral order in interpersonal interaction. Cambridge Univ. Press (2017). https://doi.org/10.1017/9781107280465

31. Kádár, D.Z., Haugh, M.: Politeness as social practice. In: Understanding Politeness, pp. 57–80. Cambridge University Press (2013). https://doi.org/10.1017/CBO9781139382717.005
32. LeCompte, T., Chen, J.: Sentiment analysis of tweets including emoji data. In: 2017 International Conference on Computational Science and Computational Intelligence. IEEE (2017). https://doi.org/10.1109/CSCI.2017.137, https://ieeexplore.ieee.org/document/8265116
33. Lewis, C., Mehmet, M.: Does the nps® reflect consumer sentiment? a qualitative examination of the nps using a sentiment analysis approach. Int. J. Mark. Res. **62**(1), 9–17 (2020). https://doi.org/10.1177/1470785319863623
34. Liang, X., et al.: An end-to-end solution for net promoter score estimation and explanation from social media using natural language processing. In: Fuzzy Systems and Data Mining IX, pp. 54–66. IOS Press (2023). https://doi.org/10.3233/FAIA231006
35. Liu, R.W., Lapinski, M.K., Kerr, J.M., Zhao, J., Bum, T., Lu, Z.: Culture and social norms: Development and application of a model for culturally contextualized communication measurement (mc3m). Front. Commun. **6** (2022). https://doi.org/10.3389/fcomm.2021.770513
36. Livingstone, S.: Igen: why today's super-connected kids are growing up less rebellious, more tolerant, less happy – and completely unprepared for adulthood. J. Child. Media **12**(1), 118–123 (2018). https://doi.org/10.1080/17482798.2017.1417091
37. Loke, R.E., Kachaniuk, O.: Sentiment polarity classification of corporate review data with a bidirectional long-short term memory (bilstm) neural network architecture. In: Proceedings of the 9th International Conference on Data Science, Technology and Applications, pp. 310–317. SCITEPRESS – Science and Technology Publications, Lda. (2020). https://doi.org/10.5220/0009892303100317
38. Loke, R.E., Pathak, S.: Decision support system for corporate reputation based social media listening using a cross-source sentiment analysis engine. In: Proceedings of the 12th International Conference on Data Science, Technology and Applications, pp. 559–567. SCITEPRESS – Science and Technology Publications, Lda. (2023). https://doi.org/10.5220/0012136400003541
39. Melnic, E.: The science of customer satisfaction in the retail banking system - a critical comparison between the two international indexes: Net promoter score (NPS) and American customer satisfaction index (acsi) (2016). https://www.etimm.ase.ro/?p=109
40. Miracula, V., Picone, A.: Unleashing the power of user reviews: Exploring airline choices at Catania airport, Italy. arXiv:2306.15541 (2023). https://arxiv.org/abs/2306.15541v1
41. Morgan, N.A., Rego, L.L.: The value of different customer satisfaction and loyalty metrics in predicting business performance. Mark. Sci. **25**(5), 426–439 (2006). https://doi.org/10.1287/mksc.1050.0180
42. Morgeson, F.V., Hult, G.T.M., Sharma, U., Fornell, C.: The American customer satisfaction index (ACSI): A sample dataset and description. Data Brief **48**, 109123 (2023). https://doi.org/10.1016/j.dib.2023.109123
43. Mukhopadhyay, M., Sahney, S.: Effect of toxic review content on overall product sentiment. J. Market. Theor. Pract. (2022). https://doi.org/10.1177/10591478241309439
44. Müller, S., Seiler, R., Völkle, M.: Should net promoter score be supplemented with other customer feedback metrics? an empirical investigation of net promoter score

and emotions in the mobile phone industry. Int. J. Market Res. **66**(2–3), 303–320 (2024). https://doi.org/10.1177/14707853231219648
45. Parasuraman, A., Berry, L.L., Zeithaml, V.A.: Refinement and reassessment of the servqual scale. J. Retail. **67**(4), 420–450 (1991)
46. Patel, N.: The benefits and importance of customer satisfaction, https://widewebadvisor.com/wp-content/uploads/2019/01/The-Benefits-and-Importance-of-Customer-Satisfaction/1851/-1.pdf. Accessed 28 Sept 2024
47. Pechter, J., Kuusik, A.: NPS from the customer's perspective: The influence of the recent experience. Int. J. Mark. Res. **66**(2–3), 261–277 (2024). https://doi.org/10.1177/14707853231214188
48. Pingitore, G., Morgan, N., Rego, L., Gigliotti, A., Meyers, J.: The single-question trap. Market. Res. **19**(2), 8–13 (2007)
49. Reddy, D., Singh, A., Chopra, R., Patel, R.: Leveraging machine learning algorithms and natural language processing for ai-enhanced social media marketing analytics. Journal of AI and Marketing (2023). https://joaimlr.com/index.php/v1/article/view/28, preprint
50. Reichheld, F.: The one number you need to grow. Harvard Business Review (December 2003). https://hbr.org/2003/12/the-one-number-you-need-to-grow
51. Sakode, H., Surekha, T.L., Kumar, G.B., Sri, M.D.: Sentiment analysis using text and emojis. In: Proceedings of the International Conference on Inventive Computation Technologies (ICICT 2023) (2023). https://doi.org/10.1109/ICICT57646.2023.10134459
52. Schulman, A., Sargeant, K.: Measuring donor loyalty beyond net promoter score (2013). https://www.nonprofitpro.com/article/measuring-donor-loyalty-beyond-net-promoter-score/
53. Sha, Y., Micallef, N., Wu, Y.: Dissecting the advocacy discourse behind the #StopAsianHate movement on X/Twitter. In: Social Networks Analysis and Mining, pp. 211–229. Springer Nature Switzerland, Cham (2025)
54. Situmorang, S.H.: Gen c and gen y: experience, net emotional value and net promoter score. In: Proceedings of ICOSOP-16, pp. 259–265 (2016). https://doi.org/10.2991/icosop-16.2017.38
55. Thelwall, M.: Sentiment strength detection for the social web. J. Am. Soc. Inform. Sci. Technol. **63**(1), 163–173 (2012). https://doi.org/10.1002/asi.21662
56. Walter, V., Kölle, M., Collmar, D.: Measuring the wisdom of the crowd: How many is enough? PFG – journal of photogrammetry. Remote Sens. Geoinform. Sci. **90**(3), 269–291 (2022). https://doi.org/10.1007/s41064-022-00202-2

# Moving Toward Natural Gesture Interaction: Understanding User Preferences in Smart Homes

Mauro Filho[✉], Ana Patrícia Rocha, Tiago Silvestre, Gonçalo Lourenço Silva, Diogo Matos, Inês Santos, Nuno Vidal, António Teixeira, and Samuel Silva

IEETA, DETI, LASI, University of Aveiro, Aveiro, Portugal
{mauro.filho,aprocha,tiago.silvestre,goncalolsilva,dftm,ismsantos,
nunovidal,ajst,sss}@ua.pt

**Abstract.** Smart environments, such as smart homes, promise to enhance our daily lives. How we interact with these spaces, which encompass a wide range of devices and functionalities, remains a challenge that research seeks to address with increasingly natural forms of interaction, such as speech. However, the latter may not be appropriate in various situations (e.g., noisy environments, speech difficulties) where gestures can be a suitable alternative (or complement). To inform our research on designing gesture-based interaction for smart environments, we conducted a focus group to gather users' views and preferences regarding the use of gestures to interact with smart home devices. Overall, gestures were found to be better suited for discrete binary commands (e.g., on/off, previous/next) and participants suggested that actions, not the controlled devices, should dictate the gestures. This study provides useful insights on users' expectations and mental models for gesture interaction in smart environments, informing future research and development.

**Keywords:** Gesture elicitation · Focus group · Human-machine interaction · Smart homes

## 1 Introduction

The environments we live in are becoming increasingly intelligent due to advancements such as the Internet of Everything and Artificial Intelligence. This transformation enables enhanced device/appliance control, promising greater convenience, efficiency, safety, and comfort. However, as these environments become smarter, they also become more complex, presenting challenges concerning natural, intuitive, and efficient interaction with them. While smart speakers incorporating assistants are a step towards addressing these challenges, speech input faces limitations related to ambient noise and accessibility for individuals with speech difficulties. In this regard, gestures offer an alternative or complement, maintaining the possibility of interaction at a distance.

Gesture interaction has some potential drawbacks, such as being influenced by ambient conditions (e.g., low light) and raising privacy concerns. However, these can be minimized by using unobtrusive sensors, such as radio frequency sensing [1]. Other challenges include low user acceptance and adoption due to a potential steep learning curve and user fatigue, requiring careful user and context consideration when designing gestural interfaces.

To address this, several gesture elicitation studies have been carried out [16,17] aimed at different applications (e.g., virtual or augmented reality [13,14], gaming [15], wheelchairs [4], displays [9,20], and smart homes [3,5–8,10–12,18,19]). Considering smart homes, while most studies explored mid-air hand/arm gestures, some considered foot gestures [7], on-skin gestures [3] or gestures involving soft surface and/or rigid objects [5,6]. Most focused on one or two specific home divisions, such as the living room [5,12], living room and home office [6], kitchen [3,10], or bathroom [7]. Gesture elicitation was typically carried out individually or in pairs, with participants being asked to suggest gestures for each predefined scenario/home division, device, and/or action.

Two exceptions are the studies by Chamunorwa et al. [6] and Hosseini et al. [11], where devices and commands were selected by participants in a focus group or individual semi-structured interviews, respectively. Nevertheless, the spaces/scenarios were still preset. Hosseini and co-workers further explored the consistency of user's suggestions when transitioning to a different scenario. Their findings show that users tend to associate given gestures with the control of different devices, with the authors suggesting universal gesture patterns.

In light of these works, and in the scope of designing novel technologies supporting gesture interaction in smart spaces and to inform further work, we aimed to understand user preferences and obtain insights on how gestures might fit different actions, in these environments. In this regard, we conducted a focus group where relevant aspects related to interaction with smart environments, focusing on gesture-based interaction, were discussed as a group, with the participants guiding the different choices. In contrast to related works, no limitations were imposed concerning specific rooms in the house.

## 2 Study Design

To better understand the preferences of users regarding gesture-based interaction within smart homes, while trying not to overly influence them, we conducted a focus group aimed at gathering insights into the following main aspects: (1) opinion on gesture use for interaction with smart environments; (2) devices and actions for which they would most likely use gesture input; (3) preferred gesture for each device and action selected by the group.

### 2.1 Apparatus

The focus group session was held in a laboratory at the Institute of Electronics and Informatics Engineering of Aveiro (IEETA), University of Aveiro (Aveiro, Portugal). Apart from the participants, the session involved three moderators: two "active" moderators who directly engaged with the participants and one "passive" moderator who enabled indirect recording of gestures suggested by the participants. The apparatus consisted of chairs, with the participants' chairs being organized in a semicircular shape and the moderators' chairs being placed in front of the participants to facilitate and encourage group interaction. The material also included a consent form and a questionnaire with questions regarding age, occupation, and area of specialization. The "active" moderators were provided with a guide to help steer a semi-structured discussion with the participants. Two smartphones were also used, one for recording the audio of the discussion (destroyed after transcription) and another to record videos of the "passive" moderator replicating the gestures proposed by the participants to avoid recording videos of the volunteers.

## 2.2 Procedure

The focus group was divided into four phases as described in Table 1. It was carried out as part of the user studies of the "OLI Health" project, which obtained clearance from our university's Ethical Committee (Reference: 49-CED/2023).

**Table 1.** Summary of the phases considered for the focus group session.

| Phase | Duration | Description |
|---|---|---|
| **Introduction** | 5 min | Presentation of the study to the participants, including its general objective and the participant's expected role, followed by the introduction of each participant. |
| **Warm-up Discussion** | 15 min | Initial discussion where participants were asked open-ended questions related to smart environments and interaction with them, including questions regarding gesture-based interaction, to better understand their preferences, perspectives, and thoughts on the topic. |
| **Main Discussion** (w/ Gesture Elicitation) | 35 min | Main discussion on gesture interaction, where participants were asked to identify devices and actions for which gesture-based interaction might be beneficial. For each device/action selected as a group, they were then asked to propose gestures and choose the most adequate one. |
| **Conclusion** | 5 min | Session wrap-up, where we thanked the volunteers. |

During the Introduction phase, the study was presented to the participants using a slide presentation as support. The participants were then encouraged to introduce themselves to the group to foster a comfortable discussion environment. Subsequently, during the Warm-Up Discussion phase, the "active" moderators used the following questions to steer the discussion:

- What do you understand as a smart environment?
- Have you ever interacted with a smart environment? (If yes) How?
- What do you think are the best ways of interacting with smart environments?

- (If no one mentions gestures) In the case of [*situation where a given method is not applicable*] you wouldn't be able to use [*method*]. Can you think of any other alternative way of achieving it?
- (If no one mentions gestures) How about using gestures for that purpose?
- What do you think of gesture interaction with smart environments? What are the pros of this type of interaction when compared to other?

This was followed by the Main Discussion, where the "active" moderators began by asking the participants to imagine that they were in a smart home and could interact with any device using gestures. The participants were then prompted to identify which devices they would like to control. The moderators compiled a list of the most mentioned devices and, for each one, asked the participants what action they would accomplish using gestures.

Participants were then asked to propose the gesture(s) they believed would be the most natural and intuitive way to achieve each indicated action. The different suggested gestures were discussed and the participants were asked to choose the most adequate one by consensus. This, we hypothesized, would trigger explicit distinction among actions that are more natural to perform using gestures and those which would not be as evident or intuitive as hinted by diverse (or the lack of) perceived affordances.

The moderators never mentioned any specific technology that enables gesture interaction. Furthermore, during gesture elicitation, to avoid capturing images of the participants, videos of the "passive" moderator mimicking the proposed gestures were recorded (with the camera facing away from the participants).

### 2.3 Participants

Besides the moderators, the focus group session involved seven participants (five female and two male), with ages ranging from 18 to 23 years old. They were recruited through personal connections, all being students at University of Aveiro (Aveiro, Portugal). No volunteer presented any speech or hearing difficulty that would affect their ability to participate in the group discussion. To involve subjects with different levels of knowledge and experience concerning smart environments and technology, we recruited students from different areas: Computer Engineering and Informatics (four volunteers); Tourism, Languages and Cultures, and Physics Engineering (one volunteer each). All participants gave informed consent and filled the demographics questionnaire.

## 3 Results

This section presents the main results obtained during the focus group. The **Warm-Up Discussion** revealed that most participants were not very familiar with smart environments or at least could not provide examples of smart environments or explain what makes an environment "smart". Instead, they focused on the benefits of technology, such as making life easier. When asked about interactions with smart environments, participants initially struggled to provide examples, mostly mentioning "ChatGPT" or "benches that charge phones". However, when specifically asked about smart homes, they mentioned controlling smart lights or blinds using smartphones or voice assistants such as Google Assistant, and using kitchen robots. Therefore, while participants may not be aware of it, they can identify interactions with smart environments, even if they do not have first-hand experience.

Concerning the best methods to interact with smart homes, the participants reiterated the use of smartphones and voice commands. They also mentioned eye tracking and movement detection, with one participant giving examples of movement-activated lighting and video game control via hand movements (using Xbox). Participants also acknowledged that gesture-based interaction has benefits, especially in noisy environments or for people with speech difficulties. However, they also pointed out drawbacks, such as the physical effort required and the risk of false positives, where everyday movements could be misinterpreted as gestures, triggering unintended actions.

Although the generic expression "smart environments" was the starting point for the warm-up discussion, the conversation converged to home device control, as described above. The **Main Discussion** thus focused on gesture interaction with smart homes. Participants began by selecting various devices with which they would like to interact. Then, for those mentioned the most, they indicated what action they would like to perform. Finally, for each device and action, participants were encouraged to propose one or more gestures and then asked to discuss them and agree on only one as a group.

Table 2 provides a summary of the results of gesture elicitation for the devices and actions for which participants agreed on a suitable gesture. Some of those gestures are illustrated in Fig. 1. Other devices/actions were discussed: controlling the blinds' height, lighting brightness, and air conditioning (AC) temperature; navigating the menu, choosing a specific channel, and increasing/decreasing the volume of a TV; locking/unlocking doors; controlling faucets (turning on/off and increasing/decreasing water temperature) and flushing the toilet in the bathroom. However, for these cases, the group could not agree on a suitable gesture, concluding it would be better to use a different interaction mode, or they considered gestures to be less intuitive and potentially more time-consuming than traditional methods (e.g., for a faucet or toilet). For security-related actions, such as (un)locking doors, the group felt that gestures was not the best option, suggesting facial recognition instead.

Participants generally found gestures to be useful for controlling lighting, TVs, AC, blinds/curtains, and doors. For most of the selected devices, several commands were initially considered. Nevertheless, for those involving a more continuous control (e.g., increasing/decreasing luminosity, temperature, or volume), it was deemed difficult to achieve using a single gesture or to easily allow a fine control using hand gestures. In the end, the gestures the group agreed on correspond to discrete binary control (e.g., open/close, on/off, next/previous).

**Table 2.** Gestures the group agreed on for different devices and actions for which they believed gesture interaction would be most useful.

| Device | Action | Gesture |
|---|---|---|
| Curtains | Open/Close | Starting with the hands together, move them away from each other, as if opening curtains, and vice versa for closing |
| Blinds | Open/Close | Move one of the hands/arms up/down, with the forearm extended and hand palm facing up/down |
| Lights | Turn on/off | Gesture similar to screwing/unscrewing a light bulb, rotating the hand once to the left/right |
| Doors | Open/Close | Mid-air swipe with one of the hands/arms to the right/left |
| Air conditioning | Turn on/off | Mid-air swipe gesture to the left/right with the index finger extended |
| TV | Turn on/off | Extend one of the arms, with the hand parallel to the chest, and then bring it closer to the chest ("push and pull" gesture) – same for on and off |
| | Navigate channels | Mid-air swipe with one of the hands/arms to the left or right (next or previous channel, respectively) |
| Gesture interaction | (De)activate | Gesture similar to locking a door using a key, by rotating the hand clockwise in the air (with the fingers pointing up) – same for activating and deactivating |

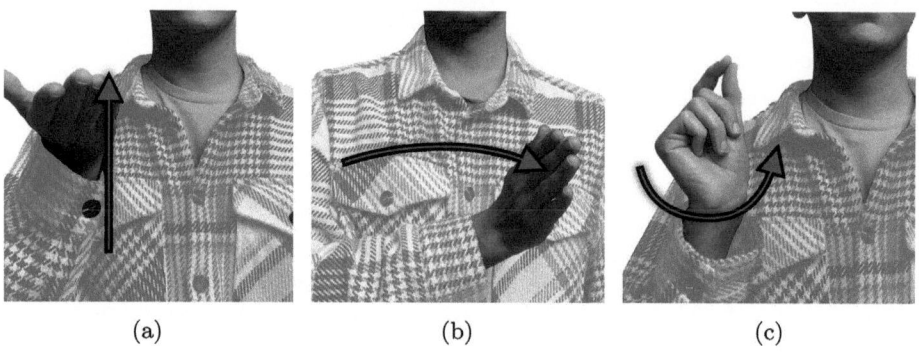

**Fig. 1.** Illustration of some of the proposed gestures for: (a) opening blinds; (b) changing to next TV channel; (c) interaction activating gesture.

It is also interesting to observe that (de)activating gesture interaction was considered a relevant feature, with participants mentioning it could help avoid confusing interaction gestures with daily life movements. For this action, the group proposed a gesture they thought would not be easily confused with other gestures: a mid-air gesture similar to locking a door (see Table 2). Concerns were also raised regarding guests' unfamiliarity with the gestures that can be used for interaction, hinting at the well-known discoverability issue in gesture interaction.

Another aspect worth mentioning is that participants tried to come up with different gestures for different devices, even if the action was similar. However, toward the end of the discussion, the participants themselves reached the conclusion that it was difficult to think of new gestures and it would probably be easier to use the same gesture for the same action even if the device is different (e.g., turning on/off any device).

## 4 Key Takeaways and Discussion

This study consisted of a single focus group with a relatively short duration, involving a reduced number of participants recruited from the same university based on personal connections, which reduces the generalization of our findings. Furthermore, the group setting may have introduced some bias. However, we believe that collaborative gesture proposal also has its benefits, such as leading to gestures that would not be suggested individually. Furthermore, the focus group also fostered a discussion that highlighted where there was easier agreement – hinting at a more intuitive association between certain gestures and actions – and a more disparate view – as a result of different perspectives or lack of adequate gestures for controlling certain aspects in a natural way.

Despite the limitations mentioned above, there are several interesting takeaways from the focus group replicating or adding to the existing studies:

- **Gestures are considered more suited for discrete binary controls.** These include turning devices on or off, opening or closing objects, or navigating to the next or previous item. These actions have clear start and end states, making them easy to map to simple gestures that users can remember and perform reliably.
- **The choice of gestures should be inspired by familiar gestures and leverage affordances.** The chosen gestures should suggest their function through physical similarity to real-world actions (i.e., they should exhibit good affordance). For example, opening/closing actual curtains maps naturally to opening/closing gestures for smart curtains; pushing a button to control a TV mimics pressing a physical button; flipping pages in a book aligns with gestures for changing TV channels. Most of the gestures in Table 2 are inspired by actions people already perform when interacting directly with such devices or similar objects.
- **Gestures should be defined for specific actions rather than devices.** This is in line with the findings by Hosseini and colleagues, which indicate that users tend to associate the same gesture(s) with identical types of control for different devices [11]. Nevertheless, in our study, it was the group discussion that led the participants to reach this conclusion.
- **There is potential in exploring gestures in tandem with methods that allow defining the interaction target.** The solution of using a given gesture for the same command implies that the smart home needs to be able to identify the target of the gesture (e.g., based on the device the user is facing or looking at), in line with the proposal by Barros et al. [2].

- **Users prefer gestures that allow movement economy and are more comfortable/ergonomic.** As it can be seen in Fig. 1, the gestures agreed by the participants commonly involve keeping the upper arm close to the body, with the movement being performed by the forearm and hand only. This hints at the importance of posture/movement naturalness for more natural gesture interaction, besides an intuitive gesture and action association.
- **Alternative modalities can be leveraged for precise or continuous control interactions.** For actions such as adjusting AC temperature or TV volume, and for operating specific devices such as faucets or toilets, gestures alone may lack precision or intuitiveness. Here, alternative or complementary input modalities – such as voice commands, touch interfaces, or physical controls – can offer more accurate, efficient, and user-friendly interaction.

Overall, by adopting the focus group method, we were able to gather new relevant information on people's preferences when it comes to gesture-based interaction with smart homes, extending the findings of previous similar works concerning mid-air hand/arm gestures that relied on individual interviews and/or focused on a specific or small set of rooms in a home [10–12,18,19].

## 5 Conclusions

To explore users' insights on the use and adequacy of gesture interaction in smart homes, we carried out a focus group with seven participants. Although gestures were not immediately mentioned as the best way to interact with smart environments, participants agreed they could be useful for some interactions, namely device control. Overall, the present study's findings provide useful insights that inform the design and implementation of gesture-based interaction towards a more natural and intuitive interaction between people and future smart homes.

To confirm and expand this study's findings, as well as compare preferences across various demographic groups, additional focus group sessions should be carried out with different groups of people (e.g., different ages, capabilities, and cultural backgrounds). It would also be important to perform follow-up studies where the environment is equipped with the devices identified in the focus groups, to further validate and explore the naturalness and acceptability, as well as the discoverability and learnability, of the elicited gestures. Considering the identified gesture limitations, it would also be interesting to investigate the combination of gestures and other modalities (e.g., speech, gaze, proximity) for target selection and/or reduction of false positives regarding interaction intention.

**Acknowledgments.** We thank the focus group participants. This work was funded by national funds through FCT - Fundação para a Ciência e a Tecnologia, I.P., in the context of project/support UID/00127. Part of the authors were funded by Project "Agenda ILLIANCE" [C644919832 00000035 – Project no 46], financed by PRR – Plano de Recuperação e Resiliência under Next Generation EU from European Union.

**Disclosure of Interests.** The authors have no competing interests to declare that are relevant to the content of this article.

# References

1. Ahmed, S., Kallu, K.D., Ahmed, S., Cho, S.H.: Hand gestures recognition using radar sensors for human-computer-interaction: a review. Remote Sensing **13**(3) (2021). https://doi.org/10.3390/rs13030527
2. Barros, F., Teixeira, A., Silva, S.: Developing a generic focus modality for multimodal interactive environments. In: Companion Publication of the 25th International Conference on Multimodal Interaction, pp. 31–35. ACM, New York, NY, USA (2023). https://doi.org/10.1145/3610661.3617165
3. Beşevli, C., Genç, H.U., Coşkun, A., Göksun, T., Yemez, Y., Özcan, O.: Gestural interaction in the kitchen: insights into designing an interactive display controlled by hand specific on-skin gestures. Des. J. **25**(3), 353–373 (2022). https://doi.org/10.1080/14606925.2022.2058444
4. Bilius, L.B., Ungurean, O.C., Vatavu, R.D.: Understanding wheelchair users' preferences for on-body, in-air, and on-wheelchair gestures. In: Proceedings of the 2023 CHI Conference on Human Factors in Computing Systems. Association for Computing Machinery, New York, NY, USA (2023). https://doi.org/10.1145/3544548.3580929
5. Chamunorwa, M., Wozniak, M.P., Krämer, S., Müller, H., Boll, S.: An empirical comparison of moderated and unmoderated gesture elicitation studies on soft surfaces and objects for smart home control. Proc. ACM Human-Comput. Interact. **7**(MHCI) (Sep 2023). https://doi.org/10.1145/3604245
6. Chamunorwa, M., Wozniak, M.P., Vöge, S., Müller, H., Boll, S.C.: Interacting with rigid and soft surfaces for smart-home control. Proc. ACM Human-Comput. Interact. **6**(MHCI) (Sept 2022). https://doi.org/10.1145/3546746
7. Chen, Z., Tu, H., Wu, H.: User-defined foot gestures for eyes-free interaction in smart shower rooms. Int. J. Human-Comput. Interact. **39**(20), 4139–4161 (2023). https://doi.org/10.1080/10447318.2022.2109260
8. Choi, E., Kwon, S., Lee, D., Lee, H., Chung, M.K.: Towards successful user interaction with systems: focusing on user-derived gestures for smart home systems. Appl. Ergon. **45**(4), 1196–1207 (2014). https://doi.org/10.1016/j.apergo.2014.02.010
9. Gentile, V., Fundarò, D., Sorce, S.: Elicitation and evaluation of zoom gestures for touchless interaction with desktop displays. In: Proceedings of the 8th ACM International Symposium on Pervasive Displays. Association for Computing Machinery, New York, NY, USA (2019). https://doi.org/10.1145/3321335.3324934
10. He, Z., Zhang, R., Liu, Z., Tan, Z.: A user-defined gesture set for natural interaction in a smart kitchen environment. In: 2020 13th International Symposium on Computational Intelligence and Design, pp. 122–125 (2020). https://doi.org/10.1109/ISCID51228.2020.00034
11. Hosseini, M., Mueller, H., Boll, S.: Controlling the rooms: How people prefer using gestures to control their smart homes. In: Proceedings of the 2024 CHI Conference on Human Factors in Computing Systems. Association for Computing Machinery, New York, NY, USA (2024). https://doi.org/10.1145/3613904.3642687
12. Lee, S.S., Chae, J., Kim, H., Lim, Y.k., Lee, K.p.: Towards more natural digital content manipulation via user freehand gestural interaction in a living room. In: Proceedings of the 2013 ACM International Joint Conference on Pervasive and Ubiquitous Computing, pp. 617–626. Association for Computing Machinery, New York, NY, USA (2013). https://doi.org/10.1145/2493432.2493480

13. Li, J., Coler, A.S., Borhani, Z., Ortega, F.R.: Collecting and analyzing the mid-air gestures data in augmented reality and user preferences in closed elicitation study. In: Chen, J.Y.C., Fragomeni, G. (eds.) Virtual, Augmented and Mixed Reality, pp. 201–215. Springer Nature Switzerland, Cham (2024). https://doi.org/10.1007/978-3-031-61044-8_15
14. Liu, Q., Li, Y., Chen, B., Wu, H., Liang, H.N.: User-defined gesture interactions for VR museums: an elicitation study. In: 2024 IEEE International Symposium on Mixed and Augmented Reality, pp. 633–642 (2024). https://doi.org/10.1109/ISMAR62088.2024.00078
15. Ng, C., Marquardt, N.: Eliciting user-defined touch and mid-air gestures for co-located mobile gaming. Proc. ACM Human-Comput. Interact. **6**(ISS) (Nov 2022). https://doi.org/10.1145/3567722
16. Villarreal-Narvaez, S., Sluÿters, A., Vanderdonckt, J., Vatavu, R.D.: Brave new ges world: A systematic literature review of gestures and referents in gesture elicitation studies. ACM Comput. Surv. **56**(5) (Jan 2024). https://doi.org/10.1145/3636458
17. Vogiatzidakis, P., Koutsabasis, P.: Gesture elicitation studies for mid-air interaction: a review. Multimodal Technol. Interact. **2**(4) (2018). https://doi.org/10.3390/mti2040065
18. Vogiatzidakis, P., Koutsabasis, P.: Frame-based elicitation of mid-air gestures for a smart home device ecosystem. Informatics **6**(2) (2019). https://doi.org/10.3390/informatics6020023
19. Vogiatzidakis, P., Koutsabasis, P.: 'Address and command': two-handed mid-air interactions with multiple home devices. Int. J. Hum Comput Stud. **159**, 102755 (2022). https://doi.org/10.1016/j.ijhcs.2021.102755
20. Wittorf, M.L., Jakobsen, M.R.: Eliciting mid-air gestures for wall-display interaction. In: Proceedings of the 9th Nordic Conference on Human-Computer Interaction. Association for Computing Machinery, New York, NY, USA (2016). https://doi.org/10.1145/2971485.2971503

# The Rhetoric of Smartness

Girish Dalvi[1]( ) and Malay Dhamelia[2]

[1] Indian Institute of Technology Bombay, Powai, Mumbai 400 076, India
girish.dalvi@iitb.ac.in
[2] Indian Institute of Technology Gandhinagar, Palaj, Gandhinagar 382 355, India
malay.dhamelia@iitgn.ac.in

**Abstract.** The idea of 'smart' is pervasive in technological landscapes. There are smartphones, smartwatches, smart refrigerators, smart mattresses and even smart bottles. This descriptor for technology has an ambiguous sense of what 'smart' implies. Its ambiguity is imaginative, allowing various interpretations, projections, meanings, and logics of 'smartness' to emerge and propagate. We attempt to capture some of the many meanings of contemporary 'smartness', including what might be called 'smart dumbness' through the examination of 'smart' as an imaginary. Three prevalent logics are proposed: the logic of augmentation, the productivity logic, and the logic of anticipation, through analysis of communication materials, device capabilities, and user practices. Our analytical observations draw attention to the different meanings of 'smartness,' the technological imaginations it creates, and the need to develop a body of work that broadens our collective imagination about technology.

**Keywords:** Smart Technology · Dumb Technology · Critical Technology · Theory · Anticipatory Systems · Technological Imagination

## 1 Introduction

Contemporary technological landscapes are saturated with a pervasive, often unexamined, rhetoric of 'smartness'. This label, liberally applied to an expanding spectrum of technologies ranging from everyday objects to complex infrastructures, has achieved near ubiquity. It is frequently presented as an imaginative descriptor filled with inherent virtues, signifying progress, efficiency, and augmented capabilities. Beneath such projections of technological advancements lies a concept ripe for critical interrogation. What precisely does it signify for a technology, an object, or a system to be designated as 'smart'? What are the conceptual underpinnings, and crucially, what are the implications of this labelling for our perceptions of technology, its societal integration, and our own evolving subjectivities? The 'smart' label increasingly influences our experiences of technology, which makes these questions important. 'Smart' resonates with an intuitive sense of advanced functionality, but the moment one attempts to formulate a precise definition, ambiguities and contradictions emerge, revealing the term's imaginative nature.

Interrogating the pervasive application of 'smartness' across objects, infrastructure, and abstract concepts reveals a generative vagueness that obfuscates complexities and contradictions. In the realm of "smart objects", the label denotes digitally-mediated capabilities like remote control, data collection in everyday objects such as bottles, refrigerators, etc. Such 'smartness' is constrained by material dependencies like batteries, power, network access, etc., raising questions about the autonomy and intelligences implied by the term. The 'smartness' of infrastructure, such as "smart homes", "smart grids", etc. shifts the concept to a systemic level, entailing abilities of sensing, processing, and responding to various events, projecting interconnectedness and optimization for infrastructure management [22]. This definition suggests efficiency and control from a centralized perspective, potentially overlooking the diverse needs and experiences of individuals within the system and even exacerbating existing inequalities. Furthermore, the application of "smartness" to abstract concepts like "smart money", "smart economy," etc. expands the term, to signify efficiency and strategic advantage. This abstract usage obscures underlying structures and biases that shape economic and perceptual landscapes.

Therefore, we argue that the frequent invocation of 'smartness', built upon fundamental ambiguities, warrants sustained questioning. Its function expands beyond projecting progress, describing technical capabilities to serve as a rhetorical tool. This tool shapes social and individual perceptions of technology, masking the inherent complexities and potential trade-offs involved. By avoiding and obscuring scrutiny of its claims to intelligence and autonomy, the 'smart' label also serves to reinforce existing ideologies and inequalities.

## 2   The Lineage of 'Smart'

Originating in Old English with connotations of physical pain ('smarting') [4], its meanings expanded over centuries, incorporating notions of intellectual sharpness (13th c.), cleverness and knowledge (17th c.), and fashionable elegance (18th c.) [4,7]. The explicit application to technology, signifying behaviour "as though guided by intelligence", is a recent phenomenon, documented around the 1970s. This trajectory, from physical sensation to intellectual acuity, and aesthetic appeal, suggests complex semantic layers informing its modern deployment. The embedded associations with 'sharp' intellect and 'elegant' design contribute to the positive, aspirational qualities that make 'smart' such a convenient label and an appealing aesthetic [17, p. 3] for technologies. Transitions in the usage of 'smart,' and the semantic possibilities these create, have allowed for the emergence of newer meanings. Smartness therefore is a generative concept that is both monolith-like in its applications and at the same time ambiguous in its nature. This semantic flexibility allows it to be molded and adapted to suit various technological contexts, and perceptual manipulation through to marketing appropriation [17, p. 11]. These appropriations become evident when examining how 'smartness' is deployed across different domains and marketing narratives.

This semantic landscape can be materially experienced and analysed through the existence and design of objects, infrastructure, abstract concepts, and campaigns to market them. Of these categories, we focus on 'smart objects' and their marketing to identify logics emerging from, and intertwined with, the generative ambiguities in the notion of smartness. It is with this focus we now turn to the specific 'imaginaries' that fuel their propagation.

## 3 The Imaginaries of Smart Technology

The rhetoric of 'smart' temporarily stabilizes the imagination of what 'smart' means, even though the term itself is ambiguous. Subjects of stabilised imaginations—researchers, technologists, designers, engineers and users—make sense of, and interpret 'smart' through its ambiguous and implied meanings. Imaginaries are tacit and embedded in our communications, concerning "the conduct of our social existence, [and] also norms about how this existence ought to be played out" [18]. In technological landscapes, such imaginaries develop into "imaginaries of smartness" which shape technological imaginations through logics which are presented by communication and marketing materials.

### 3.1 The Logic of Augmentation

A primary driver of these imaginaries is what we term the logic of augmentation, in which everyday objects and concepts are presented as fundamentally improved by adding digital capabilities. This logic manifests in the form of a narrative. The device is presented as "not only A", its traditional, perhaps 'dumb' form, "but also B", its technologically enhanced successor, endowed with a suite of novel, often interconnected, functionalities. Consider a smart water bottle [1]. It is no longer simply a vessel for carrying water (A). Instead, it becomes a multifunctional device (B) that can play music, emit colorful lights, connect to a smartphone, and send reminders to its user to stay hydrated. This "not only A but also B" logic is a catalyst in the widespread adoption of smartness. The promise of enhanced utility and an expanded role for technology, even in the most mundane aspects of our lives.

This drive to imbue objects with additional digital layers stems from desires to overcome perceived limitations of their conventional counterparts. A regular water bottle simply holds liquid; a smart one is projected as though it actively participates in the user's wellness journey, transforming from a passive container to an active health companion. This augmentation is framed as a move towards greater convenience and efficiency. The smart water bottle promises the elimination of the need to manually track hydration, listen to music via a separate device, or even remember to turn on a light. All these functions are integrated, "for convenience", into a single object, projecting a streamlined user experience and seamless interaction with their environment. This logic of bundled functionalities caters to a craving for integrated solutions, where the complexity of managing multiple devices is reduced through the convergence of features. This logic extends to the "smart home", where switches become voice-activated interfaces (B) beyond its manual function (A), and a "smart refrigerator" an inventory manager (B) in addition to a cold storage unit (A). Hill identifies a similar logic about "smart phones"—"most people do not want their phone to function [just] as a phone" [15].

The "not only A but also B" logic obscures constraints and trade-offs that accompany such technological layering. The smart bottle, for instance, is no longer a self-contained entity. Its expanded capabilities rely on factors such as power for its electronics and connectivity to a network and other devices. This introduces dependencies that were absent in its 'dumb' form. The user must now remember to charge the bottle, ensure it is within Wi-Fi or Bluetooth range, and potentially manage software updates or compatibility issues with other devices. These considerations are omitted in marketing materials, highlighting the fact that the added 'smartness' comes with its own set of demands and frustrations, transforming a once-reliable object into one that can fail in more complex ways.

Furthermore, the propagation of this logic is fueled by a marketing discourse that equates 'smart' with progress and improvement. The term 'smart' itself has become a vague imaginative label, implying a level of intelligence and sophistication that may not always be warranted. The application of this term to technology often conflates several meanings, suggesting that a device with added digital features is functionally superior and hence desirable than its 'dumb' counterpart. This rhetoric creates a sense of obsolescence for earlier objects, pressuring users to adopt the 'smarter' alternatives, even if the added functionalities are not essential or frequently utilized.

The "not only A but also B" logic also raises questions about the social valuation of everyday objects. Is the primary function of a water bottle to carry water, or is it now also expected to be a source of entertainment and a data-gathering tool? This blurring of lines can lead to functional overload, where devices attempt to fulfill multiple roles, potentially compromising their original functionality while creating complex user experiences. Moreover, this logic often prioritizes technological capabilities and market differentiation over primary user needs. The decision to add music playing or lights to a water bottle seems to be driven by technological feasibility and marketing trends rather than prioritized demands from users for such features.

The propagation of 'smartness' through the "not only A but also B" logic can also be interpreted as a manifestation of a broader techno-solutionist ideological trend. This belief that technology can and should be deployed to address a wide range of user needs and problems, including those that might be better addressed through non-technical means, such as social, cultural, or political interventions. This can lead to an over-reliance on technological fixes and a neglect of deeper structural issues. Furthermore, the data-streams generated by these 'smart' devices, including seemingly innocuous information about hydration habits or music preferences, contribute to larger patterns of surveillance and datafication. The trajectories and utilization of this data often remain opaque to users. It raises concerns about autonomy and privacy as individuals become increasingly dependent on, and shaped by, these systems.

The cognitive load of managing an expanding network of such devices, each with its own demands and idiosyncrasies, can paradoxically diminish, rather than enhance, a user's sense of control and freedom. This sets the stage for a disenchantment with the relentless pursuit of 'smartness'. Beyond merely adding features, the rhetoric of 'smartness' also heavily emphasizes an increase in user efficiency and output, leading to what we term the 'productivity logic'.

## 3.2 The Productivity Logic

The productivity logic frames devices as tools for continuous work and creation. They have the ability to transform any space into a potential workplace and any moment into an opportunity for work, regardless of context. It can be on a staircase (as observed in [9]), while rushing to the office (as observed in [11], in the kitchen, or even perched on a tree (as observed in [10]. These devices project a sense of greater user autonomy allowing them to be anywhere they choose, but mostly to work. A user can be on a tree, but with a device, engaged in a task because the device can be used anytime and anywhere. To communicate this pervasiveness, the idea of anytime and anywhere is used. However, it transforms 'any' to 'every'. Users are encouraged to use the device 'everytime' and 'everywhere', thereby intensifying the ubiquitous perception of work. This drive for productivity, tied to economic imperatives and cultural values exalting busyness, blur work-life boundaries and exacerbate performance pressures.

This logic propagates itself through a bundle of 'cans'. A user can think, can organize, can build, can draw, can click pictures, can check emails, can translate efficiently, all through a single device. The device is 'smart' because it can manage multiple tasks, and the user also becomes 'smart' through the device, as seen in campaigns like Apple's "What's a computer?" [9] or Samsung Galaxy S9's Introduction Film [23]. In the film, two interns use Galaxy's smart features like AI translation, summarization and image creation to outperform experts. This exemplifies how the rhetoric of smartness perpetuates the idea that smartness is omnipresent and it must continuously produce. The productivity logic encapsulates that smart devices are productive, and users can become more productive by integrating smart devices into their everyday tasks.

## 3.3 The Logic of Anticipation

Devices (A) augmented with sensors (B) anticipate events and announce their output, thereby making their presence felt. These devices throb with anticipations fueled by data collected through sensors. Smart refrigerators anticipate inventory requirements, smart mattresses anticipate bodily needs like sleep and exercise (as observed in [8]), smartwatches, a user's health and readiness scores (as observed in [2]), and music platforms, a user's preferred song.

An emerging logic suggests that as devices anticipate, "they know more" about users than the users themselves. This knowledge enables them to anticipate better. The smartness of an object is thus 'measured' by how well it can anticipate the user's needs and context, thereby creating an epistemic shift in how one perceives the world through augmented senses. The user need not be consciously aware of their sleep patterns, nutrition intake, and exercise routines; instead, they can rely on the device's pronouncements. Such anticipation is projected as an emancipatory experience for the user. They can run, play, and sleep without worrying about what their body experiences. Knowledge about the user's body and its activities resides not within the user, but in the device. Senses are extended to the device to such an extent that they are displaced from the user and onto the device. The user's sensory experiences become mediated by the device. This reliance on externalized, device-held knowledge about one's body and needs, fosters a shift. The logic of anticipation thereby transforms into a logic of perceived emancipation: emancipation from the burden of self-monitoring and from direct sensory engagement.

Smart devices are positioned as solutions to everyday phenomena and problems, claiming that knowledge can reside outside the user and inside the device. For instance, Sleep Number, a smart mattress, purportedly solves snoring by raising the user's head. A smart bottle problematizes hydration and presents reminders as solutions. The solution lies outside the body, accessible through the device. Smartwatches are offered as a solution to user's weakening will to exercise. This reconfigures the relationship between the smart device and the user. The logic shifts where user knowledge resides, placing it within the device and making users reliant on devices to access that knowledge. Marketing narratives position smartwatch ownership as an essential component toward fitness, implying that the device itself, rather than intrinsic motivation and habits, are the primary agents of a healthier lifestyle. These devices project a sense of freedom, as they offer to free users from the perceived burden of decision-making and constant self-awareness.

These logics, emerging through the ambiguity of 'smartness', do not represent a singular conceptual current. Their dominance and the dependencies they create allow for newer forms of smartness to emerge. We now turn to 'smart dumbness', 'dumbness', and 'dumb' devices, which are parallel concepts in this space.

## 4 Smart Dumbness

Dumbness encompasses devices and practices that attempt to perceptually detach users from the rhetoric of smartness. Practicing dumbness takes several metaphorized forms such as digital minimalism, digital detox, and digital diet. Users having experienced what they perceive as data excess, practice 'digital minimalism' to reduce their reliance on smart devices [12,26]. Methods such as the 'digital detox' aim to counter adverse effects of smartness: uncontrolled usage habits and the cognitive load of data excess. These practices frame digital excesses as detrimental to user well-being, necessitating moderation through measured approaches like a 'digital diet' [13, 14, 20], which treats digital consumption like food: necessary, but in limited and controlled quantities. To support such voluntary trimming, users adopt practices such as grayscaling their phones, using minimalist launchers, and employing blocking applications to limit usage.

Inspired by such practices, manufacturers have introduced a series of 'dumbed devices' like the reMarkable tablet and Light Phone. These devices are pre-trimmed of 'smart' features. We identify this phenomena as 'smart dumbness', where devices intentionally limit functionality while retaining certain 'smart' attributes. These devices are marketed differently. Instead of using the language of 'cans' used in smart technology, these devices are marketed with the language of 'cannots'. The explainer video for the Light Phone declares: "It can't post on social media, it can't send an email, it can't steal your data ..., it can't ... interrupt your train of thoughts ..." [21]. The Light Phone is, "designed to be used as little as possible" [3], affords users the opportunity to be "more present" [3]. It is projected as a device that can do 'just' the things required, thereby trimming features and logics augmented by smartness. Its smartness lies in its moderation of features and its design for 'presence'. This 'presence' is a projected as curated experience, shaped by user control.

A parallel logic is evident in the marketing of the reMarkable tablet. It appropriates this language of 'cannots' by explicitly weaving in the 'productivity logic'. First, a user is stabilized by the familiar: "like paper" (A). Then, the familiar is augmented with attributes: "Only Better" (B). This augmentation is operationalized into 'dumb' features like highlighting, and erasing, which projects that users can focus on "one task at a time" [5]. Ironically, while promoting single-tasking, its 'dumb smartness' still echoes the logic of augmentation which it purports to critique by consolidating multiple tools (notebooks, erasers, highlighters) into one device.

Smart objects intentionally dumbed down by trimming features require an augmented, larger-than-life position to provide a requisite experience. The logic of productivity is woven into the aesthetic of dumbness: of being present and distraction-free, through the features retained after the trimming. This trimming is used to articulate what a device "cannot" do, while simultaneously assuring users it "can" do "just the things a user needs, nothing more" [5]. This means the device's smartness can be seen in its dumbness, i.e. in its ability, through its inability to do many things. Such 'smartnesses', and 'dumbnesses' within technological landscapes are generative, but for different reasons. The ambiguity of 'smartness' comes from its polysemy, 'dumbness' becomes 'smart' because its meaning is inherently unstable and transient within the space of smartness itself.

The paradox of "smart dumbness", is that it does not resist the rhetoric of smartness; instead, it repositions it. It appropriates the language of 'cannots' to sell another product, ultimately reinforcing the very tendencies that it projects to counter. Such ideas of dumbness do not reject smartness. They occupy a paradoxical space within the two concepts. They are not 'dumb' in the way a simple object is. Instead, this curated dumbness is entirely dependent on the infrastructure of smartness. The reMarkable device requires sync and share services, and the Light Phone relies on map services, music streaming, and other dependencies to fulfill its promise. The dumbness logic positions itself as an alternative imagination, yet it borrows from and relies on the very logics of smartness it seeks to counter. This coexistence creates a fertile ground for the emergence of new meanings and evolving relationships with technology.

## 5 Conclusion

The rhetoric of 'smartness' functions as a powerful and generative force whose foundational ambiguity propagates specific technological imaginaries. The emergence of 'smart dumbness' signifies an expansion of this dominant and pervasive rhetoric. The meaning and nature of smartness have varied over time and continued to evolve with the advent of newer technologies like AI; ongoing analysis of these transitions is therefore crucial. We examine the idea of smartness concerning technology, the logics it develops, and the imaginations that it fuels. This work aims to provoke critical thought furthering what Marcuse termed 'one-dimensional' rationality and the imagination driven by it [16].

In this context, critical technological practices in Human-Computer Interaction (HCI) research that explore alternative values deserve greater attention as sites for alternative imaginations. Examples include the design of slow technology [6,19], tools for digital self-control, and research exploring diverse technological values [24,25,27]. Technological labels such as 'smartness' need further examination. We suggest the premises for such theoretical and empirical research. Theories that expand the idea of 'smartness' from objects to infrastructure and broader concepts can help articulate the underlying logics of our technological imaginations. Studying trimming practices and devices that actively modify and redefine the rhetoric of smartness, empirical research could yield results to understand user and social perceptions. Such work is required for scrutinizing the uncritical and pervasive use of technology labels like 'smart', and for advocating a more considered technological discourse.

## References

1. Aquaminder smart water bottle glows & beeps to remind you to drink more 770 ml chug cap bottle for adults and kids perfect for gift, travel, gym, yoga, black, silicone : Amazon.in: Home & kitchen. https://www.amazon.in/dp/B0DBZL2PTC?th=1
2. Fitbit charge 6: Our #1 tracker, now with google - YouTube. https://youtu.be/jbLmKWsaCvI?si=87iRJ9809fzmLQ6L
3. The light phone. https://www.thelightphone.com
4. Read this to get 'smart'. https://www.merriam-webster.com/wordplay/smart-usage-history
5. reMarkable - the future of paper is here. https://remarkable.com/
6. Slowly. https://slowly.app/de/
7. smart. https://dictionary.cambridge.org/dictionary/english/smart

8. Temperature-control mattresses for couples from sleep number - YouTube. https://youtu.be/YcwPuzUjyK0?si=zd__GJZpY3YQQIq-
9. Apple: [AD] iPad pro: How to correctly use a computer - YouTube. https://youtu.be/YcwPuzUjyK0?si=L-L7n3U4JEMOvAf5
10. Apple everyday: Ipad pro— what's a computer– apple. https://www.youtube.com/watch?v=3S5BLs51yDQ
11. Apple India: Mac | work is worth it | apple. https://www.youtube.com/watch?v=DcbvaYThJ5Y
12. Aylsworth, T., Castro, C.: Is there a duty to be a digital minimalist? **38**(4), 662–673. https://doi.org/10.1111/japp.12498. https://onlinelibrary.wiley.com/doi/abs/10.1111/japp.12498, _eprint: https://onlinelibrary.wiley.com/doi/pdf/10.1111/japp.12498
13. Brabazon, T.: Digital dieting: from information obesity to intellectual fitness. Routledge. https://doi.org/10.4324/9781315577159
14. Geddes, L.: Could a 'digital diet' help me fix my bad phone habits? https://www.theguardian.com/technology/2025/may/17/could-a-digital-diet-help-me-fix-my-bad-phone-habits
15. Hill, K.: I was addicted to my smartphone, so i switched to a flip phone for a month. https://www.nytimes.com/2024/01/06/technology/smartphone-addiction-flip-phone.html
16. Marcuse, H.: One-Dimensional Man: Studies in the Ideology of Advanced Industrial Society. Beacon Press
17. (Mireille), H.: Smart technologies. https://doi.org/10.14763/2020.4.1531, https://policyreview.info/concepts/smart-technologies, publisher: Alexander von Humboldt Institute for Internet and Society gGmbH
18. Nerlich, B.: Imagining imaginaries. https://blogs.nottingham.ac.uk/makingsciencepublic/2015/04/23/imagining-imaginaries/
19. Odom, W., Selby, M., Sellen, A., Kirk, D., Banks, R., Regan, T.: Photobox: on the design of a slow technology. In: Proceedings of the Designing Interactive Systems Conference, pp. 665–668. DIS '12, Association for Computing Machinery. https://doi.org/10.1145/2317956.2318055, https://dl.acm.org/doi/10.1145/2317956.2318055
20. Orben, A.: Digital diet: A 21st century approach to understanding digital technologies and development **31**(1), e2228. https://doi.org/10.1002/icd.2228, https://onlinelibrary.wiley.com/doi/abs/10.1002/icd.2228, _eprint: https://onlinelibrary.wiley.com/doi/pdf/10.1002/icd.2228
21. Phone, T.L.: Introducing the light phone III. https://vimeo.com/954143759
22. Ramaprasad, A., Sanchez Ortiz, A., Syn, T.: Ontological Review of Smart City Research
23. Samsung: Galaxy tab s9 series: Official introduction film i samsung. https://www.youtube.com/watch?v=ggfA3ltufPk
24. Schulz, A.S., Müller, J., Beruscha, F.: Experience by cohabitation: Living in a smart home initiated by your partner. In: Abdelnour Nocera, J., Kristín Lárusdóttir, M., Petrie, H., Piccinno, A., Winckler, M. (eds.) Human-Computer Interaction – INTERACT 2023, pp. 304–323. Springer Nature Switzerland. https://doi.org/10.1007/978-3-031-42286-7_17
25. Seo, J.A., Cho, H., Lee, S., Cheon, E.: Back to the 1990s, BeeperRedux!: revisiting retro technology to reflect communication quality and experience in the digital age. In: Proceedings of the 2025 CHI Conference on Human Factors in Computing Systems, pp. 1–19. CHI '25, Association for Computing Machinery.https://doi.org/10.1145/3706598.3713568, https://dl.acm.org/doi/10.1145/3706598.3713568

26. Skivko, M., Korneeva, E., Kolmykova, M.: Digital Minimalism as a Leading Limitation of Media Communications in the Heyday of Digital Culture. https://doi.org/10.2991/assehr.k.200526.010
27. Theus, A.L., Chiasson, S.: "a solution to a problem that didn't exist?": Exploring attitudes towards smart streetlight systems. In: Abdelnour Nocera, J., Kristín Lárusdóttir, M., Petrie, H., Piccinno, A., Winckler, M. (eds.) Human-Computer Interaction – INTERACT 2023, pp. 205–238. Springer Nature Switzerland. https://doi.org/10.1007/978-3-031-42286-7_12

# Ubiquity on the Road: Co-designing an Itinerant Ubiquitous Computing Laboratory

Josiane Rosa de Oliveira Gaia Pimenta[1,2]($\boxtimes$), Deógenes P. Junior da Silva [3], and M. Cecilia C. Baranauskas[1,3]

[1] University of Campinas, Campinas, São Paulo, Brazil
j262076@dac.unicamp.br, mccb@unicamp.br
[2] Federal Institute of São Paulo, Hortolândia, São Paulo, Brazil
[3] Federal University of Paraná, Curitiba, Paraná, Brazil
dpsjunior@inf.ufpr.br

**Abstract.** Brazil is a large and socially diverse country that could benefit from equitable access to emerging technologies, particularly in rural and remote communities. This paper addresses this challenging task by presenting the concept and design process of an itinerant ubiquitous computing laboratory, a vehicle-based environment aimed at delivering participatory learning opportunities to vulnerable populations. By using the Socially Aware Design framework, we conducted four co-design workshops with 16 specialists experienced in ubiquitous computing installations. Through some Socially Aware Design artifacts, we broadly identified in the social context 35 stakeholders, 29 challenges and 43 prospective requirements that informed the final laboratory proposal. The laboratory scenario was consolidated with low-fidelity prototypes developed through participatory techniques. Besides technical requirements, such as power sources and sensor integrations, an itinerant laboratory must also address social aspects, including community engagement and compliance with local regulations. As conceptual contributions, our paper extends ubiquitous computing beyond fixed installations by illustrating traveling interactive spaces that can bring awareness of emerging technologies with hands-on experiences that are socially relevant. As practical contributions, this paper presents some lessons learned about designing itinerant laboratories of ubiquitous computing.

**Keywords:** Ubiquitous Computing · Itinerant Laboratory · Socially Aware Design

## 1 Introduction

Brazil has a continental size with many challenging socioeconomic situations, such as isolated rural communities, indigenous people and riverside population. The diversity of situated contexts motivates the government to find strategies to bring education and information to distant populations. To overcome the barriers, some organizations in Brazil use vehicles as a place of education and access to services, such as odontological and medical care. Non-profit organizations use itinerant vehicles, such as trucks, modified to act as a classroom, or a doctor's or dentist's office, for example. The truck remains for a few days in places where these services or educational opportunities are not accessible to the population, normally in the interior of the states or in rural areas.

In this context, *"participative and universal access to knowledge for the Brazilian citizen"* was declared in 2006 as a Grand Challenge of Computer Science Research in Brazil [2]. Although some progress has been made in the last years, the challenge still remains, as Brazil deals with many inequalities of access to technology, which impacts for example their right to citizenship [15].

This work is in the context of the larger HCI4D (Human-Computer Interaction for Development) HCI area, concerned with understanding and designing technologies in the developing nations or for underserved, under-resourced, and under-represented populations [5]. The HCI4D international community argues for considering the need of understanding the local communities necessities and developing solutions in view of their needs, especially in developing countries [1]. Also, reducing inequalities is the $10^{th}$ goal of the United Nations 2030 Agenda, which target 10.2 specifies *"Promote universal social, economic and political inclusion"*[1]. Access to technology is important also as participation in the political, educational and industrial spheres of society becomes increasingly digitized. Internet of Things and Cyber-Physical Systems, for example, are placed as central in Industry 4.0 [13], and discussions about Industry 5.0 involve human-robot interaction [19]. With the emergent technologies based on Ubiquitous Computing, there can be more socioeconomic barriers that affect vulnerable populations discussing and accessing these types of technologies.

Installations are ways of providing the public with some knowledge and use of emergent technologies. Installations have been developed for spaces such as museums [8, 22], educational places [12, 21, 25], public parks and spaces [17]. However, these types of installations are more common in the global-north, or in more developed regions. Some populations living far from large and metropolitan cities usually do not have access to these types of technological machinery.

This paper is motivated by the challenge of vulnerable populations in accessing and learning about emergent technologies based on Ubiquitous Computing. We aim at creating spaces where less advantaged populations can access digital life that is shaping the future of society. The objective of this work is to discuss the design of an itinerant Ubiquitous Computing laboratory that brings access to ubiquitous computing technology and educational opportunities to the population living in the interior and rural areas of the region of Campinas, São Paulo, Brazil. Usually Ubiquitous Computing installations are stationary for long periods, fixed in rooms or spaces where interaction occurs. To the best of our

---

[1] Global Goals: $10^{th}$ - target 10.2: last access March $29^{th}$, 2025. Avaliable at <https://www.globalgoals.org/goals/10-reduced-inequalities/>.

knowledge, our paper brings a new context of investigation for understanding an interaction scenario that is movable, nomadic and socially-motivated.

The investigation is based on the Socially Aware Design (SAwD) [4]. The SAwD is a co-design framework that presents artifacts and methods to support stakeholders to create sense-making about a given domain situation and propose technological interventions aware of the situated socioeconomic situations in a participatory manner. SAwD has been already used in literature to support the design of Ubiquitous Computing installations in museums spaces [16], educational scenarios [6], and hospitals [26]. However, an itinerant and moveable installation was not yet investigated with this framework.

Considering the difference between a stationary and an itinerant ubiquitous computing installation and the new challenges that can appear in a moving space, we posed the following research questions (RQ1): *What constitutes an Itinerant Ubiquitous Computing Laboratory for the addressed context?* Drawing on the potential of SAwD to support different scenarios of design, a second research question is (RQ2): *How to approach the problem of prototyping an Itinerant Ubiquitous Computing Laboratory with the Socially Aware Design framework?*

The study involved 11 specialists experienced in the investigation and design of Ubiquitous Computing installations in four co-design sessions, supported by SAwD artifacts and methods, held in the University of Campinas - Unicamp, in the city of Campinas, São Paulo, Brazil. The first two co-design sessions helped us to understand the domain context of an itinerant ubiquitous computing laboratory in Brazil, identifying direct and indirectly affected stakeholders, their challenges, difficulties and barriers, and anticipating prospective requirements for the itinerant laboratory through SAwD artifacts. The other two co-design sessions were aimed at designing the actual itinerant laboratory in a VW bus, and educational activities to be offered in the vehicle vicinity, through Brainwriting and Braindrawing activities. In the final co-design session, a proposal of an itinerant ubiquitous computing laboratory was consolidated by the specialists.

In this paper, we present the SAwD design process carried out and its outcomes of designing the proposal of the itinerant laboratory, discussing how the mobile nature of a ubiquitous installation can bring new challenges and demands for design. We also discuss emergent themes that appeared in the specialists discussion, for example a dual nature of both space and artifact of interaction that the ubiquitous computing itinerant laboratory assumed in design. With this paper, we expect to contribute with the HCI community in broadening the way of thinking about ubiquity and interaction through the prospective itinerant scenario. Moreover, some lessons can be learned from the socially-challenging context we are addressing and how to deal with it.

This paper is organized as follows. Section 2 presents the fundamentals we draw upon, and related works of SAwD, ubiquity and itinerant environments. Section 3 presents the methodology of co-design, data collection and analysis methods. Section 4 presents results from the co-design activities in understanding the domain and ideation activities. Section 5 presents our discussions, answering the research questions and highlighting some lessons learned. Finally, Sect. 6 concludes and points to further work.

## 2 Theoretical Background and Related Works

This section presents the SAwD theoretical background used in this research, and related works regarding initiatives of itinerant technological environments.

### 2.1 Ubiquity from a Socioenactive Perspective

The socioenactive concept, proposed by Baranauskas et al. [3], studies the design of interaction in scenarios of ubiquitous technology under a phenomenological perspective. The concept highlights how people, technology and the physical world come together to shape interaction. Unlike traditional views that focus on a single person using a computer, the socioenactive perspective underscores the social and shared nature of embodied interactions. It recognizes people's actions, motivations, values and experiences deeply influenced by others and by the (technological) environment around them.

A key idea of the socioenactive approach is the tripartite coupling of Social, Physical and Digital dimensions. The Social involves the people in a scenario of interaction, their relationships, intersubjective interactions and communication. The physical dimension involves people's bodies, the tangible objects, including technology such as sensors and actuators, surfaces and spaces where the interaction takes place. The Digital dimension includes the software processing, data and computational resources of technology. In a socioenactive scenario, the three dimensions mutually affect each other.

The socioenactive concept was investigated in proposing different Ubiquitous Computing scenarios of interaction, such as museum installations [9] and educational scenarios [6]. No investigation of an itinerant or traveling ubiquitous installation has been found. Thus, this concept is underlying this research, supporting the understanding of the tripartite coupling; the Physical dimension, such as restrictions of a vehicle space, motivates the investigation of an itinerant laboratory that does not neglect the Social dimension of people and their intersubjective interactions with the physical-digital artifacts.

### 2.2 The Socially Aware Design

The Socially Aware Design (SAwD) is a framework of social understanding in design, in which meaning is approached as a social phenomenon arising from person-world relations [4]. In this framework, social understanding means the sensemaking that emerges in a design process—people interactions in a design situation for creating artifacts—for "understanding others and understanding the world through others in the design process" [4, p. 82]. The framework is based on Organizational Semiotics, Participatory Design, and Universal Design, in which these basis contribute to a participatory approach to responsibly involving interested parties with the design situation.

Underlying the SAwD framework is an understanding that technical aspects of system design depend on and impact the formal and informal aspects of organizations and society [20]. The Organizational Semiotics offer lenses and methods to approach design based on the formal, informal and technical layers of information, as a way of balancing social and technical aspects in the prospective information system [10]. Considering design only under its technically centered perspective prevents reaching a wider sense-making of the social context being handled and the technology being proposed [20].

Artifacts and methods that constitute the SAwD framework enables those involved in a design situation to create a shared sensemaking about relevant aspects of the social world, such as stakeholders challenges, expectations and socioeconomic issues. Thus, this sensemaking generates new knowledge and awareness of the social context and enables people involved in design with the access to relevant understandings of the social world, making sense to stakeholders and promoting technology acceptance and adoption [20].

The SAwD framework has already been used in the development of ubiquitous computing installations. Da Silva and Baranauskas [26] used SAwD as the framework for developing IoT installations in a hospital scenario to promote well-being to children in medical treatments. Duarte et al. [7], in turn, used SAwD to explore a situation of designing public interactive installations, such as in parks, train, bus stations, and museums.

### 2.3 Related Works: Ubiquity and Itinerant Environments

We searched for related works through an exploratory literature review in digital scientific libraries. We used the word "itinerant" as a way to represent this traveling form of using vehicles to bring information, technology and education to distant locations. In the Springer library no papers regarding the word itinerant were found in computing venues. At IEEE, two related work were found; one related work was found in SBC OpenLib[2]; in Scielo[3] we found six candidate papers, however as we read their content they were excluded for not being related to the subject of this paper; finally, at ACM we found one related work. Next, we briefly present each of these related works.

Vasconcelos et al. [27] presents the experience of the Scratch on Road project in Portugal, that aims to raise awareness and motivate students to develop digital competences using scratch programming environment. The team used a mobile technological laboratory that traveled between schools as a way to overcome material and human resources constraints. The project has made possible that more students have access to programming topics in their educational curriculum. The project increased the number of students who have the opportunity to program by 50%, and increased the school's contact with new technologies. This

---
[2] SOL OpenLib:Available at <https://sol.sbc.org.br/> access: March $29^{th}$, 2025.
[3] Scielo: Available at <https://www.scielo.br/> access: March $29^{th}$, 2025.

experience indicates the success of itinerant educational interventions. However, the laboratory is not framed as an ubiquitous installation, such as in our study, but more like a place where educational activities take place. Also, there are different challenges for design in the Brazilian context and when thinking of an itinerant laboratory as a ubiquitous computing installation.

Veiga Furtado and Rechena [28] study presents the MIRAGE project, which investigates how art practice can contribute to the empowerment, self-esteem and identity of women victims of domestic violence in Shelter Houses. The project involves co-creating a laboratory where women develop artistic projects based on their life stories. One of the objectives of MIRAGE project was to inform, sensitize and raise awareness in society about the social problem of violence against women, disseminating the artistic process results in an Itinerant Exhibition. Veiga Furtado and Rechena [28] research indicates the relevance of using an itinerant exhibition as a way to promote awareness on important themes, such as the fight against domestic violence.

Saleemi et al. [24] investigated the health care of antenatal care in rural areas in Punjab, Pakistan. The health service is itinerant in the sense of going to the houses and leaving medicines, accompanying Mom and child, vaccinating, among other tasks. To facilitate their work the results propose an ubiquitous framework to collect, organize and present the patients data. The framework was used in the wild and it facilitated the health care of antenatal patients.

Ribeiro et al. [23] proposed the use of a boat to create an Itinerant Data Center to provide internet services in remote Amazon areas. The IDC - Itinerant Data Center, was implemented in isolated communities within Amazon in Brazil. The IDC aims to allow internet connection to the communities and access to educational projects, online medical appointments, among others. The IDC is hosted inside a boat, the only way of access to these communities.

Whereas Ribeiro and colleagues [23] aimed to provide internet infrastructure, our initiative is related to access and education opportunities regarding emergent technological installations. Salemi et al. [24], in turn, wanted to improve the delivered health service with an ubiquitous computing solution. Vasconcelos et al. [27] took programming learning to different schools with an itinerant project, although without a vehicle as a laboratory but using the school infrastructure instead. Veiga Furtado and Rechena [28] worked on the co-creation of a laboratory while we worked with a co-design. Their laboratory is situated on a shelter, however they held Itinerant Exhibitions of the produced work. Our work proposes an active laboratory for teaching ubiquitous computing with a environment inside a vehicle, an itinerant laboratory. The majority of these works share a motivation of exploring an advantage of an Itinerant Laboratory: the possibility of accessing and bringing services or education to more distant areas. Our work adds to this literature, by considering the vehicle itself an artifact, aiming to spread the knowledge of ubiquitous computing, especially among people who have less opportunity to access these technologies.

## 3 Methodology

According to the SAwD framework, the design of any technology presupposes the understanding of the context domain being investigated and its socio economic realities. The design activities constituted a co-design process, meaning a "participatory sensemaking process that involves a diverse group of people who experience a design situation through coordinated action with others and with artifacts in the design environment" [4, p. 86].

The SAwD framework presents artifacts to support a socially aware understanding of the context being investigated. Three main artifacts are used to support understanding informal aspects of the domain, such as the identification of stakeholders, their challenges, needs, beliefs and values, and to identify prospective ideas and requirements for a technology being developed. The three artifacts are the Stakeholders Identification Diagram (SID), the Evaluation Frame (EF), and the Semiotic Framework (SF).

The SID artifact presents five levels of analysis for supporting the interested parties involved in a design situation to identify stakeholders that are direct or indirectly impacted by the investigated context or the technology being developed. Briefly, the five levels can be described as: i) Operation: the project under analysis; ii) Contribution: stakeholders directly affected by the domain context or the technology being developed, and those responsible for the technology development; iii) Source: customers and information providers; iv) Market: partners and competitors; v) Community: legislators, spectators, the community at large.

The EF artifact, in turn, is an artifact that extends SID levels to support identifying the stakeholders' challenges and prospective solution ideas. This artifact helps raise awareness of possible socioeconomic challenges and problems of stakeholders in the analyzed context. Possible prospective ideas or features for the technology can also be annotated.

Finally, the SF artifact supports the identification and organization of requirements in six levels of formalization that must be considered in the design of a system [4]: i) social world: the consequence of the use of signs in human activities; ii) pragmatics: intentional use of signs and the behavior of their agents; iii) semantics: relations between a sign and what it refers to; iv) syntactic: the combination of signs; v) empirics: static properties of signs; vi) physical world: physical aspects of signs. The first three levels are related to human and social aspects, whereas the last three levels are related to technical aspects.

Figure 1 represents the co-design activities and SAwD artifacts used among the four workshops. In the workshops 1 and 4 we joined HCI specialists at Unicamp (University of Campinas), in Campinas, São Paulo, Brazil. Workshops 2 and 3 were remotely conducted joining researchers of Peru and Brazil. In the first workshop we utilized the artifacts SID and EF, followed by a Braindrawing. In the second we worked on SID, EF and SF using OpenDesign[4] [14] platform. In the third we consolidated the SF in the OpenDesign. Finally, we held the last workshop with a braindraw and a proposal consolidation.

---

[4] https://opendesign.ic.unicamp.br/.

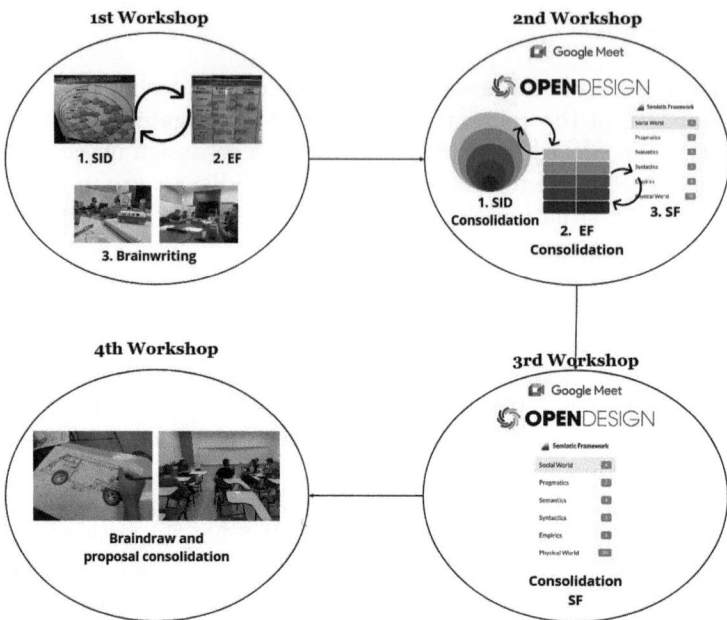

**Fig. 1.** Co-design methodology.

*Co-located in Person Workshops (1st and 4th Workshops).* Printed posters of the SID, EF and SF artifacts and post-its were used to register the participation results. The participants were free to write stakeholders, problems and ideas on post-its and stick on the printed poster of the respective artifact. The authors acted both as participators and mediators, helping in writing the result of the discussion in post-its and sticking on the poster, and helping the involved people by clarifying doubts about the artifact.

*Online orkshops (2nd and 3rd Workshops).* The Google Meets video conferencing tool was used to organize the online workshops. The participants entered in a shared room and the first author conducted the design activities through the OpenDesign platform. The OpenDesign platform [14] presents digital and interactive versions of the SAwD artifacts and methods for online and distributed participatory activities. The online platform also presents other collaborative and deliberative features, such as comments and likes for voting. Especially in online meetings, the design activities and discussions were situated through the platform. The participants discussed in the Meets room while using the OpenDesign platform to register the participants' ideas and discussion through the digital artifacts of SID, EF and SF.

The first and second workshops aimed at creating sensemaking about the context through SAwD artifacts [2]: SID, EF and SF. After understanding the context, two workshops were conducted to prototype the itinerant laboratory through Brainwriting and Braindrawing participatory methods [18]. The participants of the workshops were 16 different specialists working in a research project involved in investigating and building scenarios of ubiquitous computing installations. The specialists were involved in both theoretical and practical investigations of ubiquitous computing, with participation in regular meetings to discuss literature and practice on emergent technology and the experience of designing, evaluating or using ubiquitous installations. The specialists were invited to voluntarily participate in this work and an email described the objectives, activities and benefits of the research.

The workshop's planning, revised with at least another researcher, involved the definition of objectives and methods to be used. The data collection methods involved participatory observation, writing notes about results and discussions in the co-design sessions. The SID, EF and SF filled artifacts and materials from the workshops were collected for analysis. For data analysis, we draw on the Thematic Analysis method (Braun and Clarke, 2006). The analysis included: i) reading in its entirety the textual data; ii) generating initial codes from text; iii) revising codes with other researchers; iv) grouping codes into broader themes and producing a thematic map; v) writing discussion about themes. The data that support the findings of this study are openly available in REDU (Research Data Repository of Unicamp at https://redu.unicamp.br/, reference https://doi.org/10.25824/redu/DDXMVV. Table 1 presents a summary of the study organization, characterizing the workshops conducted, the artifacts and methods used, the number of participants and main results.

**Workshop 1.** The first workshop was an in-person meeting. After receiving and welcoming the participants, the first author presented the research social motivation of bringing ubiquitous computing knowledge to distant and challenging socioeconomic regions. The initial presentation included the premise of using vehicles as a form of enabling ubiquitous computing access and education. The first author presented her VW Bus vehicle presented in Fig. 2 called Princesa (Princess, in English) and its story of 28 years in possession of her family. This clarified the social and emotional sides involved in the project. Second, the author detailed the VW Bus vehicle in depth showing its importance in Brazil, its flexibility and adaptation for different tasks and the available space for possibly building an itinerant laboratory.

The first design activities, following the SAwD framework, were used to understand the complex socioeconomic context. The stakeholders were identified using the five levels of SID. The five levels enable identifying broadly the stakeholders that impact or are impacted in some way by the project, mitigating the risk of neglecting relevant aspects of social life.

Afterwards, we used the EF artifact to identify stakeholders' challenges and prospective ideas to tackle the challenges. Following recommendations of the literature [11], at least one stakeholder of each level must be considered when analyzing this artifact. Following the filling of the two artifacts, we used the brainwriting method [18] to identify ideas for an itinerant laboratory of Ubiquitous Computing. During one minute each person had a sheet of paper and could

**Table 1.** Summary of four co-design workshops.

| Workshops | Artifacts or Methods | Participants | Results |
|---|---|---|---|
| *Workshop 1*. April 12th, 2024. Objective: understanding the context of an itinerant laboratory. In-person meeting | SID. EF. Brainwriting | 11 participants | Identification of 35 stakeholders, 29 related challenges and 23 prospective ideas for the itinerant laboratory |
| *Workshop 2*. June 21th, 2024. Objective: consolidating the context understanding and prospecting ideas for the itinerant laboratory. Online meeting with the OpenDesign platform[7] | Consolidation of SID and EF. SF | 11 participants | Consolidation of results for the itinerant laboratory. Identification of 43 requirements for the itinerant laboratory |
| *Workshop 3*. October 16th, 2024. Objective: discussing ideas for the itinerant laboratory. Online meeting with the OpenDesign platform | Open Brainstorming for itinerant ubiquitous computing laboratory ideation | 7 participants | Consolidation of SF requirements |
| *Workshop 4*. October 18th, 2024. Objective: prototyping the itinerant laboratory. In-person meeting | Braindraw supported by vehicle mockups | 7 participants | Low-fidelity prototypes Consolidation of a proposal for the itinerant laboratory |

write her ideas. Then, we changed papers in clock-size order and the person read the preview paragraphs and continued writing, refining existing ideas or generating new ones. Brainwriting was used as a method to enable a broad and open flow of ideas about an itinerant laboratory in a participatory way. After brainwriting, an open discussion about the results were conducted. The participants highlighted and shared the ideas they found most interesting.

**Workshop 2.** The second workshop occurred online. We utilized Google Meet platform to have the HCI specialists in online design activities and discussions, and the OpenDesign platform to enable registering of the design activities results. The first author transcribed the results from the first workshop to the SAwD digital artifacts making them available on the OpenDesign platform. During this workshop, we reviewed and discussed the previous work on the Stakeholders Identification Diagram and Evaluation Frame, helping in bringing to awareness the understandings created up to that point.

**Fig. 2.** Princesa VW Bus.

Continuing the workshop, we used the digital version of the Semiotic Framework (SF) available on the OpenDesign platform to formalize into requirements the ideas previously identified in the brainwriting. By using the Semiotic Framework artifact, we can consolidate the knowledge identified in previous artifacts in a systematic way, representing human/social requirements and technical ones.

**Workshop 3.** The third workshop occurred online. As done in workshop 2, we also used Google Meet and OpenDesign platforms to bring together the HCI specialists in shared activities and synchronous discussions. The workshop aimed to consolidate initial requirements for the itinerant laboratory and to brainstorm about possible uses in the Brazilian scenario. The first author presented the Princesa vehicle space and commented about possible (and necessary) modifications to transform the vehicle in a laboratory. Having this information about the vehicle, that defined restrictions and possibilities for design, the participants reviewed and consolidated the requirements identified through the Semiotic Framework at the OpenDesign platform.

After consolidation of the requirements, the participants performed an open brainstorming about the conception of the possible purposes and uses of the Itinerant Laboratory. Finally, they discussed conceptual understandings of the laboratory as an interactive installation, and planned the next design activities for the laboratory development.

**Workshop 4.** The fourth workshop was an in-person meeting to prototype the itinerant laboratory. The method used was Braindraw [18], as it enables the participatory prototyping of technology without high cost and effort, generating various prototypes as candidates to be implemented in future.

A VW Bus mockup was used as the source of Braindrawing prototyping tool. A VW Bus mockup used in braindrawing, to illustrate the vehicle as the physical space considered in design. The basic mockup presents a 2D outline of a VW Bus, with labels identifying different vehicle parts and spaces. Finally, the participants presented and discussed the Braindraw results, consolidating a proposal of ideas to be implemented as the itinerant ubiquitous computing laboratory. The results from the workshops will be presented in the next section.

### 3.1 Ethical Considerations

In Brazil, resolution 510/2016 sets out the rules applicable to research and identifies a set of research studies that are exempt from registration and evaluation by the Research Ethics Committee system, such as the ones that "emerge spontaneously and contingently in professional practice, as long as they do not reveal data that identifies the subject". The workshops were part of the activities of a research group that brings together these specialists at the university. Thus, the participants were included in the research group's professional practice, which includes activities such as participation in co-design. Participation in the workshop was voluntary, and those who decided to attend the meetings were informed about the objectives of the research, the expected benefits and that the possible risks were no greater than those existing in everyday life. The participants were informed that they were free to stop participating and could refuse to take part in some specific activity. The identities of the participants were kept confidential. No personal data was collected from participants, nor sensitive data collection instruments were used. Whenever data revealed any aspect of the participants' identity they were anonymized . Regarding the practical activities being planned to involve people in real contexts of experimenting the products of this research, we have already the approval of a local board on research ethics (# CAAE 80397324.8.0000.5404), which will allow the conduction of evaluation activities.

## 4 Codesign Results

This section presents the results from the workshops categorized by the broad steps that guided design.

### 4.1 Context Understanding

The results from the context understanding come mainly from Workshops 1 and 2, where the participants filled and consolidated the SID and EF artifacts. Quantitatively, the understanding shared through the SID and EF artifacts resulted in 35 direct and indirect mapped stakeholders, 29 challenges and problems, and 23 prospective ideas for the itinerant laboratory.

The Operation level contains as stakeholders the maintenance professionals, the technical support and the Princess VW Bus. In the Contribution level, there are parents, children including those with disabilities, elderly, and a local laboratory involved in creating ubiquitous installations. The mapped stakeholders represent the social organizations of the countryside - centered on families. Through our analysis, we conceived the possible participants of the itinerant laboratory organized by the whole family-structure: parents, guardians, children, elderly. Although the itinerant laboratory could be focused on children, one or more members of the family could participate together in the experience, helping in creating a social experience more welcoming and significant for the participants. In this way, the laboratory could be approached as an affective and social experience, in which the whole family can participate together.

The Source level presents teachers, tutors, monitors, maker labs, schools, and community centers. These stakeholders represent entities that can contribute with important knowledge about how to create an interesting and engaging scenario that both give access and opportunities for learning about technology. Schools, maker labs and community centers highlight the social network of people that can be involved with the itinerant laboratory creation and dissemination.

The Market level has the majority of interested parties: educational, innovation and technological fairs, Furniture Manufacturers, Old cars clubs, Companies which build lab makers, Unicamp University and public funding resources, development schools, engineers, Lab Makers, public and private schools, input suppliers. The stakeholders in this level represent opportunities of partnerships: in a technical dimension, helping to implement the laboratory regarding operational aspects and infrastructure; in a social dimension, helping to spread the information to distant and isolated families, as in the countryside much of the information only reaches people with the word-of-mouth strategy of communication.

Finally, the Community level involved legislation and law providers, Ethical Research Committee, city council, Unicamp University, Women organizations, Computer Science Conferences. These represent broad and high-level entities that define regulations to be considered, such as ethical norms, and have potential interest in the technology access dissemination in Brazil.

Regarding the EF, the participants found 29 challenges to be faced in the context. In the Operation level, there were challenges such as: *"Access to electrical energy, electric extension or nobreak"* in places without infrastructure. These challenges emerge mainly because of the nature of a laboratory in the wild that could be anywhere, and not physically located in a specific place. An itinerant laboratory demands unique care and procedures, such as precautions for assembling and disassembling the laboratory, transporting equipment and technologies safely, considering the vehicle and the laboratory as a place that will be on the move, visiting several different locations. Implementation challenges also include knowing where it is possible or legal to set up the laboratory and demarcating spaces in which the laboratory will operate. This characteristic is different from an installation in a museum, for example, which already has the available limits and respective regulations related to the museum building. Being in-the-wild, in several places, legal norms and restrictions might be less known or predictable.

In the Contribution level, the participants identified challenges related to full access to the laboratory for people in its widest possible diversity, for example *"access of elderly and other people with physical limitations inside the VW Bus"*. As the motivation of the itinerant laboratory is bringing ubiquitous computing literacy to people, accessibility and access are both objectives and challenges to be considered in design. This level also identified challenges involved in how to create social experiences and not just individualistic ones, aiming to promote meaningful experiences among the participants.

At the Source level, the participants raised challenges on how to share ubiquitous computing content in an accessible and engaging way for participants and other stakeholders, such as schools. This is a challenge that reminds the necessity of thinking about accessibility not just in the physical access to the laboratory, but regarding the meanings and content being communicated. At the Market level, the participants found challenges on how to find and establish partnerships and the need for strategies to raise funds to make the laboratory viable. Finally, at the Community level, the participants identified challenges related to knowing relevant traffic regulations, ethical research standards and access to the physical spaces where the mobile laboratory could physically reach.

After understanding the socioeconomic context, the participants identified and consolidated 43 requirements distributed in six levels of formality through the SF. The *Social World* layer has four requirements that indicate values and motivations that must be considered in design. For instance, the need of considering the values of access (of knowledge, technology and technological spaces) and promoting maker culture practices.

The requirements from the *Pragmatics* layer has seven requirements that define intentions and objectives around the itinerant laboratory, regarding its accessibility, affective and cultural aspects. For instance, the itinerant laboratory must consider recommendations from equitable and inclusive design as a way to enable universal access to different participants. The experience in the itinerant laboratory must be safe, ludic, social and charming. Requirements also formalized intentions to explore affective dimensions, leveraging on memories and folklore of the Princesa story from the first author's family.

The *Semantics* layer, in turn, has four requirements related to meanings and knowledge around the itinerant laboratory. The participants defined the educational requirement of having awareness and getting to know ubiquitous computing as the main objective of the itinerant laboratory. The proposal of workshop educational activities should consider schools curricula, to align the itinerant nature with school activities and enable possible partnerships. As a way to promote meanings with different audiences, games and thematic activities (e.g., as vintage automobilism) should be explored.

The *Syntactics* layer has two requirements that define aspects regarding the form and structure of the itinerant laboratory. For example, the Brazilian State Department of Traffic (DETRAN) monitors the traffic of land vehicles and determines rules for driving vehicles. Knowing previously that this stakeholder defines important regulations and norms, the participants defined the requirement "consider the restrictions of VW Bus modifications determined by DETRAN".

The *Empirics* layer had four requirements that defined aspects of frequency, communication and noise. For instance, in terms of data communication, the VW Bus must use 4G bandwidth for connection; in terms of energy transmission, the VW Bus must make available 110/127 and 220 V to energize projects.

Finally, the *Physical World* layer had 20 requirements. The high number of requirements of the Physical World layer are related to the itinerant laboratory's unique physical nature, in which many physical and environmental aspects must be identified and specified as requirements. For example, as Ubiquitous Computing laboratory, the itinerant laboratory must use physical sensors (e.g., lightness, temperature), actuators (LEDs, Speaker, display) and microcontrollers (e.g., arduino, esp32). The laboratory must also consider physical enablers of power and energy, such as energy generators or extensions, power charger source, and stationary battery packs. The laboratory vicinity was also considered, for example providing physical ramps for wheelchair users to access the vehicle interior, providing chairs or tables to organize the space outside the VW Bus and for sitting and resting, giving people comfort.

### 4.2 A Shared Understanding for the Itinerant Laboratory

The Brainwriting generated 118 ideas from 11 participants. We analysed the generated ideas using the Thematic Analysis, that resulted in five main themes: Itinerant Laboratory, Workshop, Accessibility, Interaction, and Socioenactive. Figure 3 presents a Thematic Map illustrating the five themes and subthemes.

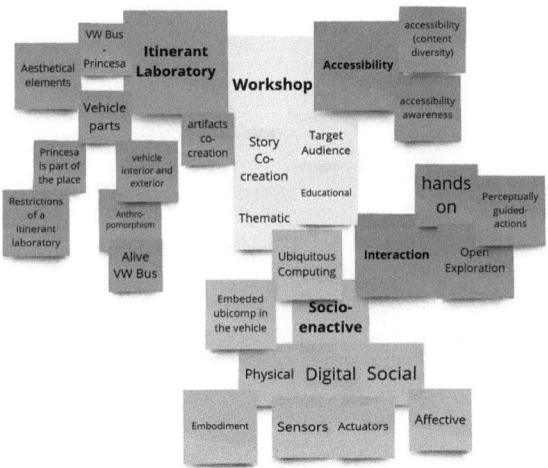

**Fig. 3.** Thematic Map of the Brainwriting.

*Itinerant Laboratory.* This theme represents the ideas that defined a proposal for a working itinerant laboratory in the VW Bus "Princesa". The laboratory should involve ubiquitous computing artifacts co-creation as a way to engage and create learning experiences from the practice, and not from a detached or mental exercise. The itinerant laboratory should be interactive, where the vehicle parts would be transformed in interactive or anthropomorphic places to stimulate interaction and help the creation of affective meanings. The idea that emerged from participants is that Princesa VW Bus is "alive", responding to people's interactions: Princesa has a heart that beats faster or slower depending on the presence of people in the vehicle; has eyes that blink when people pass by. The anthropomorphism metaphor is to help participants to create an affective relation with the VW Bus, perceiving the vehicle not as a technical neutral space, but a welcoming one—a place of intimacy, wonder and curiosity. Aesthetic elements should be considered, for instance Princesa should be aesthetically pleasing and"pretty". Finally, the itinerant laboratory should consider specific design restrictions from being "in the wild", affected by rain, wind, sun and other environmental conditions.

*Workshop.* As the Itinerant Laboratory possible uses, workshops were indicated as a form of educational practice and access to ubiquitous computing technology. The workshop idea enables the participants to co-construct meaning on situated experiences. Instead of creating a fixed installation, we can organize workshops that help people co-create meanings and experiences around ubiquitous computing in a participatory way. In this way, the diverse population to be encountered from distinct socioeconomic realities can gather together in workshops adapted to a situated socioeconomic reality.

*Accessibility* emerged as the awareness in the laboratory access, as well accessibility to the content or information presented in workshops. As a distinct physical place, and considering the motivation of bringing ubiquitous computing to a diverse audience, accessibility is a central value and requirement. When thinking about the laboratory size and dimensions, a physical accessibility nature appears. But social accessibility is also important, creating educational experiences that people can relate to their socioeconomic situations. For example, a workshop must not require participants to have smartphones to access an experience (as occurs in many museums). Considering socio economic inclusion is being aware of the physical, social and cultural dimensions of accessibility.

*Socioenactive* represents the ideas related to Physical, Digital, and Social couplings from the socioenactive concept [3]. Social dimension was explored through affective qualities: the VW Bus was not only a vehicle, but has been present for generations in the first author family, with many memories and stories. In Brazil, the VW Bus was used for social purposes, such as transporting and traveling groups and associations. This social dimension of a vehicle both familiar to Brazilian culture and present in an affective horizon of experiences of the first author was considered in design. The laboratory must also explore features that promote social activities and participatory meaning-making. The physical represent the bodies of participants that must be considered as designing whole-body interaction; it also includes the physical aspects of the laboratory, such as physicality of technology in the ubiquitous computing environment. The technology would be embedded in the very physical fabric of the vehicle, transforming it into an interactive vehicle. The digital consists in the algorithms and processing logic to make the interactive installations work as such.

*Interaction* represents approaching the itinerant laboratory as an interactive place and a place of social interaction. To help people co-create meaning, the interaction with the VW Bus should be open, where people are free to create their own stories and memories of interaction, creating meanings around the itinerant laboratory and ubiquitous computing with others. The exploration should be guided by people's perceptions and further actions, where the laboratory would respond to people's interactions, and the change in laboratory expression would provoke more actions from the public. To help engage the body, the laboratory should involve hands-on activities where people could be directly involved in the meaning making and creation of Ubiquitous Computing artifacts.

### 4.3 Building Blocks of the Itinerant Laboratory

The Braindraw generated seven low-fidelity prototypes (some illustrated in Fig. 1). In this paper, we present the participants' braindraw consolidation, where the participants shared the main prototyped aspects relevant for the itinerant laboratory. Next, we present the categories that participants themselves consolidated for the final proposal of the laboratory.

*External Spaces.* The participants prototyped benches for people to sit and tables to show interactive artifacts. Interactive "clothes" for the VW Bus could be designed, enabling technology to be coupled with different vehicle parts, such as headlights, hubcaps, and awning. The vehicle should respond to people's presence, such as playing welcoming messages. Anthropomorphism inspired behavior should be prototyped, such as making the vehicle "wake up" or "go to sleep", and "feeding" a vehicle hungry for fuel. The action should be as social as possible, exploring affective affordances that trigger social actions and interactions, such as hugs and giving hands.

*Internal Spaces.* Different sensors should be implemented inside the vehicle. For example, using pressure sensors on seats to trigger responses of the vehicle. The perception-action should be guided by anthropomorphism metaphors, such as perceiving a VW Bus "heart" inside the vehicle. Princesa stories could be presented in some internal part of the vehicle (such as the passenger seat), giving opportunities for participants to co-create stories.

*Open Questions* and answers were pointed out by the participants regarding the educational hands-on experiences. For instance, the participants raised the question "what will children learn?" and presented opportunities such as present technological components, their connections and related concepts (e.g., energy). The open questions indicate the need of defining an educational plan for workshop activities, which can be done with schools partnership.

## 5 Discussion

With this design experience and prototyping, we answer the two research questions. Regarding RQ1: *What constitutes an Itinerant Ubiquitous Computing Lab-*

*oratory for the addressed context?*, much more than technology is involved in the process as illustrated in Fig. 4.

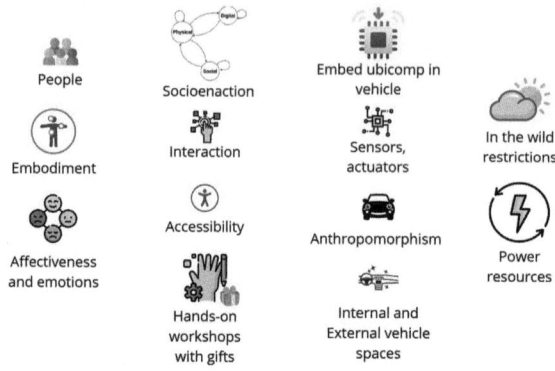

**Fig. 4.** Building blocks of the itinerant laboratory.

The itinerant laboratory structure is related to the socioenaction concept, constituted by the tripartite coupling of the Social, Physical, and Digital dimensions. These socioenactive dimensions underlie the laboratory concept, involving the social interaction to be promoted (Social), the physical aspects of the vehicle and spaces available for interaction, and the sensors and actuators to create artifacts (Physical) of an interactive laboratory (Digital). We found that the interactions are diverse and involve Embodiment, Affectiveness and Emotions. The vehicle has a story and the activities which will be held on it will create other stories. Accessibility is a main challenge in the physical internal environment of the car and the external environment as well. As a consequence, the environment inside and outside must be carefully built to be accessible. The laboratory is a practical space where people should be involved in hands-on activities and could build their own workshop gifts as a way of building engagement and affective memories with the laboratory experience. Sensors and Actuators are going to be embedded with the ubiquitous computing in the vehicle. In this case we designed anthropomorphic objects making the perception that the VW Bus is "alive" and responding to the interactions of participants individually and in groups. As in the wild restrictions we must consider the weather conditions and the local conditions where the vehicle is going to park. Finally, we depend on power resources to make the laboratory work, such as batteries, solar power, wired power, etc. All these elements together constitute the laboratory.

Regarding RQ2: *How to approach the problem of prototyping an Itinerant Ubiquitous Computing Laboratory with the Socially Aware Design?* we highlight four design recommendations:

1. Create a shared space for sense-making about the situated socioeconomic challenges that both motivates the creation of this type of laboratory (social) and affects designers capabilities of implementing the laboratory (technical)

(a) Raising and discussing the interested parties - SID;
(b) Bringing awareness about interested parties' challenges and unique socioeconomic conditions - EF;
2. Design for the body considerations when projecting sensorimotor interactions: consider bodily dimensions, space, size, body positions, and possible bodily differences of the public, such as wheelchair users;
3. Keep people mindful of the uniqueness of interaction (with a vehicle), its special characteristics, existing affordances and restrictions;
   (a) using vehicle photos and mockups to bring forth people's spatial perception to support brainwriting and braindraw;
   (b) presenting about vehicle space components, affordances and possible modifications;
4. Use participatory methods to help leverage the participants experiences and ideas, enabling the co-construction of the technology with everyone's input and consolidation;
   (a) Using brainwriting to help prospect ideas and braindrawing with consolidation to end the co-design with a concrete and visual proposal;
   (b) Using OpenDesign platform to share, evaluate and improve the content;

In our design experience, we found some surprising and challenging aspects. Surprisingly, we did not expect anthropomorphism to emerge to make the VW Bus itself alive in design. This unexpected result might be related to the affective and emotional expressions of the first author towards the vehicle which is a family 28 years old property. This anthropomorphism covers "interactive organs" (e.g. heart and stomach) and "acts of living" for instance waking up/putting the VW Bus to sleep.

Also, the duality of the VW Bus as: i) being the installation and ii) being the space which helds an installation was not expected. The initial expectative was just creating a space for helding the laboratory. During the co-design the idea evolved to make the VW Bus also a form of installation, meaning that the VW Bus should be alive and have interaction affordances, which extends its role beyond being only a physical space.

We perceived co-designers developing affective expressions for the VW Bus. The affective expression of the first participant may have acted as an emotional contagion for co-design participants, seeing the VW Bus not as a physical neutral material, but a lived and affective place.

As challenges, it was demanding to reach a consolidated proposal for the itinerant laboratory. Four workshops were necessary to consolidate a proposal. The authors have conducted co-design workshops in the past and usually two or three workshops are sufficient to reach a proposal. We attribute this challenge to the very innovative concept of an ubiquitous itinerant laboratory. 'Ubiquitous' or 'itinerant' alone are already challenging concepts. When these two particulars come together, more challenges appear with the combination of the two, such as the mobile network and integrated devices still working after the vehicle travels long distances between places (potholes as in bad quality and unpaved roads) and weather events (rain, wind). Also, it was challenging to advance the laboratory contents and its use (educational workshops) at the same time. On the one hand, only after we had an understanding about the laboratory, we could plan its use in educational activities. On the other hand, thinking in the design of educational activities also influenced the design of the laboratory, helping specify workshop benches and educational kits.

Finally, it was especially difficult to design considering socioeconomic vulnerable settings. We always have to keep in mind values such as recyclable, low-cost and accessible devices and materials, and creating activities that do not necessarily demand that users have smartphones or more sophisticated technological devices.

We believe much of our design methods could be useful for other designers with similar objectives. Much of our recommendations can apply to the global south, where there is a need to travel long distances for accessing education. Also, as for vehicles, we think that much of the recommendations could apply to vehicles in other countries with similar characteristics of a VW Bus, such as large space in the vehicle and flexibility on modification or adaptation to an itinerant laboratory. However, some countries may have restrictions on modifying vehicles to act as an itinerant laboratory. Thus, this will be dependent on local legislation. Finally, specific regional and local cultural aspects, including Brazilian ones, might indicate the need for further work to tailor the recommendations to different regional cultural needs.

The laboratory is already being developed and the VW bus has currently its interior space modified to host the educational activities, and has a powered energy system from solar energy already tested. Further operational actions include the inside laboratory furniture, lighting and sounds, and network to hold a web service dealing with the sensors, actuators among other devices. Finally, we will develop the mobile installation itself, with a narrative adjustable to a local community culture and needs. Other research steps being planned include evaluations with experts and prospective domain stakeholders as a way of refining the laboratory prior to going to the field. A partnership was made with an educational institution in the countryside to evaluate the itinerant system. We already have approved the research project by an Ethical Research Committee board, enabling the evaluation procedures (# 80397324.8.0000.5404).

Some limitations of our work so far involve: 1) Not all the participants joined all the co-design sections; 2) We achieved different prototypes, however we did not implemented a final one yet, as this will be conducted as the next steps; nevertheless, some demands for infrastructure and physical solutions for the Princesa have already been carried out (e.g., energy issues); and 3) The participants did not physically enter inside the VW Bus (it was presented in photos), but every participant had already entered or occasionally seen one of such vehicles in our streets.

## 6 Conclusion

Ubiquitous computing environments require a communication of different devices working in synchronism creating a mix of interaction possibilities that bring more complexity to these environments. An ubiquitous computing itinerant laboratory faces the ubicomp challenges plus the challenges of being in the wild and not having an specific place to stand. In this paper we presented a Co-design study using the Socially Aware Design to discuss requirements of an Itinerant Ubiquitous Computing Laboratory. The co-design resulted in ideas to design this type of laboratory in socio-situated contexts. While some aspects of infrastructure of the VW bus have been worked recently, future works involve the implementation of the prototype as a real laboratory, and experimenting with different populations, itinerantly.

**Acknowledgments.** We thank the members of the InterHAD research group who contributed to the workshops and the research being conducted. Josiane Rosa de Oliveira Gaia Pimenta thanks Unicamp and IFSP (Federal Institute of São Paulo) for supporting this research. Deógenes P. da Silva Junior thanks the Coordination for the Improvement of Higher Education Personnel - Brasil (CAPES) - Finance Code 001. M. Cecilia C. Baranauskas is a Research Productivity fellow from the Brazilian Council for Scientific and Technological Development (CNPq) (grant 309442/2023-0).

**Disclosure of Interests.** The authors have no competing interests to declare that are relevant to the content of this article.

## References

1. Abdelnour-Nocera, J., Densmore, M.: A review of perspectives and challenges for international development in information and communication technologies. Ann. Int. Commun. Assoc. **41**(3–4), 250–257 (2017)
2. Baranauskas, M.C.C., Souza, C.S.: Desafio no 4: Acesso participativo e universal do cidadão brasileiro ao conhecimento. Computação Brasil **Ano VII**(23), 7 (2006)
3. Baranauskas, M.C.C., Duarte, E.F., Valente, J.A.: Socioenactive interaction: addressing intersubjectivity in ubiquitous design scenarios. Int. J. Human-Comput. Interact. **40**(13), 3365–3380 (2024)
4. Baranauskas, M.C.C., Pereira, R., Bonacin, R.: Socially aware systems design: a perspective towards technology-society coupling. AIS Trans. Human-Comput. Interact. **16**(1), 80–109 (2024)
5. van Biljon, J., Renaud, K.: Human-computer interaction for development (HCI4D): The southern african landscape. In: IFIP Advances in Information and Communication Technology, pp. 253–266. IFIP advances in information and communication technology, Springer International Publishing, Cham (2019)
6. Caceffo, R., et al.: Collaborative meaning construction in socioenactive systems: study with the mbot. In: Learning and Collaboration Technologies. Designing Learning Experiences: 6th International Conference, LCT 2019, Held as Part of the 21st HCI International Conference, HCII 2019, Orlando, FL, USA, July 26–31, 2019, Proceedings, Part I 21. pp. 237–255. Springer (2019)

7. Duarte, E.F., Gonçalves, F.M., Baranauskas, M.C.C.: Instint: Enacting a small-scale interactive installation through co-design. In: Proceedings of the 30th Australian Conference on Computer-Human Interaction, pp. 338–348 (2018)
8. Duarte, E.F., Maike, V., Mendoza, Y.L.M., Brennand, C., Baranauskas, M.C.: " the magic of science:" beyond action, a case study on learning through socioenaction. In: Workshop de Informática na Escola (WIE), pp. 501–510. SBC (2019)
9. Duarte, E.F., Mendoza, Y.L.M., Baranauskas, M.C.C.: Instime: a case study on the co-design of interactive installations on deep time. In: Proceedings of the 2020 ACM Designing Interactive Systems Conference, pp. 231–242 (2020)
10. Espinoza, G.E.T., Baranauskas, M.C.C.: Designing socially-aware persuasive systems: a proposed framework. In: Seminário Integrado de Software e Hardware (SEMISH), pp. 234–245. SBC (2020)
11. Ferrari, B., da Silva Junior, D.P., Oliveira, C.M., Ortiz, J.S., Pereira, R.: Socially aware design of games: an early workshop for game designers. J. Interact. Syst. **11**(1), 92–109 (2020)
12. Garzotto, F., Beccaluva, E., Gianotti, M., Riccardi, F.: Interactive multisensory environments for primary school children. In: Proceedings of the 2020 CHI Conference on Human Factors in Computing Systems, pp. 1–12 (2020)
13. Goknil, A., et al.: A systematic review of data quality in CPS and IoT for industry 4.0. ACM Comput. Surv. **55**(14s), 1–38 (2023)
14. Gonçalves, F.M., Baranauskas, M.C.C.: Designing in pandemic context: scientific collaboration through the opendesign platform. Interact. Comput. **35**(2), 105–117 (2023)
15. Junqueira, L., Freire, A.P., Grützmann, A., Zitkus, E.: Challenges and barriers faced by older adults to access legislative e-participation platforms in Brazil. Electron. J. Inform. Syst. Develop. Countries **89**(5), e12274 (2023)
16. Méndez Mendoza, Y.L., C. Baranauskas, M.C.: Designing a tangible tabletop installation and enacting a socioenactive experience with tangitime. J. Brazilian Comput. Society **27**(1), 9 (2021)
17. Morgan, E., Gunes, H.: Human nonverbal behaviour understanding *in the Wild* for new media art. In: Salah, A.A., Hung, H., Aran, O., Gunes, H. (eds.) HBU 2013. LNCS, vol. 8212, pp. 27–39. Springer, Cham (2013). https://doi.org/10.1007/978-3-319-02714-2_3
18. Muller, M.J., Haslwanter, J.H., Dayton, T.: Participatory practices in the software lifecycle. In: Handbook of human-computer interaction, pp. 255–297. Elsevier (1997)
19. Patnaik, A., Dawar, S., Kudal, P.: Industry 5.0: sustainability challenges in fusion of human and AI. In: Proceedings of the 4th International Conference on Information Management Machine Intelligence, pp. 1–7 (2022)
20. Pereira, R., Baranauskas, M.C.C.: Systemic and socially aware perspective for information systems. I GranDSI-BR p. 148 (2017)
21. Pimenta, J.R., Felipe Duarte, E., Bauzer Medeiros, C., C Baranauskas, M.C.: Analyzing equitable access in a remote socio-enactive setting: A case study. J. Brazilian Comput. Society **30**(1) (2024)
22. Pimenta, J.R.d.O.G., Duarte, E.F., Baranauskas, M.C.C.: Evaluating accessibility in ubiquitous environments: a case study with museum installations. In: Seminário Integrado de Software e Hardware (SEMISH), pp. 88–96. SBC (2021)
23. Ribeiro, J.B., Borges, L., Sena, P., Pinheiro, B.A., Abelém, A.J.G.: Slices como serviço sobre um centro de dados itinerante aplicado ao cenário amazônico. In: Workshop de Teoria, Tecnologias e Aplicações de Slicing para Infraestruturas Softwarizadas (WSlice), pp. 15–27. SBC (2019)

24. Saleemi, M., Anjum, M., Rehman, M.: The ubiquitous healthcare facility framework: a proposed system for managing rural antenatal care. IEEE Access **7**, 161264–161282 (2019)
25. da Silva, D.P., Pereira, R., Baranauskas, M.C.C.: Raising awareness on bullying through a design situation and rationale. In: Proceedings of the XXIII Brazilian Symposium on Human Factors in Computing Systems, pp. 1–16 (2024)
26. da Silva, J.V., Baranauskas, M.C.C., Gonçalves, D.A., dos Santos, A.C.: Building a space for the human in IoT: Contributions of a design process. J. Braz. Comput. Soc. **28**(1), 80–95 (2022)
27. Vasconcelos, V., Bigotte, E., Marques, L., Almeida, R.: Make a lab–a project focused on the gender gap in stem fields. In: 2022 31st Annual Conference of the European Association for Education in Electrical and Information Engineering (EAEEIE), pp. 1–5. IEEE (2022)
28. Veiga Furtado, T., Rechena, A.: Mirage-the social function of artistic practice as a tool for empowerment. creative net art projects with women in shelters. In: Proceedings of the 10th International Conference on Digital and Interactive Arts, pp. 1–9 (2021)

# Designing for Identity, Safety, and Cultural Values

# Dancing with Data: Privacy Compromises of Egyptian Women Reconciling Westernized Social Media Sharing with Local Cultural Values

Mennatallah Saleh[1(✉)], Shaun Macdonald[2], and Christian Sturm[3]

[1] Technical University of Berlin, Berlin, Germany
menna.esaleh@gmail.com
[2] University of Glasgow, Glasgow, Scotland
[3] Technical University of Inglostadt, Ingolstadt, Germany
christian.sturm@thi.de

**Abstract.** Social media sharing is ubiquitous. Privacy control, however, does not serve all users equally. Previous research has focused on the cultural experience of rich, western, industrialized and educated populations. Meanwhile, the privacy experiences and the impact of social media on those in globally under-represented cultures are poorly understood. To address this, we conducted detailed interviews exploring how 45 Egyptian women navigate the competing pressures that social media and collectivist, patriarchal Arab cultural norms place on their privacy, and how they share information. Our qualitative analysis revealed four key topics: *Culture, Personal Information Control and Loss, Sharing Attitudes* and *Technical Features*. We further identified seven pain points describing how current social media fail to serve this community, ranging from conflicting pressures between platforms and cultural values, to vulnerabilities in crucial technical features like private Facebook Groups. Finally, we advocate for research to further explore the unique privacy experiences of under-represented groups.

**Keywords:** Privacy · Social Media · Cross Cultural Studies

## 1 Introduction

Participating in the social media ecosystem leads to loss of privacy by incentivizing users to share personal information they would otherwise protect [38]. While prior work has demonstrated this *privacy paradox* [9,70], it disproportionately explores Western, Educated, Industrialized, Rich, Democratic (WEIRD) experiences [29,40]. With many globally prominent social media platforms designed in WEIRD countries, understanding of the impact of privacy loss on under-represented non-WEIRD cultures and groups is limited. We explore the experiences of Egyptian women as a prime example of such an under-represented group. Egyptian women face distinct pressures on their privacy practices when compared to their WEIRD counterparts [43], such as being targeted to defame familial reputation, patriarchal control of their sharing, and balancing a communal desire to share with cultural taboos. In the social media domain, which incentivizes sharing, these pressures are felt in new ways. Social media use is also prominent in Egypt, with social, communal and cultural factors all motivating the need to stay connected and in the loop, making abstinence difficult [72]. Thus, Egyptian women are compelled by market and social forces to grapple with unique privacy concerns on platforms not designed for this purpose, which can force them to negotiate, distort or abandon their ways of life. By investigating the privacy attitudes and social media sharing these users exhibit, we can inform how these experiences could be better tailored for Egyptian women, as well as advocate for future usable security research investigating the experiences of similarly under-represented users.

Researchers have documented Egyptian cultural values that impact privacy and sharing, identifying core factors including reputation and defamation [42], male-dominance [13] and concepts such as the *evil eye* [18]. Prior HCI research explored usable security models of privacy [56,69], identifying usability as a crucial factor in system security [8] and promoting inherent privacy considerations with the concept of *privacy by design* [12]. The impact of social media on users' needs, wants, and privacy has also been examined [50,53], but predominantly conducted in WEIRD contexts [40]. While Egypt is second in internet usage in North Africa and the Middle East, with prominent social media use [35], understanding of Egyptians' unique experiences on these platforms is lacking. In particular, how Egyptian women navigate desires to share online while upholding contradictory cultural values around privacy is not well understood.

To address this gap, we conducted 55 in-depth interviews with women from three distinct backgrounds: higher socioeconomic Egyptians (HSE), lower socioeconomic Egyptians (LSE) and higher socioeconomic Germans (HSG) to allow comparison with WEIRD perspectives. These interviews explored users' attitudes and beliefs regarding privacy in the social media age, the impact of cultural norms, and the workarounds they use for information sharing and privacy management on platforms designed without their needs in mind. Using inductive qualitative analysis, we describe the findings from these interviews and identify the underlying phenomena, informing future understanding and design.

We identified four key aspects of attitudes and experiences toward privacy and social media information sharing, which encompasses public posts, private groups and direct messages. These aspects were *cultural influences, personal information control and loss, sharing attitude* and *technical features*. Within each aspect, we mapped the factors and phenomena that drive user beliefs and behavior around information sharing, coalescing into seven pain points that encapsulate how current social media design undermines the needs and wants of Egyptian women in regard to privacy. We then use our findings to inform a set of actionable recommendations for designers to address these core user grievances.

Furthermore, we discuss how the global propagation of technology and social media designed by WEIRD cultures enacts a form of technocolonialism [37], incentivizing the disparagement and abandonment of cultural values to more effectively utilize these ubiquitous platforms, a divide we observed between HSE and LSE participants. Our work identifies the gaps found between WEIRD system design and the cultural requirements for the privacy of Egyptian women, motivating future researchers to seek to understand and serve the perspectives of similar under-represented groups whose cultural identity risks erosion.

### 1.1 Contributions

We make the following contributions in this work:

1. The first comprehensive investigation of the attitudes of Egyptian women toward social media sharing and privacy;
2. We present the key factors that differentiate social media use by Egyptian women of different socioeconomic backgrounds and Western users to identify core pain points these users experience when managing their online privacy;
3. We contribute actionable recommendations to better support the cultural relationship Egyptian women have with privacy and information sharing.

## 2 Related Work

### 2.1 Egyptian Cultural Factors

A deeply rooted cultural belief in Egypt is the *evil eye*. The *evil eye* is the belief that harm will be bestowed upon oneself due to the envy of others [46]. When others look at the blessings that you have with ill intentions, the blessings will be gone. This causes many Egyptians to hide blessings in an attempt to protect themselves from the harms of envy. This practice in itself is a reason for Egyptians to value privacy, especially in sensitive matters such as bearing children, possible marriages, new employment, financial gain, or even simple achievements like getting a good grade. Despite this belief, Egyptian society is collectivist and communal by nature when compared to WEIRD cultures [32, 33]. This collectivism motivates Egyptians to share good news with others, but directly conflicts with hiding one's blessings due to the *evil eye*, resulting in a *privacy paradox* [50]. It is sometimes perceived that Egyptians lack privacy, due to the imposition of strangers on personal affairs and the lack of secrets within families. However, the principles of privacy are understood and practiced differently in Egypt [63], and what is considered private to an individual of a Western culture does not necessarily translate into a private affair in Egypt.

Furthermore, the social landscape in Egypt features a clear socioeconomic divide that influences all cultural attitudes and norms. This class distinction is a spectrum differentiating between more traditional lower socioeconomic groups and more Westernized higher socioeconomic groups, leaving the country in a split [31]. This divide is propagated by public and private schooling systems [5], where private schooling systems that focus on the English language are a symbol of status. Therefore, students who attend private schools are more Westernized and experience a form of acculturation, moving away from traditional values, which may influence their privacy practices. In order to best capture Egyptian behavior and perspectives, therefore, we recruited participants from both ends of this polarized socioeconomic spectrum to observe how balancing the use of Westernized sharing platforms with traditional cultural values varies.

## 2.2 Pressures of Gender, Family and Reputation

Perhaps the most controversial issue in Egyptian culture is gender [2]. This gender-focused culture can be perceived as a form of respect or, alternatively, a form of suppression to Arabic women. Regardless, such societies have patriarchal tendencies that influence cultural norms [52]. One such example is the concept of *'ird*, where the family name and reputation are defined by the reputation of its women [19]. Therefore, any public action of a woman outside the cultural norm directly influences her family. This has been directly linked to defamation where, if someone wants to attack a family, they target the reputation of its women [19]. This in turn leads women to focus on keeping much of their activity secret to protect their families. Therefore, the privacy of women is crucial in this culture, as it influences personal and familial positions in society. The abundance of communication technology adds further privacy complications to this ecosystem, presenting fresh defamation vectors to attack women's reputations, such as fabricating photos or exposing private chats [55]. Therefore, understanding this space and its important social implications is necessary for technology researchers to be able to protect vulnerable users and restrict harmful behavior.

## 2.3 WEIRD Privacy and Technology Design

As with other facets of technology, WEIRD culture prevails in digital space design [28,61]. Research has found a track record of technological norms being built in Western WEIRD cultures, then copied and barely adapted worldwide [34]. This is also reflected in privacy design, where system design is heavily influenced by privacy norms in WEIRD cultures. Much of modern information privacy policy is heavily influenced by the foundational privacy protection advocacy by Westin [68] in his book "Privacy and Freedom". In this work, he states: *"the firm expectation of having privacy for permissible deviations is a distinguishing characteristic of life in a free society."*

To promote the protection of users' privacy, researchers and designers have advocated for protective design philosophies such as privacy by design. Privacy by design is a term coined by Cavoukian [12] that encourages designers to develop a privacy mindset when creating their products. It extends the notion that privacy is a cultural practice into becoming a legal framework and a requirement in all modern-day designs. The principle is broken down into seven components, for example: Privacy as the default, Visibility and Transparency, Respect for User Privacy and others, which inspire the recommendations for this work.

While privacy is a vital issue in the technological era, the way in which it impacts users' experience of a platform in terms of usability is also important and can cause some platforms to hesitate in prioritizing it in the design process. The concept of incorporating usability into privacy and security was introduced by Saltzer and Schroeder [56]. They explained how, without usability, the security of systems may be threatened. According to Birge [8], there are five categories of research in the current literature on usable privacy, three of which were particularly relevant for this work, including:

1. **Trust and Ethical Studies:** Exploring concepts such as "trust" and "privacy" from ethical and practical perspectives.
2. **Security and Privacy Experience Studies:** These are investigations into current experiences with security and privacy in existing products and services, in order to evaluate privacy perceptions and attitudes.
3. **Modeling and Guidelines:** Research focused on developing design guidelines to produce usable privacy-centered systems from initial design phases.

Privacy on social media has been studied using different lenses, such as data mining [60], employee data privacy [22], the privacy paradox [50], and security practices [30]. However, most of this literature tends to take a WEIRD or culturally agnostic lens and is not inclusive of non-WEIRD populations. Researchers have explored the influence that social media success metrics, such as 'Likes', can have on technology-mediated dangerous behavior or neural reward processing in WEIRD or unspecified populations [62,66]. Others have specifically explored social media sharing and privacy, such as Gruzd et al., who found that Canadian users showed no difference in self-disclosure from public or private accounts [25].

## 2.4 Non-WEIRD Privacy and Technology

Past work has demonstrated the importance of studying Westernised technology in under-studied cultures, as differences in attitude, cultural influence or even legal regulations can have dramatic effects [51]. These impact not only the way technology is used but also the quality of life of users. While the research on privacy outside the WEIRD context is still in its early stages, there have been several significant studies that showcase the value and nuanced implications of the domain. Ahmed et al. showcase how gender and religion [4] influence privacy concerns in Bangladesh, where the hierarchical social structure was also highlighted [21]. Nemati et al. found that collectivist Chinese users were more likely to inadvertently share private information than their US counterparts [26]. Research suggests that women are more vulnerable on social media outside the West, with experiences being strongly linked to reputation as well as sexual and physical violence [55,57]. Furthermore, they are reported as often being surveilled, and forced to share personal devices, data or accounts with males in the family, influencing their perception of privacy [54,58].

Haque et al. [27] investigate the workarounds users create from unconventional backgrounds to protect their privacy online by manipulating existing frameworks. They report the conservative nature of the Global South leading to the development of secret communication codes, for example, on taboo words or topics. The field has also explored the role Religion plays in the approach to online privacy, such as Muslim American women being under higher scrutiny by their cultural community simply because of their background [3], a trend we expected to expand to Muslim women in Egypt as well which is the majority of Egypt's population. Others explored how literacy and technological awareness impacted privacy protection, such as in a study reporting that Kenyan participants asked the owner of a cyber-cafe to set their passwords for them, because interacting as a novice user can be stressful [47]. It is important to note, however, that little to no research focuses on Egyptian women within this context, and so, while findings can be compared, it is still essential to study this culture.

## 3 Methodology

In an age of globalization, it is critical to understand the needs of underrepresented populations. Egyptian women heavily use social media, and their specific needs are understudied and therefore under-served. This study formulates an understanding of what privacy means to Egyptian women and how technology can be designed to accommodate their experiences and requirements. To gain a holistic understanding, we used in-depth interviews to investigate the experiences and attitudes that Egyptian women from both high and low socioeconomic backgrounds exhibit towards privacy and information sharing, and contrasted them with women from a WEIRD background. We sampled both socioeconomic statuses (SES) from the Egyptian culture to investigate the impact of Westernization on sharing between low-income and high-income Egyptian women [31]. We chose German participants with high SES to act as a control group that represented WEIRD attributes. The insights we constructed from participants were then used to inform how systems can respect the needs of Egyptian women.

**Researcher Positionality:** This research was led by the first and last authors, an Egyptian woman and a German man. As an Egyptian woman researching Egyptian participants, the first author brought an insider perspective, offering cultural and linguistic familiarity. This allowed them to build a strong rapport with the participants and establish trust. In their time in Egypt, they occasionallyÂăexperienced cultural pressure on their own sharing. However, they consistently observed these pressures acting upon friends, colleagues and acquaintances in their everyday experiences from afar. These observations were a key motivator to conduct this research. Further, they led to the authors' initial expectation that differences would be observed between all three user groups, although the nuances and implications of these differences were not yet clear. In particular, this research sought to understand the role technology plays in the lives of LSE women, which was ambiguous.

The last author's research career has consistently explored cross-cultural practices. They provided an outsider perspective in this work, as a German man. While the first author's experiences were key in motivating these under-explored research areas, the authors engaged in reflexive activities, including memoing and debriefing sessions with the outsider researcher. Their integration in both societies allowed for careful observations of nuances and the ability to discuss in the native language where needed. Furthermore, we follow Grounded Theory practices to engage with community experts and iterative data collection and analysis to reduce bias.

### 3.1 Qualitative Analysis Procedure

We analyzed rich qualitative data with an inductive grounded theory analysis approach to construct new understanding of Egyptian women's sharing behavior, experiences and privacy beliefs [24]. Data was collected and coded iteratively. Related categories and concepts were then constructed, informing future iterations of data collection, coding and concept construction via constant comparison.

Grounded theory coding followed a three-step process. First, open coding was conducted to identify pertinent concepts. This followed a line-by-line approach for the first third of interviews to develop an initial scheme of *in vivo* and constructed codes, as well as understand how participants defined concepts [23]. Based on this coding, paragraph-by-paragraph coding was then used after consistency was found between the code assignment of the two approaches. Axial coding was then conducted with a set of affinity diagrams to support the identification of code categories and relationships. Codes were placed on a map and categories, relationships and interactions were created and evaluated iteratively, guided by expert interviews and Corbin and Strauss' assertion that three major relationship types need to be considered: *conditions*, *interactions* and *outcomes* [15]. Finally, selective coding was used to identify core phenomena that describe the findings, presented as a series of descriptive *pain points* our participants experienced, supported by relevant quotations. This framework can enable future researchers to better understand and address their concerns about privacy and the use of social technologies [45]. To improve validity [15], we conducted interviews with four experts from Germany and Egypt who consulted on the relationships during axial coding to discuss the validity of the assumptions, connections made, and core phenomena identified. As proposed by grounded theory methodology we selected experts who were older individuals with extensive cultural experience and involvement within their community, granting them the key characteristics of theoretical relevance and experience-based expertise [15], with one also being a sociologist.

### 3.2 Interview Guides

Interview guides were developed iteratively via stepwise refinement of previous interviews and codes [39]. The initial guides featured open questions and a rough guideline inspired by related work [55], while the final guideline was semi-structured with over 35 questions. Not all questions were asked during each interview, as the discussions were open-ended allowing probing and re-routing *ad hoc*. The guide was divided into five sections: (1) Privacy of Information, (2) Sharing with Others and Platforms, (3) Privacy Invasion and Protection, (4) Consequences and Reaction and (5) a miscellaneous exploration section.

### 3.3 Participants and Recruitment

Following ethical approval per institution policy, 55 participants were recruited. We recruited 45 Egyptian women, 20 from higher socioeconomic backgrounds (HSE) with a mean age of 27.7 ($\sigma = 1.19$, range: 25–30). Only 6 HSE participants were married, with prevalent occupations being engineer (9) and manager (4). 14 of the 25 women from lower socioeconomic backgrounds (LSE) were married. Their mean age was 33.4 ($\sigma = 11.8$, range: 18–53) and their most common occupations were nurse (18) and student (7). Sample sizes were selected to reach a level of theoretical satisfaction from each user group independently based on the conversations that were conducted [65]. In addition, 10 German women from high socioeconomic backgrounds (HSG) participants were recruited from university channels. (mean age = 22.5, $\sigma = 6.43$, range: 18–40) in order to observe how WEIRD perspectives contrasted with those of our Egyptian participants.

Recruitment proved challenging due to concerns around sharing that our participants highlighted in interviews. We utilized snowball convenience sampling for HSE participants on social media and LSE participants recruited via a gatekeeper at a local hospital. Both groups were properly screened against our criteria (women, heavy social media users). Despite this, there may be biases introduced by this sampling, and our results should be understood in this context. Criteria for inclusion in HSE or LSE were based on self-reported level of education and family income, however, targeted recruitment was necessary before filtration. Participants signed a consent form and could opt out at any time. Egyptian participants were incentivized with a gift card worth 200 Egyptian Pounds. Interviews were face-to-face, lasted between 45–90 min and were recorded, transcribed and anonymized by an independent transcriber who signed a non-disclosure form. Interviews in Egypt were conducted in Arabic, translated into English by the transcriber and verified by the transcriber and researcher, both native Arabic and fluent English speakers. Interviews in Germany were conducted in English with fluent participants. Participants were encouraged to express themselves openly and discuss their perceptions of privacy and information sharing, whether online or offline. They were not coerced or forced to answer questions.

## 4 Results

This section overviews codes, categories and relationships resulting from open and axial coding, before describing the themes which emerged as pain points.

## 4.1 Step 1: Open Coding and Categories

After some codes were altered, merged or removed throughout the process, a total of 199 codes remained. The following section will give an overview of the five most prominent categories and constituent codes before discussing axial coding.

The most prominent category, constructed from 179 statements, was **Facebook/Instagram Behavior**, encapsulating codes such as *Types and Frequency of posts (58)*, *Fake Names on Facebook (28)* and if social media could be used to infer *Personalities or Identities (14)*. The category **Sharing Style (163)** described how participants engaged in social media sharing, such as in *Arguments and Debate (36)*, who they *Shared information With (25)*, or if they engaged in *Minimal Sharing (17)*. Participants also discussed online or offline **Venues of Sharing (160)**, their *Reasoning for their Satisfaction with Different Communication Venues (38)*, use of different *Platforms (31)* and whether a venue was *Documented (40)*. Participants' **Motivation for Sharing (144)** encompassed codes including *Meaningful Social Interaction and Deepening Personal Connections (49)*, *Self Expression or Venting Negative Feelings (26)* and *Seeking Advice or Experience (22)*. Finally, the topic of **Cultural Norms (141)** was identified, such the *Evil Eye (108)*, *Collectivism (48)*, and how these norms could limit participants due to factors like *Restrictions from Male Figures (22)*, leading to some acting *Outside of the Cultural Norm (48)*.

## 4.2 Step 2: Axial Coding and Affinity Diagrams

Axial coding resulted in the identification of four major topics: *Culture*, *Personal Information Control and Loss*, *Sharing Attitude* and *Technical Features*. Each topic, their constituent codes, and the relationships between them are organized on a series of four axial maps, which we will now briefly overview before taking a deep dive into six key pain points we identified via selective coding.

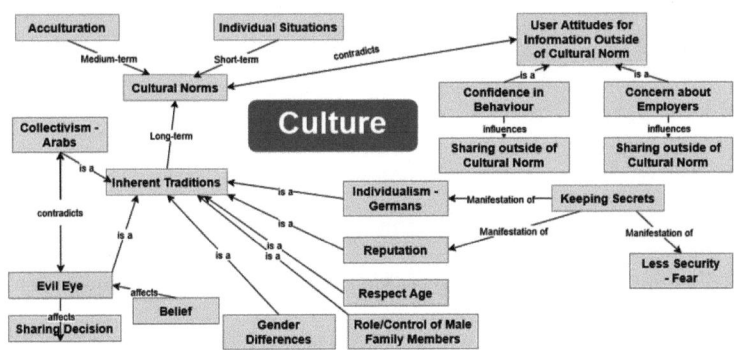

**Fig. 1.** Axial coding map of the major topic *Culture*.

**Axial Map - Culture.** This topic collated codes and categories that described how cultural factors and patriarchal power structures exerted control and provided competing pressures on women's sharing (see Fig. 1). The decision to adhere to these pressures or deny them was a prominent topic in every interview.

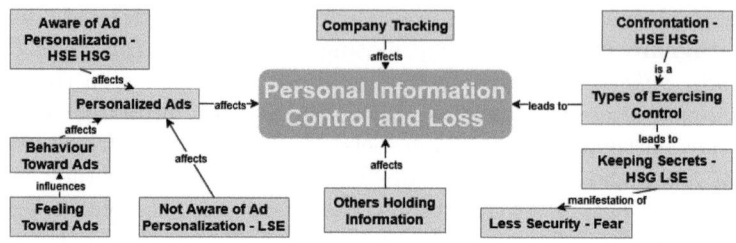

**Fig. 2.** Axial coding map of the major topic *Personal Information Control & Loss*.

**Axial Map - Personal Information Control and Loss.** This topic contained codes and categories related to control of personal information (see Fig. 2). This encompassed personalized adverts, documentation of private sharing and ways of exercising control, such as tag approvals, social contracts or secrets.

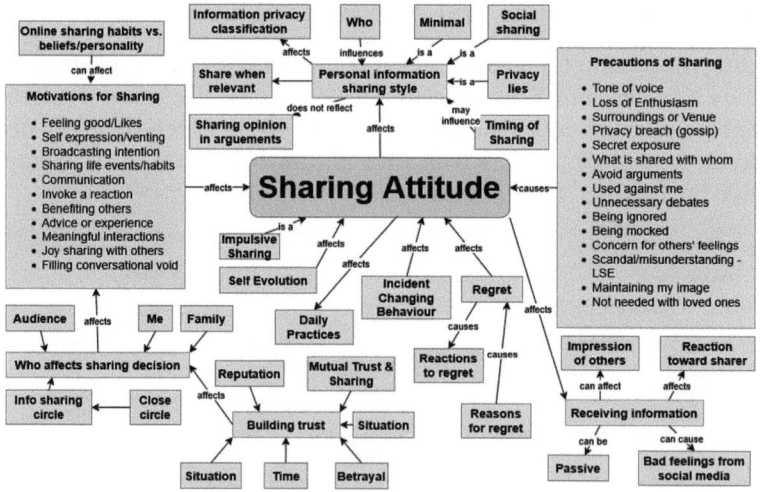

**Fig. 3.** Axial coding map of the major topic *Sharing Attitude*.

**Axial Map - Sharing Attitude.** These codes described participants' motivations for sharing, as well as their approach and attitudes. Participants described precautions of sharing that affected their attitude, such as the need to protect reputation (full list in Fig. 3). Motivations for sharing included seeking advice or experience or sharing life events. Regret had an important relationship with sharing style: participants regretted being either too open or too minimal, which in turn influenced their future sharing as they tried to find the right balance.

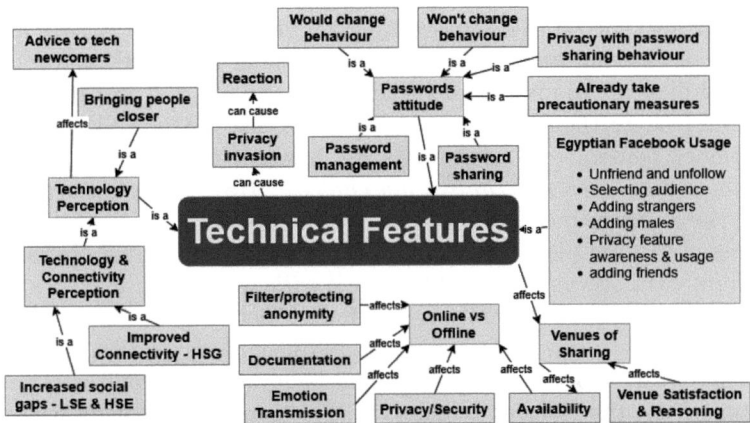

**Fig. 4.** Axial coding map of the major topic *Technical Features*.

**Axial Map - Technical Features.** Categories and codes about technical features revealed the biggest divide in Egyptian and German perspectives (see Fig. 4). Germans felt technology increased their connectivity, but Egyptians felt it increased social gaps with less meaningful interaction. However, Egyptians had high Facebook usage, in particular Facebook groups. Egyptians also described sharing passwords with family, colleagues or friends, in contrast to Germans.

### 4.3 Selective Coding - User's Pain Points

Next, we used selective coding to identify a series of seven descriptive themes as core user **pain points** for our participants when sharing information online.

**1. The In-Between.** Egyptian women were caught between the cultural values of *collectivism*, which encourages sharing, and the evil eye, reputation protection and male control, which discourage it. Navigating this conflict, especially online, was treacherous. HSE and LSE participants both felt pressured by cultural norms. For example, P314 described how the patriarch or their household controlled the ability of their daughters to share information: *"we didn't have internet until they got engaged. Their father is a bit strict. Only when they got engaged, did he allow the internet to be installed"*. Meanwhile, P210 (HSE) said their family was *"more of a trustworthy environment so, if we said something, we say it because we want to"*. P318 (LSE) disparaged this norm - *"I get annoyed from the Egyptian norms so, I don't care"*, but respected familial approval: *"my* mother and my father are OK with it and this is the most important thing. I don't care about what people will say".

*Restrictions from Male Figures* put another pressure on Egyptian women's sharing habits. This particularly impacted LSE women, such as P323 (LSE) who, after their friend shared pictures of eating during Ramadan, said: "*my husband is on my page so I can't share the pictures.*" As in prior work, the gender of a sharing recipient was also key [1] as discussed by P301 (LSE): "*if it is a work problem, I share with my husband because he has experience in this part*", and by P214: "I used to send pictures to my [female] friends without my veil and I was confident they wouldn't share them with anyone". Others, like P319 (LSE), felt they did not experience control: "*he never asks me where I went as he already knows where I go and he does not control my choices*". HSE women more commonly expressed the desire to increase self-liberation from older traditions, such as P213 who discussed sharing pictures of themselves wearing 'revealing' clothing: "*think I won't share with everyone but, I'll share it with people who are open-minded*".

The most complicated relationship found between these traditions was between arab collectivism and the *evil eye*. While collectivism encouraged Egyptians to share life events with others, some believed in the evil eye; that harm would result from the envy of others [18]. This impacted sharing decisions, for example by communicating in non-explicit terms [73]. There was a split in participant belief in the *evil eye*, from important cultural value to bygone superstition, but no clear divide between LSE and HSE participants. Overall, the decision of how an Egyptian woman will share information is complex and discretionary, when balancing *collectivism* with conflicting cultural values, such as protecting *reputation*, the *evil eye* and control by *older* or *male* family members.

**2. Data Privacy is Unresolved.** Most LSE participants were unaware of online data tracking and personalized adverts, resulting in these facts having no impact on their sharing behaviors, theoretically leaving them open to exploitation and uninformed sharing decisions. HSE users predominantly understood the current landscape of personal data tracking and personalized content, but were not comfortable with that status quo, developing a *negative reaction to personalized adverts*. While upset, some felt there was little to nothing they could do, while others chose to adopt a "nothing to hide" attitude. When asked about technology companies tracking data, P219 responded "*I don't think it's their right but, it's a fact and I made peace with it*", while P201 said: "*my data is not that valuable...let them track it.*" In general, despite a difference in awareness of data tracking across LSE and HSE participants, the issue remains unresolved.

**3. Privacy Invasions.** These were of great concern to participants, and many had experienced them. While Germans described mild consequences such as embarrassment, the pressure on Egyptian women was highlighted by the increasingly serious consequences for HSE and LSE participants, including loss of trust, ruined relationships, defamation and even divorce. LSE participants in particular had experience with attacks involving impersonation or defamation. Such experiences motivated changes to future behavior, such as P305 who reported "*I certainly made sure I'd log off properly from public computers*" or P304 who stated *"Yes, I always read every possible setting for privacy on social networks now"*. There are, however, inherent vulnerabilities to the venues (e.g., Facebook groups) and cultural practices (e.g., password sharing) that make the threat and heightened consequences of privacy invasions hard for individuals to prevent.

**4. Privacy Lies.** In the face of the consequences of privacy invasion, both HSE and LSE women described using privacy lies. When considered in the context of this statement by P310: *"we're an open book. What we say is what we do"*, this practice was an uncomfortable contradiction, particularly for LSE participants. Despite this, however, Egyptian women employed this strategy to engage in online communities or discussions without risk. P320 (LSE) used a second account to hide their identity from their family as *"if I post something political and I'm criticizing something and they may get upset because of this concept so, why would I cause myself problems?"* while P317 (LSE) highlighted the difference in online freedoms between men and women: *" We women use fake names, but men use their real names"*. The difference between HSE and LSE experiences regarding privacy lies was exemplified by an HSE expert interview with P201: *"It is also okay* [for HSE Egyptian women] *to share photos or have male friends on any platform, but for the lower socioeconomic status, it is not the case"*. The prevalence of privacy lies demonstrates the clash of cultural norms Egyptian women face and the need for a solution that allows comfort and security.

**5. Password Sharing.** Both HSE and LSE women commonly shared passwords with trusted family, friends and colleagues, in stark contrast to Germans. Rationale for this was described by P202: *"In our home there isn't such a thing that you have a password. Everyone at home should know your password because what do you have to hide from your family"*. This practice highlights the cultural value of the family unit in Egypt [64] and the difficulty that Egyptian women may have in sharing or expressing views that stray from those of their family.

Notably, participants were asked if they had considered that recipients of their messages may also share their passwords, potentially leading to individuals outside their trusted circle reading their messages. Some restricted the content they shared as a precautionary measure, and others would not change their behavior in light of this possibility. Most, however, similar to findings by [54], had not considered this, and many felt it would change their future sharing behavior. Given the potential damage unintended disclosure could do to one's reputation, particularly in Egyptian culture, the phenomenon of password sharing illustrates how the current platforms do not account for these users' circumstances, particularly as most senders are unaware of the password-sharing behavior of recipients.

**6. Facebook Groups.** Facebook groups, particularly women-only groups, were a crucial resource for many interviewees, facilitating relief, support, community and meaningful interactions. These groups host questions, discussions and sharing for women which fall outside of acceptable cultural sharing. P204 described this as seeking advice from an *"inner circle"*. In particular, these groups allowed sharing of photos which P302 described as "very sensitive in our culture", with several participants describing how photos of them engaging in 'unacceptable' fashion or activities led to conflict with male family members. Despite their importance, however, these reservoirs of discrete discussion are also major privacy risks. Trusted communication is impeded by the possibility of fake identities, defamatory screenshots or abusive actors. When discussing online groups, P205 commented: *"in a physical environment, I am more likely to share my opinion, because it is not documented."* This risk incentivizes privacy lies and motivates using other platforms like Instagram which are perceived as '*safer*'.

**7. Pressure to Share on Social Media.** Social media is a ubiquitous force in Egyptian society, pressuring women to share online and pushing them into conflict with cultural values. Social media generally incentivizes sharing via numerical engagement metrics [14], but our participants also felt motivated by other needs to share on social media, such as the desire for personal connection: *"if we're sharing interests like if someone is listening to the same type of music that I listen to so, we send things that we like to each other so, it's more of like an exchange platform. It brings people closer"* (P208). Social pressure was also a factor: *"there's like peer pressure so, you want to appear cool"* (P218). P201 was motivated to share on social media to curate their public image: *"I think that social media does affect my image and it helps me show the side of me that I want people to see"*, while P206 was motivated by supportive interactions: *"I was a bit scared of posting but, one day I remember OK, I'm proud of it, I can show myself [...] and I remember I grew because of that like my confidence grew as I was like this is who I am and people were 'like this is so pretty' and I really met a few people online and we messaged each other's since then".*

# 5 Discussion

Following our analysis, we discuss the most pertinent leaps in understanding this research contributes and offer a series of actionable design recommendations.

## 5.1 Cultural Conflicts

When compared to WEIRD users, Egyptian women are continually working to balance many cultural norms that impact their social media use. Strongly defined gender roles were particularly influential, despite Egyptian culture trending toward female empowerment [20] and men being viewed more as protectors of family [6] than oppressors. Awareness of male presence caused Egyptian women to reconsider and limit how or what they shared online to avoid the risk of conflict or familial defamation, echoing prior studies of Pakistani women also prioritizing familial reputation when choosing social engagements [48]. Offsetting this risk requires women to invest effort in identifying trustworthy confidants or spaces as outlets for potentially contentious sharing, with no guarantee of discretion.

Perhaps the most delicate balance for Egyptian women was adhering to the clashing cultural values of collectivism and the *evil eye*. Participants were unwilling to share achievements for fear of drawing envy but, felt that withholding them was dishonest and non-communal. Social media has exacerbated this conflict, incentivizing more frequent and public sharing without offering women culturally suitable privacy management tools. This conflict was strongest among LSE participants who adhered more to traditional cultural values, but even impacted HSE, who felt the norms were antiquated. For comparison, WEIRD worries about over-sharing personal information primarily regarding employment prospects. While some Egyptian participants acted outside their norms, doing so was still seen as a deliberate or rebellious decision. This highlights the extra tension these users must shoulder when using social media.

## 5.2 Sharing and Secrets

Egyptian women showed different sharing attitudes and behaviors to WEIRD women, often rooted in cultural exposure. For example, German participants were more accepting of privacy lies than Egyptian participants, which prior social media research suggests this difference may be rooted in how serious a sin lying is considered in Islamic culture [67]. Lying to platforms themselves, however, such as signing up with a false age or gender, was not viewed with the same disdain as lying to another person. Islamic teachings advise to keep one's plans a secret until they are fulfilled, to avoid drawing the *evil eye* or forfeiting one's desires, and this motivated secretive sharing styles from Egyptian participants, consistent with prior work [44]. Once events or plans were complete, however, collectivist Egyptian participants felt compelled to share them, despite wariness of the *evil eye*, as sharing information could be seen as a lie. Some adopt a 'share when asked' approach, but this conflicts with social media incentives. These behaviors contrast with WEIRD German women, who felt more able to share as they wished on social media. Germans withheld some matters as private and shared achievements without cultural pressure, although they also engaged in less casual interpersonal discussion than their Egyptian counterparts.

Social media is also hosting a growing socioeconomic divide in sharing agency. HSG and HSE participants made individual decisions to share, albeit perhaps only with trusted recipients. By contrast, only one LSE participant shared content on their own (using a fake identity), rather than deciding alongside family or friends. This echoes a trend from prior work: the influence of male control is fading from HSE society but remains much stronger for LSE women [71]. Egyptian women reported sharing more with friends and family and less in public than WEIRD users, similarly to other collectivist cultures such as China [41]. Both cultures place greater relative importance on relationships than individual success. While Chinese users were observed showing higher levels of trust online, Egyptian women (particularly LSE) contending with familial control and defamation risks work hard to identify trusted confidants and otherwise carefully cultivate or obfuscate their image by choosing what not to share [16]. Private data breaches can be especially harmful to these users, simultaneously shattering the trust that is painstakingly established and potentially damaging the reputation of a whole family. This can prompt offline discussion of sensitive topics, such as non/pre-marital relationships. Some women simply avoid sharing personal information in any documentable form to avoid repercussions, in line with prior theories suggesting communication modes are selected based on expected outcomes [10]. Generally the maintenance of personal data security, image and reputation, is a minefield Egyptian women must navigate when using social media platforms that incentivize open sharing to drive engagement.

### 5.3 Technology Use and Understanding

The specific requirements of Egyptian women prompted them to use novel workarounds within the constraints of social media platforms. Understanding these workarounds informs how designers could proactively support these users in future. Similar to Afnan et al. [3], users' navigation of online technology varied based on their demographic, but here primarily on socioeconomic basis rather than religiosity. HSE made common use of curated friend lists to limit sharing recipients to trusted friends or to exclude men. In addition, LSE considered adding males as friends or contacts on these platforms to be taboo and shameful, although most HSE women felt more able to do so. Participants also curated their audiences with private groups that host advice, advocacy, venting and sharing away from public viewing. These groups naturally become vulnerable to data breaches and abuses of power, however, as they are operated and moderated by other users rather than the platform itself. Screenshots of private conversations within these safe spaces can be extremely damaging. Some users went a step further to guarantee privacy by using fake names, profile pictures and personal information to make posts/messages that could not be traced back to them. We further observed overlap with the work of Haque et al. [27] who explored the usage of secret codes and languages to discuss taboo topics. Participants described substituting names or using "Franco Arab", Arabic words written in English letters as a popular method of communication for HSE youth. This creates a barrier with LSE users who do not frequently use this language. While effective, these strategies conflict with cultural values for truth and interpersonal trust, making them uncomfortable solutions. The fact that, despite this discomfort, some still utilize this strategy illustrates the difficulty faced by this group in the simultaneous search for self-expression and cultural compliance.

Compared to HSE and HSG users, LSE users are unaware of how their data is exploited by corporations and often feel helpless in the face of privacy invasions facilitated by technology. This lower technological awareness leads to increased vulnerability to attacks, such as phishing or hacking [36], and increased fear of future privacy invasions [55]. LSE participants did not feel social media platforms enabled them to understand these threats or protect themselves, and were less aware of how to exploit features like friend lists or groups, resulting in some favoring offline communication to guarantee security from snooping.

Generally, Egyptian participants felt technology had widened social gaps, replacing the more intimate modes of communication they shared with family and friends, while Germans instead felt technology had improved their connectivity with friends and family, a finding consistent with prior work [17]. A final way this lack of awareness of security threats manifested was in the practice of account sharing, which was exclusive to Egyptian participants. Collectivist participants would share accounts with their trusted family or friends, feeling they had nothing to hide. They did not always, however, consider that those they shared with may also share their accounts, leading to unwanted disclosure outside of trusted confidant circles. This behavior, which was habitually performed by Egyptian users as influenced by local cultural factors, can have unexpected consequences when the platform they use is not designed with these users in mind.

### 5.4 Social Media as Technocolonialism

Throughout this work, we observed a spectrum of attitudes and actions regarding sharing and privacy. While traditional cultural exposure caused LSE users to exhibit very different behaviors on social media platforms than WEIRD users, HSE users appeared to be experiencing a state of transition. While they were aware of Egyptian traditional values, they found themselves moving closer toward WEIRD behaviors, either by using workarounds or simply abandoning their cultural norms. This echoes a wider trend in Egyptian culture. Across all economic classes in Egypt, there exists a phenomenon called "*Okdet Alkhawaja*", or 'foreign complex', whereby Egyptians admire Western culture and view it as superior to local practices [49]. Class divide then plays a role, as HSE users are more likely to have learned English in school and visited Western countries, resulting in acculturation towards a "better" culture for HSE and the desire for LSE to climb the socioeconomic ladder away from their "worse" traditional cultural background. Ubiquitous social media platforms, built to accommodate the cultural values and expectations of WEIRD users, may be exacerbating this effect. By incentivizing sharing behavior that conflicts with local cultural norms, and lacking accommodations to combat the discomfort these conflicts cause, platforms could enact a form of Technocolonialism, eroding local traditions as they push Egyptian users to assimilate into the Westernized global experience offered. Our results echo prior works which raised concerns about potential or observed cultural pressure and homogenization driven by global social and digital media distribution [7,11]. Egypt is a culturally polarised nation whose upper classes populate a "westernized Egypt" that mixes both cultures and traditions, while lower classes are left to maintain traditional values. This is an illustrative case study of how Westernized technology can enact or worsen internal strife and cultural erosion across the globe, highlighting the importance of research which explores the experiences and perspectives of under-represented groups, enabling the localization of these ubiquitous platforms for different cultural groups.

## 6 Design Recommendations

In light of our findings, we provide six actionable design guidelines to protect and respect the privacy of Egyptian women and improve privacy options at large.

1. **Facilitate Selective Sharing** (Pain Point 1): We found that Egyptian women are stuck between their wish to share and their need to grapple with specific cultural consequences. Safe spaces that allow selective sharing are, therefore, a necessity to avoid sharing beyond a set of trusted confidants. While features exist to support this concept, such as sharing with a restricted friend list, selective sharing could be further facilitated using culturally appropriate preset lists, such as automatically generated female-only lists that aren't as vulnerable to abusive actors as female-only groups.
2. **Protect Online Support Communities** (Pain Point 6): We found Facebook groups to be vital safe spaces for sharing, but also found they can be fraught with unwanted disclosure and abuses of power. We propose further work exploring how these spaces can be systematically protected and better serve Egyptian women. For example, automatic obfuscation of screenshots, or detection of fake accounts. There have been positive steps in this direction, as the Facebook platform has added the ability to post anonymously with admin permission, which helps users share while controlling their disclosure.
3. **Reduce the Need for Privacy Lies** (Pain Point 4): Privacy lies are increasingly common for online data protection [59] but our participants found keeping these lies was uncomfortable, as they had to balance their moral compass, cultural norms and data protection. We propose that applications reduce the amount of personal data users must provide, such as not requiring surnames or only requiring the birth year rather than date for age checks. The ability to post anonymously to Facebook groups presents an alternative.
4. **Explore Social Media Measures of Successes** (Pain Point 7): Many of our participants reported a minimal or discrete sharing style in order to avoid the risks of cultural transgression, which resulted in them not achieving numerical measures of social media success (i.e., number of likes, shares and comments received). More inclusive and less quantitative measures of success should be explored that allow different styles of sharing to feel rewarding. For example, platforms could reward recommendations from friends, engaging in longer conversational interactions, which our participants found more meaningful, rather than short interactions (e.g., likes).
5. **Facilitate Control of Sensitive Data** (Pain Point 5): The cultural practice of password sharing opens the door to unwanted or unexpected sharing of sensitive content, but there are tools designers could apply to account for this phenomenon. Some applications already feature systems that automatically delete data, such as stories, after a set time. This could be repurposed to instead delete private messages after a certain time if either user engages in password sharing. The platforms could also facilitate automated warnings to users based on the level of password sharing their conversation partner engages in. Password sharing could be detected using either self-reporting or automatically detected via biometrics.
6. **Raising Data Exploitation Awareness via Design** (Pain Point 2): A major finding was LSE participants' almost uniform lack of awareness about how their data is being exploited on online platforms. Platforms had not succeeded in raising awareness for these users; they do not 'speak their language'

and rather just seek to receive their consent. Designers should leverage the interfaces they craft to raise awareness about privacy features and data usage to protect users, to avoid dissatisfaction that can lead to long-term user loss, especially as new platforms become available. For example, privacy policies could be designed with an interactive component, allowing users to explore and observe how their data is obtained and what personal data informs the targeted ads in their feeds. Some platforms have begun to address this issue, such as Facebook adding a link titled 'Why Am I Seeing This Ad?' to adverts, which links information and ad personalization settings. While HSE users who were aware of these policies were often still unsatisfied with the status quo, having awareness still gave them the opportunity to reduce or change their platform usage as they wished.

# 7 Conclusions

This paper presents a ground theory analysis of Egyptian women's experiences as they attempt to control their privacy on social media while managing the unique factors that impact sharing decisions. We interviewed 45 women from higher and lower socioeconomic groups in Egypt, and 10 women from a WEIRD country, Germany, to compare attitudes and experiences. Using axial coding to construct four core topics from 199 codes. Selective coding was used to identify six pain points these women experience when balancing the desire to share content in a collectivist, social media-enabled culture with cultural pressures such as the *evil eye*, patriarchy and reputation. We found these users make unusual use of social media platforms' technical features as workarounds to facilitate their ways of life but could be better supported if research and design focused more on their unique cultural experiences. Given this, we make a series of recommendations to inform the design of tailored and respectful social media experiences for this group. Furthermore, we use this as a case study to advocate for further research to investigate under-represented groups, as we found that forced compliance with Western cultural values via dominant Western social media platforms can enact a form of technocolonialism and lead to cultural erosion.

# References

1. Abokhodair, N., Vieweg, S.: Privacy & social media in the context of the Arab gulf. In: Proceedings of the 2016 ACM Conference on Designing Interactive Systems, pp. 672–683 (2016)
2. Abu-Lughod, L.: "Orientalism" and middle east feminist studies (2001)
3. Afnan, T., Zou, Y., Mustafa, M., Naseem, M., Schaub, F.: Aunties, strangers, and the FBI: online privacy concerns and experiences of Muslim-American women. In: Eighteenth Symposium on Usable Privacy and Security (SOUPS 2022), pp. 387–406 (2022)
4. Ahmed, S.I., Haque, M.R., Chen, J., Dell, N.: Digital privacy challenges with shared mobile phone use in Bangladesh. Proc. ACM Hum.-Comput. Interact. 1(CSCW), 1–20 (2017)

5. Assaad, R., Krafft, C.: Is free basic education in Egypt a reality or a myth? Int. J. Educ. Dev. **45**, 16–30 (2015)
6. Badran, M.: Islam, patriarchy, and feminism in the middle east. Trends Hist. **4**(1), 49–71 (1986)
7. Bansal, G.: Reprogramming the software of the mind: a new framework for cultural homogenization. J. Glob. Inf. Technol. Manag. **27**(1), 1–7 (2024)
8. Birge, C.: Enhancing research into usable privacy and security. In: Proceedings of the 27th ACM International Conference on Design of Communication, pp. 221–226 (2009)
9. Blank, G., Bolsover, G., Dubois, E.: A new privacy paradox: young people and privacy on social network sites. In: Prepared for the Annual Meeting of the American Sociological Association, vol. 17 (2014)
10. Blumler, J.G., Katz, E.: The uses of mass communications: current perspectives on gratifications research. Sage Ann. Rev. Commun. Res. Vol. III (1974)
11. Bourreau, M., Moreau, F., Wikström, P.: Does digitization lead to the homogenization of cultural content? Econ. Inq. **60**(1), 427–453 (2022)
12. Cavoukian, A., et al.: Privacy by design: The 7 foundational principles **5**, 12 (2009). Information and Privacy Commissioner of Ontario, Canada
13. Cihangir, S.: Gender specific honor codes and cultural change. Group Processes Intergroup Relat. **16**(3), 319–333 (2013)
14. Cingel, D.P., Carter, M.C., Krause, H.V.: Social media and self-esteem. Curr. Opin. Psychol. **45**, 101304 (2022)
15. Corbin, J., Strauss, A.: Basics of Qualitative Research: Techniques and Procedures for Developing Grounded Theory. Sage Publications (2014)
16. Costa, C., Torres, R.: To be or not to be, the importance of digital identity in the networked society. Educação, Formação & Tecnologias (Specia) (2011)
17. Darwish, A.F.E., Huber, G.L.: Individualism vs collectivism in different cultures: a cross-cultural study. Intercult. Educ. **14**(1), 47–56 (2003)
18. Elworthy, F.T.: The evil eye: an account of this ancient and widespread superstition. J. Murray (1895)
19. Feghali, E.: Arab cultural communication patterns. Int. J. Intercult. Relat. **21**(3), 345–378 (1997)
20. Fernea, R.: Gender, sexuality and patriarchy in modern Egypt. Critique Crit. Middle Eastern Stud. **12**(2), 141–153 (2003)
21. Gankovsky, Y.V.: The social structure of society in the People's Republic of Bangladesh. Asian Surv. **14**(3), 220–230 (1974)
22. Ghoshray, S.: Employer surveillance versus employee privacy: the new reality of social media and workplace privacy. N. Ky. L. Rev. **40**, 593 (2013)
23. Glaser, B.G.: Open coding descriptions. Grounded Theor. Rev. **15**(2), 108–110 (2016)
24. Glaser, B.G., Strauss, A.L.: The Discovery of Grounded Theory: Strategies for Qualitative Research. Routledge (2017)
25. Gruzd, A., Hernández-García, A.: Privacy concerns and self-disclosure in private and public uses of social media. Cyberpsychol. Behav. Soc. Netw. **21**(7), 418–428 (2018)
26. Hamid Nemati, J.D.W., Chow, A.: Privacy coping and information-sharing behaviors in social media: a comparison of Chinese and U.S. users. J. Glob. Inf. Technol. Manag. **17**(4), 228–249 (2014)

27. Haque, S.T., Saha, P., Rahman, M.S., Ahmed, S.I.: Of Ulti,'Hajano', and "Matachetar otanetak datam" exploring local practices of exchanging confidential and sensitive information in urban Bangladesh. Proc. ACM Hum.-Comput. Interact. **3**(CSCW), 1–22 (2019)
28. Henrich, J., Heine, S.J., Norenzayan, A.: Most people are not weird. Nature **466**(7302), 29 (2010)
29. Henrich, J., Heine, S.J., Norenzayan, A.: The weirdest people in the world? Behav. Brain Sci. **33**(2–3), 61–83 (2010)
30. Herath, T.B., Khanna, P., Ahmed, M.: Cybersecurity practices for social media users: a systematic literature review. J. Cybersecur. Priv. **2**(1), 1–18 (2022)
31. Hinnebusch, R.A.: Children of the elite: political attitudes of the westernized bourgeoisie in contemporary Egypt. Middle East J. **36**(4) (1982)
32. Hofstede, G.: Cultural dimensions in management and planning. Asia Pac. J. Manag. **1**(2), 81–99 (1984)
33. Hoodfar, H.: Return to the veil: personal strategy and public participation in Egypt. In: Working Women, pp. 115–136. Routledge (2005)
34. Howell, B.: Weird? Institutions and consumers' perceptions of artificial intelligence in 31 countries. AI & Soc., 1–23 (2025)
35. Internet World Stats: Internet world stats: usage and population statistics. https://www.internetworldstats.com/stats5.htm. Accessed 9 June 2022
36. Krishnan, S.: Exploitation of human trust, curiosity and ignorance by malware. arXiv preprint arXiv:2002.11805 (2020)
37. Kwet, M.: Digital colonialism: US empire and the new imperialism in the global south. Race Class **60**(4), 3–26 (2019)
38. Liao, Y.: Sharing personal health information on social media: balancing self-presentation and privacy. In: Proceedings of the 10th International Conference on Social Media and Society, pp. 194–204 (2019)
39. Lingard, L., Albert, M., Levinson, W.: Grounded theory, mixed methods, and action research. BMJ **337** (2008)
40. Linxen, S., Sturm, C., Brühlmann, F., Cassau, V., Opwis, K., Reinecke, K.: How WEIRD is CHI? In: Proceedings of the 2021 CHI Conference on Human Factors in Computing Systems, pp. 1–14 (2021)
41. Liu, J., Rau, P.L.P., Wendler, N.: Trust and online information-sharing in close relationships: a cross-cultural perspective. Behav. Inf. Technol. **34**(4), 363–374 (2015)
42. Löwstedt, A.: Do we still adhere to the norms of ancient Egypt? A comparison of Ptahhotep's communication ethics with current regulatory principles. Int. Commun. Gaz. **81**(6–8), 493–517 (2019)
43. Mitri, K.: In the gender war, was patriarchy victorious? Theoretical concepts of gender discrimination in patriarchal societies and solutions. J. ISSN **259**, 9953 (2022)
44. Mohd, K.B.: The integrity of fintech in information security from Islamic perspective. Editorial Board **61** (2019)
45. Molich, R.: Are usability evaluations reproducible? Interactions **25**(6), 82–85 (2018)
46. Mughazy, M.A.E.: Pragmatics of the evil eye in Egyptian Arabaic (2000)
47. Munyendo, C.W., Acar, Y., Aviv, A.J.: "In eighty percent of the cases, I select the password for them": security and privacy challenges, advice, and opportunities at cybercafes in Kenya. In: 2023 IEEE Symposium on Security and Privacy (SP), pp. 570–587. IEEE (2023)

48. Mustafa, M., Asad, A.M., Hassan, S., Haider, U., Durrani, Z., Krombholz, K.: Pakistani teens and privacy-how gender disparities, religion and family values impact the privacy design space. In: Proceedings of the 2023 ACM SIGSAC Conference on Computer and Communications Security (2023)
49. Naguib, A.M.: Ketabat fel mogtamaa wal iqtisad-masr (writings about society and economy-Egypt) (2006)
50. Norberg, P.A., Horne, D.R., Horne, D.A.: The privacy paradox: personal information disclosure intentions versus behaviors. J. Consum. Aff. **41**(1), 100–126 (2007)
51. Nourian, L., Shinohara, K., Tigwell, G.W.: Digital accessibility in Iran: an investigation focusing on Iran's national policies on accessibility and disability support. In: Proceedings of the 24th International ACM SIGACCESS Conference on Computers and Accessibility, pp. 1–5 (2022)
52. Pratt, N.: Popular culture, gender, and revolution in Egypt. J. Middle East Women's Stud. **17**(1), 137–146 (2021)
53. Riva, G., Wiederhold, B.K., Cipresso, P.: Psychology of social media: from technology to identity. In: The Psychology of Social Networking, vol. 1, pp. 4–14. De Gruyter Open Poland (2016)
54. Saleh, M., Elagroudy, P., Lukowicz, P., Sturm, C.: Ghost readers of the Nile: decrypting password sharing habits in chatting applications among Egyptian women. Proc. ACM Hum.-Comput. Interact. **8**(MHCI), 1–43 (2024)
55. Saleh, M., Khamis, M., Sturm, C.: What about My privacy, Habibi? In: Lamas, D., Loizides, F., Nacke, L., Petrie, H., Winckler, M., Zaphiris, P. (eds.) INTERACT 2019. LNCS, vol. 11748, pp. 67–87. Springer, Cham (2019). https://doi.org/10.1007/978-3-030-29387-1_5
56. Saltzer, J.H., Schroeder, M.D.: The protection of information in computer systems. Proc. IEEE **63**(9), 1278–1308 (1975)
57. Sambasivan, N., et al.: "They don't leave us alone anywhere we go" gender and digital abuse in south Asia. In: Proceedings of the 2019 CHI Conference on Human Factors in Computing Systems, pp. 1–14 (2019)
58. Sambasivan, N., et al.: "Privacy is not for Me, it's for those rich women": performative privacy practices on mobile phones by women in south Asia. In: Fourteenth Symposium on Usable Privacy and Security (SOUPS 2018), pp. 127–142 (2018)
59. Sannon, S., Bazarova, N.N., Cosley, D.: Privacy lies: understanding how, when, and why people lie to protect their privacy in multiple online contexts. In: Proceedings of the 2018 CHI Conference on Human Factors in Computing Systems, pp. 1–13 (2018)
60. Saravanakumar, K., Deepa, K., et al.: On privacy and security in social media–a comprehensive study. Procedia Comput. Sci. **78** (2016)
61. Sengupta, N., Subramanian, V., Mukhopadhyay, A., Scaria, A.G.: A global south perspective for ethical algorithms and the state. Nat. Mach. Intell. **5**(3), 184–186 (2023)
62. Sherman, L.E., Hernandez, L.M., Greenfield, P.M., Dapretto, M.: What the brain 'Likes': neural correlates of providing feedback on social media. Soc. Cogn. Affect. Neurosci. **13**(7), 699–707 (2018)
63. Stevens, P.B.: The pragmatics of street hustlers' English in Egypt. World Englishes **13**(1), 61–73 (1994)
64. Tarek Okasha, H.E., El-Ghamry, R.: Overview of the family structure in Egypt and its relation to psychiatry. Int. Rev. Psychiatry **24**(2) (2012). pMID: 22515467
65. Thomson, S.B.: Sample size and grounded theory. Thomson, SB (2010). Grounded theory-sample size. J. Adm. Gov. **5**(1), 45–52 (2010)

66. Turel, O., Qahri-Saremi, H.: Role of "likes" and "dislikes" in influencing user behaviors on social media. J. Manag. Inf. Syst. **41**(2), 515–545 (2024)
67. Usmani, S.A.A., Shahzad, M.: Sharing/spreading non-verified information on social media in the light of Quran and Sunnah. The Islamic Culture "As-Saqafat-ul Islamia" Al Thaqafa Al Islamiyah-Res. J.-Sheikh Zayed Islamic Centre University of Karachi **43** (2020)
68. Westin, A.F.: Privacy and freedom. Washington Lee Law Rev. **25**(1), 166 (1968)
69. Whitten, A., Tygar, J.D.: Why Johnny can't encrypt: a usability evaluation of PGP 5.0. In: USENIX Security Symposium, vol. 348, pp. 169–184 (1999)
70. Wu, P.F.: The privacy paradox in the context of online social networking: a self-identity perspective. J. Am. Soc. Inf. Sci. **70**(3), 207–217 (2019)
71. Yamin, S.: Challenging patriarchy: Pakistan, Egypt, and Turkey. In: Women Waging War and Peace: International Perspectives of Women's roles in Conflict and Post-Conflict Reconstruction (2011)
72. Yin, L., Wang, P., Nie, J., Guo, J., Feng, J., Lei, L.: Social networking sites addiction and FoMo: the mediating role of envy and the moderating role of need to belong. Curr. Psychol. **40**(8), 3879–3887 (2021)
73. Zakaria, N., Stanton, J.M., Sarkar-Barney, S.T.: Designing and implementing culturally-sensitive it applications: the interaction of culture values and privacy issues in the middle east. Inf. Technol. People (2003)

# Towards Design Guidelines for Safety Experience in Mobile Applications for Tourism

Minna Virkkula[1]( ), Siiri Paananen[2], and Jonna Häkkilä[2]

[1] Oulu University of Applied Sciences, Oulu, Finland
minna.virkkula@oamk.fi
[2] University of Lapland, Rovaniemi, Finland
{siiri.paananen,jonna.hakkila}@ulapland.fi

**Abstract.** In the service industry, ensuring user safety experience is a central factor in building trust and promoting positive user experiences. When designing mobile applications for outdoor and community activities, it is essential to prioritise awareness of safety as a part of social sustainability. In this paper, we present a set of design guidelines for enhancing the safety experience in mobile applications in the context of tourism, as well as an evaluation of the guidelines. A design thinking approach is utilised as a framework for understanding users' safety needs, reviewing key design theories, developing a set of safety guidelines, and evaluating and redefining guidelines. The collected data and prototypes were analysed by identifying common themes and key insights using qualitative content analysis. As a salient finding, we report how each guideline was applied and how different safety aspects were integrated into the application designs. The results of the study indicate that applying the guidelines enhanced the design process by maintaining the focus on users' safety aspects and integration in design. Community-based aspects were part of the guidelines with an emphasis on safety and social sustainability. Adapting psychological and social safety aspects into specific features proved to be the most challenging, highlighting the need to expand the guidelines with additional support and examples to improve clarity. This research adds value by highlighting users' safety in mobile application design by developing a novel set of five safety guidelines. Integrating these guidelines aims to enhance the user experience of safety and encourage social engagement.

**Keywords:** Design thinking · Design guidelines · Mobile application design · Safety design

## 1 Introduction

In today's service landscape, there is a growing need to focus on user safety and to shift the mindset towards sustainable practices in building trust and promoting positive user experiences. In the context of tourism, this means focusing on approaches that contribute to the overall satisfaction of visitors and maintaining responsible actions, both in user guidance and in promoting desired user behaviour.

Matiza and Slabbert [20] explore aspects of safety in tourism, highlighting both objective and subjective dimensions. They identify three main categories: psychological, physical, and social safety. Psychological safety includes the mental well-being of tourists influenced by awareness of risks and perceptions. Physical safety pertains to objective measures to minimise physical harm. Protection from social threats and fostering a sense of community are part of social safety, both objective and subjective concerns [20]. As mobile applications can support outdoor and community-based activities [1,3,11], users' safety needs to be considered on a subjective level and taking into account different themes [34], including the above-mentioned physical safety, psychological safety, and social aspects. Identifying these dimensions in design not only enhances the user experience but also emphasises the importance of safety as a part of social sustainability [23].

In this paper, the process is applied to develop safety guidelines for mobile applications, aiming to ensure they are simple and effective to use. The objective of the study was to utilise the Design Thinking process [7] in the application of customer safety aspects to formulate, specify, and refine design guidelines for mobile applications in an outdoor context. The development of the set of safety guidelines involves understanding customer safety concerns, identifying key theories, generating ideas, developing prototypes, and gathering feedback to refine the guidelines.

The research phase reviewed best practices in user experience (UX) guidelines [31], design heuristics [24], and the latest trends [26] in mobile design. Three researchers created the initial safety guidelines, focusing on simplicity. Interaction design students (n = 15) from the University of Lapland, Finland, designed a mobile application following these guidelines. Four high-fidelity prototypes were developed for an application that allows users to plan outdoor activities and receive feedback on trail conditions. Students evaluated the guidelines through a survey, and the guidelines were refined based on the analysis of feedback. In addition, two researchers examined the UI prototypes and analysed their content against the guidelines using qualitative content analysis.

As a key finding, we report how each guideline was applied and how different safety aspects were integrated into the design. The guidelines helped the designers to maintain the focus on the primary functionalities of safety. Psychological and social safety aspects were reported as the most challenging to apply, indicating that additional support is needed. Examples were requested to improve the clarity of the guidelines. This research contributes to recognising customers' safety aspects and developing a novel set of five practical guidelines for designing safety experiences in mobile applications. They provide a user-focused approach and guidance to help design teams prioritise safety and social sustainability in mobile apps for outdoor and community-based activities.

Firstly, the paper provides an overview of recent literature on safety and UX design for mobile applications. Secondly, a set of five design guidelines is presented for safety and utilised in design tasks through which the usage of the guidelines is evaluated. In the results section, we report on the application of the guidelines in the design process and the perceived benefits and limitations of usage.

## 2 Related Work

### 2.1 Background and Context of the Study

There is an increasing need to emphasise the importance of the behaviour of tourists with respect to sustainability. Sustainable tourism is building on established approaches of regulation and development control, but also seeking innovative methods to identify ways to secure positive benefits [2]. In addition, awareness of the need for sustainability actions is increasing [33]. Sajid et al. [29] have reported how awareness of positive consequences on tourists' environmentally responsible intention was found to be stronger than that of negative consequences, highlighting the importance of showing positive consequences of sustainability actions. Consequences refer to the environmental outcomes of tourist behaviour, including positive ones such as supporting conservation and negative ones like contributing to pollution. Also, the results of the study conducted on tourists in Kuala Lumpur indicated that sociocultural and technological sustainability impacted tourists' satisfaction and revisit intention both directly and indirectly [28].

Sustainability factors are especially relevant for our research and local hikers on trails in order to increase awareness of safety and sustainable practices. The study by Zhang et al. [37] examines various sustainable factors that influence tourists' intentions to engage environmentally responsibly when visiting forest trails. The findings emphasise the importance of awareness, education, and community involvement in encouraging behaviours that protect the environment and hikers using these trails. By fostering a culture of safety and responsibility, the overall experience can be enhanced [37]. When comparing hikers and tourists, hikers have been reported to have more perceived connections to nature, and thus, their pro-environmental attitude was stronger [38]. Integrating sustainability targets involves educating hikers about following rules and focusing on personal safety. Adhering to rules helps ensure that outdoor activities are safe for everyone and that the environment remains undamaged. Moreover, practices aimed at minimising environmental impact and fostering a sense of community among trail users enhance both safety and sustainability [37].

The research by Shale et al. [30] examines the connection between tourist safety and their overall experience at attractions and accommodations. The study aims to identify gaps between these two aspects and how safety can enhance the tourist experience. Results suggest feeling unsafe impacts enjoyment and satisfaction, even if actual safety measures are in place. Being informed and prepared leads to positive experiences, and understanding local customs and conditions can enhance the experience.

## 2.2 Tourism and Mobile Applications

User experience, going beyond usability, includes both the hedonic and pragmatic sides when interacting with a system [13]. Research on tourism and mobile application design prioritises user experience by presenting intuitive user interfaces and personalised content, enhancing the experience to make applications more inviting for users. Applications integrate with smart technologies, for example, the Internet of Things (IoT), to provide real-time information related to cities and travel [36]. Some applications promote sustainable aspects of tourism to environmentally conscious travel. In addition, technologies such as VR and AR are increasingly used in pre-planning and onsite information. Artificial intelligence (AI) and machine learning algorithms are used to discover personalised preferences, for example, activities to enhance the travel experience [5]. Safety and interaction in UX design are seen as a continuous experience and interaction with the technology, involving periods before and after [12]. This approach includes concepts such as expectations, features that offer value, and emotions. Integrating safety features into the design targets to meet the needs of the users and to ensure a positive experience.

The outdoors use context has gained more attention during the past years among HCI research [16,22]. Jones et al. discuss the design for outdoor recreation and emphasise the engagement with place, time, and community [15]. Seeking for solitude has frequently been reported as an important part of nature experience [15,27], even up to designing technology to deliberately avoid people [27]. Shrestha et al. [32] focus on the development of a mobile application designed to improve the safety and security of tourists. The paper outlines key design requirements for application design, including authentication and data privacy. The study also highlights the importance of real-time location tracking and emergency alert functionalities. It also emphasises the need for a user-friendly interface that is easy to use even in stressful situations.

Research related to the safety and use of mobile applications when hiking or skiing outdoors has brought up themes such as being aware of friends when separated on the mountains [14], and using crowd-sourcing for reporting maintenance requirements along hiking routes [3,18]. The research conducted in warm and humid environmental conditions focuses on investigating how the design of mobile applications can enhance safety, especially by addressing health risks with heat exposure and environmental hazards. The designed mobile solution plays a role in developing smarter tourism ecosystems by integrating real-time data, an intuitive user interface, and an emergency assistance feature [4]. Despite the growing amount of prior research in HCI outdoors, the studies have focused mostly on case studies when addressing safety themes. So far, the research has yet to consider holistic UX design and design guideline development for safety in the context of outdoor tourism mobile applications.

## 3 Methodology

### 3.1 Design Thinking Approach

The method used in this study to create safety guidelines followed a Design Thinking process and its phases. Design thinking is a user-centered approach to problem-solving that consists of five stages: empathise, define, ideate, prototype, and test [21]. Through these phases, as depicted in Fig. 1, the study aims to develop a comprehensive set of safety guidelines for mobile applications. The first stage focuses on understanding customers' safety concerns in application settings. This involves identifying and reviewing key theories relevant to designing guidelines and safety. In the second stage, ideas are generated to develop safety guidelines. This stage first aims to produce a wide range of potential solutions before final design guidelines are prioritised for the next phase. The next stage involves prioritising the guidelines using research triangulation as a method. The design task of developing initial prototypes of the application while utilising the guidelines in the design was part of the testing phase. Prototypes visualise and concretise the ideas used in UI designs. The feedback on the usage of the guidelines was included in the evaluation, and afterwards, the guidelines were refined accordingly. The design thinking process emphasises users' perspective and provides structure and experimentation, aiming to lead to meaningful solutions [6,17].

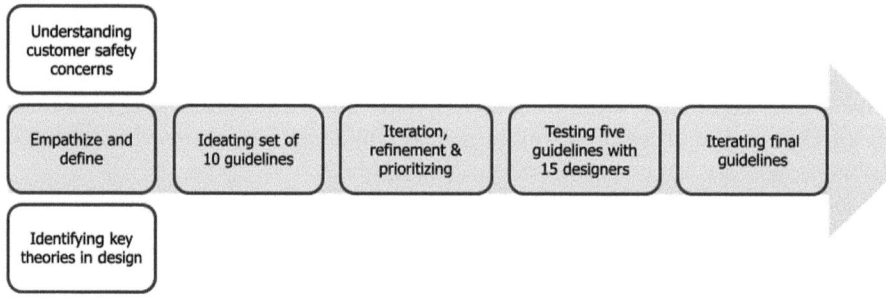

**Fig. 1.** The overall design process of developing the guidelines.

### 3.2 Key Theories Applied in UX Guideline Design

The research phase involved reviewing best practices of user experience guidelines and studying recent trends in the design of mobile applications. Furthermore, guidelines are linked to users' safety perception, and this perspective should be taken into account in their design.

Generally, key theories in designing mobile applications focus on design principles, usability, and the challenges of understanding user perception. Nielsen's [24] heuristics provides a foundation set of principles for designing user-friendly interfaces. Shneiderman's [31] eight golden rules are vital for designing effective user interfaces (UI). Similarities in these theories are that they both emphasise the importance of consistency in aiding users in predicting and comprehending the interface. They take different users into account in design while highlighting the need for users to feel in control and navigate freely. Furthermore, they bring in simple and informative feedback and reduce the cognitive load of users by providing clear and concise information [24,31]. The study of Garcia-Lopez et al. (2021) is grounded in identifying common usability issues and proposing practical usability recommendations for mobile tourist applications. They redefine further general heuristics that are fundamentally important for user-centric design [10].

The document by SINTEF [25] offers practical advice for developing user-friendly mobile applications, addressing critical issues such as screen space utilisation, interaction mechanisms, and overall design. In contrast, the paper by Fang et al. [8] focuses on user-centered design principles, discussing usability and user perception issues across various mobile platforms. Generally, guidelines cover design issues related to input, display, navigation, and feedback. The latest research related to UX design in mobile applications has focused on several key areas, such as improving user experience, engaging the user, and considering recent trends that enhance the aforementioned aspects [19]. Generally, the quality of the user experience design fails to follow design principles and optimise performance.

Suggestions to improve designs in mobile applications include recommendations highlighting personalisation features, adopting mobile-first design principles, having continuous feedback loops triggered by the user, and incorporating emerging technologies in a user-friendly manner [26]. These principles and trends have demonstrated the ability to enhance user engagement and satisfaction.

### 3.3 Ideation of User Experience Guidelines for Safety

Design principles, current trends in mobile design, and user safety aspects are crucial in developing effective mobile applications for the outdoors. These principles are the basis for the creation of user experience guidelines that emphasise safety. Consistency in maintenance activities and environmental stewardship relates to the consistent use of indications and information retrieval. Ensuring system status visibility helps users stay informed regarding the latest safety updates and trail conditions. User control, for example, reporting and editing trail issues, combined with informative feedback, ensures the application remains up-to-date.

According to Okonkwo [26], trends in mobile design include personalisation, mobile-first design principles, and emerging technologies. Design for safety should incorporate these trends to enhance the user experience. Additionally, guidelines must address users' psychological, physical, and social safety, as highlighted by [20]. Understanding users' safety concerns is essential for user-centered design [34,35]. Previous studies indicate that prioritising safety aspects fosters trust and a positive experience. Psychological safety can be achieved by managing cognitive load, physical safety by providing necessary information and real-time feedback, and social safety through sharing and community-based features. Comprehensive safety considerations ultimately enhance user experience and application effectiveness.

The research through design methodology, implemented through project work, serves as the foundation of the design knowledge related to the user safety experience. The initial set of various and detailed level guidelines was proposed among researchers. Subsequently, three researchers used researcher triangulation to create the prioritised version of the safety guidelines, focusing on simplicity in mobile application designs. The authors comprise a senior lecturer in UX design with over 15 years in UX and service design, a university teacher with a decade of experience in interaction and UX design, and a professor of industrial design with extensive leadership in UX research across academia and industry. All authors reviewed the guidelines, while the first and second authors evaluated the UI designs.

### 3.4 Applying Design Guidelines in Practice

After finalising and contributing the guidelines, interaction design master-level students (n = 15) from the University of Lapland were tasked to design a mobile application using these guidelines as a framework during the course assignment. The course cohort comprised both local students from Finland (6) and exchange students from Europe and Asia (9). Four student groups each designed a prototype of the application that enables users to plan outdoor activities, provide feedback on trail conditions, and contribute to environmental and social good actions. The design process included collecting background information, competitor analysis, interviews with users, and reviewing the high-fidelity prototypes of the application with other groups and researchers. After completing the assignment and the final presentation of the application, each student evaluated the use of design guidelines through a survey, providing feedback on the guidelines' clarity and usefulness in application design. Collected data was analysed by identifying common themes and key insights, and used to refine and improve guidelines. In addition, two researchers reviewed the UI prototypes and reflected on their content in relation to the guidelines in qualitative content analysis.

## 4 Results

Overall, based on the analysis of the questionnaire, the design guidelines were seen as clear, helpful, and key to maintaining focus in the design process and organising content, ensuring that all necessary aspects of safety were taken into account in the design of the application. Groups described the goals of the application in various ways, including feeling safe in outdoor activities, encouraging participation in trail maintenance, having information related to preparedness and sustainable practices, engaging users with rewards, and being part of the community.

## 4.1 Insights of the Guidelines' Usage

Based on experiences in the design task and responses collected from the questionnaires on guidelines, many of the participants found them clear and easy to understand. The average score for the question related to understanding the guidelines was 4.1 out of 5 on the Likert scale (1 = strongly disagree, 5 = strongly agree), with responses in this sample ranging from 3 to 5. This indicates that simple guidelines assisted in focusing on the essentials, what needed to be included and what kind of features to focus on during the design process as the participants commented: *"The design guidelines were quite easy to apply and helped to identify what should be focused on while designing the app"* (P10), *"The guidelines were pretty clear and helpful"* (P8).

The average response to the question "The guidelines were useful in the design task" was 4.2 on the same Likert scale (responses also ranged from 3 to 5). Additional comments highlighted that guidelines were used in benchmarking and when designing information architecture for the application. Also, having guidelines available throughout the whole process helped keep safety aspects in focus and integrate needed aspects into the design. This helped in brainstorming, idea generation, and seeing the bigger picture when having background information from the beginning of the project. Comments from participants about applying guidelines were: *"They made it easier to focus on the main things on the app. It is easy to start making lots of cool-looking things, but forget the most important parts"* (P4). *"There was a lot to consider in the application design, but the clear DGs helped us progress through the project without losing our way"* (P8). *"I think that, yes, it was easy to apply. Guidelines helped in seeing the bigger picture of the project instead of making everything from scratch"* (P9). *"All the time when we designed things for the app, we discussed how this feature affects physical or psychological safety"* (P12). Moreover, the feedback included the idea of viewing the design task from different perspectives based on guidelines that enrich the process.

In addition, specific guidelines on environmental care and safety provided a solid foundation for developing sustainable and safety-focused characteristics. These functions were brought to the main view (Fig. 2), enabling their efficient use. An open-ended question that invited detailed responses related to parts that were particularly difficult to understand or to apply in the design guidelines got mainly responses to social and psychological aspects of safety. Addressing psychological safety was seen as challenging in translating ideas into specific features and making applications comfortable to use. As an issue related to applying social aspects, it was not easy because they wanted to have a simple, easy-to-use application. Some also felt that social sustainability as part of safety should have been considered more broadly in design. Here are examples of collected feedback that brought up these issues: *"Addressing psychological safety was the hardest one for me personally. I tried to apply it by making the app as simple to use as possible"* (P4). *"Maybe the social side was the hardest to apply since our app left a lot of social aspects out to keep the usage as fast as possible (no account option to discuss or comment with other users)"* (P5). Furthermore, other men-

**Fig. 2.** Examples of quick functions and dynamic icons on the map in the groups' UI designs

tioned difficulties were related to clarifying the target audience (tourist/local), balancing user group needs, and understanding administrative roles. However, some found the guidelines clear and did not encounter significant issues.

In general, based on the analysis of the questionnaire, the guidelines were applied throughout the application design. The guideline used most frequently in application design was 'Encouraging trail maintenance and environmental stewardship', which was a primary focus of application design. The prototypes had similarities in features due to the descriptions of the guidelines above. Addressing psychological safety and social factors posed more challenges due to the complexity of integrating these aspects into a simple application. Social factors were also considered to enhance user interaction and community engagement linked to community contributions via feedback and rewards related to reports.

In addition to the survey responses, two researchers reviewed the prototypes of the groups and compared them to the guidelines, conducting qualitative content analysis. The following results are based on the expert evaluation of the prototypes. The UI layouts incorporate features focused on safety and sustainability, highlighting users' need to feel safe in outdoor activities and encouraging participation in maintaining trail conditions and being aware and prepared to explore trails and nature safely. Table 1 presents the key features concerning different safety aspects, assembled from application designs of student groups.

Safety in outdoor activities is enhanced in designs through quick functions and dynamic icons on the map, as well as trails without issues. To encourage participation in trail maintenance and reporting, the UI design includes features

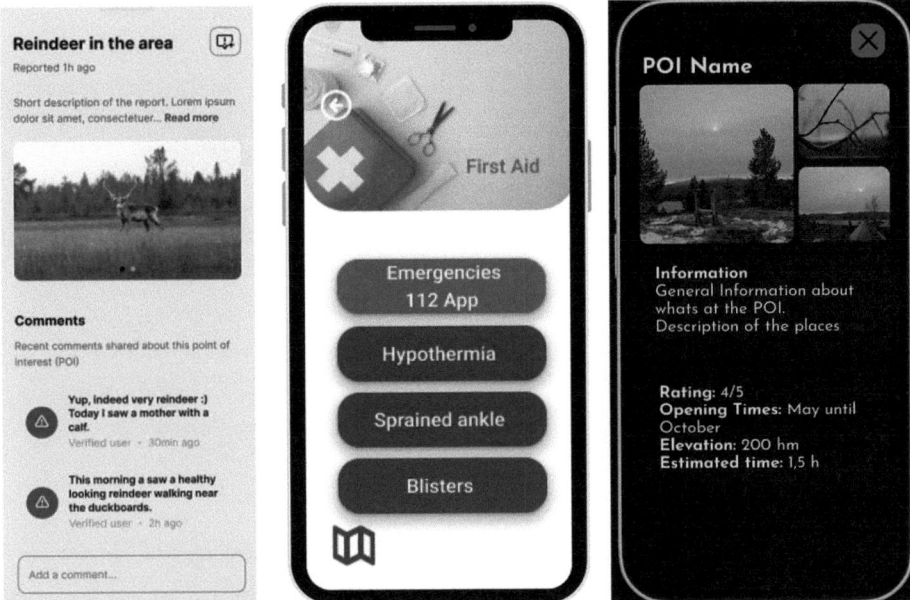

**Fig. 3.** Examples of the features applied in the UI designs related to safety and trail conditions.

to report various issues such as littering, things to be fixed, unusual sights, and warnings with varying levels of urgency. Information related to preparedness is provided, covering topics related to first aid, weather, coordinates, and information on facility details. Visual examples of application features (Fig. 2) show the domains of physical, psychological, and social safety of the designs. A clear user interface with quick functions, such as an emergency button, is related to physical safety, allowing quick action. They also connect to psychological safety by minimising cognitive load and improving the user's sense of control. Visual indicators of dangerous conditions, facilities, and trail difficulty provide support and serve a dual function; they assist in physical planning and reduce psychological stress by setting realistic expectations. Furthermore, Fig. 3 shows examples of different features applied in UI designs based on guidelines. Instructions for emergency preparedness provide users with actionable knowledge that supports both physical readiness and psychological reassurance. Lastly, features that enable the sharing of points of interest and user-generated comments foster the building of social trust and community engagement. Social sustainability is also promoted by informing users about everyman's rights and having a rulebook for nature etiquette that might be unfamiliar to visitors. Users are involved in action through rewards and positive feedback, fostering a sense of community by allowing them to see and discuss others' comments, as demonstrated in Table 1.

**Table 1.** Usage of the guidelines in application design

| Guideline | Design Focus | Description of used feature |
|---|---|---|
| 1. Encouraging trail maintenance | Primary focus | Users can report issues and points of interest<br>Achievements reward users for exploring<br>Feedback encourages detailed reports |
| 2. Up-to-date safety info | Primary focus | Quick reporting for trail issues<br>Real-time and dynamic notifications on conditions<br>Users can check and update reports |
| 3. Physical safety | Moderate use | Emergency button for quick access<br>Report button is always accessible<br>Information on weather, difficulty, and best visiting times<br>Notifications inform users about issues |
| 4. Psychological safety | Moderate use | Safety features include emergency contacts<br>Instructions for emergency preparedness<br>Users can share reports for improved safety<br>Design prioritises ease of use |
| 5. Social factors | Moderate use | User reviews build trust in high-ranked trails<br>Community interaction via shared reports and comments<br>Feedback and rewards encourage engagement<br>Moderation by admins is part of the design |

## 4.2 Implication of the Results

The guidelines were generally seen to be clear and helpful in the design process. The improvement ideas collected from the questionnaires indicate that some guidelines could benefit from allowing space for alternative features. Some guidelines, on the other hand, should have more detailed descriptions and a broader understanding of their purpose and context of use by having practical examples. The following guidelines proposal for improvement has been formed based on feedback received regarding their usage and reflection on UIs by researchers as a third iteration round. Survey quotes illustrate the feedback; *"Maybe a little explanation, for example, what addressing physiological safety means, maybe an example"* (P5). *"The design guidelines could be improved by providing more specific examples for each guideline, making them easier to apply in real-world scenarios"* (P13). *"In some cases, the guidelines were a bit too specific, more like a solution"* (P1).

**Overly Specific Guidelines.** In summary, some guidelines should offer more flexibility in order to encourage creativity, according to some participants, and not propose the exact solution. The *"Encouraging trail maintenance and environmental stewardship"* guideline was considered too prescriptive in how users should report and maintain trails, potentially limiting novel approaches. Additionally, being up-to-date with safety factors on the trail is too limited, and there should be more room for alternative features to ensure safety. An improvement idea for these is to present these guidelines as a flexible tool rather than a finished solution in order to encourage designers to explore creative ideation of features while keeping safety in mind.

**Incorporate Examples of the Guidelines.** Many participants suggested including examples of each guideline to make them easier to apply and more actionable. In order to improve this, general advice is needed for each guideline to understand the usage of the guideline better.

**Clarification of Contextual Understanding.** Include additional context-based information, for example, *"What does safety as a part of social sustainability mean?"* to clarify the concept and deepen the knowledge about the subject. This highlights the importance of gathering enough background information about the topic and the area designers are working on. Improvement ideas for the future could be having background information on user safety experience and sustainable practices.

**Best Practices and Real-World Application.** Deepening knowledge around underlying concepts and desired real-world examples was mentioned a few times. This was especially related to social safety guidelines, which were a bit challenging to understand. An improvement idea was to include a new guideline for the desired scenario of usage and apply the guidelines to real-world situations by offering best practices and specific examples.

**Improved Guidelines for Designing a Safe Experience in Mobile Applications**

1. **Promote user engagement in trail maintenance and environmental care**
   - Include ways for users to participate.
   - Include responses related to user interactions, visual clues, and notifications.
   - Consider using gamification, such as rewards and achievements.
2. **Ensure user access to the latest safety information on trails**
   - Provide a mechanism for real-time updates on the trail and other conditions.
   - Include safety tips, resources, and emergency information.
3. **Enhance physical safety and well-being**
   - Provide quick access to information related to emergency contacts.
   - Support physical well-being by minimising the risks of injuries.
   - Consider having information on preparation for the activity.
   - Offer information on trails, trail difficulty, conditions, infrastructure, and services.

4. **Promote users' psychological safety and comfort**
   - Offer clear and concise information to support decision-making.
   - Provide clear instructions for emergencies to reduce cognitive load.
   - Provide information on encountering unfamiliar situations, environments, and nature.
   - Encourage transparent communication and feedback.
5. **Foster social safety through trust and community engagement**
   - Encourage social interactions and collaborations among users and the community.
   - Include reviews and shared experiences.
   - Consider users' diverse backgrounds in the design.

In general, utilising the provided guidelines was considered valuable and was widely utilised in the design process. They were particularly beneficial in keeping users up-to-date with safety factors and increasing awareness, promoting trail maintenance and environmental stewardship, and engaging the community.

## 5 Discussion

Existing research on design guidelines for safety has been mainly targeted for the design process in health and patient safety, increasing the importance of addressing safety in the predesign of facilities [9]. There is a lack of research in the area of user experience related to safety in mobile applications. Addressing this subject is the focus of this study, aiming to improve the overall experience and promote sustainable practices.

The purpose of the study was to create a set of safety guidelines for design and evaluate the usage of the guidelines in the design process of outdoor applications. Additionally, we propose further improvements to enhance the application of guidelines in design. The goal of the designed UI prototypes in this study included focusing on safety aspects, creating a simple and effective user interface, and fostering user engagement with social interaction.

By integrating safety aspects into design guidelines for mobile applications, we must consider the physical, psychological, and social aspects from the user's perspective. Physical safety and users' well-being were part of the application concepts by minimising physical risks, enabling quick response, providing guidance, and preparing for physical situations. Psychological safety includes reducing uncertainty and stress, and supporting decision making. A user-friendly interface reduces the user's cognitive load by easy access and keeping users informed at all times, which can be highly appropriate in an outdoor setting. Other aspects include up-to-date and transparent information and precise instructions in unexpected or unfamiliar situations, environments, and nature. Moreover, in this context, mobile-first principles apply to ensure that the application is straightforward to use. Social aspects include creating a sense of community, enabling interaction, and building trust. The guideline for social safety was the least used and most difficult concept for participants to understand. Encouraging social interaction and connecting users with locals sharing experiences fosters user engagement and creates a sense of belonging to the community in unfamiliar situations. Features include user-generated reviews and mechanisms to participate and provide support. Taking inclusivity into account, incorporating positive reinforcement and feedback into design fosters trust and sustained user engagement. To improve UI designs, a continuous feedback loop and a focus on personalisation [26] are essential aspects of designs and should be examined more closely to determine how they can be incorporated into safety guidelines. Simplicity, efficiency, and consistency are common principles in UI design [24]. Taking these into account in design and emphasising consistency enhances the overall safety experience and creates a more predictable environment for those involved.

The established set of safety guidelines is based on the Design Thinking process and was developed in collaboration with design students from the University of Lapland. The paper presents a first-stage study to propose and evaluate safety design guidelines from the design process point of view. The early maturity of the prototypes guided the testing to evaluate the application features and user experience at a higher level, addressing safety as a design objective rather than a matter of usability. However, the entire design process should be applied; user interaction with designed prototypes and usability testing are lacking in the process. This phase will provide insight into optimising the overall experience and exploring how designs meet user needs. This approach aids in identifying potential issues in the application of safety guidelines and in gathering comprehensive feedback on the areas for improvement, based on real-world experiences.

The study indicates that by utilising these guidelines, designers can focus on UI design that includes user safety expectations and needs in mobile applications. Implementing a set of safety guidelines leads to improving safety practices and community actions as a part of sustainability.

## 6 Conclusion

The findings of the study suggest that implementing a defined set of safety design guidelines enhances the design process by maintaining a focus on safety aspects. Moreover, guidelines were helpful in ensuring that necessary safety considerations were integrated into the whole application design. Design guidelines prioritise safety and sustainability, with a strong emphasis on community-based aspects. However, results indicate that adapting psychological safety into specific features of the application presented challenges for participants. Additionally, including social safety aspects was demanding due to the preference for a simple and easy-to-use application.

In the future, research should investigate how the set of safety guidelines would function across the stages of implementation and in real-world settings. This examination aims to understand the adaptability of the safety guidelines and to ensure that the guidelines are continuously refined and beneficial within different contexts, enhancing overall safety and user experience.

The design of safety is closely linked to social sustainability. In the future, guidelines can be expanded further to include user safety experience and sustainable practices related to, for example, company engagement and local community well-being in ensuring overall customer satisfaction. This set of design guidelines focuses on ensuring user safety while fostering environmental responsibility and creating a collaborative community around outdoor exploration. By utilising safety guidelines in design, the application becomes a comprehensive tool for considering both the needs and preferences of personal safety, as well as environmental stewardship.

**Acknowledgments.** This work has received support from the projects 'Regenerative services and local collaboration as enablers of attractiveness in rural areas (EHOMPI)', implemented in collaboration with Oulu University of Applied Sciences and the University of Lapland. The project is co-funded by the European Agricultural Fund for Rural Development, and the funding is granted by the Centre for Economic Development, Transport and the Environment of Northern Ostrobothnia. 'Xstory - Lapland narratives with experience technologies', co-funded by ERDF and the Regional Council of Lapland. We thank the students on the Interaction Design course for their contribution.

**Disclosure of Interests.** The authors have no competing interests to declare that are relevant to the content of this article.

# References

1. Anderson, Z., Jones, M.: Rethinking the role of a mobile computing in recreational hiking. In: McCrickard, D.S., Jones, M., Stelter, T.L. (eds.) HCI Outdoors: Theory, Design, Methods and Applications. HIS, pp. 291–305. Springer, Cham (2020). https://doi.org/10.1007/978-3-030-45289-6_16
2. Bramwell, B., and, B.L.: Towards innovation in sustainable tourism research? J. Sustain. Tourism **20**(1), 1–7 (2012). https://doi.org/10.1080/09669582.2011.641559
3. Cheverst, K.W.J., Gregory, I.N., Turner, H.: Encouraging visitor engagement and reflection with the landscape of the English lake district: exploring the potential of locative media. In: International Workshop on 'Unobtrusive User Experiences with Technology in Nature', pp. 1–5 (2016)
4. Dinkoksung, S., et al.: A mobile solution for enhancing tourist safety in warm and humid destinations. Appl. Sci. **13**(15) (2023). https://doi.org/10.3390/app13159027
5. Dorcic, J., Komsic, J., Markovic, S.: Mobile technologies and applications towards smart tourism-state of the art. Tourism Rev. **74**(1), 82–103 (2019). https://doi.org/10.1108/TR-07-2017-0121
6. Dorst, K.: The nature of design thinking. In: Proceedings of the 8th Design Thinking Research Symposium (DTRS8) Interpreting Design Thinking, Sydney, 19–20 October 2010, pp. 131–139 (2010). https://cir.nii.ac.jp/crid/1571417124270201344
7. Dorst, K.: The core of 'design thinking' and its application. Des. Stud. **32**(6), 521–532 (2011). https://doi.org/10.1016/j.destud.2011.07.006
8. Fang, X., Chan, S., Brzezinski, J., Xu, S., Lam, J.: User-centered guidelines for design of mobile applications (2004)

9. Freeman, W.: Designing for patient safety: developing methods to integrate patient safety concerns in the design process. In: Proceedings of the AHRQ Conference on Designing for Patient Safety, pp. 11–12. Centers for Disease Control and Prevention Atlanta, GA, Atlanta, GA (2002)
10. Garcia-Lopez, E., Garcia-Cabot, A., de Marcos, L., Moreira-Teixeira, A.: An experiment to discover usability guidelines for designing mobile tourist apps. Wirel. Commun. Mob. Comput. **2021**(1), 2824632 (2021). https://doi.org/10.1155/2021/2824632
11. Häkkilä, J., et al.: Reflections on the NatureCHI workshop series: unobtrusive user experiences with technology in nature. Int. J. Mob. Hum. Comput. Interact. (IJMHCI) **10**(3), 1–9 (2018). https://doi.org/10.4018/IJMHCI.2018070101
12. Hassenzahl, M.: Experience Design: Technology for All the Right Reasons. Morgan & Claypool Publishers (2010). https://doi.org/10.1007/978-3-031-02191-6
13. Hassenzahl, M., Tractinsky, N.: User experience-a research agenda. Behav. Inf. Technol. **25**(2), 91–97 (2006). https://doi.org/10.1080/01449290500330331
14. Hurtig, K., Colley, J., Jones, M., Häkkilä, J.: Glove navigator for skiing in the mountains. In: Proceedings of the 22nd International Conference on Mobile and Ubiquitous Multimedia, pp. 509–511 (2023). https://doi.org/10.1145/3626705.3631791
15. Jones, M., et al.: Toward a framework for the design of interactive technology for nature recreation. Int. J. Hum.-Comput. Interact., 1–21 (2024). https://doi.org/10.1080/10447318.2024.2443808
16. Jones, M.D., Anderson, Z., Häkkilä, J., Cheverst, K., Daiber, F.: HCI outdoors: understanding human-computer interaction in outdoor recreation. In: Extended Abstracts of the 2018 CHI Conference on Human Factors in Computing Systems, pp. 1–8 (2018). https://doi.org/10.1145/3170427.3170624
17. Kimbell, L.: Rethinking design thinking: Part I. Des. Cult. **3**(3), 285–306 (2011). https://doi.org/10.2752/175470811X13071166525216
18. Kotut, L., Horning, M., Stelter, T.L., McCrickard, D.S.: Preparing for the unexpected: community framework for social media use and social support by trail thru-hikers. In: Proceedings of the 2020 CHI Conference on Human Factors in Computing Systems, pp. 1–13 (2020). https://doi.org/10.1145/3313831.3376391
19. Kumar, B.A., Goundar, M.S., Chand, S.S.: Usability guideline for mobile learning applications: an update. Educ. Inf. Technol. **24**(6), 3537–3553 (2019). https://doi.org/10.1007/s10639-019-09937-9
20. Matiza, T., Slabbert, E.: Tourism is too dangerous! Perceived risk and the subjective safety of tourism activity in the era of covid-19. Geo J. Tourism Geosites **36**, 580–588 (2021). https://doi.org/10.30892/gtg.362spl04-686
21. Meinel, C., Leifer, L., Plattner, H.: Design Thinking: Understand – Improve – Apply. Understanding Innovation, 1 edn. Springer, Heidelberg (2011). https://doi.org/10.1007/978-3-642-13757-0
22. Mencarini, E., et al.: Designing for/with/around nature: exploring new frontiers of outdoor-related HCI. In: Proceedings of the 14th Biannual Conference of the Italian SIGCHI Chapter, pp. 1–2 (2021). https://doi.org/10.1145/3464385.3467687
23. Nawaz, W., Linke, P., Koc, M.: Safety and sustainability nexus: a review and appraisal. J. Clean. Prod. **216**, 74–87 (2019). https://doi.org/10.1016/j.jclepro.2019.01.167
24. Nielsen, J.: Enhancing the explanatory power of usability heuristics. In: Proceedings of the SIGCHI Conference on Human Factors in Computing Systems, pp. 152–158 (1994). https://doi.org/10.1145/191666.191729

25. Nilsson, E.G.: Design guidelines for mobile applications. SINTEF ICT, June 2008
26. Okonkwo, C.: Assessment of user experience (UX) design trends in mobile applications. J. Technol. Syst. **6**(5), 29–41 (2024)
27. Posti, M., Schöning, J., Häkkilä, J.: Unexpected journeys with the hobbit: the design and evaluation of an asocial hiking app. In: Proceedings of the 2014 Conference on Designing Interactive Systems, pp. 637–646 (2014). https://doi.org/10.1145/2598510.2598592
28. Rasoolimanesh, S.M., Chee, S.Y., Ari Ragavan, N.: Tourists' perceptions of the sustainability of destination, satisfaction, and revisit intention. Tourism Recreation Res., 1–20 (2023). https://doi.org/10.1080/02508281.2023.2230762
29. Sajid, M., Zakkariya, K., Surira, M.D., Peethambaran, M.: Flipping the script: how awareness of positive consequences outweigh negative in encouraging tourists' environmentally responsible behavior? J. Sustain. Tour. **32**(7), 1350–1369 (2024). https://doi.org/10.1080/09669582.2023.2227776
30. Shale, S.J., Nthebe, S.S., Swart, M.P.: Exploring the relationship between tourist safety and tourist experience: theories from accommodation establishments and attractions. In: Katsoni, V. (ed.) IACuDiT 2022. Springer Proceedings in Business and Economics, pp. 579–591. Springer, Cham (2022). https://doi.org/10.1007/978-3-031-29426-6_36
31. Shneiderman, B., Plaisant, C.: Designing the User Interface: Strategies for Effective Human-Computer Interaction. Pearson Education India (2010)
32. Shrestha, D., Wenan, T., Adhikari, B., Shrestha, D., Khadka, A., Jeong, S.R.: Design and analysis of mobile-based tourism security application: concepts, artifacts and challenges. In: Bindhu, V., Tavares, J.M.R.S., Boulogeorgos, A.-A.A., Vuppalapati, C. (eds.) International Conference on Communication, Computing and Electronics Systems. LNEE, vol. 733, pp. 201–219. Springer, Singapore (2021). https://doi.org/10.1007/978-981-33-4909-4_15
33. Sumardi, R., Mahomed, A., Najib, M.: Sustainable tourism recommendations: systematic literature review. In: Proceedings of the 1st International Conference on Sustainable Management and Innovation, ICoSMI 2020, 14–16 September 2020, Bogor, West Java, Indonesia. EAI (2021). https://doi.org/10.4108/eai.14-9-2020.2304433
34. Virkkula, M., Hokkanen, L., Häkkilä, J.: Making visitors feel safe-design students' perspectives on safety concerns when designing future tourism services for north. In: Global Sustainable Tourism Council Academic Symposium. Purdue University Press (2024)
35. Virkkula, M., Hokkanen, L., Häkkilä, J., Aro, P.: Improving the festival safety management through design approach. In: DMI: Academic Design Management Conference, pp. 815–824. Design Management Institute (2024)
36. Zaoui, S., Denaib, I., Kouhili, M., et al.: Design and implementation of a tourism mobile application in the context of smart cities. Ph.D. thesis, Ahmed Draia University-Adrar (2019)
37. Zhang, Q., Popa, A., Sun, H., Guo, W., Meng, F.: Tourists' intention of undertaking environmentally responsible behavior in national forest trails: a comparative study. Sustainability **14**(9), 5542 (2022). https://doi.org/10.3390/su14095542
38. Zhang, Q., Sun, H., Peng, X., Lin, Q.: Who behaves more pro-environmental in the national parks: a comparison of the tourist and the hiker. PLoS ONE **18**(6), e0287227 (2023). https://doi.org/10.1371/journal.pone.0287227

# Who We Are and What We Mean: a Scoping Review of Concepts and Terminology on Digital Legacy

Cristiano Maciel[1]([✉])[iD], Vinícius Carvalho Pereira[1][iD],
Francisco Wesley Gomes Bezerra[2][iD], and Tânia Saraiva de Melo Pinheiro[3][iD]

[1] Universidade Federal do Mato Grosso, Cuiabá, MT, Brazil
{cristiano.maciel,vinicius.pereira}@ufmt.br
[2] Centro Universitário Dr. Leão Sampaio, Juazeiro do Norte, CE, Brazil
wesleybezerra@leaosampaio.edu.br
[3] Campus Quixadá, Universidade Federal do Ceará, Quixadá, CE, Brazil
taniapinheiro@ufc.br

**Abstract.** As the volume of online interactions and digital assets grows, so does the challenge of addressing what happens to these data after a user's death—that is, the user's digital legacy. Based on an initial analysis of the limitations found in literature reviews on digital legacy within the field of Human-Computer Interaction, we formulated the following research questions: What researcher cluster formations could facilitate the identification of predominant sub-themes in the area of interactive technologies related to digital legacy? What regularities can be identified through the terminologies emerging from different researcher clusters? In search of these answers, the general objective of this study was defined as mapping predominant sub-themes and the terminology of published studies through the analysis of researcher clusters that, at some point, co-published within the collected sample, whether on digital legacy or other topics. We carried out a Scoping Review using the PRISMA-ScR (Preferred Reporting Items for Systematic Reviews and Meta-Analyses extension for Scoping Reviews) method. The analyses involved a preparatory stage for identifying key concepts, followed by the use of clustering techniques based on co-authorship to identify connections between authors and terminologies used in the field. Two emerging categories are explored in this paper. The first, *timeline*, indicates that empirical studies are situated at specific moments in relation to a user's life (or death). The second category concerns the use of terms that appear to be fundamental to the field: *legacy* and *digital legacy*.

**Keywords:** Legacy · Digital legacy · Digital asset · Death · Afterlife

## 1 Introduction

The fate of user data after their death is a question that has driven efforts to conceptualize and develop systems and functionalities designed to address these unique challenges, although such solutions remain scarce and often unexplored.

Data generated within organizations belong to them, and when a person leaves, the data they have produced typically remains as part of the organization's legacy. However, there is another category of legacy data that is not automatically transferable: personally owned data linked to individuals. In cases of death, such data take on a distinct significance. Unlike organizational legacies, personal data—closely tied to an individual's identity, such as social media profiles, personal email accounts, or photos stored in the cloud—lacks an automatic recipient in most systems. Thus, digital legacy becomes part of the remains users leave behind after death, introducing new challenges for these systems.

As the volume of online interactions and digital assets grows, so does the challenge of addressing what happens to these data after a user's death. This issue extends beyond the field of human-computer interaction (HCI) and affects other communities, such as information systems, influencing the technological structures necessary to manage these legacies responsibly.

In an initial analysis of works in the field of HCI that address digital legacy through broader literature reviews [13,23], and based on the gaps highlighted by these studies, we observed a proliferation of concepts and terms within this field and formulated the central research problem guiding this study. In this context, the following research questions emerge: **Q1** – What researcher cluster formations could facilitate the identification of predominant sub-themes in the field of interactive technologies related to digital legacy?; **Q2** – What regularities can be identified in the terminologies emerging from different researcher clusters?

The **general objective** of this study is to map predominant sub-themes and the terminology used in studies on digital legacy. As a **methodology**, a bibliographic study was conducted using a Scoping Review approach, following the model of [2] and as described in [18]. The PRISMA-ScR method (Preferred Reporting Items for Systematic Reviews and Meta-Analyses extension for Scoping Reviews) was adopted along with its checklist. The analyses included a preparatory phase to explore key concepts from the perspective of a user's timeline stages (life, dying, death, post-mortem, and beyond), followed by the application of clustering techniques based on co-authorship branches to identify connections between authors and the terminologies used in the field.

This mapping represents another step toward understanding this emerging field. Until a mature mapping is achieved—marking the transition from an emerging area to a more established one—we continue to face fundamental challenges, such as consolidating a definition for digital legacy and its related nomenclature. We do not expect to arrive at a prescriptive systematization of concepts and terminology, which may not even be possible given the strong cultural component associated with the topic of death. However, we aim to systematize our thinking with a minimal theoretical framework that enables better navigation among the scholarship produced by different research groups.

This article is organized as follows: After this introduction, Sect. 2 discusses the scope review, including its preparatory phase and the methodology adopted during the review process. Section 3 presents the researcher clusters and articles identified in the scope review stage, while Sect. 4 focuses on mapping two variables in the reviewed articles: (1) the point in the user's life/death timeline that each legacy study addresses and (2) the terminology—"legacy" or "digital legacy"—used in each work to refer to key concepts in the field. Section 5 presents the final remarks of the study, followed by references. As the authors of this paper are not native speakers of the English language, the text was written in Portuguese, translated using ChatGPT, and finally edited by the authors.

## 2 Scoping Review

In this section, we describe, in phases, the methodological procedures for data collection and analysis adopted. From a methodological perspective, this is a bibliographic study conducted through a Scoping Review [2,18], with analyses incorporating a preparatory phase to explore key concepts from the perspective of a user's timeline stages (life, dying, death, post-mortem, and beyond), followed by the use of clustering techniques based on co-authorship branches to identify connections between authors and terminologies used in the field. For the scope review, the PRISMA-ScR method (Preferred Reporting Items for Systematic Reviews and Meta-Analyses extension for Scoping Reviews) was adopted, following the items outlined in its checklist [18]. This study expands on [2], which focused on mapping practices for a "good death" using technologies, rather than on themes related to the technologies themselves, as is the case in our research. For example, the authors excluded papers that "do not address how people experience the end of life".

### 2.1 Preparatory Phase

We began this study with a classic literature review, revisiting scientific publications about what happens to users' digital legacy after their death. Although we have been studying this topic for a few years, we decided to adopt the perspective of newcomers to the field, which was facilitated by the recent addition of new members to the research group, including the first author of this article. For someone entering the field of digital legacy, how can we present what the field is, and what are the reference studies and key terms used by different authors to designate the central concepts?

In an attempt to answer this question, we started with an overview analysis of the papers already in use by the research group, aiming to trace the development of the field as well as the definition of key concepts and the negotiation of its terminology among researchers. To do so, we examined these papers, trying to follow the chronology of the earliest publications.

Doyle and Brubaker [13] argue that, up until the time of their publication, digital legacy had been studied for about two decades in the fields of HCI and Social Computing. According to the exploratory search we conducted, 2009 can be considered a landmark for the beginning of studies on the topic, although there were already tangential studies in the field of death and technology, but with distinct approaches. In the area of HCI, an extended paper published by

Massime and Charisi in 2009 [25] discusses the concepts of dying, death, and mortality, proposing ways to address thanatosensitivity in HCI. For the authors, "mortality is 'the condition of being mortal or subject to death' [1]. We refer to death as 'the act or fact of dying; the end of life' [1]. [...] Thus mortality is an intrinsic and ongoing state over the entire lifespan of all persons. Death, on the other hand, is a singular and temporally constrained occurrence." As the theoretical foundation for their research, the authors used Humanistic Approaches, including those that relate death and writing. Among the article's contributions, subfields of HCI are identified, along with research questions uncovered by a cursory thanatosensitive analysis, namely: user-centered design, user modeling, intelligent agents, research methodology, and privacy. In the conclusions, the authors emphasize that "HCI research must contend with the fact that users eventually die."

In 2010, continuing this work, in the subsequent edition of the Conference on Human Factors in Computing Systems (CHI), Massimi, Odom, Kirk, and Banks [29] proposed a workshop that included potential topics (but not limited to them): "devices for reflection and meaning-making across multiple lifespans; interdisciplinary practices surrounding mortality, dying, and death; technology heirlooms; digital rights management; and methodological approaches to researching end-of-life technology issues." As primary goals for the workshop, the proponents indicated "to identify and share common research interests in this area" and "to draw attention to this topic as an emergent strand of research," highlighting how the field was being shaped.

The following year, these same authors published a new study proposing "the end of life as another period of the human lifespan that merits consideration" [26]. They contrast the tradition of HCI working with living people and propose a "lifespan-oriented approach." They expand the timeline perspective of HCI studies, typically situated at specific moments of the user's life (or death).

In 2012 [27], Massimi, Odom, Kirk, and Banks continued the workshop, with the inclusion of Moncour. In addition to the workshops themselves, we identified that the different institutional affiliations of at least two of these authors over the years seem to have contributed to the dissemination of the field. It is worth noting that, although we have been studying the topic for over a decade, we are not affiliated with these groups of scholars, which might give us a better perspective on how relevant these two calls for papers were in the early organization of the field. Unfortunately, the websites for these workshops are no longer available, but the call can be found in [28].

By extending the exploratory search to books in the field, it was possible to identify that researchers from various countries who participated in the 2012 workshop are contributors to the book *Digital Legacy and Interaction: Post-Mortem Issues* [24], which, in its introduction, states:"we would like to thank the organizers of the workshop 'Memento Mori: Technology for the End of Life,' which took place at CHI 2012 [27]. That workshop permitted us to deepen the discussion herein presented and put us in contact with some of the authors of this book." The book was edited by Brazilian researchers Cristiano Maciel and

Vinicius Pereira, with contributors from different universities in the UK and the USA. The book documents part of the discussions from the event, maybe as the first volume on the topic in HCI.

Another work published in book form that can be considered a milestone in the conceptualization of digital legacy is Your Digital Afterlife: When Facebook, Flickr, and Twitter Are Your Estate, What's Your Legacy?, authored by Evan Carroll and John Romano, in 2011 [11]. The book includes sections such as "Your Digital Life, Death, and Beyond," and "Securing Your Digital Legacy." Regarding the concept of Digital Legacy, the following definition appears on page 3: "When you pass away you will leave behind your digital content. Taken as a whole, this content is your digital legacy."

Maciel and Pereira [23] also conducted a literature review. The authors proposed a categorization of information systems sensitive to digital legacy issues, defining requirements based on their research with different user groups and analyzing existing systems. The study considered other efforts to categorize these systems, such as in [19], which analyzed 75 systems that, at the time of the study, had begun to play some role in practices related to "death, legacy, bereavement, and remembrance." Also, they mention [35], who expanded the discussion of these systems in a commercial context and coined the term Digital Afterlife Industry (DAI).

Finally, there is a Grounded Theory Literature Review conducted by [13], who "argue that it is time to take stock of digital legacy" studies. They identified four foci in digital legacy research: "how identity is navigated in the passing of digital legacy, how digital legacies are engaged with, how digital legacies are put to rest, and how technology interfaces with offline legacy technologies."

Doyle and Brubaker [13] tried to establish some concepts, including digital legacy. The authors [13] mention that "Legacy materials that get passed down can include values, wishes, identities, objects, digital content, heirlooms, or many other meaningful items. [...] When taken as a whole, digital legacy materials such as data and accounts form a digital legacy that is passed down between individuals. Similar to other legacy materials (e.g., physical heirlooms), digital legacy materials (e.g., social media accounts, collections of passwords, or digital archives of files or media) can carry values and meaning that are passed down." Likewise, [19] states that "A person's legacy, which is composed of some combination of material and immaterial things, is one of the primary ways in which people think about how their life will have a lasting influence."

In other studies the term "digital asset" is used. For [30], digital assets refer to any multimedia content posted on the web or social networking services, including photos, music, videos, and documents. These assets remain accessible even after a user's death, which may raise issues related to privacy, inheritance, and misuse. The study, which excludes offline digital assets—such as those saved on a user's machine—proposes post-mortem management systems for online digital assets, called Digital Asset Management Systems (DAMS), allowing designated heirs to manage the content in a controlled manner.

Following the search for the history of the emergence of the digital legacy theme in HCI publications, we proceeded with deepening the preparatory phase by studying two literature reviews: [13,23].

Doyle and Brubaker [13] sought to take stock of digital legacy research, selecting papers on this topic written in English, published in SIGCHI Proceedings or other top 20 HCI venues, with no time restriction, and containing the strings "digital legacy," "memorial," "heirloom," "inheritance," and "stewardship" within the titles of publications or abstracts. This paper conducts a grounded theory literature review, aiming to analyze the themes emphasized in the literature.

In turn, [23] aimed at a categorization of information systems for digital legacy. For their literature review, the authors formulated search strings relating to the topic ("digital immortality," "digital culture," "human values," and "sociotechnical issues"), and they were inserted in the Google Scholar search engine looking for papers published between 2011 and 2021.

Although these reviews followed different paths and objectives, they had six references in common, which drew our attention to the authors and topics addressed: Joachim Pfister [38]; William Odom, Richard Banks, David Kirk, Richard Harper, Siân Lindley, and Abigail Sellen [32]; Rebecca Gulotta, David B. Gerritsen, Aisling Kelliher, and Jodi Forlizzi [19]; Rebecca Gulotta, William Odom, Haakon Faste, and Jodi Forlizzi [20]; Jack Holt, James Nicholson, and Jan David Smeddinck [21]; and Jed R. Brubaker, Lynn S. Dombrowski, Anita M. Gilbert, Nafiri Kusumakaulika, and Gillian R. Hayes [5].

Still considering both literature reviews, we examined their limitations, based on the assumption that, in systematic reviews, the limitations of a paper can be understood as limitations of the field. The limitations addressed by [13,23] allowed us to formulate our research questions.

Maciel and Pereira [23] sought to explore legacy aspects in information systems from theoretical, systemic, and user perspectives. The theoretical perspective aimed to investigate theories related to systems with legacy-related functionalities. The systemic perspective examined existing practices and implementations of Legacy Management Systems (i.e., systems that help users manage their digital legacy) in real-world scenarios. The user perspective focused on studies analyzing how individuals perceive activities related to legacy management information. However, perhaps due to the topic still being emergent, the authors report as the first research limitation that the theoretical study began to resemble the study of real-world experiences. Even though several papers had already presented concepts and categorizations, no structuring theoretical guidelines for the field had been identified.

Another research limitation was pointed out by [13]. The authors state that their "literature review was intentionally focused on HCI scholarship to summarize the current scholarship on user experiences and design considerations for digital legacy." Additionally, they suggest that expanding the investigation to other disciplines that "may be influential to digital legacy scholarship" would be relevant. They conclude that "future work would benefit from incorporating additional perspectives from adjacent literature."

Based on these reflections and as an output of the preparatory phase of our research, we formulated two research questions that guided the scope review detailed in this article: **Q1** – What researcher cluster formations could facilitate the identification of predominant sub-themes in the field of interactive technologies related to digital legacy?; **Q2** – What regularities can be identified through the terminologies emerging from different researcher clusters? The answers would emerge in the next stage of our review as detailed below.

## 2.2 Scoping Review Process

To achieve the research objectives, the scoping review methodology was adopted, following the PRISMA-ScR procedure, as also applied by [2] and conducted according to the checklist presented in [18]. According to [12], "scoping studies aim to map the literature [...] and provide an opportunity to identify key concepts; gaps in the research; and types and sources of evidence to inform practice, policymaking, and research."

It is worth noting that many of the procedures used in scoping reviews also apply to systematic reviews. However, the latter follow stricter protocols, whereas the former allow for greater flexibility, the inclusion of gray literature, and do not necessarily prioritize the quality assessment of the studies included in the sample [3]. According to [16], in the synthesis phase, this method is "typically tabular with some narrative commentary," as also found in our study.

Since this methodology involves mapping themes, we added a complement: the analysis of authors addressing the mapped themes and the terminology they employ. We proceeded in this way because we understand that it is the authors who establish the interdisciplinary connection, not the fields themselves. Interdisciplinarity arises not only from content but also through individual intentions, although authors and content are by no means mutually exclusive. It happens only when people actively work to establish what [39] calls interdisciplinary bridges and involves defining a common vocabulary.

Given this context, our task was not only to analyze published papers but also to identify "who is talking about what" and "how are they talking about it" in the field of digital legacy.

**Strategy for Selecting Articles.** We could have adopted more common strategies for selecting reviewed texts, such as those paths employed by [13,23], who used inclusion criteria such as publication channels, time frames, and search strings. However, we sought to address gaps that the previous reviews had not been able to fill, which required us to seek complementary strategies for article selection. We needed a path that would also take us "outside the box," as we intended to reach authors from other fields. These authors might not be publishing in the same venues as those in the HCI field.

In an attempt to select texts based on content similarities, we decided to use the ConnectedPapers tool, which shows related publications through semantic analysis, co-citations, and bibliographic coupling. In brief, the user enters a search keyword, and in response, they receive a graph and/or a list of 40 related texts, regardless of the level of impact, trust, or relevance of the articles. In the interface, there is an indicator of how similar each text is to the original, but this indicator was disregarded in our search because we aimed to include the "non-obvious" texts. Therefore, we were able to reach researchers publishing in other fields, such as Health, for example, in works with terminally ill patients regarding digital legacy configuration.

The search keyword chosen to start our investigation in this stage was "digital legacy", selected because of its frequency in the six common references identified in the preparatory phase. Initially, we were unsure if "digital legacy" would be a good starting point, given the thematic bias of the six references. But, since any choice would be subject to some bias, we proceeded down this path, keeping its validation pending until the final clustering of the authors. As the research progressed, it became evident that the text selection strategy indeed led us to reach the main authors in the field (those who publish in greater volume and gather the greatest number of authors around them).

**Collecting and Organizing the Articles.** The article collection in ConnectedPapers was conducted with data generated on January 4th and 5th, 2025, using the paid version (which generates graphs updated at the time of the query). The collected material was organized in a spreadsheet. Initially, the metadata collected for each article were: *Title*, *Authors*, and *Year*. Later, *link*, *abstract*, and *DOI*, as well as *reference*, and the *institutional affiliation of the authors* found in the texts were manually collected. The list generated by the ConnectedPapers platform also includes data on the number of *Citations*, *References*, and an indicator of *Similarity to origin*. These data were collected but disregarded when we removed title duplicates, a procedure described later.

In the first search, using the string "digital legacy", a list of results with publications related to the topic appeared. Then, we clicked on the first result in the list [13], and the platform generated a graph with 40 nodes centered on that paper, with each node representing a publication related to it. One of the nodes was disregarded because it was a duplicate of a text resulting from a small change in the title spelling. Therefore, 40 texts remained in the graph: the original one and 39 others related to it.

Next, new graphs were generated centered on each of these 39 already selected papers, with 40 new nodes for each one. Potentially, if there were no repetitions between the graphs of different publications, we could reach up to 1600 texts: 40 (first graph) + (39*40) = 1600. The Prisma-ScR Flow Diagram (Fig. 2 visually describes the process of selecting the studies included for the scoping review.

The next step was the organization of the data: 1. Removal of new text duplications due to orthographic fluctuations, leaving 359 titles (only 22.4% of the total collected); 2. Manual inclusion of the publication date of 6 papers. 3. Standardization of author names when there were fluctuations in abbreviations.

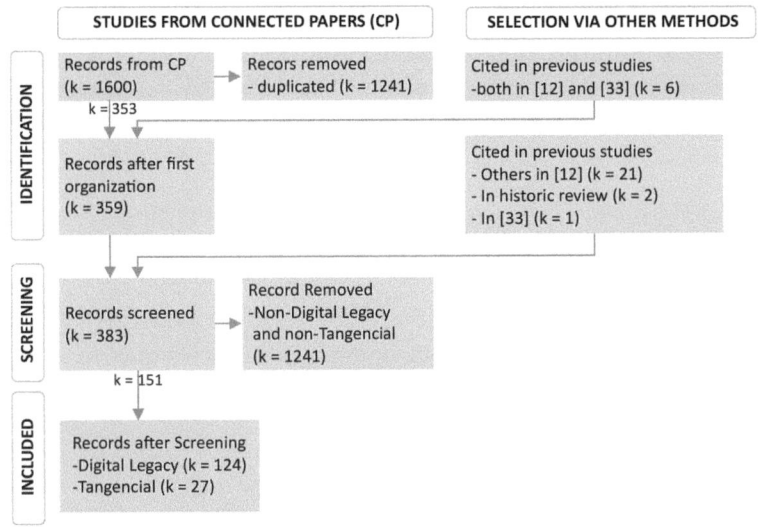

**Fig. 1.** PRISMA ScR Flow Diagram.

A total of 24 references were added, bringing the total to 383 for this study. Of these, 21 are from [13] that had not yet been included[1]. Another added reference was [29], cited in [27], which describes the event that seems to have marked the beginning of the field. Others come from a book that helped us trace the history of the digital legacy field [11]. Finally, [35] was included. It discusses the concept of Economy of Death, cited in [23].

Next, a reduction of the sample by subject was carried out, which required important decision-making. We could not remove all studies that were not directly related because we were seeking research that could contribute to the field, even if from tangential perspectives. The texts were then classified as follows: 1. NO for those that were excluded; 2. TANG for those with topics tangential to digital legacy studies; and 3. YES for those directly about digital legacy. This classification was carried out based on reading titles. In cases of doubt, the abstract was also considered. In two cases where the abstracts were unclear, the full text was checked.

This classification was reviewed at every stage of the research, with the final version showing the following quantities: of the 383 titles analyzed, 232 were excluded, leaving 151 in the sample. The excluded texts addressed topics not directly related to what happens to user data after death, namely: art, automation, blindness, blockchain, business, calculus/math, climate change, cybersecurity, decentralized data in AI, digital health, dignity therapy, drones, education, emerging technologies, energy, finance, forensics, immigrants, interactive devices, interface, IoT, non-digital, others, paperless, psychology, robotics, slowness, spirituality, telecommunication, and tourism.

---

[1] From this article, only references related to its research methodology were excluded.

We tried to start the analysis by themes, but we encountered the same difficulty as previous literature reviews: we got lost in the enormous variety of terms that sometimes seemed to be just different names for the same objects, but at other times, seemed to refer to different objects altogether. Examples include "digital legacy," "digital remains," "digital heritage," "digital assets," etc.

The solution found was to organize groups of authors, with the expectation of simplifying the categorization of terminology. Given the lack of terminological standardization in the research community on the topic, we began to examine the lexical items used by each group of researchers separately.

**Authors Clustering.** The first step in author clustering was to organize the data obtained from ConnectedPapers into a spreadsheet. The author field was broken down into separate rows, formatted as a database. We also collected the institution of each researcher, which sometimes changed over time.

New metadata were added to the spreadsheet, such as a unique abbreviation for authors and institutions, article identification codes, grouping information, and the number of texts per author. The data in this study will be fully available online in the final version of the article, following open science best practices.

The first attempt at data analysis consisted of creating a ranking based on the number of titles for each of the 278 authors identified in the sample. However, it was observed that this was not a good indicator of these authors' relevance to the field, since some authors with few titles played a more significant role in relation to other articles. The first such case is [38], who, despite having only one publication, is cited in the two references that led to this study. We also have the example of [43], with a total of 12 texts collected, of which only 4 were selected for this stage of the study. The distinguishing feature of this author is his vast production on the physical, the digital, and their integration.

Next, an attempt was made to group the authors by their institutions, but this was not possible because some authors list different institutions in different papers. In some cases, this may be due to a change of institutional affiliation over the years, but in others, the duplication remains up to the present day, possibly due to specific research partnerships.

Noticing that there seemed to be regularities in co-authorship, even when the co-authors were from different institutions, we changed our strategy to make associations based solely on co-authorship. At this point, we began using the term "cluster," rather than "research group," because we grouped researchers in a more flexible way, focusing only on the publications in our data sample. From this perspective, co-authors of a paper might, in practice, belong to different research groups, having only participated in a single publication together.

In establishing the author clusters, we assumed that each author belongs to a single cluster and that, to belong to a cluster, there must be at least one co-authorship with another person from the same cluster, and none with authors from other clusters. According to this logic, two types of clusters were established, as detailed and quantified in Sect. 3.

**Terminology Mapping.** The terminology mapping work analyzed the titles of the selected articles, as this paratextual element is usually indicative of the work's theme. In only 10 cases, when the titles did not clearly identify the theme, the abstracts were also analyzed. The process is described in Fig. 2.

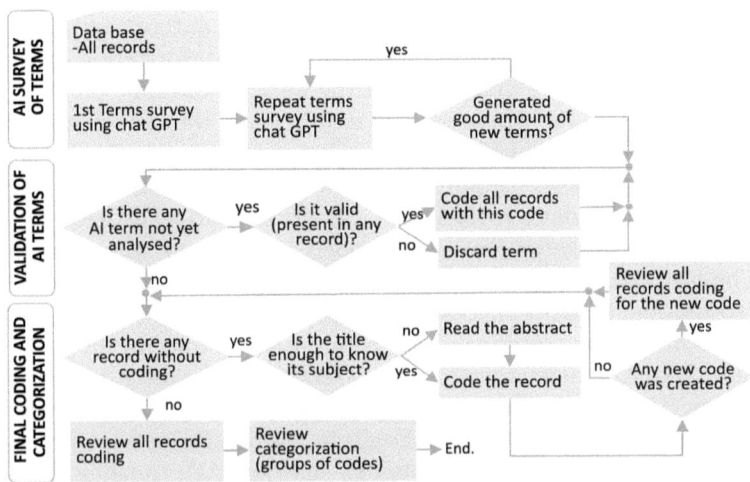

**Fig. 2.** Terminology Mapping Process.

To facilitate the manual processing of the data, ChatGPT was asked to follow the prompt: "Please provide a list of all the nouns from the following titles, including adjectives that accompany them, whenever present." Examples of nouns and adjectives that emerged from the responses include "network" ("social network", "networked grief") and "possessions" ("virtual possessions", "digital possessions"). The request was made three times. At each time, a different set of terms was provided as a response, along with some errors. Despite these issues, the approximate total of 250 terms was considered satisfactory for this stage.

Next, each of the terms identified by the Artificial Intelligence was searched in all the titles of the articles. This was done manually, by using filters in the spreadsheet. Whenever a term, or one of its variations, was located, it would be categorized as a code in the classification. It is important to highlight that this mapping focused on the words (occurrences in the terminology) and not on the concepts (conventional meanings assigned to the terms). Thus, we adopted a communicative perspective of terminology, according to which a term is a lexical unit (word or phrase) that acquires a specialized and specific value in the communication between specialists in a field [7–9]. For example, at this stage, it was important to verify that some papers use "digital legacy," while others only use "legacy," without delving into the differences in meaning and context of these uses. The categorization of the terminology aimed to rely minimally on our prior knowledge of the subject, in order to reduce biases in the final categorization. At this point, having a new member in the research group was very helpful.

After a complete categorization of the main terms, we reviewed the whole process again during the next stage, when the terms were related to the authors who employed them. Whenever there were terms divergent from those already mapped for a particular cluster or author, the work was revisited.

**Who is Talking About What.** Having mapped the authors and the terms for key concepts of each article, the next step was the categorization of the terms, for subsequent comparative analysis with the author clusters.

The categorization used three pairs of new fields in the spreadsheet. The first pair contained the following collected data: terms (such as "legacy," "mourning," "digital legacy," or "legacy," "family," "YouTube") and sample (a slightly longer excerpt from the raw data to facilitate categorization). The second pair was related to the categorization: codes (mapped terms) and category (groups of codes). The last pair contained fields for auxiliary notes: meaning (the meaning of some words) and insights (necessary for notes during categorization).

Here are some of the categories and, in parentheses, some of the codes defined to represent the terminology found: context/culture (religiosity, values, multicultural), design/HCI/process (research agenda, framework); people (user, family, stewards, etc.); platforms (Facebook, YouTube, web, information systems); technology (automation, display, music, photos, chatbot, AI); timeline (life, mortality/dying, death/loss, post-mortem, digital life, final disposition); and legacy (digital legacy, legacy).

For the writing of this article, the last two categories (timeline and legacy) were selected for analysis because they led us to results that more directly address the questions of this research. The in-depth analysis allowed for a revision of the conceptualization of some terms, since we "knew" better the approach of the researcher clusters. The meaning of some terms became clearer when considered in the context of the different works published within each cluster.

The final step was to transform the spreadsheet data into an interactive visualization analytic tool to enhance both analysis and accessibility. For this purpose, we employed a data analytics tool, namely Looker Studio by Google, though any comparable platform could serve the same purpose. This interactive map is especially valuable for researchers interested in the topic of digital legacy, as it enables them to explore patterns, clusters, and terminologies according to their own analytical focus.

The visualization is publicly accessible and available via the website of the research group Dados Além da Vida - DAVI (Data Beyond Life), which works in this research field: https://lavi.ic.ufmt.br/davi/artefatos/. Fig. 3 illustrates two screens of the tool's interface.

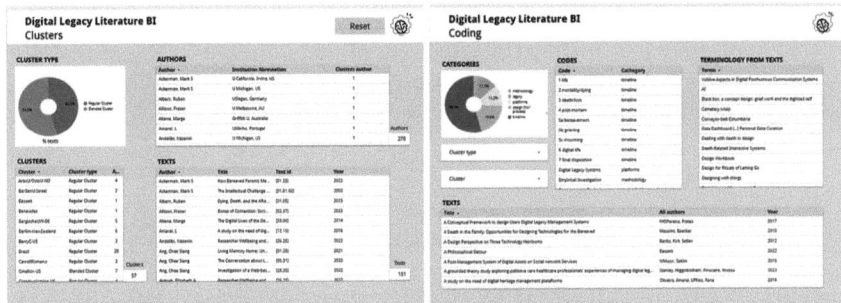

**Fig. 3.** Data analytics tool interface.

## 3  Who We Are: Clustering of Researchers

The authors were grouped into 57 clusters, classified as Regular Clusters or Blended Clusters, according to co-authorship branches. The clustering process was conducted in 2 stages: (a) manual grouping based on co-authorship patterns, and (b) verification through pivot tables. Each author belongs to one cluster, encompassing all their co-authors.

Each cluster has a name that we believe best represents the group of authors, noting that names similar to those of institutions do not mean that all authors in the cluster are affiliated with the same institution.

45 Regular Clusters were formed, including 158 authors. Below is the list of Regular Clusters and the number of authors in each: ArticU/OsloU-NO (4), BarIlanU-Israel (2), Bassett (1), Benavides (1), BergischeUW-DE (5), Berlim-NewZealand (6), BerryC-US (2), Brazil (20), CarrollRomano (2), Communication-US (4), Cornell Med/others (13), CornellU-US (8), CornellUIthaca-US (6), Google-DE (3), Gotved (1), GriffithU-AU (3), Harbinja (1), Health-Seattle-US (3), Health/Liverpool-UK (4), Hjorth (1), HSKelly (1), Indiana-US (5), IndianaU-US (3), ITUCopenhagen-DK (2), Kaptelinin (1), KIM/HannamU-KR (2), Kneese (1), LancasterU-UK (2), LaplandU-FI (8), Michigan-US (2), North-Carolina-US (3), OxfordU-UK (3), Pfister (1), SGray (1), SheffieldHallamU-UK (2), StockholmU-SE (2), UInsubria-IT (3), UMich-US (4), UMinho/UPorto-PT (4), UNIST-Korea (5), UOCatalunya-ES (2), USalford-UK (3), USiegen-DE (4), USunshineCoast-AU (2), and UWashington-US (2).

In addition, 12 Blended Clusters were formed, named as follows: Cmellon-US, Microsoft-UK, NewcastleU-UK, NorthumbriaU-UK, SFU-Canadá, UBC-Canadá, UCaliforniaIrvine, UColorado, Udundee-UK, UMelbourne-AU, UTokyo, UToronto. There are a total of 120 authors involved, but it is not possible to precisely distinguish the number of authors per cluster, because of their blended nature. In this context, "blended" means that this type does not follow the original principle of the cluster concept, as there are co-authorships between its authors. As shown in Fig. 1, the Blended Cluster has a large and interesting web of co-authorship branches centered on the researchers who organized the thematic sessions on death and digital technologies at the CHI events in

2010 [29] and 2012 [28]: William Odom, HCI Institute, Carnegie Mellon University, USA; David Kirk, Culture Lab, Newcastle University, UK; Richard Banks, Microsoft Research, Cambridge, UK; Michael Massimi, University of Toronto, Canadá; and Wendy Moncur, School of Computing, University of Dundee, UK.

Odom, Kirk, and Massimi published together in 2010, without any other co-authors. In 2011, there was a paper by them and additional input from Massimi. In 2012, a paper added Moncur, bringing all five together. They co-authored a call for publications for a workshop at CHI 12, with the theme "Memento Mori: technology design for the end of life" [27]. The fact that Odom and Brubaker changed institutions over time further expanded the web of co-authorships.

The clusters with these authors were grouped into the Blended Cluster, containing clusters that could have common authors. The result of this Blended Cluster is shown in Fig. 4, which highlights connections between authors across blended clusters while excluding self-citations. It is important to note that for the Regular Cluster, no image was generated because no co-authorship relationships were identified between them. From each cluster, Fig. 4 illustrates only those who participate in more than one cluster. The interconnection between Odom, Kirk, Banks, Massimi, and Moncour is highlighted. Also noteworthy is Odom's participation initially as a member of CMellon, and later at SFU-Canada, as well as with Brubaker, who also shows indications of changing institutions. In both cases, joint publications with researchers from both institutions remain.

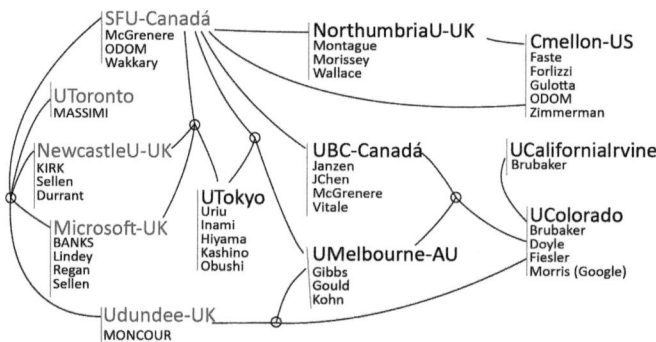

**Fig. 4.** Blended Clusters.

The author clustering was an auxiliary step to reach the scoping review in its intended expanded format, not only mapping themes but also grouping them by authors. The following section addresses the Scoping Review and, later on, the analysis includes a reinterpretation in light of the author clusters.

## 4  What Are We Talking About

In the methodology section, we described the main categories coded in this study and indicated that two of them were selected to represent the main results. The first, *timeline*, refers to the fact that empirical studies are situated at specific moments in the user's life (or death), such as, for example, end of life, death, or afterlife. The second category refers to the use of terms that seem to be more fundamental to the field: "legacy" and "digital legacy".

## 4.1 Timeline Category

We identified another way to define the theme each cluster refers to. We chose to analyze them according to the user's life stages in relation to their mortality. The category named *timeline* contains the codes related to this sequence of stages, as shown in Fig. 5: *1 life*; *2 mortality/dying*; *3 death/loss*; *4 post-mortem*; *5 bereavement, grieving, and mourning*; *6 digital life*; and *7 final disposal*.

Different authors use different terminologies to designate each stage. Below are the main terminological variations found in the scoping review: *1 life* ("across time", "encounters", "life", "living", "present moment"); *2 mortality/dying* ("dying", "end of life", "mortality", "palliative care", "serious illness"); *3 death/loss* ("death", "death online", "deceased", "loss", "the inevitable"); *4 post-mortem* ("after death", "afterlife", "beyond life", "beyond the grave", "posthumous", "post-mortem"); *5a bereavement* ("bereavement", "ongoingness", "the bereaved"); *5b grieving* ("grief", "grieve", "grieving"); *5c mourning* ("death rituals", "mourn", "mourning", "ritual"); *6 digital life* ("'AI", "automated mourning", "avatars", "communicating with the dead", "digital life", "grievable lives", "interactions with deceased", "messengers of/from the dead", "relationship with the deceased"); and *7 final disposal* ("digital death", "final disposition", "profile deletion", "second loss").

The categorization was carried out using the words from the article titles, with the use of 10 abstracts to better identify the study stage in terms of the timeline. Some studies were classified into more than one stage, and many did not point to specific moments on the timeline.

The analysis of the stage *1 life* inspires us to the following reflection: what if we start prioritizing studies with practices during life, when the user is not yet in a terminal state (*end of life*)? Part of the studies is related to data organization practices with teenagers [33], young adults [36], or the elderly [41], but without direct reference to death. Such studies contribute, even if indirectly, to better future management of potential legacy data.

The stage *2 mortality/dying* [14,40] differs from *1 life* by adding the aspect of mortality, a stage in which users realize that they are continuously approaching the deadline to organize their legacy. A certain emotional burden and sense of urgency begin, which intensify in studies that adopt terms such as *end of life* [44], or *serious illness* [17]. One term that was unexpected was palliative care, as in [40], describing that patients in palliative care (terminal patients) are demanding support from health professionals "to manage their digital legacy."

The strategy used for text selection in Connected Papers allowed us to reach tangential papers that had not been published in the HCI field. For example, the data show that this topic is being addressed by multidisciplinary clusters with researchers and professionals from the Healthcare field, such as [17]. Such articles might not have been included in the sample if we had searched in events with specific themes using common procedures for systematic reviews. With the terminology mapping, perhaps in future research, these articles can be found using strings like *palliative care* or *end of life*, combined with the term *digital*. This is a vast field to be explored multidisciplinarily, as the texts reveal.

Articles on stage *3 death* refer to more general topics, such as HCI practices for dealing with death and what happens to a user's data at the time of death [34]. Notable are multicultural studies [42], considering the different meanings that death and its taboos can assume in distinct societies [37].

Stage *4 post-mortem* [22] corresponds to the persistence of data beyond the limits of the user's physical life, as indicated by terms such as "posthumous", "after death", "afterlife", "beyond life", "beyond the grave", and "post-mortem". Living users interact with the data of the deceased in this stage. Recent research has addressed the themes of afterlife, digital remains, or end-of-life data in the field of artificial intelligence.

In turn, stage 5 concerns the time living users spend emotionally processing the passing of other users. Although different languages do not always distinguish between these processes in the same way, we opted for a subclassification based on English terminology, which differentiates: *5a bereavement* (associated with the terms "bereavement", "ongoingness", "the bereaved"); *5b grieving* (including "grief", "grieve", and "grieving"); and *5c mourning* (with "memorialization", "death rituals", "mourn", "mourning", and "ritual").

There is also stage *6 digital life*, which closely relates to post-mortem but is understood here more specifically as cases where the original data owner's content is re-edited for purposes of continued existence. Additionally, there are more complex cases involving the generation of posthumous content through generative AI [6]. This latter case prompted the separation of stage *6 digital life* from stage *4 post mortem*, as it gives the impression of creating an entirely new stage of a person's life, even if artificially. This is suggested by phrases such as "generative ghosts" [31], "non-living 'ghosts' and non-human networks" [40].

Stage *7 final disposition* comprises studies that go beyond post-mortem, addressing *profile deletion* and *second loss*—moments when data ceases to be accessible. One particular study proposes rituals to formally close online profiles and delete data [15], aligning with the right to be forgotten, similarly to the exhumation of a user's data.

The presentation of the results in this subsection aligns with the proposal by [26], who considered "the end of life as another period of the human lifespan that merits consideration." In their article, the researchers challenge the tradition in HCI of working only with living users, instead proposing a "lifespan-oriented approach." The *timeline* category analyzed here helps systematize this approach, especially following the survey of terminology used in studies on the subject, as discussed in the next section.

| Regular Clusters | 1 Life | 2 Mortality/Dying | 3 Death/Loss | 4 Post-Mortem | 5a Bereavement | 5b Grieving | 5c Mourning | 6 Digital Life | 7 Final Disposition |
|---|---|---|---|---|---|---|---|---|---|
| BarIlanU-Israel | - | - | - | - | - | - | • | - | - |
| Bassett | • | • | - | • | - | • | - | • | • |
| Benavides | - | - | - | - | - | - | - | - | - |
| BergischeUW-DE | - | - | • | - | • | - | • | - | - |
| Berlim-NewZealand | - | • | - | - | - | - | - | - | - |
| BerryC-US | - | - | - | - | • | • | - | - | - |
| Brazil | - | - | • | - | - | • | - | - | - |
| CarrollRomano | • | - | - | • | - | - | - | - | - |
| Communication-US | - | - | - | - | - | - | • | - | - |
| Cornell Med/others | - | - | • | - | • | - | • | - | - |
| CornellUIthaca-US | - | - | • | - | • | - | - | - | - |
| Google-DE | • | - | - | - | - | - | - | - | - |
| GriffithU-AU | - | - | • | - | • | - | • | • | - |
| Health/Liverpool-UK | • | - | - | - | - | - | • | - | - |
| Health-Seattle-US | - | • | - | - | - | - | - | - | - |
| Hjorth | • | - | • | • | - | - | - | - | - |
| Indiana-US | - | - | - | - | • | • | - | - | - |
| IndianaU-US | - | - | - | - | - | • | - | - | - |
| Kaptelinin | - | • | • | - | - | - | - | - | - |
| KIM/HannamU-KR | • | - | - | - | - | - | - | - | - |
| Kneese | • | - | - | - | - | - | - | - | - |
| NorthCarolina-US | - | - | • | - | - | - | - | - | - |
| OxfordU-UK | - | - | • | - | - | - | - | - | - |
| SGray | - | - | - | - | - | - | • | - | - |
| StockholmU-SE | - | - | - | - | - | • | - | - | - |
| UInsubria-IT | • | - | - | • | - | - | - | - | - |

| Regular Clusters (continued) | 1 Life | 2 Mortality/Dying | 3 Death/Loss | 4 Post-Mortem | 5a Bereavement | 5b Grieving | 5c Mourning | 6 Digital Life | 7 Final Disposition |
|---|---|---|---|---|---|---|---|---|---|
| UMich-US | - | - | - | • | - | - | - | - | - |
| UNIST-Korea | • | - | - | - | - | - | - | - | - |
| UOCatalunya-ES | - | - | - | - | • | - | • | - | - |
| USiegen-DE | - | • | • | • | - | - | - | - | - |
| USunshineCoast-AU | - | - | - | - | • | - | • | - | - |
| UWashington-US | - | - | - | - | - | - | • | - | - |

| Blended Clusters | 1 Life | 2 Mortality/Dying | 3 Death/Loss | 4 Post-Mortem | 5a Bereavement | 5b Grieving | 5c Mourning | 6 Digital Life | 7 Final Disposition |
|---|---|---|---|---|---|---|---|---|---|
| Cmellon-US | - | - | - | • | - | - | - | - | - |
| Microsoft-UK | - | • | - | - | - | - | - | - | - |
| NewcastleU-UK | - | - | • | - | - | - | - | - | - |
| NorthumbriaU-UK | • | • | - | • | - | - | • | • | - |
| SFU-Canada | - | - | • | - | • | - | - | - | - |
| UBC-Canada | - | • | - | - | - | - | - | - | - |
| UCaliforniaIrvine | - | - | • | • | • | - | - | - | - |
| UColorado | - | • | - | • | - | - | - | • | • |
| Udundee-UK | - | • | - | • | - | - | • | - | - |
| UMelbourne-AU | - | • | - | • | - | - | - | - | - |
| UTokyo | - | • | - | • | - | • | - | - | - |
| UToronto | • | • | - | • | - | - | - | - | - |

**Fig. 5.** Who is talking about what moment in the timeline.

### 4.2 Legacy Vs. Digital Legacy Category

To discuss the correlations between themes and authors, we revisit the issue raised by [13] regarding the difficulty of standardizing terminology in the field, particularly concerning the key terms "legacy" and "digital legacy." The analyzed data suggest that these terms are indeed central, sometimes used as synonyms and sometimes with different nuances by various authors. For this reason, we present below a proposal for defining and applying them.

By analyzing only the etymology and morphosyntax of the terms "legacy" and "digital legacy," we can infer some aspects of their meanings, which will be further refined by considering their usage in the studies in this scope review.

According to the Online Etymology Dictionary citeetymonline, "legacy" derives from the Proto-Indo-European root *leg-, which meant "to collect, gather." This root is also present in terms such as "collect," "collegial," "election" and "legal," reflecting the idea of selection, transmission, or delegation of something. The Oxford Dictionary [10] states the word can be used as a noun (as it is frequently found in the papers analyzed in this scope review) meaning "money or property that you receive from someone after they die" or "something that is a part of your history or that remains from an earlier time". It can also be used as an adjective in phrases like "legacy app" or "legacy media", "used to describe something such as technology which still exists or is still used, but is from an earlier time than other similar things which have since been invented". This use is common in areas such as History of Computing, or Media Archeology, but not in Digital Legacy studies. In turn, "digital legacy" is a phrase in which the adjective "digital" restricts the semantic scope of the noun "legacy", designating a specific case of legacy composed of digital items. In our sample, the word "legacy"—without the accompanying adjective "digital"—has been more commonly applied to studies with a more social perspective, whereas "digital legacy" appears more frequently in studies specifically focused on the technological context.

In our sample, authors who use "legacy" also employ terms such as "legacy-making", as seen in [19], who study Digital Legacy Systems in a similar way to authors who use "digital legacy", such as [23]. In addition to the latter, other authors prefer "digital legacy", bringing important social issues into the discussion, as in (? ). As socio-technical systems, many challenging issues emerge in this field and have been investigated by different research groups, particularly in the field of HCI. These include privacy, usability, communicability, accessibility, transparency, system security and trust, the roles of stakeholders, collaboration practices, and adherence to legal aspects, especially those related to application terms of use and national legislation.

Table 1. Distribution of "legacy" and "digital legacy" in the sample

| Regular Clusters | Codes | Terms used by authors |
|---|---|---|
| BergischeUW-DE | legacy | legacy |
| Brazil | digital legacy | digital legacy |
| Harbinja | digital legacy | inheritance of digital media |
| Health-Seattle-US | legacy | legacy |
| Health/Liverpool-UK | digital legacy | digital legacy |
| ITUCopenhagen-DK | legacy | legacy |
| Kaptelinin | digital legacy | Technological Givens of Existence |
| LaplandU-FI | legacy | cultural heritage experiences |
| Pfister | digital legacy | digital legacy |
| SGray | digital legacy | digital legacy, memory remains (within the network), remains in the network |
| UMinho/UPorto-PT | digital legacy | digital heritage |
| UNIST-Korea | legacy | Reminiscence Experiences |
| Blended Clusters | Codes | Terms used by authors |
| Cmellon-US | legacy | legacy, legacy making |
| Microsoft-UK | legacy | heritage of death |
| NewcastleU-UK | digital legacy | digital legacy |
| NorthumbriaU-UK | digital legacy | digital legacy |
| SFU-Canada | digital legacy | digital materials, passing on with interactive Technologies |
| UColorado | digital legacy | digital legacy, legacy (digital) |
| Udundee-UK | digital legacy | digital legacy |

The data reveal that the distinction between "legacy" and "digital legacy" appears to be merely a terminological variation, influenced by the choices of each research group, without any real conceptual distinction. Since this study analyzed the network of authorship among scholars researching legacy-related issues in a digital context, the expression "digital legacy" naturally appeared more frequently. In Tab. 1, each cluster has its defined nomenclature.

Observing the table and the different uses of these terms, it is striking to note the provocation made by [13], that "A concise definition of 'digital legacy' across much of the literature is surprisingly elusive as most scholars have left the definition implicit."

Throughout this article, and particularly in the preparatory stage, several definitions of these concepts were identified. In general, the usage suggests that a legacy refers to what remains for others after an individual's death. According to [11], a legacy is a digital legacy if what "you leave behind" is "digital content".

Taking a broader analysis of the usage of the terms 'legacy' and 'digital legacy' in the articles, it is important to correlate their distribution with the data from the *timeline* category. Considering the codes from the *timeline* category, the term "legacy" is used in studies addressing the stage *3 death* or stages occurring after the user's death. Studies focusing on a period before death generally discuss legacy preparation. In studies about the stages *1 life* and *2 mortality/dying*, the term "digital assets" is used, for example, referring to digital goods or assets that users have during their lifetime. "Digital remains", on the other hand, is another concept that arises, but it is not associated with a specific stage of the users' life/death. Its meaning is more general, linked to the idea of remnants or what remains, without necessarily being restricted to what remains after death.

Gulotta, Gerritsen, Kelliher and Forlizzi [19] presents the perspective of "legacy-making," related to the process of creating digital data (potential future legacies) during the stages when the user is alive. "As people age, many take steps to prepare for their death. One significant way in which people do so is by crafting a legacy that they hope will shape how they are remembered after they have passed away [82]". For the authors, "Legacy-making, for example, is often viewed as a communicative activity".

In other publications, such as [4], the noun "estate" is used, which is not yet a legacy, as it refers to the possession of assets during life, especially land and property in the physical world. However, in the legal context, "estate" can be used to designate "everything that a person owns when they die", according to the Oxford Dictionary. [4] uses "estate", sometimes referring to online data, which we codified as digital legacy, and at other times discussing social aspects.

Thus, the studied sample reveals a terminological fluctuation in designating assets (digital or otherwise) produced during life and left to third parties after the owner's death. As in any emerging field, there is still a proliferation of concepts and terminologies, as well as a certain degree of imprecision, partly due to subjectivity and contextual usage. This underscores the need for further theoretical studies. At this stage of the field's development, for authors who prefer to be specific when referring to digital data after a user's death, we propose revisiting the conceptualization of digital legacy introduced in the foundational work of [11], as well as the discussions presented in the preparatory phase of this study.

## 5 Final Remarks

In this bibliographic research, a scoping review was conducted to map: (1) the predominant subthemes concerning the stage in the life/death timeline of users as addressed in the studies within the sample; and (2) the terminology used ("legacy" vs. "digital legacy") in these same studies. The analysis was based on clusters of researchers identified through co-authored publications. In this process, we found studies that explore different aspects of the topic, delineating an emerging field with a body of knowledge and technical lexicon still in formation, aligning with the challenges mentioned by [13]. Each study is an effort to map an uncharted territory with its concepts, and directions for future development.

At the same time, various technologies are continuously being developed, influencing how people incorporate them into cultural practices related to death and legacy, thereby shaping and reinterpreting concepts in this field. This evolution not only impacts the design of computational artifacts but also informs legal understandings in the domain. Consequently, the mapping of concepts and terminology is both necessary and valuable—whether for newcomers to the field or for researchers seeking a stronger theoretical foundation.

Through the scoping review, this study makes the following key contributions to the theoretical field: a) A historical review of the concepts of legacy and digital legacy; b) The clustering of authors based on co-authorship networks (Regular Cluster vs. Blended Cluster); c) The coding of the *timeline* category, which identifies empirical studies situated at specific moments in a user's life (or death); d) A mapping of the uses of the terms "legacy" and "digital legacy," along with a discussion of related concepts in the analyzed studies.

In the field of open science, another contribution is the provision of raw data, organized in a table and accompanied by a graphical visualization in BI (Business Intelligence). The analysis of the data and the clusters allows the identification of professionals working in specific sub-areas, facilitating partnerships for research in the field.

From a methodological standpoint, the design of a scope review through the analysis of connections between papers, grouped around specific concepts/ terminologies (in this case, using ConnectedPapers), is an original contribution and can be replicated by other studies. While we recognize the volatility of AI-driven tools and their algorithmic opacity, we opted to include this tool due to its potential to expand the scope beyond traditional searches. Additionally, the findings of this work help define descriptors for systematic reviews in the field.

Limitations of the study include the fact that little attention was given to the publication dates of the articles that formed the clusters. Additionally, the evaluation of the clusters was carried out solely by the authors of the study, and the abstracts were not assessed. These limitations can be addressed in future work, which should also include the building of a glossary based on the terminology identified, encompassing the terms that make up the codes in the *timeline* category. This glossary could be made available alongside the data visualization in the BI tool, to be shared on the research project's website. NLP-based clustering is also a promising future direction if we expand our team to include such expertise. Finally, a procedure should be defined for receiving suggestions for corrections or the inclusion of new papers, a need that may arise as the data starts to be used by the community.

**Acknowledgments.** The authors are grateful for the research grants from the National Council for Scientific and Technological Development (CNPq).

**Disclosure of Interests.** The authors have no competing interests to declare that are relevant to the content of this article.

# References

1. Oxford English Dictionary Online. Oxford University Press (nd). https://www.oed.com/
2. Albers, R., Sadeghian, S., Laschke, M., Hassenzahl, M.: Dying, death, and the afterlife in human-computer interaction. a scoping review. In: Proceedings of the 2023 CHI Conference on Human Factors in Computing Systems, pp. Article 302, 1–16. CHI '23, Association for Computing Machinery, New York, NY, USA (2023). https://doi.org/10.1145/3544548.3581199
3. Arksey, H., O'Malley, L.: Scoping studies: towards a methodological framework. Int. J. Soc. Res. Methodol. **8**(1), 19–32 (2005). https://doi.org/10.1080/1364557032000119616
4. Bahri, L., Carminati, B., Ferrari, E.: What happens to my online social estate when i am gone? an integrated approach to posthumous online data management. In: Proceedings of the 2015 IEEE International Conference on Information Reuse and Integration (IRI), pp. 31–38. IEEE (2015). https://doi.org/10.1109/IRI.2015.16
5. Brubaker, J.R., Dombrowski, L.S., Gilbert, A.M., Kusumakaulika, N., Hayes, G.R.: Stewarding a legacy: Responsibilities and relationships in the management of post-mortem data. In: Proceedings of the SIGCHI Conference on Human Factors in Computing Systems, pp. 4157–4166. ACM, Toronto, Ontario, Canada (2014). https://doi.org/10.1145/2556288.2557059
6. Brubaker, J.R., Morris, M.R., Doyle, D.T., Fiesler, C., Gibbs, M., McGrenere, J.: AI and the afterlife. In: Extended Abstracts of the CHI Conference on Human Factors in Computing Systems (CHI EA '24), pp. 458:1–458:5. ACM, New York, NY, USA (2024). https://doi.org/10.1145/3613905.3636321
7. Cabré, M.T.: Terminologie et linguistique: la théorie des portes. Terminologies Nouvelles (21), 10–15 (2000). https://pascal-francis.inist.fr/vibad/index.php?action=getRecordDetail&idt=14204702
8. Cabré, M.T.: Theories of terminology: their description, prescription and explanation. Terminology **9**(2), 163–199 (2003). https://doi.org/10.1075/term.9.2.03cab
9. Cabré, M.T.: La teoría comunicativa de la terminología: una aproximación lingüística a los términos. Revue française de linguistique appliquée **14**(2), 9–15 (2009). https://www.cairn.info/revue-francaise-de-linguistique-appliquee-2009-2-page-9.htm

10. Cambridge Dictionary: Legacy - definition in the cambridge english dictionary. https://dictionary.cambridge.org/dictionary/english/legacy (2024). Accessed 18 Feb 2024
11. Carroll, E., Romano, J.: Your Digital Afterlife: When Facebook, Flickr and Twitter Are Your Estate, What's Your Legacy? New Riders (2010)
12. Daudt, H.M.L., van Mossel, C., Scott, S.J.: Enhancing the scoping study methodology: A large, inter-professional team's experience with Arksey and O'malley's framework. BMC Med. Res. Methodol. **13**, 48 (2013). https://doi.org/10.1186/1471-2288-13-48
13. Doyle, D.T., Brubaker, J.R.: Digital legacy: a systematic literature review. Proc. ACM Human-Comput. Interact. **7**(CSCW2), 268:1–268:26 (2023). https://doi.org/10.1145/3610059
14. Figueroa Gray, M., Banegas, M.P., Henrikson, N.B.: Conceptions of legacy among people making treatment choices for serious illness: protocol for a scoping review. JMIR Res. Protocols **11**(12), e40791 (2022). https://doi.org/10.2196/40791
15. Gach, K.Z., Brubaker, J.R.: Designing postmortem profile deletion as a community ritual. In: CHI 2020 Workshop: HCI at End-of-Life and Beyond. ACM (2020). https://cmci.colorado.edu/idlab/assets/bibliography/pdf/gach-chi2020.pdf
16. Grant, M.J., Booth, A.: A typology of reviews: an analysis of 14 review types and associated methodologies. Health Inform. Libr. J. **26**(2), 91–108 (2009). https://doi.org/10.1111/j.1471-1842.2009.00848.x
17. Gray, M.F., Banegas, M.P., Henrikson, N.B.: Conceptions of legacy among people making treatment choices for serious illness: Protocol for a scoping review. JMIR Res. Prot. **11**(12), e40791 (2022). https://doi.org/10.2196/40791
18. Group, P.: Prisma for scoping reviews (2024). https://www.prisma-statement.org/scoping. Accessed 2024
19. Gulotta, R., Gerritsen, D.B., Kelliher, A., Forlizzi, J.: Engaging with death online: An analysis of systems that support legacy-making, bereavement, and remembrance. In: Proceedings of the 2016 ACM Conference on Designing Interactive Systems pp. 736–748. ACM, New York, NY, USA (2016). https://doi.org/10.1145/2901790.2901802
20. Gulotta, R., Odom, W., Faste, H., Forlizzi, J.: Legacy in the age of the internet: Reflections on how interactive systems shape how we are remembered. In: Proceedings of the 2014 Conference on Designing Interactive Systems, pp. 975–984. ACM, New York, NY, USA (2014). https://doi.org/10.1145/2598510.2598579
21. Holt, J., Nicholson, J., Smeddinck, J.D.: From personal data to digital legacy: Exploring conflicts in the sharing, security and privacy of post-mortem data. In: Proceedings of the Web Conference 2021, pp. 2745–2756. ACM, New York, NY, USA (2021). https://doi.org/10.1145/3442381.3450030
22. Holt, J., Smeddinck, J.D., Nicholson, J., Vlachokyriakos, V., Durrant, A.C.: Postmortem information management: exploring contextual factors in appropriate personal data access after death. Human–Computer Interaction, pp. 1–36 (2024). https://doi.org/10.1080/07370024.2023.2300792
23. Maciel, C., Mendes, F.F., Pereira, V.C., Yamauchi, E.A.: Defining digital legacy management systems' requirements. In: Enterprise Information Systems. Lecture Notes in Business Information Processing, vol. 455, pp. 256–279. Springer, Cham (2022). https://doi.org/10.1007/978-3-031-08965-7_13
24. Maciel, C., Pereira, V.C. (eds.): Digital Legacy and Interaction: Post-Mortem Issues. Human–Computer Interaction Series, Springer, Heidelberg, Germany (2013). https://doi.org/10.1007/978-3-319-01631-3

25. Massimi, M., Charise, A.: Dying, death, and mortality: towards thanatosensitivity in hci. Association for Computing Machinery, New York, NY, USA (2009). https://doi.org/10.1145/1520340.1520349
26. Massimi, M., Odom, W., Banks, R., Kirk, D.: Matters of life and death: locating the end of life in lifespan-oriented hci research. In: Proceedings of the SIGCHI Conference on Human Factors in Computing Systems, pp. 987–996. ACM, New York, NY, USA (2011). https://doi.org/10.1145/1978942.1979090
27. Massimi, M., Odom, W., Banks, R., Kirk, D.: Memento mori: Technology design for the end of life. In: CHI '12 Extended Abstracts on Human Factors in Computing Systems, pp. 2759–2762. ACM, New York, NY, USA (2012). https://doi.org/10.1145/2212776.2212714
28. Massimi, M., Odom, W., Banks, R., Kirk, D.: Memento mori: Technology design for the end of life (2012). www.researchgate.net/publication/_technology_design_for_the_end_of_life, call for Participation, CHI 2012 Workshop
29. Massimi, M., Odom, W., Kirk, D., Banks, R.: Hci at the end of life: understanding death, dying, and the digital. in: chi '10 extended abstracts on human factors in computing systems (CHI EA '10), pp. 4477–4480. Association for Computing Machinery, New York, NY, USA (2010). https://doi.org/10.1145/1753846.1754178
30. Moon, W., Kim, S.: A post-management system of digital assets on social network services. J. Digital Converg. **13**(3), 209–214 (2015). https://www.koreascience.or.kr/article/JAKO201509163113534.page
31. Morris, M.R., Brubaker, J.R.: Generative ghosts: anticipating benefits and risks of AI afterlives. In: arXiv preprint arXiv:2402.01662 (2024). https://doi.org/10.48550/arXiv.2402.01662
32. Odom, W., Banks, R., Kirk, D., Harper, R., Lindley, S., Sellen, A.: Technology heirlooms?: Considerations for passing down and inheriting digital materials. In: Proceedings of the SIGCHI Conference on Human Factors in Computing Systems, pp. 337–346. ACM, New York, NY, USA (2012). https://doi.org/10.1145/2207676.2207723
33. Odom, W., Zimmerman, J., Forlizzi, J.: Teenagers and their virtual possessions: Design opportunities and issues. In: Proceedings of the SIGCHI Conference on Human Factors in Computing Systems, pp. 1491–1500. ACM, New York, NY, USA (2011). https://doi.org/10.1145/1978942.1979161
34. Ohman, C.: From bones to bytes: A new chapter in the history of death. In: Savin-Baden, M., Mason-Robbie, V. (eds.) The Digital Afterlife: Death Matters in a Digital Age, pp. 17–30. CRC Press (2019). https://www.researchgate.net/publication/336428482_From_Bones_to_Bytes_A_New_Chapter_in_the_History_of_Death
35. Öhman, C., Floridi, L.: The political economy of death in the age of information: a critical approach to the digital afterlife industry. Mind. Mach. **27**(4), 639–662 (2017). https://doi.org/10.1007/s11023-017-9445-2
36. Pereira, F.H., Tempesta, F., Pimentel, C., Prates, R.O.: Exploring young adults' understanding and experience with a digital legacy management system. J. Interact. Syst. **10**, 50–69 (2019). https://doi.org/10.5753/jis.2019.553
37. Pereira, V.C., Maciel, C., Leitão, C.F.: The design of digital memorials: Scaffolds for multicultural communication based on a semiotic analysis of tombs. In: Proceedings of the 15th Brazilian Symposium on Human Factors in Computing Systems, pp. 1–10. Association for Computing Machinery, New York, NY, USA (2016). https://doi.org/10.1145/3033701.3033726

38. Pfister, J.: "this will cause a lot of work": coping with transferring files and passwords as part of a personal digital legacy. In: Proceedings of the 2017 ACM Conference on Computer Supported Cooperative Work and Social Computing, pp. 1123–1138. ACM, New York, NY, USA (2017). https://doi.org/10.1145/2998181.2998262
39. Pinheiro, T.S.M.: Como pensar e estruturar projetos com propósito, direção e impacto. Expressão, Fortaleza (2024)
40. Stanley, S., Higginbotham, K., Finucane, A., Nwosu, A.C.: A grounded theory study exploring palliative care healthcare professionals' experiences of managing digital legacy as part of advance care planning for people receiving palliative care. Palliat. Med. **37**(9), 1424–1433 (2023). https://doi.org/10.1177/02692163231194198
41. Thomas, L.A., Briggs, P.: An older adult perspective on digital legacy. In: Proceedings of the 8th Nordic Conference on Human-Computer Interaction: Fun, Fast, Foundational, pp. 237–246. ACM, New York, NY, USA (2014). https://doi.org/10.1145/2639189.2639485
42. Uriu, D., Ko, J.K., Chen, B.Y., Hiyama, A., Inami, M.: Digital memorialization in death-ridden societies: How HCI could contribute to death rituals in taiwan and japan. In: Proceedings of the 21st International Conference on Human-Computer Interaction, pp. 532–550. Springer (2019). https://doi.org/10.1007/978-3-030-22012-9_38
43. Uriu, D., Okude, N.: Thanatofenestra: Photographic family altar supporting a ritual to pray for the deceased. In: Proceedings of the 8th ACM Conference on Designing Interactive Systems, pp. 422–425. ACM, New York, NY, USA (2010). https://doi.org/10.1145/1858171.1858253
44. Wallace, J., et al.: HCI at end of life & beyond. In: Extended Abstracts of the 2020 CHI Conference on Human Factors in Computing Systems, pp. 1–8. Association for Computing Machinery, New York, NY, USA (2020). https://doi.org/10.1145/3334480.3375143

# Emotionally-Informed Design

# Applying the Laws of Simplicity to Redesign an Educational Social Network

Jonas Lopes Guerra(✉), Deógenes P. Junior da Silva, Krissia M. L. Menezes, and Roberto Pereira

Federal University of Paraná, Curitiba, Brazil
{jlguerra,dpsjunior,kmlmenezes,rpereira}@inf.ufpr.br

**Abstract.** This paper investigates the potential of John Maeda's Laws of Simplicity to inform user experience redesign, discussing how the laws were applied, an approach not explored in previous studies. We drew on the laws to inform the redesign of an educational social network developed for teachers, students, and other stakeholders interested in education. The redesign was a challenging task because it involved a legacy system combining social networking and repository features, and should meet the needs of various stakeholders in a socioeconomically diverse reality with different barriers to accessing information and knowledge. Adopting Action Research as the research method, we applied the Laws of Simplicity and conducted five Thinking Aloud sessions over six months in focus groups with a total of 21 participants. The application of the Laws of Simplicity to inform the user experience redesign resulted in a simpler system interface, reducing the time required to complete tasks and making the social network easier to navigate. The findings led to a discussion of the benefits and challenges of applying the Laws of Simplicity to support user experience redesign and to the formulation of guiding questions for using these laws. Finally, we conclude that the Laws of Simplicity can effectively inform user experience redesign, and we encourage further studies to explore their application in different HCI contexts.

**Keywords:** Laws of Simplicity · User Experience Design · MEC RED

## 1 Introduction

The Laws of Simplicity, proposed by John Maeda [15] in 2006, aim to reduce complexity and promote simplicity in interface design, and have been applied in HCI studies to simplify interfaces and interactions. In a context of information overload [2], simplicity offers a crucial path to fostering a good user experience. Mark Weiser [30], while proposing ubiquitous computing, also highlighted the dilemma of information overload: *"[t]here is more information available at our fingertips during a walk in the woods than in any computer system, yet people find a walk among trees relaxing and computers frustrating."* The presence of numerous features, the bombardment of information, and interactions demanding excessive user attention can negatively impact user experience, leading to what Weiser called "frustrating" and Maeda [15, p. i] described as "uncomfortably full."

The complexity and information overload challenge remains current. Even searching for favorite items (e.g., books, music, movies) on the internet can be a time-consuming process [25]. Users often face "cluttered" and overloaded experiences when browsing online [14]. Information overload is also cited as affecting users' well-being [13] and is related to misinformation and the dissemination of fake news [1,2], especially since the COVID-19 pandemic.

Challenges related to interaction complexity and information overload, and their impact on UX, motivate our research into simplicity. We specifically investigate a "simplicity-oriented design" space, exploring opportunities for using the Laws of Simplicity as a basis to inform UX design. This is particularly relevant in redesign contexts, where existing websites and legacy systems often face complexity in information, presentation, navigability and functionality. The existing HCI literature on the Laws of Simplicity [4,17,23] already exemplifies a developing field of simplicity in HCI, which we intend to explore and expand.

In this research, we investigate the Laws of Simplicity to inform the redesign of the MEC Digital Educational Resources social network (MEC RED). MEC RED is an educational social network for sharing open educational resources. The system presented significant complexity challenges, including numerous pages, information overload, inconsistent interface design, confusing features and labels, and excessive interaction possibilities. These issues notably affected users' ability to interact fluidly and meaningfully on the network, impacting their capacity to build and share educational materials, make sense of content, and create meaningful connections with other users. We used MEC RED as the redesign context to explore simplicity as a framework to deal with complexity issues. To address the issues and redesign needs, this research explored the potential of John Maeda's Laws of Simplicity to inform the MEC RED user experience redesign, striving for a simplicity-oriented redesign.

This paper presents a critical analysis of the Laws of Simplicity and their application to MEC RED's redesign, offering a set of recommendations that inform the use of these Laws, and discussing their potential to inform user experience redesign. We hope this paper contributes to the HCI community by presenting both the rationale and practical experience of applying these Laws in a real-world setting. Therefore, we articulate our experience through a set of simplicity-focused guiding questions, intended to support the iterative design prototyping process. Drawing on this rationale and experience, we introduce simplicity as a relevant conceptual framework that can inform the redesign of user experience in systems facing interaction complexity.

This paper is organized as follows: Sect. 2 presents a background on the Laws of Simplicity, simplicity in HCI, and provides the context of the MEC RED social network and the requirements for its redesign. Section 3 explains the methods used and the undertaken design activities. Section 4 presents the main results, and Sect. 5 discusses the challenges and benefits of using the Laws to inform MEC RED's redesign, presenting recommendations for applying the Laws of

Simplicity in redesigning an interactive system. Finally, Sect. 6 presents our final considerations and provides suggestions for future studies.

## 2 Background

In his 2006 book, "The Laws of Simplicity" [15], MIT scientist and professor John Maeda introduces ten laws and three "keys" for simplifying design, technology, business, and life. He categorizes these laws by their conditions of simplicity: basic simplicity (Laws 1 to 3), intermediate simplicity (Laws 4 to 6), and deep simplicity (Laws 7 to 10).

**Law 01 – Reduce.** *"The simplest way to achieve simplicity is through thoughtful reduction"* [15, p. 1]. Maeda outlines three methods for reducing elements to achieve simplicity: shrink, hide, and embody. This law emphasizes that simplicity can be attained by eliminating excess (of information or objects) without compromising project quality.

**Law 02 – Organize.** *"Organization makes a system of many appear fewer"* [15, p. 11]. For this law, Maeda describes a method for organizing elements to achieve a system's simplicity: select, label, integrate, and prioritize.

**Law 03 – Time.** *"Savings in time feel like simplicity"* [15, p. 23]. Maeda argues that shortening the user's perceived time is a key aspect of simplicity, thereby enriching their experience with the system.

**Law 04 – Learn.** *"Knowledge makes everything simpler"* [15, p. 33]. This fourth law marks the beginning of his discussion on intermediate simplicity laws. Maeda explains how knowledge simplifies tasks through the steps: relate–translate–surprise. He demonstrates how icons and symbols can facilitate interface comprehension without requiring users to fully read an instruction manual, as prior knowledge of symbols and their associated meanings helps users identify an icon's function in interface design.

**Law 05 – Differences.** *"Simplicity and complexity need each other"* [15, p. 45]. This fifth law highlights the necessity of balancing simplicity with complexity, as the presence of more complex elements and functions enables the user to perceive simplicity. This contrast is crucial to maintain the user's sense of simplicity. Analogous to how music relies on different rhythms, organizing sounds and silences, interfaces can also provide varying rhythms for users through the organization and ordering of elements, features, and actions.

**Law 06 – Context.** *"What lies in the periphery of simplicity is definitely not peripheral"* [15, p. 53]. This sixth law emphasizes that during the simplification process, one must always remain aware of the broader context in which the object of study or work is situated.

**Law 07 – Emotion.** *"More emotions are better than fewer"* [15, p. 63]. This law introduces the deep laws and advocates for adding "more love, more care, and more meaningful actions" [15, p. 71] to products, processes, and systems.

**Law 08 – Trust.** *"In simplicity we trust"* [15, p. 73]. This law explains that simplicity is also perceived when users can rest and relax while products and systems perform tasks. However, this is only possible when such products and systems function without compromising the user's experience. Another crucial aspect of trust, regarding simplicity, is the ability to undo actions.

**Law 09 – Failure.** "*Some things can never be made simple*" [15, p. 83]. In this ninth law, Maeda revisits his set of laws, acknowledging that there are situations where complete simplification is impossible. He also reflects on Law 05, "Differences," which states that simplicity and complexity need one another.

**Law 10 – The One.** "*Simplicity is about subtracting the obvious and adding the meaningful*" [15, p. 89]. This tenth law, considered the "master law" by Maeda, indicates that simplicity is "*hopelessly subtle, and many of its defining characteristics are implicit*" [15, p. 89].

## 2.1 Laws of Simplicity in HCI

In the field of interactive computational systems design, John Maeda's Laws of Simplicity [15] have been employed to think about, understand, create, and evaluate products and interfaces with the ultimate goal of simplifying the final artifact. Developing simpler interfaces makes us less vulnerable to errors, saves us time, facilitates learning, strengthens trust, and connects us with what is essential [15]. Some studies reference The Laws of Simplicity to discuss, argue for, or reinforce ideas related to the concept of simplicity [5,7,10,12,16,26,28,29]. Other works cite the book as the source to evaluate UX design, propose new solutions, and analyze these laws in design practice [4,6,17,23,24]. Here, we briefly discuss three main studies particularly relevant to this research, as they applied the Laws of Simplicity in the context of prototypes and user interfaces.

Canal et al. [4] introduced the Laws of Simplicity to evaluators of both the industrial design and interface design of the OLPC Laptop. Through the application of these Laws, they identified problems and proposed solutions. Furthermore, they suggested that future work could develop methods utilizing the Laws of Simplicity to aid in the design and evaluation of digital artifacts.

Menezes and Baranauskas [17] used the Laws of Simplicity to evaluate navigable prototypes for mobile devices. In their study, the participants evaluated the prototypes according to the Laws, producing relevant insights such as: (i) only 29% of the participants evaluated the prototypes explicitly using the Laws; (ii) on average, participants employed only 3 of the Laws; (iii) no participant used Law 9 (Failure) or Law 10 (The One); and (iv) Laws 1 (Reduce), 2 (Organize), and 3 (Time) were the most frequently used. The researchers concluded that the students likely lacked sufficient time to apply all the Laws, given the need to perform evaluations with other methods within the experiment schedule.

Pereira and Baranauskas [23] employed the Laws of Simplicity to evaluate a mobile application. They concluded that the Laws of Simplicity supported reflection and assessment of the application, and raised questions about user privacy, comfort, and autonomy. However, they also noted that comprehending the Laws of Simplicity is not immediate and can be confusing even for experts.

Despite the existence of literature applying Maeda's Laws of Simplicity for supporting both design and evaluation, few studies document and focus on analyzing the application of all ten laws. Instead, most papers invoke only selected laws, often through brief excerpts that reinforce or justify isolated design choices. This gap suggests an opportunity of applying and reflecting on the full set of Laws of Simplicity in a complex, real-world UX scenario. In this paper, we discuss such experience, aiming to help designers understand the practical value of simplicity, and propose guiding-questions as a way for integrating simplicity laws into interactive system redesign.

## 3 The MEC RED Social Network: Context and Redesign Challenges

The MEC RED educational social network is designed for teachers, students, school administrators, and other individuals interested in the relationship between education and digital culture. Its initial version was launched in 2015 [19,22] and reached 43416 users in its current version[1]. It primarily offers features related to searching, accessing, publishing, and sharing educational resources across various subject areas, including teaching materials, lesson plans, presentations, and multimedia instructional content. Users can create, evaluate, comment on, and favorite resources to foster a community of practice on the network. Regarding content curation, users can create personal resource collections and make them public, sharing these collections or individual resources with colleagues, and maintain a personal profile on the network.

Due to shifts in Brazil's political landscape, the social network entered a maintenance phase focused on preserving existing functionality, without significant technological advancements. Almost a decade after MEC RED's conception and initial release, its technological infrastructure required updates, necessitating the replacement of many legacy technologies. Concurrently, the National Strategy for Connected Schools [20] expanded the demand for the Digital Educational Resources to include "*diverse and high-quality resources aligned with the Common National Curriculum Base (BNCC), available to students and teachers.*" In this way, MEC RED was positioned as an important social network to support interested parties from educational contexts in their everyday practice, when planning, conducting and evaluating educational activities, and also sharing lessons learned and best practices.

For the social network to effectively fulfill its purpose and meet these new demands, the research project "*Enhancing the MEC RED Integrated Platform: Research, Innovation and Improvement of the Educational Experience through the Integration of Social Networks and Content Search Engines*" was initiated, funded by the Brazilian Ministry of Education. The project aim was to improve the user experience, enhancing the quality of interaction with the MEC RED social network by using innovative Human–Computer Interaction approaches that increase user engagement and participation through a sociotechnical understanding of requirements. An evaluation study [18] was conducted to identify potential problems and interaction barriers on the MEC RED existing interface.

---

[1] Available at https://mecred.mec.gov.br (accessed June 9, 2025).

Through a heuristic evaluation by UX specialists, a user test, and a focus group, 19 main groups of issues were identified for improving the social network. Among the recommendations, the following were highlighted: (i) fixes and adjustments to existing features, (ii) redesign points to enhance a new version of the social network, and (iii) proposals for new features. While (i) fixes and adjustments involve targeted interface modifications (e.g., correcting bugs and broken links), (ii) and (iii) required substantial changes to the interface and interaction model.

This research specifically focuses on point (ii): the redesign to enhance existing features and improve the UX in a new version of the social network. As part of this redesign, improvements and enhancements were recommended for system navigability, interface (aesthetics, style, and standards), the search and sharing features for educational resources, interaction and operations involving resources (e.g., favoriting and evaluating educational items), and user profiles.

Given the goals and challenges of the MEC RED social network, its redesign presented a suitable real-world scenario for investigating the potential of the Laws of Simplicity to support user experience (re)design. The issues identified in the initial evaluation [18] served as a starting point for MEC RED's redesign, guided by the Laws of Simplicity. Through collaborative activities and the investigation of simplicity as a lens for improving the social network, other relevant elements for the redesign also emerged.

## 4 Research Method

To develop the new version of MEC RED, we drew on the Action Research method, which is *"an approach to research that involves engaging with a community to address some problem or challenge and through this problem solving to develop scholarly knowledge"* [8, p. 49]. As illustrated in Fig. 1, the method was based on two major stages according to the Action Research framework.

The first stage investigated the current situation with stakeholders in the problem (i.e., teachers, Ministry of Education professionals) and the solution domain (i.e., HCI professionals and software developers). The second stage intervened in the current situation: redesigning the MEC RED social network, resulting in a new version with improvements in presentation, organization, navigation, and existing functionalities.

Regardless of the stage, the designer (first author) engaged in a "reflective practice," assuming the posture of a designer in reflective conversation with the design situation [27]. This reflective practice with the other authors and the project participants took place in such a way that the insights and knowledge emerging from the social redesign process were (re)generated and analyzed in light of John Maeda's theory of simplicity.

As illustrated in Fig. 1, the two stages did not unfold sequentially but rather iteratively. The research involved diagnostic cycles, which informed intervention cycles of modifying the current situation, and vice versa.

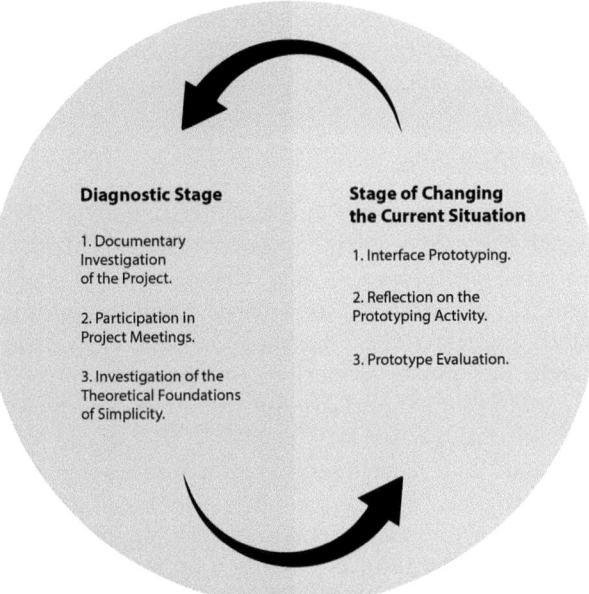

**Fig. 1.** Research method.

## 4.1 Diagnostic Stage

The diagnostic stage involved three main activities, described below along with the input materials and the corresponding outputs (results).

*1. Documentary Investigation of the Project.* Input: MEC RED social network UX evaluation report [18]; executive project report. Description: We analyzed project documents to identify the project's goals, priorities, and needs, which established the social network as an important tool within the Brazilian education policy. We also examined the results of studies evaluating MEC RED's UX to compile existing problems affecting interaction on the network. Output: (i) A compilation of goals and objectives to be achieved; (ii) A compilation of already identified interaction problems and barriers.

*2. Participation in Project Meetings.* Input: Project demands. Description: Participation in the meetings allowed the researcher to integrate into the project's shared (social) space as an active participant, rather than remaining an external observer. Output: Established interpersonal relationships with team members, with the researcher acting as an active participant in the project.

*3. Investigation of the Foundations of Simplicity.* Input: Maeda's laws [15] and related literature in HCI [4,17,23]. Description: Each law of simplicity was investigated in terms of (i) its definition, (ii) its description, and (iii) illustrative examples. During this investigation, the first author recognized the need to gather the information that allowed to use the Laws of Simplicity to inform the prototyping of the MEC RED's redesign. A set of guiding questions was distilled from the compiled content and the practical knowledge. Output: An initial version of guiding questions related to the Laws of Simplicity to support their practical application.

### 4.2 Intervention Stage

The intervention stage changed the current situation (Fig. 1), involving three main activities aimed at prototyping the new version of MEC RED and iteratively evaluating these prototypes as they were created. Following a reflective practice approach [27], the first author recorded reflections during each prototyping cycle, which informed the refinement of artifacts emerging from both diagnostic (research) and practical (action) processes.

*1. Interface Prototyping.* Input: Guiding questions derived from the Laws of Simplicity; the current version of the MEC RED social network (prior to redesign). Description: This activity involved planning the prototyping effort with the development team. Weekly team meetings focused on discussing priorities for which areas of the existing social network should be prototyped. Once priorities were set, the first author, leveraging a professional design background, created the interface prototypes guided by the Laws of Simplicity, operationalized through the guiding questions. The prototypes were developed using Adobe XD (version 58.0.12). Different versions of the redesigned MEC RED interface were stored to document the evolution of the redesign, with a total of five versions produced over the course of prototyping. Output: Versioned medium-fidelity prototypes (v1 to v5) of the new MEC RED social network.

*2. Reflection on the Prototyping Activity.* Input: Practical experience of prototyping informed by the Laws of Simplicity. Description: Inspired by reflective design practice, the first author recorded spontaneous insights, reflections, and questions that arose during the prototyping process in personal notes. These experiences and insights were subsequently shared with two other researchers (second and third authors) in informal meetings. The two researchers, in turn, provided feedback and helped refine the sense-making generated by the first author, which took shape in the guiding questions. Thus, the guiding questions were refined based on the first author's practical prototyping experience and discussions with two researchers. Needs, questions, and challenges during prototyping served as sources for refining these guiding questions, which were revisited in light of the demands of prototyping and interface simplification. Output: Refined versions of the simplicity-focused guiding questions.

*3. Prototype Evaluation.* Medium-fidelity prototypes developed in Adobe XD. Description: Team members were invited via email to attend, in-person, prototype evaluation sessions. The stakeholders included five individuals from the Brazilian Ministry of Education and eleven members from UFPR's Center for Scientific Computing and Free Software (C3SL): three professors, two graduate, and six undergraduate students. All the UFPR members were involved in MEC RED's development, for example working in coding and testing activities. During these sessions, team members simulated using the new interface by interacting with a navigable prototype. Throughout the simulation, participants were asked to "speak their thoughts" [3] so that their interaction logic and any barriers or misunderstandings could be identified. Participants simulated the interaction during the meeting. Following the simulation, the participants discussed the prototypes in a focus group [11], aiming to share opinions and suggest improvements. The narration and group discussion were documented by the first author, providing insights into potential areas for improvement in the interface, navigation, and proposed features. Output: Suggestions for improving the prototypes and prototypes validated by the project team.

## 5 Results

Prototyping resulted in a medium-fidelity navigable prototype. Considering its last version, 67 modifications were inspired by the Laws of Simplicity, which were organized into three important parts of the redesign: (1) changes to aesthetics, style, and visual patterns; (2) changes to navigational structure and information hierarchy; and (3) changes to the structure of the MEC RED's core functionalities, such as searching for and accessing educational resources.

All these changes are documented and available online[2]. To illustrate how the Laws of Simplicity were used, we focus on the "Resource Access" screen, demonstrating how all ten laws were applied at different points of user interaction with the system, including the interface (aesthetics, style, and patterns), web navigation, and resource interaction (like liking, commenting, sharing). Figure 2 shows the resource screen old version, and Fig. 3 shows the new version.

In the old version (Fig. 2, indication #1), the menu relied on dropdown buttons for navigation only, and the available interaction options did not truly show what was important about the social network or the interface. In the new version (Fig. 3), a left-side menu clearly shows MEC RED's most important actions, like sharing resources and making social connections. Icons were added to quickly show what each action means, and they are easy to access with a single click. The menu uses specific colors and sizes so it stays on the edge of users' attention—it never pulls too much focus but is always available when needed. This approach connects to Law 1 (Reduce).

At indication #2 in both Figures, the search function was highlighted to show how important user exploration is on the social network. This approach shows what is most important and valuable about the network. It also simplifies interaction by putting more emphasis on the search feature and accessibility functions in the search bar. Indications #3, #4, and #7 illustrate how information about educational resources has changed. In the old interface, text was presented as if it were the most important element, often making things complex (for example, large blocks of text with nothing highlighted). In the new interface, Law 2 – Organize helped structure the information by using tabs and menus. This created whole gestalts of information in grouped signs, and made the title clickable, an option that was not there before.

---

[2] Available at https://figshare.com/s/a0feb4dadd5de4f5bd47 (accessed June 9, 2025).

**Fig. 2.** Resource Screen in the Old Version

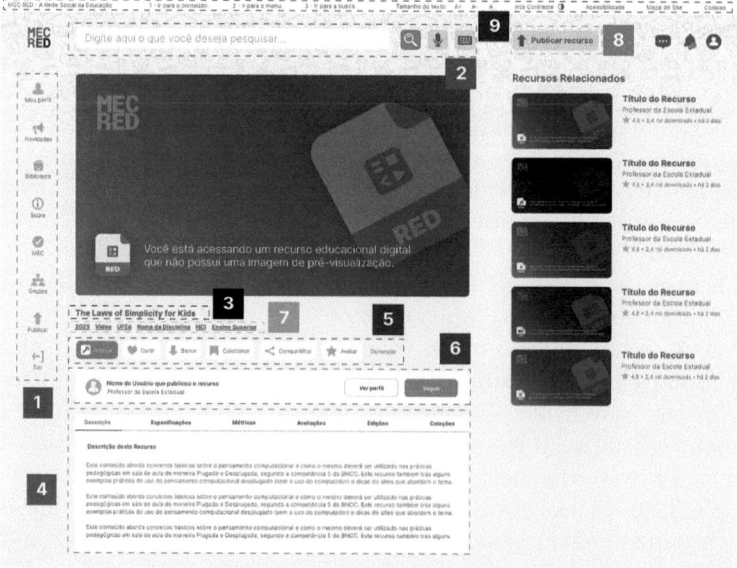

**Fig. 3.** Resource Screen in the New Version

Table 1 presents a summary of the modifications presented in Fig. 2 and 3, indicating the simplicity law used to inform the redesign. Indication #5 relates to resource features. In the original setup for resource actions, the elements organization did not clearly show how they relate to each other. It also put more emphasis on reporting things instead of sharing or saving resources. In the new interface (#5 in Fig. 3), we put actions like accessing, liking, downloading, and saving resources first.

**Table 1.** Summary of simplicity motivated redesign in MEC RED interface.

| Fig. 2 and 3 | Modifications on MEC RED | Simplicity laws used |
|---|---|---|
| #1 | Listing the main pages in the new menu | 2. Organize |
| #1 | Transforming the menu into a side menu, ensuring that it is visible at all times and accessible with just a single click | 4. Learn |
| #1 | Adding icons to the menu so that the user can easily identify the function of each menu item | 3. Time |
| #2 | Search function has become a fixed search bar at the top, eliminating the need to find the functionality and perform a click to perform a search | 3. Time |
| #2 | Keeping the search bar always visible, informing the user that searching (for resources, collections, etc.) is one of the basic functions | 6 - Context |
| #3, #4, #7 | Aligning all possibilities of interaction of a resource in a single place (access, download, like, comment, collect, share, evaluate and report resource); Organize, grouping user features by similar characteristics ("Description", "Specifications" and "Metrics" of a resource) | 2. Organize |
| #3, #4, #7 | Highlighting the main action button (access or download) in the Resource page with a highlighted color | 5. Differences |
| #3, #4, #7 | Hiding part of the information, displaying it by group only when the respective group (tab menu) is selected | 1. Reduction |
| #5 | Comments in resources with other users as a way of creating social bonds and emotional expressions of gratitude | 7. Emotions |
| #6 | Changing the Reviews section to Comments section, as Reviews did not allow interaction with other users, whereas Comments enables the sharing of ideas and fostering bonds | 10. The One |
| #8 | Keeping the "Publish" button feature in the same place as the previous version, preventing the user from having to figure out where to find it | 4. Learn |
| #9 | Adding essential features to the website such as an accessibility bar and features | 10. The One |

Indication #6 shows how we made user information stand out more, offering more ways for people to connect socially – highlighting the social network's most important actions. Indication #8, in turn, illustrates something that did not change in the interface as a decision of simplicity. The old and the new version both share the same position for the button feature (interface top-right area), in an area with prominence in the interface that needs to be easily findable. As "publish resource" is an important feature of MEC RED, we did not change its location to not make users need to learn the location of this important feature. Finally, indication #9 represents the changes we made to actions tied to accessibility features. We included an accessibility bar (not available in the old version) and the user can navigate with just a few tab-clicks. Users can, for example, access the last accessibility option only with 9 tab-clicks. With this feature, persons with disabilities have significant features to simplify their interaction with MEC RED.

## 6 Discussion

Below, we present and explain how each law was applied and helped guide a simplicity-oriented redesign.

**Law 1 – Reduce:** This law helped us simplify complexity, especially concerning the excessive use of colors in backgrounds, buttons, and text. The old version overused symbols to convey information, and this law guided us in reducing an overload of meanings. For example, we reduced background colors from four to just one. For typography, we cut the number of text colors from eight to four. Also, some resource information is now hidden and only shown through a tabbed menu, as seen at indication #4 in Fig. 3.

**Law 2 – Organize:** This law informed various ways of structuring information on the interface. It helped reduce complexity by organizing, categorizing, or putting elements into intuitive groups. These groups are designed to match how people naturally perceive different gestalts. For instance, in object/content boxes, we grouped similar information sets under one label, as shown at #5 in Fig. 3. Buttons were also labeled and standardized in color for different system functions and states.

**Law 3 – Time:** This law guided the redesign to cut down on the time and effort needed on the social network. For example, the sidebar menu now lets users access the MEC RED's main features with a single click. This means they do not have to navigate through many menus and submenus to find what they need, as indicated by #1 in Fig. 3. We also improved the resource preview feature. Now, users can save time by previewing a resource without having to download and open a file just to see what it is about.

**Law 4 – Learn:** This law guided our strategy to use signs and patterns already common in social networks when redesigning the interface. This makes the environment more familiar to Brazilian users. Icons, buttons, and interaction patterns were reviewed. For instance, button colors were matched to conventional meanings (like red for danger), and we added icons to the menu so users can easily tell what each item does, as shown at #1 and #5 in Fig. 3.

**Law 5 – Differences:** This law highlighted the need to make the important interaction options on the social network stand out more. For example, we made it clearer which icons and text are clickable and which are not. We also improved the information hierarchy and changed how less-used functions are presented so they do not draw unnecessary attention.

**Law 6 – Context:** This law pointed to the need for adding symbols that reinforce the system's status and connect to the educational and cultural background of MEC RED. This helps bring in user experiences tied to the educational context. For instance, we added a school-themed pattern to the background to show the system's main theme. We also changed button colors to indicate when a component or function is active, as seen at #4 in Fig. 3.

**Law 7 – Emotion:** This law informed the choice of a visual style that brings up positive feelings related to a school environment, using icons and images. We moved away from an old, more bureaucratic style that could have made the interface feel complex. For example, we prioritized the commenting feature to encourage social relationships and expressing feelings. We also added icons to the menu to make the experience feel lighter, as shown at #1 in Fig. 3.

**Law 8 – Trust:** This law informed design choices meant to build user confidence when interacting with the social network. For instance, we chose a typeface that conveys the seriousness and security expected from an official government network. We also standardized and improved an accessibility bar on it, making it easier for people with disabilities to access, as indicated at #9 in Fig. 3.

**Law 9 – Failure:** This law highlighted that, sometimes, we need to go against Law 1 (Reduce). This means keeping or even adding more information and interaction options. We made this choice to make users feel more secure, ensure accessibility for users with different needs, and prevent them from getting lost while using the system. For example, we kept text on buttons to ensure accessibility, as seen at #5 in Fig. 3. We also kept extra functions always visible in the menu to prevent users from getting lost, as shown at #1 in Fig. 3. And we kept all extra resource information to make users feel secure when dealing with a resource, as indicated at #4 in Fig. 3.

**Law 10 – The One:** This law guided the redesign to focus on what's truly important in the interaction. For instance, we reinforced MEC RED's branding through the colors and symbols used. We also put more emphasis on social relationships and on accessing and sharing educational resources.

In general, the Laws of Simplicity allowed the designer to make quick decisions. When examining an interface or a component, the designer might ask, "*By applying the Laws of Simplicity, how can I simplify this component to enhance the user experience?*" For example, regarding Law 1 – Reduce, the question might be, "*Using the Law of Reduction, how can I simplify the main menu in such a way that the user experience is not compromised?*" Applying the Laws of Simplicity is not a linear process, but rather an iterative and incremental one. During prototype development, it became clear that a single application of the Laws of Simplicity would not suffice to achieve the desired simplicity. Additional analysis and design alternatives informed by the Laws were required to ensure the user experience was not undermined.

Throughout the process, we also reflected on the difference between a simple interface and a minimalist interface [21]. In some cases, pushing simplification to the extreme paradoxically made the interface more complex. This can be illustrated by the redesign of buttons: removing the text from buttons and leaving only icons would yield a cleaner interface with fewer elements, yet it would become more complex for people who do not recognize those icons. To avoid scenarios like this, the team consistently referred to the project requirements to ensure that design decisions did not lead to interfaces failing to meet the needs of a diverse user base, spanning different age groups and varying levels of digital literacy. In this sense, we view the requirements as a "benchmark" for simplicity, helping the development team decide when the user experience is truly simple or overly complex.

During the redesign, we observed that applying the basic simplicity laws (Reduce, Organize, Time) is more intuitive and easier, as noted by Maeda [15] and by Menezes and Baranauskas [17]. One possible explanation is that these laws produce immediate effects on simplification, correlating with natural human strategies for handling complexity. The intermediate simplicity laws (Learn, Differences, Context) demand more attention as they seem conceptually close to each other. For instance, Law 5 – Differences and Law 6 – Context can sometimes be confused, and applying either one has mutual implications. The deep simplicity laws (Emotion, Trust, Failure, The One), on the other hand, require more time to apply because they evoke deeper reflection than the other laws. One likely reason is that they are more closely tied to intimate aspects of the human experience, such as aesthetics, value, affection, security, and well-being.

A difficulty when applying the Laws was finding literature that not only cited the Laws but also offered insights for their application. Papers that mention the Laws of Simplicity tend to reinforce concepts or justifications, as noted earlier. Therefore, this paper presents the Laws while also reflecting on the rationale for their application, including practical examples. In our view, the Laws of Simplicity have special potential in redesign scenarios, particularly when a system already deals with complexity issues that affect UX. Drawing on Menezes and Baranauskas [17], Pereira and Baranauskas [23], and Canal et al. [4], we observed that the Laws can function as evaluation guidelines as well as support (re)design by informing possible solutions when dealing with complexity. Hence, rather than using the Laws merely as a way to assess the user experience (diagnosis), we used them as a means to transform the user experience (redesign).

Another difficulty was the need to revisit and remember the recommendations associated with all ten Laws. Ideally, it should not be necessary to memorize every aspect of the Laws of Simplicity to make an interface simpler. Nevertheless, it was often necessary to consult the book repeatedly to apply the Laws, which interrupted the reflective process and made the design work more tiring.

Because the Laws cover broad concepts, they offer the designer considerable flexibility in how they are applied, fostering creativity in questioning how to design the user experience. For example, instead of reflecting on Dieter Rams' statement that "Good design is less design" [9], one might use Law 1 – Reduce as a starting point to ask, "*Will shrinking this component harm the user experience?*" or "*Which items can be temporarily hidden to improve the user experience?*" Such questions were compiled and presented in Sect. 6.1 as guiding questions to support the simplicity-oriented UX (re)design.

## 6.1 Guiding Questions for a Simplicity-Oriented UX (re)Design

Based on the reflections presented, we put together a set of questions to help HCI professionals to apply the Laws of Simplicity during the user experience design or redesign. These questions can be used as triggers for prototyping and to guide design, or to check if a prototype already considers different aspects of the ten Laws of Simplicity.

### Law 1 – Reduce

- Are the sizes of on-screen elements appropriate, or should they be smaller?
- Are there elements that must stay visible at all times?
- Are there pieces of information that can be hidden and only shown at certain moments, based on user preference or specific conditions?

### Law 2 – Organize

- Which items should show up in the main menu?
- Which layout elements let the user contact system support?
- Which ones are about user information?
- After grouping these elements for the project's needs, can they be put together and then prioritized by importance?
- Is it possible to combine pages into one menu (like a dropdown)?
- Which functions can go into a micro-interactions menu?
- Which button should be the default for a certain action?
- Which items need to be at the top of a list, page, or form?

### Law 3 – Time

- How many clicks do users need to get where they want to go?
- How many pages or screens must they go through to finish their task?
- Are the interfaces light, with few images or effects that load fast?
- Can the user go back to the homepage or a previous screen or state in just one click?
- What happens when users have to wait for the system to do something?
- Is there a progress bar?
- What can we do to make this waiting time okay?

### Law 4 – Learn

- When we compare our system to ones people commonly use, do we use the same signs to send the same messages?
- Are contact forms, confirmation buttons, and icons for sharing, liking, and saving put in places in the layout where users would expect them, based on other systems?

### Law 5 – Differences

- Does the system show a sequence of complex layouts, or is there a mix of complex ones with simpler ones in between?

- Can hard tasks be broken down into smaller steps?
- Which interfaces can be taken apart and redesigned with contrast and rhythm so users can have a better experience?

### Law 6 – Context

- Should interface elements always keep the same color and size when accessed, or can they act differently depending on the situation?
- How can the interface clearly tell the user what they need to do during different tasks?
- Is there a way to show users where they are in their journey (like progress indicators)?
- Do the interface elements fit with the main purpose, or are there some that don't belong in the context?
- Does the interface help the user stay focused, or does it have distracting parts?

### Law 7 – Emotion

- What emotion do we expect users to feel?
- Are the interface texts impersonal, or do they show personality and empathy?
- Does the interface let users express their own emotions and personality?
- Can users change the interface to feel more connected to the system or the task they're doing?

### Law 8 – Trust

- Does the interface make users feel like they can trust it?
- Do the instructions and feedback messages make users feel secure when using the system?
- Do users feel in control of their actions, with the power to undo anything they've done?
- Are the options to go back, cancel, undo, contact support, file a complaint, or exit easy to find?
- Are cookie policies, privacy statements, and terms of use clear and visible to users?

### Law 9 – Failure

- What could go wrong if a process is made simpler?
- Will users understand and manage this interface if it gets simpler?
- Do we have enough time and other resources to really make things simple in this part of the project?

### Law 10 – The One

- Which elements are important to users but are missing or not being clearly shown?
- What kind of messages, images, or animations can take the place of text to make the user experience with the software easier?
- Which elements in the interface are useless?
- What truly adds value to the user's experience?

## 7 Conclusion

This paper investigated the potential of the Laws of Simplicity to inform user experience design, using as context the redesign of an educational social network that faced complexity challenges. John Maeda does not propose clear instructions in his book on how to apply the Laws of Simplicity, leaving designers to interpret and apply them according to their understanding. In the absence of supporting artifacts and tools, designers may feel discouraged or at a loss, failing to see the possibilities the Laws of Simplicity can bring to their projects.

From applying the laws in the context of redesigning the MEC RED social network, we observed that the application of the laws follows an iterative and incremental process, and the Laws provide designers with flexibility and freedom to exercise creativity in addressing problems. The laws also helped us in decision-making and the system's requirements can define the boundary between simplicity and minimalism. Relying only on the book as a reference throughout the design process can be labor-intensive, and for this we proposed and used guiding questions to facilitate the practical application of the laws. However, applying the intermediate and deep simplicity laws requires more time and effort than the basic simplicity laws. As contributions, this paper adds to the literature by presenting practical results of the Laws' application, acting as a guide for applying the Laws in practical contexts, and providing a tool, via guiding questions, to facilitate the application process – i.e., helping to advance towards a simplicity-oriented redesign.

This study has some limitations that should be addressed in future research. The purpose of the study was not to generalize the results, but to explore the laws of simplicity and discuss their potential regarding the (re)design of UX. As future works, we indicate evaluating MEC RED with diverse users (e.g., teachers and students), and conducting quantitative and comparative studies, for example, evaluating usability and UX metrics as an indication of the effectiveness of the Laws of Simplicity when redesigning interfaces. In the same way, other elements of the user experience, such as responsiveness, animations, sounds, and music, warrant further investigation. Beyond the ten Laws, Maeda also proposes three "keys" that can complement and support simplification, which calls for additional exploration. The guiding questions emerged from our redesign practice and experience. Although they were shared and refined in meetings with other researchers, they still need to be tested in different contexts and with other participants to assess their potential for supporting learning and application of the Laws. Finally, this study focused on the redesign of a legacy system, meaning certain patterns from the old version had to be retained. Therefore, exploring simplicity in designing a brand-new interface, with no reference to a previous version, presents another research opportunity stemming from our experience.

We conclude that the Laws of Simplicity show promise for reducing interaction problems in scenarios with numerous interfaces, complex navigation, and a variety of signs being communicated to the user. Specific examples of their potential for informing user experience design oriented toward simplicity include: i) helping select a color palette that is contextual and conveys positive and negative actions to the user; ii) supporting the structuring of the information hierarchy; iii) guiding the selection of graphical elements like icons, illustrations, and photographs to represent ideas; iv) aiding in the choice of a typeface versatile enough to meet the system's communication needs; v) supporting the standardization of system states; vi) guiding user flow design; vii) defining the system's textual tone of voice; viii) crafting the system's instructions; ix) measuring how much effort the user needs to invest to interact with the system; and x) developing strategies to ensure the user feels safe when interacting with the system.

Finally, we understand that the concept of simplicity can offer valuable insights to the HCI research community, and we see new avenues for investigation based on the experiences shared in this paper. Among these possibilities are associating simplicity with cultural issues, understanding how the Laws might affect people's interpretation and interaction across different countries and customs, and investigating what are the limitations of simplicity when it comes to UX design. Likewise, a research gap exists in exploring the relationship between simplicity and accessibility to understand how simplicity influences the design of accessible interfaces. The Laws of Simplicity should also be investigated in the context of emerging HCI technologies, such as conversational interfaces, artificial intelligence, and ubiquitous computing, to examine how simplicity takes shape in non-traditional interface scenarios, including voice-based interfaces and context-aware systems.

**Acknowledgments.** The authors would like to thank the entire team that participated in the studies and worked on MEC RED redesign: C3SL and MEC team, and consultants. This study was financed in part by the Coordination for the Improvement of Higher Education Personnel - Brasil (CAPES) - Finance Code 001. The Project "Potencializando a Plataforma Integrada MEC RED: Pesquisa, Inovação e Melhoria da Experiência Educacional através da Integração de Redes Sociais e Mecanismos de Busca de Conteúdo" is funded by the MEC (Ministério da Educação) and FNDE (Fundo Nacional de Desenvolvimento da Educação). Roberto Pereira is a Research Productivity fellow from the Brazilian Council for Scientific and Technological Development (CNPq) (grant 306423/2023-5).

**Disclosure of Interests.** The authors have no competing interests to declare that are relevant to the content of this article.

# References

1. Apuke, O.D., Omar, B.: Social media affordances and information abundance: enabling fake news sharing during the covid-19 health crisis. Health Inform. J. **27**(3), 14604582211021470 (2021). https://doi.org/10.1177/14604582211021470
2. Bawden, D., Robinson, L.: Information Overload: An Introduction. In: Oxford Research Encyclopedia of Politics (2020)
3. Boren, T., Ramey, J.: Thinking aloud: reconciling theory and practice. IEEE Trans. Prof. Commun. **43**(3), 261–278 (2000). https://doi.org/10.1109/47.867942

4. Canal, M.C., de Miranda, L.C., Almeida, L.D.A., Baranauskas, M.C.C.: Analisando a simplicidade do laptop da olpc: Desafios e propostas de soluções de design. In: Seminário Integrado de Software e Hardware (SEMISH), pp. 1250–1264. SBC (2011). https://sol.sbc.org.br/index.php/semish/article/view/29210
5. Choi, J.H., Lee, H.J.: Facets of simplicity for the smartphone interface: a structural model. Int. J. Hum. Comput. Stud. **70**(2), 129–142 (2012). https://doi.org/10.1016/j.ijhcs.2011.09.002
6. Cysne, C., Schramm, L., RIOS, R.: As leis da simplicidade: Análise dos portais jangadeiro online e o povo (2010)
7. Eytam, E., Tractinsky, N., Lowengart, O.: The paradox of simplicity: effects of role on the preference and choice of product visual simplicity level. Int. J. Hum. Comput. Stud. **105**, 43–55 (2017). https://doi.org/10.1016/j.ijhcs.2017.04.001
8. Hayes, G.R.: Knowing by doing: action research as an approach to HCI. In: Olson, J.S., Kellogg, W.A. (eds.) Ways of Knowing in HCI, pp. 49–68. Springer, New York (2014). https://doi.org/10.1007/978-1-4939-0378-8_3
9. de Jong, C.W., Klemp, K., Mattie, E., Goodwin, D.: Ten principles for good design: dieter Rams: the Jorrit Maan collection. Prestel, Munich (2017)
10. Joshi, S.G.: Designing for experienced simplicity. why analytic and imagined simplicity fail in design of assistive technology. Int. J. Adv. Intell. Syst. **8**(3-4), 324–338 (2015)
11. Lazar, J., Feng, J.H., Hochheiser, H.: Research Methods in Human-Computer Interaction. Morgan Kaufmann (2017)
12. Lee, D.W., Moon, J.H., Kim, Y.J.: The effects of simplicity and interactivity in blog services, pp. 488–493 (2007)
13. Li, X., Chan, M.: Smartphone uses and emotional and psychological well-being in china: the attenuating role of perceived information overload. Behav. Inf. Technol. **41**(11), 2427–2437 (2022). https://doi.org/10.1080/0144929X.2021.1929489
14. Ma, R., Lassila, H., Nurgalieva, L., Lindqvist, J.: When browsing gets cluttered: exploring and modeling interactions of browsing clutter, browsing habits, and coping. In: Proceedings of the 2023 CHI Conference on Human Factors in Computing Systems, pp. 1–29 (2023). https://doi.org/10.1145/3544548.3580690
15. Maeda, J.: The Laws of Simplicity. MIT Press (2006)
16. Margaria, T., Floyd, B.D.: Simplicity in it: a chance for a new kind of design and process science. J. Integr. Des. Process. Sci. **17**(3), 1–7 (2013)
17. Menezes, E.M.D., Baranauskas, M.C.C.: O uso de mensageiros instantâneos móveis pode ser formal? um estudo situado no contexto educacional. In: Sánchez, J. (ed.) Nuevas ideas en informática educativa, vol. 12, pp. 294–304. Santiago de Chile (2016)
18. Menezes, K., Pereira, R., Bona, L.C., Reis, R., Todt, E.: Avaliação da plataforma mec red por especialistas (2024). https://doi.org/10.13140/RG.2.2.13129.56162
19. Menezes, K.M.L., Ortiz, J.S., Pereira, R.: Avaliando a acessibilidade a partir de uma perspectiva inclusiva: o caso da plataforma mec de recursos educacionais digitais. In: Simpósio Brasileiro de Informática na Educação (SBIE), pp. 1018–1029. SBC (2023). https://doi.org/10.5753/sbie.2023.234693
20. Ministério da Educação: Enec: Estratégia nacional de escolas conectadas. https://www.gov.br/mec/pt-br/escolas-conectadas. Accessed
21. Nielsen, J.: Enhancing the explanatory power of usability heuristics. In: Proceedings of the SIGCHI conference on Human Factors in Computing Systems, pp. 152–158. Association for Computing Machinery, New York, NY, USA (1994). https://doi.org/10.1145/191666.191729

22. de Oliveira, M.R., et al.: Open educational resources platform based on collective intelligence. In: 2018 IEEE 4th International Conference on Collaboration and Internet Computing (CIC), pp. 346–353. IEEE (2018). https://doi.org/10.1109/CIC.2018.00053
23. Pereira, G.C., Baranauskas, M.C.C.: Empowering lesbian, gay, bisexual, and transgender (LGBT) people with codesign: a critical evaluation through the lens of simplicity. In: Marcus, A., Wang, W. (eds.) DUXU 2018. LNCS, vol. 10918, pp. 153–164. Springer, Cham (2018). https://doi.org/10.1007/978-3-319-91797-9_12
24. Pinto, N.N.C., Mota, S.C.: Prototipação e validação multifásica de instrumento avaliativo para ensino de jovens e adultos| prototyping and multiphasic validation of an evaluation tool for youth and adult education. InfoDesign-Revista Brasileira de Design da Informação **17**(2), 49–65 (2020). https://doi.org/10.51358/id.v17i2.819
25. Pu, Q., Hu, B.: Intelligent movie recommendation system based on hybrid recommendation algorithms. In: 2023 International Conference on Ambient Intelligence, Knowledge Informatics and Industrial Electronics (AIKIIE), pp. 1–5. IEEE (2023). https://doi.org/10.1109/AIKIIE60097.2023.10389982
26. Resatsch, F., Sandner, U., Michelis, D., Hoechst, C., Schildhauer, T.: Everyday simplicity: the implications of everyday tasks for ubiquitous computing applications (2007)
27. Schon, D.A.: Designing as reflective conversation with the materials of a design situation. Res. Eng. Des. **3**(3), 131–147 (1992). https://doi.org/10.1016/0950-7051(92)90020-G
28. da Silva Araujo, J.I., Moser, P.C., Domingos, E.R., Afonso, V.A.S.D., Barbosa, J.F.: Benefícios e limitações da simplicidade em projetos inovadores de software: uma revisão sistemática da literatura. GESTÃO. Org **16**(7), 279–292 (2018). https://doi.org/10.21714/1679-18272018v16Ed.p279-292
29. Verkijika, S.F., De Wet, L.: Understanding word-of-mouth (WOM) intentions of mobile app users: the role of simplicity and emotions during the first interaction. Telematics Inform. **41**, 218–228 (2019). https://doi.org/10.1016/j.tele.2019.05.003
30. Weiser, M.: The computer for the 21st century. Sci. Am. **265**(3), 94–105 (1991)

# Designing for *Einfühlung:* Strategies for Embodied Sensitivity in Interactive Spaces

Maja Fagerberg Ranten[1](✉) 📵, Mads Hobye[1] 📵, Troels Andreasen[1] 📵, Karen Eide Bøen[2], and Lise Aagaard Knudsen[3]

[1] Roskilde University, Universitetsvej 1, 4000 Roskilde, Denmark
{mranten,troels}@ruc.dk, mads@hobye.dk
[2] Bergen, Norway
[3] Copenhagen, Denmark

**Abstract.** This paper explores strategies for designing interactive spaces that cultivate *Einfühlung* - an embodied sensitivity to feeling into others' experiences. While prior work has explored the designer's embodied role, we focus on how interactive technologies can engage participants' bodily experience to foster affective and relational resonance. Through a series of research-through-design experiments with the Memory Mechanics installation, a virtual archive of embodied memories, we investigate how spatial, gestural, and affective interactions can evoke bodily resonance. Drawing on these experiences, we identify four key strategies for supporting embodied sensibility and collective reflection. We propose that *Einfühlung* is not a fixed trait, but an emergent quality shaped through interactive engagement. These strategies offer conceptual tools for designing technologies that foster intimacy, sensitivity, and meaning over control and efficiency in interactive spaces.

**Keywords:** Einfühlung · Embodied Sensitivity · Embodied Interaction · Phenomenology · Soma Design · Interactive Art · Computer Vision · Machine Learning

## 1 Introduction

When designing interactive experiences, qualities such as slowness, sensibility, and reflection are often overlooked in favour of excitement, novelty, and engagement as primary qualities for capturing people's attention [1]. This paper explores how to design for *embodied sensibility* —a bodily and affective attunement to others' experience, through the concept of *Einfühlung,* a German term loosely translated to empathy, but more precisely meaning "feeling into" another's experience. This concept provides a lens for

---

K. E. Bøen —Independent choreographer.
L. A. Knudsen—Independent performer.

---

**Supplementary Information** The online version contains supplementary material available at https://doi.org/10.1007/978-3-032-05002-1_15.

exploring how interactive systems might invite participants to connect with the embodied experiences of others in subtle, reflective ways. Our research is situated within a programmatic design approach [4, 37, 38]. We ask: *How can we design interactive spaces that invite us to feel the embodied memories of others?* To explore this, we present *Memory Mechanics*, an interactive installation that stores participants' spoken memories alongside the bodily poses in which they were shared.

This paper builds on phenomenology and embodied approaches, aligning with the somatic turn within third-wave HCI, a shift that foregrounds lived, felt experience as central to interaction design [9, 15, 24, 28, 41, 45]. It contributes with four design considerations for crafting interactive spaces that support embodied sensitivity and shared reflection.

## 2 *Einfühlung*: Embodying Sensitivity

This section lays the conceptual foundation for our analytical work by rearticulating *Einfühlung* as a form of embodied sensitivity, engaging with others through affective, bodily, and relational resonance. Rather than treating empathy as a cognitive or representational process, we draw from phenomenology [19, 31, 32], affect theory [10, 30], and somatic design [6, 17, 18, 25, 26, 40, 47] to frame *Einfühlung* as a situated, lived experience that unfolds through movement, posture, and gesture in technological environments. *Einfühlung* is historically rooted in aesthetic theory, initially describing the projection of feeling into art objects [34]. Husserl [20] later framed it as recognising the other's subjectivity through bodily distinction. Both emphasise *feeling into* another being or form rather than thinking about it. In interaction design, we reposition *Einfühlung*'s historical roots in aesthetics and psychology to a contemporary understanding of embodied, intuitive sensitivity, cultivated through bodily awareness and perceptual engagement with others in interactive installations. This orientation privileges slowness, affective resonance, and relational experience over cognitive control. It is shaped in-between bodies, mediated by rhythm, gesture, and space. We structure our conceptual framework of *Einfühlung* around three interconnected themes we termed: *Embodied Resonance, Movement and Mirroring*, and *Relational and Situated Attunement*.

**Embodied Resonance** draws on Debes' [8] reading of early phenomenological and psychological theories of empathy, revisiting Lipps' idea of *Einfühlung* as combining *projection* and *motor imitation*. When observing others or objects, we project *kinesthetic feelings* back into them, producing felt resonance. This embodied feedback, rather than cognitive interference, is foundational to *Einfühlung*. This informs our view of empathy in interactive environments as enacted through bodily movement and gesture. We align this with *somatic empathy*—visceral, embodied resonance with another's state—as discussed by Singer & Lamm's [43], emphasising affective sharing and self-other distinction.

**Movement and Mirroring:** From dance and performance studies, *kinaesthetic empathy* describes the ability to feel and understand others' experiences or emotions through shared movement and rhythm [42]. In HCI, *kinesthetic interaction* [10, 33] highlights how bodily motion, shaped by environmental or technological stimuli, enables people to perceive and respond to one another. Concepts such as *inner imitation* and *motor* *mimicry* [5, 34] explain how unconscious bodily mirroring can establish empathetic links. Not empathy through language, but through gesture and motion. Together, these perspectives show how *Movement and Mirroring* enable a form of empathy grounded in bodily resonance.

**Relational and Situated Attunement:** Empathy is increasingly recognised as central to experience-centred design. Wright and McCarthy [49] describe empathy as key to connecting with users' felt experiences. Loke and Robertson's [27] propose *kinesthetic movement* and "making strange" to disrupt habitual movements and provoke new relational awareness. Our installation builds on this, treating empathy as an emergent, bodily process involving humans and their entanglement with technology and the environment. This highlights Einfühlung as *Relational and Situated Attunement*. Zigon's [50] notion of *empathic attunement* reinforces this, viewing empathy as arising through dynamic affective relations. While technology lacks embodied relationality, it mediates affective or sensory cues and supports empathic attunement. In the installation, memories are recalled not through explicit selection, but by adopting bodily postures that echo others' gestures, triggering shared, embodied experience.

While empathy in HCI is often approached through three dimensions: somatic, affective and cognitive [36], most studies treat it as an internal, individual process. We challenge this by drawing on Genç and Verma's [13] critique of individualistic empathy, proposing instead a collective, spatially mediated view enacted through bodily movement and affective feedback loops between people and technologies.

Based on these three interconnected themes, we frame *Einfühlung* within interaction design as embodied sensitivity, grounded in movement, affect, and relational resonance, offering a conceptual framework—rooted in phenomenology, aesthetic theory, and somatic design—for analysing and designing interactive systems that evoke empathetic engagement.

## 3 Methodology: Situated Disseminations as a Field Lab

This research follows a programmatic approach [4, 37, 38] grounded in research through design [11, 16, 37, 51], where knowledge is generated through iterative making, reflection, and situated engagement. Our process involves cycles of digital sketching and prototyping [35], and experience-based refinement to explore how memories, bodily awareness, and digital mediation can be meaningfully intertwined. Central is a designerly mode of inquiry –understanding through doing and making– where the installation is not conceived as an outcome, but as a vehicle for inquiry, contributing knowledge through its experiential, performative, and technical qualities.

The project has unfolded through lab- and field-based development [14, 22, 23], with the touring of the installation across diverse venues and contexts acting as methods of inquiry[1]. These situated experiments allowed us to trace interaction strategies through our field-informed situated knowledge of observing and being with the installation and participants. Across varied contexts, spatial setups, algorithmic behaviours, and interaction rituals, we observed how such variations shaped the participants' embodied interaction and informed ongoing design adjustments. Participants were primarily digitally literate adults (25–65) from Western European backgrounds, with mixed gender representation and generally unrestricted mobility.

In line with Höök et al. [17], we invited participants to engage with the installation and qualitatively analyse their embodied experience – not to provide full accounts, but to surface design-relevant qualities [29] and opportunities [46]. Central to this evaluation was sustained participant engagement across diverse contexts. Through informal dialogue and co-presence, recurring patterns emerged. These were distilled into four interrelated design strategies, not as prescriptive rules, but as generative strategies for future work on bodily and affective interaction. While insightful, further exploration of individual experience remains a potential avenue.

## 4 Memory Mechanics: An Interactive Installation

The system uses real-time computer vision to track participants' poses and gestures within a dedicated space, transforming bodily movement into a medium for recording and recalling memories. The experience has two modes of operation:

**Mode #1: Collecting Memories Anchored in the Body.** A process was developed that guided the participants into this relationship. The process consisted of the following steps: *1. Connecting to early memories*: participants were invited to recall and draw on their earliest childhood memories. *2. Guided movement*: with eyes closed, they were gently led through the interactive space, encouraged to surrender to being guided. *3. Guided positioning*: The facilitator then placed them in a pose. *4. Sharing a memory:* participants were invited to share a memory (out loud) that arose in the pose. 5. Repetition: steps 2–4 were repeated a few times (see Fig. 1).

Through these steps, each participant is guided to find a pose that stimulates a memory, experience or sensation to surface. The participant is then invited to voice the invoked memory. Often, these were forgotten or emotionally charged memories that surfaced through embodied exploration. This process created space for vulnerability, reflection, and affective resonance. Whenever a sharing surfaced, the participants voice and the pose they stood in were recorded. This was done either automatically through the interactive system or manually, using an audio recorder and annotating the pose by hand for later training in the system.

---

[1] The installation has been showcased in a series of exhibition venues and contexts: 2020 Ars Electronica Festival, Kepler's Gardens (online); 2021 CLICK AI Days at the Culture Yard, Helsingør (old Shipyard venue); 2021 NOVA Festival, in Bucharest (gallery); 2021 HAUT Works-in-progress festival, Copenhagen (theatre black box); 2022 NOFOD conference: Moving, relating, commanding, Choreographies for bodies, identities and ecologies, Copenhagen (conference room); 2022 Piksel Festival, Bergen (gallery); and 2024 eCommemoration Convention, Hamburg (convention space).

   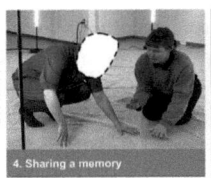 

**Fig. 1.** *Memory Mechanics* installation & illustration: The different steps to retrieve a memory.

**Mode #2: Exploring the Memories in the Interactive Space.** In the second mode of operation, the participants can explore the collected memories by moving through the space, experimenting with different poses. When a participant adopts a pose similar to one held by another who shared a memory, the voiced recording will be played.

A ritual around the installation was created to help participants connect with the space and approach the stories with sensitivity, offering an experiential framework through four stages: *1. Transitioning,* where participants removed their shoes and put on wireless headphones to enter an individual, focused space; *2. Dormant,* where a chorus of overlapping voices created a sense of memory traces awaiting attention (the system would stay in the dormant mode until the participants managed to tune into a specific memory and thus pose); *3. Tuning in,* where matching a recorded pose amplified a single memory while others faded (hence the participant had to stay in the pose to keep hearing the memory); and *4. Repeating,* where moving out of the pose returned to dormancy, inviting continued exploration through new postures.

From a technical perspective, the system uses computer vision for real-time tracking of participants' poses in the space and an incremental supervised machine learning model to classify the poses. The classes in the model corresponds to each memory recorded during Mode #1, and classification thus corresponds to a mapping from a pose to a spoken memory. During the recording of a memory, a series of labelled input samples (poses with class labels) for the memory are stored. These represent the natural variation of the pose the participant has while simultaneously speaking and maintaining the chosen pose, and they provide training data for the specific classification. Further, a collection of samples (poses) not corresponding to a specific memory was used for rejection classification. When a participant steps into the installation, the machine learning model (in real time) estimates the similarity (in percentage) of the current participant's pose to each pose in the collection (see Fig. 2).

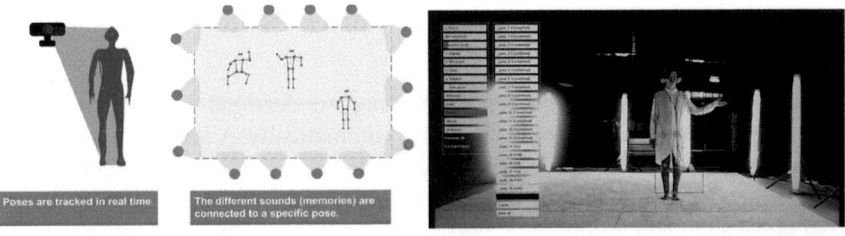

**Fig. 2.** *Memory Mechanics* Screen & Illustration: The technical setup of the installation.

If the rejection classification scored above 50%, all samples were raised to a medium volume (dormant state). If one of the other poses scored highest, the volume of each sound sample of the memories is adjusted according to this classification (tuning in stage). The sounds were either played through wireless headphones or a speaker system[2].

## 5 Findings: Four Strategies for Designing for Einfühlung in an Interactive Space

The following outlines the four design strategies that emerged from the series of explorations in the field (see the Sect. 5.1, 5.2, 5.3, 5.4):

### 5.1 Strategy 1: Recognise and Navigate Multiple Modes of User Engagement

Participants brought a range of orientations to *Memory Mechanics*, revealing a tension between the designed ideal of a deep, embodied experience and the diverse ways people actually engaged. From a phenomenological perspective, each participant's lifeworld [19] shapes their perceptions and interactions.

We identified four user archetypes: *1. The Technically Curious*, who explored the system's mechanics; *2. The Unaware Observer* didn't realise the installation was interactive; *3. The Empathetic Resonator* connected emotionally through gesture and memory; *4. The Playful Explorer* interacted expressively, but with a limited engagement with content.

These modes reflect different starting points for approaching the installation. Some participants remained with visual feedback (on the stick figure on the monitor), framing the installation as task-based or representational. Others engaged through kinesthetic and auditory feedback, exploring the space affectively and experientially.

Designing for *Einfühlung* requires accommodating this variability. Systems should offer layered entry points that support kinesthetic exploration and movement-based attunement, enabling transitions from cognitive to affective and embodied engagement. This supports *Embodied Resonance*, as users connect to the system through bodily projection and affective feedback. *Relational and Situated Attunement* is co-shaped by the user's relational stance and prior experiences as a form of interaction. This aligns with third-wave HCI and phenomenological perspectives that see meaning as emerging through embodied interaction-in-context [2, 9, 32, 46, 48].

### 5.2 Strategy 2: Use Ritual and Spatial Framing to Support Transitions for Embodied Sensitivity

In *Memory Mechanics*, we found that *Einfühlung*—understood as the capacity to feel into the experience of another—does not arise automatically. A set of rituals and spatial cues helped the participants to shift towards a slower, more reflective, and embodied mode of being. These transitional rituals [21] included *putting on headphones* to block external noise and enter an intimate, personal soundscape; *removing shoes* to heighten

---

[2] See a video of the installation.

a kinesthetic awareness of your feet touching the ground; *stepping onto a soft carpet* that evoked a homely, tactile transition; and *moving into dim inward-facing lightning* that marked a clear boundary between being outside and inside, reinforcing the enclosed atmosphere of the space.

These design choices framed the space as distinct, inviting participants to leave behind distractions and enter a more vulnerable, resonant bodily state. This aligns with *Embodied Resonance*, as participants attune to space through kinesthetic and sensory projection, and *Movement and Mirroring*, as inner imitation and bodily gestures activate empathetic engagement.

Phenomenologically, this reflects Merleau-Ponty's [31] notion that the body is the primary site of perception. These spatial and sensory cues became part of the *inner imitation* process [5], and the shift in posture, tempo, and sensory input supported a reorientation toward bodily sensing, enhancing the possibility for empathetic mirroring.

The move from speakers to personal headphones marked a crucial transition: from public performance [7] to private resonance. In contrast, headphones encouraged intimate engagement and inward orientation, deepening relational sensitivity through intimate engagement. Thus, *Einfühlung* is shaped partly by the designed atmosphere and embodied rituals supporting attunement.

### 5.3 Strategy 3: Attend to Situated Context as Co-shapers of Empathy

As established in third-wave HCI [2, 3], interaction is always situated, emerging through the interplay between people, material configurations, and sociocultural settings. While this is widely acknowledged [9, 39], our work reaffirmed that empathetic engagement unfolds through contextually framed bodily experience.

Context co-constructs meaning, pace, and affective tone. Participants' prior experiences, interests, and worldviews are not separate from the interaction but deeply entangled with the setting in which it unfolds. In the formal atmosphere of a *gallery setting*, the setting fostered ritualistic, reflective engagement. At the *thematic conferences*, participants were guided by each event's focus: at eCommemoration, the installation was seen as a speculative archive of intangible traces, while at NOFOD, it was approached as a choreographic interface; and at the Piksel *art + tech festival*, interaction was driven by curiosity about the system's technical behaviour. Each situation invited different forms of relational and embodied sensitivity.

This speaks directly to *Relational and Situated Attunement* as the capacity to feel into the installation emerged through a shared spatial-temporal atmosphere. *Memory Mechanics* functions as a living archive, a space shaped by the contributions of many. Participants do not merely encounter data but attune to resonant traces of others, accessed through gesture and sound. This evokes Merleau-Ponty's notion of intercorporelity [32], where meaning arises *between* bodies in shared space. The facilitator's role was to initiate engagement, with participants often mirroring the performer's gentle vibe (in Mode #1). As Höök et al. [18] note, guidance must be subtle, directing attention without seizing it. Still, the reliance on guided movement potentially raises concerns about reproducibility and bias, underscoring the need to examine the facilitator's influence more closely in future development of design strategies for *Einfühlung*.

Designing for *Einfühlung* in this context means treating memory not as static content to retrieve but as relational and embodied, emerging through contextually framed bodily engagement. It involves crafting spaces that feel collectively owned, emotionally resonant, and alive with the presence of others in an augmented, intersubjective space. This design strategy underscores the importance of contextual resonance: empathy does not emerge universally, but through situated bodily experience.

### 5.4 Strategy 4: Embrace Algorithmic Openness Through Affective Feedback Loops

*Memory Mechanics* was not designed for precision but for embodied resonance. The system embraced the inherent fuzziness of machine learning (ML), not as a flaw, but as a feature that enabled ambiguity [12, 44], openness, and embodied exploration.

Through bodily gestures and postures—stretching an arm, shifting stance—participants activated fragments of memory. These gestures formed a collective choreography, a growing archive of memories. By preserving uncertainty in how movement is mapped to memory, the system shifted focus from task completion to felt sensitivity. The algorithm acted as a responsive co-performer, inviting misinterpretation, surprise, and exploration, rather than serving as a strict evaluator. Because of the ML fuzziness and the algorithmic principles of volume adjustment between dormant and tuning in the participants had to "tune in"—like adjusting a radio—to subtle bodily cues, often maintaining postures to keep the memory alive, engaging the whole body in sensing and listening. This supported *Movement and Mirroring*, as the interaction unfolded through dynamic feedback, unconscious mimicry [5, 34], and *Embodied Resonance*, when participants tuned into the system to sustain memory traces.

The design strategies fostered moments of affective feedback loops involving the participant's movement, evolving soundscapes, and bodily awareness. The system did not interpret but co-responded and supported situated *Einfühlung* to memory traces.

## 6 Conclusion

In this paper, we explored how interactive installations can foster *Einfühlung* —as an embodied sensitivity that enables participants to *feel into* others' experiences through movement, gesture, and attunement. Through research-through-design experiments with the *Memory Mechanics* installation, we identified four interrelated design strategies for crafting interactive spaces that support empathic, bodily engagement.

These design strategies emerged through iterative practice and are grounded in phenomenology, affect theory, and embodied and somatic interaction design. They show how empathy can be fostered through spatial framing, transitional rituals, ambiguous feedback, and affective bodily interaction. Our contribution lies in articulating *Einfühlung* as an emergent, relational quality—shared through interaction, space, and the lived body—rather than a fixed capacity or cognitive function. We argue for embracing ambiguity, slowness, and rituals as conditions for fostering embodied empathy. We acknowledge that cultural, gendered, and bodily differences influence embodiment, and that our design reflects assumptions. Future work should involve participants with diverse embodiments—not just as users, but also as potential co-designers—to support more inclusive and culturally sensitive interaction design.

The strategies are not prescriptive formulas, but conceptual tools —design qualities that can guide interaction designers to support intimacy, reflection, and attunement over control and efficiency. We offer them as prompts for further exploration, reconfiguration, and reflection towards designing for *Einfühlung*.

**Acknowledgments.** Memory Mechanics is created by Maja Fagerberg Ranten, Mads Hobye, Troels Andreasen, Karen Eide Bøen, and Lise Aagaard Knudsen. Memory Mechanics was initiated as part of the Staging the Future of Technologies (SFT) vol. 2 project, by CLICK, HAUT, and Catch. SFT was funded by Bikubenfonden & Copenhagen Municipality. Memory Mechanics has been showcased in 2020 at Ars Electronica Festival, Kepler's Gardens; 2021 CLICK AI Days at the Culture Yard, Helsingør; 2021 NOVA Festival, in Bucharest; 2021 HAUT Works-in-progress festival, Copenhagen; 2022 NOFOD conference: Moving, relating, commanding, Choreographies for bodies, identities and ecologies, Copenhagen; 2022 Piksel Festival, Bergen; and 2024 eCommemoration Convention, Hamburg.

**Disclosure of Interests.** The authors have no competing interests to declare that are relevant to the content of this article.

# References

1. Benford, S., et al.: From interaction to trajectories: designing coherent journeys through user experiences. In: Proceedings of the SIGCHI Conference on Human Factors in Computing Systems. ACM, New York, NY, USA (2009). https://doi.org/10.1145/1518701.1518812
2. Bødker, S.: Third-wave HCI, 10 years later - Participation and sharing. Interactions (2015). https://doi.org/10.1145/2804405
3. Bødker, S.: When second wave HCI meets third wave challenges. In: ACM International Conference Proceeding Series. (2006). https://doi.org/10.1145/1182475.1182476
4. Brandt, E., et al.: XLAB. Danish Design School Press (2011)
5. Burns, T.: Theodor Lipps on the concept of Einfühlung (Empathy). In: Theodor Lipps (1851–1914): Psychologie, Philosophie, Esthétique, Langage/Psychology, Philosophy, Aesthetics, Language. SDVIG Press (2022)
6. Candau, Y., et al.: Designing from embodied knowing: practice-based research at the intersection between embodied interaction and somatics. In: Filimowicz, M., Tzankova, V. (eds.) Human–Computer Interaction Series. pp. 203–230 Springer, Cham (2018). https://doi.org/10.1007/978-3-319-73374-6_11
7. Dalsgaard, P., Hansen, L.K.: Performing perception—staging aesthetics of interaction. ACM Trans. Comput. Hum. Interact. **15**(3), 1–33 (2008)
8. Debes, R.: From einfühlung to empathy. In: Sympathy. pp. 286–322 Oxford University Press (2015)
9. Dourish, P.: Where the Action Is: The Foundations of Embodied Interaction. MIT Press (2001)
10. Fogtmann, M.H., et al.: Kinesthetic interaction. In: Proceedings of the 20th Australasian Conference on Computer-Human Interaction: Designing for Habitus and Habitat, New York, NY, USA. ACM (2008). https://doi.org/10.1145/1517744.1517770
11. Frayling, C.: Research in art and design. Royal College of Art (1993)
12. Gaver, W.W., et al.: Ambiguity as a resource for design. In: Conference on Human Factors in Computing Systems - Proceedings (2003). https://doi.org/10.1145/642611.642653

13. Genç, U., Verma, H.: Situating empathy in HCI/CSCW: a scoping review. Proc. ACM Hum. Comput. Interact. **8**(CSCW2), 1–37 (2024). https://doi.org/10.1145/3687052
14. Hobye, M.: Playing with fire: Collaborating through digital sketching in a creative community. In: Making Futures. pp. 131–152 The MIT Press (2014)
15. Höök, K.: Designing with the Body. The MIT Press (2018)
16. Höök, K., et al.: Knowledge Production in Interaction Design. Presented at the (2015). https://doi.org/10.1145/2702613.2702653
17. Höök, K. et al.: Move to be moved. In: Conference on Human Factors in Computing Systems - Proceedings (2016). https://doi.org/10.1145/2851581.2856470
18. Höök, K. et al.: Somaesthetic appreciation design. In: Proceedings of the 2016 CHI Conference on Human Factors in Computing Systems, New York, NY, USA. ACM (2016). https://doi.org/10.1145/2858036.2858583
19. Husserl, E.: Cartesian Meditations. Springer, Dordrecht (1960). https://doi.org/10.1007/978-94-017-4952-7
20. Husserl, E.: Ideas pertaining pure phenomenology phenomenological philosophy. Second book: Studies phenomenology constitution (R). Studies phenomenology constitution (R. Rojcewicz & Schuwer, Trans.) (1989)
21. Klüber, S. et al.: Designing ritual artifacts for technology-mediated relationship transitions. In: Proceedings of the Fourteenth International Conference on Tangible, Embedded, and Embodied Interaction, New York, NY, US. ACMA (2020). https://doi.org/10.1145/3374920.3374937
22. Koskinen, I., et al.: Design research through practice: from the lab, field, and showroom. IEEE Trans. Prof. Commun. (2013). https://doi.org/10.1109/tpc.2013.2274109
23. Koskinen, I., et al.: Lab, field, gallery, and beyond1. Artifact. **2**(1), 46–57 (2008)
24. Kozel, S.: Closer: Performance, Technologies, Phenomenology Massachusetts (2007)
25. Kozel, S. et al.: the weird giggle: attending to affect in virtual reality **31**, 31 (2018)
26. Loke, L., Núñez-Pacheco, C.: Developing somatic sensibilities for practices of discernment in interaction design. Senses Soc. **13**(2), 219–231 (2018). https://doi.org/10.1080/17458927.2018.1468690
27. Loke, L., Robertson, T.: Moving and making strange: an embodied approach to movement-based interaction design. ACM Trans. Comput. Hum. Interact. (2013). https://doi.org/10.1145/2442106.2442113
28. Loke, L., Robertson, T.: The lived body in design. Presented at the (2011). https://doi.org/10.1145/2071536.2071565
29. Löwgren, J.: The use qualities of digital designs. Knowledge Creation Diffusion Utilization. (2002)
30. Massumi, B.: Politics of Affect. Polity Press, Oxford, England (2015)
31. Merleau-Ponty, M.: Phenomenology of Perception. Routledge, London, England (1962). https://doi.org/10.4324/9780203720714
32. Merleau-Ponty, M.: The Visible and the Invisible: Followed by Working Notes. Northwestern University Press (1968)
33. Moen, J.: From Hand-Held to Body-Worn: Embodied Experiences of the Design and Use of a Wearable Movement-Based Interaction Concept. 15–17 (2007). https://doi.org/10.1145/3337722.3337733
34. Montag, C.M., et al.: Theodor Lipps and the concept of empathy: 1851–1914. Am. J. Psychiatry **165**(10), 1261–1261 (2008)
35. Padfield, N., et al.: Empowering academia through modern fabrication practices. Fablearn Europe (2014)
36. Price, A., Dambha-Miller, H.: Empathy as a state beyond feeling: a patient and clinician perspective. J. Roy. Soc. Med. **112**, 2 (2019)

37. Redström, J.: Making Design Theory. The MIT Press (2017)
38. Redström, J.: Some Notes on Program/Experiment Dialectics, 1–8 (2011)
39. Robertson, T., Loke, L.: Designing situations. In: Proceedings of the 21st Annual Conference of the Australian Computer-Human Interaction Special Interest Group - Design: Open 24/7, OZCHI '09. (2009). https://doi.org/10.1145/1738826.1738828
40. Schiphorst, T.: Soft(n): toward a somaesthetics of touch. In: Conference on Human Factors in Computing Systems - Proceedings. (2009). https://doi.org/10.1145/1520340.1520345
41. Schiphorst, T., Loke, L.: The somatic turn in human-computer interaction. Interactions (2018). https://doi.org/10.1145/3236675
42. Sheets-Johnstone, M.: The Primacy of Movement. John Benjamins Publishing, Amsterdam, Netherlands (1999)
43. Singer, T., Lamm, C.: The social neuroscience of empathy. Ann. N. Y. Acad. Sci. **1156**(1), 81–96 (2009)
44. Sivertsen, C., et al.: Machine learning processes as sources of ambiguity: Insights from AI art. In: Proceedings of the CHI Conference on Human Factors in Computing Systems, pp. 1–14, New York, NY, USA. ACM (2024). https://doi.org/10.1145/3613904.3642855
45. Svanæs, D.: Dag: Interaction design for and with *the lived body*. ACM Trans. Comput. Hum. Interact. **20**(1), 1–30 (2013). https://doi.org/10.1145/2442106.2442114
46. Tomico, O., Wilde, D.: Soft, embodied, situated & connected. In: MobileHCI 2015 - Proceedings of the 17th International Conference on Human-Computer Interaction with Mobile Devices and Services Adjunct (2015). https://doi.org/10.1145/2786567.2794351
47. Tsaknaki, V., et al.: Feeling the sensor feeling you: a Soma design exploration on sensing non-habitual breathing. In: Proceedings of the 2021 CHI Conference on Human Factors in Computing Systems, New York, NY, USA. ACM (2021). https://doi.org/10.1145/3411764.3445628
48. Vallgarda, A., et al.: Material programming. Interactions (2017). https://doi.org/10.1145/3057277
49. Wright, P., McCarthy, J.: Empathy and experience in HCI. In: Proceedings of the SIGCHI Conference on Human Factors in Computing Systems, New York, NY, USA. ACM (2008). https://doi.org/10.1145/1357054.1357156
50. Zigon, J.: Can machines be ethical? On the necessity of relational ethics and empathic attunement for data-centric technologies. Soc. Res. Int. Quart. **86**(4), 1001–1022 (2019)
51. Zimmerman, J., et al.: Research Through Design As a Method for Interaction Design Research in HCI. In: Proceedings of the SIGCHI Conference on Human Factors in Computing Systems. pp. 493–502 ACM, New York, NY, USA (2007). https://doi.org/10.1145/1240624.1240704

# Framing the Risk: A Large-Scale Field Experiment on Risk Communication in Responsible Gambling

Carly Grace Allen[1,2](✉), Tanja Sveen[1], Frode Volden[2], and Yavuz Inal[2]

[1] Norsk Tipping AS, 2315 Hamar, Norway
[2] Department of Design, Norwegian University of Science and Technology, 2815 Gjovik, Norway
carly-grace.allen@norsk-tipping.no, carly.g.allen@ntnu.no

**Abstract.** As more people participate in gambling online, adding focus to the interaction design aspect of responsible gambling and related tools can improve their use and the goal of reducing gambling harm. An example of such an experiment was conducted to explore how receiving a message about a recent increase in risky gambling behavior can potentially influence and encourage players to set or change playing limits, take a break from playing, or complete a self-assessment. The message was set up as an A/B test with two types of message framing without a control group and was carried out live on the Norsk Tipping app and website, sent to 122,214 players over the span of two and a half months. The results show that roughly one in three went on to get further information, with more players doing so of those who received a message using general framing than negative framing, and one in ten decided to take some form of action based on the information they received, with negative framing being more effective in this percentage wise.

**Keywords:** Interaction design · Responsible gambling · Player experience · Risk communication · Behavioral tracking · Duty of care

## 1 Introduction

Responsible gambling encompasses both practices and policies that focus on three primary aspects: consumer protection, harm minimization, and harm reduction [1]. Research in responsible gambling sometimes looks at tools that can be used by players [2], and some focuses on communicating with players in real-time game sessions [3] or other forms of interventions. Due to the increase in the amount of online gambling and a higher propensity to become a problem gambler that has followed [4], the need for design to be taken into account grows to see how it can help responsible gambling efforts by increasing visibility, understanding, and access. One example of a responsible gambling tool that can be tested is in risk monitoring and messaging.

Informing players and motivating them to reduce their risk is one of the purposes of risk monitoring tools. By understanding their risk [5], players can more easily choose to make a change to help either keep control or take back control of their gambling and reduce their risk of developing gambling problems or addiction. Early intervention has shown promising results in that it can "reduce gambling symptoms, harm and behaviors" [6, p.968], and to do so on a large scale within a short time frame may increase the impact of responsible gambling measures.

When discussing communication of information, decision-making processes should be considered. Three relevant theories within behavioral design and economics are *prospect theory*, *framing*, and *self-determination*. Prospect theory focuses on how decision-making processes are based on a variety of biases, including frame dependence and availability biases, as well as cognitive differences [7]. It looks at how people often evaluate gains and losses in relation to a reference point, not the final gains or losses. This is especially true in the context of risk.

Framing theory is rooted in prospect theory, in which the way information is framed can have an impact on decision-making [8]. It can be used as a way to create a storyline to describe what a problem is about [9]. This is in opposition to more "traditional economic models" [8] that assume people are rational beings that make rational decisions based solely on facts. The most common types of framing focus on what is called "positive" (this is good) or "negative" (this is bad) framing. In self-determination theory, motivation "emerge as a function of the interaction between basic psychological needs and the social contexts that either support or thwart them" [10, p.1598]. Self-determination focuses on internal versus external motivation [11], and there is a potential in responsible gambling to evoke autonomy as a way to encourage intrinsic motivation to make a positive change in gambling behavior [10].

Some gambling companies desire to encourage autonomy and a positive change in gambling behavior. There are several European countries, including Norway, that have laws or principles on what is called "duty of care" [12, p.2], and these regulators "rely heavily on operators to design and implement these duty of care models". Norsk Tipping has the prerogative to test new responsible gambling features and tools in their goal of reducing gambling harm among their players [13]. Previously at Norsk Tipping, messages about a player having a recent increase in risky gambling behavior were sent as a push notification, and push notifications in general can have a click-through rate of 4–8% [14]. In our study, in an effort to improve these push notifications, an A/B test was conducted in the Norsk Tipping app and website. The objective of this test was to examine how different types of framing an initial message about a change or increase in risky gambling behavior can influence whether a player decides to use a responsible gambling tool, such as setting or changing gambling limits, taking a play break, or completing a self-assessment. These messages were formed as a message that would be shown in full screen on a mobile phone, as it can increase visibility and access to responsible gambling tools and potentially increase usage to help reduce and prevent future increases in risky gambling behaviors.

## 2 Methods

In a test about communication styles with players about a recent increase in risky gambling behavior, players were randomly assigned in an A/B test with no control group to receive a message about their recent change. The test was conducted live in the Norsk Tipping app and website as a part of the customer journey. It was designed for a per protocol analysis, which focuses on investigating the effect of receiving a treatment [15], or in this case, information via one of two messages about a recent negative change in behavior. These messages were generated weekly at 06:00 every Monday when the risk monitoring tool updated players' risk scores. This message pops up when a customer logs in after the message has been generated, and the message follows the already established internal design system used by Norsk Tipping.

### 2.1 Design of Intervention

Figure 1 shows the test set-up and flow of the messages. The texts behind these messages are connected to prospect theory [7] and framing [8], where the goal of the experiment was to test how possible communication of information in an initial message could influence the decision-making process in the following steps.

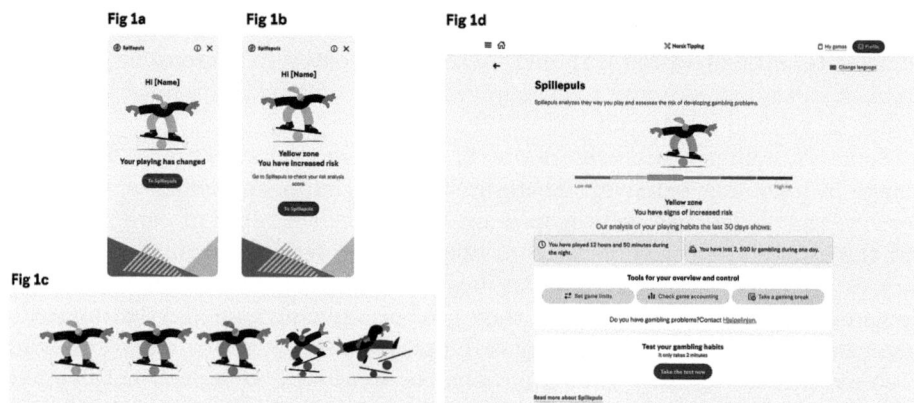

**Fig. 1.** Image with the general framing message (**1a**) and negative framing message (**1b**), a picture of the 5 different figures a player can be shown based on their risk score (**1c**), and the landing page that both messages took players to when they clicked the button to find more information (**1d**) (Color figure online)

The two types of framing used here were a "general frame", where the focus was on the fact that there had been a recent change in how they played, and a "negative frame", where the focus was on a recent change in their playing in a potentially detrimental way. The first message said "Hi [Player name]. Your playing has changed" (Fig. 1a) which will from here on out be referred to as general framing, and the other message said "Hi [Player name]. [Yellow or Red] zone. You have increased risk. Go to Spillepuls to check your risk analysis" (Fig. 1b) which will be from here on out referred to as negative framing. Even though positive framing is one of the two primary methods of framing used, it was not realistic in this context, as the reason for receiving one of these messages was a negative change in playing behavior. Both messages had a button that said "Go to Spillepuls" that led to the risk monitoring tool where players could get more information. The reasoning behind this button and messaging was an attempt to invoke intrinsic motivation, which is a large aspect of self-determination theory [10]. Finally, both messages used the same illustrations and graphic elements.

## 2.2 Participants

More than 2 million players were registered with Norsk Tipping as of January 1, 2025. Players are assigned a risk score that is based on a scale of 0–6, where 0 means that a player has not played enough to receive a risk score within the previous 5 weeks, 1 is considered low risk (or green), 2–4 are considered medium risk (or yellow) with medium-low, medium, or medium-high (collectively called medium here), and 5–6 considered high risk (or red) with high- or very-high (collectively called high here). Participants in this study were players who had a recent increase in their risk score from 0 or 1 (green) to 2–6 (yellow or red), or from 2–4 (yellow) to 5–6 (red) during the data collection period. A total of 122,214 messages were generated, and after removing those aged 18–19 due to having a lower maximum limit and removing invalid message triggers, the total number of players was reduced to 115,077. The analysis done here focused solely on those players who clicked the button for more information, totaling 42,459, shown in Table 1 (ref 1a and 1b, "To Spillepuls").

**Table 1.** Demographic distribution of players who received a message and clicked the button for more information

| Category | Variable | Respondents | Share of total |
|---|---|---|---|
| Gender | Female | 10,705 | 25.2% |
| | Male | 31,754 | 74.8% |
| Age interval | 20–24 | 9,231 | 21.7% |
| | 25–35 | 12,955 | 30.5% |
| | 36–45 | 8,417 | 19.8% |
| | 46–60 | 7,852 | 18.5% |
| | 61+ | 4,004 | 9.4% |
| Risk score | Medium | 33,315 | 78.5% |
| | High | 9,144 | 21.5% |
| Game risk score | Low | 7,343 | 17.3% |
| | Medium | 14,904 | 35.1% |
| | High | 20,212 | 47.6% |

## 2.3 Data Collection Procedure and Analysis

The analysis of this A/B test aimed to see if: (a) players who received one of the two messages either set a new limit, took a play break, or took a self-assessment; (b) differences in age, gender, risk score, or primary gambling risk category influenced the usage of these tools; and (c) there were differences between the two message variants in the usage of tools described in (a). The data collected was from November 1, 2024 to January 12, 2025, and was cleaned to remove invalid data, such as those for whom a trigger to receive a message was created and then nullified due to a change in their gambling behavior, making the message irrelevant.

SPSS version 30.0.0.0 (172) was used to perform the analysis. Pearson's Chi-square was used to test for independence and statistical significance throughout the analysis, as well as Cramér's V for effect-size to understand how potential significance could be impacted by the sample size.

# 3 Results

## 3.1 Click or Skip: How Framing Affects Initial Engagement

For the general framing message, 39.6% (n = 22,796) of players clicked the button for more information, compared to 34.2% (n = 19,693) for the negative framing message. The results of the Pearson's Chi-square independence test show significant effects ($x^2 = 349.065$, df = 1, n = 115.133, $p < 0.001$) towards the general framing message being more effective in leading more players to click the button. However, there is likely little association between framing and button clicks (Cramér's V = 0.055), meaning that the results may be predominantly due to sample size. Overall, the results show that the general framing message in absolute numbers outperforms the negative framing message in the initial step of clicking the button for more information.

## 3.2 General vs Negative Framing

The primary dependent variable looked at in this study was whether a player who received a message about increased risk and clicked to go further for more information changed their gambling limits, took a play break, or completed a self-assessment. These three actions were combined into one variable called "action", whereby the results are divided into "took action" or "did not take action".

When focusing only on those players who clicked the button, the general and negative framed messages were compared against each other (Table 2). The results show a significant relationship ($x^2 = 25.609$, df = 1, n = 42,459, $p < 0.001$) towards the negative framing message outperforming the general framing message. However, the small effect size indicates a very small relationship between framing and taking action (Cramér's V = 0.054), meaning the negative framing message may perform statistically better, predominantly due to sample size.

**Table 2.** Distribution of players who either changed their limits, took a play break, completed a self-assessment, or none of the above by message variant

| Message variant | Took action | | Did not take action | |
|---|---|---|---|---|
| General framing | 4,023 | 17.7% | 18,760 | 82.3% |
| Negative framing | 3,851 | 19.6% | 15,825 | 80.4% |

### 3.3 Gender and Age with Framing

Next, framing and action-taking based on gender and age were evaluated. Results for both demographics show significant effects towards the negative framing message (Gender: $x^2 = 231.187$, df $= 1$, n $= 42,459$, p $< 0.001$, and age: $x^2 = 517.952$, df $= 4$, n $= 42,459$, p $< 0.001$).

Regarding gender, although the results are significant, there is likely little association between framing and gender (Cramér's V $= 0.074$), meaning that gender does not likely play a differentiating role in which message would perform better. And across both message variants, women were more likely to take action than men. On the other hand, there is a small to medium tendency for certain types of messages to be associated with the different age groups, and the older a player was, the more likely they were to take action.

### 3.4 Player Risk Score and Framing

Following the previous demographics, framing and action-taking was compared based on player risk score (Table 3). Risk status 2, 3, and 4 were combined into one (medium risk) as they are all evaluated as yellow, or medium risk, at Norsk Tipping, and risk status 5 and 6 were combined into one (high risk) as they are both evaluated as red, or high risk, at Norsk Tipping. The results show significant effects ($x^2 = 868.595$, df $= 1$, n $= 42,459$, p $< 0.001$). There is a weak to moderate association between framing and player risk score (Cramér's V $= 0.143$), meaning that there may be a relationship between the two risk scores and a negatively framed message. The higher risk players were in general slightly more likely to take action in the negative framing message.

**Table 3.** Distribution of players who either changed their limits, took a play break, or completed a self-assessment, or none of the above by player risk score (medium is yellow, high is red)

| Risk score | General framing | | | Negative framing | | |
|---|---|---|---|---|---|---|
| | Took action | Did not | | Took action | Did not | |
| Medium | 2,607 | 15,233 | 14.6% | 2,601 | 12,874 | 16.8% |
| High | 1,416 | 3,527 | 28.6% | 1,250 | 2,951 | 29.8% |

## 3.5 Game Category Risk Score and Framing

Finally, game risk category was looked at in relation to message framing and action-taking (Table 4). The findings show significant effects ($x^2 = 1,424.334$, df = 2, n = 42,459, p < 0.001), and there is a weak to moderate tendency (Cramér's V = 0.182) for each game category risk to lean more towards the negative framing message. The findings also show that the higher the game risk level, the more likely a player is to take some form of action. The players who participated in higher-risk games were more likely to take some form of action than those who predominantly played lower-risk games.

**Table 4.** Distribution of players who either changed their limits, took a play break, completed a self-assessment of the above by game risk score

|           | General framing | | | Negative framing | | |
|-----------|-----------------|---|---|------------------|---|---|
| Game risk | Took action | Did not | | Took action | Did not | |
| Low    | 372   | 3,570 | 9.4%  | 367   | 3.034 | 10.8% |
| Medium | 950   | 7,027 | 11.9% | 939   | 5,988 | 13.6% |
| High   | 2,701 | 8,163 | 24.9% | 2,545 | 6,803 | 27.2% |

## 4 Discussion and Conclusion

Study results obtained from the A/B test indicate two primary outcomes. First, when attempting to communicate a recent increase in risky gambling behavior to players, a general framing message is statistically likely to get more players to take the first step in finding out more information. Second, a negative framing message is statistically likely to get more of those players who took a first step to then take a second step and use responsible gambling tools that are readily available, such as limits, play breaks, and self-assessments. This was true across all demographics analyzed, including age, gender, player risk score, and game risk score. In addition, across both message variants, the higher the game category risk a player primarily played or the older the player, the more likely they were to take some form of action, and men were less likely than women to take action, even though women were in the minority of this study. Seeing that both younger players as well as men were less likely to take action is something that should be researched, as there has been a higher prevalence for problem gambling and addiction among young men in recent years [16].

Having a general framing message as an initial point of contact can open up a player up for possible future decision-making in an easier way than a negative framing message. On the other hand, a negative framing message may create a stronger pull towards a basic psychological need to be safe, thus encouraging more players statistically to complete some form of action than a general framing message.

However, reflecting back on the tables provided in the results, it is clear that due to more players clicking the button in the general framing message than the negative framing message, the absolute number of players who took some form of action was slightly higher in the general framing message. This is a limitation of the test, and to better understand the effects of framing, there are multiple analyses that could be done, including delving deeper into demographics and finding out what the players did in the following weeks, as well as for those who may receive a message more than once. The overall small effect size is also a limitation of this test, yet when looking at the broader picture of how many players can be reached and over such a short period of time, it can be up for discussion as to if that can make up for the small effect size.

Finally, conducting tests online and on a large scale can provide additional insight into early prevention. This is in comparison to some of the risk communication research in responsible gambling that focuses for example on direct communication via email or telephone [17,18] which requires manpower and time, or pop-up messages that are done "in the moment" [3] and often with higher-risk gambling behavior. How risk is framed and on what scale it is communicated can potentially reduce the number of players seen becoming higher-risk players, thus reducing costs in society related to gambling harm and addiction. With gambling moving even more to the online realm, it is increasingly important to test future features and tools, especially in the realm of prevention, and having industry and research collaborate can increase the validity of results. Without clearly communicating recent increased risk, the chances of a player taking some form of action are much smaller, and there is an increased likelihood that a player does so only after their gambling has started to become problematic.

**Disclosure of Interests.** The first and second authors are employees at Norsk Tipping and the first author is also an industrial ph.d. candidate at Norsk Tipping.

# References

1. Blaszczynski, A., et al.: Responsible gambling: general principles and minimal requirements. J. Gambl. Stud. **27**(4), 565–573 (2011)
2. Reynolds, J., Kairouz, S., Ilacqua, S., French, M.: Responsible gambling: a scoping review. Crit. Gambl. Stud. **1**(1), 23–39 (2020)
3. Bjørseth, B., et al.: The effects of responsible gambling pop-up messages on gambling behaviors and cognitions: a systematic review and meta-analysis. Front. Psychiatry. **11**, 601800 (2020)
4. Ghelfi, M., Scattola, P., Giudici, G., Velasco, V.: Online gambling: a systematic review of risk and protective factors in the adult population. J. Gambl. Stud. **40**(2), 673–699 (2024)
5. Griffiths, M., Whitty, M.: Online behavioural tracking in Internet gambling research: ethical and methodological issues. Int. J. Internet Res. Ethics **3**, 104–117 (2010)
6. Rodda, S.N.: A systematic review of internet delivered interventions for gambling: prevention, harm reduction and early intervention. J. Gambl. Stud. **38**(3), 967–991 (2022)

7. Pan, Z.: A review of prospect theory. J. Hum. Resour. Sustain. Stud. **07**(01), 98–107 (2019)
8. Zhao, R.: A holistic review of framing effect: theories and applications. In: Striełkowski, W., et al. (eds.) Advances in Social Science, Education and Humanities Research, pp. 1634–1643. Atlantis Press, Paris (2022)
9. Joseph, E., Hughes, K., Thompson, J.: Investigating the framing effect in social and behavioral science research: potential influences on behavior, cognition and emotion. Soc. Behav. Res. Pract. - Open J. **1**(1), 34–37 (2016)
10. Rodriguez, L.M., Neighbors, C., Rinker, D.V., Tackett, J.L.: Motivational profiles of gambling behavior: self-determination theory, gambling motives, and gambling behavior. J. Gambl. Stud. **31**(4), 1597–1615 (2015)
11. Uysal, A., Yildirim, I.: Self-determination theory in digital games. In: Advances in Social Science, Education and Humanities Research, pp. 123–135. Atlantis Press SARL, Paris (2016)
12. Marionneau, V., Ristolainen, K., Roukka, T.: Duty of care, data science, and gambling harm: a scoping review of risk assessment models. Comput. Hum. Behav. Rep., 100644 (2025)
13. Ministry of Culture, Norwegian Goverment: The role of Norsk Tipping— regjeringen.no
14. Saikia, P., Cheung, M., She, J., Park, S.: Effectiveness of mobile notification delivery. In: 2017 18th IEEE International Conference on Mobile Data Management (MDM). IEEE, Daejeon, South Korea (2017)
15. Tripepi, G., Chesnaye, N.C., Dekker, F.W., Zoccali, C., Jager, K.J.: Intention to treat and per protocol analysis in clinical trials. Nephrology (Carlton) **25**(7), 513–517 (2020)
16. Richard, J., King, S.M.: Annual research review: emergence of problem gambling from childhood to emerging adulthood: a systematic review. J. Child Psychol. Psychiatry **64**(4), 645–688 (2023)
17. Jonsson, J., Hodgins, D.C., Munck, I., Carlbring, P.: Reaching out to big losers leads to sustained reductions in gambling over 1 year: a randomized controlled trial of brief motivational contact. Addiction **115**(8), 1522–1531 (2020). http://creativecommons.org/licenses/by-nc/4.0/
18. Auer, M., Griffiths, M.D.: The impact of personalized feedback interventions by a gambling operator on subsequent gambling expenditure in a sample of Dutch online gamblers. J. Gambl. Stud. **39**(2), 929–946 (2023)

**Open Access** This chapter is licensed under the terms of the Creative Commons Attribution 4.0 International License (http://creativecommons.org/licenses/by/4.0/), which permits use, sharing, adaptation, distribution and reproduction in any medium or format, as long as you give appropriate credit to the original author(s) and the source, provide a link to the Creative Commons license and indicate if changes were made.

The images or other third party material in this chapter are included in the chapter's Creative Commons license, unless indicated otherwise in a credit line to the material. If material is not included in the chapter's Creative Commons license and your intended use is not permitted by statutory regulation or exceeds the permitted use, you will need to obtain permission directly from the copyright holder.

# Towards Smart Workplaces: Understanding Mood-Influencing Factors of the Physical Workspace in Collaborative Group Settings

Tzu-Hui Wu[✉], Sebastian Cmentowski, Yunyin Lou, Jun Hu, and Regina Bernhaupt

Eindhoven University of Technology, Eindhoven, The Netherlands
{t.wu2,s.cmentowski,j.hu,r.bernhaupt}@tue.nl, y.lou@student.tue.nl

**Abstract.** Group mood plays a crucial role in shaping workspace experiences, influencing group dynamics, team performance, and creativity. The perceived group mood depends on many, often subconscious, aspects such as individual emotional states or group life, which make it challenging to maintain a positive atmosphere. Intelligent technology could support mood regulation in physical office environments, for example, as adaptive ambient lighting for mood regulation. However, little is known about the relationship between the physical workspace and group mood dynamics. To address this knowledge gap, we conducted a qualitative user study ($N = 8$ workgroups and overall 26 participants) to explore how the physical workspace shapes group mood experiences and investigate employees' perspectives on intelligent mood-aware technologies. Our findings reveal key factors influencing group mood, and participants' expectations for supportive technology to preserve privacy and autonomy. Our work highlights the potential of adaptive and responsive workspaces while also emphasizing the need for human-centered, technology-driven interventions that benefit group well-being.

**Keywords:** Group Mood · Shared Experience · Group Dynamics · Physical Workspace · Intelligent Technology · Office Well-being

## 1 Introduction

When a group works with a collective purpose [47], group mood refers to the shared affective atmosphere experienced by the group members in response to a specific event [26]. This affective sharing process shapes the dynamic, intertwined pattern of emotions within the group [17]. Studies have shown how collective-level affective experiences influence group dynamics in organizational functioning: group effectiveness in decision-making, the attitudes and behaviors of group members, team performance and creativity tasks [14]. Therefore, fostering "positive workplace vibes" has become a popular topic in organizational management.

In this context, the physical workspace environment can be seen as a complex system encompassing all objects and stimuli that employees encounter and perceive in their work [6]. Prior work leverages intelligent measurements and interventions to mediate mood experiences and support positive ways of working in office environments. Some tools visualize a user's arousal level to support a productive vibe [46]. Other researchers designed systems that collect individual data and transform the datasets into collective visualizations to create a reflective process for complete teamwork [52,53]. However, research on understanding the relationship between the group's experiences and their work environment is limited, with a focus mainly on the individual lens, ignoring the reflection from the collective lens. There is currently no explicit knowledge available to assess the workplace's impact on employees' group experiences. It remains unclear what factors could affect group mood and whether intelligent technology can play a meaningful role in fostering beneficial group moods in work settings.

To address this research gap, we conducted an exploratory study to gain a deep understanding of the potential influence of physical workplace shaping group mood experiences, and participants' expectations and concerns regarding the use of intelligent technology in fostering positive group moods. Specifically, we adopted the user experience curve method and combined it with semi-structured interviews to obtain user responses and envisions based on their lived experiences of complex and multimodal mood experiences. After asking members of 8 workgroups to sketch their meeting mood states, we conducted in-depth interviews to investigate the mood-influencing factors of the workplace and expand on the participants' ideas of how technology can contribute to office well-being.

The results of our thematic analysis provides an understanding of how the physical workplace influences group mood dynamics, yielding insights that are directly applicable to human-computer interaction (HCI) and workplace design. Specifically, we identified three key aspects at the group level linked to positive mood patterns in office environments: well-structured and low-hierarchy meetings, strong interpersonal connections, and optimal environmental conditions with flexible physical settings. Importantly, these factors are double-edged; if not managed appropriately, they can negatively impact the perception and experience of group mood. These findings offer an experience-oriented perspective grounded in real-world settings. Our analysis also highlights user concerns regarding the integration of intelligent technologies in workspaces, particularly the balance between privacy, autonomy, and system adaptability. In summary, our paper contributes in two ways: (1) An understanding of relevant aspects in the workplace environment that affect group mood patterns; and (2) Promising design directions based on participants' expectations and concerns about intelligent technology supporting group mood experiences in physical workspace.

## 2 Related Work

### 2.1 Group Mood

Group mood can be defined as a pervasive affective atmosphere experienced by group members during a group activity [47], which emerges within a group, shaped by the interaction and reciprocal influence between individuals [17]. Group affect includes both immediate shared emotional reactions (group emotion) and more enduring shared mood experiences (group mood) [47]. While group emotion refers to direct responses to specific stimuli [23], group mood encompasses all consistent or uniform emotional responses, representing the general emotional tone [3,34].

Recently, group mood has been explored within the fields of organizational sciences and human psychology. Prior research focuses mainly on classifying the types and dimensions of mood [47]. Additionally, group mood is generally assessed through self-reported measurements, using the average score to represent the overall group mood [19,51]. However, these studies may not fully capture the collective experience, potentially overlooking the contextual factors, especially the physical workspace, that shape group dynamics. In this research, we focus on group moods in the physical workspace as diffuse and enduring affective states that are shared by group members.

### 2.2 HCI and Mood Research

With the help of HCI approaches, users could receive data-driven self-insights to help optimize their behavioral patterns according to mood patterns [43]. Currently, HCI research uses physiological or behavioral indicators to detect moods. Physiological signals include skin temperature [25,46] and heart rate variability [53,54], while behavioral signals include facial or verbal expressions [21,40,50], gestural or bodily movements [33], and user-product interaction behaviors [1]. Another approach to detecting mood is to use sentiment analysis, inferring moods from texts posted on social media [35]. In addition, several studies enable the detection of mood-related contextual data, such as date and time, location, or weather [24].

A recurring challenge in the literature is the lack of reliability in mood-related data. Physiological signals, commonly used as proxies for mood, are often unstable due to factors such as sensor invasiveness [22,32] and variable environmental conditions [38], which undermines their reliability. Additionally, mood self-tracking methods are inherently subjective [22], and users may inadvertently misrepresent their emotions and experiences [28]. To enhance reliability, some studies have proposed combining automated sensor technology with self-tracking approaches [2,18]. Consequently, researchers have increasingly employed sensor-based systems in physical environments to detect and respond to human emotional states [48]. However, our understanding of how environmental factors relate to mood remains limited. Moreover, concerns about system surveillance and user privacy are widespread, with users often feeling overly monitored by technology [5,35] and expressing apprehension regarding the security and privacy of their mood data [25]. Therefore, it necessitates a deeper understanding of how physical workplace characteristics influence group mood, and for the development of measurement and intervention strategies that enhance mood regulation without compromising user privacy or comfort.

## 2.3 Physical Workspace for Office Well-Being

Previous studies explored the potential influence of physical workspace characteristics (e.g., light, sound, air quality) on employees' mental health [6]. The workplace environment is a complex system that encompasses not only objective physical stimuli at work, but also the ways in which individual occupants subjectively perceive these stimuli [42]. For example, research found that exposure to daylight could increase productivity, mood, and reduce fatigue [8]. Increased background noise can also relate to reduced productivity, concentration, and well-being. Although employees prefer to work in an open work environment [15,29], disturbing background noise could negatively influence peoples' mental health [7,15]. It also seems that products and the spatial features of a room can contribute to certain group moods by affording or limiting interactions. For example, being physically distant from the center of a clustering activity caused some participants to feel "out of the group vibe" [47]. A presentation screen also contributed to the group mood by attracting the group's attention.

## 2.4 Intelligent Technology in Physical Workplace for Promoting Office Well-Being

In recent years, many academic disciplines have taken advantage of technologies to promote office well-being. Office well-being covers both psychological and physical aspects, which is considered crucial to work performance, job satisfaction, and employee health [37,44,49]. Intelligent technology has significantly transformed the physical workplace, enabling dynamic interactions that influence office well-being. Enhancing physical activity and reducing mental health problems has become a top priority in the workplace [6,16]. Interactive environments utilize smart devices and responsive systems to facilitate collaboration, adapt to users' needs, and create an active atmosphere, such as visualizing computer-based activity on ambient displays to reduce sedentary behavior [13], or facilitating walking using interactive screens [20]. Ambient intelligence extends these capabilities by embedding context-aware technologies into the environment, allowing workplaces to sense and respond to users through data collected from internet of things (IoT) devices. For example, personalized ambient lighting systems were used to reduce distraction [39], and twinkly lights on ambient installation to nudge people to change their behavior [41]. Additionally, digital twins further enhance workplace intelligence by creating virtual replicas of physical spaces [45]. These replicas allow real-time monitoring of the workplace, providing insights into how spatial arrangements, environmental factors (e.g., light, sound, and air quality), and user interactions impact office well-being [12].

# 3 Research Focus

The goal of our study is to gain a deeper understanding of how the physical workplace shapes group mood dynamics and how intelligent technology could

support positive group mood experiences. Prior research highlights the importance of environmental and social factors in influencing office well-being, yet a comprehensive exploration of these influences in real-world office settings remains limited. To design intelligent mood-aware technologies that foster positive group moods, it is essential to first understand users' perceptions on how the physical workplace influences their group mood. Accordingly, our research question is:
**RQ1: How does the physical workspace influence group mood?**
To answer this question, we subdivide it into three sub-questions that focus on the general factors, the influence of meeting stages, and the impact on the group mood:

- **RQ1a:** Which factors of the physical workspace influence group mood?
- **RQ1b:** Which factors are important during which stage of group work?
- **RQ1c:** Which factors are facilitators or inhibitors for group mood?

Additionally, previous research has extensively explored both group mood definitions and intelligent workplace technologies as separate domains. However, the intersection of these two areas—how intelligent technology can actively shape and support group mood in office environments—remains underexplored. Existing studies on workplace technology primarily focus on individual well-being and productivity, often overlooking the collective emotional experience of workgroups. Therefore, our research investigates employees' expectations and concerns towards the integration of intelligent technology in fostering positive group moods. This leads us to our second research question:
**RQ2: How do users perceive the potential of Mood-Aware Workspace Environment (MAWEs) for enhancing mood and well-being in group scenarios?**
Our exploration is a crucial first step toward designing intelligent interventions to enhance office well-being. By identifying the mood-influencing factors and understanding participants' expectations towards intelligent technologies, we aim to develop actionable guidelines for creating mood-aware workspace environments that foster a positive atmosphere and promote office well-being.

## 4 Method

For our user study, we combined two methodologies, the user experience curve (UX Curve) and semi-structured interviews, to answer our research questions (see Fig. 1). The UX Curve is "a method to support users in retrospectively reporting how their experience changed over time" [31]. It helps capture subjective and self-reported experiences with a product. The goal is to gather reports of the experience as it unfolds, thereby supporting memory reconstruction. In this study, group members self-reported their experienced group mood development based on their actual meeting. In this context, the UX curve can reveal subtle mood changes over the course of an experience, providing rich contextual insights. Using these sketches as a starting point, we then conducted in-depth interviews to explore the factors influencing group mood patterns and delve deeper into participants' perspectives on how technology could enhance their office well-being. The combination of UX curves and semi-structured interviews captures both immediate mood experiences and deeper insights behind these experiences.

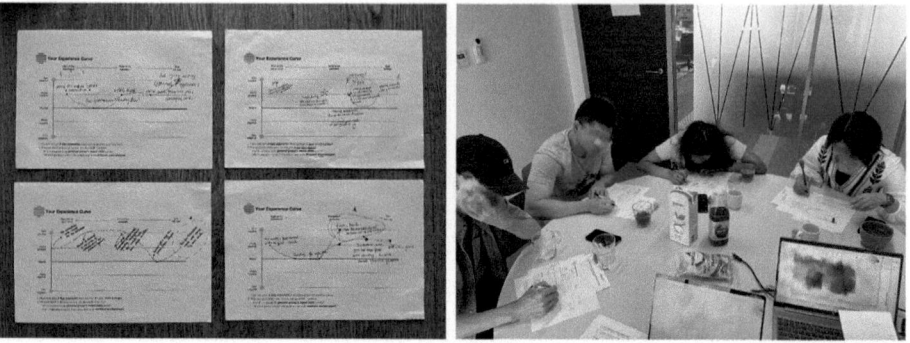

**Fig. 1.** Research materials used for self-reporting: The experience curve (left) and study setting (right).

### 4.1 Participant

For our study, we recruited 8 groups (a total of 26 participants) engaged in ongoing group projects from the University. Our sample size aligns with prior qualitative research norms by Braun and Clarke [10,11], who indicate that thematic saturation is typically reached with 12–25 participants. Three of the groups consisted of PhD staff who met regularly for academic research. The other groups were ongoing student design teams working on group assignments in workshops or focus groups. To accurately capture group mood experiences, we established sampling criteria based on factors that influence mood convergence in workgroups [3,4]: Membership stability, task interdependence, and social interdependence. Additionally, when groups exceed six members, individuals are less likely to engage in collective interactions that foster mood homogeneity [30,47]. Based on these criteria, we selected groups with a maximum of 6 members, who engaged in an ongoing project (membership stability), performed distinct tasks while collaborating within the group (task interdependence), and had established familiarity with one another (social interdependence). Our final set comprised 8 groups with 3–4 participants each, who engaged in 60–90 min of group work.

We recognize the importance of personal and contextual factors in influencing group mood. To control for external influences, we collected detailed contextual information, including meeting type, physical environment, and collaboration duration. Table 1 gives an overview of the demographic and contextual information of participants.

**Table 1.** Participant group profiles: group number, size, participants (coded), meeting types, environment, collaboration, participant roles in each session.

| Number | Size | Meeting type | Environment | Duration | Participant Roles |
|---|---|---|---|---|---|
| Group 1 | 3 | Focus group | Meeting room | <3 months | 1 facilitator, 2 members |
| Group 2 | 4 | Student project | Open space | One month | 4 members |
| Group 3 | 3 | Academic meeting | Meeting room | >6 months | 2 supervisors, 1 PhD |
| Group 4 | 3 | Academic meeting | Meeting room | >3 months | 2 supervisors, 1 PhD |
| Group 5 | 3 | Academic meeting | Meeting room | >6 months | 1 supervisor, 2 PhD |
| Group 6 | 4 | Focus group | Meeting room | >6 months | 1 facilitator, 3 members |
| Group 7 | 3 | Workshop | Open space | >6 months | 1 facilitator, 2 members |
| Group 8 | 3 | Focus group | Meeting room | <3 months | 1 facilitator, 2 members |

## 4.2 Research Procedure and Materials

The procedure of this study is described in Fig. 2. Following each group meeting, the 3–4 participants attended a shared interview session with the first author. We deliberately chose group interviews as they encourage participants to build on each other's ideas, revealing insights that might not emerge in isolation. While one-on-one sessions allow for deep personal reflections, they might fail to capture the ideas that emerge from dynamic collaborative discussion. These sessions lasted 60–70 min and consisted of two parts: First, participants recalled their meeting by sketching and describing their perception of the group mood development using a pen-and-paper experience curve. Afterwards, the researcher conducted a semi-structured interview session to explore commonalities and distinctions between group members' mood perceptions and their perspectives on intelligent mood-aware technologies. In detail, our interview session used the following structure:

**Part 1: Retrospecting the Actual Meetings and Sketching the Experience Curve.** This first part aimed to understand the actual experiences of group collaboration. We introduced the experience curve to the participants and asked them to share their collaboration experiences by sketching the perceived group mood development and identifying five key moments where they perceived a significant change in group mood. Data collection in this phase consisted of their sketches and descriptions.

**Part 2: Semi-structured Interview.** The second part focused on understanding the group mood patterns and exploring participants' views on using intelligent technologies to enhance group office well-being. The first part aimed to explore the factors shaping group mood dynamics in the workplace. We asked guiding questions about their experience curves, such as "What do you think caused the change in group mood at this key moment?", "Do you observe any connection between this key moment and the surrounding context?", and "What do you see as a main trigger in the physical workplace that affects your group mood?". We also explored participants' differing perceptions of the experience curves, asking follow-up questions to understand the factors influencing their varied interpretations of group mood. For example, we inquired, "Why did you choose a different group mood state at this moment?". For the second part of the interview, we introduced the concept of a "Mood-Aware Workspace Environment" (MAWEs) and invited participants to share their perspectives. We asked open-ended questions such as "What are your thoughts on integrating intelligent technologies into the workplace to create a mood-aware environment? How might these technologies impact your experience?".

Naturally, qualitative data like ours is specific to the interviewed participants and might be influenced by personal circumstances and external events. We took particular care to minimize these influences by framing the interview questions explicitly on mood-related factors of the physical workplace, distinguishing them from external events, and asking participants to focus primarily on environmental factors. When external influences were reported, we separated these cases in our analysis, ensuring that only mood changes attributed to workspace conditions were captured. All participants provided with informed consent prior to the study. Upon the consent of the participants, all the sessions were voice recorded.

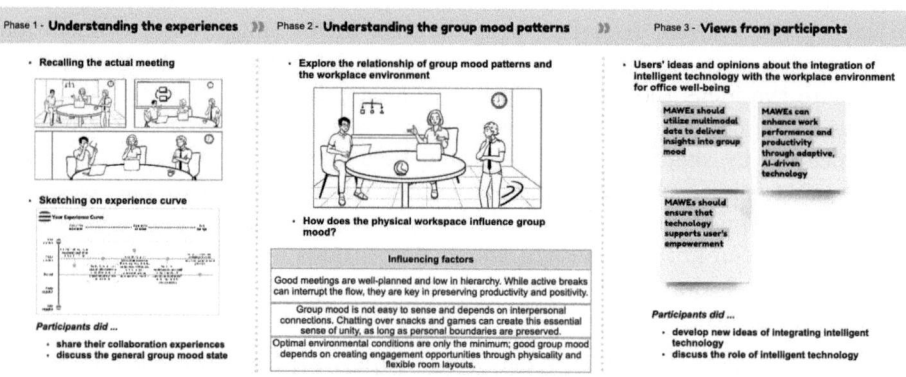

**Fig. 2.** A visual outline of the study, including provided materials, tasks for participants, and transcribed data in each phase.

### 4.3 Data Analysis

For data analysis, the main author first transcribed the audio recordings using Microsoft Teams[1], then reviewed and cleaned the original transcripts before initiating the analysis. For the subsequent coding of both the interview data and the experience curve sketches, we used the online platform Dovetail[2]. Therefore, we followed a six-step thematic analysis process originally outlined by Braun

---

[1] https://www.microsoft.com/en-us/microsoft-teams/group-chat-software.
[2] https://dovetail.com/.

and Clarke [9]. While we consider our analysis procedure generally as "reflexive", marked by iterations in which the codes evolve and change during the analysis [11], we also incorporated aspects of other strains of thematic analysis: two researchers coded all data independently (i.e., coding reliability) and iteratively reviewed and aligned the results codes frequently (i.e., codebook approach). To start the process, we first derived an initial codebook deductively, drawing from group-mood-influencing factors reported in prior literature [47]. Additionally, we tagged the identified factors according to their occurrence in the meeting (e.g., beginning, middle, end) and their impact on the experience curve (i.e., facilitating or inhibiting group mood). For the perceptions of mood-aware systems, we solely relied on inductive codes.

Two researchers independently coded 25% of the interview data before meeting with a third, more senior author to discuss and unify the resulting codebook. Afterwards, we repeated the same procedure for the next 25% of the data, further refining the codebook. For the remaining data, the two main coders followed this procedure without the involvement of the third author. At each discussion stage, we discussed all coded data, resolved any coding differences, and revised/consolidated the codebook. Please refer to Appendix for a picture of the final codebook. After finalizing coding, the first author used an affinity mapping approach to group the codes and generate initial themes. Subsequently, the three primarily involved authors discussed and refined the results to establish the final theme definitions. The analysis aimed to achieve two objectives: (1) identifying factors that shape group mood dynamics in the workspace, and (2) investigating participants' expectations regarding intelligent technology that support group experiences in workspace settings.

## 5 Results

In this section, we present the six main themes we identified within the data through thematic analysis (see Table 2). In the following parts, we will elaborate each theme and participant quotes. Participants are labeled "P" followed by group number, for example, "P3-2" for the second participant in the third group.

### 5.1 Theme 1: Good Meetings Are Well-Planned and Low in Hierarchy. While Active Breaks Can Interrupt the Flow, They Are Key in Preserving Productivity and Positivity

**Subtheme 1.1: The Meeting Type and Organization Determines the Importance and Direction of Group Mood Developments.** Most participants emphasized that the structure and type of meetings significantly determine how group mood evolves: *"Perception of group mood would change depending on whether the meeting is more casual or formal"* (**P5-2**). Participants also reported that well-organized meetings with a clear agenda and low hierarchy not only promote inclusivity, but also shape the emotional tone of the group. For example, participants' experiences and perceptions of the group mood and dynamics could

**Table 2.** Table of the six main themes extracted from the data alongside their related subthemes, separated by research question.

| Themes | Subthemes |
| --- | --- |
| (1) Good meetings are well-planned and low in hierarchy. While active breaks can interrupt the flow, they are key in preserving productivity and positivity | 1.1. The meeting type and organization determines the importance and direction of group mood developments; 1.2. Breaks, Surprises, and Physical Activity are important but can be distracting |
| (2) Group mood is not easy to sense and depends on interpersonal connections. Chatting over snacks and games can create this essential sense of unity, as long as personal boundaries are preserved | 2.1. Perceiving group mood is hard but communication and social bonds lead to mood convergence eventually; 2.2. Communication, informal chats, and group interactions are essential for creating a productive environment |
| (3) Optimal environmental conditions are only the minimum; positive group mood depends on creating engagement opportunities through physicality and flexible room layouts. | 3.1. Calm, well-lit, and ventilated rooms are basic requirements for productive work; 3.2. Working with physical materials and communication tools creates an engaging atmosphere; 3.3. Room layouts are a two-edged sword: adaptable layouts benefit while unfamiliarity hinders engagement |
| (4) MAWEs should utilize multimodal data to deliver insights into group mood, ensuring context-aware communication of mood to enhance understanding and cohesion | 4.1. MAWEs should leverage multimodal data to gain comprehensive insights into group mood dynamics; 4.2. MAWEs should support context-aware and subtle communication of emotional sharing |
| (5) MAWEs can enhance work performance and productivity through adaptive, AI-driven technology while ensuring explainable and transparent communication to understand system's behaviors | 5.1. Adaptive interventions in MAWEs boost energy and re-engage individuals, thereby enhancing work performance; 5.2. AI meeting tools in MAWEs boost productivity with effective time tracking and management 5.3. MAWEs should offer flexible, explainable, and transparent information to ensure understanding in system decisions |
| (6) MAWEs should ensure that technology supports user empowerment in environmental control without compromising ethical and privacy concerns | 6.1. MAWEs should empower users to control environmental settings, balancing automated regulation with group consensus; 6.2. Ensuring clear social boundaries and carefully managing sensitive data are crucial for addressing ethical and privacy concerns in MAWEs |

vary depending on their specific role (e.g., moderator/instructor). In contrast, group mood suffers from low energy levels due to long meetings with excessive workload and poor scheduling: *"Busted for a long time period"* (**P2-4**) and *"Getting tired due to the intense discussion"* (**P2-1**).

**Subtheme 1.2: Breaks, Surprises, and Physical Activity Are Important but Can Be Distracting.** While many participants recognized that breaks, surprises, and physical activity are critical to recharging and energizing the group, they also mentioned that these elements can sometimes be distracting if not well-timed. Participants noted that incorporating physical activity during meetings is key to maintaining a positive mood and gauging individual engagement: *"It's positive because we were moving around rather than just staying in the same place"* (**P1-1**), highlighting how even small bursts of body movement can enhance the overall atmosphere. Similarly, breaks, though sometimes reluctant, were seen as necessary for recharging energy: *"When we come back from the break, we felt a bit more relaxed"* (**P8-3**). However, novelty and relief during meetings is a double-edged sword. While participants appreciated surprises to break the routine, several noted that unanticipated challenges could disturb the workflow: *"Our workshop was interrupted because other people also want to use the table"* (**P7-1**).

## 5.2 Theme 2: Group Mood Is Not Easy to Sense and Depends on Interpersonal Connections. Chatting over Snacks and Games Can Create This Essential Sense of Unity, as Long as Personal Boundaries Are Preserved

**Subtheme 2.1: Perceiving Group Mood Is Hard but Communication and Social Bonds Lead to Mood Convergence Eventually.** Participants expressed that discerning individual and group mood can be challenging, as it is a complex combination of individual moods and how they affect the group dynamics: *"It was really hard to differentiate my own mood from the group mood"* (**P4-3**). However, they also highlighted that effective communication—positive feedback, supportive tone, timely rewards, and successful outcomes—can significantly enhance the perception of group mood: *"Our moods were influenced by the tone of the instructor's speech and outcomes"* (**P6-2**). Furthermore, strong team bonds, shared backgrounds, and compatible personalities were also identified as critical factors that minimize information gaps. Through consistent communication and the strengthening of social bonds, individual moods eventually align: *"Our mood gradually aligned to a similar level in group meeting"* (**P3-2**). This convergence highlights the gradual but powerful role of interpersonal communication in shaping a shared emotional atmosphere.

**Subtheme 2.2: Communication, Informal Chats, and Group Interactions Are Essential for Creating a Productive Environment.** Some participants pointed out that informal interactions are essential for fostering unity. They noted that active social engagement and regular group interactions with lightweight, positive topics tend to elevate group mood: *"The vibe was pretty positive, ending with the fun interaction and discussion with memes card"* (**P2-4**). While sensitive or intrusive conversations related to *"more personal things"*

**(P1-2)** can lead to discomfort. Participants also highlighted shared interests and mutual expectations as key to creating a sense of unity, thereby enhancing communication: *"The important thing is that we have a really clear goal, [...] so everything just smoothly."* **(P2-3)**. This shows that while group mood is hard to capture, it can be nurtured through intentional, informal communication and strong social bonds, which in turn contribute to a more productive work environment. Providing snacks and games fosters a relaxed atmosphere, encouraging group members to connect on a more personal level.

### 5.3 Theme 3: Optimal Environmental Conditions Are only the Minimum; Good Group Mood Depends on Creating Engagement Opportunities Through Physicality and Flexible Room Layouts

**Subtheme 3.1: Calm, Well-Lit, and Ventilated Environments Are Basic Requirements for Productive Work.** Participants stressed that optimal environmental conditions—such as thermal comfort, optimal lighting, and fresh air—play a crucial role in promoting relaxation and elevating group mood. One participant explained that *"The air is becoming not good at all, [...] staying here in a hot environment, which is not helpful for attention and mood"* **(P3-2)**, illustrating the direct impact of environmental conditions on concentration. Additionally, while ambient sounds and background music can stimulate creativity, excessive noise was described as a major distraction undermining group mood and productivity: *"It's ok if there just regular ambient sound, but I get distracted if someone is screaming"* **(P7-1)**. These conditions, although fundamental, are viewed as minimum requirements for a productive work environment.

**Subtheme 3.2: Working with Physical Materials and Communication Tools Creates an Engaging Atmosphere.** Beyond the basic conditions, participants highlighted the use of physical materials, such as cards and sticky notes, to be engaging and helpful in facilitating the group discussion and problem solving process. They felt that the tangible nature of these materials allowed them to better organize their thoughts and collaborate effectively: *"fun interaction with memes cards and stickers"* **(P2-4)**. Likewise, the use of shared communication tools, like collaborative whiteboards and digital displays, was also noted as a key factor in fostering active participation: *"When we start to open or use some cooperative tools, like using the Miro or whiteboard, [...] that's quite a positive atmosphere"* **(P5-2)**. Integrating both physical materials and collaborative tools can sustain group engagement and creativity.

**Subtheme 3.3: Room Layouts Are a Double-Edged Sword: Adaptable Layouts Benefit While Unfamiliarity Hinders Engagement.** Most participants discussed the role of room layouts, revealing a double-edged effect. On the one hand, flexible configuration and adaptable layouts benefit engagement, communication, and concentration. For example, a U-shaped or circular table arrangement **(P4-3)** promotes interaction, as it encourages participants to face each other and engage in more discussions. On the other hand, unfamiliar environments and physical distance impact the individual perception of the group mood. Getting used to the environment **(P5-3)** and collaborating to address issues contributed to an improved group dynamic over time. Conversely, physical distant affects the perception: *"I feel distancing, [...] feel a little bit bad"* **(P4-1)**. Maintaining a sense of familiarity is important to ensure a positive atmosphere.

### 5.4 Theme 4: MAWEs Should Utilize Multimodal Data to Deliver Insights Into Group Mood, Ensuring Context-Aware Communication of Mood to Enhance Understanding and Cohesion

**Subtheme 4.1. MAWEs Should Leverage Multimodal Data to Gain Comprehensive Insights Into Group Mood Dynamics.** Participants proposed some examples of using various sensors and data points, such as group distribution and positioning, physiological indicators like heart rate and skin conductance, sound, body status and behaviors, to infer group atmosphere. They believe that these physical cues can provide insights into the overall group dynamics. Some participants also suggested the possibility of allowing people to self-report their emotional states: *"Self-rating emotions could help, [...] offer some insights"* **(P5-1)**. But there are concerns about the reliability of self-reporting, as people may not always accurately perceive or be willing to share their true emotional state. In addition, some participants highlighted the role of embodied physical objects in capturing interactive mood-related data. For example, *"talking objects"* **(P8-2)** and *"perceptible plants"* **(P8-3)** could display a general group mood indicator without being too invasive.

**Subtheme 4.2. MAWEs Should Support Context-Aware and Subtle Communication of Emotional Sharing.** Participants wished for systems that are be able to identify when individuals are inclined to share personal information and are willing to reveal their feelings. They expressed a desire to know others' moods, as it could help them gauge if they have done something wrong or if the other person is upset: *"I want to know people's feelings when I'm suspicious or I do something wrong"* **(P2-3)**. However, there are also concerns about the sensitivity of sharing emotions, especially if it could be recognized by supervisors or used for performance evaluations: *"Mood should not always be visible. When you had difficult conversation with your supervisor, I'm not sure if you want them to know that you're uncomfortable in the moment"* **(P4-3)**. The overall sentiment is that while knowing others' moods could be beneficial in some situations, people should still have control over whether they want to share their emotions. Some participants explore ideas like using plants or other representations to provide subtle cues about the group mood or energy levels. These insights indicate that context-aware emotional communication not only preserve personal boundaries but also enhances team cohesion by facilitating a balance between individual privacy and group mood awareness.

## 5.5 Theme 5: MAWEs Can Enhance Work Performance and Productivity Through Adaptive, AI-Driven Technology While Ensuring Explainable and Transparent Communication to Understand System's Behaviors

**Subtheme 5.1. Adaptive Interventions in MAWEs Boost Energy and Re-Engage Individuals, Thereby Enhancing Work Performance.** Participants envisioned adaptive intelligent interventions that could dynamically adjust to their needs, reducing friction in collaborative work. As articulated by **P4-2**, physical settings adjusting automatically can boost energy levels. Some noted MAWEs should support adaptive workspaces: *"The chairs or tables in the room can automatically be configured depending on what we need"* (**P4-2**). Some participants also noted that adaptive interventions, including physical activity suggestions, mood-tailored music, and the display of mood changes, help re-engage distracted individuals. However, concerns about automation were raised, with participants preferring that systems act as "assistants" rather than imposing mandatory interventions.

**Subtheme 5.2. AI Meeting Tools in MAWEs Boost Productivity with Effective Time Tracking and Management.** Participants want AI-powered features that can manage real-time meeting processes, such as summarizing discussions or searching for information, to enhance meeting productivity. **P3-2** envisioned a virtual facilitator that summarizes key points and suggests discussion topics for the group, helping to maintain a productive meeting atmosphere. They also emphasize the importance of having reminder systems (**P7-1**) to help keep meetings on track and ensure engagement, especially in larger group settings where it can be difficult to interrupt someone who is taking too long.

**Subtheme 5.3. MAWEs Should Offer Flexible, Explainable, and Transparent Information to Ensure Understanding in System Decisions.** Most participants highlighted the desire for physical workspaces that provide both flexibility and explainable information to support understanding. The potential for MAWEs, such as automated curtains, to act unpredictably or annoying users is a concern, especially when their actions lack clear explanations: *"It might be nice if it could indicate in some way why the curtains are closing or opening"* (**P4-2**). Participants also noted need for flexibility and transparency in the work environment, such as information on how each person's state affects the overall group dynamics. Group level is a complex social phenomenon, with certain individuals having a stronger influence on the group mood than others.

## 5.6 Theme 6: MAWEs Should Ensure that Technology Supports User's Empowerment in Environmental Control Without Compromising Ethical and Privacy Concerns

**Subtheme 6.1. MAWEs Should Empower Users to Control Environmental Settings, Balancing Automated Regulation with Group Consensus.** Some participants pointed out the challenges of MAWEs that need to be addressed. Users expressed frustration with the automated curtain and lighting system in their office. They found the curtains to be either too bright or too dark, and the automatic adjustments to be disruptive, especially during meetings. There is a lack of group control over the curtains, leading to conflicts between colleagues who have different preferences for lighting. Users suggest that a more customizable or zoned lighting system could help address these issues and better accommodate the diverse needs of office workers **(P1-2)**. The concept of user control in group settings raises the question of whether intelligent technologies can enhance group mood dynamics without undermining individual autonomy. One participant explained that *"The environment could understand the general mood in the office, but it shouldn't force interactions or mood changes"* **(P6-2)**.

**Subtheme 6.2. Ensuring Clear Social Boundaries and Carefully Managing Sensitive Data Is Crucial for Addressing Ethical and Privacy Concerns in MAWEs.** Most participants were concerned about privacy issues relating to sharing personal information, such as heart rate and mood, with a smart environment. They preferred that the environment provides only abstract or general information about mood levels, rather than specific personal details, ensuring the social boundaries. Intelligent technologies should provide sufficient flexibility and options to allow teams to decide when and how interventions or information occur. **P6-1** noted, *"I don't want to let environment knows my personal information like heart rate"*. Participants were also concerned about the sensitivity of personal information, especially in a work context where it could be accessed by leader and potentially influence perceptions or decisions.

## 6 Discussion

The results in Sect. 5 summarize our findings regarding the relevant aspects in the workplace environment that shape the group mood patterns, as well as participants' expectation and concerns about MAWEs. In this section we discuss the interpretation and application of these results.

### 6.1 RQ1: How Does the Physical Workspace Influence Group Mood?

**Theme 1** reveals that the type of meeting and its organizational structure fundamentally shape the group's emotional tone. This finding is supported by existing literature: the meeting type, group leadership and attendee roles may determine the expected group mood [3,47]. However, our study extends these insights by highlighting the role of physical activities and breaks in sustaining productivity and positivity. According to our participants, the structure of a meeting, combined with observable physical activities, provides valuable cues about individual and collective status, enabling designers to better infer the overall group atmosphere. Breaks and surprise elements serve as facilitator, energizing participants and reinforcing a positive group vibe. But if breaks and unexpected challenges are not well-timed, they could be inhibitors of group mood. **Theme 2** also identifies that perceiving group mood is difficult, yet strong interpersonal interactions and social bonds foster a productive environment that gradually leads to mood convergence. This finding is in line with prior work by Chung and Grèzes [17], who demonstrate how individual emotions, through continuous emotional interactions, align into a unified group mood. Answering **RQ1c**, we identified that effective group interactions and chatting over snacks and games can serve as facilitators for building familiarity and team cohesion, not only boosting group mood but also creating a strong sense of unity. At the same time, personal boundaries can lower group mood, as sensitive or intrusive discussions can lead to discomfort. **Theme 3** emphasizes the importance of creating engagement through physicality and flexible room layouts while maintaining optimal environmental conditions. This finding resonate with prior research: physical workplace characteristics significantly impact employees' mental health (e.g. stress, fatigue, or mood) [6]. But our results extend the literature by revealing that adaptive, interactive workspaces act as a double-edged sword: when well-managed, they facilitate positive group dynamics, but an unfamiliar workspace can hinder productivity. With regards to **RQ1a**, we expand our understanding of factors influencing group mood by revealing that specific physical workplace elements, well-structured and low-hierarchy meetings, strong interpersonal connections, and optimal environmental conditions paired with flexible physical settings, play a crucial role in shaping group mood.

Furthermore, our analysis reveals that the significance of these factors fluctuates over time (**RQ1b**). The initial stage of group work is especially sensitive to the meeting type and the clarity of its structure (**Theme 1**), with a sense of novelty providing an additional energy boost. Participants noted that the meeting types and initial tasks establish the foundational emotional tone for the group. Interestingly, many described the default state at the beginning as a neutral mood—neither distinctly positive nor negative—serving as a baseline from which emotions and engagement can later shift up or down depending on the group dynamics and activities. Conversely, during the middle and later stages of group work, the physical environment and collaborative tools take on an essential role in fostering engagement and interactivity. Participants indicated that optimal environmental conditions, the use of physical materials, and well-designed room layouts create an atmosphere that not only fosters interaction but also re-energizes the group (**Theme 3**). Additionally, effective communication, robust group interactions, and strong social bonds become more vital for sustaining energy in the later stages (**Theme 2**). However, these factors are not isolated.

They are intricately intertwined, collectively shaping the dynamic fluctuations of group mood and lead to mood alignment eventually.

## 6.2 RQ2: How Do Users Perceive the Potential of MAWEs for Enhancing Mood and Well-Being in Group Scenarios?

Participants have two expectations for MAWEs: utilizing multimodal data to infer and communicate group mood, discussed in **Theme 4**, and leveraging AI-driven technology to enhance work performance, discussed in **Theme 5**. These expectations demonstrate promising examples of using various sensors to infer and interpret group mood. Our discussion also highlights potential challenges and limitations of these approaches, including the difficulty in accurately interpreting emotional states, the risk of making incorrect assumptions, and the necessity of balancing privacy concerns with the goal of fostering a responsive and supportive work environment. Embodied physical objects that combine sensors and self-reporting methods can provide a more precise assessment of group mood. Theme 5 also emphasized adaptive and AI-driven technology to improve office well-being and productivity in a shared work setting by monitoring and responding to their emotional and energy states. Sometimes we passively accept the system's information and interventions, overlooking the autonomy individuals should have in the physical workspace. In such cases, MAWEs look like a black box, hiding the reasons behind their actions and leaving users in the dark about system's behaviors. This opacity not only undermines trust, but also hinders understanding of the technology. Participants also raised challenges of MAWEs: supporting user empowerment in environmental control without compromising ethical and privacy concerns, discussed in **Theme 6**. Privacy, transparency, and user autonomy remain key concerns. Although users are generally open to smart, adaptive workspaces, their effectiveness depends on a balance between automated regulation, user empowerment, and robust ethical data management. Achieving this balance is essential for building trust and ensuring technology supports, rather than undermine, human interaction and agency.

## 6.3 Design Implications

Finally, we propose actionable recommendations for designing effective MAWEs based on our findings.

**Enhancing Group Mood Monitoring with Reliability and Privacy Control.** Our findings suggest that designers can combine a diverse array of data, including physiological signals, spatial positioning, audio cues, self-reports, body language, posture, and interactions with furniture or devices, to accurately capture group mood (**Subtheme 4.1**). Previous work highlights that mood detection via sensors or self-tracking is often unreliable, as physiological and behavioral signals can be unstable across contexts and users [38]. By integrating this heterogeneous data using advanced analytics, MAWEs can identify subtle emotional shifts and trigger adaptive interventions when energy levels drop or stress increases. Prior research has used "SocialStools" to promote group cohesion through embodied interaction by measuring the distance, orientation and interaction among group members [27]. However, designers should address privacy concerns: "always-on" mood tracking could lead to perceived privacy invasion **(Subtheme 6.2)**. To protect user comfort and agency, we propose the anonymous sharing of physiological data and the use of non-intrusive, ambient sensors or indirect mood indicators (e.g., behavior patterns or embodied physical objects), which can infer group mood without collecting sensitive personal data.

**Fostering Mood Alignment.** Our qualitative findings suggest facilitating the alignment of individual moods into a group emotional state through intentional design interventions. Mood alignment, a specific kind of group dynamics, cultivates a sense of togetherness and strengthens collaborative efforts [17,27]. Possible interventions could aim for more mood awareness in collaborative settings, which can trigger reflection [35], lead to behavioral mimicry, and ultimately foster mood alignment among team members [36]. Additionally, designers could define appropriate timing and prompt cues to invite participants to share their feelings at predetermined moments **(Subtheme 4.2)**. By guiding when and how group express themselves, whether via physical tools or digital notifications, these measures help team members adjust their behaviors in response to others, fostering a stronger sense of unity and enhancing collaboration.

**Empowering Group Control in Adaptive Workspaces.** The feedback from our participants also suggests empowering groups through shared, adaptive control over their workspace environments, ensuring interventions align with collective preferences and individual comfort **(Subthemes 5.1, 6.1)**. Mood-regulating recommendations should be context-aware and sensitive to individual differences, allowing groups to modify interventions according to their preferences. A collaborative control interface, such as a group dashboard or mobile app, that presents information about ambient conditions (e.g., light level, temperature, noise) allows team members to suggest or vote on adjustments, which fosters transparency and group consensus, reducing the feeling of control by automated systems. In addition, although automated adaptations can be effective in regulating group mood, designers should consider system intrusiveness and unintended disruptions to workflow or mood. Previous research has shown that unobtrusive ambient displays can effectively regulate affect without distracting users [39]. To address these concerns, interventions should aim for seamless integration into existing work routines or unobtrusive ambient mood indicators, minimizing distraction and avoiding unnecessary interactions.

### 6.4 Future Work and Limitation

While our findings offer valuable insights into how the physical workspace influences group mood, this qualitative study has limitations. Primarily, qualitative methods may not fully capture the variability in group experiences across diverse real-life settings. Our participant pool ($N = 26$ across 8 groups) was relatively homogeneous, potentially limiting the generalizability of our conclusions. Given that no new codes or themes emerged during analysis of the final two interviews, we are confident saturation was reached; however, larger and more varied samples could offer additional knowledge. Additionally, our analysis could reflect interpretive biases given our diverse academic backgrounds: two authors were from industrial design and the third from computer science with experience in VR gaming research. While these backgrounds potentially introduced biases, they also provided a comprehensive understanding of group mood dynamics. Future research should incorporate larger, diverse participant groups to enhance generalizability and use controlled experiments to empirically validate specific environmental and interpersonal factors identified in this study. Addressing privacy concerns, we recommend developing privacy-preserving behavioral analysis methods to infer group mood, using anonymized data on posture, spatial positioning, and interaction patterns. Validation studies involving controlled experiments and longitudinal field studies in realistic workplace environments are also recommended to evaluate the effectiveness and long-term impacts of workspace interventions on group mood dynamics.

## 7 Conclusion

Group mood in the workspace is inherently difficult to describe, making it equally challenging to measure or design for. While prior research has largely focused on individual experiences, the impact of physical workspaces on collaborative group affect remains underexplored. Our study addresses this gap by uncovering how workspace features shape group dynamics. Before we can design interventions that can enhance group mood, we must first understand the underlying factors and expectations. Our qualitative findings provide this foundational knowledge. Through an exploratory study employing the experience curve and semi-structured interviews with eight groups, our analysis revealed that a variety of factors, i.e., well-structured and low-hierarchy meetings, strong interpersonal connections, and optimal environmental conditions paired with flexible physical settings, significantly influence group mood. Our findings further emphasized the temporal differences of mood fluctuations, highlighting how these factors can either facilitate or inhibit group dynamics. These factors should not be seen in isolation, but as interconnected forces shaping the emergence of group mood. Subsequently, we explored the potential of intelligent technologies to support mood-aware workspaces, suggesting that effective MAWEs must balance adaptive, automated interventions with strong user autonomy and transparent communication. Based on participants' feedback, we propose a set of design implications aimed at guiding future efforts in multimodal data assessment, mood alignment, and the empowerment of autonomy. In the context of HCI research, our study contributes a novel perspective on group well-being in shared environments. It offers practical value for researchers and designers through actionable insights and design recommendations, particularly around how smart technologies might support communication and adapt dynamically to group mood.

**Acknowledgments.** The first author is partially supported by the Guangzhou Elites Scholarship Council.

# References

1. Alonso, M.B., Keyson, D.V., Hummels, C.C.: Squeeze, rock, and roll; can tangible interaction with affective products support stress reduction? In: Proceedings of the 2nd International Conference on Tangible and Embedded Interaction, pp. 105–108 (2008)
2. Balaam, M., Fitzpatrick, G., Good, J., Luckin, R.: Exploring affective technologies for the classroom with the subtle stone. In: Proceedings of the SIGCHI Conference on Human Factors in Computing Systems, pp. 1623–1632 (2010)
3. Barsade, S.G., Knight, A.P.: Group affect. Annu. Rev. Organ. Psychol. Organ. Behav. **2**(1), 21–46 (2015)
4. Bartel, C., Saavedra, R.: The collective construction of work group moods. Admin. Sci. Quart. **45**, 197–231 (2000). https://doi.org/10.2307/2667070
5. Benke, I., Knierim, M.T., Maedche, A.: Chatbot-based emotion management for distributed teams: a participatory design study. Proc. ACM Hum.-Comput. Interact. **4**(CSCW2), 1–30 (2020)
6. Bergefurt, L., Weijs-Perrée, M., Appel-Meulenbroek, R., Arentze, T.: The physical office workplace as a resource for mental health-a systematic scoping review. Build. Environ. **207**, 108505 (2022)
7. Berry, D.: Office noise and employee concentration: identifying causes of disruption and potential improvements. Ergonomics **48**, 25–37 (2005). https://doi.org/10.1080/00140130412331311390
8. Boubekri, M., et al.: The impact of optimized daylight and views on the sleep duration and cognitive performance of office workers. Int. J. Environ. Res. Public Health **17**, 3219 (2020). https://doi.org/10.3390/ijerph17093219
9. Braun, V., Clarke, V.: Using thematic analysis in psychology. Qual. Res. Psychol. **3**(2), 77–101 (2006)
10. Braun, V., Clarke, V.: Reflecting on reflexive thematic analysis. Qual. Res. Sport Exerc. Health **11**(4), 589–597 (2019)
11. Braun, V., Clarke, V.: One size fits all? What counts as quality practice in (reflexive) thematic analysis? Qual. Res. Psychol. **18**(3), 328–352 (2021)
12. Brombacher, H., Houben, S., Vos, S.: Tangible interventions for office work well-being: approaches, classification, and design considerations. Behav. Inf. Technol. **43**, 1–25 (2023). https://doi.org/10.1080/0144929X.2023.2241561
13. Brombacher, H., Ren, X., Vos, S., Lallemand, C.: Visualizing computer-based activity on ambient displays to reduce sedentary behavior at work. In: Proceedings of the 32nd Australian Conference on Human-Computer Interaction, OzCHI 2020, pp. 760–764. Association for Computing Machinery, New York, NY, USA (2021). https://doi.org/10.1145/3441000.3441022
14. Cernea, D., Ebert, A., Kerren, A.: Visualizing group affective tone in collaborative scenarios. In: Poster Abstracts of the Eurographics Conference on Visualization (EUROVIS 2014), p. 3 (2014)
15. Chadburn, A., Smith, J., Milan, J.: Productivity drivers of knowledge workers in the central London office environment. J. Corp. Real Estate **19** (2017). https://doi.org/10.1108/JCRE-12-2015-0047

16. Chau, J.Y., et al.: Are workplace interventions to reduce sitting effective? A systematic review. Prev. Med. **51**(5), 352–356 (2010)
17. Chung, V., Grèzes, J., Pacherie, E.: Collective emotion: a framework for experimental research. Emot. Rev. **16**(1), 28–45 (2024)
18. Church, K., Hoggan, E., Oliver, N.: A study of mobile mood awareness and communication through MobiMood. In: Proceedings of the 6th Nordic Conference on Human-Computer Interaction: Extending Boundaries, pp. 128–137 (2010)
19. Collins, A.L., Lawrence, S.A., Troth, A.C., Jordan, P.J.: Group affective tone: a review and future research directions. J. Organ. Behav. **34**(S1), S43–S62 (2013)
20. Damen, I., Kok, A., Vink, B., Brombacher, H., Vos, S., Lallemand, C.: The hub: facilitating walking meetings through a network of interactive devices. In: Companion Publication of the 2020 ACM Designing Interactive Systems Conference, DIS 2020 Companion, pp. 19–24. Association for Computing Machinery, New York, NY, USA (2020). https://doi.org/10.1145/3393914.3395876
21. Dang, C.T., Aslan, I., Lingenfelser, F., Baur, T., André, E.: Towards somaesthetic smarthome designs: exploring potentials and limitations of an affective mirror. In: Proceedings of the 9th International Conference on the Internet of Things, pp. 1–8 (2019)
22. Lera, E.: Emotion-Centered-Design (ECD) new approach for designing interactions that matter. In: Marcus, A. (ed.) DUXU 2015. LNCS, vol. 9186, pp. 406–416. Springer, Cham (2015). https://doi.org/10.1007/978-3-319-20886-2_38
23. George, J.M.: Personality, affect, and behavior in groups. J. Appl. Psychol. **75**(2), 107 (1990)
24. Ghandeharioun, A., McDuff, D., Czerwinski, M., Rowan, K.: EMMA: an emotion-aware wellbeing chatbot. In: 2019 8th International Conference on Affective Computing and Intelligent Interaction (ACII), pp. 1–7. IEEE (2019)
25. Gluhak, A., Presser, M., Zhu, L., Esfandiyari, S., Kupschick, S.: Towards mood based mobile services and applications. In: Kortuem, G., Finney, J., Lea, R., Sundramoorthy, V. (eds.) EuroSSC 2007. LNCS, vol. 4793, pp. 159–174. Springer, Heidelberg (2007). https://doi.org/10.1007/978-3-540-75696-5_10
26. Goldenberg, A., Garcia, D., Halperin, E., Gross, J.J.: Collective emotions. Curr. Dir. Psychol. Sci. **29**(2), 154–160 (2020)
27. Guo, G., Leshed, G., Green, K.E.: "I normally wouldn't talk with strangers": introducing a socio-spatial interface for fostering togetherness between strangers. In: Proceedings of the 2023 CHI Conference on Human Factors in Computing Systems, pp. 1–20 (2023)
28. Guribye, F., Gjøsæter, T., Bjartli, C.: Designing for tangible affective interaction. In: Proceedings of the 9th Nordic Conference on Human-Computer Interaction, pp. 1–10 (2016)
29. Hsiao, L., Hsiao, M.C., Wang, Y.L.: Effects of office space and colour on knowledge sharing and work stress. S. Afr. J. Econ. Manag. Sci. **16**, 42–53 (2013). https://doi.org/10.4102/sajems.v16i5.668
30. Kelly, J.R.: Mood and emotion in groups. In: Blackwell Handbook of Social Psychology: Group Processes, pp. 164–181 (2001)
31. Kujala, S., Roto, V., Väänänen, K., Karapanos, E., Sinnelä, A.: UX curve: a method for evaluating long-term user experience. Interact. Comput. **23**, 473–483 (2011). https://doi.org/10.1016/j.intcom.2011.06.005
32. LiKamWa, R., Liu, Y., Lane, N.D., Zhong, L.: MoodScope: building a mood sensor from smartphone usage patterns. In: Proceeding of the 11th Annual International Conference on Mobile Systems, Applications, and Services, pp. 389–402 (2013)

33. Lindström, M., et al.: Affective diary: designing for bodily expressiveness and self-reflection. In: CHI 2006 Extended Abstracts on Human Factors in Computing Systems, pp. 1037–1042 (2006)
34. Menges, J.I., Kilduff, M.: Group emotions: cutting the Gordian knots concerning terms, levels of analysis, and processes. Acad. Manag. Ann. **9**(1), 845–928 (2015)
35. Mora, S., Rivera-Pelayo, V., Müller, L.: Supporting mood awareness in collaborative settings. In: 7th International Conference on Collaborative Computing: Networking, Applications and Worksharing (CollaborateCom), pp. 268–277. IEEE (2011)
36. Nanninga, M.C., Zhang, Y., Lehmann-Willenbrock, N., Szlávik, Z., Hung, H.: Estimating verbal expressions of task and social cohesion in meetings by quantifying paralinguistic mimicry. In: Proceedings of the 19th ACM International Conference on Multimodal Interaction, pp. 206–215 (2017)
37. Peeters, M.M.R., Megens, C.J.P.G.: Experiential design landscapes: how to design for behaviour change, towards an active lifestyle. Ph.D. thesis, Zechnische Universiteit Eindhoven, Industrial Design (2014). https://doi.org/10.6100/IR771700
38. Peng, Z., Desmet, P.M., Xue, H.: Mood in experience design: a scoping review. She Ji J. Des. Econ. Innov. **9**(3), 330–378 (2023)
39. Pereira, E., et al.: Stars: enlightenment in the office space for behavioral change. In: Proceedings of the 2016 ACM International Joint Conference on Pervasive and Ubiquitous Computing: Adjunct, UbiComp 2016, pp. 1640–1645. Association for Computing Machinery, New York, NY, USA (2016). https://doi.org/10.1145/2968219.2968527
40. Rajcic, N., McCormack, J.: Mirror ritual: an affective interface for emotional self-reflection. In: Proceedings of the 2020 CHI Conference on Human Factors in Computing Systems, pp. 1–13 (2020)
41. Rogers, Y., Hazlewood, W.R., Marshall, P., Dalton, N., Hertrich, S.: Ambient influence: can twinkly lights lure and abstract representations trigger behavioral change? In: Proceedings of the 12th ACM International Conference on Ubiquitous Computing, UbiComp 2010, pp. 261–270. Association for Computing Machinery, New York, NY, USA (2010). https://doi.org/10.1145/1864349.1864372
42. Roskams, M., Haynes, B.: Salutogenic workplace design: a conceptual framework for supporting sense of coherence through environmental resources. J. Corp. Real Estate (2019). https://doi.org/10.1108/JCRE-01-2019-0001
43. Saldaña, J.: The Coding Manual for Qualitative Researchers, 5th edn. SAGE Publications, London, England (2025)
44. Sandblad, B., et al.: Work environment and computer systems development. Behav. Inf. Technol. **22**(6), 375–387 (2003)
45. Semeraro, C., Lezoche, M., Panetto, H., Dassisti, M.: Digital twin paradigm: a systematic literature review. Comput. Ind. **130** (2021). https://doi.org/10.1016/j.compind.2021.103469
46. Snyder, J., et al.: MoodLight: exploring personal and social implications of ambient display of biosensor data. In: Proceedings of the 18th ACM Conference on Computer Supported Cooperative Work & Social Computing, pp. 143–153 (2015)
47. Sönmez, A., Desmet, P.M., Herrera, N.R.: Chill, fiery, slack, and five other vibes: a phenomenological inquiry into group mood. She Ji J. Des. Econ. Innov. **8**(1), 93–117 (2022)
48. Stangl, A., Wepman, J., White, D.: MoodCasting: home as shared emotional space. In: CHI 2012 Extended Abstracts on Human Factors in Computing Systems, CHI EA 2012, pp. 1303–1308. Association for Computing Machinery, New York, NY, USA (2012). https://doi.org/10.1145/2212776.2212444

49. Tabassum, U., Khan, B., Sherani, A.W., Khan, I.: The relationship between job satisfaction and job performance among employees: a case of commercial banks in Punjab city, Pakistan. PM World J. **5**(8), 1–17 (2016)
50. Tsujita, H., Rekimoto, J.: HappinessCounter: smile-encouraging appliance to increase positive mood. In: CHI 2011 Extended Abstracts on Human Factors in Computing Systems, CHI EA 2011, pp. 117–126. Association for Computing Machinery, New York, NY, USA (2011). https://doi.org/10.1145/1979742.1979608
51. Wood, S., Leoni, S., Ladley, D.: Comparisons of the effects of individual and collective performance-related pay on performance: a review. Hum. Resource Manag. Rev., 100982 (2023)
52. Xue, M., Liang, J., Hu, J., Feijs, L.: ClockViz: designing public visualization for coping with collective stress in teamwork. In: 10th International Conference on Design and Semantics of Form and Movement (DeSForM 2017): Sense and Sensivity, pp. 67–78 (2017)
53. Xue, M., Liang, R.H., Yu, B., Funk, M., Hu, J., Feijs, L.: AffectiveWall: designing collective stress-related physiological data visualization for reflection. IEEE Access **7**, 131289–131303 (2019)
54. Yu, B., Zhang, B., An, P., Xu, L., Xue, M., Hu, J.: An unobtrusive stress recognition system for the smart office. In: 2019 41st Annual International Conference of the IEEE Engineering in Medicine and Biology Society (EMBC), pp. 1326–1329. IEEE (2019)

# When Motivation Can Be More Than a Message: Designing Agents to Boost Physical Activity

Alessandro Silacci[1,2](✉), Maurizio Caon[2], and Mauro Cherubini[1]

[1] Persuasive Technology Lab, University of Lausanne, Lausanne, Switzerland
{alessandro.silacci,mauro.cherubini}@unil.ch
[2] School of Management of Fribourg, HES-SO University of Applied Sciences and Arts of Western Switzerland, Fribourg, Switzerland
{alessandro.silacci,maurizio.caon}@hes-so.ch

**Abstract.** Virtual agents are commonly used in physical activity interventions to support behavior change, often taking the role of coaches that deliver encouragement and feedback. While effective for compliance, this role typically lacks relational depth. This pilot study explores how such agents might be perceived not just as instructors, but as co-participants: entities that appear to exert effort alongside users. Drawing on thematic analysis of semi-structured interviews with 12 participants from a prior physical activity intervention, we examine how users interpret and evaluate agent effort in social comparison contexts. Our findings reveal a recurring tension between perceived performance and authenticity. Participants valued social features when they believed others were genuinely trying. In contrast, ambiguous or implausible activity levels undermined trust and motivation. Many participants expressed skepticism toward virtual agents unless their actions reflected visible effort or were grounded in relatable human benchmarks. Based on these insights, we propose early design directions for fostering co-experienced exertion in agents, including behavioral cues, narrative grounding, and personalized performance. These insights contribute to the design of more engaging, socially resonant agents capable of supporting co-experienced physical activity.

**Keywords:** co-experience · human-agent interaction · motivation · perceived effort · physical activity · social comparison

## 1 Introduction

In Human-Computer Interaction (HCI), intelligent agents have long been used to support behavior change, especially in physical activity contexts where they often take the form of virtual coaches, delivering encouragement, tracking performance, and offering feedback [2,4,13,17,19]. While this role is effective for promoting compliance [13,19], it remains limited in depth, focusing on instruction rather than fostering richer, more relational forms of interaction [2,4,17].

Agents are uniquely positioned to influence motivation through not just informational support but also social presence, a factor known to sustain long-term engagement [22,25]. However, current designs rarely leverage this potential to create a sense of shared experience, particularly in the expression of effort.

Recent advancements in Large Language Models (LLMs) have expanded the capabilities of virtual agents, enabling more fluid, context-sensitive, and empathetic interactions [15]. However, in the realm of physical activity interventions, these agents currently remain confined to traditional coaching models providing textual support, missing opportunities to foster deeper engagement through shared experiences and co-participation.

In contrast, agents in video games are often designed as opponents, companions, or mirrors of the player – roles that foster emotional connection, narrative engagement, and meaningful social dynamics. Concepts like Simulated Exercising Peers (SEPs) have begun to explore similar dynamics in physical activity contexts [24], but it remains unclear how users perceive an agent's effort, or what makes that effort feel believable and motivating.

A key challenge is how agents can meaningfully convey exertion. Unlike humans, they do not visibly struggle or tire, and users may not naturally attribute effort to them. Identifying the cues, behaviors, and design elements that make an agent's effort feel believable, motivating, and shared with the user is a key challenge for future agent-based interventions.

The aim of this pilot study is to explore how virtual agents might be perceived as co-participants in physical activity interventions – engaging not only as coaches, but as entities that appear to share the user's effort. We are particularly interested in how users interpret agent behavior as indicative of exertion or collaboration. To guide this investigation, we ask: *How do users perceive and evaluate virtual agents' effort in the context of social physical activity interventions?* Through a series of qualitative interviews, we examine the cues, expectations, and conditions that shape these perceptions, and consider how such insights might inform the design of more socially resonant and relational agent interactions.

## 2 Background

Sustaining physical activity remains a persistent challenge, despite interventions grounded in motivational theories such as SDT and SCT, which emphasize relatedness, autonomy, and social modeling [1,9]. One of the strategy has been to embed social mechanisms such as support, feedback, and peer comparison, into interventions aiming to enhance motivation through interpersonal dynamics [25].

However, coordinating group-based activity poses practical challenges, often sustained engagement and synchronized schedules. To address these limitations, researchers have turned to virtual agents, including conversational and embodied forms, as scalable alternatives that simulate social presence. These agents can personalize feedback and interaction timing while maintaining a sense of continuity and responsiveness.

Yet, systems that incorporate social comparison present a double-edged sword: while motivating for some, they can discourage others when competition feels unfair or unbalanced [12,21]. This tension is particularly relevant for Simulated Exercising Peers (SEPs), agents designed to support human teammates through social support and physical effort simulation [24]. In this work, we explore how agents might go beyond comparison and coaching by fostering a perception of effort, enabling more engaging and cooperative interactions.

## 2.1 Effort, Embodiment, and Perception

While social comparison can motivate physical activity, it also risks unfair competition and reduced self-confidence, particularly when performance disparities are pronounced [12,21]. These risks extend to agent-based systems [27], including SEPs [24], which must balance challenge and fairness. To avoid replicating the pitfalls of human competition, agent design should shift from emphasizing performance outcomes to supporting perceived effort – both in the user and in the agent.

Cognitive science and psychology emphasize that effort is not simply a measure of physical strain, but a subjective experience – a felt cost associated with continuing an action [3]. This internal sense of effort helps guide decisions about persistence, disengagement, and intensity. Crucially, motivation depends not only on how difficult a task is in objective terms, but on how demanding it feels. This logic extends to social contexts, where perceiving effort in others can influence commitment and engagement in cooperative activities.

Empirical studies support this view. Users invest more effort when they believe a partner is exerting themselves [7], and subtle cues of agent commitment – even without performance data – enhance perseverance [26]. Responsiveness and socially supportive behaviors further increase users' feelings of closeness and engagement [27]. Yet current physical activity agents rarely communicate effort in socially meaningful ways. This presents a key opportunity to design agents not just to act, but to be seen as trying – fostering a sense of co-experienced exertion between human and machine.

## 2.2 Roles of Agents in Physical Activity

In physical activity interventions, virtual agents are most commonly cast in the role of coaches – providing encouragement, guiding goal setting, and offering educational support to help users build healthier habits [13,15,17,19]. These agents do more than dispense advice; by engaging users in sustained dialogue, they can foster relational bonds that support behavior change over time [4]. These agents can increase user adherence by facilitating conversation and building strong relational ties [5]. As these relationships develop, users often come to see the agent as a collaborative partner – a dynamic described in therapeutic contexts as a working alliance, built on shared goals, trust, and mutual engagement [2].

Although coaching agents are often preferred for their structure and expertise [14], companions provide alternative forms of support. These agents, often imagined as animals, cyborgs, or abstract creatures, use informal communication and can appear more emotionally responsive [24]. Their design enables users to influence the agent's state, such as its health [16] or mood [18], promoting a more reciprocal dynamic.

The role an agent plays has significant implications for interaction design. Coaches tend to function as authoritative figures, directing tasks and goals [20], which can streamline structure but may limit relational flexibility [23]. Companion agents, in contrast, support more emotionally resonant and socially dynamic relationships [16,18]. Their informality allows for increased social presence and vulnerability, making them especially promising for scenarios involving shared struggle or exertion. Critically, while coaches often monitor user effort, companion agents may better support the perception of agent effort – enabling richer, more immersive experiences of co-experienced physical activity [24].

While companion agents may help convey a sense of shared effort, it remains unclear what cues lead users to perceive such exertion – a gap this pilot study explores.

## 3 Methods

To investigate how users perceive virtual agents' physical effort, we conducted semi-structured interviews with 12 participants from an inter-group competition experiment promoting physical activity. The six-month study involved a prototype app where participants viewed their own and teammates' daily step counts on a leaderboard. Each team competed weekly against another, with access to both intra-team and opponent leaderboards.

We collected qualitative data through post-experiment interviews, focusing on how participants interpreted teammate behavior and how they envisioned virtual agents fitting into such settings. Our goal was not to assess performance outcomes, but to identify early themes in how effort is perceived – and which design elements might support or hinder that perception.

### 3.1 Recruitment

Participants for the interviews were selected from a larger ongoing experiment at the University of Lausanne, specifically those exposed to features designed to provide social connectedness (e.g., a team leaderboard and user profiles). As the intervention used cumulative weekly step counts as a proxy for physical performance, we aimed to recruit participants representing a range of activity levels: below, at, and above the median step count. Recruitment was conducted via email from the University of Lausanne's ORSEE participant pool, which includes over 8,000 volunteers, primarily university students. A total of 96 participants were eligible for inclusion.

## 3.2 Participants

We selected 37 eligible participants based on their willingness to participate, availability and their fluency in French, of which 13 agreed to participate. One was excluded due to consent form issues, resulting in a final sample of $N = 12$ (8 female, $M_{age} = 23\ years$). All participants had previously engaged in an intervention that tracked weekly step counts as a performance measure, and put them in an inter-group competition setup. The median weekly count was 31259.5; among interviewees, $N_{higher} = 3$ had values above the median and $N_{lower} = 9$ below. A detailed selection notebook is available in our Open Science Framework (OSF) repository[1].

## 3.3 Procedure

We conducted one-hour semi-structured interviews with participants previously involved in a mobile intervention at University of Lausanne, each of whom received a compensation of USD 27 (CHF 25). The first part of the interview focused on two app features: a team leaderboard that displayed weekly step counts to elicit social comparison [12], and user profiles with avatars, pseudonyms, hobbies, and preferred sports. We asked how these features shaped engagement, teammate comparisons, and users' sense of relatedness within the app's coopetitive structure (intra-team collaboration, inter-group competition).

In the second part, we explored perceptions of virtual agents. Participants were asked how such agents might complement existing features, what traits would make them credible or relatable, and how they would feel about collaborating or competing with AI teammates. Special attention was given to how agent effort might be perceived and expressed, and whether such agents could meaningfully participate in social dynamics around physical activity.

Interviews were continued until saturation of the data was evident, characterized by the consistent identification of previously established patterns and the emergence of no novel insights or information.

## 3.4 Analysis

Content generated through the interviews was analyzed using thematic analysis [6] to examine how participants interpreted social dynamics, perceived effort, and the potential role of agents in physical activity contexts. Our analysis was guided by the research question: *How do users perceive and evaluate virtual agents' effort in the context of social physical activity interventions?*

We used a primarily inductive, semantic coding approach. After jointly reviewing a subset of transcripts, two researchers collaboratively developed an initial set of 22 initial codes and 8 sub-themes grounded in the data. The progression of this coding process, from initial codes to emerging themes, is visually represented in Fig. 1. For inter-coder consistency, the two researchers independently

---

[1] See: https://doi.org/10.17605/OSF.IO/B2Y9N, last accessed June 2025.

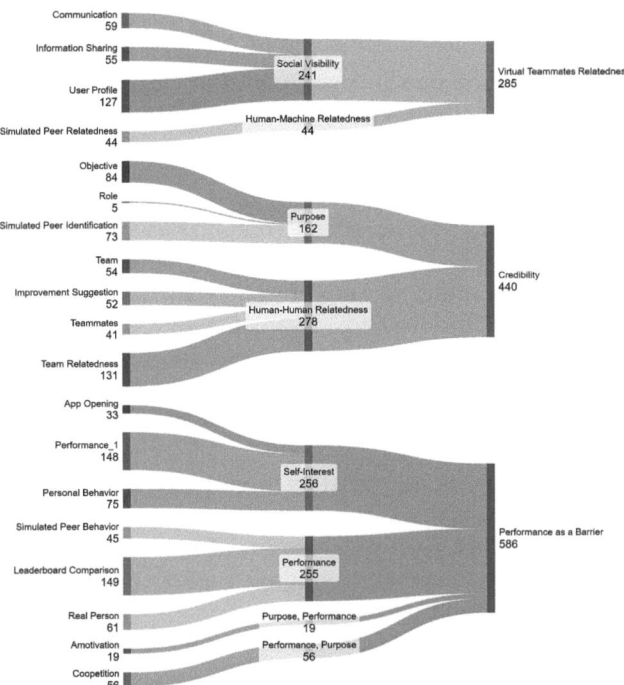

**Fig. 1.** This Sankey diagram visually illustrates the progression of our thematic analysis, mapping the aggregation of initial codes (left-most column, representing individual concepts or aspects from the data) into intermediary sub-themes (center column), and finally into overarching main themes (right-most column). The width of the flows (lines) and the nodes (boxes) represents the frequency or volume of data contributing to each code and theme. This visualization enhances transparency by showing how granular data insights were synthesized into broader analytical patterns.

coded 10% of the interviews, resulting in a Cohen's Kappa score of 0.83, which was deemed sufficient. Subsequent coding proceeded with continuous refinement of these codes through regular meetings as new patterns and nuances emerged during full dataset analysis. The complete codebook and thematic structure are available in our OSF repository[2].

### 3.5 Ethical Consideration

The Institutional Review Board (IRB) of the University of Lausanne approved our study. Interviews were conducted online and participants were provided with a link to the online meeting and could join as anonymous guests. We ensured anonymity of the data by replacing the used names of the interviewees with anonymous identifiers (e.g., P1, P2, etc.).

---

[2] See: https://doi.org/10.17605/OSF.IO/B2Y9N, last accessed June 2025.

## 4 Results

We identified three main themes in the qualitative data, reflecting how participants perceived social dynamics, effort, and credibility within the intervention.

### 4.1 Competition as a Potential Barrier

Participants frequently engaged in social comparison, often aspiring to match high-performing teammates. However, this same dynamic could become demotivating when perceived as unfair or unrepresentative. Technical issues (e.g., lost data) and contextual disruptions (e.g., exams) made some feel their effort was invisible. One participant, after losing progress due to app failure, remarked, *"It's just that when I saw that I was losing everything [because of the app tracking issues] I was there: Well I, mean I walk quite a bit, so..."* – reflecting both frustration and resignation.

Perceptions of inactive or implausibly high-performing teammates further eroded trust. Some questioned whether certain users were even real, speculating that a teammate *"may have been a computer."* This ambiguity led to what we interpret as a breakdown in social grounding – participants could not reliably assess others' effort or contextualize their own.

To cope with underperformance, some participants withdrew from the app, hid it, or avoided checking the leaderboard. These avoidance behaviors suggest a self-protective response to upward comparison, consistent with prior work showing that such comparisons can backfire when users lack control or credibility cues [12, 21].

Overall, while competition initially drove engagement, it also risked triggering guilt and disengagement. These findings underscore the need for systems to represent effort fairly and transparently to sustain motivation.

### 4.2 Credibility and the Search for Explanations

Participants often assessed teammates' profiles not for social connection, but to determine whether their activity levels were believable. They scanned details like age, hobbies, and listed sports to evaluate whether performance on the leaderboard made sense. As one participant put it, seeing a teammate *"doing 20,000 steps per day"* led them to assume that person *"must have been a runner."* Such inferences illustrate how users constructed plausible narratives to make comparative data feel credible.

This interpretive work reflects a deeper need to validate the fairness of social comparisons. When profile cues matched expectations, users were more likely to trust others' effort. When data seemed implausible or lacked context, participants grew skeptical – in some cases questioning whether certain users were even real. This credibility gap weakened trust in the system and diminished the motivational value of the leaderboard.

In short, participants used personal plausibility as a stand-in for perceived effort, anchoring trust in social data through coherence between identity and performance.

## 4.3 Skepticism Toward Agent Effort and Authenticity

When analyzing the relatedness between the participants and their virtual peers, a recurring source of frustration among participants was the lack of concrete information about their teammates, which created uncertainty about whether those users were real. Some described the experience as *"dehumanized"* or *"very anonymous,"* noting that pseudonyms and avatars alone were not enough to establish genuine social presence. This was particularly problematic when performances were extreme – either very high or unusually low – which participants found difficult to contextualize without additional background.

This skepticism extended to the idea of integrating virtual agents. Many participants expressed discomfort with the notion that teammates might be computer-controlled, stating that it would undermine the sense of authentic competition. As one participant put it, *"the competition is between the people,"* suggesting that human agency was essential to the leaderboard's motivational effect. Others noted that knowing an agent was *"just a program"* would render its performance meaningless, as it wouldn't reflect real physical effort – just *"a number that is useless."*

Despite this skepticism, several participants proposed ways that agents could still contribute meaningfully. One common idea was to use the agent as a daily step target or motivational benchmark. As one described, it could serve as *"a motor for motivation,"* offering inspiration rather than competition. Others suggested that grounding the agent's behavior in the identity or performance of a real person – such as an athlete or public figure – could make its actions feel more credible and aspirational.

## 5 Discussion and Conclusion

Our findings point to a recurring tension between performance and perceived effort. Participants valued social features when they felt that their teammates' activity reflected real exertion – a dynamic that virtual agents currently struggle to convey. If an agent's behavior is interpreted as effortless or artificial, its motivational credibility diminishes. This highlights a key challenge for the design of agents in physical activity contexts: not just how they act, but how they appear to try.

Insights from game design may help illuminate this challenge. In video games, agents – whether companions or opponents – are often designed to exhibit adaptive difficulty, emotional expression, or visible struggle [8,11]. These features are not only aesthetic but functional: they signal effort, fallibility, and investment, which foster engagement and emotional connection. For example, when game agents exhibit emotional expressiveness and vulnerability – such as fatigue or personality-driven responses – players report greater immersion and social connection [8].

Conversely, when agents are perceived as infallible or overpowered, the relationship can break. The case of AlphaGo is illustrative: despite its technical mastery, human players found its style demotivating, in part because its moves

**Table 1.** Summary of the main themes and their design implications

| Main Theme | Design Implications |
|---|---|
| 1. Competition as a Potential Barrier | **Make agent effort visible:** Agents should actively display signs of exertion (e.g., slowed movement, visual fatigue, or verbal cues) to signal they are "working" too. This can strengthen believability and mutual challenge, addressing user frustration from invisible or arbitrary effort. |
| 2. Credibility and the Search for Explanations | **Use human-like performance benchmarks:** Agent behavior should reflect realistic human standards (e.g., average step counts or variability) to avoid appearing unfair or artificially perfect. This fosters trust in social comparison by helping users interpret the agent's effort as credible. |
| 3. Skepticism Toward Agent Effort and Authenticity | **Personalize for co-engagement:** Agents can foster connection by adjusting to the user's pace or progressing in sync. Such alignment supports the illusion of shared effort and builds relational depth, moving beyond a simple coach role toward more resonant partnerships. |

appeared opaque and devoid of struggle [10]. In our pilot study, participants expressed a similar unease when they imagined competing against virtual teammates whose step counts were *"just a number"* – lacking context, backstory, or any sign of exertion.

These parallels suggest that designers of physical activity agents might draw on game-based conventions to reinforce perceptions of effort and co-experience. Agents could, for instance, visibly slow down when the user is inactive, display fatigue when achieving high step counts, or adapt their pacing to mirror the user's progress. By signaling effort through expressive behavior, narrative grounding, or performance variability, agents might move beyond role-based interactions (e.g., coach) toward more emotionally resonant partnerships. Based on our findings, we suggest three preliminary design directions to inform future agent development, as detailed in Table 1. These directions include making agent effort visible, using human-like performance benchmarks, and personalizing for co-engagement. The design directions established in this work open up several promising avenues for future research into co-experienced exertion. A primary research question is how to effectively translate the conceptual principles of co-experienced exertion into system designs that align with users' subjective expectations. Investigating this question could involve participatory design methodologies, not merely to refine predefined concepts, but to fundamentally explore the design space of how users perceive and value the expression of effort from an agent. For example, future studies could explore the nuances of how users interpret different modalities of an agent's "fatigue" – be it through visual cues, auditory feedback, or changes in behavior.

Furthermore, a significant area for inquiry lies in understanding the dynamic and reciprocal nature of the user-agent relationship. This raises questions about how an agent's "pace" and "effort" should be algorithmically adapted to a user's real-time activity and psychological state to foster a genuine sense of partnership. Exploring this could involve comparative studies, such as A/B tests, to analyze the differential impacts of various adaptive algorithms on user motivation, trust, and the perception of effort. Beyond quantitative metrics, in-depth qualitative studies are needed to uncover the lived experiences of users interacting with these systems over time. Such a research program, integrating both quantitative and qualitative approaches, would be crucial for developing a comprehensive theoretical framework of co-experienced exertion in physical activity interventions.

**Limitations.** While these insights offer promising directions for design, several limitations should be noted in interpreting the findings. As an exploratory pilot, our findings are based on a small and relatively homogeneous sample of university students, which impacts the generalizability of our results to a wider population. Data was drawn from semi-structured interviews, relying on participant imagination rather than live interaction with functioning agents. We also did not triangulate interview responses with behavioral or usage data, which could have added further depth and validation. Future research should involve interactive prototypes and broader participant samples to better understand how perceptions of agent effort play out in real-world settings.

Moving forward, the challenge is to bridge imagined potential with embodied design – creating agents that can visibly participate in effort, adapt to users, and foster sustained motivation through shared experience.

**Acknowledgments.** The authors acknowledge financial support from the HEC Faculty at the University of Lausanne, which funded participant compensation.

**Disclosure of Interests.** The authors have no competing interests to declare that are relevant to the content of this article.

# References

1. Bandura, A.: Health promotion from the perspective of social cognitive theory. Psychol. Health **13**(4), 623–649 (1998). https://doi.org/10.1080/08870449808407422
2. Bennett, J.K., Fuertes, J.N., Keitel, M., Phillips, R.: The role of patient attachment and working alliance on patient adherence, satisfaction, and health-related quality

of life in lupus treatment. Patient Educ. Couns. **85**(1), 53–59 (2011). https://doi.org/10.1016/j.pec.2010.08.005
3. Bermúdez, J.P.: What is the feeling of effort about? Australas. J. Philos. **103**(1), 88–105 (2025). https://doi.org/10.1080/00048402.2024.2351208
4. Bickmore, T., Gruber, A., Picard, R.: Establishing the computer-patient working alliance in automated health behavior change interventions. Patient Educ. Couns. **59**(1), 21–30 (2005). https://doi.org/10.1016/j.pec.2004.09.008
5. Bickmore, T.W., Picard, R.W.: Establishing and maintaining long-term human-computer relationships. ACM Trans. Comput.-Hum. Interact. **12**(2), 293–327 (2005). https://doi.org/10.1145/1067860.1067867
6. Braun, V., Clarke, V.: Using thematic analysis in psychology. Qual. Res. Psychol. **3**(2), 77–101 (2006). https://doi.org/10.1191/1478088706qp063oa
7. Chennells, M., Michael, J.: Effort and performance in a cooperative activity are boosted by perception of a partner's effort. Sci. Rep. **8**(1), 15692 (2018). https://doi.org/10.1038/s41598-018-34096-1
8. Chowanda, A., Flintham, M., Blanchfield, P., Valstar, M.: Playing with social and emotional game companions. In: Traum, D., Swartout, W., Khooshabeh, P., Kopp, S., Scherer, S., Leuski, A. (eds.) IVA 2016. LNCS (LNAI), vol. 10011, pp. 85–95. Springer, Cham (2016). https://doi.org/10.1007/978-3-319-47665-0_8
9. Deci, E.L., Ryan, R.M.: The "what" and "why" of goal pursuits: human needs and the self-determination of behavior. Psychol. Inq. **11**(4), 227–268 (2000). https://doi.org/10.1207/S15327965PLI1104_01
10. Egri-Nagy, A., Törmänen, A.: The game is not over yet–go in the post-Alphago era. Philosophies **5**(4), 37 (2020). https://doi.org/10.3390/philosophies5040037
11. Emmerich, K., Ring, P., Masuch, M.: I'm Glad You Are on My Side: How to Design Compelling Game Companions. In: Proceedings of the 2018 Annual Symposium on Computer-Human Interaction in Play. CHI PLAY '18, New York, NY, USA, pp. 141–152. Association for Computing Machinery (2018). https://doi.org/10.1145/3242671.3242709
12. Estabrooks, P.A., Harden, S.M., Burke, S.M.: Group dynamics in physical activity promotion: what works? Soc. Pers. Psychol. Compass **6**(1), 18–40 (2012). https://doi.org/10.1111/j.1751-9004.2011.00409.x
13. Fadhil, A., Wang, Y., Reiterer, H.: Assistive conversational agent for health coaching: a validation study. Methods Inf. Med. **58**(01), 009–023 (2019). https://doi.org/10.1055/s-0039-1688757
14. Griffiths, S., et al.: Exercise with social robots: companion or coach? In: Proceedings of Workshop on Personal Robots for Exercising and Coaching at the HRI 2018 (HRI2018) (2018)
15. Jörke, M., et al.: GPTCoach: towards LLM-based physical activity coaching. In: Proceedings of the 2025 CHI Conference on Human Factors in Computing Systems, Yokohama Japan, pp. 1–46. ACM (2025). https://doi.org/10.1145/3706598.3713819
16. Kniestedt, I., Gómez Maureira, M.A.: Little fitness dragon: a gamified activity tracker. In: Wallner, G., Kriglstein, S., Hlavacs, H., Malaka, R., Lugmayr, A., Yang, H.-S. (eds.) ICEC 2016. LNCS, vol. 9926, pp. 205–210. Springer, Cham (2016). https://doi.org/10.1007/978-3-319-46100-7_18
17. Kocielnik, R., Xiao, L., Avrahami, D., Hsieh, G.: Reflection companion: a conversational system for engaging users in reflection on physical activity. Proc. ACM Interact. Mob. Wearable Ubiquitous Technol. **2**(2), 70:1–70:26 (2018). https://doi.org/10.1145/3214273

18. Lin, J.J., Mamykina, L., Lindtner, S., Delajoux, G., Strub, H.B.: Fish'n'Steps: encouraging physical activity with an interactive computer game. In: Dourish, P., Friday, A. (eds.) UbiComp 2006. LNCS, vol. 4206, pp. 261–278. Springer, Heidelberg (2006). https://doi.org/10.1007/11853565_16
19. Maher, C.A., Davis, C.R., Curtis, R.G., Short, C.E., Murphy, K.J.: A physical activity and diet program delivered by artificially intelligent virtual health coach: proof-of-concept study. JMIR Mhealth Uhealth **8**(7), e17558 (2020). https://doi.org/10.2196/17558
20. Mohan, S., Venkatakrishnan, A., Hartzler, A.L.: Designing an AI health coach and studying its utility in promoting regular aerobic exercise. ACM Trans. Interact. Intell. Syst. **10**(2) (2020). https://doi.org/10.1145/3366501
21. Mollee, J.S., Klein, M.C.A.: the effectiveness of upward and downward social comparison of physical activity in an online intervention. In: 2016 15th International Conference on Ubiquitous Computing and Communications and 2016 International Symposium on Cyberspace and Security (IUCC-CSS), pp. 109–115 (2016). https://doi.org/10.1109/IUCC-CSS.2016.023
22. Ren, X., Yu, B., Lu, Y., Brombacher, A.: Exploring cooperative fitness tracking to encourage physical activity among office workers. Proc. ACM Hum.-Comput. Interact. **2**(CSCW), 146:1–146:20 (2018). https://doi.org/10.1145/3274415
23. Salman, S., Richards, D., Dras, M.: Identifying which relational cues users find helpful to allow tailoring of e-coach dialogues. Multimodal Technol. Interact. **7**(10), 93 (2023). https://doi.org/10.3390/mti7100093
24. Silacci, A., Cherubini, M., Caon, M.: Navigating the design of simulated exercising peers: insights from a participatory design study. Front. Dig. Health **7–2025** (2025). https://doi.org/10.3389/fdgth.2025.1551966
25. Stragier, J., Mechant, P., De Marez, L., Cardon, G.: Computer-mediated social support for physical activity: a content analysis. Health Educ. Beh. **45**(1), 124–131 (2018). https://doi.org/10.1177/1090198117703055
26. Székely, M., Powell, H., Vannucci, F., Rea, F., Sciutti, A., Michael, J.: The perception of a robot partner's effort elicits a sense of commitment to human-robot interaction. Interact. Stud. **20**(2), 234–255 (2019). https://doi.org/10.1075/is.18001.sze
27. Zhou, C., Bian, Y., Zhang, S., Zhang, Z., Wang, Y., Liu, Y.J.: Exploring user experience and performance of a tedious task through human-agent relationship. Sci. Rep. **13**(1), 2995 (2023). https://doi.org/10.1038/s41598-023-29874-5

# HCD for Mission-Critical Systems

# Before It Falls: Supporting Drone Fleet Management Through Battery Visualizations

Maria-Theresa Bahodi[1](✉), Nathan Lau[2], Niels van Berkel[1], Kasper Andreas Rømer Grøntved[3], Mikael B. Skov[1], and Timothy Merritt[1]

[1] Human Centered Computing, Department of Computer Science, Aalborg University, Aalborg, Denmark
merritt@cs.aau.dk
[2] Grado Department of Industrial and Systems Engineering, Virginia Tech, Blacksburg, VA, USA
[3] SDU Drone Center, University of Southern Denmark, Odense, Denmark

**Abstract.** Battery life is a critical constraint in drone operations, directly impacting a flight's success and operations. Drone operators need to interpret battery information when deciding on their mission's subsequent steps. This decision-making involves maximizing mission completion while ensuring the drones can safely return to base. In this paper, we present a $2 \times 2$ within-subject design, where we compare two mission displays and enabled notifications that appear when the estimated battery level at the base reaches 15% or 5%. The first display follows traditional interfaces, representing battery levels through icons and percentages. The other follows Ecological Interface Design (EID), where the battery level is conveyed as the remaining range on the mission path. We measured performance metrics, cognitive load, and mental workload for each condition. Our results indicate that the EID-based interface resulted in higher mission completion rates, while the notifications significantly reduced their perceived cognitive load and mental workload.

## 1 Introduction

Unmanned aerial vehicles (UAVs), more commonly known as drones, have been used in various contexts, such as military, security, and emergency efforts. Drones have the added advantage of being much cheaper and more flexible in providing additional and vital aerial data for further contexts of the mission compared to larger manned aircraft like helicopters [26].

Despite the benefits, UAVs suffer from some technical limitations that dictate how useful they can be in a given situation. For example, environmental conditions have a significant influence on their performance [21]. In the case of weather, strong winds, precipitation, and temperature can all affect the UAV's

---

The original version of the chapter has been revised. A correction to this chapter can be found at https://doi.org/10.1007/978-3-032-05002-1_34

mobility and battery level, thereby limiting the UAV's range and airtime. These factors subsequently affect drone operators' ability to plan and execute a mission. Battery level is one of the main considerations for an operator when planning and executing a task. Currently, most UAV user interfaces display the battery level through an icon with percentage [1,4], but some also display the estimated remaining flight time based on the flight behavior, such as the speed of the drone[1]. These displays still require the drone operator to use their experience and cognitive resources to project how far the UAVs can go before they need to return to their landing space, something that can be very difficult if a person is not experienced with the effects of the environment on the UAVs.

The mental demand of the drone operator increases substantially in multi-UAV operations [27,28]. Deploying a fleet or swarm of drones has the added benefit of completing a task faster compared to a single UAV, and they provide more information simultaneously. With the increased complexity of more tasks and information in multi-drone missions, research has been investigating how to support operators at higher levels of automation. The operator should no longer act as a pilot flying each UAV separately but rather become a supervisor of the fleet, processing the information and taking corrective actions as needed to ensure that the UAVs are able to carry out their mission [10]. Yet research indicates the need to retain some levels of user control and balance (machine) autonomy with user intervention for certain tasks and scenarios such as task planning and manual control if the UAVs are behaving in an unexpected way [27]. For current drone systems, drones automatically attempt to return to base when a set threshold has been reached, but the user can decide to override it if the landing space is not safe or if they deem it safe to continue the flight. In a multi-UAV system, a user should still be capable of overriding the autonomous behavior. However, as the mental and cognitive demands increase due to the higher number of UAVs, exponentially more information and decisions need to be managed by the future user, and systems need to be designed to support the change properly [9].

While many user interfaces display the battery level through the current percentage, there are opportunities to go beyond conventional displays and reduce the cognitive effort needed to perform a task. Previous research has explored how the ecological interface design (EID) framework can help design interfaces that reduce the cognitive workload required to maintain a system [43] and design future UAV displays [20]. Moreover, a multi-UAV system requires extensive autonomy, and as the operator takes on the role of a supervisor, the user needs to be continuously updated on the current state of the system, which includes the battery level. Incorporating explicit system notifications has shown to be highly valuable for helping users maintain systems with multiple moving entities [6,29].

In this paper, we examine the difference in user behavior when given an interface inspired by current battery display design practices compared to an interface inspired by design guidance from EID. We also explore how system notifications, notifying the expected battery at landing, affect user decisions in regards to returning a drone back to the base. Our results indicate that using an

---

[1] https://www.dji.com/dk/downloads/djiapp/dji-fly.

EID-inspired display, where the UAV's ability to return home is visualized on its flight path, makes the user more willing to allow the UAVs to complete more of their mission. Moreover, we found that enabled notifications reduce the number of UAV crashes as well as reduce the cognitive load and mental workload of the user.

## 2 Related Work

Our work is grounded in human-battery interaction and ecological interface design (EID) for UAV systems. We build on studies that reveal how users interpret battery information and manage energy levels, highlighting key design-behavior dynamics. EID research suggests that visually integrating energy information enhances situational awareness and decision-making.

### 2.1 Human-Battery Interaction Research

Human-battery interaction (HBI) [37] explores how people operate their devices with respect to the battery level and how their behavior reflects particular concerns. Research has focused on how users manage the battery level of their portable devices, from their personal devices such as mobile phones and laptops to the more critical range concerns with battery electric vehicles (BEVs) [17] and drones [20]. For personal devices, users adopt strategies to manage the battery level either charging the device regularly without monitoring the level closely or responding to battery level visualizations and alarm notifications [7,13,34,37,42]. Researchers have also experimented with performance and functionality trade-offs users would be willing to make when trying to extend their battery level [48], emphasizing the need to understand user goals and context.

Design approaches to battery level displays in research and industry follow a few strategies [19,24,37,41]. The primary way of displaying battery levels for smartphones has been through icons and percentages, which give an instantaneous estimate of the current battery level, yet more advanced visualizations show the history of the battery depletion and estimated remaining time [5,13]. Findings from mobile battery management suggest that the design of battery visualizations and notifications is crucial in supporting the user in managing battery levels [14].

The consequences of running out of power when driving a vehicle or when flying a drone are far more serious. Research has examined how battery level affects users of battery electric vehicles (BEVs) such as cars [17,38]. Here, the phenomenon of *range stress* or *range anxiety* (RA) has been a prominent topic [18,19]. RA describes the driver's fear of getting stranded in the middle of their trip due to insufficient battery, often leading to the driver taking shorter trips than what the vehicle is capable of [35,36,41]. Yet research suggests that with more experience, RA decreases [16]. Managing the battery level is critical for drone missions, and research has examined technical improvements for optimizing flight planning based on the battery level [1,4] and creating models for predicting available battery [11,25].

## 2.2 Ecological Interface Design

Human-Drone research often adopts a user-centered or participatory approach to design future systems [1,3,4,26]. However, relying on experts or users has some limitations. First, users and sometimes experts may not be able to articulate their needs. Second, users or experts may have mental models that imperfectly represent the systems or real world, especially when operating experience is limited or sometimes absent for novel systems. Finally, the user-centered approach does not systematically address unanticipated events that are not brought up by the users or operators by definition. Ecological Interface Design (EID) directly addresses the challenge of supporting operators during unanticipated events [47]. EID prescribes work domain analysis to thoroughly understand the work domain and generate information requirements that can complement the design inputs from the users on the tasks they need to complete. The work domain analysis typically involves modeling the system with an abstraction hierarchy (AH) [40], a multi-level knowledge representation framework that helps identify system constraints. AH is characterized by the structural means-end relation between levels in that an object in one level is a mean to another object in a higher level, *why*, and an end to another object at a lower level, *how*.

EID is also based on the skills, rules, and knowledge (SRK) taxonomy [39], which describes the three levels of cognitive control a person can exhibit with respect to how they interpret information in the form of signals, signs, and symbols. Information interpreted as signals, signs, or symbols subsequently dictates whether skill-based behavior (SBB), rule-based behavior (RBB), or knowledge-based behavior (KBB) is engaged and, thus, what cognitive performance can manifest. While KBB allows the person to handle novel situations, it is also the slowest way of processing information. One can argue that displaying the battery level as an icon and percentage aims to activate RBB but results only in KBB since the operators must process the battery information in conjunction with weather conditions, which change very rapidly. In other words, the display has not sufficiently integrated multiple information elements, so operators would still need to analyze the situation further to reach an assessment of the battery level for the mission. To activate the lower levels of cognitive control more readily to improve operator performance, the user interface not only needs to include the necessary information but also visualize the information relevant to the system's purpose or mission objective.

EID has been applied to develop user interfaces for managing multiple entities simultaneously [8,15,30]. Specifically for flight systems, EID can support experts in better and safer decision-making [8,33,46]. Fuchs et al. [20] adopted EID to develop an alternative UAV display and found that representing the remaining range communicated through the path's color was the most useful out of all the display elements. However, their evaluation did not compare the effectiveness of the new interface against any of the existing solutions.

## 3 System Design

Recognizing that previous studies have not examined battery management for multi-drone systems and lack direct comparisons between traditional displays and EID, we developed a simulation platform to study this empirically. We developed a web application where eight simulated UAVs follow a predetermined parallel track mission. The interface can be seen in Fig. 1. The flight paths for the missions were computed based on the coverage algorithm by Grøntved et al. [22], which decomposes a polygonal area into lines that are allocated to the UAVs in the environment through a group of flight paths for each UAV that minimizes the distance between the tasks.

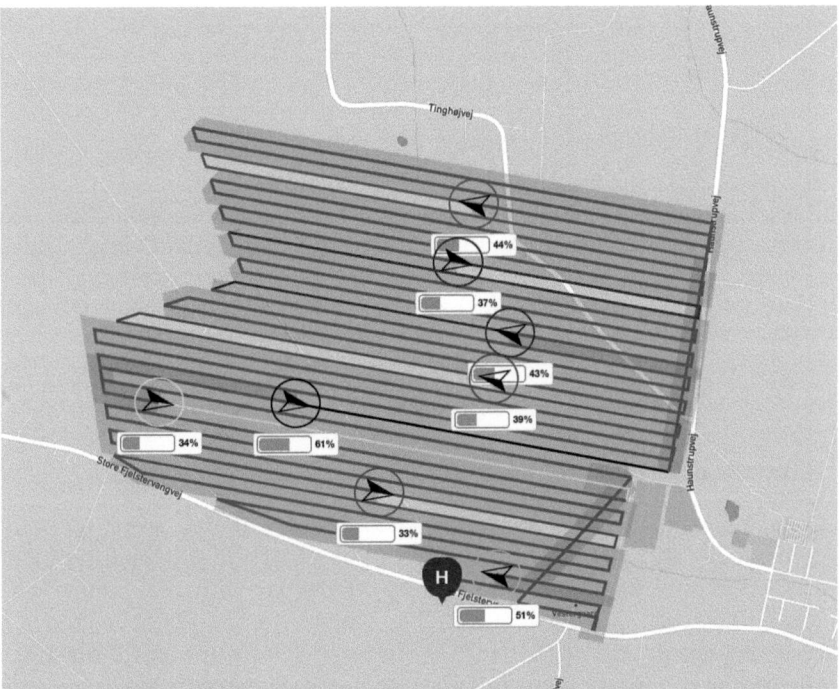

**Fig. 1.** Full screen view of the study platform with eight UAVs indicated by an arrow pointing in the direction of movement following their respective color-coded flight paths. The home location is indicated with the pin marked with an 'H.'

We designed the interface to incorporate a non-interactive map to ensure that all UAVs were visible. This removed the possibility for the participants to accidentally move the map, which resulted in UAVs being outside the participant's view. Therefore, the study could be completed on a screen of 14" or above, allowing our participants to participate on their personal computers.

To return a UAV to the base, the user had to select it on the map and select 'Return home' as shown in Fig. 2C. If the condition involved notifications, the UAV could also be returned to base by accepting the notification. We decided on this simplified way of interacting with the UAVs to emulate how UAVs are returned to the base on current drone devices, where a 'return to home' command can be activated through a button on a physical controller.

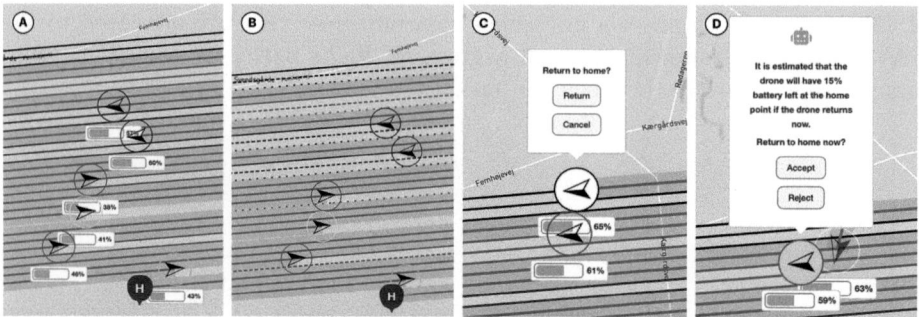

**Fig. 2.** The interface of the study platform. **A. Traditional display:** Battery icons and percentages follow the individual UAVs. **B. EID display:** No battery icons are displayed, instead the path follows the design on Fig. 3. **C. Manual return:** A dialogue box appears on top of the selected UAV. **D. Notifications:** A dialogue box appears automatically when the estimated battery level is 15% and 5% at landing.

### 3.1 Traditional Display

Traditional battery displays usually visualize battery charge levels numerically as a percentage, and also graphically with the color fill corresponding to the percentage. We implemented the TRADITIONAL display with both numerical and graphical indicators, as shown in Fig. 2A, whereas a battery icon and a percentage is displayed. Although the UAV battery level is usually displayed in a separate graphical element from the map, such as a side menu, we opted to have the battery level following the position of the UAV on the map. This decision was based on recent work that suggests the need to incorporate essential information together with the immediate UAV position to motivate a holistic view of the system [6, 29, 31].

### 3.2 Ecological Interface Design (EID)

One of the proposed benefits of adopting EID is that ecological interfaces explicitly support the system operator in handling novel events, since the connection between the constraints and properties of the system is made explicit for adaptive problem solving [47]. This differs from more traditional interfaces that do not explicitly depict the system properties for the operator, who would then have to rely on their own experience and knowledge. The design of the EID display is inspired by the work of Fuchs et al. [20] whereas battery levels are indicated by line types for each segment of the flight path in the mission as shown in Fig. 2B. In the weeks prior to the study reported her, we conducted pilot studies with three drone experts to refine the design of the paths when multiple UAVs have tightly packed flight paths typical for a search and rescue mission. Instead of using colors to represent whether a UAV would be able to reach its next waypoint [20], we decided to use the line stroke of the flight path to visualize the range of the UAV as seen in Fig. 3. We used unique colors for the flight paths matching the respective UAVs to show which mission belonged to which UAV.

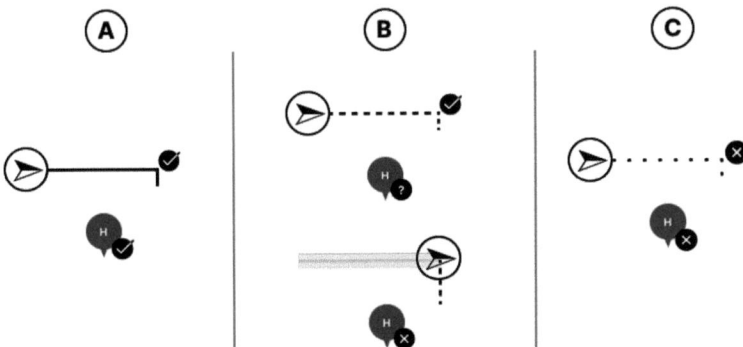

**Fig. 3.** The redesigned battery display inspired by Fuchs et al. [20]. **A. Solid path until the next waypoint:** The UAV can reach both the next waypoint and the home point from its current position. **B. Dashed path until next waypoint:** The UAV can reach the next waypoint, but it is unknown how much of the path the UAV can complete until it is no longer able to reach home. It is only certain that if the waypoint has been reached, the homepoint *cannot* be reached. **C. Dotted path until next waypoint:** Neither the next waypoint nor the home point can be reached any longer.

### 3.3 Notifications

In addition to the persistent battery level displays, we were interested in whether explicit notifications that suggest returning a UAV to the base would affect user decisions when monitoring a fleet of UAVs. As support systems can calculate how much battery a UAV will likely have left to return to base at a given time, the system can suggest when a UAV should return. The operator can consequently determine both from their understanding of the situation and the display whether a UAV should return to base or continue its mission.

In conditions where notifications were ENABLED, a dialogue box would appear, asking if the participant would like to return a UAV based on the estimated battery level at base if returned immediately as shown in Fig. 2D. The notification would appear twice. The first appeared when the estimated battery level would be 15%, and a second when the level would be 5%. The notification would not disappear until the participant had actively accepted or rejected the notification to ensure they had seen it. The persistence of the notification was chosen to ensure that the participant had time to see it and make a conscious decision from the notification. For the notifications DISABLED condition, notifications would not be displayed, and the participant must manually select individual UAVs to return any to base.

## 4 Method

We conducted a user study to empirically investigate differences in the management of a fleet of drones with traditional and EID battery displays and the impact of explicit system notifcations using the simulation platform. This study has the following three hypotheses:

- H1: *There is a decreased risk of a UAV crashing when* DISPLAY *is* EID *since the EID display explicitly visualizes range capabilities of the drone through the flight path, more clearly indicating where in the mission there is increased risk that a UAV cannot return home.* The expectation is that EID enables the user to simply scan the screen and engage in rule based behavior (RBB), which is faster and involves lower cognitive load compared to the traditional display that requires the user engage in knowledge-based behavior (KBB) to read and interpret symbols for the battery levels and then examine the remaining flight path.
- H2: *The UAV will have completed a higher percentage of its mission when* DISPLAY *is* TRADITIONAL *compared to* EID; *however, that would be at the expense of the risk of decreasing a UAV's ability to return safely to base.* The expectation here is that the EID design provides a more conservative estimate of range and would offer the user an opportunity to send a UAV home according to the path, which involves RBB or simple pattern matching and lower levels of cognitive load.
- H3: *The UAVs will complete more of their mission when notifications are enabled than when they are not.* When users know that the system will notify them when to return UAVs home, we expect them to wait for the notification rather than manually monitor and evaluate when to return a UAV.

### 4.1 Participants

We calculated a sample size of 24 participants with an a priori power calculation using G*Power [12], where we used a small effect size $f = 0.2$, a significance level of $\alpha = 0.05$, and a power of 0.8. We recruited 24 participants, twelve of whom had little to no drone experience, while the remaining twelve participants had flown drones as part of their work or hobby, with an experience range between

10 to 500 h ($SD = 175.6, mean = 152.08$). Participants' mean age was 29 years. We recruited both novices and experienced drone users, where familiarity with flying drones was the primary distinction between the groups. The experienced participants all actively work with drones as their main occupation or use them in their spare time. As the EID display will be novel to both groups, there could be differences in opinions and preferences on a given display design or notifications.

We expect experienced participants to be familiar with the issues of maintaining sufficient battery to ensure the drones can safely return to base. They could have experienced scenarios where they were at risk of losing a drone due to a lack of foresight in the amount of battery level needed for a task. Their experience provides insight into how professionals determine when drones should return or continue their mission and also how the alternative EID approach would benefit or hinder their work. Novices do not have as strong of a prenotion of battery level as experts but might benefit more from the additional support provided.

### 4.2 Study Design and Procedure

This study adopted a within-subjects design with two independent variables: DISPLAY with two levels (TRADITIONAL, EID) and NOTIFICATION with two levels (ENABLED, DISABLED).

The participants completed the study either in-person or online through Teams or Zoom. All novice participants completed the study in-person on their personal laptop or researcher's laptop. Most experienced participants completed the study online, as some did not reside near the study location while others did not have the time to attend in-person. Online participants shared their screens so that the researcher could observe their actions and ensure that everything was displayed correctly.

Before the participants performed the tasks, we introduced them to the project and the subject matter of battery level in UAVs. If the participant had experience with using UAVs, we asked them a set of questions related to how they currently managed battery level. The study sessions were set up in the following way:

1. **Introduction.** On the landing page, the participant was welcomed with an introduction to the study and the context of the tasks they were to complete. We framed the context as a surveillance mission where the UAVs had been programmed to conduct a parallel search, and the participant was to monitor and ensure that the UAVs would return to base safely while covering the assigned flight path as much as possible. After the brief introduction, the participants were asked to sign a consent, which they needed to accept to continue with the study. Upon giving their consent, they were asked to enter their age, occupation, and an approximation of their total flight hours with UAVs.
2. **Tutorial.** After the introduction, participants were presented with an interactive tutorial in which they learned how to return the UAVs (with and without notifications) and the two approaches in which the battery level would

be presented to them. We counterbalanced which display was given first in the tutorial phase to mitigate potential order bias.
3. **Experimental Tasks.** Throughout the study, participants completed four missions, once for each of the four conditions (all possible permutations of DISPLAY and NOTIFICATION). The ordering of these followed a Latin square to prevent the possibility of ordering bias. A unique mission map was used for each of the four conditions so that participants did not learn a specific location or shape. While we designed the maps to be of similar size and complexity, the assignment of the maps to the conditions was also counterbalanced, such that any differences in difficulty of a mission did not affect our overall study results. Figure 4 Prior to each condition, we showed the participants what display would be presented in the upcoming task and whether notifications would appear. We reminded participants that their main task was to ensure that all eight UAVs could return to base safely but also aim to cover the area as much as possible. In each condition, participants monitored the simulated UAVs until all the UAVs had been returned to base safely or had stopped due to the battery level reaching 0. After each condition, the participants completed a NASA-TLX assessment [23] as well as a modified Naïve Rating Questionnaire [32] to capture their perceived cognitive load and mental workload.

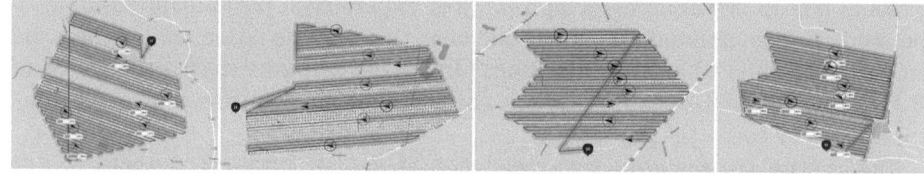

**Fig. 4.** Overview of the four unique mission map shapes used in the study. The four study conditions were assigned using a latin square to account for order effects.

After completing all conditions, we ended the study session with a semi-structured interview about their experience with the different display approaches and notifications and which considerations they had when estimating when to return the UAVs to base.

### 4.3 Measures

We collected several data points that captured the participants' performance in each condition.

*Safe Landing of a UAV:* Binary value of whether a drone reached the base with a battery level above 0%. When the battery level is 0%, we interpret it as the drone has crashed.

*Battery Level when Landing (%):* Remaining battery level of the UAVs when they have landed.

*Mission Completion (%):* Percentage of the mission the UAVs completed before they were instructed to return.

*Mental Workload and Cognitive Load:* Perceived mental workload using the NASA-TLX [23] and cognitive load using a modified Naïve Rating Questionnaire [32]. We removed questions on learning deemed irrelevant for this study, as we did not incorporate any learning tasks. We purposefully incorporated a higher amount of UAVs compared to previous studies to assess whether the EID interface helps lower the cognitive load and workload, as previously indicated by Schewe and Vollrath [43]. We incorporated both questionnaires as the mental workload can examine how much information and how many actions a person can process and perform simultaneously [49], while cognitive load examines how information is processed as well as the source of the load (intrinsic, extraneous, and germane) [32,45].

## 5 Results

We present the results gathered throughout the study and report those that showed a significant main effect or interaction effect. The significance level is set to $\alpha < 0.05$ for all effects. Participant experience level did not have any significant effect on performance or subjective measures.

### 5.1 Safe Landing

We fitted a generalized linear mixed model to our data, which showed whether a drone had crashed in a given condition or not. The model revealed that there was a significant main effect of NOTIFICATION, $\beta = 1.23, SE = 0.26, p < .001$, and indicates that when notifications are ENABLED the likelihood of a drone landing safely is increased. We performed a post-hoc pairwise comparison with Tukey adjustment, and again, we found that all conditions with ENABLED notifications had significantly fewer crashes than conditions with notifications DISABLED, which is also visible in Table 1.

To analyze the battery level data at landing, we first computed the mean value of the battery level of the eight UAVs in each condition. The Shapiro-Wilk test on the mean values revealed that the data was normally distributed. The two-way ANOVA revealed no significant effects across conditions. As seen in Fig. 5, the mean values of the battery values are very similar both for the different displays and whether notifications are enabled or disabled.

### 5.2 Mission Coverage

Similar to the battery level analysis, we calculated the mean percentages completed for the mission across the eight UAVs. The Shapiro-Wilk test revealed that

**Table 1.** Total number of UAV crashes across conditions, where 86 out of the 768 UAVs (11.2%) did not make it to base.

|  | DISPLAY | | |
|---|---|---|---|
| NOTIFICATION | TRADITIONAL | EID | Total |
| DISABLED | 36 | 28 | 64 |
| ENABLED | 9 | 13 | 22 |
| Total | 45 | 41 | |

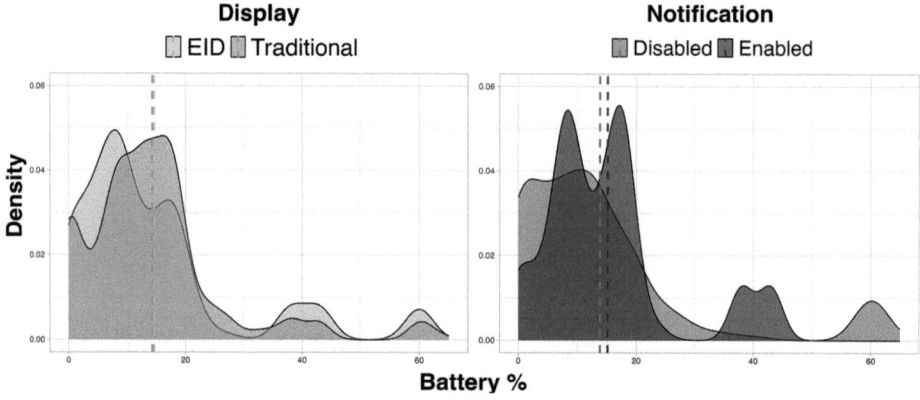

**Fig. 5.** Battery level when the UAVs had landed. Vertical lines represent the mean value of the two plots.

the data was not normally distributed. Therefore, we performed an ART procedure revealing significant main effects of DISPLAY, $F(1, 92) = 23.604, p < .001$ and NOTIFICATION, $F(1, 92) = 265.056, p < .001$. When DISPLAY is TRADITIONAL, the UAVs completed on average 77.5% of their mission, whereas with EID, UAVs completed 83.3% on average as illustrated in Fig. 6. When notifications were ENABLED, UAVs would complete 91.2% of their mission, whereas 69.6% when DISABLED.

An interaction effect was also found for the independent variables, $F(1, 92) = 4.175, p = .044$. A contrast test revealed that the effect was present across all interactions as all had $p < .001$. As seen in Fig. 7, conditions where DISPLAY is EID, UAVs completed more of their mission compared to TRADITIONAL; however, the most significant change happened when enabling notifications. Our results indicate that notifications enhance the participants' task completion and do not diminish the positive effect EID originally had.

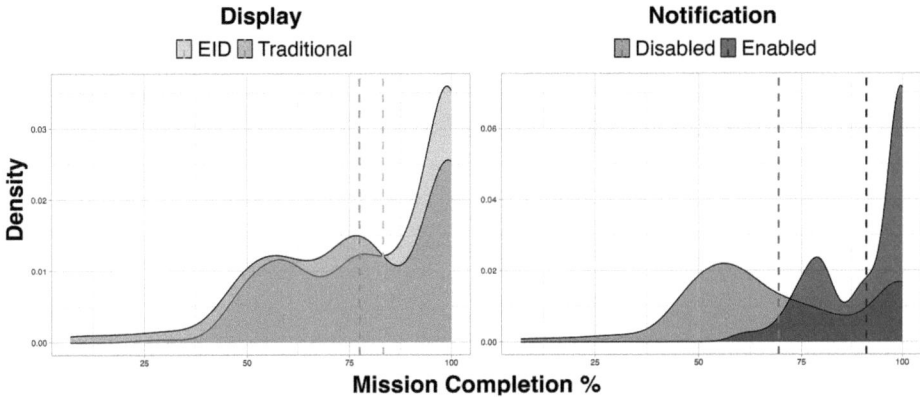

**Fig. 6.** Percentage of the mission the UAVs completed. Vertical lines represent the mean value of the two plots.

### 5.3 Questionnaire Responses

**Cognitive Load.** The ANOVA revealed that a significant main effect of NOTIFICATION on extraneous cognitive load (ECL), $F(1, 92) = 8.018, p = .006$, and intrinsic cognitive load (ICL), $F(1, 92) = 13.278, p < .001$. For ECL, when notifications were ENABLED, the average score given was 2.98 compared to 3.72 when DISABLED. For ICL, when notifications were ENABLED, the average score given was 3.53 compared to 4.53 when DISABLED. Both of these results suggest that the notifications reduced their perceived cognitive load (Fig. 8).

**Mental Workload.** For the NASA-TLX responses, three of the dimensions displayed a significant main effect of NOTIFICATION: mental demand. $F(1, 92) = 5.223, p = .0236$, performance, $F(1, 92) = 8.407, p = .005$ and effort, $F(1, 92) = 12.999, p < .001$. For these three dimensions, the participants gave a lower score when NOTIFICATION was ENABLED, indicating that the participants felt those tasks required less active thinking while also feeling their performance improved (Fig. 9).

### 5.4 Interview Responses

We asked the participants directly about their preference for the display approach. Thirteen participants preferred the TRADITIONAL approach, while nine of the participants preferred EID. Two participants saw strengths in both and thought that a combination of the two would be optimal.

With the TRADITIONAL display, the participants would continuously evaluate the battery level depletion rate in relation to the distance it had flown to estimate how much battery level was needed to cover the current distance to the base. Four participants (P3,11,16,18) claimed they would also look at the heading of the UAV because if the UAV was heading in the direction of the base, they would

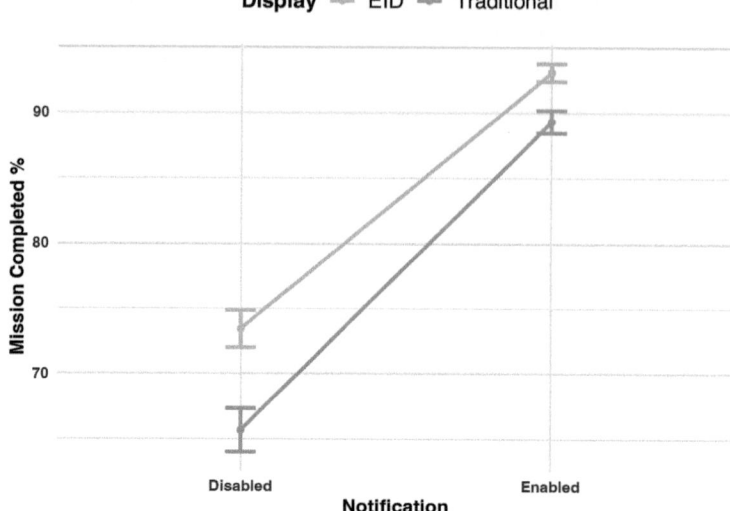

**Fig. 7.** Interaction between DISPLAY and NOTIFICATION.

let the UAV complete part of the remaining missions until the UAV was as close to the base as possible.

For conditions with EID, participants would observe where the solid lines would stop, and if they saw that the whole flight path was solid, they would de-prioritize the UAV. If a UAV entered a dashed line type, three participants (P5,8,16) claimed to calculate the distance to the next waypoint and the base. When the distance was approximately equal, they would instruct the UAV to return. Six other participants (P4,6,7,10,13,20) claimed they would allow the UAV to complete a certain percentage of the dashed section before returning.

**Preference in Displays.** Participants who preferred the traditional display, where the battery level was shown with a percentage and icon, felt that the precision and specificity gave them a better chance to estimate how far the UAV could fly before returning to the base was necessary. One participant said, *"[...]I can estimate how far the drones can fly, perhaps not incredibly precise, but I don't feel it has the same uncertainty as me saying, now I am beginning on a dashed line, how far can I reach[...]"*(P11). All thirteen who preferred the traditional display made claims that they could better strategize and plan when they had the percentage directly shown. Especially when comparing the traditional interface with the EID-inspired one, seven claimed they felt uncertain about how the EID display represented the UAVs entering a path with dashed lines and did not indicate how much of the dashed path could be covered for the given battery level. Ten participants mentioend that their experience with UAVs made them feel more confident in their estimation skills. Five of the experienced drone pilots preferred the traditional display, claiming that it felt more intuitive to them, and

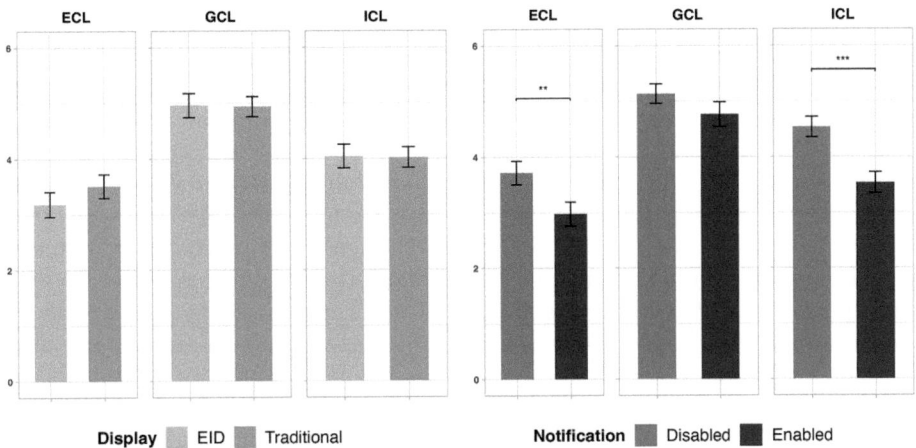

**Fig. 8.** Mean score levels (± standard error) for the Naïve Ratings Questionnaire [32] for each condition. Bars represent the average score, while error bars indicate the standard error of the mean (SEM). ECL = extraneous cognitive load; GCL = germane cognitive load; ICL = intrinsic cognitive load.

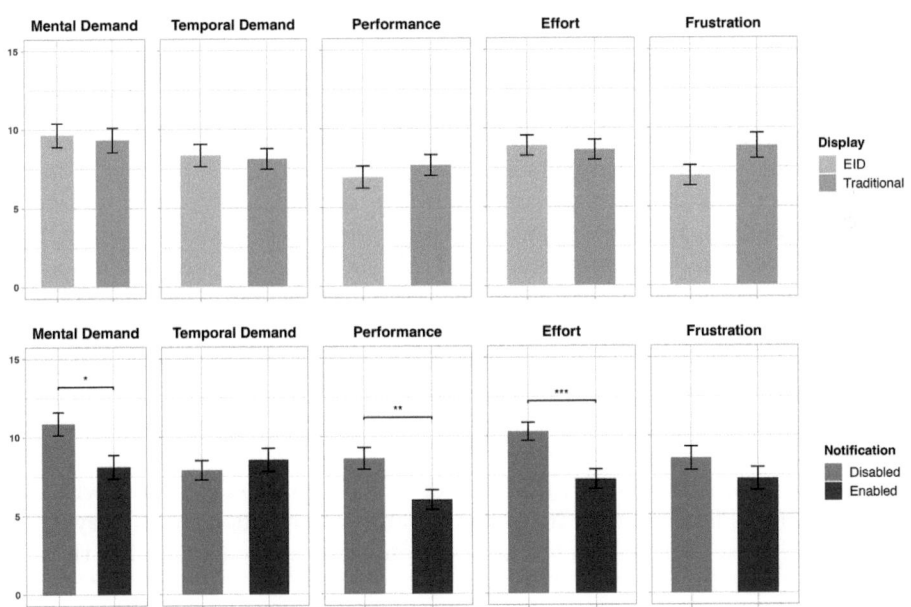

**Fig. 9.** Mean score levels (± standard error) for the NASA-TLX for each condition. Bars represent the average score, while error bars indicate the standard error of the mean (SEM).

all of these mentioned that they would prefer if data, such as mission coverage and estimated battery level at the base, were shown persistently. The novice users did not raise the need for more persistent data about the mission.

Participants preferred the EID-inspired display because they had a better overview of the overall situation and did not have to continuously calculate how much battery was needed to return to base. The line stroke served as a reminder of where there was an increased risk of not being able to return. One participant noted, *"[...]the extra battery information is nice, but I feel the other one [EID display] is better suited for the task[...]"*(P8) where their sentiment was due to them feeling the traditional display encouraged them to be too risky. Another participant said, *"It annoyed me that I did not know the battery level with the one with the routes [EID-display], but it is the one that is[...]most safe and gives the most information[...]"*(P24).

While some participants preferred the traditional display, four (P3,15,17,20) explicitly mentioned that they would prefer the EID display when there would be more significant consequences in real-life missions where UAV crashes could be catastrophic and where the weather conditions can be dynamic or unpredictable.

**Usage of Notifications.** When asked about their usage of the notifications, multiple factors influenced whether they would accept or reject the notifications. Seven claimed they would immediately reject the first notification at 15%, as they knew about an upcoming notification for 5%. However, four mentioned they would accept the first if they could see the UAV was further away from the base because they interpreted the notification as an estimation and thus was not exact. A participant said in regards to not accepting the last pop-up for a UAV, *"[...]because these 5% would have been enough to go home[...]"*(P20), which was similar to what other participants shared.

When asked whether they primarily used the notifications to activate returns or their estimation, ten participants said that they used a combination. Often, the participants had an idea of when the UAV should return, and when a notification appeared and was in line with their own expectations, they would immediately accept it. However, there were moments when they felt they might have missed a notification and would rely on their internal calculations rather than waiting for the next notification. One participant noted, *"I thought I had not seen the pop-up and that it might have been there and I had just missed it since there was only 10% charge and it [the drone] still had a bit left [flight path]. Here, I trusted my own instincts."*(P9). Moreover, if a notification appeared when the UAV was almost finished with its mission, four participants claimed they would allow the UAV to continue, as the notification acted as a confirmation that the UAV could make it.

Eight of the participants noted that notifications could be overwhelming and, at times, even frustrating. This was especially the case when they would appear at once or if they felt they already had a good grasp of the situation and the notifications felt excessive. In relation to using notifications with the EID-inspired display, one participant stated, *"If the task requires me to go home* at 15% then this [the notifications] is something super useful, but if it does not need that[...]then I actually found it less useful[...]it asks me to consider me something I already know[...]"(P17). As an alternative, instead of dialogue boxes, six participants noted that they would appreciate deciding whether they needed to see the estimated battery level at landing instead of being forced to see it and also suggested that it could be a constantly updating value.

## 6 Discussion

Our results show significant main effects and interaction effects for the various measurements, especially with respect to NOTIFICATION.

We reject H1, as there were no significant main effects of DISPLAY with regard to crashes and the battery level at the base. This implies that the display approach did not influence the number of UAVs that crashed or the battery level of the UAV when they landed at the base.

We found a significant main effect for DISPLAY for the mission completion, contrary to expectation, thus rejecting H2. From the interviews, we found that many participants would let the drone complete some part of the dashed line, even with uncertainty about whether the drone could return to base. This implies that the EID display appears to provide better battery level estimation for the participants, enabling the drones to complete more of the mission before returning to base. However, some participants noted that their behavior would differ if they were in a real-life situation where the risk of damaging property, technology, or people is real.

When notifications were ENABLED, the participants allowed the drones to complete a greater proportion of their mission than when it was DISABLED. As hypothesized in H3, when participants knew that they would be notified on when to return to base, they would wait until the notifications appeared and rarely return the drone to base prior. The interviews revealed that upon receiving the second notification if the UAV were close to completing its mission, the participants would allow the UAV to finish. There were a few occasions when they felt uncomfortable waiting for the notification as the battery level appeared very low, and they returned the drone to the base manually. This was especially the case when the drone was on a trajectory leading further away from the base, which increased the risk of a crash.

### 6.1 Cognitive Load and Mental Workload

Our results show that the two displays did not significantly differ in the participants' perceived cognitive load or mental workload. Instead, the notifications had a positive effect on cognitive load and mental workload and exhibited a positive impact on the participants' performance.

Relating the results to the SRK taxonomy [39], we argue that the decrease in both cognitive load and mental workload is because the participants engaged in more RBB. Many participants created their own return to base strategy: they would reject the first notification and accept the second unless the mission was almost finished. Without notifications, participants appeared to be more likely to engage in KBB more frequently to estimate the risk of how much longer to continue the mission. They directly stated in the interviews that they would estimate the most optimal decision based on multiple variables, such as battery depletion rate and distance from base, among other factors.

Our results also showed that with the EID-inspired display, the UAVs completed more of their mission without having a significant difference in the battery level when landing at the base. This indicates that using the EID display allowed the participants to efficiently use the remaining energy without introducing more risks. Together with notifications, the participants mentioned that they would use the line type as an indicator of when to expect a notification to appear, which can be interpreted as a "sign" inducing RBB, as they created a routine of using the lines to prioritize which drone should be attended to and which could safely be ignored.

## 6.2 Displays to Support Battery Management & Safe Flight

The study aimed to discover if an EID-inspired display and notifications could better support a person when monitoring a UAV fleet and managing the battery levels to ensure a safe return while completing as much of their flight mission as possible. Our results indicate that using the design inspired by Fuchs et al. [20] with explicit notification of expected battery levels for a return to base successfully supports users in completing their tasks more efficiently.

Although range anxiety was not explicitly investigated in this study, participants completed less of the flight mission when shown the display with icons and percentages compared to the EID-inspired display. This implies that participants were more cautious when only provided with battery percentages, while with the other visualization, they were confident in the UAV's range, and their decisions on when to return to base improved. As mentioned in Sect. 2, HBI research on portable devices showed that projecting future energy consumption helped users optimize battery usage [14]. The EID-inspired display provided a similar feature, as users could directly see when the UAV would have a lower battery level given the current conditions. Participants noted that the 'expected battery level at base' data displayed in notifications could be changed to a continuously decreasing value, adding another value that shows the expected battery level.

While participants reported that they could see a benefit when using the EID-inspired display, a majority still preferred the more traditional approach with icons and percentages. Relying only on the line types added some uncertainty as it was not as precise and concrete, which made it challenging to understand the drone's current state. This, in turn, made it more difficult to leverage their estimation skills, which added to the uncertainty since there was no indication of how much of the dashed line the drones could complete. Welber et al. [48] mentioned that users would consider trade-offs when trying to extend their battery consumption, and removing the percentage indicator could potentially diminish their ability to do so. However, this problem might not be as apparent when notifications were included in the user interface. Our findings reveal potential user preference conflicts and a mismatch in EID performance, suggesting a potential barrier to acceptance of the new designs that could be due to familiarity bias. Additional studies could explore this further.

While notifications clearly impacted performance, perceived cognitive load, and mental workload, participants mentioned some inconveniences caused by the notifications. Some participants noted that on different occasions, they were unsure if they had seen a notification, which almost resulted in the drone not being able to return. Suppose notifications were not to appear, and the display did not show any concrete data, such as battery level; one can argue that this could limit a person's decision-making abilities and lead to a higher risk of not landing safely. Participants mentioned giving a person the option to display more data so that they can engage in KBB or if they are uncertain about the current system status.

Our study did not include environmental effects such as weather, which makes it more challenging to estimate the remaining range when shown the traditional display if participants take a similar estimation strategy as reported in Sect. 5.4. However, calculations of the line types in the EID-inspired display consider all factors that affect the drone's capability to return to base. Research has also shown that EID is not as impacted by noise that affects the quality of the incoming data as much as conventional displays [44]. Therefore, we do not expect task difficulty to increase when using the EID-display. Future research needs to explore more realistic systems with critical factors to UAV flight and investigate the differences between the displays further.

### 6.3 Limitations

It was essential for us to include experienced drone pilots in this study to explore how different representations of the remaining battery level might affect a person who already has extensive domain knowledge. Many of our participants lived overseas, which resulted in having to conduct some studies online. While in-person research could be more controlled, we ensured that online participants had a similar experience to each another by designing the study platform so that it could be completed on a relatively small screen. Moreover, we asked participants to share their screens so that we could observe their actions and ensure that things were displayed correctly.

As noted by some of the participants, their choices in this study did not necessarily reflect how they would behave in a real-life scenario due to the lack of consequences of losing a drone. If they had a closer relationship with the equipment and the situation, they would have likely taken a more cautious approach and utilized the EID display to their advantage. Our results, therefore, do not entirely reflect the behavior of a user in a more realistic scenario. However, the current study still provides insights into user strategies when exposed to different displays, the presence of notifications, and how they affect their monitoring behavior in a multi-UAV system. In addition to increased realism, future studies should include more experts and explore how experience affects preferences and trust across visualization types [2]. Ideally, longitudinal studies can be conducted to account for learning effects.

## 7 Conclusion

In this paper, we conducted a $2 \times 2$ within-subjects design to explore whether two different representations of a drone's battery level could influence a person's ability to optimize mission completion while ensuring the safe return of a fleet of drones. The first display was inspired by conventional battery level displays that are currently used in single and multi-drone systems, where the battery level is represented through symbols and percentages. The other display was inspired by a display designed with the ecological interface design (EID) framework, where a drone's ability to return home is represented on the paths line types (solid, dashed, and dotted). We also studied the influence of battery level notifications and whether they could add extra support for decision-making and task completion.

In a simulated environment, 24 participants were asked to complete four experimental tasks followed by a short interview. In each task, they were instructed to monitor a fleet of drones and ensure that each would complete as much of their mission as possible while still being able to land at the base. Our results revealed that the EID-inspired display increased mission completion without adding any significant reduction to task completion. Enabling notifications had a greater impact, reducing the number of UAV crashes, increasing mission completion, and significantly reducing cognitive load and mental workload. Our work shows that ecological interface design and notifications that project the future system health can enhance decision support in a multi-UAV system and pave the way for more intuitive and resilient interfaces that improve human-autonomy collaboration.

Despite demonstrating benefits of EID, our qualitative data revealed a notable tension: a majority of participants still preferred the traditional percentage display. Participants often cited familiarity and perceived greater precision with numerical values, suggesting that performance benefits alone may not guarantee user acceptance. This highlights that future interfaces should consider integrating elements from both display types or allowing user control over information presentation to address preferences and support more cautious decision-making in real-world, high-consequence scenarios where behavior may differ from a simulation.

**Acknowledgments.** This work is supported by the Innovation Fund Denmark for the project DIREC (9142-00001B).

**Disclosure of Interests.** The authors have no competing interests to declare that are relevant to the content of this article.

# References

1. Agrawal, A., et al.: The next generation of human-drone partnerships: co-designing an emergency response system. In: Proceedings of the 2020 CHI Conference on Human Factors in Computing Systems, pp. 1–13. CHI '20, Association for Computing Machinery, New York, NY, USA (2020). https://doi.org/10.1145/3313831.3376825
2. Ahlskog, J., Bahodi, M.T., Lugmayr, A., Merritt, T.: Fostering trust through user interface design in multi-drone search and rescue. In: Proceedings of the Second International Symposium on Trustworthy Autonomous Systems. TAS '24, Association for Computing Machinery, New York, NY, USA (2024). https://doi.org/10.1145/3686038.3686052
3. Alon, O., Rabinovich, S., Fyodorov, C., Cauchard, J.R.: Drones in firefighting: a user-centered design perspective. In: Proceedings of the 23rd International Conference on Mobile Human-Computer Interaction, pp. 1–11. ACM, Toulouse & Virtual France (2021). https://doi.org/10.1145/3447526.3472030
4. Alyassi, R., Khonji, M., Karapetyan, A., Chau, S.C.K., Elbassioni, K., Tseng, C.M.: Autonomous recharging and flight mission planning for battery-operated autonomous drones. IEEE Trans. Autom. Sci. Eng. **20**(2), 1034–1046 (2023). https://doi.org/10.1109/TASE.2022.3175565
5. Athukorala, K., et al.: How carat affects user behavior: implications for mobile battery awareness applications. In: Proceedings of the SIGCHI Conference on Human Factors in Computing Systems, pp. 1029–1038. ACM, Toronto Ontario Canada (2014). https://doi.org/10.1145/2556288.2557271
6. Bahodi, M.T., Van Berkel, N., Skov, M., Merritt, T.: Show me what's wrong: impact of explicit alerts on novice supervisors of a multi-robot monitoring system. In: Proceedings of the Second International Symposium on Trustworthy Autonomous Systems, pp. 1–17. ACM, Austin TX USA (2024). https://doi.org/10.1145/3686038.3686069
7. Banerjee, N., Rahmati, A., Corner, M.D., Rollins, S., Zhong, L.: Users and batteries: interactions and adaptive energy management in mobile systems. In: Krumm, J., Abowd, G.D., Seneviratne, A., Strang, T. (eds) UbiComp 2007: Ubiquitous Computing, vol. 4717, pp. 217–234. Springer Berlin Heidelberg, Berlin, Heidelberg (2007). https://doi.org/10.1007/978-3-540-74853-3_13
8. Borst, C., Bijsterbosch, V.A., van Paassen, M.M., Mulder, M.: Ecological interface design: supporting fault diagnosis of automated advice in a supervisory air traffic control task. Cogn. Technol. Work **19**(4), 545–560 (2017). https://doi.org/10.1007/s10111-017-0438-y
9. Breslow, L.A., Gartenberg, D., McCurry, J.M., Gregory Trafton, J.: Dynamic operator overload: a model for predicting workload during supervisory control. IEEE Trans. Hum. Mach. Syst. **44**(1), 30–40 (2014). https://doi.org/10.1109/TSMC.2013.2293317
10. Chen, J.Y.C., Barnes, M.J.: Human-agent teaming for multirobot control: a review of human factors issues. IEEE Trans. Hum. Mach. Syst. **44**(1), 13–29 (2014). https://doi.org/10.1109/THMS.2013.2293535
11. Chen, Y., Baek, D., Bocca, A., Macii, A., Macii, E., Poncino, M.: A case for a battery-aware model of drone energy consumption. In: 2018 IEEE International Telecommunications Energy Conference (INTELEC), pp. 1–8. IEEE, Turin (2018). https://doi.org/10.1109/INTLEC.2018.8612333

12. Faul, F., Erdfelder, E., Buchner, A., Lang, A.G.: Statistical power analyses using G*Power 3.1: tests for correlation and regression analyses. Beh. Res. Methods **41**(4), 1149–1160 (2009). https://doi.org/10.3758/BRM.41.4.1149
13. Ferreira, D., Dey, A., Kostakos, V.: Understanding human-smartphone concerns: a study of battery. Life (2011). https://doi.org/10.1007/978-3-642-21726-5_2
14. Ferreira, D., Ferreira, E., Goncalves, J., Kostakos, V., Dey, A.K.: Revisiting human-battery interaction with an interactive battery interface. In: Proceedings of the 2013 ACM International Joint Conference on Pervasive and Ubiquitous Computing, pp. 563–572. UbiComp '13, Association for Computing Machinery, New York, NY, USA (2013). https://doi.org/10.1145/2493432.2493465
15. Feuerstack, S., Saager, M.: Ecological interface design for efficient maritime traffic supervision. In: Proceedings of the 33rd European Conference on Cognitive Ergonomics, pp. 1–4. ACM, Kaiserslautern Germany (2022). https://doi.org/10.1145/3552327.3552335
16. Franke, T., Günther, M., Trantow, M., Krems, J.F.: Does this range suit me? Range satisfaction of battery electric vehicle users. Appl. Ergon. **65**, 191–199 (2017). https://doi.org/10.1016/j.apergo.2017.06.013
17. Franke, T., Krems, J.F.: Interacting with limited mobility resources: psychological range levels in electric vehicle use. Transp. Res. Part A: Policy Pract. **48**, 109–122 (2013). https://doi.org/10.1016/j.tra.2012.10.010
18. Franke, T., Neumann, I., Bühler, F., Cocron, P., Krems, J.F.: Experiencing range in an electric vehicle: understanding psychological barriers. Appl. Psychol. **61**(3), 368–391 (2012). https://doi.org/10.1111/j.1464-0597.2011.00474.x
19. Frankea, T., Günthera, M., Trantowa, M., F. Kremsa, J.: Examining User-Range Interaction in Battery Electric Vehicles – a Field Study Approach (2021). https://doi.org/10.54941/ahfe100697
20. Fuchs, C., Borst, C., de Croon, G.C.H.E., van Paassen, M.M.R., Mulder, M.: An ecological approach to the supervisory control of UAV swarms. Int. J. Micro Air Veh. **6**(4), 211–229 (2014). https://doi.org/10.1260/1756-8293.6.4.211
21. Gao, M., Hugenholtz, C.H., Fox, T.A., Kucharczyk, M., Barchyn, T.E., Nesbit, P.R.: Weather constraints on global drone flyability. Sci. Rep. **11**(1), 12092 (2021). https://doi.org/10.1038/s41598-021-91325-w
22. Grøntved, K.A.R., Lundquist, U.P.S., Christensen, A.L.: Decentralized multi-UAV trajectory task allocation in search and rescue applications. In: 2023 21st International Conference on Advanced Robotics (ICAR), pp. 35–41 (2023). https://doi.org/10.1109/ICAR58858.2023.10406912
23. Hart, S.G.: NASA Task Load Index (TLX): Computerized Version - Volume 1.0 (1986)
24. Harter, T., Vroegindeweij, S., Geelhoed, E., Manahan, M., Ranganathan, P.: Energy-aware user interfaces: an evaluation of user acceptance. In: Proceedings of the SIGCHI Conference on Human Factors in Computing Systems, pp. 199–206. CHI '04, Association for Computing Machinery, New York, NY, USA (2004). https://doi.org/10.1145/985692.985718
25. Hashemi, S.R., et al.: New intelligent battery management system for drones. In: Volume 6: Energy, p. V006T06A028. American Society of Mechanical Engineers, Salt Lake City, Utah, USA (2019). https://doi.org/10.1115/IMECE2019-10479
26. Herdel, V., Yamin, L.J., Cauchard, J.R.: Above and beyond: a scoping review of domains and applications for human-drone interaction. In: CHI Conference on Human Factors in Computing Systems, pp. 1–22. CHI '22, Association for Computing Machinery, New York, NY, USA (2022). https://doi.org/10.1145/3491102.3501881

27. Hoang, M.T.O., van Berkel, N., Skov, M.B., Merritt, T.R.: Challenges and requirements in multi-drone interfaces. In: Extended Abstracts of the 2023 CHI Conference on Human Factors in Computing Systems, pp. 1–9. CHI EA '23, Association for Computing Machinery, New York, NY, USA (2023). https://doi.org/10.1145/3544549.3585673
28. Hoang, M.T.O., Grøntved, K.A.R., Van Berkel, N., Skov, M.B., Christensen, A.L., Merritt, T.: Drone swarms to support search and rescue operations: opportunities and challenges. In: Dunstan, B.J., Koh, J.T.K.V., Turnbull Tillman, D., Brown, S.A. (eds.) Cultural Robotics: Social Robots and Their Emergent Cultural Ecologies, pp. 163–176. Springer International Publishing, Cham (2023). https://doi.org/10.1007/978-3-031-28138-9_11
29. Imbert, J.P., Hodgetts, H.M., Parise, R., Vachon, F., Dehais, F., Tremblay, S.: Attentional costs and failures in air traffic control notifications. Ergonomics **57**(12), 1817–1832 (2014). https://doi.org/10.1080/00140139.2014.952680
30. Janisch, D., Aken, D., Borst, C.: Ecological collaborative interface for unmanned aerial vehicle traffic management and tower control. J. Air Transp. **30**, 1–16 (2022). https://doi.org/10.2514/1.D0295
31. Kearney, P., Li, W.C., Yu, C.S., Braithwaite, G.: The impact of alerting designs on air traffic controller's eye movement patterns and situation awareness. Ergonomics **62**(2), 305–318 (2019). https://doi.org/10.1080/00140139.2018.1493151
32. Klepsch, M., Schmitz, F., Seufert, T.: Development and validation of two instruments measuring intrinsic, extraneous, and germane cognitive load. Front. Psychol. **8** (2017). https://doi.org/10.3389/fpsyg.2017.01997
33. Klomp, R., Borst, C., Van Paassen, M.M., Mulder, M.: Expertise level, control strategies, and robustness in future air traffic control decision aiding. IEEE Trans. Hum. Mach. Syst. **46**, 1–12 (2015). https://doi.org/10.1109/THMS.2015.2417535
34. Min, C., et al.: Exploring current practices for battery use and management of smartwatches. In: Proceedings of the 2015 ACM International Symposium on Wearable Computers - ISWC '15, pp. 11–18. ACM Press, Osaka, Japan (2015). https://doi.org/10.1145/2802083.2802085
35. Neubauer, J., Wood, E.: The impact of range anxiety and home, workplace, and public charging infrastructure on simulated battery electric vehicle lifetime utility. J. Power Sources **257**, 12–20 (2014). https://doi.org/10.1016/j.jpowsour.2014.01.075
36. Philipsen, R., Brell, T., Biermann, H., Ziefle, M.: Under pressure-users' perception of range stress in the context of charging and traditional refueling. World Electric Veh. J. **10**(3), 50 (2019). https://doi.org/10.3390/wevj10030050
37. Rahmati, A., Qian, A., Zhong, L.: Understanding human-battery interaction on mobile phones. In: Proceedings of the 9th International Conference on Human Computer Interaction with Mobile Devices and Services, pp. 265–272. ACM, Singapore (2007). https://doi.org/10.1145/1377999.1378017
38. Rainieri, G., Buizza, C., Ghilardi, A.: The psychological, human factors and sociotechnical contribution: a systematic review towards range anxiety of battery electric vehicles' drivers. Transport. Res. F: Traffic Psychol. Behav. **99**, 52–70 (2023). https://doi.org/10.1016/j.trf.2023.10.001
39. Rasmussen, J.: Skills, rules, and knowledge; signals, signs, and symbols, and other distinctions in human performance models. IEEE Trans. Syst. Man Cybern. **SMC-13**(3), 257–266 (1983). https://doi.org/10.1109/TSMC.1983.6313160
40. Rasmussen, J.: The role of hierarchical knowledge representation in decision making and system management. IEEE Trans. Syst. Man Cybern. **SMC-15**(2), 234–243 (1985). https://doi.org/10.1109/TSMC.1985.6313353

41. Rauh, N., Franke, T., Krems, J.F.: Understanding the impact of electric vehicle driving experience on range anxiety. Hum. Factors **57**(1), 177–187 (2015). https://doi.org/10.1177/0018720814546372
42. Saxena, S., Sanchez, G., Pecht, M.: Batteries in portable electronic devices: a user's perspective. IEEE Ind. Electron. Mag. **11**(2), 35–44 (2017). https://doi.org/10.1109/MIE.2017.2688483
43. Schewe, F., Vollrath, M.: Ecological interface design effectively reduces cognitive workload – the example of HMIs for speed control. Transport. Res. F: Traffic Psychol. Behav. **72**, 155–170 (2020). https://doi.org/10.1016/j.trf.2020.05.009
44. St-Cyr, O., Jamieson, G.A., Vicente, K.J.: Ecological interface design and sensor noise. Int. J. Hum. Comput. Stud. **71**(11), 1056–1068 (2013). https://doi.org/10.1016/j.ijhcs.2013.08.005
45. Sweller, J.: Cognitive load theory. In: Psychology of Learning and Motivation, vol. 55, pp. 37–76. Elsevier (2011). https://doi.org/10.1016/B978-0-12-387691-1.00002-8
46. Van Dam, S.B.J., Mulder, M., van Paassen, M.M.: Ecological interface design of a tactical airborne separation assistance tool. IEEE Trans. Syst. Man Cybern. - Part A: Syst. Hum. **38**(6), 1221–1233 (2008). https://doi.org/10.1109/TSMCA.2008.2001069
47. Vicente, K., Rasmussen, J.: Ecological interface design: theoretical foundations. IEEE Trans. Syst. Man Cybern. **22**(4), 589–606 (1992). https://doi.org/10.1109/21.156574
48. Welber, S., Zhao, V., Dolin, C., Morkved, O., Hoffmann, H., Ur, B.: Do users have contextual preferencesfor smartphone power management? In: Proceedings of the 29th ACM Conference on User Modeling, Adaptation and Personalization, pp. 44–54. UMAP '21, Association for Computing Machinery, New York, NY, USA (2021). https://doi.org/10.1145/3450613.3456813
49. Young, M.S., Brookhuis, K.A., Wickens, C.D., Hancock, P.A.: State of science: mental workload in ergonomics. Ergonomics **58**(1), 1–17 (2015). https://doi.org/10.1080/00140139.2014.956151

# Multi-Variant UCD - A Process for the Design of Interactive System Variants: Application to Launch Vehicles Flight Safety Operations

Daniel Rodriguez-Hernando[1,2](✉) [iD], Célia Martinie[2] [iD], Philippe Palanque[2] [iD], and Sandra Steere[1] [iD]

[1] CSG, CNES, Kourou, France
{daniel.rodriguez-hernando,sandra.steere}@cnes.fr
[2] ICS-IRIT, Université de Toulouse, Toulouse, France
{celia.martinie,philippe.palanque}@irit.fr

**Abstract.** Command-and-control interactive systems support generic activities of operators such as monitoring, forecasting, decision making and controlling systems. When belonging to the same application domain, those generic activities are even more alike, leading to very similar user interfaces of those interactive systems. Despite those similarities, differences remain, which are mostly due to the intrinsic capabilities and performances of the system under control. Actual UCD approaches do not address the challenge of developing multiple user interfaces for the same user or user groups when the systems under control share common characteristics yet also have distinct, identifiable parts. This paper proposes a systematic process for producing variants of such user interfaces. This systematic process is a refined version of the UCD process dedicated to the design of multiple usable systems with a high degree of similarity. This process aims to produce variants of user interface for a same user group in order to avoid human errors and simplify training. The approach is demonstrated on two variants of user interfaces for flight safety operations in the space domain.

**Keywords:** User interfaces for safety-critical systems · task models · human errors

## 1 Introduction

Command-and-control systems (CCSs) are a widely deployed type of interactive systems where a group of trained and qualified operators manage missions and supervise the status of a controlled system. In particular, command-and-control interactive systems for mission execution support generic activities of operators such as monitoring, forecasting, decision making and controlling systems. When belonging to the same application domain, those generic activities are even more alike, leading to very similar user interfaces of those interactive systems. Despite those similarities, differences remain, which are mostly due to the intrinsic capabilities and performances of the system under control.

An important aspect when designing User Interfaces (UI) is the application of processes and techniques to ensure their usability (defined as *"the extent to which a product can be used by specified users to achieve specified goals with effectiveness, efficiency, and satisfaction in a specified context of use"* in the ISO 9241 standard [22]). Beyond individual UI properties like usability, across systems properties [6] and in particular similarity [29] have also to been studied to support, for example, the comparison of the *"distance between several interfaces in terms of orientation, order and density of their items"* [19]. The similarity property can inform the design decisions, in particular for safety-critical systems, when a same user group may use a variant of an already used UI [6], to avoid user confusion [29], and limit training changes [6]. Actual User Centered Design (UCD) approaches do not address explicitly the design of multiple variants of UI for the same user or user group when those systems share common characteristics yet also have distinct, identifiable parts. In this paper, we present a refined UCD process to support the design of multiple usable systems having a high degree of similarity. The main goal is to avoid human errors and to simplify training for users. We applied this process to the design of two UI variants for the Flight Safety Operations CCS of Europe's Spaceport. Each UI variant allows operators to monitor a specific launch vehicle and its associated systems. While these systems share certain commonalities, they also exhibit distinct characteristics that are essential for fulfilling specific mission requirements. Nevertheless, the Flight Safety Operations team requires the use of consistent command-and-control user interfaces across all operations to effectively manage each launch in accordance with established regulations. The remainder of the paper is organized as follows. Next section provides the background for our research. The third section presents the case study of the design of prototypes of user interfaces for Flight Safety Operations at the French Guiana Europe's Spaceport Operation Center. The fourth section presents the multi-variant UCD process. Section 5 presents the results of applying the multi-variant UCD process to produce two UI variants for Flight Safety Operations. Section 6 discusses the benefits and the limitations of the work presented in the paper. Section 7 concludes the paper highlighting the contributions of the multi-variant UCD process, and describing directions for future work.

## 2 Background: Existing Approaches Limitations and Foundational Methods

This section highlights limitations of UCD methodologies and model-driven approaches in supporting the design of multiple variants of UI for the same user or user group when those systems share common characteristics yet also have distinct, identifiable parts. The second part of this section presents the methods and framework that are the foundation for our work.

### 2.1 Related Work on UCD and Revisions

The UCD process, as defined in ISO 9241 Part 210 [21], allows designers to effectively create individual, usable systems, for an identified user or user group. In response to emerging challenges and contexts beyond the scope of UCD, the process has been revised and integrated with other methodologies. This evolution highlights the ongoing necessity to refine and expand the UCD framework to include new problem domains and technological advancements. Fleury et al. [15] proposed a generalized framework for enhancing the UCD process, introducing a multi-user centered design process for multi-user technologies and the complexities of interaction among multiple users. Cockton et al. [12] and Hussian et al. [20] explored the integration of the UCD process with Agile development approaches. Bouzekri et al. [7] presented a system-centered process in complement to the UCD process for the design of CCSs. Although these revisions and integrations allows to expand the initial purpose of the UCD process —for example, by providing a framework for designing shared interactive systems for multiple users with similar or different roles [15], enabling the creation of unique interactive systems for identified users or user groups following a user-centered agile approach [12] [20], or facilitating the design of a single, reliable, and safe interactive CCSs [7]— none of them covers the design of interactive system variants that share common characteristics yet also have distinct, identifiable parts.

### 2.2 Related Work on the Design of Multiple Variants of Interactive Systems

Even if not directly addressed by already proposed UCD revisions, the design and development of multi-variant interactive systems—particularly their UI aspects— have been addressed by the combination of model-driven approaches that are Software Product Lines (SPL) and Model-Based User Interface Design (MBUID). Pleuss et al. [32, 33] proposed several approaches, based on the Cameleon Reference Framework (CRF) [9, 34], to model and generate user interface variants, associated to an application logic by configuration, for various target platforms (e.g., mobile devices or personal computers, different operating systems, etc.). Their work enables UI customization at design time (e.g., changing UI elements position or size, or referencing to a style definition stylesheet). Sboui et al. [36] introduce a semi-automatic approach for generating UI variants that adapt to the context of use (the triplet < user, platform, environment > [9]) during runtime. Their approach allows for UI customizations based on potential context changes to be defined and implemented during the design phase, covering multiple UI aspects such as structure, layout, visual appearance, and behavior. Fadhlillah et al. [14] propose an approach for managing customizations of generated UI variants through interchangeable collections of styles, which define a global visual theme that specifies UI elements, color schemes, and layouts for a particular UI variant within a web application product line. However, these model-driven approaches generate UI variants without explicit user needs analysis or iterative identification of optimal design options. While they allow for UI customizations like behavioral changes, color themes, etc., particularly for simple WIMP interfaces, they lack the user-centered focus of the traditional UCD process.

It is essential to highlight that the issue of the impact of similarity and differences on dependability has been raised in [29], and a notation has been proposed to represent theirs contributing factor when comparing several UI elements [6]. However, these works do not support the application of the full UCD process.

## 2.3 Foundational Methods Exploited in This Paper

The work presented in this paper is grounded in several methods and framework. We have adopted the UCD process as the primary methodological basis for this research due to its established reputation as a standard that emphasizes the importance of designing for and involving users in the development of interactive systems. The advantage of the UCD process, compared to other methodologies such as Ecological Interface Design (EID) [18], lies in its standardized framework, as outlined in ISO 9241 Part 210 [21].

CCSs are complex socio-technical systems whose complexity is accurately characterized by the POISE framework [31]. This framework systematically decomposes interactive socio-technical systems into four distinct yet interconnected components:

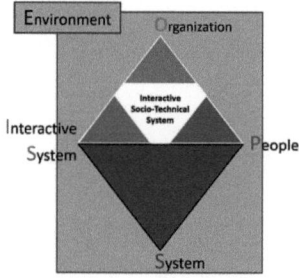

**Fig. 1.** POISE-S extended from (from [31])

- "People": several people are usually involved in command-and-control of physically dispersed systems, services and staff. Each of them is in charge of a specific role and performing specific tasks for this role.
- "Organization": the CCSs may involve staff that belong to several different organizations (e.g. national organizations, and industrial partners), and who apply work organization processes and define training needs for operators. Processes documents define and describe the operations in the control centers [24] [25].
- "Interactive systems" (e.g. workstations, displays, and input devices): they present information about the systems, services and information that are being monitored and controlled. These interactive systems and technologies support crewmembers in performing their tasks and to support the stakeholder organizations' objectives.
- "Environment": the CCSs are operated within an environment in which the computing systems, humans and organization stand (represented by the gray rectangle surrounding the diamond of in Fig. 1). The environment has an impact on their behavior (e.g. a very noisy environment may cause an operator to badly hear an instruction).

In this paper we extend the original POISE framework by making explicit the underlying system being controlled by the operator. As an illustrative example, the aircraft cockpit is the command-and-control system while the aircraft engine is one of the underlying systems being controlled. Consequently, a fifth component can be added to the POISE framework, the System, to form the POISE-S extension (Fig. 1). This fifth component allows for the identification and description of the system managed and operated by the people, organization and interactive systems (and that may be composed of a set of physically dispersed systems). The top triangle of Fig. 1 shows the POISE framework standing on top of the System (bottom triangle of Fig. 1), to represent the fact that the people, organization and interactive systems support the management and operation of the System.

Finally, to effectively capture the goals and tasks that users perform within a CCS—a crucial aspect for understanding system usability and design requirements—we adopt the HAMSTERS notation and its associated eponym modeling tool [27]. HAMSTERS embeds the elements required to describe user tasks, while also enabling detailed specification of interactions with the user interface, including the refinement of interactive tasks and required UI elements required to perform the tasks. Historically, HAMSTERS is a refinement of the notation used to describe tasks in the Hierarchical Task Analysis method [1]. Furthermore, similar to Goal-directed Task Analysis [5], HAMSTERS enables to identify and describe decision tasks. Similarly, the integration of HAMSTERS with the organizational aspect introduced in POISE addresses the same concerns as Cognitive Work Analysis [40]. However, HAMSTERS also covers aspects of interaction design and command-and-control systems [30], as well as training engineering [26].

## 3 The Concrete Design Context of Launch Vehicle Flight Safety Operations

At the French Guiana Europe's Spaceport, a new operations center (called the CDO [37]) is being developed to provide a flexible and open spaceport for launch vehicles. The new operations center is renewing all Core Launch Range systems and services, including all the IT and operational equipment that is necessary to support the execution of the launch campaigns. The key objectives are to increase the launch frequency by reducing the time needed to reconfigure the whole base, thereby being able to launch different vehicles in a short period; and facilitate the operators' system adaptation to switch from one position to another with minimum training required. To address the broad and complex nature of the Core Launch Range systems and services, and more specifically the Flight Safety Operations CCS, we employ POISE-S (presented in Sect. 2) to provide a detailed description of our case study's design context.

### 3.1 People

Launch operations are monitored and controlled by several persons who each have a particular role, and associated tasks. The presented work focuses on the Flight Safety Officer (FSO), whose role is to monitor the launch vehicle and to send a command on board (e.g., to neutralize the launch vehicle if the safety of the population is at stake). In particular, the Flight Safety Officer must, at any time:

- assess the dangerous nature of the launch vehicle in flight:
  - by supervising its horizontal and vertical trajectory;
  - by analyzing the status of the resources contributing to this mission;

- intervene if necessary to neutralize the launch vehicle or deactivate the onboard neutralization system (outside the phases of overflight of foreign territorial lands and seas).

Operators who are assigned the role of FSO have to follow a specific training process and have to be qualified before being assigned to a mission. A FSO may be assigned several missions, for different launch vehicles.

### 3.2 Organization

Several organizations are involved in operations for the launch of a vehicle (e.g. the manufacturer of the launch vehicle, the spaceport leading organization...). The presented work focuses on the spaceport leading organization, who is responsible for the safety of operations. The Flight Safety Operations must respect the French law that governs space activities in France, i.e. "the French Space Operation Act" [10], and the derived document "Order Regulating the Operation of Installations of the Guyana Space Center" [11]. According to these laws, the Flight Safety team must carry out different missions to ensure the safety of populations and properties, the protection of public health, and the protection of the environment on the Earth's surface against any damage that may result from the in-flight operation of the said vehicle. The Flight Safety team is composed of several operators, in addition to the already mentioned FSO, including a substitute for the FSO.

The case study presented only covers one of the many missions of the Flight Safety team, which is the "Safety and intervention mission" (also called MSI, described in article 63 of [11]).

### 3.3 Interactive System

FSO interacts with a ground segment interactive CCS for the monitoring of the launch vehicle trajectory and for the possible neutralization of the launch vehicle. Depending on the type of launch vehicles and ground segment systems, the monitoring UI may differ (e.g. additional warning UI element for an additional ground station antenna). FSO also interacts with a physical control panel for the activation/deactivation of the launch vehicle on board neutralization system.

### 3.4 Systems

Along with the renewal of the Guiana Space Europe's Spaceport, there are new "classic" launch vehicles like Ariane 6 [2] or Vega-C [38], but also reusable vehicles like CALLISTO [8] and other micro vehicles. Each launch vehicle has its proper characteristics that have a direct impact on which Flight Safety command-and-control ground system data and services are needed by the FSO and his respective UI to complete the MSI. For example, the Ariane 6 heavy launch vehicle has two different versions depending on the performance required: a version with two boosters, called Ariane 62, and Ariane 64 with four boosters. Overall, the average height of Ariane 6 launch vehicles is around 62m having a 3500kN of maximal thrust. This launch vehicle brings new constraints to the Flight Safety CCS, including:

- A particular configuration of launcher tracking and command-and-control means that have to be reflected on the UI;
- Two different flight phases, each one changing the tasks the Flight Safety team must do with the system;
- A ballistic trajectory (East, North-East, or North) with static trajectory limits to evaluate launch vehicle deviations;

The second system we use in the paper concerns the reusable launch vehicle CALLISTO. This vertical take-off/vertical landing launch vehicle demonstrator of about 13 m of height and 46 kN of maximal thrust also brings new constraints to the Flight Safety command-and-control ground system, including:

- A particular configuration of localization and command-and-control means that have to be reflected on the UI;
- Three different flight phases, including one with a very short reaction time to manage potential trajectory deviations, which could lead to decision aid UI elements;
- A vertical trajectory with dynamic trajectory limits to evaluate launch vehicle deviations.

### 3.5 Environment

The environment in which the FSO operates is static and controlled (dedicated room with limited light source in the spaceport facilities). There may be some possible perception of tremor once the launch vehicle takes off (video flow from the launch pad), but not intense enough to influence operations.

## 4 The Multi-Variant UCD Process

This section presents a revised UCD approach that enables designers to account for the variability involved in developing multiple interactive system variants for a single user or user group. The goal is to create multiple usable systems with a high degree of similarity, thereby reducing human errors [35] (e.g., capture or interference) and simplifying training, ideally requiring only differential training [23].

### 4.1 Identification of the Variants

Before exploring the design of multiple interactive systems with shared characteristics for a single user or user group, hereafter referred to as "interactive system variants", we must clearly define the types of variants we intend to address. Consider, for example, two interactive systems, A and B. Several scenarios are possible:

- No Shared Characteristics (Fig. 2, disk 1): A (left) and B (right) are entirely distinct systems. In this case, no interactive system variants exist.
- Identical Systems (Fig. 2, disk 2): A is identical to B. Again, no system variants exist.
- Superset (and equivalent Subset) Relationship (Fig. 2, disk 3): A (left) encompasses all the functionality of B (right). No system variants are considered.

- Partial Overlap (Fig. 2, disk 4): A (left) and B (right) share some characteristics but also have distinct parts. This scenario represents two distinct variants (A and B), and it will be the focus of this paper. Throughout this paper, we will use the following notation A - B (or B - A) to denote the characteristics unique to system A (or B), representing the differences between the systems (as illustrated in the top right and bottom right portions of Fig. 2). The shared characteristics of both systems will be represented by A ∩ B, the intersection (middle right portion of Fig. 2).

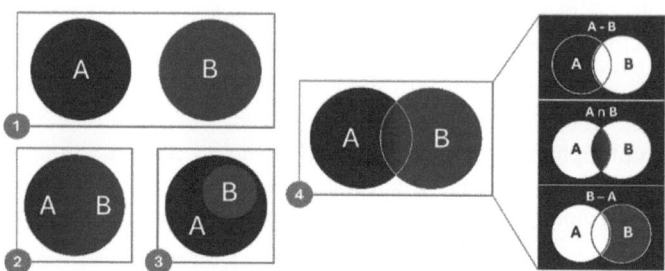

**Fig. 2.** Interactive systems variability represented using Venn's Diagrams [39]

To promote a clearer understanding of the similarities and differences between interactive system variants, the above schema makes use of the Venn's diagrams [39]. These diagrams serve to depict an overview of the shared and unique characteristics of each interactive system variant, allowing to visually represent the relationships between different systems variants and better navigate the complexities of variability.

After identifying the target variant scenarios, we must consider the variability of all POISE-S components across the interactive system variants. For brevity, we will convert the Venn diagrams into matrices to provide a concise overview of variant component combinations.

The matrix in Fig. 3 shows all possible POISE-S component combinations for two interactive system variants, subject to the following constraints:

- Both variants are designed for the same user or user group. Therefore, the "P(People)" column reflects that the users of System 1 (S1), including the Interactive System 1 (IS1), who can perform user-system Tasks 1 (T1), are the same across all components of the second system. This constraint arises because variants intended for different users or user groups can be handled by the classic UCD process described in [21].
- The Environment and Organization components are also shared between the two variants and are therefore omitted from Fig. 3.
- Combinations where only the system and the interactive system differs (e.g., S1 – S2, considering only the distinct parts of S1, and IS2 – IS1, considering only the distinct parts of IS2) are excluded as they are considered configuration errors. Similarly, combinations differing only in the interactive system and user-system tasks (e.g. IS1 – IS2, considering only the distinct parts of IS1, and T2 – T1, considering only the tasks feasible on the IS2) are excluded as they are considered procedural errors.

These procedural errors represent a user attempting a task intended for a unique part of IS1 on IS2, where that specific IS1 part does not exist.

| | P (PEOPLE)<br>- P1<br>- P2 | S (SYSTEM)<br>- S1<br>- S2 | IS (INTERACTIVE SYSTEM)<br>- IS1<br>- IS2 | T (TASKS)<br>- T1<br>- T2 | |
|---|---|---|---|---|---|
| #DesignChoice1 | P1 = P2 | S1 - S2 | IS1 - IS2 | T1 - T2 | |
| | | S2 - S1 | IS2 - IS1 | T2 - T1 | |
| #DesignChoice2 | P1 = P2 | S1 - S2 | IS1 - IS2 | T1 ∩ T2 | |
| | | S2 - S1 | IS2 - IS1 | | |
| #DesignChoice3 | P1 = P2 | S1 - S2 | IS1 ∩ IS2 | T1 - T2 | POSSIBLE USABILITY ISSUES |
| | | S2 - S1 | | T2 - T1 | |
| #DesignChoice4 | P1 = P2 | S1 - S2 | IS1 ∩ IS2 | T1 ∩ T2 | |
| | | S2 - S1 | | | |
| #DesignChoice5 | P1 = P2 | S1 ∩ S2 | IS1 - IS2 | T1 - T2 | POSSIBLE USABILITY ISSUES |
| | | | IS2 - IS1 | T2 - T1 | |
| #DesignChoice6 | P1 = P2 | S1 ∩ S2 | IS1 - IS2 | T1 ∩ T2 | |
| | | | IS2 - IS1 | | |
| #DesignChoice7 | P1 = P2 | S1 ∩ S2 | IS1 ∩ IS2 | T1 - T2 | POSSIBLE USABILITY ISSUES |
| | | | | T2 - T1 | |
| #DesignChoice8 | P1 = P2 | S1 ∩ S2 | IS1 ∩ IS2 | T1 ∩ T2 | |

**Fig. 3.** A matrix view on the Venn's Diagrams.

In this matrix, green lines represent combinations considered feasible by default. The design team will determine their actual applicability to the systems under development. Red lines also represent feasible combinations but may introduce usability issues, which will be discussed in the next section.

### 4.2 A Generic UCD Process for Multi-Variants Management

As far as the UCD process [21] does not target the design of interactive system variants for a common user or user group, we propose several extensions to support variability identification and to ensure the consistency and validity of proposed solutions in relation to tasks, design choices, and constraints. These extensions primarily refine two UCD process activities:

- "Specify User Requirements": We add a sub-activity, "Identify Global Design Choices and Constraints", which will help identify which design choices, as outlined in the matrix from Fig. 3, will be addressed in the design solutions. During this phase, it is crucial to clearly define constraints, such as similarity constraints. For example, shared information between variants must be represented using at least one common visual variable [3].
- "Evaluate Designs Against Requirements": We add a sub-activity, "Verify Conformance and Validity of Design Choices", to assess whether all identified user-system tasks are feasible with the created design solutions, and whether these solutions adhere to the design choices and constraints established by the design team.

These sub-activities are shown as dark gray rectangles below the activities they refine in Fig. 4, disk a. For easier navigation, schemas illustrating the extended UCD process will follow the visual presentation exemplified in Fig. 4, disk b.

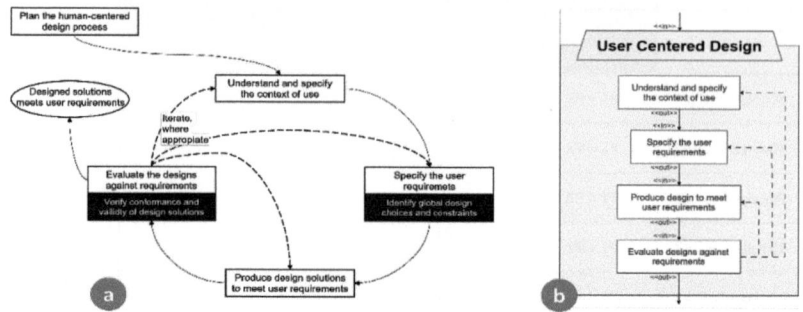

**Fig. 4.** Generic UCD process for multi-variants management

Figure 5 details the extended UCD process. Elements highlighted in dark gray represent the proposed artifacts for managing variant variability. This extended process takes as input a matrix of design choices (similar to the one shown in Fig. 3) and a comprehensive description of all common and distinct data and services of the systems (the POISE-S "S" component), which may be used later in the interactive system variants design. New modifications and additions to the UCD process [21] are described below:

- In the initial step of the process (Fig. 5, disk 1), it is crucial to identify all information that can be shared between interactive system variants, as well as information that are unique to each variant. This should be done while considering the overall goals and tasks that both users and the system must accomplish in each variant.
- During the specification of requirements (Fig. 5, disk 2), designers must instantiate the matrix in Fig. 3 with the respective POISE-S components for their target variants. As mentioned previously, this step also requires identifying constraints, which further limit the scope of managed variability.
- To capture the variability of the interactive system variants, design solutions for each variant must be analyzed and broken down into common and distinct layouts, visual appearances, and behaviors of interactors and input/output devices. This provides a complete description of interactive system variants according to the user-system tasks the user or user group performs with each variant (Fig. 5, disk 3).
- Finally, if the design solutions do not conform to the user-system tasks or fail to meet the designers' intended choices and constraints, they must be reworked until full compliance is achieved (Fig. 5, disk 4).

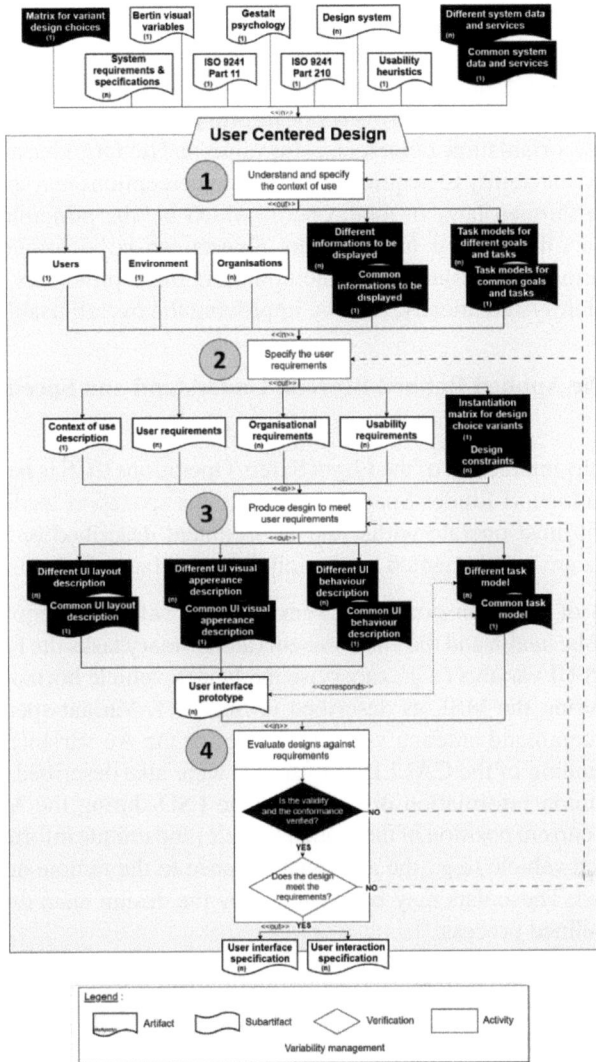

**Fig. 5.** Detailed multi-variant UCD process

## 5 Application of the Refined UCD Process to UI Design of Flight Safety Operations CCS

This section details the refined UCD process instantiated to design two of the CCS UIs for the multi-launch vehicle Flight Safety Operations of Europe Spaceport. Using the case study introduced in Sect. 3, we describe the outcome of the application of each step of the process to create both UIs: a UI variant for the Ariane 6 launch vehicle and a UI variant for the CALLISTO reusable launch vehicle. Due to space constraints, a visual representation of the instantiation of the refined UCD process for the case study is provided in Fig. 13.

It is essential to highlight that our approach for designing and evaluating the design solutions is grounded in theoretical design principles, particularly on Bertin's visual variables [3] and the Gestalt principles [17]. Bertin's visual variables [3] identify six graphic dimensions that can be used to encode information when creating a visualization, namely size, shape, orientation, color hue, color value, and texture. Gestalt principles [17] aim to understand the ability to acquire and maintain perceptions in a seemingly chaotic world. There are thirteen laws in total, one of which is "the principle of invariance" addressing the fact that similar and different objects can be identified independently of the scale, rotation, or translation. By incorporating these principles, it is possible to encode information systematically, thereby improving the overall usability of a system.

### 5.1 Step 1 of the Applied Refined Process: Understand and Specify the Context of Use

The content and the interaction of the Flight Safety Operations CCS is heavily influenced by the Centre National d'Études Spatiales (CNES), the spaceport leading organization (Sect. 3.2), and it must operate within the environment described in Sect. 3.5. These contextual details are supplemented by the following artifacts (Fig. 13, disk 1):

- A description of common goals (e.g., ensuring the safety of people and property, protecting public health and the environment) and primary tasks the FSO will perform using the CCS UI variants (e.g., supervise the launch vehicle horizontal and vertical trajectory;) during the MSI, as described in Sect. 3.1. Variant-specific goals (e.g., visualize the command antenna visibility range for the A6 variant) and tasks (e.g., monitor the landing of the CALLISTO variant) were also described.
- A list of common information displayed to the FSO during the MSI for both UI variants (e.g., current position of the launch vehicle) and unique information displayed for each launch vehicle (e.g., the approach distance to the remote antenna range for the A6 variant). These lists may be expanded by the design team during the second phase of the refined process.

These artifacts are developed by considering the common data and services available from the Ariane 6 launch vehicle and its ground segment systems, and from the CALLISTO launch vehicle and its ground segment systems, that the FSO can leverage to achieve the expected goals and tasks for each variant (Sect. 3.4). Input and output devices and associated interaction techniques are also an essential part of the interactive CCSs [13], but they will not be discussed further on this paper.

### 5.2 Step 2 of the Applied Refined Process: Specify the User Requirements

We defined the user requirements (e.g., #REQ_1: the symbology used to encode information on the two variants must be similar enough to be recognizable from a UI variant to the other), organizational requirements (e.g., #REQ_2: CCS UIs must cover all the activities described in article 63 of [11] regarding the MSI), and usability requirements (e.g., #REQ_3: FSO must be able to perceive information displayed, analyze it and act in a few seconds). Figure 6 presents the instantiated matrix for the two proposed variants: "A6" for the launch vehicle Ariane 6, and "CAL" for the reusable launch vehicle

CALLISTO. Design choice 5 (#DesignChoice5 of Fig. 6) was dismissed in the instantiated matrix because we don't want to address differently the similarities between the systems for A6 and CAL (SA6 ∩ SCAL) in the FSO user interfaces and their associated tasks (e.g., in the Airbus vs. Boeing case, one employs a sidestick to adjust the aircraft's attitude, while the other uses a yoke). Additionally, design choices 3 and 7 were rejected due to potential usability issues: even if there is a shared part between the user interface variants for A6 and for CAL (ISA6 ∩ ISCAL), the tasks associated with these parts differ. This discrepancy may arise from the way common information is designed to be interpreted across the user interfaces variants (for instance, FSO could be trained to view all green elements as hazardous on the A6 UI variant, whereas he could be trained to see them as nominal on the CALLISTO UI variant). All other design choices in the instantiated matrix were approved for further investigation in steps 3 and 4 of the refined process.

From the instantiated matrix in Fig. 6, several constraints for proposing design solutions were identified. An example of constraint is to ensure the across-system similarity property [6] for both variants, and for this purpose, it is essential that "shared information between variants must be represented using at least the same color hue and color value visual variables". Another example of constraint, deducted directly from design choices 3 and 7, is that "if a part of a user interface is shared between the two variants (ISA6 ∩ ISCAL), the associated tasks must also be shared (TA6 ∩ CAL)".

|  | P (PEOPLE)<br>- PA6 (P of Ariane 6)<br>- PCAL(P of CALLISTO) | S (SYSTEM)<br>- SA6 (S of Ariane 6)<br>- SCAL (S of CALLISTO) | IS (INTERACTIVE SYSTEM)<br>- ISA6 (IS of Ariane6)<br>- ISCAL (IS of CALLISTO) | T (TASKS)<br>- TA6 (T of Ariane6)<br>- TCAL (T of CALLISTO) | ACCEPTATION FOR CASE STUDY |
|---|---|---|---|---|---|
| #DesignChoice1 | PA6 = PCAL | SA6 - SCAL<br>SCAL - SA6 | ISA6 - ISCAL<br>ISCAL - ISA6 | TA6 - TCAL<br>TCAL - TA6 | ACCEPTED |
| #DesignChoice2 | PA6 = PCAL | SA6 - SCAL<br>SCAL - SA6 | ISA6 - ISCAL<br>ISCAL - ISA6 | TA6 ∩ TCAL | ACCEPTED |
| #DesignChoice3 | PA6 = PCAL | SA6 - SCAL<br>SCAL - SA6 | ISA6 ∩ ISCAL | TA6 - TCAL<br>TCAL - TA6 | NOT ACCEPTED |
| #DesignChoice4 | PA6 = PCAL | SA6 - SCAL<br>SCAL - SA6 | ISA6 ∩ ISCAL | TA6 ∩ TCAL | ACCEPTED |
| #DesignChoice5 | PA6 = PCAL | SA6 ∩ SCAL | ISA6 - ISCAL<br>ISCAL - ISA6 | TA6 - TCAL<br>TCAL - TA6 | NOT ACCEPTED |
| #DesignChoice6 | PA6 = PCAL | SA6 ∩ SCAL | ISA6 - ISCAL<br>ISCAL - ISA6 | TA6 ∩ TCAL | ACCEPTED |
| #DesignChoice7 | PA6 = PCAL | SA6 ∩ SCAL | ISA6 ∩ ISCAL | TA6 - TCAL<br>TCAL - TA6 | NOT ACCEPTED |
| #DesignChoice8 | PA6 = PCAL | SA6 ∩ SCAL | ISA6 ∩ ISCAL | TA6 ∩ TCAL | ACCEPTED |

**Fig. 6.** Design Choices Matrix Instantiated for the Case Study.

## 5.3 Step 3 of the Applied Refined Process: Produce Design Solutions

Multiple design solutions, i.e. UI prototypes, were created during the application of the refined UCD process to our case study. The A6 UI prototype, presented in Fig. 7, has two different display screens. The left display screen, presented on the left side of Fig. 7, is used to monitor the horizontal trajectory of the launch vehicle; and the right display screen, presented on the right side of Fig. 7, is used to monitor the vertical trajectory. Disk 3 of Fig. 7 presents a specific UI element (a well identified part of the UI prototype) from the A6 UI prototype used to visualize the remaining distance between the current launch vehicle position and the command antenna end of visibility.

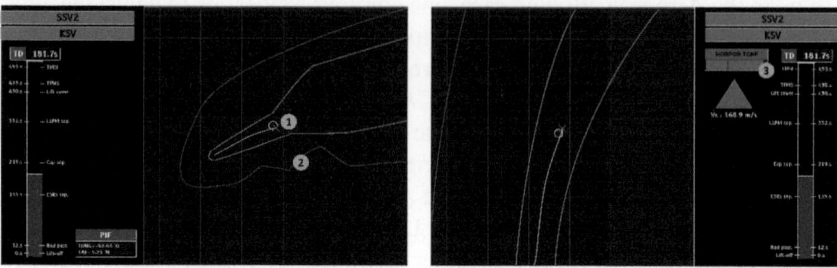

**Fig. 7.** Ariane 6 UI Prototype - Left screen of the UI for the supervision of the launch vehicle horizontal position – Right screen of the UI for the supervision of the launch vehicle verticality.

The CALLISTO UI prototype (Fig. 8) has a single screen. The main design decision for this UI prototype was to display information's within a relatively small area of focus (all UI elements centered) due to the take-off and landing on the same position of CALLISTO (Sect. 3.4).

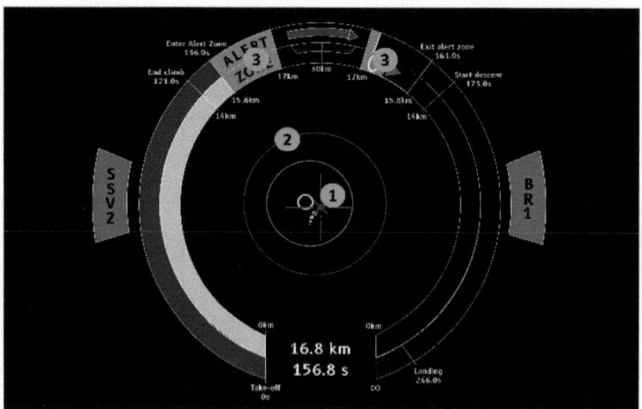

**Fig. 8.** CALLISTO UI Prototype - UI for the supervision of the reusable launch vehicle horizontal and vertical position.

There are also two graphs on this UI prototype. The horizontal trajectory is displayed in the center of the UI. The vertical trajectory is represented by a circular progress bar that moves from left to right, reaching its maximum possible altitude at 20km (and beyond if necessary). Disk 3 of Fig. 8 presents a specific UI element from the CALLISTO UI prototype used to visualize the alert zone, a flight zone on which FSO has a very little time to react to a possible launch vehicle deviation.

For each information identified during step 1 of the refined process, and displayed to the FSO in each UI prototype via an UI element, the following categorization was made:

- Layout of the UI elements presenting the information in the UI prototype, considering logical properties like the order, for UI elements with a layered layout; the arrangement (their x and y coordinates on a container); and the size of the UI element.
- Visual appearance of the UI element presenting the information in the UI prototype, considering visual properties like the color value (having multiple colors if the UI element has multiple states), and the shape of the UI element, among others [3].
- Behavior of the UI element presenting the information in the UI prototype. This behavior can be managed internally to the UI element or externally, by the global behavior of the application [13].

During this categorization, the design team stipulated that if one of the aspects "visual appearance" or "behavior" of the UI prototype is dissimilar for a shared information between variants (as these aspects were deemed most impactful than "layout" according to the Gestalt's principle of invariance), then the respective UI element is considered as dissimilar. This reasoning is useful during step 4 for the verification of the respect of the accepted design choices (Fig. 6) and the identified design constraints.

| UI PROTOTYPE INFORMATION UIPIA6 (for the Ariane 6 variant) UIPICAL (for the CALLISTO variant) | UI PROTOTYPE LAYOUT UIPLA6 (for the Ariane 6 variant) UIPLCAL (for the CALLISTO variant) | UI PROTOTYPE VISUAL APPERANCE UIPVAA6 (for the Ariane 6 variant) UIPVACAL (for the CALLISTO variant) | UI PROTOTYPE BEHAVIOUR UIPBA6 (for the Ariane 6 variant) UIPBCAL (for the CALLISTO variant) |
|---|---|---|---|
| UIPIA6 ∩ UIPICAL Current position | UIPLA6 - UIPLCAL Horizontality graph (current position): Order = (0), Arrangement = (x=598, y=0), Size = (width=1085, height=1077) | UIPVAA6 - UIPVACAL Color = Green, Shape = Cross | UIPBA6 ∩ UIPBCAL Always in the center of the horizontality graph. It correspond to the center of the viewport. |
|  | UIPLCAL - UIPLA6 Horizontality graph (current position) : Order = (0), Arrangement = (x=465, y=145), Size = (width=745, height=760) | UIPVACAL - UIPVAA6 Color = Green, Shape = Crosshair |  |
| UIPIA6 ∩ UIPICAL Horizontality intervention limit | UIPLA6 - UIPLCAL Horizontality graph (horizontality intervention limit) : Order = (2), Arrangement = (x=598, y=0), Size = (width=1085, height=1077) | UIPVACAL ∩ UIPVAA6 Color = Red, Shape = Polygon | UIPBCAL ∩ UIPBA6 It visually changes position when the viewport change |
|  | UIPLCAL - UIPLA6 Horizontality graph (horizontality intervention limit) : Order = (2), Arrangement = (x=465, y=145), Size = (width=745, height=760) |  |  |

**Fig. 9.** Extract of the outcome of the categorization.

Figure 9 presents two examples of information categorization. The first one, the "Current position" (second row of Fig. 9), corresponds to the launch vehicle's current position in the horizontal trajectory graph and has different layout and visual appearance for each UI prototype. For the A6 UI prototype, the current position is represented by a green cross (inherited from the Ariane 5 UI) and is placed in the center of the prototype's horizontal graph (Fig. 7, disk 1), while for the CALLISTO UI prototype, it is represented by a green crosshair (to simulate the crosshair of a sight) and is also placed in the center of the prototype's horizontal graph (Fig. 8, disk 1). The current position in both UI prototypes is encoded in green. This color code comes from the CNES current design system, aligning with the Gestalt principle of past experiences which states that elements can be perceived according to human past experiences. The second example concerns the "Horizontality intervention limit" (third row of Fig. 9), indicating the limit beyond which the monitored launch vehicle represents a danger to the people, properties and environment, and beyond which it must be neutralized. In this second example, the visual appearance between UI prototypes is shared (requirement imposed by the FSO), while only the layout changes (Fig. 7, disk 2 for the A6 UI prototype and Fig. 8, disk 2 for the CALLISTO UI prototype).

Each of the presented UI prototypes must correspond to a common task model, for all the shared tasks done by the FSO on both UI prototypes (ensuring the coverage of similarities [29]), and to a specific task model for each variant, where unique information's for each variant, like the remaining distance to the command antenna end of visibility for the Ariane 6 launch vehicle (Fig. 7, disk 3), or the alert zone engagement status for the CALLISTO launch vehicle (Fig. 8, disk 3), must be covered by several variant-specific tasks (ensuring the coverage of dissimilarities [29]). As operators' tasks are usually numerous, the task models are quite large. In this paper, we present only excerpts of these task models, done using the HAMSTERS notation and the associated modeling tool [27]. It is important to note that the task models produced in this process step represent a more detailed and concrete version of the task models presented briefly during step 1 (Sect. 5.1).

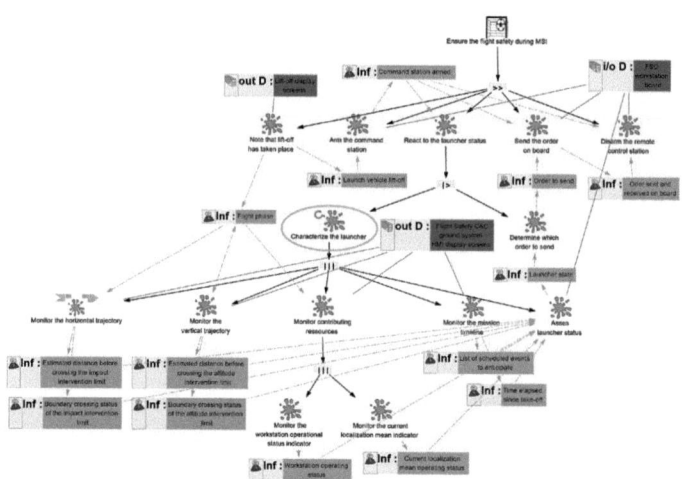

**Fig. 10.** Common "Ensure the flight safety during MSI" task model for the two variants.

Figure 10 presents the task model of the common tasks that the FSO can perform using any UI prototype, regardless of the launch vehicle for which they must ensure the MSI. It reads in the following way: the main goal is to "Ensure the flight safety during MSI". It consists of the sequence of abstract tasks: "Note that the lift-off has taken place", "Arm the remote-control station", "React to launch vehicle status", "Send the order on board" and "Disarm the remote-control station". Each one of these abstract tasks must be refined for each variant, but due to space limitations, only the sub-task of "React to launch vehicle status" called "Characterize the launcher" (Fig. 10, highlighted in blue) will be detailed, which corresponds to the assessment of the potential risks with the launch vehicle. This task can be decomposed into several concurrent tasks, notably the "Monitor the launch vehicle trajectory" abstract task (Fig. 10, disc 2), to supervise the horizontal and vertical trajectory of the launch vehicle.

At this level of refinement, we can already spot some differences on the task's models of the two variants, exposed on Fig. 11. For example, for the A6 UI prototype, several information's (e.g., "Inf: Boundary crossing status of the alert limit") related to specific launch vehicle and ground segment characteristics, and requirements, are specific to the A6 task model (Fig. 11, disk 1). New abstract tasks are also introduced (e.g., "Monitor the command antenna visibility range", Fig. 11, disk 2), related to the specific UI element of the A6 UI prototype (Fig. 7, disk 3, thus corresponding to the #DesignChoice1 of the Fig. 6). On the other hand, for the CALLISTO UI prototype, the addition of information is also remarkable, notably the information "Inf: Alert zone engagement status" (Fig. 11, disk 3). The addition or removal of information of a common abstract task implies variant specific changes of the refined sub-tasks, which could be modelled as the addition of new possible tasks and information's, or the removal of some existent.

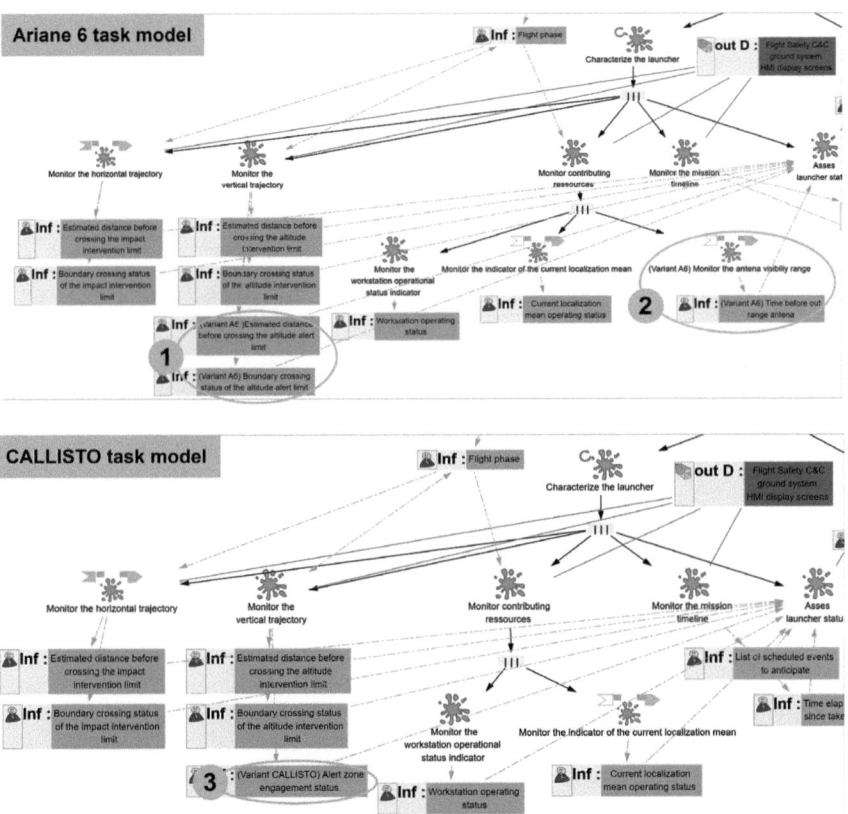

**Fig. 11.** Specific "Characterize the launch vehicle" task models for Ariane 6 (top side) and CALLISTO (bottom side) variants.

Going further on the task refinement, if we take for example the abstract task "Monitor the horizontal trajectory", to track the use of different graphical representations on each UI prototype for a shared information, the task model must be refined for each variant UI prototype to point out the graphical representation of the UI elements used to perform the tasks.

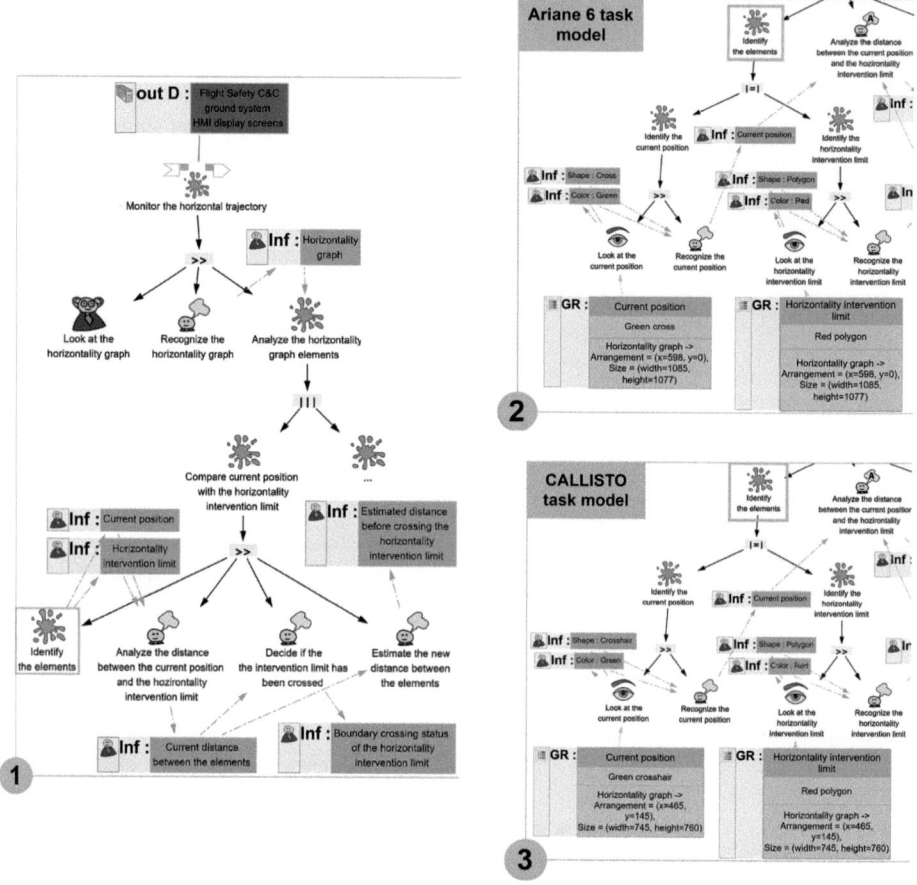

**Fig. 12.** Common "Monitor the horizontal trajectory" task model (disk 1). Common "Identify the elements" task model for the A6 variant (disk 2), and the CALLISTO variant (disk 3).

This tracking is done in the task models using the symbol "GR" (GR for Graphical Representation), followed by a label indicating the name of the UI element, making it possible to identify the visual appearance and the layout of an UI element used by a task or a group of tasks. For example, starting from the "Monitor the horizontal trajectory" sub-task "Compare current position with horizontality intervention limit"; to describe the graphical representation of the UI element showing the information "Inf: Current position", used in the common task "Identify the elements" (Fig. 12, disk 1), two symbol labels are used for the A6 UI element, presented in the task model of Fig. 12, disk 2 ("GR: Visual appearance of current position: green cross" and "GR: Layout of current position: center of the horizontal trajectory graph"). They indicate that the perceptive task "Identify current position" (Fig. 12, disk 2) is performed using a specific UI element that displays the current position in the form of a green cross located in the horizontality trajectory graph. Similarly, to represent the graphical representation of the UI element for the CALLISTO UI prototype, two symbol labels are also used, which are presented in the task model of Fig. 12, disk 3 ("GR: Visual appearance of current position: green crosshair" and "GR: Layout of current position: center of the horizontal trajectory graph"). In this way, we use task models to trace the use of specific UI element graphical representations, allowing to describe precisely how the identification of UI elements that shows the same information differs for each variant.Even if not covered in the presented examples, the behavior of UI elements can be also modelled by having an information of the state of the UI element deducted from its graphical representation. This information implies having several tasks, connected by a choice operator, executed depending on the UI element state information.

At last, the consistency between the UI prototypes for A6 and CALLISTO and their corresponding common and specific task models is verified during the concurrent and synchronized development of UI prototypes and task models (as illustrated in Fig. 13).

## 5.4 Step 4 of the Applied Refined Process: Evaluate Designs Against Requirements

We achieved the conformance checking between the UI prototypes and the POISE-S components by conducting a detailed decomposition of the POISE-S components for both variants, allowing us to verify the alignment of the common and specific elements of each component across all components, while considering the instantiated design choices and constraints (Fig. 13, disk 4). An example of this decomposition is illustrated in Fig. 14.

**Table 1.** Extract of the outcome of requirements verification

| ID | Short title | Fulfillment |
| --- | --- | --- |
| #REQ_1 | The symbology must be similar enough | Yes, for both UI prototypes (same color hue and value, shapes that are identical or close) |
| #REQ_2 | The UI variants must cover all the activities | Yes, by both prototypes (Fig. 7 and Fig. 8), which match all the identified tasks described in task models (extracts of these task models are presented in Fig. 10, Fig. 11 and Fig. 12) |
| #REQ_3 | FSO must be able to treat information under seconds | Yes, from user testing with a group of FSOs |

This complete conformance verification also serves to ensure that the design choices and constraints established in step 2 have been respected. For instance, during an iteration of the UI prototype for A6, the current position was indicated by a yellow cross (ISA6 - ISCAL), whereas in the UI prototype for CALLISTO, it was represented by a green crosshair (ISCAL – ISA6). Given that the "System" component related to the current position is shared between both variants, SA6 ∩ SCAL (the ground segment subsystem responsible for retrieving the launch vehicle's position from radars and converting it into coordinates usable by the interactive CCS), this discrepancy violates the constraint established in step 2 "shared information between variants must be represented using at least the same color hue and color value visual variables", while respecting the #DesignChoice6 of Fig. 6.

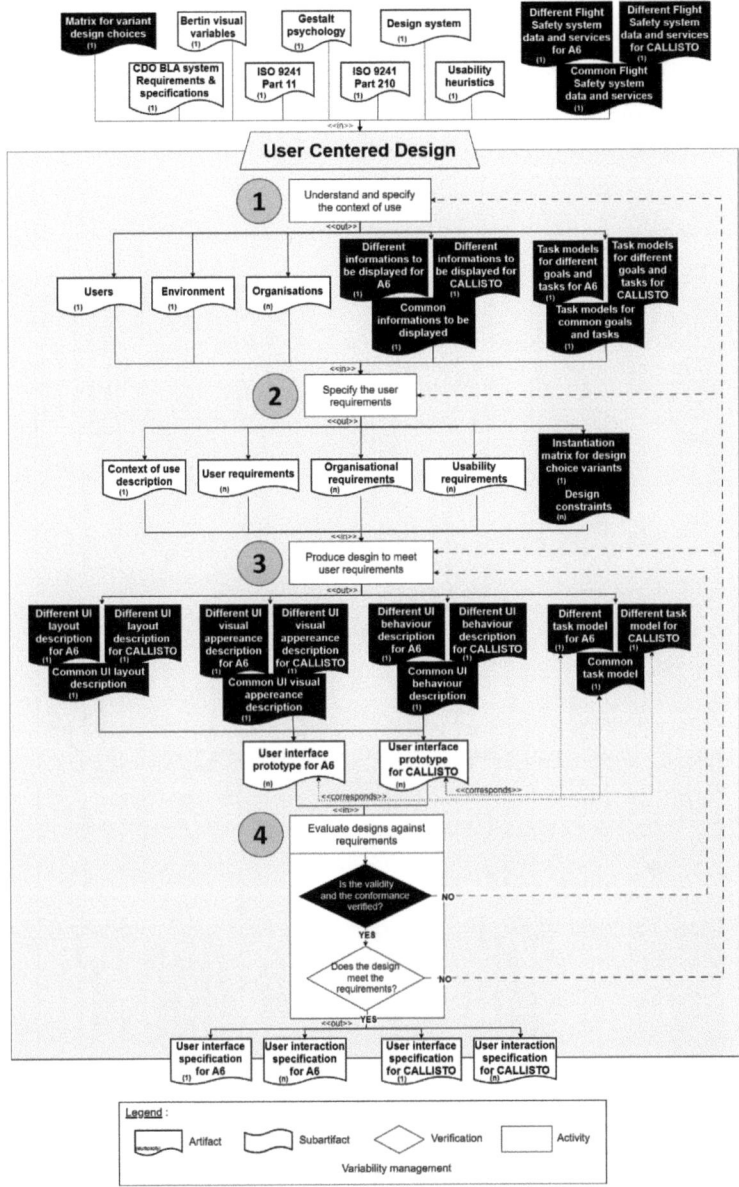

**Fig. 13.** Detailed multi-variant UCD process instantiated for the FSO case study.

Once the design solutions were fully compliant with the accepted design choices and overall conformance was achieved, we evaluated these solutions against the requirements established in step 2 (Fig. 13, disk 4). Table 1 presents an extract of the outcome of the verification.

| SYSTEM<br>SA6 (for the Ariane 6 variant)<br>SCAL (for the CALLISTO variant) | | INTERACTIVE C&C SYSTEM (*Only the UI part*)<br>UIPA6 (for the Ariane 6 variant)<br>UIPCAL (for the CALLISTO variant) | | | | TASKS<br>TA6 (for the Ariane 6 variant)<br>TCAL (for the CALLISTO variant) | ASSOCIATED DESGIN CHOICE |
|---|---|---|---|---|---|---|---|
| LAUNCHER SYSTEM<br>LSA6 (for the Ariane 6 variant)<br>LSCAL (for the CALLISTO variant) | GROUND SEGMENT SYSTEM<br>GSSA6 (for the Ariane 6 variant)<br>GSSCAL (for the CALLISTO variant) | UI PROTOTYPE INFORMATION<br>UIPIA6 (for the Ariane 6 variant)<br>UIPICAL (for the CALLISTO variant) | UI PROTOTYPE LAYOUT<br>UIPLA6 (for the Ariane 6 variant)<br>UIPLCAL (for the CALLISTO variant) | UI PROTOTYPE VISUAL APPEREANCE<br>UIPVAA6 (for the Ariane 6 variant)<br>UIPVACAL (for the CALLISTO variant) | UI PROTOTYPE BEHAVIOUR<br>UIPBA6 (for the Ariane 6 variant)<br>UIPBCAL (for the CALLISTO variant) | | |
| **SA6 ∩ SCAL** | | **ISA6 - ISCAL**<br>**ISCAL - ISA6** | | | | **TA6 ∩ TCAL** | |
| **LSA6 ∩ LSCAL**<br>System responsible for cummunicaiting launch vehicle position to radars | **GSSA6 ∩ GSSCAL**<br>System responsible for retrieving the launch vehicle's position from radars and converting it into coordinates | **UIPIA6 ∩ UIPICAL**<br>Current position | **UIPLA6 - UIPLCAL**<br>Horizontality graph (**current position**): Order = (0), Arrangement = (x=598, y=0), Size = (width=1085, height=1077)<br>**UIPLCAL - UIPLA6**<br>Horizontality graph (**current position**) : Order = (0), Arrangement = (x=465, y=145), Size = (width=745, height=760) | **UIPVAA6 - UIPVACAL**<br>Color = Green, Shape = Cross<br>**UIPVACAL - UIPVAA6**<br>Color = Green, Shape = Crosshair | **UIPBA6 ∩ UIPBCAL**<br>Always in the center of the horizontality graph. It correspond to the center of the viewport. | **TA6 ∩ TCAL**<br>Look at the current position | **#DesginChoice6** |
| **SA6 - SCAL**<br>**SCAL - SA6** | | **ISA6 ∩ ISCAL** | | | | **TA6 ∩ TCAL** | |
| **LSA6 ∩ LSCAL**<br>*No associated system* | **GSSA6 - GSSCAL**<br>System responsible for recovering the horizontality intervention limit data from A6 configuration files<br>**GSSCAL - GSSA6**<br>System responsible for recovering the horizontality intervention limit data from CALLISTO configuration files | **UIPIA6 ∩ UIPICAL**<br>Horizontality intervention limit | **UIPLA6 - UIPLCAL**<br>Horizontality graph (**horizontality intervention limit**) : Order = (2), Arrangement = (x=598, y=0), Size = (width=1085, height=1077)<br>**UIPLCAL - UIPLA6**<br>Horizontality graph (**horizontality intervention limit**) : Order = (2), Arrangement = (x=465, y=145), Size = (width=745, height=760) | **UIPVAA6 ∩ UIPVACAL**<br>Color = Red, Shape = Polygon | **UIPBA6 ∩ UIPBCAL**<br>It visually changes position when the viewport change | **TA6 ∩ TCAL**<br>Look at the horizontality intervention limit | **#DesginChoice4** |
| **SA6 ∩ SCAL** | | **ISA6 ∩ ISCAL** | | | | **TA6 ∩ TCAL** | |
| **LSA6 ∩ LSCAL**<br>System responsible for the reception of commands | **GSSA6 ∩ GSSCAL**<br>System responsible for sending the commands on board | **UIPIA6 ∩ UIPICAL**<br>Deactivation button | **UIPLA6 ∩ UIPLCAL**<br>Order = (None), Arrangement = (x=1100, y=1000), Size = (width=20, height=20) | **UIPVAA6 ∩ UIPVACAL**<br>Color = Yellow, Shape = Circle | **UIPBA6 ∩ UIPBCAL**<br>It sinks when pressed, sending the deactivation command on board, and it returns to the initial state when released | **TA6 ∩ TCAL**<br>Send the order on board | **#DesginChoice8** |

**Fig. 14.** Excerpt of the detailed decomposition of the POISE-S components for both variants.

## 6 Discussion and Lessons Learnt

This paper has proposed several contributions, including a revised UCD process (addressing the property of similarity between interactive systems) called the Multi-Variant UCD process. This process addresses the challenges related to the design of usable and similar interactive systems variants, where those variants will be used by the same user(s). This similarity property (between several interactive systems) is not addressed by standard UCD approaches.

In this paper, the revised UCD process is detailed by means of stepwise process identifying precisely the activities to be performed as well as the artifacts/information needed and produced for each activity. This detailed stepwise process is made concrete on a real-life case study in the area of space launch operations considering both an extant and a future system. Following the Mutli-Variant UCD process, the presented variants have been designed by producing and selecting the UI prototypes the most adapted to user tasks, design choices, constraints, and requirements using several new artifacts. This work has been led in an industrial context in which the careful production of UI variants of CCSs are key to support training, cross-qualification of operators, ensure performance and tasks feasibility as well as reduction of operators' errors (especially interference errors occurring with dissimilar UIs). Reusing part of the designs and the application code of the variants reduces the associate costs, including testing and maintenance costs.

There are some limitations to the work presented in this paper. The first limitation is related to the characteristics of the application we used to make the process concrete. This application is mainly focused on monitoring activities (i.e. operators checking values of information on the display). Interaction is limited to zooming. More complex interaction techniques should have been presented to demonstrate the applicability of the process on this specific part of an interactive system. This leads to the second limitation related to the validation of the revised UCD process. So far, validation has only been done on case studies in the area of space ground segments where operators are trained and people life is at stake. More mundane areas (e.g. mobile applications) have to be considered to demonstrate its applicability and value in other contexts. The third limitation lies in the fact that most of the inter-variants' verification has to be done manually. Automating them would avoid human errors and ensure exhaustiveness.

## 7 Conclusion and Perspectives

This paper proposes a solution to the problem of operators using similar in some parts and different in other parts applications in safety critical contexts. Similarity of the user interface will support operators in reusing knowledge from one application to the other ones as well as reducing training costs. However, the dissimilar parts are likely to induce interference and capture errors from operators. To both ensure the benefits and avoid the drawbacks of this work context we presented a revised UCD process, the Multi-Variant UCD process.

The presented variants have been designed by producing and selecting the UI prototypes the most adapted to user tasks, design choices, constraints, and requirements using several new artifacts. This work has been led in an industrial context in which the careful production of UI variants of CCSs are key to support training, cross-qualification of operators, ensure performance and tasks feasibility as well as reduction of operators' errors.

In order to support and validate this process further work has to be performed. On the design side, there is a need to be able to describe in a systematic way the user interface as well as the interaction techniques. Indeed, similarity and dissimilarity might take place on every aspect of an interactive system. Without a precise and unambiguous description of these elements, some similarities and dissimilarities might be overlooked. Future work targets the development of these UI variants using existing interactive system standards, such as the User Interface Description Language (UIDL) UsiXML and Petri net based behavioral descriptions [4]. On the engineering side, the benefits from reusing parts of the interactive system which are similar requires software tools and techniques supporting such reuse. Future work will encompass component-based engineering of interactive systems both at operators' tasks descriptions [16] and UI widgets [28].

## References

1. Annett, J., Duncan, K.D.: Task analysis and training design. J. Occupat. Psychol. (41) (1967)
2. Ariane 6 launch vehicle webpage, https://cnes.fr/en/projects/ariane-6. Accessed Dec 2024
3. Bertin, J.: Semiology of Graphics: Diagrams, Networks, Maps. ESRI Press (2010)
4. Barboni, E., Martinie, C., Navarre, D., Palanque, P., Winckler, M.: Bridging the gap between a behavioural formal description technique and a user interface description language: Enhancing ICO with a graphical user interface markup language. Sci. Comput. Program. **86**, 3–29 (2014). https://doi.org/10.1016/j.scico.2013.04.001
5. Bolstad, C.A., Riley, J.M., Jones, D.G., Endsley, M.R.: Using goal directed task analysis with army brigade officer teams. Proc. Hum. Fact. Ergon. Soc. Ann. Meet. **46**(3), 472–476 (2002). https://doi.org/10.1177/154193120204600354
6. Bouzekri, E., Canny, A., Martinie, C., Palanque, P.: Characterizing sets of systems: representation and analysis of across-systems properties. In: Abdelnour Nocera, J., et al. (eds.) Beyond interactions. INTERACT 2019. LNCS, vol. 11930, pp. 84–96. Springer, Cham (2020). https://doi.org/10.1007/978-3-030-46540-7_9
7. Bouzekri, E., Canny, A., Martinie, C., Palanque, P., Gris, C.: Deep system knowledge required: revisiting UCD contribution in the design of complex command and control systems. In: Lamas, D., Loizides, F., Nacke, L., Petrie, H., Winckler, M., Zaphiris, P. (eds.) INTERACT 2019, Part I 17. LNCS, vol. 11746, pp. 699–720. Springer, Cham (2019). https://doi.org/10.1007/978-3-030-29381-9_42
8. CALLISTO launch vehicle webpage. https://cnes.fr/en/projects/callisto. Accessed Dec 2024
9. Calvary, G., Coutaz, J., Thevenin, D., Limbourg, Q., Bouillon, L., Vanderdonckt, J.: A unifying reference framework for multi-target user interfaces. Interact. Comput. **15**, 289–308 (2003)
10. CNES. French Space Operations Act. N° 2008-518 (2008)
11. CNES. Order Regulating the Operation of Installations of the Guyana Space Center. CNES/P/2010-1 (2010)
12. Cockton, G., Lárusdóttir, M., Gregory, P., Cajander, Å.: Integrating user-centred design in agile development. In: Cockton, G., Lárusdóttir, M., Gregory, P., Cajander, Å. (eds.) Integrating User-Centred Design in Agile Development. Human–Computer Interaction Series. Springer, Cham (2016). https://doi.org/10.1007/978-3-319-32165-3_1
13. Cronel, M., Dumas, B., Palanque, P., Canny, A.: MIODMIT: a generic architecture for dynamic multimodal interactive systems. In: Bogdan, C., Kuusinen, K., Lárusdóttir, M., Palanque, P., Winckler, M. (eds.) HCSE 2018. LNCS, vol. 11262, pp. 109–129. Springer, Cham (2019). https://doi.org/10.1007/978-3-030-05909-5_7
14. Fadhlillah, H.S., Setyautami, M.R.A., Rohma, I.A., Budiardjo, E.K.: Managing customizable user interface for web application product lines using delta modeling. In: Proceedings of the 18th International Working Conference on Variability Modelling of Software-Intensive Systems, Bern, Switzerland, pp 61–70. Association for Computing Machinery (2024)

15. Fleury, S., Chaniaud, N.: Multi-user centered design: acceptance, user experience, user research and user testing. Theor. Issues Ergon. Sci. **25**, 209–224 (2024). https://doi.org/10.1080/1463922X.2023.2166623
16. Forbrig, P., Martinie, C., Palanque, P., Winckler, M., Fahssi, R.: Rapid task-models development using sub-models, sub-routines and generic components. In: Sauer, S., Bogdan, C., Forbrig, P., Bernhaupt, R., Winckler, M. (eds.) HCSE 2014. LNCS, vol 8742, pp. 144–163. Springer, Cham (2014). https://doi.org/10.1007/978-3-662-44811-3_9
17. Graham, L.: Gestalt theory in interactive media design. J. Hum. Soc. Sci. **2**(1) (2008)
18. Gibson, J.J.: The Ecological Approach to Visual Perception: Classic Edition, 1st edn. Psychology Press (2014). https://doi.org/10.4324/9781315740218
19. Heil, S., Bakaev, M., Gaedke, M.: Measuring and ensuring similarity of user interfaces: the impact of web layout. In: Cellary, W., Mokbel, M.F., Wang, J., Wang, H., Zhou, R., Zhang, Y. (eds.) Web Information Systems Engineering – WISE 2016. LNCS, vol. 10041, pp. 252–260. Springer, Cham (2016). https://doi.org/10.1007/978-3-319-48740-3_18
20. Hussain, Z., et al.: Integrating extreme programming and user-centered design. In: PPIG, pp 107–113(2008)
21. International Standard Organization. 2019. ISO 9241–210:2019(en), Ergonomics of human-system interaction — Part 210: Human-centred design for interactive systems. https://www.iso.org/obp/ui/#iso:std:iso:9241:-210:ed-2:v1:en
22. International Standard Organization. 2019. ISO 9241–11:2018(en), Ergonomics of human-system interaction — Part 11: Usability: Definitions and concepts. https://www.iso.org/obp/ui/#iso:std:iso:9241:-11:ed-2:v1:en
23. Jennions, I.: The World of Civil Aerospace. SAE International (2019)
24. Kitamura, M., Fujita, Y., Yoshikawa, H.: Review of international standards related to the design for control rooms on nuclear power plants. J. Nuclear Sci. Technol. **42**(4), 406–417. https://doi.org/10.1080/18811248.2005.972640
25. Kuch, T., Sabath, D.: The columbus-CC—operating the European laboratory at ISS. Acta Astronautica **63**(1–4), 204–212 (2008). ISSN 0094–5765, https://doi.org/10.1016/j.actaastro.2007.12.041
26. Martinie C., Navarre D., Palanque P., Barboni E., Steere S. Engineering operations-based training. Proc. ACM Hum. Comput. Interact. **6**(EICS), 164:1–164:25 (2022)
27. Martinie, C., Palanque, P., Bouzekri, E., Cockburn, A., Canny, A., Barboni, E.: Analysing and demonstrating tool-supported customizable task notations. Proc. ACM Hum.-Comput. Interact. **3**(EICS) (2019). Article 12, 26 pages. https://doi.org/10.1145/3331154
28. Navarre, D., Palanque, P., Bastide, R., Sy, O.: Structuring interactive systems specifications for executability and prototypability. In: Palanque, P., Paternò, F. (eds.) DSV-IS 2000. LNCS, vol. 1946, pp. 97–119. Springer, Heidelberg (2000)
29. Navarre, D., Palanque, P., Hamon, A., Della Pasqua, S.: Similarity as a design driver for user interfaces of dependable critical systems. In: Clemmensen, T., Rajamanickam, V., Dannenmann, P., Petrie, H., Winckler, M. (eds.) Global Thoughts, Local Designs. INTERACT 2017. LNCS, vol. 10774, pp. 114–122. Springer, Cham (2018). https://doi.org/10.1007/978-3-319-92081-8_11
30. Palanque, P., Schyn, A.: A model-based approach for engineering multimodal interactive. In: IFIP TC13 International Conference on Human-Computer Interaction (INTERACT 2003). IOS Press (2003)
31. Palanque, P.: POISE: a framework for designing perfect interactive systems with and for imperfect people. In: Ardito, C., et al. (eds.) INTERACT 2021. LNCS, vol. 12932, pp. 39–59. Springer, Cham (2021). https://doi.org/10.1007/978-3-030-85623-6_5

32. Pleuss, A., Wollny, S., Botterweck., G.: Model-driven development and evolution of customized user interfaces. In: Proceedings of the 5th ACM SIGCHI Symposium on Engineering Interactive Computing Systems. Association for Computing Machinery, London, United Kingdom, pp. 13–22 (2013)
33. Pleuss, A., Hauptmann, B., Dhungana, D., Botterweck, G.: User interface engineering for software product lines: the dilemma between automation and usability. In: Proceedings of the 4th ACM SIGCHI Symposium on Engineering Interactive Computing Systems. Association for Computing Machinery, Copenhagen, Denmark, pp 25–34 (2012)
34. Poskin., L., Vanderdonckt, J.: The Cameleon Reference Framework: A Systematic Mapping Study (2024). http://hdl.handle.net/2078.1/thesis:47354
35. Reason, J.: Human Error. Cambridge University Press (1990)
36. Sboui, T., Ben Ayed, M., Alimi, A.M.: A UI-DSPL approach for the development of context-adaptable user interfaces. IEEE Access. **6**, 7066–7081 (2018). https://doi.org/10.1109/ACCESS.2017.2782880
37. Steere, S., Julien, E., Manon, F.: The CDO: an innovative, flexible and modern operations Control Centre for Europe's spaceport, French Guiana: Ground system architecture, resilience & operational excellence. J. Space Saf. Eng. **11**(2), 301–310 (2024). https://doi.org/10.1016/j.jsse.2024.04.006
38. Vega-C launch vehicle webpage. https://cnes.fr/en/projects/vega-c. Accessed Dec 2024
39. Venn, J.: On the diagrammatic and mechanical representation of propositions and reasonings. Philos Mag J Sci. **9**, 1–18 (1880). https://doi.org/10.1080/14786448008626791
40. Vicente, K.J.: Cognitive Work Analysis: Toward Safe, Productive, and Healthy Computer-Based Work. CRC Press (1999)

# HCI in Formal and Inclusive Learning Contexts

# Designing from Within: HCI4D and PD4D in Sahrawi Refugee Camps

Daniel Cabezas[1(✉)], Enric Mor[1], José Luis Abdelnour-Nocera[2], and Clara Amorim[3]

[1] Universitat Oberta de Catalunya, Rambla del Poblenou, 154-156, 08018 Barcelona, Spain
dcabezasl@uoc.edu
[2] University of West London, St Mary's Road, London W5 5RF, UK
[3] Instituto Politécnico Viana do Castelo, Praça Gen. Barbosa 44, 4900-347 Viana do Castelo, Portugal

**Abstract.** This article presents preliminary findings from the second phase of a broader study exploring the potential of situated design and mobile learning (m-learning) in contexts of protracted displacement, through the case of the Sahrawi Refugee Camps (SRC) in Tindouf, Algeria. Drawing on a qualitative methodology based on contextual ethnography and co-design workshops, the study analyzes the structural, cultural, and gender-related conditions that shape the self-managed Sahrawi educational system, as well as the training needs of primary school teachers, particularly women. The article examines the methodological and socio-political implications of conducting fieldwork in an environment marked by technological precarity, traditional gender norms, and strong community ties. It discusses the challenges and lessons learned from implementing Human Computer Interaction for Development (HCI4D) and Participatory Design (PD) approaches, with special attention to the role of culture in politics in shaping collaborative processes. Ultimately, the article argues that ethnography and situated design provide a frameworks for co-creating culturally relevant and sustainable educational technologies in complex and marginalized contexts.

**Keywords:** HCI4D · PD · Ethnography · Western Sahara

## 1 Introduction

Despite global advances in access to education, learning poverty, defined as the inability to understand a simple text by age 10, continues to affect a significant proportion of children in developing countries [1]. According to the World Bank [2], over 70% of children in low- and middle-income countries fail to reach this basic literacy threshold, undermining their educational trajectories and perpetuating intergenerational inequalities. In response, mobile technologies have been proposed as an accessible and scalable solution to expand access to educational content and strengthen teacher training opportunities [3]. However, mobile learning faces technical, contextual, and pedagogical limitations, especially in remote areas where connectivity, digital literacy, technological sustainability, and cultural relevance remain persistent barriers [4].

This article is part of a broader study exploring the possibilities and tensions of m-learning in the continuing education of teachers in remote areas. The case study is located in the SRC in Tindouf, Algeria, one of the harshest regions in the Western Sahara desert, where over 50 years of displacement have created unique challenges for educational access, infrastructure, and continuity.

To address this complexity, our study draws on the situated design approach [5, 6], which recognizes that the practices and uses of technology are deeply shaped by the surrounding social, cultural, and historical context. Unlike universalist frameworks, situated design argues that technological solutions must emerge from within the environments in which they will be used, responding to local values, relationships, and knowledge systems.

In collaboration with teachers and inspectors, our study addresses two key questions: what role can situated design play in contexts of protracted displacement and limited educational infrastructure? and how can educational technologies be designed to respond both to contextual constraints and to teachers' aspirations?

Our research follows an research methodology structured in four phases: (1) a systematic literature review on m-learning in the Global South [7]; (2) an ethnographic study and co-creation workshops to identify challenges and opportunities (focus of this article); (3) a participatory design phase scheduled for November 2025; and (4) validation through user testing. This article presents preliminary findings from the second phase, based on qualitative fieldwork with a mixed-methods approach combining ethnographic techniques and participatory dynamics. The methodology included participant observation, semi-structured interviews, focus groups, user journey mapping, forms, and co-design sessions with local educators. The goal is to identify the cultural, social, and environmental factors that should be considered in the design of relevant, sustainable educational technologies. The following sections review the literature on m-learning in rural areas of the Global South, outline the study's methodology, present initial findings, and discuss implications for research in HCI4D and PD.

## 2 HCI4D and Mobile Learning in Rural Contexts

Over the past two decades, HCI4D has emerged as a key discipline for addressing challenges in structurally and technologically constrained settings, particularly in low and middle-income countries (LMICs) [8]. Within this field, education has become a central area of application, with growing interest in designing mobile learning (m-learning) solutions tailored to the realities of rural communities and educators working in resource-limited environments [9–13]. These initiatives aim not only to improve access to training and knowledge but also to promote participatory and sustainable approaches that reflect the concrete needs of end users [14].

In the first phase of our research, we conducted a systematic review using PRISMA guidelines, identifying 52 key studies published between 2014 and 2024 [7]. These works provide a detailed snapshot of the current state of mobile technology design for primary school teachers in rural LMICs. The review is structured around four core dimensions: research topics, geographic coverage, methodological approaches, and technologies used. Below we summarize the key outcomes of that review.

Over half of the reviewed studies focus on user acceptance of mobile learning, mainly using the Technology Acceptance Model (TAM), and on pedagogical strategies involving mobile technologies. Topics like usability, accessibility, and theoretical perspectives from HCI4D and participatory design are less common, while newer approaches such as AI, gamification, or extended reality are rarely addressed, especially in rural teacher training.

Research is geographically concentrated in Sub-Saharan Africa, with less attention to regions like North Africa, the Middle East, and Latin America—areas including the Sahrawi Refugee Camps (SRC) in Algeria, which remain largely overlooked despite their significance.

Most studies use quantitative methods, with fewer employing mixed or qualitative approaches. Although local context and user experience are acknowledged, participatory design is underutilized, and few m-learning platforms incorporate HCI or culturally adaptive frameworks. This highlights the need for more user-centered, context-sensitive designs, including AI integration through Learning Experience Projects (LXP). Our study addresses these gaps through ethnographic research and co-design with Sahrawi teachers, aiming to inform the creation of more just, adaptive, and culturally relevant educational technologies for local communities.

## 3 Methodology

This study took place in the Sahrawi Refugee Camps (SRC) in Tindouf, Algeria, where over 170,000 people live in displacement and teachers face challenges such as geographic isolation, limited technology, and harsh climate. To address the complex, resource-scarce, and self-managed educational context, researchers used a qualitative, mixed-methods approach combining contextual ethnography with co-design workshops, following PD and HCI4D principles. The main goal was to understand female teachers' training experiences and collaboratively identify key challenges to propose culturally relevant technological interventions. Fieldwork, conducted from March 1 to April 26, 2025, included classroom and community observations, interviews, focus groups, field diaries, and four co-design sessions with local teachers and inspectors. This article details the methods used and the methodological challenges encountered during this collaborative process.

The process was structured into two interrelated modules (see Fig. 1). The first focused on ethnographic analysis, centered on the functioning of the educational system and the cultural dynamics of teachers and inspectors. The second module consisted of co-design workshops, where collaborative interactions were used to identify needs and generate solution ideas.

## Phase 2: Discovering and Defining

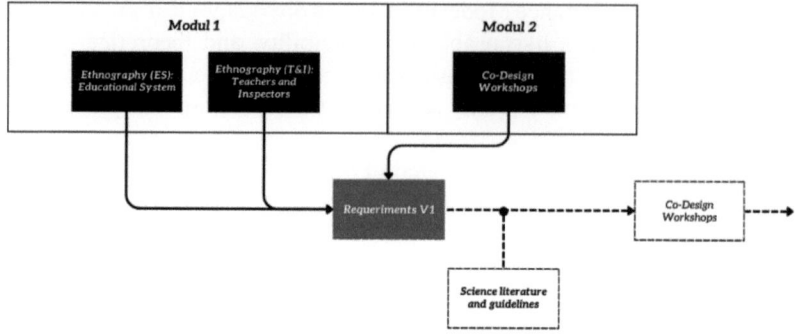

**Fig. 1.** Phase 2: Discovering and Defining

The ethnographic work was carried out primarily in the wilaya of Auserd through full immersion of the research team in the local educational environment. A total of 13 female teachers and 4 inspectors participated. This approach enabled observation of practices, values, and work dynamics through participant observation, interviews, focus groups, and contextual analysis.

Following Joshi et al. [15], ethnography is not merely a data collection technique, but an interpretative approach that reveals aspects of technology use and social relations that other methods may overlook. The study employed an analytical ethnography, focused on the situated knowledge that shapes everyday educational practices—an essential foundation for designing context-sensitive technologies.

The second module involved two co-design workshops held at the General Education Center in Auserd. These aimed to build a shared understanding of the challenges of teacher training. Participatory Design served as the guiding methodology, promoting collaboration between non-expert users and designers through reciprocal learning and democratic decision-making.

The workshops drew on the framework proposed by Bird et al. [16], which outlines a three-stage co-design methodology for complex social contexts: Pre-design (contextual research and participant preparation), Co-design (problem framing, idea generation, and solution visualization), and Post-design (data analysis and translation into technical requirements). This structure was adapted to fit the local environment.

The workshops pursued two operational goals: to analyze group dynamics in collaborative work and to collectively identify key challenges in continuing education. Initial ideas generated during the sessions served as a foundation for defining functional requirements for a future mobile learning application.

A total of 17 Sahrawi participants were involved: 13 female teachers (ages 18–40) and 4 inspectors (three men and one woman, aged 45–55). The teachers were all from Auserd, while the inspectors came from the four wilayas with primary education centers: Auserd, Cabo Bojador, El Aaiún, and Smara.

Auserd was selected as the main site due to its connection with the RASDELE [17] project by the University of Seville, which has supported Spanish language teacher training since 2023. This collaboration facilitated initial institutional and logistical contacts.

Additional local support for field preparation and meetings with educators was arranged through the University of Tifariti.

The research team chose to stay with local families rather than in the designated housing for international cooperants, which allowed for deeper immersion in Sahrawi daily life. Hospitality, a core element of local culture, enabled relationships of trust and community integration. Despite the economic hardship, teacher salaries are below €50 per month and paid quarterly, hosting cooperants provides families with a valuable source of supplementary income.

It is worth noting that fieldwork coincided with the month of Ramadan, which significantly reduced formal work activity. However, the general inspector of the wilaya arranged introductory meetings that enabled the research team to present the project, distribute informed consent forms, and recruit participants for the co-design sessions.

## 4 Ethnographic Findings and Co-design Sessions

Designing and implementing educational technologies in specific sociocultural settings requires not only technical considerations but also a deep understanding of social structures, cultural values, and local forms of knowledge. In this regard, a context-sensitive design approach is essential, arguing that technological solutions must be rooted in the social, political, and cultural realities of the environments where they are deployed [18]. This perspective is particularly relevant in collectivist communities such as the Sahrawi camps, where decision-making, cooperation, and social hierarchies are shaped by group affiliations.

### 4.1 Educational-Context Realities

Ethnography revealed a self-managed educational system marked by fragile infrastructure, scarce material and technological resources, and multiple structural weaknesses, despite a highly hierarchical organization. Responsibility for education falls mainly on women in a context where gender roles are sharply divided: men focus on securing economic resources, while women handle household management and family care. These divisions stem from entrenched patriarchal structures that limit women's public participation [19]. Economic precariousness, teacher salaries are under €50 a month, paid quarterly, imposes a double burden on female teachers: formal teaching and unpaid domestic labor. In low-income settings this feminization of teaching is often accompanied by social and economic devaluation of the profession [20]. Many women therefore leave teaching when they marry, pressured by social norms that reinforce domestic roles, a phenomenon described as "gendered dropout" [21]. High staff turnover brings in young, inexperienced women with limited subject mastery, destabilizing school staffing and lowering primary-level quality [22].

Although the Polisario Front's constitution formally abolished tribal structures to foster unity, tribal relationships persist, especially in the domestic sphere. This endurance operates within a strongly collectivist culture in which individuals maintain close interdependence with extended family, tribe, or daira, shaping behavior according to shared norms and expectations [23]. Group goals tend to prevail over individual interests, influencing educational dynamics, community participation, and leadership styles.

From an intercultural standpoint, education and technological development must be approached with epistemological, political, and cultural sensitivity. Interculturality, understood as a symmetrical dialogue of knowledge [24], demands that local cultural frameworks become constitutive elements of design. This shifts the focus from user-centered to situated design, recognizing culture as an active system of meaning and promoting deep collaboration with local actors to define problems and co-create solutions [25, 26].

For Sahrawi teachers, this approach recognizes how local gender roles, community, and teaching practices shape technology use, and promotes intercultural co-design over imposing external models.

### 4.2 Insights from the Co-design Workshops

The workshops featured two methodological components. The first two sessions used group dynamics organized into three structures: (1) Mixed groups of female teachers and inspectors (men and women), (2) Role-segregated groups, one of teachers (all women) and one of inspectors (mixed-gender). (3) Gender-segregated groups, composed exclusively of men or women. These configurations allowed exploration of how power, gender, and professional role shaped interaction and emergent content.

The third and fourth sessions focused on individual contributions moderated by a researcher, capturing perspectives free from group pressure. Each session ended with individual self-assessments and group reflections to review functioning, dialogue quality, and participation, fostering metacognition and methodological adjustment.

Distinct patterns emerged. In mixed groups, senior men assumed leadership without consensus, monopolizing discussion, interrupting female colleagues, and delegitimizing other voices, behavior replicated in the inspector group, where women were virtually silent. In contrast, the all-women teacher group showed no explicit leadership; dialogue was horizontal, encouraging collaboration and mutual respect.

Gender-segregated sessions sharpened these contrasts [27, 28]. The women's group chose no formal leader; discussion was balanced, and the spokesperson was selected by consensus for her ability to articulate collective ideas, evidence of distributed leadership aligned with horizontal approaches [29]. In the men's group the highest-ranking participant again self-appointed as leader, though dialogue was more open and peer opinions better accepted than in mixed groups.

These observations mirror well-documented patterns of informal leadership, gender, and participation. In hierarchical, patriarchal contexts, leadership is typically claimed by those with greater symbolic capital, perpetuating female exclusion [30]. Conversely, non-hierarchical or women-only settings foster collaborative practices that enhance inclusion and active participation.

Such findings have sociocultural value and provide crucial input for participatory technology design. Understanding how gender and hierarchy shape interaction enables adaptation of co-design methodologies to create more inclusive environments where historically marginalized voices, such as female teachers, actively influence decision-making and the development of contextualized technological solutions (Table 1).

**Table 1.** Comparison of Dynamics According to Group Configuration

| Group Configuration | Leadership Dynamics | Female Participation | Discussion Style |
|---|---|---|---|
| Mixed (Inspectors and Teachers) | Leadership automatically assumed by highest-ranking men | Strongly inhibited; female opinions ignored or dismissed | Directive, hierarchical, with frequent interruptions |
| Hierarchical – Inspectors (Mixed) | Men lead without consensus; female inspectors do not participate | Silenced; women have no active voice in the discussion | Authoritarian, centered on male figures |
| Hierarchical – Teachers (Women Only) | No explicit leadership; equitable dialogue | Active and horizontal | Egalitarian, with balanced speaking time |
| Gender-Segregated – Women | No leader designated; spokesperson chosen by consensus | Free and collaborative participation | Fluid, open, without dominant voices |
| Gender-Segregated – Men | Leadership self-assumed by highest-ranking member, though peers are heard | Not applicable (men-only group) | Moderately hierarchical, but with accepted dialogue |

In sessions three and four, moderated by a research-team member, self-appointed leadership declined markedly. The moderator's presence balanced participation, although some higher-status participants still sought authoritative positions. Self-evaluations showed positive evolution: most participants engaged more equitably and increasingly acknowledged weaknesses that, through mutual support, became strengths. In contrast, unilateral leaders tended to avoid responsibility, blaming external factors for shortcomings.

## 5 Discussion: Power, Culture, and Collaboration in Co-design Processes

The ethnographic and workshop results indicate that designing educational technologies in protracted displacement contexts must be sensitive to the social, symbolic, and cultural fabrics structuring daily life. From a situated-design perspective [28, 31], knowledge is neither transferable in the abstract nor universalizable; it is deeply anchored in local practices, values, and relationships. Recent work reinforces this view, emphasizing that co-design approaches in such settings must account for the power dynamics that mediate speech, knowledge, and legitimacy. Continuous-training technologies cannot be dissociated from these dynamics and must be developed through participatory methods that reflect the lived experiences of displaced communities.

Ethnography exposed a self-managed education system constrained by structural limitations, resource scarcity, and economic precarity. Women teachers, facing a dual workload (teaching and domestic duties), low professional status, and sociocultural pressure to leave teaching after marriage, are particularly affected. Informal power structures, tribal and gender hierarchies, determine who may speak, decide, or lead, re-emerging during workshops, especially in hierarchical or mixed configurations.

Interaction analysis showed senior men automatically assuming leadership and silencing women, even in participatory settings, an expression of Bourdieu's symbolic violence. By contrast, women-only groups created horizontal dialogue, effective collaboration, and leadership distributed through mutual recognition.

These findings call into question the actual inclusivity of participatory processes. While co-design is promoted as democratizing [32], workshops reveal that symbolic exclusions persist unless dominant structures are actively challenged. As Winschiers-Theophilus et al. [33] argue, participation alone does not guarantee equity; power asymmetries are often reproduced within co-design settings unless deliberately addressed. External moderation in later sessions was crucial for redistributing speaking time and fostering more equitable reflection, yet some participants continued asserting authority, evidencing entrenched hierarchies.

Self-evaluations were valuable for fostering group reflexivity. Most participants improved in collaboration and recognition of weaknesses, converted into strengths through peer support, whereas unilateral leaders tended to shirk responsibility, attributing failures to external factors. This contrast underscores the need for methods that not only capture local voices but also transform power relations and representation.

In sum, designing educational technologies for the SRC cannot be reduced to technical concerns. It requires a situated, intersectional, and critical approach that accounts for historical, social, and gendered conditions shaping life and knowledge. Co-design methodologies must adapt to physical as well as symbolic, relational, and political contexts to produce truly inclusive, relevant, and sustainable educational solutions.

## 6 Conclusions and Future Work

This study reveals that designing educational technologies in protracted displacement settings requires deep sensitivity to local social, cultural, and political realities [18]. In the Sahrawi camps, fragile infrastructure and entrenched gender roles place a heavy burden on women teachers, affecting education quality and staff retention [19].

Co-design workshops showed that male-dominated leadership and power hierarchies often silence women in mixed groups, while women-only groups foster more collaborative and inclusive dialogue. External moderation and self-reflection helped balance participation but did not fully eliminate entrenched authority [32, 34].

Methodologically, combining ethnography with co-design highlighted how knowledge and legitimacy are rooted in local practices and power dynamics [28, 31]. Future phases will co-develop a mobile app, explore hybrid learning, and evaluate inclusion in participatory design, aiming to create educational technologies that empower marginalized voices and transform power relations in displacement contexts.

## References

1. How to tackle Learning Poverty? Delivering education's promise to children across the world. World Bank Blogs. https://blogs.worldbank.org/en/education/how-tackle-learning-poverty-delivering-educations-promise-children-across-world. Accessed 10 Apr 2024
2. The State of Global Learning Poverty: 2022 Update. World Bank. https://www.worldbank.org/en/topic/education/publication/state-of-global-learning-poverty. Accessed 10 Apr 2024
3. Varanasi, R.A., Vashistha, A., Parikh, T., Dell, N.: Challenges and issues integrating smartphones into teacher support programs in India. In: Proceedings 2020 … (2020). https://doi.org/10.1145/3392561.3394638
4. Whale, A.M., Scholtz, B.M., Calitz, A.P.: Components of e-learning for enterprise systems' education in developing countries. In: Proceedings of the 9th IDIA Conference. Citeseer (2015). https://citeseerx.ist.psu.edu/document?repid=rep1&type=pdf&doi=f90cf502bbec835313437cde33425da05bf78dd7
5. Situated Design Methods, MIT Press. https://mitpress.mit.edu/9780262544726/situated-design-methods/. Access 20 Jun 2025
6. Cronholm, S., Neubauer, M., Stary, C.: Guiding situated method transfer in design and evaluation. Univers. Access Inf. Soc. 14(2), pp. 151–168, jun. 2015, https://doi.org/10.1007/s10209-013-0336-x
7. Cabezas-López, D., Mor-Pera, E., Abdelnour-Nocera, J.L., Clara Figueiredo Amorim, M.: Culture. Conference on Interaction Design and International Development, Mumbai, India • November 7–9, 2024, Revised Selected Papers. IFIP Advances in Information and Communication Technology, vol. 727, Springer, Cham (2024)
8. Abdelnour-Nocera, J., Densmore, M.: A review of perspectives and challenges for international development in information and communication technologies. Ann. Int. Commun. Assoc. **41**(3–4), 250–257 (2017). https://doi.org/10.1080/23808985.2017.1392252
9. Abachi, H.R., Muhammad, G.: The impact of m-learning technology on students and educators. Comput. Hum. Behav. **30**, 491–496 (2014). https://doi.org/10.1016/j.chb.2013.06.018
10. Ahmadi, A.R., Paracha, S., Sokout, H., et al.: Mobile mediated learning and teachers education in less resourced region. International Journal of …. academia.edu (2015). https://www.academia.edu/download/92304094/10000487.pdf
11. Akurigo, M.A.: The use of mobile phone technology as an instructional tool for lesson delivery at abura Asebu Kwamankese District. ir.ucc.edu.gh (2019). https://ir.ucc.edu.gh/xmlui/handle/123456789/4270
12. Erasmus, R.: A framework for designing South African mobile learning experiences through a participatory design process. scholar.sun.ac.za (2022). https://scholar.sun.ac.za/handle/10019.1/124819
13. Nicholson, R., Strachan, R., Dele-Ajayi, O., Fasae, K.: Emergency remote education in nigeria: challenges and design opportunities. In: Proceedings of the 2024 CHI Conference on Human Factors in Computing Systems, en CHI '24. New York, NY, USA, pp. 1–14. Association for Computing Machinery (2024). https://doi.org/10.1145/3613904.3641921
14. Muhammad, G.: Challenges in development of eLearning systems in higher education of the developing countries. London Journal of Research in Humanities …. journalspress.com (2017). https://journalspress.com/LJRHSS_Volume17/142_Challenges-in-Development-of-eLearning-Systems-in-Higher-Education-of-the-Developing-Countries.pdf
15. Joshi, T., Biggs, H., Bardzell, J., Bardzell, S.: Who is 'I'?: Subjectivity and Ethnography in HCI. In: Proceedings of the 2024 CHI Conference on Human Factors in Computing Systems, en CHI '24. New York, NY, USA, pp. 1–15. Association for Computing Machinery (2024). https://doi.org/10.1145/3613904.3642727

16. Bird, M., et al.: A generative co-design framework for healthcare innovation: development and application of an end-user engagement framework. Res. Involv. Engagem. **7**(1), 12 (2021). https://doi.org/10.1186/s40900-021-00252-7
17. III Curso de Formación y Sensibilización para la cooperación al desarrollo: enseñanza de español en los campamentos de refugiados saharauis | Universidad de Sevilla. https://www.us.es/eventos/agenda/iii-curso-de-formacion-y-sensibilizacion-para-la-cooperacion-al-desarrollo-ensenanza. Accessed 20 Jun 2025
18. Oyugi, C., Abdelnour-Nocera, J., Clemmensen, T.: Harambee: a novel usability evaluation method for low-end users in Kenya. In: Proceedings of the 8th Nordic Conference on Human-Computer Interaction: Fun, Fast, Foundational, en NordiCHI '14. New York, NY, USA, pp. 179–188. Association for Computing Machinery, (2014). https://doi.org/10.1145/2639189.2639227
19. Roy, A.: Gender, Sexuality, Decolonization: South Asia in the World Perspective. Oxford, UNITED KINGDOM: Taylor & Francis Group (2020). [Online]. http://ebookcentral.proquest.com/lib/bibliouocsp-ebooks/detail.action?docID=6419124. Accessed 19 May 2025
20. Kabeer, N.: Gender, schooling and global social justice. Comput. Educ. **47**(2), 283–284 (2011). https://doi.org/10.1080/03050068.2011.555142
21. Dunne, M.: Beyond access: transforming policy and practice for gender equality in education. Comput. J. Comp. Int. Educ. **38**(5), 643–645 (2008). https://doi.org/10.1080/03057920802351499
22. Tikly, L.: Towards a framework for researching the quality of education in low-income countries. Comp. Educ. **47**(1), 1–23 (2011). https://doi.org/10.1080/03050068.2011.541671
23. Cheng, A., et al.: Individualism vs. Collectivism, pp. 287–297 (2020). https://doi.org/10.1002/9781119547181.ch313
24. Moreno, Ó.J.C.: Consideraciones sobre educación, interculturalidad y la perspectiva decolonial. Rev. Investig. UNAD **9**(1), 217 (2010). https://doi.org/10.22490/25391887.661
25. Proceedings of the 14th Participatory Design Conference: Short Papers, Interactive Exhibitions, Workshops - Volume 2, vol. 2. New York, NY, USA: Association for Computing Machinery (2016)
26. Suchman, L.: Located accountabilities in technology production. Scand. J. Inf. Syst. **14**(2) (2002). https://www.proquest.com/docview/2632386451/abstract/213884F453E343A8PQ/1. Accessed 19 May 2025
27. Balka, E.: Participatory design in women's organizations: the social world of organizational structure and the gendered nature of expertise. Gend. Work Organ. **4**(2), 99–115 (1997). https://doi.org/10.1111/1468-0432.00027
28. Taylor, H., Williamson, S.: Co-design to evaluate the impact of gender equality initiatives: lessons for practitioners, evaluators and researchers. Qual. Rep. **29**(7), 2067–2088 (2024). https://doi.org/10.46743/2160-3715/2024.6779
29. Creating Leaderful Organizations: How to Bring Out Leadership in Everyone | Request PDF», ResearchGate. https://www.researchgate.net/publication/278100196_Creating_Leaderful_Organizations_How_to_Bring_Out_Leadership_in_Everyone. Access: 19 May 2025
30. Acuña Ferreira, V.: Gendered talk at work. Constructing gender identity through workplace discourse. Janet Holmes (2006). Socioling. Stud. **3** (2009). https://doi.org/10.1558/sols.v3i1.115
31. Dourish, P.: What we talk about when we talk about context. Pers. Ubiquitous Comput. **8**(1), 19–30 (2004). https://doi.org/10.1007/s00779-003-0253-8
32. Urbaniak, A., Wanka, A. (eds.): Routledge International Handbook of Participatory Approaches in Ageing Research. Routledge, London (2023). https://doi.org/10.4324/9781003254829

33. Winschiers-Theophilus, H., Chivuno-Kuria, S., Kapuire, G.K., Bidwell, N.J., Blake, E.: Being participated: a community approach. In: Proceedings of the 11th Biennial Participatory Design Conference, en PDC '10. New York, NY, USA, pp. 1–10. Association for Computing Machinery (2010). https://doi.org/10.1145/1900441.1900443
34. Nunes, F., et al.: African co-design: past, present, and emerging. In: Proceedings of the 4th African Human Computer Interaction Conference, en AfriCHI '23. New York, NY, USA: Association for Computing Machinery, ene. 2024, pp. 316–318 (2024). https://doi.org/10.1145/3628096.3629080

# From Design to Evaluation: A Case Study on Learner Experience

Deivid Silva[1]([✉]), Tayna Conte[2], Guilherme Guerino[3], and Natasha M. C. Valentim[4]

[1] Federal University of Western Pará (UFOPA), Oriximinrá, Brazil
deivid.silva@ufopa.edu.br
[2] Federal University of Amazonas (UFAM), Manaus, Brazil
tayana@icomp.ufam.edu.br
[3] State University of Paraná (UNESPAR), Apucarana, Brazil
guilherme.guerino@ies.unespar.edu.br
[4] Federal University of Paraná (UFPR), Curitiba, Brazil
natasha@inf.ufpr.br

**Abstract.** Learner Experience (LX) focuses on learners' perceptions and responses when using computational resources in education. To support teachers (or others designers) in LX design and evaluation, we proposed the LEDEF conceptual framework. This paper presents a case study evaluating LEDEF's applicability, including its design guidelines and evaluation model, in a real learning context. Learners and a teacher at a Brazilian university participated in this study. The teacher, responsible for designing and redesigning the activity, assessed the entire LX process. Results were analyzed quantitatively and qualitatively. The findings indicate that interactions with computational resources were positive, enhancing efficiency and satisfaction. However, social interactions presented challenges—even in a setting where learners felt comfortable with technology, interpersonal skills and communication difficulties negatively impacted their experience. LEDEF allowed the teacher to identify these aspects and implement small interventions throughout the learning process. This study highlights how LEDEF supports iterative LX design, evaluation, and redesign, addressing both technological and social dimensions of learning experiences.

**Keywords:** Learner eXperience · LX Evaluation · LX design

## 1 Introduction

The concept of Learner eXperience (LX) can be understood as learners' perceptions and responses when participating in activities with computational resources [7,9,14], extending the concept of User Experience (UX) to the educational context [7]. The literature defines UX as the preferences, perceptions, emotions, and physical and psychological responses of the user that occur before, during, and after use [3]. Thus, LX and UX are two concepts related to the quality of the experience an individual has when interacting with computational resources.

Similar to UX, LX comprises elements that refer to the components that guide the design and evaluation of LX, allowing for the inclusion and verification of experience characteristics, including feelings and emotions in learning. Within the stages of the LX life cycle, a greater emphasis was noted on the design and evaluation phases, which are believed to be the most critical, because directly impacting the quality of the educational experience. For example, the study by Arachchi et al. [1] showed that LX design can have a positive impact on usability, accessibility and learning, elements that influence educational experiences. Furthermore, Magyar and Haley [11] demonstrated that evaluation contributes to identifying and correcting LX design problems, preventing them from negatively impacting learners.

From this perspective, the LEDEF conceptual framework was proposed, which LX design and evaluation. According to Pawson and Tilley [13], a conceptual framework is a guide for action that directs decision-making and the implementation of interventions in different contexts. It provides principles and guidelines for professional practice, promoting coherence and effectiveness in actions. LEDEF is composed of two technologies, one entitled LEDG design guidelines and the other LEEM evaluation model. To evaluate LX in a real context using LEDEF, a case study was carried out. The research question of this study is: "Does LEDEF support the design and evaluation, and improvement of LX during a real educational activity using computational resource?".

Nineteen learners and one teacher from the first period of the Algorithms and Programming Techniques course in Computer Science of State University of Paraná (UNESPAR) in Brazil participated in this study. The teacher was selected for convenience, and the choice of class and course was under his responsibility. The teacher designed an educational activity using LEDG to support programming instruction, incorporating computational resources suggested by the framework, such as Notion (for organizing and submitting reports) and PowerPoint, Prezi, Google Slides, or Genially (for presentations). Additionally, tools already used in the course, including Code::Blocks, Visual Studio Code, Dev-C++, and the BeeCrowd platform, were also employed. The teacher received guidance on using the framework but had the freedom to make his own choices, including the design of the activity. Moreover, he filled out one of the checklists. The learners answered the checklists and set of open questions of LEEM. These data were analyzed quantitatively and qualitatively.

Overall, the case study presented in this paper contributes to the field of Human-Computer Interaction (HCI) by examining an educational activity situated within a specific context that has clear objectives, involves social interactions, and leverages computational resources. Grounded in Activity Theory [2], this study highlights that computational resources not only facilitate the development of the LX but also shape how tasks are perceived and executed. A key contribution of this study is the application of our conceptual framework, LEDEF, which explicitly addresses elements of the LX and provides a structured process for designing, evaluating, and refining educational activities. LEDEF grants teachers greater flexibility in selecting the LX components while offering a well-defined workflow with steps, goals, and artifacts that can be tailored to the educational context.

From an HCI perspective, this study benefits multiple stakeholders. For researchers, it introduces a structured approach that supports the design and evaluation of educational interactions-centered activities while providing mechanisms for evaluating LX effectiveness and satisfaction. For educators, LEDEF serves as a practical tool that helps in designing, evaluating, and refining educational activities, ensuring they align with learners' needs. Finally, for educational technology developers, the study offers insights into the design of user-centered solutions by framing the educational process within HCI principles, promoting the development of computational resources that seamlessly integrate into teaching and learning practices.

## 2 Related Work

Despite the importance of discussing LX, finding works that provide clear concepts and definitions on the topic, along with well-defined elements to be explored, remains a challenge. Based on the Systematic Mapping Studies (SMSs) used as the foundation for this research [15,16], three studies were selected for the following reasons: they (a) address both LX design and evaluation; (b) present an approach oriented toward LX elements; and (c) use computational resources as mediators of the experience.

Donelan and Kear [5] present an online group project with undergraduate learners who collaborated online to create a wiki resource on a website. The project was organized into three parts: collaboration (how learners will interact with each other), task (what learners will have to do and produce), and assessment (how to collect learner feedback and assign grades). The project lasted three weeks. Learners worked in groups of five to eight participants. After completing their tasks, learners participated in online focus groups. In qualitative analysis, it was identified that 17 learners commented on positive feelings, and five learners mentioned negative feelings. Comments related to Pleasure and Reward were fairly equivalent to those related to the collaboration process and website development task. Moreover, comments related to challenge were about collaboration, while most comments about Frustration referred to the task itself.

In the study by Papavlasopoulo et al. [12], an intervention design was developed in cycles over two years. LX design aimed to support programming workshops. Task adjustments were made to ensure suitability, including 1) an initial activity and an inspiring introduction, 2) exploration/project, 3) construction/creation of the digital artifact, and 4) evaluation/peer feedback, all done in collaboration with team members and with the support of assistants/instructors. Qualitative and quantitative data were collected during the three cycles, using various instruments, including pre- and post-knowledge acquisition tests, attitude questionnaires, eye-tracking data, semi-structured interviews, observation notes, instructor reflections, and artifacts built by learners at different stages of the process.

Zhang et al. [18] introduced a cross-stitch experiential learning model based on digital games. The LX included four distinct stages: (1) Introduction; (2) Distribution of cross-stitch materials; (3) Practical demonstration of skills, thread counting, and basic stitches; and (4) Practice time for learners. Learners were also invited to self-assess at each stage of the activity, rating Affinity, Challenge, and Frustration aspects with up to 5 stars. Additionally, a study was conducted, dividing learners into two groups, both composed of one teacher, one observer, and five learners. One group underwent the traditional cross-stitch method (Group A), while the other used a digital game (Group B). The results revealed differences between the two groups, with Group B demonstrating greater interest and engagement due to the use of the digital game, which also served as a tool to address difficulties and as a reference for learners.

Based on these studies, gaps are highlighted. Donelan and Kear [5] advocate for more personalized approaches to meet individual learner needs, noting that more experienced learners tended to express more complaints about activities, while less experienced learners found the task rewarding and conducive to learning new skills. Additionally, Papavlasopoulo et al. [12] underscore the importance of employing diverse methods to collect experiences during activities, stressing that only observations may not accurately identify programming concept learning. Finally, Zhang et al. [18] emphasize the significance of collaborating with more experienced participants in activities, highlighting that inviting skilled people could facilitate the identification of issues and aid struggling learners.

Our framework, LEDEF, not only explicitly addresses key elements of the LX, but also provides a set of LX elements, giving teachers greater flexibility in selecting which components to include in their activities. It offers a well-structured process with steps, goals, and artifacts that can be tailored to specific contexts and needs, allowing teachers to have a guided and organized path throughout the learning journey. LEDEF supports teachers to create, evaluate and adjust their activities using computational resources to meet the unique needs of their classes, while also enabling them to evaluate and refine the LX from multiple perspectives throughout its lifecycle. As no existing technology in the literature was found to encompass these characteristics, the LEDEF conceptual framework was proposed to fill this gap.

## 3 LEDEF Conceptual Framework

LEDEF conceptual framework is composed of two LX technologies, the LEDG design guidelines[1] and the LEEM evaluation model[2]. Therefore, LEDEF provides a complete cycle of LX, allowing visualization of both what is proposed activity and what is actually experienced by learners, experiences that can directly impact the learning process. The LEDEF can help identify strengths and areas

---

[1] Available at: https://sites.google.com/view/lexdg/home.
[2] Available at: https://doi.org/10.6084/m9.figshare.27146775.v1.

for improvement related to LX, enabling the redesign of activities using computational resources. As it deals with educational experiences, LEDEF can be used by all those interested in LX, such as educators, instructional designers, and developers of educational resources and materials. The LEDEF meet the following requirements: (1) Applicable to Higher Education: because the use of resources requires a certain level of learner maturity. Furthermore, the framework was developed and validated through studies conducted in this context [15,16]; (2) Possibility of Choosing LX Elements: A set of elements is provided that have been mapped and related so that the teacher can select and work on the design and evaluation of LX, with a focus on elements of LX, such as Value, Usability, Adaptability, Desirability, and Comfortability; and (3) Possibility of Choosing Computational Resources: A set of 75 tools has been compiled and categorized for use in educational experiences, as recommended by the guidelines.

It is worth noting that the technologies comprising the LEDEF can be used independently. Thus, a teacher interested in evaluating LX in their educational activities may choose to use only the LEEM. However, if the goal is also to create activities based on LX, the LEDG can be used to guide the design. Figure 1 illustrates LEDEF, considering an educational activity from beginning, where the teacher navigates and makes decisions, incorporating computational resources into their activity to provide an engaging LX. LEDEF consists of four stages (planning, design, application, and evaluation), organized into nine activities presented below.

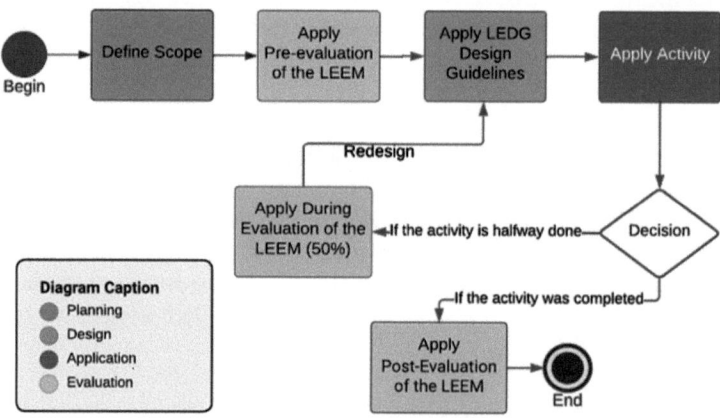

**Fig. 1.** LEDEF Conceptual Framework

In LEDEF, the teacher begins by defining the scope of the educational activity, including the focus of their discipline, the time and number of classes, the content to be covered, the participating classes, and the environment where the activity will take place, among other aspects. To better understand the learners, their difficulties, and learning preferences, the teacher administers the LEEM's pre-evaluation questionnaire. Subsequently, the teacher accesses guidelines to prepare their activity with computational resources. It is suggested that he/she uses the data collected from the pre-evaluation to guide them in choosing the LEDG guidelines [17], thus being able to apply them to define the educational activity, select the computational resource, and determine the necessary support materials. Next, the teacher implements the activity in the classroom, presenting it to the learners and providing all necessary guidance. LEDEF reserves a specific moment for LX, during which learners can actively participate and have learning experiences. When learners reach 50% of the proposed activity, the teacher conducts the during evaluation of LEEM to monitor the progress, identify any difficulties related to the activity, and use the evaluation checklist to keep a record of these experiences. If necessary, the teacher can redesign their activities to seek a more satisfactory LX in the remaining 50% of the activity. LEDEF concludes with the post-evaluation of LEEM, in which learners reflect on and share their educational experiences, participating in activities with computational resources.

LEDEF seeks to be flexible regarding this set of artifacts. Thus, the following conditions are presented: if the teacher already has the activity ready, they can use only the post-evaluation of LEEM to collect educational experiences; if the teacher already has the activity defined but does not consider it satisfactory, they can administer the during evaluation of LEEM and the guidelines of LEDG to redesign it; if they wish to make a preliminary adaptation to their activity before presenting it to the learners, they can apply only the pre-evaluation and the guidelines of LEDG; finally, if the teacher already has a ready LX evaluation process, they can use only the guidelines of LEDG to define the activity, the computational resource, and the support materials. In summary, LEDEF seeks to offer the teacher options to adapt the activity according to the needs of the learners and educational situations. Additionally, it allows for the inclusion of new guidelines and technologies as experiences are gained, offering a dynamism that can further enrich the framework and keep it relevant throughout the educational activity.

## 4 Case Study

The goal of this case study was to design and evaluate the LX and identify potential improvements through the application of the LEDEF. The study received approval from the research ethics committee at the Federal University of Paraná (UFPR) under Certificate of Presentation of Ethical Appreciation: 77365824.4.3001.9247.

**Population.** The LEDEF case study was conducted with 19 learners enrolled in the Computer Science course, specifically those attending the Algorithms and Programming Techniques class at UNESPAR, along with the course teacher. The teacher was selected for convenience and then invited to participate in the study via email, where the research guidelines were provided. After voluntarily agreeing to participate, the teacher collaborated with the researchers to extend the invitation to the learners during an in-person class session. The purpose of the study was clearly explained to the learners, and those interested were introduced to the data collection instrument by the teacher. Learners who expressed a willingness to participate were then included in the study. Characterization data of the teacher and learners can be found in Sect. 5. The study was conducted with a first-year class, focusing on the topic of recursion and recursive functions. Classes were held on Tuesdays, both in the morning and afternoon sessions.

**Context.** The goal of the practical activity carried out by the teacher was to explore the concept of recursion and the implementation of recursive functions in order to gain both practical and theoretical understanding of the topic. The educational activity was conducted collaboratively in groups of three or four learners. The groups were required to submit two deliverables: (1) Report: with a link to the detailed document on Notion, and (2) Presentation: to be prepared using one of the following tools: PowerPoint, Prezi, Google Slides, or Genially, summarizing the key points from the report (tools suggested by LEDG). The deliverables generated during the activity had to follow this structure: a) Introduction to the Topic: Definition of recursion, Explanation of recursive functions, Importance and applications of recursion in computing; b) Explained Examples of Recursive Functions, where i) each example must include: Code of the recursive function, Detailed explanation of how the recursive process works; ii) Suggested examples (choose at least 3): Factorial of a number, Fibonacci sequence, Recursive sum, Binary search, Exponentiation, Tower of Hanoi; and c) Advantages and Disadvantages of Recursion. The activity evaluation was based on the clarity of concept explanations, correctness of examples, quality of the Notion report and presentation, as well as the group's cohesion during the work. The activity lasted three weeks. The first week was dedicated to the initiation and practical execution of the coding activity. The second week was focused on completing the activity and submitting the report on Notion. During the third week, group presentations were held, with each group having a maximum of 30 min to present their findings. The data collection period took place from September 17, 2024, to October 1, 2024.

**Instruments and Procedure.** For this case study, if they agree to participate in the study, the teacher and learners signed the Informed Consent Form (ICF). Once the ICF is signed, all participants completed the characterization questionnaire, which collected demographic data for research purposes and was accessible only to the researchers. To help the teacher better understand the learners' prior experiences with computational resources, and design an activity more aligned with their needs, learners completed the Pre-Evaluation Questionnaire, which focused on LX and was available exclusively to the teacher. Following this, the teacher reviewed the learners' responses and use this information, along with the LEDG guidelines, to design a practical activity related to the Algorithms and Programming Techniques course. The guidelines followed by the teacher were: (G3: Allow learners to choose their learning space and timing; G5: Encourage learners to express themselves and ask questions; G9: Give learners the freedom to make choices; G20: Apply content to learner' daily lives; G21: Promote the exchange of experiences and knowledge). Although some guidelines can be followed in educational contexts without the use of computational resources, the content of each was designed to guide educators and structure activities for resource utilization. After this preparation, the teacher guided the learners through the practical activity, providing all necessary instructions. When the learners have completed approximately 50% of the practical work, the teacher asked them to complete the During-Activity Evaluation Questionnaire (Learners) to assess their experiences up to that point. The decision to apply the evaluation at 50% of the activity was based on two reasons: (1) to identify potential difficulties and make adjustments before the activity's completion, and (2) to reduce the need for daily evaluations in longer activities, considering the teacher's workload both inside and outside the classroom. Additionally, the teacher provided their own observations in the During-Activity Evaluation Questionnaire (Teacher). Upon completion of the practical activity, the teacher conducted a focus group where learners were encouraged, if they feel comfortable, to respond to a set of questions about their learning experiences.

**Data Analysis.** The data collected through the mentioned instruments were analyzed both quantitatively and qualitatively. For the quantitative analysis, descriptive statistics were employed using Excel, focusing on participants' responses to word pairs, the Self-Assessment Manikin (SAM), and Likert scales used during the LEEM pre-evaluation and during-evaluation stages. For the qualitative analysis, a thematic analysis was conducted using Atlas.ti [4], which allowed for the identification of patterns and emerging themes in the data. The analysis process included steps such as data familiarization, generation of initial codes, identification of potential categories, and refinement of these categories.

## 5 Results

**Learners Characterization:** In terms of gender, 68.4% (N = 13) of the learners are male, while 31.6% (N = 6) are female. Regarding age, 89.5% (N = 17) of the learners are between 17 and 19 years old, and 10.5% (N = 2) are between 20 and 30 years old. As for whether LX is evaluated in any course, 94.7% (N = 18) of the learners respond "no" while 5.3% (N = 1) answers "yes". This learner mentions that LX is evaluated in another course through a brief test.

**Teacher Characterization:** The teacher is male, aged between 20 and 30, and holds a PhD in Computer Science. Since the beginning of his teaching career, he consistently integrates various resources to support teaching and learning, including Mentimeter, WhatsApp, Moodle, Trello, Lucidchart, and Google tools. When asked if he evaluates LX in any of his courses, the teacher confirms that he does, though not systematically using specific LX elements. Instead, he evaluates the overall course experience using Google Forms. The results from the LEEM checklists and his experience with LEDG will be discussed below.

**The LEEM Pre-evaluation Checklist** consists of 12 statements with opposing word pairs. For analysis, responses to these statements were rated on a five-point scale, ranging from 1 to 5, positioned between the word pairs. The results of this pre-evaluation reveal insights into learner behavior and preferences. For the word pair "individual or in a group", 36.1% (N = 7) of learners provided a neutral response (3), indicating no strong preference. However, for the word pair "participative or shy" 47.4% (N = 9) of learners responded with a 4, leaning towards the "shy" side. In terms of engagement, 42.1% (N = 8) of learners indicated they prefer to "act rather than react" during activity. Additionally, 47.4% (N = 9) expressed a preference for practical work over theoretical tasks. Further results show that for the word pair "contribute or not impact" an overwhelming 89.5% (N = 17) of learners believe that computational resources contribute to their learning. Similarly, in the word pair "motivated or unmotivated", 89.5% (N = 17) indicated feeling motivated when using such resources. This suggests that learners largely recognize the potential of these tools to foster motivation, engagement, and meaningful learning experiences. Moreover, regarding the word pair "ease or difficulty", only 5.3% (N = 1) reported having difficulty in using computational resources. This likely reflects their familiarity with digital tools, considering they are part of a generation of digital natives who often have a high level of comfort with technology. The characterization data further supports this, showing that at least 7 participants use digital resources for more than 4 h per day. Finally, for the word pair "at home or college", 84.2% (N = 16) of learners expressed a preference for using resources at home. This may be attributed to the comfort and sense of security associated with a familiar environment, particularly since a significant portion of the class identified themselves as shy. These characteristics offer insight for educators. By identifying learners' tendencies, teachers can better observe group dynamics and provide targeted support to enhance their experience. Alternatively, this information can be used to create balanced groups, ensuring, for example, that shy learners are not all placed together, which may hinder their participation.

The **during-evaluation checklist (learner)** includes questions from Q1 to Q7 (Fig. 2) using a 9-point SAM scale, and questions from Q8 to Q23 (Fig. 3) using a 5-point Likert scale. For better visualization of the SAM scale results, the responses were categorized into three groups: sad responses (scores 1 to 3, on the left of the central column), neutral responses (scores 4 to 6, in the central column), and happy responses (scores 7 to 9, on the right). This simplified categorization was chosen to make the results more accessible and easier for teachers to interpret and use in their practice. The results of the SAM scale (Fig. 2) reveal that 15.8% (N = 3) of learners indicated feeling sad when asked how they felt emotionally on the day they completed the checklist (Q1). Conversely, 36.9% (N = 7) of learners reported feeling happy on the day they answered the checklist. Regarding how learners felt when seeking support material (Q5), only 5.3% (N = 1) indicated sadness. This is notable, as 36.9% of the class had previously indicated a preference for working individually in the pre-evaluation, and another 36.8% expressed no preference between individual and group work. Despite this, learners generally enjoyed collaborating during the activity, likely due to the challenging nature of the task, which required teamwork to divide responsibilities, brainstorm, and discuss alternative solutions. Similarly, none of the learners reported feeling sad when asked how they felt about making the improvements requested by the teacher (Q7). This indicates that learners appreciated the teacher's feedback and did not feel overwhelmed by the suggested changes. In fact, the support provided may have been particularly helpful for those struggling, especially given that the course involves coding, which can be challenging for beginners.

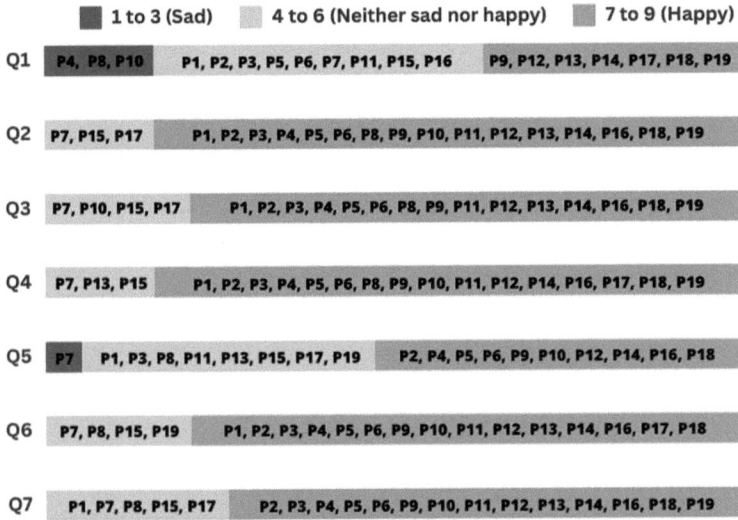

**Fig. 2.** Results of the LEEM during-evaluation checklist (learner)

Regarding the responses given using the Likert scale (Fig. 3), the results show that 5.3% (N = 1) of participants selected "Totally Disagree" for Q10, making it the only statement with at least one respondent expressing total disagreement. This may indicate that the participant was not interested in using resources beyond the Code Blocks, Visual Studio Code, Dev C++, and BeeCrowd platforms employed in the course for coding (Q10). In contrast, no participants totally disagreed with Q16, which asked whether they had learned all the content of the educational activity. However, 42.1% (N = 8) of the respondents responded neutrally to this question, suggesting that some learners may not feel entirely satisfied with their learning or the outcomes of their work. On the other hand, 47.4% (N = 9) of learners "Totally Agreed" with Q18, indicating that the resources selected for the activity were effective in supporting their understanding of the content. Finally, 63.2% (N = 12) of the respondents totally agreed that they were able to overcome obstacles during the activity (Q23), emphasizing both the complexity of the task and their determination to persevere despite the challenges. These findings highlight the significance of LX design, where the

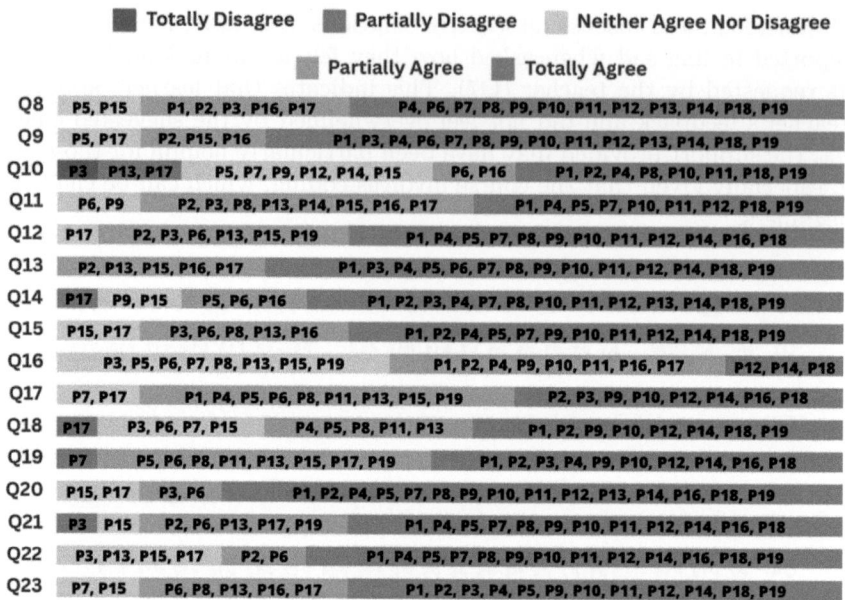

**Fig. 3.** Results of the LEEM during-evaluation checklist (learner)

teacher can transform complex subjects into more manageable and enjoyable learning experiences.

The **during-evaluation checklist (teacher)** consists of 17 statements answered on a 5-point Likert scale, ranging from Totally Disagree to Totally Agree. The teacher did not express disagreement with any of the statements. However, the teacher partially agreed with several points: that learners liked working collectively (Q3), were satisfied with the result of the educational activity (Q4), understood the content satisfactorily through the improvement suggestions provided (Q11), felt comfortable using the computational resources (Q16), and persisted without giving up when facing obstacles (Q17). It is notable that the teacher's observations during the activity align with the learners' self-assessments. For instance, many learners reported feeling neutral about fully learning the content (Q10), which was also noted by the teacher, confirming that additional activities are necessary to ensure complete understanding. The teacher's partial agreement with Q3, regarding learners' enjoyment of working collectively, further supports this, although most learners enjoyed group work. It is believed that some experienced minor conflicts, that's why none expressed total disagreement with this statement (Q3). For all other statements in the during-evaluation checklist, the teacher totally agreed, especially with elements related to Usability (concerning the ease of use, efficiency, and effectiveness of resources for completing the activity) and Adaptability (the appropriateness of the chosen resources to the context and the learner' needs in the activity). This indicates that the teacher perceived a positive and flexible learning environment, where the resources and activities effectively supported the LX.

## 6 Qualitative Analysis

In the **post-evaluation**, a set of 11 open-ended questions were qualitatively analyzed to assess learners' LX after completing the educational activity. The LX elements served as the basis for thematic analysis. The following elements were identified in the learners' responses: Value, Desirability, Adaptability, Usability, and Comfortability.

**Value Element.** Learners' perceptions of the Value element indicate that the activity provided practical and academic benefits. One participant stated that the activity using computational resources would help them better organize their daily tasks (see P6 citation). Another noted that the knowledge gained would be applicable not only in future terms of the Algorithms course but also in external situations requiring such expertise (see P11 citation). A third participant mentioned that the activity helped them tackle more challenging topics in the course by demonstrating their mastery of more basic concepts (see P15 citation). Beyond technical learning, the collaborative experience was highlighted as a positive aspect. One participant emphasized that teamwork was valuable and believed that this skill would be crucial for their professional future (see P2 citation). Another stated that the activity enhanced their group performance and expanded their proficiency with new computational tools (see P10 citation). Lastly, one participant reported personal growth, citing a significant improvement in their communication skills, which they had always found challenging (see P18 citation).

- *"The activity will help me better organize my daily tasks."* (P6)
- *"It will definitely help me in future terms of the Algorithms course and outside the university if I encounter tests or activities related to this topic."* (P11)
- *"The activity showed us that we had already mastered many basic concepts, which helped us tackle more difficult topics."* (P15)
- *"Yes, analyzing, explaining to someone, and working collectively is very beneficial. This will also be useful for my professional career."* (P2)
- *"I believe it will help me perform better in a team, just as I had to in this activity, and also to use platforms I had never used before."* (P10)
- *"I noticed significant improvement in myself. I always had difficulty speaking in public, and I feel I have matured a lot in this regard."* (P18)

These perceptions indicate that the activity provided value to the participants, impacting both their academic skills and personal development. The experience with computational resources was perceived as an asset extending beyond course content, offering support for everyday situations and future career opportunities. The integration of collaborative and communicative aspects highlights how well-structured activities can enrich learners' training, enhance their autonomy, and boost their confidence in dealing with diverse challenges. This type of activity fostered not only the assimilation of educational content but also interpersonal skills essential for academic and professional trajectories.

**Desirability Element.** Learners' perceptions of the Desirability element highlight motivations and challenges encountered throughout the educational experience. One participant mentioned that their contribution could have been better, demonstrating self-criticism and a slight sense of dissatisfaction with their performance (see P16 citation). Another shared that, despite feeling uncomfortable with presentations, they took the opportunity to research new topics of interest, such as Recursion (see P11 citation). The activity also proved stimulating for a participant who, motivated by the challenge, sought to improve and explore topics they had not previously known (see P1 citation). Additionally, the activity encouraged one participant to enhance their oral communication skills, emphasizing the positive impact on public speaking improvement (see P15 citation). Another learner commented that the research format was motivating and challenging (see P2 citation). The autonomy granted in conducting the activity was appreciated by a participant, who valued the freedom provided (see P18 citation). Finally, one participant expressed satisfaction with the teacher's approach, highlighting their guidance and problem-solving support throughout the process (see P20 citation).

- *"Not so much, I feel my contribution was good, but I also think I could have done more."* (P16)
- *"I found it very interesting. Although I don't love presenting to the class (due to shyness), I really enjoy researching new topics, especially when they are as interesting as Recursion."* (P11)
- *"I was intrigued by the challenge; it encouraged me to be better than I already was and pushed me to seek out what I didn't know."* (P1)
- *"The activity motivated me to improve my public speaking."* (P15)
- *"It was challenging because it was a 'scientific' research project, something I had never done before. It was quite challenging but also very enjoyable."* (P2)
- *"I really liked the activity and the freedom we had."* (P18)
- *"I really appreciated the teacher's work in guiding us and answering all our questions."* (P20)

These statements suggest that, even in a technical discipline like Algorithms, the activity incorporated transversal skills that increased learners' interest and motivation, enabled by the guidelines. The challenging nature of the activity and the autonomy granted contributed to a learning environment in which learners felt encouraged to explore new knowledge and develop skills beyond the course content. The teacher's shift in approach, based on the guidelines, indicates that continuous support and guidance during the activity were key factors in learners' satisfaction and engagement.

**Adaptability Element.** One participant mentioned that, although they had previously conducted seminars, they had never used tools to organize and structure their work (see P10 citation). Another participant emphasized the use of a digital platform for group work, which was a new experience for them (see P19 citation). The activity also presented a new challenge for those accustomed to similar tasks but without technological support for presentations (see P15 citation). Researching an unfamiliar topic that had not been previously taught in class provided an innovative experience for another participant, fostering independent knowledge-seeking (see P1 citation). This same participant also highlighted that prior knowledge served as a foundation, enabling a deeper understanding of the new topic (see second P1 citation).

- *"I had done some seminars before, but I had never worked in the way we did for this assignment (using some tools for organization and submission)."* (P10)
- *"I had worked in groups before, but I had never used Notion for a group project."* (P19)
- *"I had participated in similar activities, such as assignments and presentations, but they did not involve this technological approach to presenting."* (P15)
- *"Researching a topic that was not taught in class was something different that I had never experienced before."* (P1)
- *"The topics I had previously learned served as a foundation for this activity."* (P1)

Learners' reports indicate that, while the activity contained elements common to other academic practices—such as seminars, teamwork, reports, and research—it stood out due to its emphasis on computational resources. For example, the teacher, by listing on the board the resources suggested by LEDG, may have broadened learners' use of technological tools, not just for this activity but for future assignments in various disciplines. The introduction of these computational tools facilitated organization, information retrieval, and presentation, encouraging learners' adaptability in exploring new content actively, strengthening their autonomy and continuous learning skills. Thus, the Adaptability element fostered innovation in the educational process and developed competencies such as autonomy and technological proficiency.

**Usability Element.** One participant commented that they found the computational resource efficient and had never worked with it before (see P2's statement). Another participant stated that they found the resource useful and practical for collaborative activities (see P7's statement). One participant shared that they managed to learn a new tool during the activity (see P10's statement). Another said they loved it and continue to use the tool for organization (see P18's statement). Another mentioned that they enjoyed using the tools and intend to use them in the future (see P8's statement). One participant revealed that the tool makes their life easier and supports new learning (see P6's statement).

- *"Regarding computational resources, I had never worked with them before, especially Notion. I found it very efficient."* (P2)
- *"The activity introduced me to resources like Notion, which I found extremely useful and practical for collaborative work development, and I will certainly use it again in the future."* (P7)

- *"The fact that I had never used Notion before and ended up using it in this activity already shows that I learned how to use a new platform."* (P10)
- *"Yes, I didn't know Notion, for example, I loved it, and I've been using it a lot to stay organized."* (P18)
- *"I enjoyed using certain tools and will use them again."* (P8)
- *"I plan to use this at another point in my life because of how much it facilitates my tasks and contributes to new learning experiences."* (P6)

The participants' statements highlight that using resources, such as Notion, significantly contributed to their learning experience, aligning with usability criteria defined by ISO 9241-11 (2019), including ease of learning, efficiency, and satisfaction. P2 and P10's comments indicate that Notion provided an intuitive LX, allowing them to acquire new skills quickly, even without prior experience with the tool. P7 emphasizes Notion's efficiency, considering it a useful and practical resource for collaborative activities. User satisfaction is evident in P8 and P6's statements, as they expressed interest in continuing to use the tool. Thus, the activity fostered a positive interaction with computational resources, encouraging self-management and organization skills.

**Comfortability Element.** Some participants highlighted aspects that contributed to their sense of comfort or discomfort during the activity. One participant expressed that activities involving research, writing, and slide creation increased their comfort level, as they enjoy these tasks and find the experience satisfying (see P15's statement). Another participant mentioned feeling at ease using resources, indicating a level of confidence with the tools employed (see P2's statement). However, some challenges were also reported. One participant found it difficult to present in front of peers, which represents a specific discomfort related to public speaking (see P14's statement). Another described the challenge of teamwork, particularly due to misalignment in expectations and contributions among colleagues, which required additional understanding and patience (see P12's statement). There was also a participant who, despite facing communication difficulties and insecurities regarding content, felt satisfied with the outcome of their presentation (see P18's statement). Finally, one participant reported feeling discomfort when tackling an activity of unprecedented complexity, as it presented a new level of challenge for them (see P2's statement).

- *"I love challenges and conducting research; it may be hard to believe, but I find working on the dissertation satisfying. Creating slides combined areas where I feel most comfortable, so it was a very positive experience."* (P15)
- *"I felt very comfortable working with these technologies, and it encouraged me to use them even more."* (P2)
- *"Beyond the difficulties of understanding the content and worrying about not conveying incorrect information, presenting to an audience is always a challenge for me."* (P14)
- *"It was easy to complete this activity since it's a subject I am familiar with and have no difficulty in. The biggest challenge was group work because others don't always do things as expected, which requires understanding and patience."* (P12)

- *"I tried to create a very professional piece of work. Overall, I was happy with my presentation, even though I forgot some words and stuttered. So far, I think this was my best work."* (P18)
- *"I had never done an activity of this level of complexity before."* (P2)

The participants' comments show that comfort is strongly linked to familiarity with the activities and mastery of the tools used. For some, tasks such as research and slide preparation provided a positive and motivating experience, particularly when aligned with their personal interests. These aspects reinforce the importance of incorporating activities that leverage learners' skills and preferences to foster engagement and satisfaction. Conversely, factors such as public speaking and teamwork dynamics emerged as sources of discomfort, indicating that, even in a setting where students feel comfortable with technology, interpersonal and communication challenges can negatively impact their experience. The complexity of the activity suggests that adjusting the difficulty level to match students' preparedness is crucial to preventing excessive discomfort and promoting gradual learning. Thus, the perceptions of comfort and discomfort reflect a combination of personal, interpersonal, and situational factors that should be considered to enhance the educational experience.

## 7 Discussion

This case study underscores the necessity of not only considering quality criteria related to the development and use of computational resources but also addressing all factors involved during their use. This includes learner characteristics, needs, and preferences; the activities and objectives, taking into account the artifacts and systems used; and the physical, social, and cultural contexts in which learning occurs over time [8].

The analysis of participants' perceptions highlights some lessons learned that can improve educational interaction. First, giving learners autonomy can increase engagement, as they can explore tools and topics of interest. Second, the acceptance of new technologies is facilitated when digital platforms that promote organization and efficiency are used. Third, the ease of use of tools helps students learn more effectively. Finally, learners' comfort in challenging tasks can be enhanced by considering their preferences and abilities, making activities more rewarding [10].

A key distinction of the LEDEF framework is that it incorporates elements of LX, which is less common among existing technologies [16]. One of its main contributions is the ability to adapt to the evolving needs of learners and educational contexts, integrating multiple elements of the LX. LEDEF's dynamic nature allows for the inclusion of new guidelines and technologies as experiences are gained, further enriching and maintaining the framework's relevance throughout educational activities.

However, understanding learners' perspectives and assessing their self-reports can be challenging. While feedback from learners is valuable, teachers must balance this input with educational objectives when designing activities using computational resources. A task that appears aesthetically pleasing or simple may appeal to learners, but may not necessarily be the most effective option for promoting learning. Furthermore, learners' needs and perceptions may evolve over time, necessitating ongoing evaluation of the educational experience [6]. An additional limitation identified in this study was the initially extensive list of 22 guidelines and different types of assessment.

To address this, it became necessary to offer the teacher more manageable options, allowing them to choose which guidelines to apply to their activities. The guidelines were thus presented as options organized by LX elements. The teacher chose to implement five guidelines, primarily related to the element of Desirability: G3, G5, G9, G20 and G21. Nonetheless, through evaluation, other LX elements were identified as crucial in supporting learners' diverse needs, even though these were not part of the initial selection. For example, the importance of providing guidance and feedback throughout the activity - rather than leaving learners to work entirely independently - became evident (Q17, related to the element of Value). This was especially important for a class largely composed of learners who identified as shy.

Another noteworthy observation was that, while many learners initially expressed a preference for working individually, they began to enjoy group work during the activity. This demonstrates that, even when learners assess themselves in a certain way, experienced teachers can guide learners toward developing essential skills, such as teamwork, and help them gain confidence. Upon reviewing the during-evaluation checklist, the teacher recognized the need to adjust their approach to address specific areas and improve the overall LX. The iterative nature of the LEDEF framework, which alternates between design and evaluation, enabled these adjustments and facilitated the adaptation of activities to meet evolving learner needs throughout the process.

## 8 Limitations

The teacher received guidance on using the guidelines, and checklists, which can be considered a limitation, as it may have influenced its application. Additionally, weekly meetings were held to synchronize completed tasks, define upcoming actions, and provide a space for clarifying doubts. The checklists were reviewed together with the teacher before being applied, ensuring their alignment with the activity and preventing inconsistent results. The teacher was also granted autonomy to define the scope of their activity, including the amount of time and the selection of guidelines, which influenced the learners' experiences.

Another limitation was the choice of resources and guidelines familiar to the teacher, which may have limited the framework's potential for this specific activity. Additionally, learners had the freedom to form their groups based on affinity, which might have influenced the results. Although the pre-evaluation checklist could have been used to balance group dynamics, the teacher consciously chose not to interfere in this process. Furthermore, adopting alternative group formation strategies could have yielded different outcomes.

The accuracy of the collected information relied on participants' honesty, a common challenge in evaluations involving learners and teachers. Another limitation was the number of participants, as the study was conducted with a single class, without representation from other academic disciplines. Concerning construct limitations, the study employed questionnaires and interviews to gain deeper insights into the learners' and teacher's experiences. Data collection instruments previously validated in earlier studies of this research were used.

## 9 Conclusions and Future Work

This paper presented the LEDEF framework, which integrates the design and evaluation of LX. To evaluate its application, a case study was conducted with 19 learners and a teacher of an undergraduate course. The teacher used design guidelines to structure and redesign the activity, while learners provided feedback on their experiences before, during, and after the activity. This iterative process of alternating between design and evaluation of the LX proved useful both for the teacher, in refining the learning activities, and for the learners, in enhancing their engagement and practical learning. Through this process, learners were given greater autonomy, the opportunity to express themselves, and the chance to apply the course content in real-life contexts, which improved the overall LX.

The results highlighted that learners benefited from the use of technological tools such as Notion and Prezi, which enhanced organization, collaboration. These tools introduced them to new learning methods. Many learners expressed increased interest in applying these tools in future academic or professional projects. The flexibility offered by the design guidelines, allowing learners to choose their learning environment and schedule, contributed to a greater sense of autonomy and responsibility. However, the study also revealed challenges, particularly for learners who were less familiar with the required technologies. Some learners found it difficult to adapt to the new tools, which may have caused some discomfort and stress, when combined with the pressure of public presentations.

One limitation is related to the veracity of the information gathered; as with any evaluation involving learners and teachers, the accuracy of the data relied on the honesty of the participants. Additionally, learners were given the freedom to form their groups, which could have influenced the results. The pre-evaluation checklist could have been used by the teacher to balance group dynamics, but there was a conscious decision not to interfere with this process. Another limitation was the selection of participants. Since the study was conducted with learners of a class, there was no representation from other academic disciplines.

We will promote the dissemination of the LEDEF to the academic and educational community through training sessions, as well as to share practical resources and materials to support teachers in applying the framework to their activities. Also, a study is planned with learners from the Licentiate in Informatics program—future teachers in training—to explore the LEDEF's application in teacher education programs. We intended to include a larger number of students and teachers from other fields of knowledge and with diverse profiles and, to deepen the interactive systems-oriented application aspect by exploring how LX elements can be applied and analyzed in digital interaction contexts, and how UX aspects influence LX in the use of computational resources.

**Acknowledgements.** We would like to thank the financial support granted by CAPES/PROEX Finance Code 001; CNPq 314797/2023-8.

# References

1. Arachchi, T.K., Sitbon, L., Zhang, J.: Enhancing access to elearning for people with intellectual disability: integrating usability with learning. In: Bernhaupt, R., Dalvi, G., Joshi, A., Balkrishan, D.K., O'Neill, J., Winckler, M. (eds.) INTERACT 2017. LNCS, vol. 10514, pp. 13–32. Springer, Cham (2017). https://doi.org/10.1007/978-3-319-67684-5_2
2. Bertelsen, O.W., Bødker, S.: Activity theory. HCI models, theories, and frameworks: toward a multidisciplinary science, pp. 291–324 (2003)
3. Bevan, N., Carter, J., Earthy, J., Geis, T., Harker, S.: New ISO standards for usability, usability reports and usability measures. In: Kurosu, M. (ed.) HCI 2016. LNCS, vol. 9731, pp. 268–278. Springer, Cham (2016). https://doi.org/10.1007/978-3-319-39510-4_25
4. Braun, V., Clarke, V.: Using thematic analysis in psychology. Qual. Res. Psychol. **3**(2), 77–101 (2006)
5. Donelan, H., Kear, K.: Creating and collaborating: students and tutors perceptions of an online group project. Int. Rev. Res. Open Distrib. Learn. **19**(2) (2018)
6. Dos Santos, G.C., dos Santos Silva, D.E., Peres, L.M., Valentim, N.M.C.: Case study of a model that evaluates the learner experience with DICTs. In: CHI Extended Abstracts, p. 509-1 (2024)
7. Huang, R., Spector, J.M., Yang, J.: Educational technology a primer for the 21st century. Springer (2019)
8. Sharp, H., Preece, J., Rogers, Y.: Interaction Design: Beyond Human-Computer Interaction. New York (2019)
9. Koper, R.: Current research in learning design. J. Educ. Technol. Soc. **9**(1), 13–22 (2006)
10. Lammer, L., Weiss, A., Vincze, M.: The 5-step plan. In: Abascal, J., Barbosa, S., Fetter, M., Gross, T., Palanque, P., Winckler, M. (eds.) INTERACT 2015. LNCS, vol. 9297, pp. 557–564. Springer, Cham (2015). https://doi.org/10.1007/978-3-319-22668-2_43
11. Magyar, N., Haley, S.R.: Balancing learner experience and user experience in a peer feedback web application for MOOCs. In: Extended Abstracts of the 2020 CHI Conference on Human Factors in Computing Systems, pp. 1–8 (2020)
12. Papavlasopoulou, S., Giannakos, M.N., Jaccheri, L.: Exploring children's learning experience in constructionism-based coding activities through design-based research. Comput. Hum. Behav. **99**, 415–427 (2019)
13. Pawson, R., Tilley, N.: Realistic Evaluation. Sage (1997)
14. Queiros, L.M., Bouckaert, Y.H., de Oliveira, I.V., Oliveira, F.K.D., Moreira, F., Gomes, A.S.: The adoption of learning experience design tools in classroom planning activity: a systematic literature review. In: Proceedings of the Seventh International Conference on Technological Ecosystems for Enhancing Multiculturality, pp. 704–710 (2019)

15. dos Santos, G.C., Silva, D.E.D.S., Valentim, N.M.: Um mapeamento sistemático da literatura sobre iniciativas que avaliam a experiência do aprendiz. Anais do XXXIII Simpósio Brasileiro de Informática na Educação, pp. 621–633 (2022)
16. Silva, D.E.D.S., Conte, T., Valentim, N.: A systematic mapping study about learner experience design in computational systems. Inf. Educ. **23**(2), 439–478 (2024)
17. Silva, D.E.D.S., Conte, T.U., Valentim, N.M.C.: Learner experience design guidelines: proposal and a preliminary evaluation with experts. In: Simpósio Brasileiro de Informática na Educação (SBIE), pp. 2922–2930. SBC (2024)
18. Zhang, D., Yang, Y., Ji, T., Xie, H., He, Y.: Designing craft learning experience for rural children: a case study on Huayao cross-stitch in Southwest China. In: Rau, P.-L.P. (ed.) CCD 2018. LNCS, vol. 10912, pp. 117–132. Springer, Cham (2018). https://doi.org/10.1007/978-3-319-92252-2_9

# From Prototype to the Classroom: Iterative Development of Conditionals in Early Childhood Robotics

Ewelina Bakala[1], Gonzalo Tejera[1], and Juan Pablo Hourcade[2]

[1] Instituto de Computación, Universidad de la República, Montevideo, Uruguay
{ebakala,gtejera}@fing.edu.uy
[2] The University of Iowa, Iowa, USA
juanpablo-hourcade@uiowa.edu

**Abstract.** Computational thinking (CT) is widely considered an important life skill, crucial for active engagement in the digital age. Numerous studies demonstrate that CT development can begin effectively in early childhood. However, the incorporation of conditionals—a fundamental component of many CT definitions and a concept assessed in validated CT tests—into educational robotics curricula remains underexplored. This study investigates the integration of conditional programming into Robotito, an educational robot designed to teach CT to preschoolers. Across four evaluation sessions involving three experienced teachers (P1 and P2 participated in the first two sessions; P3 in the remaining ones), we identified the strengths and weaknesses of three conditionals prototypes. Based on their feedback we developed a final implementation that we evaluated with 30 preschoolers in a classroom context. This paper discusses the evaluation outcomes, emphasizing teachers' perspectives related to children's age and classroom context. Additionally, the Robotito simulator, created to facilitate prototype evaluation, was found to be a valuable tool for introducing Robotito programming to children.

**Keywords:** Computational Thinking · Conditionals · Educational Robotics · Kindergarten · Teachers' Evaluation · Classroom Evaluation

## 1 Introduction

Computational thinking (CT) is the process of formulating problems and solutions in a manner that allows a computer (whether human or machine) to effectively execute them [16]. This skill is considered essential for active participation in the digital world [9], prompting its integration into educational curricula globally [4,9,26,28]. Researchers emphasize the importance of CT learning in early childhood, as it can enhance children's analytical abilities and provide them with cognitive tools that support collaborative problem solving and self-expression [7,8,10]. Also, empirical studies confirm that it is viable to teach CT

 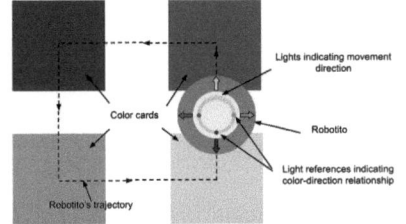 

**Fig. 1.** From left to right: Researcher simulating Robotito's movements "by hand" during the evaluation of low-fidelity prototypes; an illustration of Robotito's movements in response to color cards; teacher exploring a musical loop in the musical mode prototype.

concepts even at the preschool level [13,19,20,24]. Many of these studies use robots to teach CT, as they provide a concrete reference system for abstract problems.

Robotito is an educational robot developed by an interdisciplinary team at the Facultad de Ingeniería of the Universidad de la República in Uruguay, specifically designed to foster the development of CT skills in preschool-aged children. Unlike traditional programming tools that often rely on abstract text-based code, Robotito employs a tangible programming approach, allowing children to control the robot's movements by arranging colored cards on the floor—each color corresponding to a specific direction. It responds to color cards according to the detected color: yellow, red, blue, and green make it move forward, left, backward, and right, respectively, while purple makes it spin (see Fig. 1). This design enables young learners to grasp fundamental CT concepts such as sequencing, abstraction, and algorithmic thinking through direct, hands-on interaction.

Studies have demonstrated that such tangible interfaces are developmentally appropriate for early childhood education, promoting engagement and facilitating the representation of abstract ideas in a concrete manner [1,6,17]. The development of Robotito is grounded in the principles of open hardware and free software, ensuring accessibility and adaptability across diverse educational settings. Research conducted in Uruguayan public kindergartens has shown that children who engaged with Robotito through programming activities exhibited significant improvements in attention, motivation, and CT skills compared to peers who interacted with the robot solely through sensory-motor activities [12]. There is evidence that it is also well-suited to support groups of children learning together with one robot [2].

Robotito enables children to work on sequencing tasks that include abstraction, decomposition, route planning, and debugging. However, it consistently responds the same way to coding cards, which prevents it from addressing advanced programming concepts like conditionals.

Conditionals are an interesting concept to work on as they are a critical component of many CT definitions [11,15,25], many tools to stimulate the development of CT support conditionals (see Table 3 in [3]), and existing validated CT tests for children aged 5 to 6 [22,31] evaluate understanding of conditionals. They enable children to move beyond simple sequencing tasks by working on more advanced algorithms that involve decision-making based on specific criteria. By introducing conditionals, such as the "if-then-else" control structure, programmers can develop logical reasoning skills, allowing them to analyze situations, make decisions, and understand the consequences of those decisions. This concept also prepares students for more complex programming control structures, such as loops, by providing a clear framework for decision-making processes within algorithms.

Literature based research [23] and empirical studies [14,18,29] suggest that conditionals are accessible even to young children. Also, robotic-based CT curricula have successfully incorporated activities related to conditionals [5,27], highlighting their importance in teaching CT to preschoolers.

Recognizing the importance of conditionals, we decided to extend Robotito's capabilities to include this concept. Existing tools that incorporate conditionals are primarily commercial products designed for individual, at-home use. In contrast, Robotito has proven to be a valuable resource for fostering collaborative learning in group settings [2], and expanding its programming capabilities would provide the educational community with an open-source tool specifically designed for classroom use, supporting both basic and advanced CT concepts.

We developed three prototypes for integrating conditionals into Robotito's functionality and a screen-based simulator to illustrate these ideas. This work presents the results of a series of evaluations involving experienced teachers from an urban setting in Montevideo, Uruguay, which identified the strengths and weaknesses of each prototype. Based on their feedback, we extended Robotito's programming capabilities with conditionals and assessed the implementation with children in classroom activities. The paper discusses the outcomes of the evaluations, the feedback from teachers, and the implications for future development of Robotito's curriculum and those of similar platforms.

## 2 Conditionals Prototypes

A group of five computer scientists (two external to the Robotito team) brainstormed and refined ideas for implementing conditionals in Robotito over several weeks. As the robot's programming is event-based and its behavior changes according to the detected color card, we looked for ideas that allow the robot to respond differently to the same coding card based on the evaluation of a boolean expression. At the end of this process, we had developed three ideas: color frame, musical mode, and split card.

### 2.1 Color Frame

This prototype enables Robotito to respond differently to color cards based on the robot's current state. In addition to the standard color cards, we introduce color cards with frames and a card that changes the robot's state (see Fig. 2).

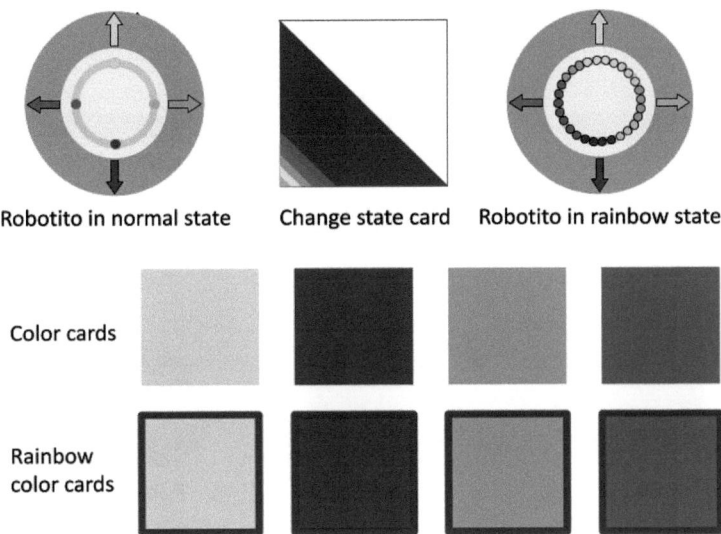

**Fig. 2.** An example of the implementation of color frame prototype. In the normal state, the robot detects only color cards; in the rainbow state, it detects only rainbow color cards. In rainbow state the led ring on the top of the robot is used to indicate robot's state.

In its normal state, Robotito detects color cards and ignores rainbow color cards[1]. In the rainbow state, Robotito does the opposite: it detects rainbow color cards and ignores color cards. The change state card is used to switch between states. Consequently, the robot behaves differently when encountering the same event, depending on its state. The conditional logic expressed by this prototype is as follows: "If the robot is in rainbow state, it will ignore color cards and detect rainbow color cards; else, it will detect color cards and ignore rainbow color cards." This logic can be represented by the following code:

**if** $state == rainbow$ **then**
    **if** $card == rainbowCard$ **then**
        $move(cardColor)$
    **end if**
**else**
    **if** $card == colorCard$ **then**
        $move(cardColor)$
    **end if**
**end if**

---

[1] The rainbow state is an example of a state the robot could implement. In our evaluations, we discussed other state changes, such as becoming angry or happy, to illustrate with a concrete example the new functionality.

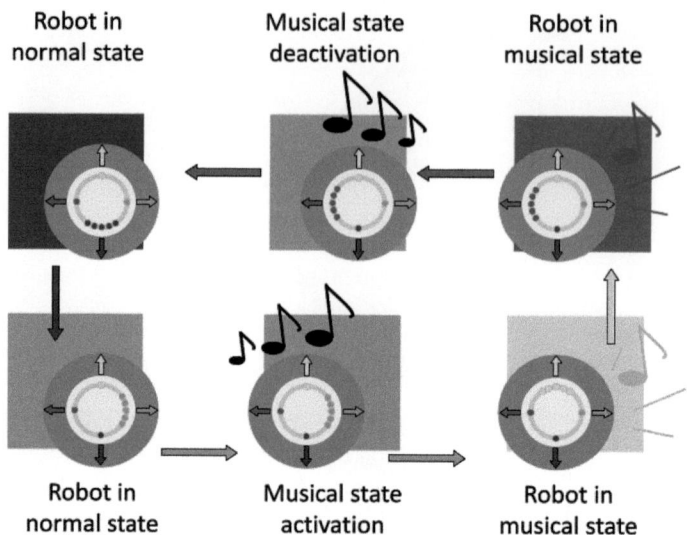

**Fig. 3.** An example of musical state activation and deactivation. The robot moves according to the color cards and produces sounds when passing over orange (activation or deactivation sound), yellow, and red cards (notes associated with the colors). (Color figure online)

### 2.2 Musical Mode

This prototype incorporates two states for the robot: the normal state and the musical state. In the musical state, the robot executes its usual direction changes in response to color cards but also produces different sounds (notes or short sounds) for each color card (see Fig. 3). The state change occurs when the robot passes over the change state card and is indicated by an activation or deactivation sound. This functionality allows the robot to perform an additional action- sound reproduction- when it is in musical state. The conditional expressed by this prototype is "if the robot is in musical state, it will also reproduce a sound when it detects a directional card." The corresponding code is:

   **if** $state == musical$ **then**
      $playSound(cardColor)$
   **end if**

### 2.3 Split Card

The split card is a multicolor card containing four sections (see Fig. 4). Each section can have a different color, although it is also possible to have sections with repeated colors. The direction in which the robot will move after detecting the card depends on the side from which the robot approaches it. This allows a single card to encode up to four different directions for the robot. The conditional

**Fig. 4.** Paper prototype of the split card. When the robot approaches the card from the bottom, it senses blue and moves in the direction indicated by the blue arrow. When it approaches from the right, it senses green and moves in the direction indicated by the green arrow. Approaching from the left, it senses yellow, and from the top, it senses red. (Color figure online)

logic expressed by this card is: "If the robot approaches the card from direction X, then it will move in direction Y," and can be expressed by the following code:

**if** $comingFrom == bottom$ **then**
    $move(bottomCardColor)$
**else if** $comingFrom == right$ **then**
    $move(rightCardColor)$
**else if** $comingFrom == left$ **then**
    $move(leftCardColor)$
**else**
    $move(topCardColor)$
**end if**

The card can be rotated to solve a programming task.

### 2.4 Robotito Simulator

The simulator is a digital version of the robot that can be deployed as a desktop or Android application. It was specifically developed to support the evaluation of conditionals prototypes for Robotito with teachers. It reflects the basic behavior of the robot (see Fig. 1) and has been extended to incorporate the additional features that we wanted to evaluate (see Fig. 5 for a concrete example). The simulator was developed using the Processing programming language.

During evaluations, we utilized the simulator as a desktop application and also used it to generate videos, which were later shared with teachers. Examples of simulations for the musical mode and split card can be found on YouTube[2].

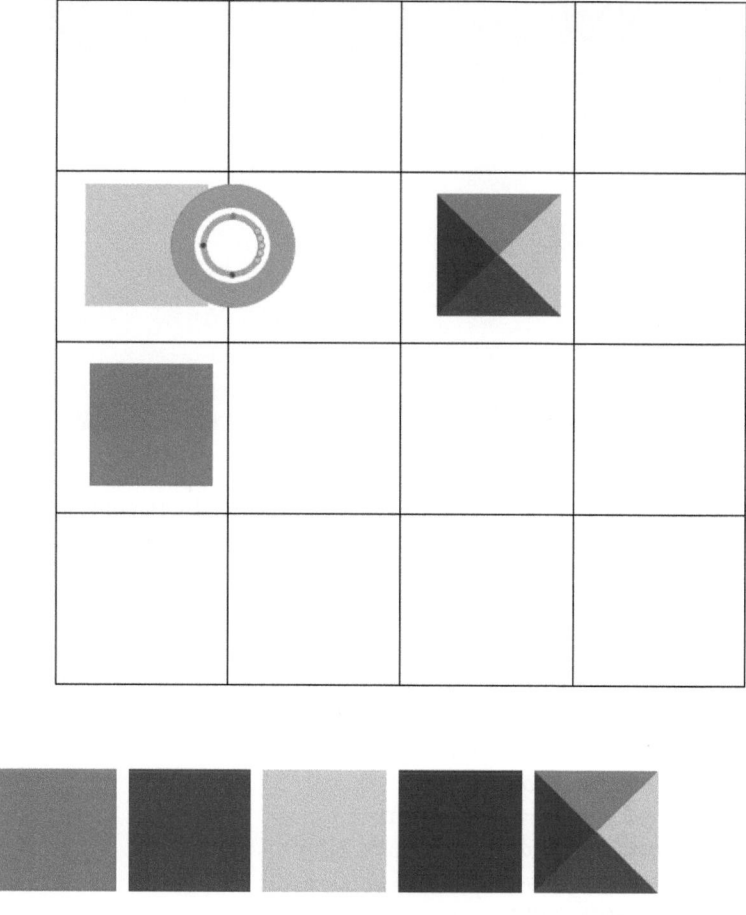

**Fig. 5.** Split card simulator. Above the working area, below the cards panel. The cards should be placed in the grid to allow their detection by the simulated robot. In this example, the green, yellow and split card were placed in the working area. Yellow lights indicate that the robot is moving right after detecting the yellow card. Approaching the split card from the left side will result in detecting the blue color and a corresponding movement to the left will be executed. (Color figure online)

---

[2] https://www.youtube.com/playlist?list=PL575oRsFVM9qjtbGgaP6RRVXiNXM176Wu.

## 3 Methodology

We conducted four prototype evaluation activities involving three teachers (see Table 1 for more details). The final implementation of conditionals for Robotito was evaluated with two classes of level 5 kindergarten students. Each activity was video recorded and analyzed.

### 3.1 Prototypes Evaluation

During the evaluations with teachers, our goal was to assess whether the proposed prototypes were age appropriate, identify aspects that required improvement for classroom use, and determine which prototype was most convincing to implement in the actual robot. Through an inductive thematic analysis of the video recordings, we identified themes related to the complexity of the prototypes and the types of activities envisioned by the teachers. The thematic analysis was conducted by one of the researchers while seeking feedback on themes from two other researchers. It involved extracting quotes from the teachers and clustering them based on similarity to arrive at themes.

**Participants.** The participants included: a computing teacher (P1) who works with preschoolers and early primary school students at a private educational center; a teacher (P2) who teaches at both public and private institutions at the preschool and primary school levels; and a preschool teacher (P3) from a public institution. P1 and P2 participated in the first two evaluation sessions, while P3 participated in the third and fourth session. All participants had more than 15 years of teaching experience, as well as experience and interest in teaching CT. They all work in schools in Montevideo, a city of about 1 million inhabitants in South America.

**Evaluation Activities.** Before evaluating the prototypes, all teachers were familiarized with Robotito and its basic behaviors. During the evaluations, we presented our ideas using various strategies: oral explanations, paper prototypes of new color cards, simulating Robotito's actions "by hand" with the robot turned off, utilizing the Robotito Simulator, video recordings of Robotito Simulator, and using Robotito itself. As we made improvements between the evaluations, each session employed different evaluation materials. Details of each session are provided in Appendix A.

### 3.2 In-Classroom Evaluation

During the in-classroom evaluation, we assessed whether the children were able to complete a task involving conditional music reproduction. Their performance was evaluated through analysis of video recordings, focusing on whether each group of children working together was able to successfully fulfill the task. We also noted any specific behaviors associated with difficulties and with overcoming them.

**Table 1.** Summary of evaluation sessions with teachers.

| Id | Date | Participants | Prototype evaluated | Evaluation type | Key Insights |
|---|---|---|---|---|---|
| 1 | 07.06.23 | P1, P2 | Color frame Musical mode Split card | Focus group with both teachers based on oral explanation, paper prototype of new cards, and a researcher simulating Robotito's actions "by hand" | Color frame prototype is difficult to understand. Split Card is attractive but requires careful preparation of the scenario. Potential problems with composing melodies when using musical mode |
| 2 | 02.08.23 | P1, P2 | Musical mode Split card | Individual interview with each teacher using on screen Robotito simulator | Musical mode is considered the most promising. Teachers recognize the simulator as a helpful tool to introduce Robotito to children |
| 3 | 15.08.23 | P3 | Musical mode | Oral explanation of the new functionality and an interactive instance with the first implementation of musical mode in Robotito | Passing in silence or making sound in some parts of the robot's route seems viable for preschoolers |
| 4 | 19.08.23 | P3 | Musical mode | Video generated using Robotito's simulator (see http://y2u.be/Ju89amk-yTs) | Absence of visual feedback to indicate whether Robotito is in musical mode |

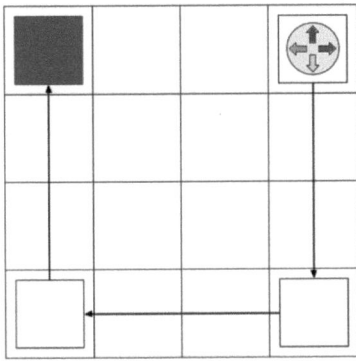 

**Fig. 6.** Left: An example of an on paper activity during session #5. Right: Session #5. Children observing the robot's behavior after passing over the orange card.

**Participants.** We worked with two classes (A1 with 17 students and A2 with 19 students) of level 5 students (5 to 6 years old) from a public kindergarten in Montevideo. A1 attended the kindergarten in the morning, and A2 was the afternoon group. None of the children had previously participated in educational robotics (ER) activities.

**ER Activities and Data Analysis.** We conducted eight ER activities with Robotito between November and December of 2023. We introduced basic Robotito programming in the first four sessions and moved to more advanced concepts in the second half of the intervention (see Appendix A for more details).

Activities #5 and #6 involved the final implementation of the musical mode—the prototype most favorably received by teachers during evaluations—and focused on conditional music reproduction. We provide a detailed description of these activities, as Activity #6 was used to assess children's performance with conditionals. During session #6 we worked with 14 children from the morning and 16 children from the afternoon group.

*Activity #5.* Total time: 40 min. The class was divided into two groups which took turns completing two activities. In one of the activities, children worked in pairs on on-paper tasks in which they had to paint already fixed coding cards with the right color to make the robot reach the purple card, or define the place and the color of the cards that direct the robot to the purple card and draw them on the paper grid (see Fig. 6).

During the other activity, children worked on a square-shaped path that was used to introduce the orange card (the one that toggles musical mode). We asked the children to imagine what the card would do, and then introduced it to the prepared path and observed how the robot responded to it (see Fig. 6). The children were invited to reflect on how to activate and deactivate sound reproduction and to propose routes that integrate sound through an orange card.

**Fig. 7.** Session #6. A group of children solving the task that required activation and deactivation of musical state.

*Activity #6.* Total time: 60 min (about 10 min per group). We formed small groups (1 to 3 children) and each group worked with Robotito for about 10 min while the rest of the class performed curricular activities with the teacher. The children in each small group were distributed around a 4 × 4 unit mat (see Fig. 7). Each child was invited to code with color cards an L-shaped path from a point near them to one of the classmates or to the researcher. The researcher determined the robot's initial orientation, starting position, and endpoint.

To increase the challenge, we introduced white cards marked with an "X," indicating that the robot could not pass through that cell. In other cases, children were asked to design a path and activate the music before reaching the endpoint. The session concluded with a collaborative task in which all group members worked together to program a longer path incorporating both music activation and deactivation. We used this final task to evaluate whether children understood how to activate and deactivate sound.

## 4 Results

Each evaluation provided valuable input, helping us identify the most appreciated ideas and focus on potential improvements for subsequent evaluations.

### 4.1 Evaluation #1 (Teachers Evaluating Low Fidelity Prototype)

**Color Frame.** The idea of additional cards and an internal state that completely alters the robot's reaction to color cards was considered complex. P2 remarked that "everything changes" and that "there are two parallel universes".

To provide a concrete example that would justify the use of color frames, P2 suggested an activity based on missions. In this scenario, the robot might fall or crash if it follows a path composed of only one type of card (either directional cards or directional rainbow cards, depending on the state). The challenge would be to change the robot's state at the appropriate moment to avoid these unwanted situations and achieve the goal, although P2 admitted, "Still, it is difficult." P1 envisioned that borders could have textures influencing the robot's behavior, such as a green border with a grass texture that slows the robot down. She suggested that patterns on the borders could be more concrete and have an immediate effect that is easily understood at the preschool level.

**Split Card.** P1 questioned the benefits and new challenges introduced by the split card: "In the end, it does the same as if you put this (blue card) here. Why do you divide it into four? What makes it different?" P2 suggested that "Perhaps you can give the card with four colors to the child and the child has to decide how to rotate it". They noted that the robot's starting position and orientation should be predefined so the child can solve the task. P2 observed, "I have to consider where it starts, what will be the first color that it senses, and which direction it will go." Additionally, they mentioned the need to account for the number of coding cards or obstacles to ensure the children would use the split card. Both teachers admitted that using the split card was not straightforward. P2 stated, "You have to think well about the tasks," and P1 added, "You have to consider the context." P2 summarized these considerations by stating, "The use of the (split) card is somehow forced".

Despite these concerns, P2 remarked that she really liked this idea and P1 found it attractive.

**Musical Mode.** After the researcher's explanation, the teachers immediately focused on the idea of creating melodies using color cards. We discussed potential issues, such as when the robot should repeat two notes, causing it to loop between two cards, and then play a new note. In this scenario, the card with the new note should be placed while the robot is moving to interrupt the loop. P1 suggested that when the robot is in musical mode, it could maintain a fixed movement direction and only read the notes: "Do not modify the route/direction variable, leave it fixed." She was enthusiastic about working on sequencing using popular melodies or songs, such as "Baby Shark." She stated, "The song guides the order," and "the ear corrects you."

**Summary.** All the prototypes presented challenges that were noted by the teachers. They proposed various ideas to overcome these challenges and considered classroom activities that could employ each prototype.

The color frame prototype was the only one that did not receive positive feedback, and the potential activities with it were considered difficult. Therefore, we focused further evaluations on the split card and musical mode.

## 4.2 Evaluation #2 (Teachers Interacting with Simulator)

During the second evaluation, we used the simulator to provide an interactive experience with the musical mode and split card prototypes.

**Musical Mode.** In the digital version of the musical mode, the card used to activate and deactivate musical state would make a sound corresponding to on or off, with musical state adding a musical note to the change of direction. This implementation of the musical mode was easily understood by both teachers. P1 remarked, "Ah! It [the color card] converts into notes. In addition to direction, it is a note." She also commented on the clarity of the activation and deactivation sound: "It is understandable that the sound is turning on and off. It's very clear" She was confident that children would understand the musical mode: "The only thing that changes is that it incorporates sound. It is not a substantial change. [...] It doesn't confuse, doesn't dazzle, this is what I'm saying."

Both teachers agreed that activating and deactivating the musical state with the same card was a good idea. P1 noted, "with the same [card] it's easier, more practical."

P1 envisioned composing simple melodies as a sequencing exercise. Although only four notes can be used with four colors, she did not see this as a problem: "At the initial level we do simple things," and "more sequence is more abstraction and more difficulty." She saw composing as engaging and emphasized that "when they [the children] are motivated they will want to spend more time working with the code."

P2 also showed interest in programming simple songs but saw working with only four sounds as a limitation. She revisited the idea from the first evaluation session, where the robot in musical state does not change its direction but only reads the color cards as notes. This way, the robot would move as usual with color cards or go in a straight line while reproducing the sounds associated with the color cards. She considered combining these two modes challenging: "We are dividing [children's] attention between two different things, and we are working with young children." However, she saw it as viable for level 5 kindergarten (children aged 5 to 6) after some initial work with the concepts. The basic version of the prototype, in which the robot moves with the colors and in musical state also reproduces the sound, was considered easy to understand: "The only thing that you add is that it makes sound, the movements do not change" (P2). An exercise where the children have to activate and deactivate the sound to create silence or sound in specific parts of the route was considered viable: "It's a good proposal," stated P2.

**Split Card.** The split card prototype was not discussed as much. P1 considered it accessible for the children since they only need to apply the color-direction rule that they already know. She imagined an introductory exercise where the normal color card is replaced by the split card to demonstrate that "it is the same".

P2 was more enthusiastic, stating, "It's incredible, I love it." She found it suitable for preschoolers as it allows working on problems using a trial-and-error strategy.

**Prototypes' Ranking.** We asked the teachers to rank the prototypes based on their suitability for preschool-level education.

P1 found both ideas attractive for preschoolers. Regarding which prototype would allow her to offer more engaging activities, her preference was musical mode. While she found the split card idea attractive, she noted its limitation, stating, "It is not more than changing the direction."

P2 shared the same preferences, stating, "I would start with the musical one; I really like the musical one. Then the split card; I really like that one too."

**Robotito Presentation.** Both teachers spontaneously mentioned that the Robotito simulator could be used to introduce Robotito to children before working with the real robot. P1 commented on the benefit of having both digital and tangible formats: "If I have to work on it, I would like to explain a little bit of theory, [...] let them see it first [on the screen], and then we do it [with the robot]. This way, their anxiety decreases since they have already seen it and know how it works, and the child is more self-regulated." P2 found that "it [the simulator] is excellent to work beforehand" and "[in the simulator] we observe what it does and then, we translate it into the [robot's] trajectory".

When asked if the drawing was understandable or perhaps too abstract, both agreed that the representation of the robot and the mat were appropriate. P1 remarked, "No, it is perfect, less is more."

**Summary.** Both teachers ranked musical mode as their preferred prototype for preschoolers due to its engaging activities involving sound and movement. It was deemed more engaging compared to solely focusing on directional changes, as seen with the split card.

Surprisingly, both teachers highlighted the benefits of using the Robotito simulator to introduce Robotito to children before engaging with the physical robot. They appreciated the dual approach of digital and tangible formats to reduce anxiety and enhance understanding among young learners.

### 4.3 Evaluation #3 (Teacher Using High Fidelity Prototype)

During the third evaluation, the researcher presented the in-robot implementation of musical mode. The teacher (P3) spontaneously began interacting with the robot, attempting to make it play the first part of Beethoven's composition "Für Elise." The challenge of composing a melody with four notes while the robot changes direction with each color was considered complicated. "It is too much," stated P3. She acknowledged that "they [the children] will love it" and that it "sparks creativity," but felt it was too complex for kindergarten.

The researcher mentioned that in previous evaluations, the idea of fixing the movement direction in musical state had been proposed so that children could focus on the notes without needing to think about direction changes. However, this idea did not convince P3. She found using the same cards for both directions and music confusing. She explained that the idea could work "if these cards had a drawing of a musical note or something to differentiate them from the others, otherwise, it's a mess."

P3 considered the concept of passing in silence or making sound in some parts of the robot's route much more viable: "[The option] to go with sound or without sound is great." She was undecided on whether there should be two separate cards to activate and deactivate the musical mode, or if one card would suffice.

**Summary.** During the third evaluation, the teacher found the musical mode engaging but too complex if the objective is composing melodies while managing direction changes. The idea of fixing the robot's direction in musical state to focus on notes was not convincing. The concept of the robot passing in silence or making sound at specific points was seen as more viable. There was uncertainty about whether one or two cards should be used to activate and deactivate the musical mode.

## 4.4 Evaluation #4 (Teacher Watching Simulator's Video)

The video of the musical mode simulator was deemed "super clear." P3 found that it accurately reflects Robotito's behavior that she experienced in the previous evaluation session: "I think I was watching exactly how the robot works." However, she noted the absence of visual feedback to indicate whether Robotito is in musical mode: "What caught my attention [...] is that there's nothing visually indicating that it's in musical mode. I didn't see any different light turning on; you can only tell if you hear the sound or not."

## 4.5 Evaluation #5 (In-Classroom Evaluation with Children)

We assessed children's understanding of the musical mode during Activity #6, with 11 groups of children (30 children in total) participating—five in the morning and six in the afternoon.

Each group was tasked with conditional music reproduction, requiring them to navigate the robot through trajectory sections with and without sound (see an example in Fig. 7). The children recalled from the previous session that the orange card activated the sound, but not all remembered how to deactivate the musical mode. After some trial and error with the orange card, all groups except one successfully completed the task. In the group that did not, the two participants mistakenly believed that you should remove the orange card from the floor to deactivate the sound.

During other tasks when they were not asked to use musical mode, some children spontaneously added the orange card that activates musical mode.

## 5 Discussion

### 5.1 Conditionals Implementation

Incorporating conditionals into Robotito's programming raised many questions about what constitutes a conditional. Given that Robotito's behavior is event-based, conceptualizing conditionals in this context was challenging for the teachers. P2 questioned whether Robotito's behavior of sensing a color and responding accordingly could already be considered a conditional, noting, "If it sees yellow, it does this thing [actions related to yellow color detection]." The teachers were familiar with procedural programs where an explicit boolean expression is evaluated, and based on the result, the robot either executes or skips an additional set of instructions. Our prototypes functioned slightly differently, enabling Robotito to respond differently to the same coding card based on the evaluation of an implicit boolean expression. Despite adhering to this definition, understanding conditionals for Robotito remained difficult, leading to doubts like "Is it conditional or a rule?" (P1 regarding the color frame prototype) and "I associate it more with an event than with a conditional" (P2 on the musical mode).

To further consider teachers' concerns we reviewed how conditionals have been introduced in educational robotic activities. We found that definitions of conditionals for robots used in early childhood are sparse [3,6,21,30] and sometimes contentious. The definitions of Bers et al. [6] ("Decisions related to events or actions.") and Pugnali et al. [21] ("Making decisions based on certain factors or events.") are not very specific and focused on the tools applied in their studies (KIBO[3] and ScratchJr[4]). Yu and Roque [30] include in their definition of conditionals implicit conditionals based on planning trajectories to avoid (or pass through) certain spots on the map, resulting in a sequence of movements that respects these invented restrictions but lacks conditionals at the code level. Bakala et al. [3] consider "blocking the program execution until some event occurs" a form of expressing conditionals, though this could be viewed more as a while loop than a traditional conditional. Regardless of the definition, programming Robotito with the option of musical mode is a more complex task than programming Robotito without the option of a musical mode.

As mentioned in the introduction, conditionals are important programming concepts that help children develop advanced algorithms. We believe it is important to integrate conditionals into the educational robotics curriculum at the preschool level. Establishing how to introduce this concept to this age group is a necessary starting point that should be explored in future research. More specifically, it would be useful to better understand what type of activities are more likely to help children transition to procedural programming using if-then-else type conditionals.

---

[3] https://kinderlabrobotics.com/kibo/.
[4] https://www.scratchjr.org/.

## 5.2 Prototypes

All the prototypes we evaluated presented certain challenges, and exchanges with the teachers helped us focus on the most viable ideas and incorporate improvements.

The color frame prototype was considered too demanding, as it relied on an if-then-else condition that would require children to manage "two parallel universes," each with a different set of coding cards. In contrast, the other prototypes were simpler, requiring only one additional coding card. Both were found attractive, but the decisive factor in the teachers' preferences was the potential to explore new actions in musical mode. Sound reproduction was considered engaging, and activities involving passing through certain parts of the robot's route in silence or with sound were seen as accessible for preschoolers. While the teachers were enthusiastic about composing melodies, they were also aware of the difficulties associated with combining sound and direction or separating the musical mode from the directional mode. The viability of music composition should be validated in future studies.

The interaction with the teachers helped validate specific aspects of the musical mode implementation. For example, the teachers suggested using a single card to activate and deactivate the mode. They also provided examples of activities and identified potential improvements, such as adding visual cues to indicate whether the robot is in musical mode.

## 5.3 In-Classroom Evaluation

The fact that 10 out of 11 groups were able to successfully complete tasks that require conditional music reproduction is encouraging. We believe it bodes well for the activities being appropriate for children in similar settings.

A positive aspect of conditional music reproduction was that it was a good fit for group activities. The children with a better understanding of the functionality of the orange card helped more confused children to complete the tasks. They provided comments such as, "You have to put the orange card back so the sound turns off," or "To stop the sound, put it back again."

We believe it is important to support CT and ER activities that can be experienced in groups because they may be a better fit in schools where it is not possible to afford one robot per child. Such activities may also be a better fit in schools with a greater emphasis on group work, social skills, and children learning together rather than more individualized approaches.

## 5.4 Simulator

The teachers saw the simulator as a valuable tool for introducing Robotito to children. They noted that presenting the robot on a screen or projecting it onto a whiteboard would be less distracting for the children since it cannot be touched or grabbed. They envisioned using it to explain the color-direction relationship or introduce a specific activity before interacting with the real robot, thereby reducing children's anxiety.

The enthusiastic reaction of the teachers helped researchers envision the simulator's use as a tool not only for introducing the robot but also for practicing programming individually. The same code used to generate the desktop simulation can be deployed as an Android application, allowing interaction with digital coding cards and an on-screen Robotito by dragging them with a finger. Given that each public preschool in the country where the research was conducted is equipped with Android tablets, we began considering incorporating programming Robotito on the tablet as part of Robotito's curriculum.

Although the simulator can help in practicing robot programming individually, it is essential to combine its use with hands-on experiences with the actual robot. While the simulated Robotito scenario is useful for practicing trajectory programming, it lacks the ability to incorporate new elements, making it challenging to engage children through activities like personalizing the robot or adding characters and decorations to build a narrative. The limited flexibility of the simulated scenario also hampers integration with preschool curricula.

We consider that simulators can reinforce the learning experience, but they should be complemented by tangible robots that offer concrete materials and greater flexibility for incorporating new elements.

## 5.5 Limitations

Despite the valuable insights gained from our work, several limitations should be acknowledged.

One of the main constraints was the small sample size of teachers, as only three participated in the evaluation of the prototypes. While this is a limited number, we believe that their feedback was valuable since they were experienced professionals who regularly use robots in their classrooms. Moreover, the four evaluation sessions involved different participants—teachers P1 and P2 attended the first two evaluations, while only P3 participated in evaluations three and four. This inconsistency may have introduced bias, as each teacher's unique experiences and perspectives could have influenced the feedback. Despite the small sample size and participant variation, the activities with children confirmed that the gathered insights contributed to a solution that is accessible to children and can be successfully implemented in a classroom setting.

Regarding the evaluation with children, the study was conducted in a group setting, which encouraged collaborative problem-solving but did not allow us to determine whether each child fully understood the concept of conditionals. While group-based evaluations are valuable for assessing collective performance and social learning, they are not sufficient for evaluating individual comprehension. In this context, individual assessments are necessary to accurately assess each child's internalization of conditionals. Additionally, the task used to evaluate conditionals was primarily designed to reinforce previously learned concepts rather than formally assess children's performance. It included researchers' scaffolding, as well as revision and repetition of the previously learned contents. As a result, the study does not provide a precise measure of children's comprehension. Although our evaluation was group-based and subjective, the preliminary results are encouraging, as they suggest that the proposed solution aligns well with preschool children's cognitive abilities. Future research could incorporate individual assessments to gain a clearer understanding of each child's level of comprehension, thereby complementing group-based evaluations with data unaffected by peer influence.

By acknowledging these limitations, we aim to highlight areas for improvement in future research and emphasize the need for broader studies to refine and expand our findings.

## 6 Conclusion

In this study, we explored various prototypes for incorporating conditionals into Robotito's programming to facilitate the teaching of advanced programming concepts in early childhood education. We obtained feedback on the color frame, musical mode, and split card prototypes, each offering distinct implementations of conditionals. Through multiple evaluations involving experienced teachers, we identified the strengths and weaknesses of each prototype. The color frame prototype was deemed too complex, while the musical mode and split card were found to be more accessible for preschoolers. The musical mode, in particular, was favored for introducing a new output modality- sound. The in-classroom evaluation of the musical mode confirmed that it can be successfully used at the kindergarten level.

Teachers also highlighted the simulator's value as a tool for introducing Robotito and working on programming tasks in a less distracting environment before using the real robot. Based on these insights, we recognized the importance of integrating the simulator into Robotito's curriculum, especially given the widespread availability of Android tablets in public preschools in the location where the research is being conducted. This study underscores the need for guidelines for implementing conditionals in early childhood robotics education and highlights the importance of iterative prototype evaluation with educator input.

**Acknowledgments.** This work was supported by Agencia Nacional de Investigación e Innovación, Uruguay (FSED_2_2021_1_169697) and a PhD scholarship from CAP Uruguay. We would like to express our sincere gratitude to the teachers that participated in the study and to the principal, children, and teachers of Jardín 216, Montevideo.

**Disclosure of Interests.** The authors have no competing interests to declare that are relevant to the content.

## A Activities

**Table 2.** Summary of ER sessions.

| Activity | Date, class (nr of children) | Modality of work | Main goal of the session |
|---|---|---|---|
| #1 | 06.11.23 A1 (14)<br>06.11.23 A2 (18) | Whole class together. | To introduce Robotito and how it moves with yellow, red, green and blue color cards. |
| #2 | 10.11.23 A1 (16)<br>10.11.23 A2 (18) | The class split in two groups. | To reinforce how the robot responds to color cards through an embodied experience. To observe that the color cards should be placed in the robot's trajectory. |
| #3 | 20.11.23 A1 (16)<br>17.11.23 A2 (18) | The class split in two groups. | To understand that directing the robot depends on the color of the coding card and the robot's rotation. To reinforce that the color cards should be placed in the robot's trajectory. |
| #4 | 22.11.23 A1 (16)<br>20.11.23 A2 (19) | Whole class together. | To reinforce how the robot responds to color cards through more individual interaction with Robotito's simulator. To practice route planning, sequencing and sequence decomposition. |
| #5 | 24.11.23 A1 (15)<br>24.11.23 A2 (15) | The class split in two groups. | To plan Robotito's trajectories, select the corresponding color cards, and place them. To introduce conditional music reproduction using the orange card. |
| #6 | 27.11.23 A1 (14)<br>24.11.23 A2 (16) | The class split into small groups. | To practice coding Robotito's routes and evaluate understanding of musical mode. |
| #7 | 29.11.23 A1 (14)<br>29.11.23 A2 (17) | The class split in two groups. | To introduce a pink card that makes the robot execute a prerecorded sequence of movements and stop. |
| #8 | 04.12.23 A1 (14)<br>04.12.23 A2 (18) | The class split into small groups. | To reinforce how the robot responds to the pink card and practice combining it with the other coding cards. |

## References

1. Angeli, C., Giannakos, M.: Computational thinking education: issues and challenges. Comput. Hum. Behav. **105**, 106185 (2020)
2. Bakala, E., Gerosa, A., Hourcade, J.P., Pascale, M., Hergatacorzian, C., Tejera, G.: Design factors affecting the social use of programmable robots to learn computational thinking in kindergarten. In: Proceedings of the 21st Annual ACM Interaction Design and Children Conference, pp. 422–429 (2022)
3. Bakala, E., Gerosa, A., Hourcade, J.P., Tejera, G., Peterman, K., Trinidad, G.: A systematic review of technologies to teach control structures in preschool education. Front. Psychol. **13**, 911057 (2022)
4. Belmar, H.: Review on the teaching of programming and computational thinking in the world. Front. Comput. Sci. **4**, 997222 (2022)
5. Benetti, E., Mazzini, G.: Coding training proposal for kindergarten. In: 2020 International Conference on Software, Telecommunications and Computer Networks (SoftCOM), pp. 1–5. IEEE (2020)
6. Bers, M.U., González-González, C., Armas-Torres, M.B.: Coding as a playground: promoting positive learning experiences in childhood classrooms. Comput. Educ. **138**, 130–145 (2019)

7. Bers, M.U.: Coding and computational thinking in early childhood: the impact of Scratchjr in Europe. Eur. J. STEM Educ. **3**(3), 8 (2018)
8. Bers, M.U.: Coding as a playground: programming and computational thinking in the early childhood classroom. Routledge (2020)
9. Bocconi, S., et al.: Reviewing computational thinking in compulsory education. Scientific analysis or review KJ-06-22-069-EN-N (online), Luxembourg (Luxembourg) (2022). https://doi.org/10.2760/126955
10. Botički, I., Kovačević, P., Pivalica, D., Seow, P.: Identifying patterns in computational thinking problem solving in early primary education. In: Proceedings of the 26th International Conference on Computers in Education, p. 6 (2018)
11. Brennan, K., Resnick, M.: New frameworks for studying and assessing the development of computational thinking. In: Proceedings of the 2012 Annual Meeting of the American Educational Research Association, Vancouver, Canada, vol. 1, p. 25 (2012)
12. Gerosa, A., Koleszar, V., Tejera, G., Gómez-Sena, L., Carboni, A.: Educational robotics intervention to foster computational thinking in preschoolers: effects of children's task engagement. Front. Psychol. **13**, 904761 (2022)
13. Glezou, K.V.: Fostering computational thinking and creativity in early childhood education: play-learn-construct-program-collaborate. In: Mobile Learning Applications in Early Childhood Education, pp. 324–347. IGI Global (2020)
14. Gomes, T.C.S., Falcão, T.P., Tedesco, P.C.d.A.R.: Exploring an approach based on digital games for teaching programming concepts to young children. Int. J. Child-Comput. Interact. **16**, 77–84 (2018)
15. Grover, S., Pea, R.: Computational thinking in K-12: a review of the state of the field. Educ. Res. **42**(1), 38–43 (2013)
16. Grover, S., Pea, R.: Computational thinking: a competency whose time has come. Comput. Sci. Educ. Perspect. Teach. Learn. Sch. **19**(1), 19–38 (2018)
17. Khoo, K.Y.: A case study on how children develop computational thinking collaboratively with robotics toys. Int. J. Educ. Technol. Learn. **9**(1), 39–51 (2020)
18. Martinez, C., Gomez, M.J., Benotti, L.: A comparison of preschool and elementary school children learning computer science concepts through a multilanguage robot programming platform. In: Proceedings of the 2015 ACM Conference on Innovation and Technology in Computer Science Education, pp. 159–164 (2015)
19. Papadakis, S., Kalogiannakis, M.: Learning computational thinking development in young children with bee-bot educational robotics. In: Handbook of Research on Tools for Teaching Computational Thinking in P-12 Education, pp. 289–309. IGI Global (2020)
20. Papadakis, S., Kalogiannakis, M., Zaranis, N.: Developing fundamental programming concepts and computational thinking with scratchjr in preschool education: a case study. Int. J. Mob. Learn. Organ. **10**(3), 187–202 (2016)
21. Pugnali, A., Sullivan, A., Bers, M.U.: The impact of user interface on young children s computational thinking. J. Inf. Technol. Educ. Innov. Pract. **16**, 171 (2017)
22. Relkin, E., Bers, M.: Techcheck-k: a measure of computational thinking for kindergarten children. In: 2021 IEEE Global Engineering Education Conference (EDUCON), pp. 1696–1702. IEEE (2021)
23. Rich, K.M., Strickland, C., Binkowski, T.A., Moran, C., Franklin, D.: K-8 learning trajectories derived from research literature: sequence, repetition, conditionals. In: Proceedings of the 2017 ACM Conference on International Computing Education Research, pp. 182–190 (2017)

24. Roussou, E., Rangoussi, M.: On the use of robotics for the development of computational thinking in kindergarten: educational intervention and evaluation. In: Merdan, M., Lepuschitz, W., Koppensteiner, G., Balogh, R., Obdržálek, D. (eds.) RiE 2019. AISC, vol. 1023, pp. 31–44. Springer, Cham (2020). https://doi.org/10.1007/978-3-030-26945-6_3
25. Shute, V.J., Sun, C., Asbell-Clarke, J.: Demystifying computational thinking. Educ. Res. Rev. **22**, 142–158 (2017)
26. So, H.J., Jong, M.S.Y., Liu, C.C.: Computational thinking education in the Asian pacific region. Asia Pac. Educ. Res. **29**, 1–8 (2020)
27. Sullivan, A., Bers, M.U.: Dancing robots: integrating art, music, and robotics in Singapore's early childhood centers. Int. J. Technol. Des. Educ. **28**, 325–346 (2018)
28. Uscanga, E.A.V., Bottamedi, J., Brizuela, M.L.: Pensamiento computacional en el aula: el desafío en los sistemas educativos de latinoamérica. Revista Interuniversitaria de Investigación en Tecnología Educativa (2019)
29. Wyeth, P.: How young children learn to program with sensor, action, and logic blocks. J. Learn. Sci. **17**(4), 517–550 (2008)
30. Yu, J., Roque, R.: A review of computational toys and kits for young children. Int. J. Child-Comput. Interact. **21**, 17–36 (2019)
31. Zapata-Cáceres, M., Martín-Barroso, E., Román-González, M.: Computational thinking test for beginners: design and content validation. In: 2020 IEEE Global Engineering Education Conference (EDUCON), pp. 1905–1914. IEEE (2020)

# Serious Games Development by Educators: Opportunities and Challenges

Joana Gabriela Ribeiro de Souza(✉), Letícia da Silva Macedo Alves,
Marcos Vinícius Caldeira Pacheco, Lucas Xavier Veneroso,
and Raquel Oliveira Prates

Fededral University of Minas Gerais, Av. Antônio Carlos, 6627,
Belo Horizonte, Brazil
{joana.souza,leticia.alves,marcospacheco,lucasxv,rprates}@dcc.ufmg.br

**Abstract.** The increasing accessibility of technology has fueled the rise of EUD, allowing educators to create and modify digital games for learning. Despite advancements in user-friendly game design tools, challenges persist in balancing usability, customization, and pedagogical effectiveness. In this work, we conduct a SLR to investigate the support available for educators in game development, identifying key trends and limitations. Many tools favor ease of use over flexibility, offering limited customization, weak LMS integration, and insufficient analytics. Additionally, the limited involvement of educators in tool development raises concerns about usability and alignment with real-world needs. A significant research gap exists in artificial intelligence integration for adaptive learning and procedural content generation. Furthermore, few studies assess the long-term impact of these tools on teaching effectiveness. By mapping the current state of art and highlighting existing challenges, this review provides insights to guide future advancements in educational game design, emphasizing the need for improved accessibility, usability, and pedagogical value to support non-technical users in creating effective learning experiences.

**Keywords:** Educational games · Authoring Tools · End-User Development

## 1 Introduction

In recent years, increased access to technology has led to greater user demand, driving the growth of End-User Development (EUD). Over the past two decades, numerous tools have emerged to support end users in various contexts [20,59], ranging from domain experts, such as administrators using spreadsheets, to lay users who want to automate personal robots using rule-based systems [8]. One prominent area where end users are becoming creators rather than just consumers is game design and extension. This shift has fueled the development of game engines specifically tailored for non-developers [22,49,53].

This trend has significant implications for education, where digital games are increasingly recognized as valuable teaching tools [12]. Games are intrinsically engaging, and their use in the educational context has been used for many years with both physical and digital games. Thus, investigating how to support educators in game creation is not new. For instance, in 1980, Malone identified three categories that motivate learning – challenge, fantasy, and curiosity – and based on them, proposed a set of heuristics to design instructional games [38]. Since then, other works have been developed to use and democratize the use of games as learning tools [15,29]. In this direction, simplified game design tools have been developed to make game creation more accessible to non-professionals [6,13,18]. Despite these efforts, even such tools may be challenging for educators [51].

The difficulties faced by educators in creating their own games align with broader discussions in the field of EUD, a relevant area in Human-Computer Interaction (HCI) as it empowers users to tailor or develop applications specific to their needs [16]. Several literature mappings have been conducted to define and structure the EUD domain [8,32,46,55], covering areas such as End-User Software Engineering (EUSE) and meta-design. However, these studies do not specifically address game development, a field that presents unique challenges even for professional developers [26,44].

A deeper understanding of EUD in the context of game creation could help clarify the state-of-the-art and identify gaps in existing tools, particularly in educational settings, where accessibility, ease of use for non-programmers, and pedagogical effectiveness are key considerations. In this direction, [2] provided a mapping of authoring tools (AT) for serious games (SG) related to instructional design principles. However, there is still a need to complement this research by further exploring how EUD principles can enhance game development for non-experts. Particularly considering that previous studies have identified that teachers can have many difficulties when using general AT to create educational games [51], and other digital medias [5].

Based on the literature, we noticed a lack of studies investigating tools that enable the creation, extension, and modification of educational games by end-users, in particular by educators – defined here as teachers or individuals acting in instructional roles. Thus, this study conducts a Systematic Literature Review (SLR) to identify relevant approaches and techniques. It aims to answer the research question: *"What support do platforms aimed at educators who want to create educational games offer?"*.

This study examines tools, challenges, and opportunities in the development of educational games by educators described in the literature. Key findings include the rise of user-friendly AT, limited customization, and gaps in AI integration. The study highlights opportunities to improve accessibility, usability, and pedagogical effectiveness, offering insights to guide future research in educational game design for non-technical users. These results are useful not only to researchers and developers interested in the topic, but it can also support educators in finding tools that suit their needs and skills.

The organization of this paper is as follows. Section 2 presents the related work. Next, we describe the methodology adopted to carry out our SLR. In Sect. 4 we present the results obtained from the analysis. In Sect. 5 we discuss the main findings, implications, and limitations. Finally, Sect. 6 presents the conclusions of the work.

## 2 Related Works

The considerable growth in the use of personal computers with graphical user interfaces and tools for personal use has created the need to create environments that allow people with little to no programming experience to design their software solutions [46]. From this need, strategies and solutions were developed to provide this support to end-users (or programmers with no experience).

Several surveys have explored different aspects of end-user involvement in software development. Ko et al. [32] focused on EUSE, classifying research in the field and discussing key factors such as risk, reward, domain complexity, and self-efficacy in tool design. Paternò [46] examined EUD, highlighting its motivations, application environments (especially web and mobile), and future directions. Later, Tetteroo and Markopoulos [55] conducted an SLR of 93 studies, covering EUD, End-User Programming (EUP), EUSE, and meta-design, identifying trends and open challenges. Unlike these works, the present study focuses on EUD and EUP in the context of game development. More recently, Barricelli et al. [8] conducted an SLR on EUD, EUP, and EUSE, categorizing solutions by techniques, application domains, and target audiences, with a broad scope including the Internet of Things. In contrast, this study focuses on game design and extension, addressing a research gap. Furthermore, their review covered work published until May 2017, leaving more recent studies unexamined.

Gajewski, El Mawas and Heutte [17] conducted an SLR to identify and compare game design tools, assisting users in selecting the most suitable option. It identified 12 tools, including general-purpose platforms like AgentSheets and Scratch, as well as professional engines such as Unity and Unreal Engine. Whereas their work takes into consideration any end-user, our focuses on solutions tailored for educators without programming expertise to produce games emphasizing ease of use in educational contexts.

Ahmad et al. [2] conducted a systematic literature review of AT for SG integrated with instructional design. Their study resulted in the analysis of the following aspects related to the eight selected articles: the role of the teacher for SG design, gameplay structuring, learning strategies, application domain, academic levels, and the genre of the games. They focused in investigate those features related to the AT capability. Differently from the SLR produced in [2], this work performs a broader (and more recent) analysis of tools.

Finally, (in 2023), Ahmad et al. [1] published another literature review focusing on educator-oriented ATs for developing Rich Educational Media (REM), including SG. Their study highlighted the challenges of REM creation, which often requires expertise in programming and digital art, as well as specialized tools like game engines and 3D modeling software. To address these complexities, educator-focused ATs aim to simplify development and reduce reliance on technical experts. Unlike the present work, which focuses primarily on AT to create SG, their review covered a broader range of technologies, as virtual, augmented, and mixed reality tools to create REM using general purpose ATs.

## 3 Methodology

In order to answer our research question (RQ) we conducted an SLR. The SLR's goal was to identify approaches, methods, and tools that allow users (educators) without prior programming or game design knowledge to create their own educational games. This method aims to capture a comprehensive set of relevant publications on the topic while ensuring the reproducibility and integrity of the search process [31]. To guide the SLR, we established a research protocol, describing the research questions (RQs), digital libraries used, study period, search string, inclusion and exclusion criteria, quality assessment measures and data extraction procedures from the publications found.

As the main objective of this study was to identify approaches that enable game development without prior programming knowledge, our research question was *"What support do platforms aimed at educators who want to create educational games offer?"* Based on this RQ, we decompose it into five specific questions that focus on aspects of the tools and the support available. Thus, the specific questions (SQ) are:

- [SQ1] What are the types of overall approaches proposed?
- [SQ2] What are the user development strategies adopted?
- [SQ3] What are the existing tools?
- [SQ4] What learning support is offered to users?
- [SQ5] Have the tools been evaluated?

SQ1 aimed to identify and understand the overall approaches regarding the type of end-user game creation being offered to users (educators). For SQ2, we looked at which end-user programming strategy was adopted (e.g., programming by template, example, and/or rules) in the solution presented. With SQ3, we identified the existing tools and whether they are available to use. SQ4 focused on examining the support offered to users to learn and interact with the proposed systems, and how to apply educational objectives into games. Finally, with SQ5 we verified whether the tools described underwent any evaluation, either of the development tool or the games generated using them.

To answer these questions, our research string (RS) includes three sets of terms related to serious games, educators, and end-user support strategy. Thus, the research string is depicted below:

*("educational games" OR "serious games" OR "game-based learning")* **AND** *("educator" OR "teacher" OR "instructor")* **AND** *("end-user development" OR EUD OR EUP OR "End-user programming" OR "authoring tool" OR "game design" OR "authoring platform" OR "Authoring system")*

Our search was conducted in the following repositories: ACM Digital Library, ScienceDirect, IEEE Xplore and Google Scholar. We limited our search to the period from January 2014 to July 2024 (when the search was carried out). The period of 10 years chosen was intended to select more recent works that describe technologies with a higher chance of being available for use.

The search with our RS, returned 2872 results. We then proceeded to pre-process the list, to generate a set of interest. To do so, we removed publications that were repeated (i.e. same title), book chapters, event sessions, and workshops. At the end our set contained 2845 articles: 951 from ACM Digital Library, 842 from IEEE Xplore, 709 from ScienceDirect, and 343 from Google Scholar.

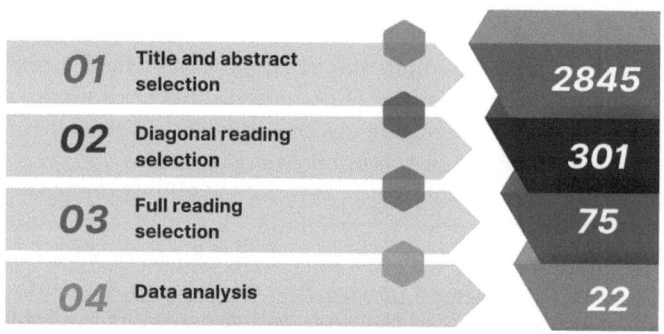

**Fig. 1.** Methodology adopted by the authors

The selection process consisted of three phases, followed by a data analysis phase. Figure 1 depicts the methodology adopted in this paper. First, the reviewers screened these 2,845 publications based on titles and abstracts (phase 1). During this step, they excluded publications whose title and abstract were not in English or Portuguese, or which made clear in the abstract that they were not related to end-user game development. At the end, the number of publications was reduced to 301. Next, in phase 2, a diagonal reading (introduction, key topics, and conclusion) was conducted, further filtering out articles unrelated to the RQ and SQs, as well as excluding extended abstracts, demonstrations, and general programming platforms, narrowing the selection to 75.

Finally, in phase 3, the articles were read in full, and the relevant data extracted and registered for each one, and the quality and relevance of the article to the SQs were assessed. To do so, we considered four questions: (C1) Does the study clearly define the purpose of the research?; (C2) Does the study discuss related work?; (C3) Does the study clarify the results and contributions?; and (C4) Does the study address the proposed SQs and RQ for the SLR? For each article, its quality was assigned a value between 0 and 1 (where 1 means that the aspect is fully covered). To be selected, the article had to meet criterion 4 and reach a minimum of 2.5 points. Our goal was to focus on tools aimed at enabling teachers to create educational games with this purpose, so we excluded platforms that only allowed storytelling as if it were an interactive book or general-purpose tools whose focus was not educational games. As result, we selected 22 articles.

In total, 5 people participated in the research. One acted as the supervisor, and the other four were responsible for conducting the steps. We followed a research protocol where in each SLR phase, at least two researchers evaluated each article. At the end of all phases, after an individual evaluation of each article by at least two researchers, a consolidation meeting with all participants was conducted. The goal was to discuss potential different views about an article and come to a consensus on whether it should be excluded or included in the next phase of the study. If there were any doubts about an article, it was forwarded to the next phase for a more thorough evaluation.

## 4 Results

In this section, we present the results of our analysis of the 22 selected articles. First we present an overview of the work published on the topic of end-user game development for educators. We then present the answers to each of the 5 specific questions (SQs) posed. Notice that, as we present the results, we refer to the papers that composed our selected set through its ID in the study, as depicted in Table 1 in Appendix A.

### 4.1 Overview

Analyzing how the work on end-user game development for educators is distributed in the last 10 years, we notice that it has been explored throughout this period of time with at least one article published per year, with the maximum of five published in 2021, three in 2014, 2016 and 2022 (see Table 1 in Appendix A). As for publication forums, the articles were distributed in 20 different forums focused on distinct areas (e.g. education, visual languages, and games), IEEE Access being the only one that has published 2 of the selected articles (see Table 1 in Appendix A). A geographical analysis of author affiliations indicates that most contributions originated in Spain (5), followed by France (3), Canada (2), Mexico (2), and the United States (2).

We classified the proposed solutions regarding the platform in which they could be executed. In general, we identified three types of tool in the studies:

- **Desktop-based solutions:** These tools require installation on a computer and often provide more complex functionalities, supporting detailed game design and richer interactions [5 articles: A8, A15, A17, A18, A21].
- **Mobile-based solutions:** These platforms are optimized for smartphones and tablets, enabling educators to create and manage games on the go. Notable examples include ZeusAR [A7], which integrates augmented reality, and JEM Inventor [A5], which allows for location-based learning experiences [6 articles: A2, A3, A5, A7, A8, and A10].

– **Web-based solutions:** These tools provide ease of access through browsers, eliminating the need for installation. Platforms such as Escapp [A9] and Moirai [A1] exemplify this category, offering intuitive interfaces for educators and students [16 articles: A1, A2, A3, A4, A6, A7, A8, A9, A10, A11, A14, A16, A18, A19, A20, and A22].

Some systems offer more than one way to access the application, allowing users to explore the tool on the web, desktop or mobile. The prevalence of web-based and mobile-friendly solutions suggests an emphasis on ease of access and of deployment. However, desktop-based tools still play a role in providing advanced functionalities of some web-based tools or as plug-ins to other applications, such as Unity [A8]. Future research could explore how cross-platform environments that integrate desktop, mobile, and web could enhance the adaptability of serious game development platforms.

### 4.2 What are the Types of Overall Approaches Proposed?

Our analysis of the selected articles indicated that EUP and EUD approaches were adopted by authors. According to Ko et al. [32], EUP refers to programming intended primarily to fulfill personal needs rather than creating broadly applicable solutions, distinguishing it from general programming. In contrast, EUD, as defined by Lieberman et al. [35], encompasses methods, techniques, and tools that enable non-professional developers to create, modify, and extend software solutions, not only for their own use but to be used by others as well.

Only A3, which presents the RUFUS tool, describes that the platform provides EUP for healthcare professionals. The tool has a web interface where games are created and customized, and a mobile interface where games are played. RUFUS allows the creation of five types of games step-by-step using a simplified graphic interface. Papers A6 and A11 acknowledge EUD as a field enabling domain specialists to develop applications without programming expertise and emphasize the need for further advancements in the growing area. Although not explicitly proposing EUD-based technologies, their discussions imply alignment with this approach.

The remaining papers do not explicitly classify their research within the EUP or EUD approaches. However, they incorporate strategies commonly associated with these approaches (e.g. programming by example and wizard-based), which will be detailed in Sect. 4.3.

### 4.3 What are the User Development Strategies Adopted?

Analyzing our second specific question, we identified the strategies employed by the authors as a means of enabling game development and extension. The sum is greater than the number of papers because in several works more than one strategy was used. Thus, we will present the 7 strategies identified in the tools as presented below.

**Wizard-Based:** This type of interaction appeared in one article and is usually adopted in situations where the task can be divided into a sequence of steps to guide users to reach their goal. ZeusAR [A7] presents a user interface (UI) based on a wizard that guides users and helps automate the development of augmented reality games.

**Templates:** Templates appear as a way of to make it easier for users to create software. They allow users to configure aspects of the game using a predefined scheme, minimizing the error rate of the game creation process. The use of customizable templates, as in SGAME [A11] and JEM Inventor [A5], is also an example of an approach to simplify game creation.

**Visual Programming:** Used in 12 of the papers reviewed [A1, A2, A3, A5, A6, A8, A10, A12, A13, A15, A17 and A19]. Different from textual programming languages, visual programming enables the user to specify a program in two or more dimensions rather than the compiler or interpreter processing the commands as a one-dimensional sequence [43]. Thus, visual programming allows the user to describe a process that makes sense to humans rather than in a way that the user has to think about how the computer would perform a function, tending to make it easier for end-users to program. We considered block-programming as a variation of visual programming. Tools such as ARQS (Authentic Role-playing game Quest System) [A1] use block-based programming, enabling the creation of 2D serious RPG games through a visual interface. Domain-Specific Visual Languages (DSVLs) are used by projects such as uAdventure [A8], allowing educators and content experts to create games without the need for textual programming, focusing on their content expertise.

**Frameworks and Diagrams:** Both tools help visualize information and concepts and are used in the articles as a way to define the logic and structure of the game [A1, A10, and A16]. We considered diagrams as a simplified drawing showing a schematic representation of something. The tool presented in A16 uses finite state machines to define the order that events occur and tables to configure game rules that will be interpreted by a game engine.

**Programming by Demonstration (PBD):** This technique appears in the tool SKETCH'NDO [A17]. In programming by demonstration/example, the system records the actions performed by the user in the interface and produces a generalized program that can be used later in an analogous example [35]. Thus, a central point is how to describe the actions and objects selected by the user so that the system can determine the type of generalization that is possible.

**Programming by Rules:** It appears in 8 papers [A1, A2, A5, A6, A7, A8, A14 and A16]. In this case, developers create a set of rules that end-users must use to construct their systems [10]. StickAndClick [A14] is an example, which uses simple conditional rules to define actions when clicking on screen elements.

**Textual Programming:** We found some works that use textual programming, either in conjunction with other techniques or as the main strategy to configure games. Textual programming, *i.e.* using a sequence of commands to create a program, is the most common in professional programming environments. A textual language can also be a scripting or a natural language, which in general is simpler for end-users [A6, A12, A14 and A22].

Most articles adopted two interaction strategies: direct manipulation and Window, Icon, Menu, Pointing (WIMP). Interaction using direct manipulation are those that lets users interact with on-screen objects directly [25] [A1, A2, A3, A4, A5, A6, A8, A9, A10, A11, A12, A14, A15, A17, A19 and A21]. For instance, RUFUS [A3], allows users to drag and drop actors in the scene of narrative games, add and drag items in the scenario of fitting puzzles. The WIMP interaction is a graphical user interface (GUI) style that uses these elements to create a visual way to interact with a computer [30]. Direct manipulation and WIMP appear in most articles [A2, A3, A5, A6, A7, A8, A11, A13, A14, A15, A18, A20 and A21]. Tools like JEM Inventor [A5] use menus for selecting predefined components.

One approach to allowing end-users to create games worth mentioning is the no-code approach[1] For instance, the Moirai platform [A1 and A6] allows the creation and modification of dialogue-based serious games without programming. The no-code approach was used across many of the strategies identified: wizard-based, templates, visual programming, frameworks and diagrams, and PBD.

### 4.4 What are the Existing Tools?

Various tools have been developed to support the creation of educational games, each with distinct features and purposes. These tools aim to simplify the game design process while ensuring educational effectiveness and user engagement.

SGAME [A11] is an authoring tool designed for teachers, which allows them to combine web-based games with SCORM learning objects. For example, a teacher could create a quiz game that tracks student progress using SCORM standards but presents it as an interactive narrative experience. Similarly, Moirai [A1 and A6] is a no-code platform that empowers non-technical users, such as healthcare professionals and educators, to design virtual serious games without requiring programming skills. This platform emphasizes ease of use, enabling users to focus on educational outcomes rather than technical complexities.

RUFUS [A3] offers a specialized platform for creating digital therapeutic or educational games. In the healthcare context, it prioritizes clinical effectiveness over technical accuracy, allowing therapists to develop cognitive rehabilitation games that adapt to patient performance while using simplified graphics and interactions. Meanwhile, uAdventure [A8 and A15] focuses on point-and-click adventure games, emphasizing storytelling and dialogue over visual fidelity. Educators can use this tool to create branching story games that teach historical events through character conversations between actors and scene exploration.

In the realm of card games, MOLEGA [A10] provides a Domain-Specific Modeling Language (DSML) to design educational card games. It emphasizes game mechanics and rules over graphical design, enabling teachers to create games

---

[1] No-code is a software development approach that enables users to create applications and automate business processes without writing code. source: https://www.ibm.com/think/topics/no-code.

that teach math concepts using abstract symbols and simple rules. On the other hand, ZeusAR [A7] is a tool for creating serious games with augmented reality, focusing on educational content over technological limitations. For instance, students can use smartphones to interact with virtual objects overlaid on real-world environments while learning complex scientific concepts.

JEM Inventor [A5] is a location-based learning AT that enables teachers to create mobile learning games. It emphasizes real-world integration over virtual simulation, allowing educators to design scavenger hunt games that use GPS data to teach geography while simplifying map representations. Similarly, Escapp [A9] is a web platform for managing educational escape rooms, focusing on puzzle design and teamwork over physical constraints. Students can solve virtual puzzles collaboratively, experiencing them as immersive challenges.

ARLearn [A18] is an open-source mobile application platform that emphasizes real-world scenarios over fictional narratives, enabling students to role-play historical figures in virtual environments while learning factual information through interactive dialogues. For collaborative design, ADDEGames [A13] provides a support environment that emphasizes user engagement over technical specifications. Teachers and students can co-design games that teach programming concepts through interactive storytelling.

For rapid prototyping, the work in A4 (no name provided) used GDevelop as a game engine that simplifies game development, emphasizing quick creation over polished production. Students can use drag-and-drop mechanics to create simple games that teach physics concepts, even if the games lack advanced graphics. On the other hand, APOGEE [A22] is an online software platform for the automated creation of 3D maze video games. It emphasizes educational purposes, allowing teachers to create games that teach geometry concepts using 3D mazes, even if the games lack advanced graphics.

StickAndClick [A14] is a tool designed to assist teachers and students in creating simple interactive digital content. It focuses on the creative and design aspects of computational thinking, allowing students to create games that teach logic concepts using drag-and-drop programming. Meanwhile, the tool in A16 (no name provided) enables teachers to design 3D learning environments, import learning elements (text, images, videos), and integrate game design elements (points, badges, rankings). For example, a teacher could create a virtual classroom that tracks student progress using points but uses simple 3D models.

For treasure hunt-type games, LMAC [A20] is an online tool that facilitates the creation of location-based mobile applications. It focuses on educational content over technical complexity, enabling teachers to create games that use GPS data to teach local ecology while simplifying map representations. Similarly, YOUth Go [A2] is an open-source platform designed to simplify the creation of location-based educational games (LBGs). It emphasizes simplicity over complexity, enabling teachers to create games that use GPS data to teach local history with minimal technical skills.

For professional training, SKETCH'NDO [A17] is a platform for the interactive creation of task-based serious games in 3D virtual environments. It focuses on immersive scenarios, enabling trainees to role-play complex situations while receiving real-time feedback from instructors. Finally, MAT for ARLearn [A18] is an educational content creation tool for mobile devices, designed for authentic learning environments. It emphasizes interactive augmented reality games, allowing students to interact with virtual objects overlaid on real-world environments while learning complex scientific concepts.

Analyzing the 18 tools (some articles referred to the same tool), we see they are aimed at different specific domains such as health [A1, A3, A6] mathematics [A10 and A18], vocational training [A17], and many of them aimed at learning computational thinking [A2, A4, A7, A8, A12, A13, A14, A15, A19, A21]. They generally focus on one [A1, A5, A6, A8, A15, A18, A20, and A21] or a few (2 to 3) types of games (other articles), limiting the customization of games to predefined mechanics. The vast majority of articles are not available for access. Articles A3 and A11 offer access to the tool created, and articles A6, A8, A9, A11, A15, and A18 present the repository of the project as open-source initiatives.

## 4.5 What Learning Support is Offered to Users?

The support provided to users varies across different tools but generally includes several key aspects designed to enhance usability, ease of access, and effectiveness. Many tools prioritize intuitive and no-code interfaces [A1, A3 and A6], making them accessible to non-technical users. These platforms often feature visual interfaces that eliminate the need for programming skills, enabling educators to focus on designing engaging learning experiences rather than grappling with technical complexities. For example, tools like Moirai [A1 and A6] and Rufus [A3] allow healthcare professionals and teachers to create games without writing a single line of code.

To further simplify the game creation process, many tools offer predefined templates and models [A1, A4, A5, A10, A11 and A14]. These templates provide a structured starting point, reducing the time and effort required to design games from scratch. For instance, JEM Inventor [A5] uses basic game models for location-based learning games, while MOLEGA [A10] provides templates for creating educational card games.

Comprehensive tutorials and documentation appears strongly in uAdventure [A8 and A15], helping users learn how to use the tool effectively. The resources include step-by-step guides, video tutorials, and FAQs, ensuring that even novice users can quickly become proficient.

Another important aspect is multimedia support [A2, A3, A4, A5, A14, A16 and A18], which allows users to incorporate images, audio, and video into their games. This feature enhances the interactivity and engagement of the learning experience. Tools like the one proposed in [A16] enable teachers to design 3D learning environments enriched with multimedia elements, making lessons more dynamic and immersive.

Some platforms also provide feedback and positive reinforcement for players [A2, A3, A5, A9, A16 and A17], which can enhance motivation and learning. For example, games created with Escapp [A9] often include mechanisms for rewarding players as they progress through challenges, fostering a sense of achievement.

Flexibility and customization are also key features, allowing users to personalize games with different themes, levels, and challenges [A3, A5, A6, A7, A10, A14, A15, A17, A19, A20, A21 and A22]. This adaptability ensures that games can be tailored to specific educational goals and learner needs. Many tools support different game types, such as platforms, card games, narrative-driven games, and escape rooms. This versatility allows educators to choose the most suitable format for their teaching objectives. For example, ZeusAR [A7] supports the creation of augmented reality games, while StickAndClick [A14] focuses on simple interactive digital content.

To accommodate users with varying levels of experience, two systems JEM Inventor [A5] and SGAME [A11] offer differentiated user modes. For instance, JEM Inventor provides basic, intermediate, and expert modes, ensuring that both beginners and advanced users can effectively utilize the platform.

Resource reuse is another valuable feature [A2, A11, A18 and A22], enabling users to repurpose existing learning materials. For example, MAT for ARLearn [A18] allows educators to reuse and recontextualize learning resources, saving time and effort while maintaining educational relevance. Additionally, some tools support mobile authoring, allowing users to create learning resources directly on mobile devices. This feature is particularly useful for educators who need to design content on the go.

Finally, many tools offer integration with Learning Management Systems (LMS) [A1, A4, A5, A8, A11 and A18], facilitating the seamless incorporation of games into existing educational workflows. For example, SGAME [A11] allows games to be exported as SCORM packages, making them compatible with a wide range of LMS platforms.

These features collectively ensure that educational game design tools are accessible, versatile, and effective, empowering educators to create engaging and impactful learning experiences for their students.

### 4.6 Have the Tools Been Evaluated?

Analyzing the evaluation initiatives reported in the studies, we notice that there are different criteria being considered (usability, user experience, learning effectiveness and performance), and with different stakeholders (teachers, students and other players). Next we describe the main different evaluation focuses and methods found.

The most common assessment is usability testing [A1, A2, A3, A4, A5, A6, A7, A11, A12, A16, A17 and A18], which focuses on evaluating the ease of use and overall user experience of the tools. The System Usability Scale (SUS) is frequently employed as a standardized method to measure usability. For example, tools like SGAME [A11] and Rufus [A3] have undergone usability testing to ensure they are intuitive and accessible for non-technical users, such as teachers and healthcare professionals. Some of these tools selected teachers [A4, A5, A7, A8 and A10], who play a central role in assessing the tools and creating educational games. Teachers provide valuable feedback on the practicality and effectiveness of the tools in real-world educational settings. For instance, platforms like MOLEGA [A10] and uAdventure [A8] have been tested by educators to ensure they align with pedagogical goals and classroom requirements.

Focus groups are used to gather detailed insights from participants about the games created with the tools [A4, A14 and A17]. This qualitative method allows researchers to explore users' perceptions, preferences, and suggestions for improvement. For example, focus groups have been conducted to evaluate games developed with StickAndClick [A14] and SKETCH'NDO [A17], providing valuable feedback on their design and effectiveness.

Evaluation of games with students [A4, A5, A9, A12] also appeared, as students are the primary end-users of the games created with these tools. Students play the games and provide feedback on their engagement, enjoyment, and learning experience. This feedback helps refine the tools to better meet the needs of learners. For example, games developed with JEM Inventor [A5] and Escapp [A9] have been tested by students to assess their educational value and appeal.

To measure the impact of the games on learning outcomes, some studies conduct measurement of learning effectiveness through pre- and post-tests [A7 and A18]. These tests evaluate whether students have achieved the intended learning objectives after playing the games created by educators. For instance, games created with ZeusAR [A7] and MAT for ARLearn [A18] have been assessed for their ability to enhance students' understanding of complex scientific concepts.

Questionnaire application is another widely used method for collecting data to validate and evaluate the developed tools [A1, A2, A4, A5, A6, A7, A9, A11, A16, and A18]. These questionnaires gather feedback from users on various aspects of the tools, such as usability, functionality, and educational value. For example, [A16] and MAT for ARLearn [A18] have been evaluated using questionnaires to ensure they meet the needs of educators and students.

Finally, performance analyses were also conducted to assess the technical efficiency and reliability of the tools [A4 and A7]. For instance, the performance of ZeusAR [A7] has been analyzed to ensure it can handle the computational demands of augmented reality games without compromising user experience.

Although none of the papers evaluated all the possible criteria with all possible stakeholders, all of them (except one - [A22]) conducted an assessment of their proposal. Many of them did include evaluation of one or more criteria [A1, A2, A4, A5, A6, A7, A8, A9, A11, A13, A14, A15, A18, and A21]. Furthermore, 19 out of 22 conducted some type of user evaluation.

## 5 Discussion

The answers to our SQs in the previous section are summarized in the next Subsect. 5.1 presenting the answer to our general research question: *"What support do platforms aimed at educators who want to create educational games offer?"*. Based on the results presented, in this section, we discuss the main contributions, challenges, and opportunities for the current state-of-the-art of end-user game development/programming aimed at educators, as well as the limitations of this work.

## 5.1 Main Contributions

The environments described in the selected papers limited the types of games end-users could create using them. The most common types of games allowed by the environments are quiz (10) and narratives (5). We also highlight treasure hunt, adventure, and puzzle games (featured in 4 works each), which have simple rules, use familiar dynamics, and aim to test knowledge or explore a subject. It is important to note that adventure games, treasure hunts, and other games generally involve the player carrying out actions related to the game's mechanics.

However, there is almost always a question component for the player to answer or solve a puzzle to advance. The solutions usually aim to test the student's knowledge of a specific content. Games that involve location are usually treasure hunts and involve more exploration than just answering questions, but they also have these characteristics. This possibility of adding questions in different parts of the game is mapped as a resource aimed at educators who constantly use games to test students' knowledge.

It raises the question of why most of the environments found do not encourage the creation of games with dynamics and mechanics that allow for greater exploration and motivate discovery and creativity. Instead, they focus more on testing knowledge. Only in A13 authors present ADDEGames, which allows teachers to create epistemic games that provide more freedom in defining game mechanics.

The papers make important contributions by offering more usable AT for educators that simplify the creation of games, such as the Moirai [A1 and A6], RUFUS [A3], SGAME [A11] and ADDEGames [A13] platforms, among others, which allow teachers to create games without the need for advanced programming. The articles also contributed to providing automatic generation of games from specifications, allowing games to be created semi-automatically using diagrams, examples, and scripting languages for this purpose [A4, A10, A17, A21, and A22]. As the aim of the users is not to be game developers, but to create games quickly for educational purposes, these strategies are especially interesting for this audience.

The possibility of adding multimedia and interactive elements appears in almost all works; tools such as YOUth Go [A2] and other platforms allow adding videos, quizzes, and external content to games. The adoption of geolocation and augmented reality (AR) appears in some works, making it possible to create interactive experiences based on location [A2, A8, A15, and A20] using augmented reality [A5, A7, A18]. Games using AR and geolocation are generally of treasure hunt and adventure type.

An interesting contribution is presented in article A18 with the MAT for ARLearn tool, which aims to provide an open environment to facilitate any user (teacher or student) to create, share, edit, and recontextualize educational resources to promote universal access. They have merged eight educational resource ATs to enable the creation of more content, the editing and recontextualization of games, and the selection of licenses to promote the reuse, revision, and distribution of educational materials. This initiative shows an attempt to unify efforts since finding assets to create games can be difficult. This possibility is especially interesting for educators who often have a lack of time as a limiting factor in using active methodologies [52].

Additionally, usability remains a crucial factor. While most tools simplify game creation, the complexity of game mechanics and interface design still poses a barrier for many educators. Providing comprehensive documentation, intuitive user interfaces, and guided workflows could improve adoption rates among teachers who lack technical expertise.

## 5.2 Challenges and Opportunities

Most ATs for educational games prioritize ease of use for educators with minimal programming experience, often at the cost of expressiveness and flexibility. Thus, the vast majority of works limit the users to the use of templates and visual programming languages, using no-code platforms where they can customize a few aspects of the games. Only A12 explores the creation of games in a more complex way, not least because its focus users are computer science teachers who would create games to facilitate the teaching of programming. It is a challenge to find a balance between high levels of expressiveness and ease of use for end-users in game creation. As presented in the Sect. 4.6, authors have made an effort to evaluate their tools with users, and these studies show that even with simplified tools, users face difficulties. Training and making available support materials can mitigate those problems but might increase the necessary time users have to dedicate to learning the system.

An important limitation is the possibility of creating different types of games on the same platform. According to the results (see Sect. 4.4) the tools usually allow for the creation of a single type of game or a few. Only A11 (SGAME) and A18 (Mat for ARLearn) offer the opportunity to create several different types of games. The first is tied to the game template, which a developer built previously. The second is tied to the ability to create different types of games in a math context. It is directly related to the level of customization allowed in the tool. We noticed that platforms where educators can create one type of game [A1, A5, A6, A7, A10, A18 and A20] allow them to customize more game aspects making them more personalized. On the other hand, tools that allow for the creation of different types of games generally allow less customization in the games, using as a strategy the adoption of templates to customize some specific parameters of the games, as we can see in A3 and A11. With this, allowing educators to create different types of games and modify their mechanics is a limitation of the works and one that can be explored in improvements to the tools or new platforms.

We noticed a low take-up of multiplayer games. Playing games in the classroom by dividing them into pairs or groups is standard practice. Teachers tend to prefer games that do not focus on excessive competition [52], which may help explain why only two tools of this type appear [A2 and A9]. We also noticed that there are no tools for creating open-ended games. For both types of games, it can be complex for this audience to develop them, as lack of time is considered one of the main limitations for educators to not adopt new resources [7,19,52]. Another point is that if they are not players themselves, it is unlikely that they will be able to create games without stimuli such as training. In addition, it can be more complex to develop authoring tools that allow such mechanics. So it can be an opportunity to create this kind of resource.

Some tools allow exporting to LMS, but integration and interoperability with educational systems are still challenges. Environments have attempted to export games to formats such as SCORM, which allows games to run on LMSs such as Moodle [A1, A6, A8, A11, and A15]. However, there is no information on configuring this in educational environments. Especially in the educational context, offering support to export games to be used in LMSs is important for educators who want to make games part of their educational resources. Although this would relevant, most authors have opted to create web-based platforms, which can also facilitate their adoption [A2, A3, A4, A5, A7, A8, A10, A12, A14, A15, A16, A17, A19 and A21].

Few tools incorporate advanced analytics to track student progress. Only A8 and A9 (uAdventure and EscApp) emphasize real-time analytics for teacher support. Only SKETCH'NDO [A17] claims to offer a mechanism for monitoring and evaluating student performance that allows for an accurate assessment of the learning process. It offers a range of assistance levels that can be set by educators or automatically adjusted to the student's abilities. Given that educational games commonly assess students' knowledge [3,24,34], the lack of data collection features, such as tracking player choices and time spent, represents a significant gap. Thus, generating meaningful reports to support teachers remains a challenge.

The articles often lack documentation on how to use or adapt the tool. Articles A3, A4, A6, A8, A9, A11, A15, and A18 provide links to access the tool or the project repository, but only articles A8 and A15 (uAdventure and Simva) have more detailed documentation. As the aim is to democratize the creation of educational games by educators, allowing projects to be open source and available on the internet is necessary for improving and creating educational game ATs. In addition, only the authors of A13 offered a game design support to help teachers think about building the game, *i.e.*, a step back before using the AT, which can help educators choose the best type of game and mechanics based on their instructional objectives. Providing this support can contribute to teachers' game design process.

Most tools undergo user testing, but their impact on learning is rarely examined in depth. Few studies assess long-term effects. The articles do not address longitudinal studies that evaluate both the teacher using the tool and their impression of the engagement and game effectiveness with their students. This gap limits our understanding of how these tools support educators. Additionally, some platforms have been discontinued or lack clear information on availability and technical support. Also related to the validation and evaluation, the studies are not concerned with the accessibility of the tools. In the tests carried out, no article reports an evaluation using WCAG[2], for example, even though there are several web platforms or other evaluations. Only the authors of RUFUS [A3] mention that the work has no accessibility requirements. The other papers do not mention accessibility assessments or anything in that direction, and when they consider the term accessibility it means "having access to the platform".

Another gap identified from the works analyzed is the lack of integration of the tools with Artificial Intelligence (AI). Considering that generative AI has been on the rise for the last 4 years [11], there is an opportunity to investigate how it may help teachers create content, assets, or even the structure of complete games. It could also be useful to investigate how AI could support personalizing the students' experience.

### 5.3 Limitations

While this study provides valuable insights into the current landscape of educational game ATs, it has several limitations. First, the review primarily focuses on published academic works, which may not capture commercial or emerging tools that have not been documented in academic literature. Future studies should include a broader range of tools to provide a more comprehensive understanding of available solutions as Educandy[3] and Educaplay[4] .

Second, we limited our search from January 2014 to July 2024. We selected this interval to narrow down our search and focus on more recent solutions that were still active. We limited our search to July 2024 so that we could analyze the papers, which took a few months. Thus, new relevant articles could have been published up to the submission of this article.

Third, using our search strategy (presented in Sect. 3), we found 2845 articles. After the search, we applied some exclusion criteria to identify papers that answered our research question. However, this choice may, for example, have excluded original ideas present in theses and dissertations and in other digital libraries.

Potential inaccuracies in data extraction and classification may arise due to researchers' varied backgrounds. To mitigate this, two researchers analyzed each paper, with disagreements leading to its inclusion in the next SLR phase. During the full reading stage, meetings were held to consolidate data and resolve conflicts. However, as an interpretative analysis, different researchers might derive varying insights.

---

[2] https://www.w3.org/TR/WCAG21/.
[3] https://www.educandy.com.
[4] https://www.educaplay.com.

## 6 Conclusion

Based on the trend to empower end-users, specifically educators, to customize and create their educational games, we conducted an SLR considering the research question *"What support do platforms aimed at educators who want to create educational games offer?"*. Since we found no current research answering this question, we followed the methodology of Kitchenham [31] to conduct the study. We analyzed 22 articles out of 2845 articles collected using our RS.

Most tools prioritize ease of use over flexibility, limiting customization and innovation. Key challenges include the absence of open-world and multiplayer support, insufficient LMS integration, and underdeveloped analytics for student tracking. Educators' limited involvement in tool design affects usability, and few studies assess long-term educational impact. The lack of AI integration for adaptive learning presents a key research gap, highlighting opportunities for future improvements in usability and pedagogical effectiveness.

This study provides valuable insights for researchers, educators, and developers involved in educational game design. Researchers can reflect on possible improvements and research directions, such as thinking about educational aspects related to the tools and the introduction of generative AI to support game creation. Educators can benefit by learning about existing tools and their limitations, which can help choose if any are interesting to be used in their context. They can also advocate for features that enhance customization, integration with LMS, and student progress tracking. Developers can use these findings to refine game authoring platforms, prioritizing accessibility while improving flexibility, and analytics. By identifying gaps and challenges, this work can guide studies in the design and evaluation of more effective educational game development tools, fostering more engaging and pedagogically sound learning experiences.

Future research should explore AI-assisted game generation, adaptive learning experiences, and the feasibility of open-world and multiplayer educational games. Longitudinal studies assessing the pedagogical impact of these tools would provide deeper insights into their effectiveness. Broadening the analysis to also consider software not presented in academic articles is a step to be taken. Another future project is the construction of a tool that allows the creation of educational games in a more flexible style, allowing the creation of different types of games and the use of different mechanics.

# Appendix A

Table 1 describes the ID or the code of each article, the title, reference, year, country of authors and the forum where they were published.

**Table 1.** Articles selected and analyzed.

| ID | Title | Reference | Year | Country | Venue |
|---|---|---|---|---|---|
| A1 | Examining the Usability of the Moirai Serious Game Authoring Platform | [57] | 2024 | Canada | Journal IEEE Transactions on Games |
| A2 | In-service school teachers' evaluation of YOUth Go, a platform for easily creating educational location-based games that require players' physical activity | [27] | 2024 | Greece | Journal Education and Information Technologies |
| A3 | Design and Evaluation of an Authoring Platform for Therapeutic Digital Games | [23] | 2023 | Brazil | Journal Interacting with Computers |
| A4 | Model for Semi-Automatic Serious Games Generation | [50] | 2023 | Mexico | Journal Applied Sciences |
| A5 | JEM Inventor: a mobile learning game authoring tool based on a nested design approach | [28] | 2022 | France | Journal Interactive Learning Environments |
| A6 | Moirai: a no-code virtual serious game authoring platform | [56] | 2022 | Canada | Journal Virtual Worlds |
| A7 | ZeusAR: a process and an architecture to automate the development of augmented reality serious games | [40] | 2022 | Mexico | Journal Multimedia Tools and Applications |
| A8 | A Tool Supported Approach for Teaching Serious Game Learning Analytics | [47] | 2021 | Spain | Conference IEEE Frontiers in Education Conference |
| A9 | Escapp: A Web Platform for Conducting Educational Escape Rooms | [36] | 2021 | Spain | IEEE Access |
| A10 | MOLEGA: modeling language for educational card games | [9] | 2021 | USA | Conference SIGPLAN International Workshop on Domain-Specific Modeling |
| A11 | SGAME: An Authoring Tool to Easily Create Educational Video Games by Integrating SCORM-Compliant Learning Objects | [21] | 2021 | Spain | IEEE Access |
| A12 | Supporting CS1 Instructors: Design and Evaluation of a Game Generator | [4] | 2021 | South Africa | Conference Innovation and Technology in Computer Science Education |
| A13 | From design to management of digital epistemic games | [45] | 2020 | France and Switzerland | International Journal of Serious Games |
| A14 | StickAndClick âĂŞ Sticking and Composing Simple Games as a Learning Activity | [58] | 2020 | Denmark | Conference Learning and Collaboration Technologies. Human and Technology Ecosystems |
| A15 | Simplifying the creation of adventure serious games with educational-oriented features | [39] | 2019 | Spain | Journal Educational Technology & Society |
| A16 | Interactive Digital Storytelling Based Educational Games: Formalise, Author, Play, Educate and Enjoy! - The Edugames4all Project Framework | [41] | 2016 | United Kingdom | Proceedings of Transactions on Edutainment XII |
| A17 | SKETCH'NDO: A framework for the creation of task-based serious games | [42] | 2016 | Spain | Journal of Visual Languages and Computing |
| A18 | Mobile authoring of open educational resources for authentic learning scenarios | [54] | 2016 | Netherlands | Journal Universal Access in the Information Society |
| A19 | Towards a new web-based serious games generator based on fuzzy expert system | [37] | 2015 | Morocco | Journal of Theoretical and Applied Information Technology |
| A20 | Location-based Mobile Application Creator creating educational mobile scavenger hunts | [48] | 2014 | Austria, Australia and Guatemala | International Conference on Interactive Mobile Communication Technologies and Learning (IMCL) |
| A21 | Toward the Adaptive and Context-Aware Serious Game Design | [33] | 2014 | France | International Conference on Advanced Learning Technologies |
| A22 | Towards a lightweight approach for modding serious educational games: Assisting novice designers | [14] | 2014 | USA | International Conference on Distributed Multimedia Systems |

# References

1. Ahmad, A., Elaklouk, A.M.S., Edris, I., Salleh, D.: Educator-oriented authoring tools to develop rich educational media: a systematic review. In: 2023 6th ACIIS, pp. 1–6 (2023). https://doi.org/10.1109/ACIIS59385.2023.10367320
2. Ahmad, A., Law, E.L., Moseley, A.: Integrating instructional design principles in serious games authoring tools: insights from systematic literature review. In: Proceedings of the 11th NordiCHI, pp. 1–12 (2020)
3. Aloisio, A., Marzano, G., Bonanni, R., Ricci, M.: Serious games for ADHD: a narrative review. In: Proceedings of DILeND 2024, Rome, Italy, pp. 24–25 (2023)
4. Anyango, J.T., Suleman, H.: Supporting cs1 instructors: design and evaluation of a game generator. In: Proceedings of the 26th ACM ITiCSE, pp. 115–121 (2021)
5. Araújo, I., Carvalho, A.A.: Enablers and difficulties in the implementation of gamification: a case study with teachers. Educ. Sci. **12**(3), 191 (2022)
6. Barianos, K.A.: Thimel-content: an inclusive content creation, game customization and gameplay personalization tool (2021)
7. Barney, D.C., Leavitt, T.: A qualitative investigation of PE teachers perceptions of introductory/warm-up activities in K-12 PE. Phys. Educ. **76**(1) (2019)
8. Barricelli, B.R., Cassano, F., Fogli, D., Piccinno, A.: End-user development, end-user programming and end-user software engineering: a systematic mapping study. J. Syst. Softw. **149**, 101–137 (2019)
9. Borror, K., Rapos, E.J.: MOLEGA: modeling language for educational card games. In: Proceedings of the 18th ACM SIGPLAN, pp. 1–10 (2021)
10. Cabitza, F., Gesso, I., et al.: Rule-based programming as easy as a child's play. A user study on active documents. In: IHCI 2012: IADIS 2012 Lisbon, Portugal, vol. 21, pp. 73–80 (2012)
11. Cao, Y., et al.: A comprehensive survey of AI-generated content (AIGC): a history of generative AI from GAN to ChatGPT. arXiv preprint arXiv:2303.04226 (2023)
12. Chaidi, I., Drigas, A.: Digital games & special education. Technium Soc. Sci. J. **34**, 214 (2022)
13. Chover, M., Marín, C., Rebollo, C., Remolar, I.: A game engine designed to simplify 2D video game development. Multimedia Tools Appl. **79**(17), 12307–12328 (2020)
14. Dahleen, J., Hunsberger, A., Weber, R., Brylow, D., Longstreet, C.S., Cooper, K.M.: Towards a lightweight approach for modding serious educational games: assisting novice designers. In: Proceedings of the 20th DMS. Knowledge Systems Institute (2014)
15. De Freitas, S.: Are games effective learning tools? A review of educational games. ET&S **21**(2), 74–84 (2018)
16. Fischer, G.: End-user development: empowering stakeholders with artificial intelligence, meta-design, and cultures of participation. In: Fogli, D., Tetteroo, D., Barricelli, B.R., Borsci, S., Markopoulos, P., Papadopoulos, G.A. (eds.) IS-EUD 2021. LNCS, vol. 12724, pp. 3–16. Springer, Cham (2021). https://doi.org/10.1007/978-3-030-79840-6_1
17. Gajewski, S., El Mawas, N., Heutte, J.: A systematic literature review of game design tools. In: Actes de la 14e Conférence internationale sur l'éducation assistée par ordinateur, vol. 2, pp. 404–414. A Distance, France (2022). https://doi.org/10.5220/0011137800003182. https://hal.science/hal-04056449
18. Gazis, A., Katsiri, E.: Serious games in digital gaming: a comprehensive review of applications, game engines and advancements. arXiv preprint arXiv:2311.03384 (2023)

19. Gibbs, K.: Voices in practice: challenges to implementing differentiated instruction by teachers and school leaders in an Australian mainstream secondary school. AARE **50**(4), 1217–1232 (2023)
20. Good, J., Howland, K.: Programming language, natural language? Supporting the diverse computational activities of novice programmers. J. Vis. Lang. Comput. **39**, 78–92 (2017)
21. Gordillo, A., Barra, E., Quemada, J.: SGAME: an authoring tool to easily create educational video games by integrating SCORM-compliant learning objects. IEEE Access **9**, 126414–126430 (2021)
22. Hashim, S.H.M., Diah, N.M.: Game engine framework for non-programming background. In: 2015 IEEE ICOS, pp. 18–21 (2015). https://doi.org/10.1109/ICOS.2015.7377271
23. da Hora Rodrigues, K.R., et al.: Design and evaluation of an authoring platform for therapeutic digital games. https://doi.org/10.1093/iwc/iwac045
24. Hu, L., et al.: NEOGAMES: a serious computer game that improves long-term knowledge retention of neonatal resuscitation in undergraduate medical students. Front. Pediatr. **9**, 645776 (2021)
25. Hutchins, E.L., Hollan, J.D., Norman, D.A.: Direct manipulation interfaces. Hum.-Comput. Interact. **1**(4), 311–338 (1985)
26. Kanode, C.M., Haddad, H.M.: Software engineering challenges in game development. In: 2009 Sixth ITNG, pp. 260–265. IEEE (2009)
27. Karanasios, S., Papastergiou, M.: In-service school teachers' evaluation of youth go, a platform for easily creating educational location-based games that require players' physical activity. Educ. Inf. Technol., 1–32 (2024)
28. Karoui, A., Marfisi-Schottman, I., George, S.: JEM inventor: a mobile learning game authoring tool based on a nested design approach. ILE **30**(10), 1851–1878 (2022)
29. Ke, F.: A qualitative meta-analysis of computer games as learning tools. In: Gaming and Simulations: Concepts, Methodologies, Tools and Applications, pp. 1619–1665 (2011)
30. Kimani, S.: WIMP Interfaces, pp. 3529–3533. Springer US, Boston, MA (2009).https://doi.org/10.1007/978-0-387-39940-9_467
31. Kitchenham, B.: Procedures for performing systematic reviews. Keele UK Keele Univ. **33**(2004), 1–26 (2004)
32. Ko, A.J., et al.: The state of the art in end-user software engineering. ACM CSUR **43**(3), 1–44 (2011)
33. Leclet-Groux, D., Caron, G.: Toward the adaptive and context-aware serious game design. In: 2014 IEEE 14th ICALT, pp. 242–243. IEEE (2014)
34. Leong, E.Y.X., Toh, T.L.: Game based assessment in the mathematics classroom. IJTLM (2021)
35. Lieberman, H., Paternò, F., Klann, M., Wulf, V.: End-user development: an emerging paradigm. In: Lieberman, H., Paternò, F., Wulf, V. (eds.) End user Development, vol. 9, pp. 1–8. Springer, Dordrecht (2006). https://doi.org/10.1007/1-4020-5386-X_1
36. López-Pernas, S., Gordillo, A., Barra, E., Quemada, J.: Escapp: a web platform for conducting educational escape rooms. IEEE Access **9**, 38062–38077 (2021)
37. Lotfi, E., Belahbib, A., Bouhorma, M.: Towards a new web-based serious games generator based on fuzzy expert system. JATIT **76**(2) (2015)
38. Malone, T.W.: What makes things fun to learn? A study of intrinsically motivating computer games. Stanford University (1980)

39. Manuel, P.C.V., José, P.C.I., Manuel, F.M., Iván, M.O., Baltasar, F.M.: Simplifying the creation of adventure serious games with educational-oriented features. J. ET&S **22**(3), 32–46 (2019). https://www.jstor.org/stable/26896708
40. Marin-Vega, H., Alor-Hernandez, G., Colombo-Mendoza, L.O., Bustos-Lopez, M., Zatarain-Cabada, R.: ZeusAR: a process and an architecture to automate the development of augmented reality serious games. Multimedia Tools Appl. **81**(2), 2901–2935 (2022)
41. Molnar, A., Kostkova, P.: Interactive digital storytelling based educational games: formalise, author, play, educate and enjoy! - the edugames4all project framework. Trans. Edutainment **12**, 1–20 (2016). https://api.semanticscholar.org/CorpusID:13541566
42. Moya, S., Tost, D., Grau, S., von Barnekow, A., Felix, E.: SKETCH'NDO: a framework for the creation of task-based serious games. JVL&C **34**, 1–10 (2016)
43. Myers, B.A.: Visual programming, programming by example, and program visualization: a taxonomy. ACM SIGCHI Bull. **17**(4), 59–66 (1986)
44. Newell, K., Patel, K., Lindén, M., Demetriou, M.K., Huk, M., Mahmoud, M.: Evolution of software development in the video game industry. In: 2021 CSCI, pp. 1989–1996 (2021). https://doi.org/10.1109/CSCI54926.2021.00367
45. Oubahssi, L., Piau-Toffolon, C., Loup, G., Sanchez, É.: From design to management of digital epistemic games. IJSG **7**(1), 23–46 (2020). https://doi.org/10.17083/ijsg.v7i1.336. https://journal.seriousgamessociety.org/index.php/IJSG/article/view/336
46. Paternò, F.: End user development: survey of an emerging field for empowering people. ISRN Softw. Eng. **2013** (2013)
47. Pérez-Colado, V.M., Pérez-Colado, I.J., Freire-Morán, M., Martinez-Ortiz, I., Fernandez-Manjón, B.: A tool supported approach for teaching serious game learning analytics. In: 2021 IEEE FIE, pp. 1–8. IEEE (2021)
48. Pirker, J., Gütl, C., Weiner, P., Garcia-Barrios, V.M., Tomintz, M.: Location-based mobile application creator creating educational mobile scavenger hunts. In: 2014 IMCL2014, pp. 160–164. IEEE (2014)
49. Rouly, J.M., Orbeck, J.D., Syriani, E.: Usability and suitability survey of features in visual ides for non-programmers. In: Proceedings of the 5th Workshop on Evaluation and Usability of Programming Languages and Tools, pp. 31–42 (2014)
50. Silva-Vásquez, P.O., Rosales-Morales, V.Y., Benítez-Guerrero, E., Alor-Hernández, G., Mezura-Godoy, C., Montané-Jiménez, L.G.: Model for semi-automatic serious games generation. Appl. Sci. **13**(8), 5158 (2023)
51. Souza, J.G.R.D., Prates, R.: Identifying challenges for elementary school teachers in building digital games through a workshop. JIS **15**, 362–374 (2024). https://doi.org/10.5753/jis.2024.3951
52. de Souza, J.G.R., Prates, R.O.: Professores do ensino fundamental: contexto social em que estao inseridos e a relaç ao com jogos educacionais. In: 2022 20lh SBGames. IEEE (2022)
53. Sumner, M., Saini, V., Guzdial, M.J.: Mechanic maker: accessible game development via symbolic learning program synthesis (2024)
54. Tabuenca, B., Kalz, M., Ternier, S., Specht, M.: Mobile authoring of open educational resources for authentic learning scenarios. Univ. Access Inf. Soc. **15**, 329–343 (2016)
55. Tetteroo, D., Markopoulos, P.: A review of research methods in end user development. In: Díaz, P., Pipek, V., Ardito, C., Jensen, C., Aedo, I., Boden, A. (eds.) IS-EUD 2015. LNCS, vol. 9083, pp. 58–75. Springer, Cham (2015). https://doi.org/10.1007/978-3-319-18425-8_5

56. Torres, A., Kapralos, B., Da Silva, C., Peisachovich, E., Dubrowski, A.: Moirai: a no-code virtual serious game authoring platform. In: Virtual Worlds, vol. 1, pp. 147–171. MDPI (2022)
57. Torres, A., Kapralos, B., Dubrowski, A.: Examining the usability of the Moirai serious game authoring platform. IEEE Trans. Games (2024)
58. Valente, A., Marchetti, E.: StickAndClick – sticking and composing simple games as a learning activity. In: Zaphiris, P., Ioannou, A. (eds.) HCII 2020. LNCS, vol. 12206, pp. 333–352. Springer, Cham (2020). https://doi.org/10.1007/978-3-030-50506-6_24
59. Valtolina, S., Matamoros, R.A.: EUD strategy in the education field for supporting teachers in creating digital courses. In: Spano, L.D., Schmidt, A., Santoro, C., Stumpf, S. (eds.) IS-EUD 2023. LNCS, vol. 13917, pp. 250–267. Springer, Cham (2023). https://doi.org/10.1007/978-3-031-34433-6_17

# HCI in Healthcare and Wellbeing

# Design of Temporal Interfaces of Digital Twins in Domestic Energy Consumption

Yaxin Zheng[1,2](✉), Harm van Essen[1], Scott Mitchell[2], Liam Fennessy[2], Laurene Vaughan[2], and Regina Bernhaupt[1]

[1] Eindhoven University of Technology, Eindhoven, The Netherlands
{h.a.v.essen,r.bernhaupt,y.zheng}@tue.nl
[2] RMIT University, Melbourne, Australia
{scott.mitchell,liam.fennessy,laurene.vaughan}@rmit.edu.au

**Abstract.** Digital Twins (DTs) evolve beyond their current usage as tools for experts into tools for the everyday lives of everyday people. How designers and researchers approach DT design in intelligible ways for non-expert users will be critical. This paper explores the temporal dimension of DTs in the context of domestic energy consumption. We develop a "Time Machine" analogy, as a conceptual tool, to describe the role of DTs, highlighting their capacity to navigate past, present, and future (predictive) data. With this tool, we developed three temporal interfaces for the domestic environment that allow users to navigate and view their energy usage. We evaluated those interfaces with 18 participants through semi-structured interviews and questionnaires. Our findings show that temporal forms of representation effect how users understand time and patterns in their energy usage, with linear presentations excelling in trend visualization, calendars aligning with familiar schedules, and spiral forms highlighting cyclical patterns and routines. Similarly, various data types influence the depth of user insights, with consumption data providing precise but abstract metrics, activity-based representations connecting energy use to specific actions, and context offering a comprehensive understanding of energy usage.

**Keywords:** Temporal Interface · Digital Twin · Energy Consumption · Context-awareness

## 1 Introduction

Designing systems that promote and facilitate sustainable energy use has become a significant focus within human-computer interaction (HCI) research [28]. Energy consumption information is traditionally presented in static forms alongside billing information at monthly, quarterly, or yearly intervals, often leading to a delayed understanding of energy usage [10,36]. This disconnection from real-time data limits user engagement and awareness, potentially leading to higher energy costs and less environmentally friendly choices [14].

Recent advancements in real-time energy dashboards, as part of the broader smart home vision, enhance energy awareness by providing users with immediate and actionable insights into their energy consumption [26]. The focus of energy consumption is often on metrics such as kilowatt-hours, emissions, and electricity costs, rather than on everyday activities such as laundry, home comfort, and meal preparation [34]. Although these metrics offer precise measurements, they might fail to make energy use tangible and relatable for users, limiting their ability to connect consumption with daily behaviors. As a result, users may struggle to identify specific actions that contribute to high energy usage or to make informed decisions about reducing waste.

In addition to this, smart home systems often struggle to interpret user intentions due to the unpredictability of users' situated actions, which are often improvised and not easily discernible from sensor data [7,35]. This need for greater contextual awareness within domestic energy monitoring and control may be satisfied by the incorporation of DTs. Being more than virtual replicas of products, processes, or services, DTs can provide real-time monitoring [39], to produce evolving models that adapt to environmental and operational changes [18].

DTs have been proposed as a way to understand user behavior in the context of smart homes [21]. To achieve this however, the concept of DTs must evolve beyond their current use as expert-centric tools for planning, optimization, and simulation [11]. Future DTs need to be able to sense and process the users' dynamic environment, proactively exchange information, make decisions to achieve individual or shared goals, and adapt themselves and their physical counterparts accordingly, which means, future DTs should be context-aware and adaptive [13].

This study examines the temporal dimension of DTs, highlighting their ability to make past, present, and future (predictive) energy usage available to users. The study conceptualizes the DT as a "Time Machine", a tool for navigating through time, and proposes three distinct temporal interfaces that may be used to explore domestic energy usage. By aligning digital representations of resource usage with user's real-world schedules and activities, these interfaces could facilitate greater understanding and energy awareness in users.

Rather than aiming to determine the best or most effective interface design, our goal is to explore how different forms of representation resonate with users, allowing us to gather insights into how temporal representations influence user's understanding of energy usage. Accordingly, our research question (RQ) is as follows: **How do temporal representations of energy consumption influence people's understanding of their domestic energy usage?** In addressing this RQ we respond to the following three sub-questions:

- RQ1.1: What role might digital twins play in shaping the temporal representations of domestic energy consumption?
- RQ1.2: How might we design different temporal representations in interfaces?
- RQ1.3: How do people understand temporal representations of domestic energy usage?

To answer RQ1.1, a conceptual tool, the "Time Machine" analogy, was proposed to help identify DTs unique capabilities in monitoring and controlling systems. To answer RQ1.2, we designed three distinct temporal interfaces based on the "Time Machine" analogy: Linear Energy Consumption interface, Calendar Energy Activity interface, and Spiral Energy Context interface. To answer RQ1.3, we evaluated interfaces with potential end-users (N = 18) to know users' understanding of temporal representations in the domestic energy context.

The main contributions of this paper are 1) the development of the "Time Machine" analogy, a conceptual tool that amplifies the temporal nature of DTs and assists designers in exploring DTs role in diverse contexts; 2) the design of three distinct propositional temporal interfaces that explore different temporal representations, integrating DT capabilities within a domestic energy context; 3) insights into user's understanding of these temporal representations of domestic energy usage.

## 2 Theoretical Background and Related Work

In the following Sect. 2.1, we explore DTs and context-aware interfaces for smart homes, focusing on their role in real-time simulation, prediction, and adaptive energy management. Section 2.2 focuses on temporal interfaces, examining how different representations of time influence user perception and interaction.

### 2.1 Digital Twins and Context-Aware Interfaces for Smart Homes

DTs are realistic digital representations that can serve as comprehensive sources of information about their physical counterparts [13]. They are regarded as living models, adaptable to environmental or operational changes through real-time sensor data, with the capacity to run simulations and make predictions about the future for their corresponding physical assets [13,18,29]. DTs have seen early adoption in aerospace and medical fields where they assist experts in simulating extreme scenarios [33]. In city management, DTs have been proposed to improve services and increase safety and security for citizens by simulating people movements and emergency evacuations and modeling road traffic and air quality [25,32]. In building management, the DT platforms can indicate the status of the ambient temperature and humidity through color-coded signals [19]. However, the application of DTs in smart homes might differ from aerospace, city management, or building management due to the home's private and complex nature. Unlike controlled environments, domestic settings require a more *context-aware* approach to capture and respond to dynamic household interactions. As Strengers [34] emphasized, daily activities (such as laundry, heating, and cooling) are also important for how energy is perceived and engaged with through these practices in the ever-changing context of the home.

DTs' ability to process large amounts of data make them well suited to bring *context awareness* to complex monitoring and control systems. *Context-awareness* is the ability of a system or component to adapt its behavior based on its context, making it more effective and relevant to the situation [13,20]. *Context* refers to any information that helps define or describe the situation of an entity, classified into external and internal context [1]. The *external* context includes environment, user, devices, location, and time [1,16]. The *internal* context includes user's goals, tasks, work context, business processes, communication, and emotional and physical states [1]. Lee at al. [17] present a framework for context-aware energy management systems in smart factories that intelligently monitors and analyzes energy usage, allowing users to efficiently control their utilities and equipment. They claim that by adapting to real-time data and user behaviors, a context-aware system can provide insights that help optimize their energy consumption, reduce waste, and improve efficiency [17]. Similarly, Marcello et al. [21] propose a DT framework that incorporates context-aware, user-centric, perspectives to enhance ambient assisted living systems and improve energy management in smart homes.

## 2.2 Temporal Interfaces

Time shapes the structure of human lives, and the impact of technology on this structure has drawn much attention from HCI researchers. Fraisse [6] highlighted that time as a succession of events is a necessary part of our daily life experience. As Gibson [9] stated, "Events are perceivable, but time is not." Time is a subjective phenomenon, indicating that there is a need to design interactions and representations tailored to subjective experiences of time [38].

Numerous interfaces have been proposed for domestic energy systems that make time perceivable through tracking and displaying energy events. Common amongst these are timeline views that display energy consumption data as a graphed time series. One example, of this seemingly ubiquitous representation, can be found in Paredes-Valverde et al. [27] *IntelliHome* interface. In contrast, Mennicken et al. [22,23] designed *Casalendar* based on a calendar metaphor, to enable users to compare and align household routines with home automation activities, and Schrammel et al. [30] designed the *FORE-Watch*, a clock face tool, to visualize the historical, current, and predictive energy consumption. For more novel temporal interfaces, we need to look beyond domestic energy systems. Of particular interest for this research is Mirlacher et al. [24] circular-shape user interface named *The Black Hole* designed for navigating temporal information in a digital TV guide.

## 3 Methodology

Analogies play a key role in design heuristics [5], helping translate concrete objects into abstract requirements [3] and enabling mental model refinement through concept generalization [8]. To answer RQ1.1, we used analogical thinking in conceptualizing how DTs could be applied within a domestic environment. For RQ1.2 and RQ1.3, we used a standard iterative, user-centered design process [12] for conceptualizing interface design and validating user understanding of temporal representations. Conceptual prototypes could efficiently allow for early-stage exploration of various interface designs in the design process without requiring a fully functional system [12]. They could facilitate gathering user perceptions and understandings, providing valuable insights for refining design concepts before implementing them in a functional real-world DT system.

The research was undertaken in four stages, as follows: 1) Assess the novel qualities of DTs and conceptualize their role within the domestic environment. 2) Document one-week energy activities. This self-recorded data provided insights into the contextual dimension of energy usage and served as the dataset for the temporal interfaces. 3) Design three propositional temporal interfaces. 4) Evaluate users' understandings of the three interfaces.

## 4 Stage 1: Assess the Qualities of DTs and Conceptualize Their Role Within the Domestic Environment

To identify and assess the novel qualities that DTs may bring to the domestic environment, we examined their current use within manufacturing and building management fields. From this we developed the "Time Machine" analogy to help conceptualize the role that DTs play in complex analysis and control systems. This analogy highlights past (data storage), present (real-time data collection), and future (predictive) qualities that DTs possess. Rather than physically traveling through time, DTs simulate and influence future scenarios based on systematic analysis.

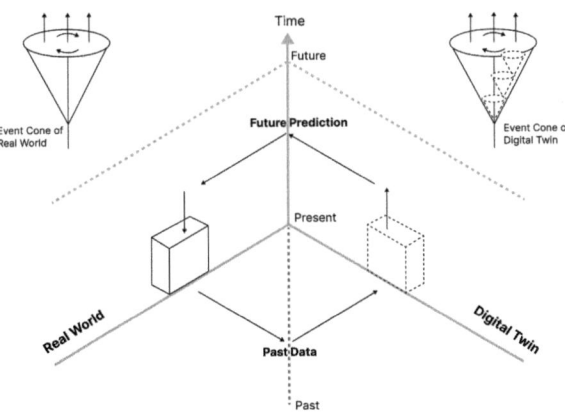

**Fig. 1.** "Time Machine" Analogy for Conception of Digital Twins

Figure 1 shows the "Time Machine" analogy to inform this research. It illustrates the relationship between the real world and a DT over time, specifically focusing on future predictions based on past data. The time axis represents past, present, and future, with past data feeding into DT models for prediction. The event cones, inspired by Voros [37], visualize possible future outcomes, incorporating cyclical patterns (e.g., daily or seasonal trends) within a linear progression. The diagram highlights DTs' predictive capacity that links past insights, present monitoring, and future possibilities.

The "Time Machine" analogy suggests that DTs may be provided with an interface for navigating through these three distinct time frames. Informed by this logic, we formulated four key design considerations for DT-based temporal interfaces:

1. Presenting Information Across Time (Past, Present, Future). DTs have capabilities to store past data, monitor current situations, and predict possible futures. Users should easily interpret what has happened (past), what is currently happening (present), and what is expected to happen (future).
2. Connecting Data Across Timeframes. Temporal interfaces should show how past events impact the present and how current actions shape future outcomes, reinforcing causal relationships in temporal data.
3. Scheduling and Time Management. Temporal interfaces should support planning and organizing tasks, aligning event schedules with user needs while providing structured timelines.
4. Encouraging Active User Interaction. Interfaces should prompt users to actively engage with time-based data by exploring trends, adjusting inputs, and making informed decisions based on temporal insights.

By applying these four design considerations, we aim to create interfaces that leverage DTs unique advantages and enhance user engagement with domestic energy systems.

## 5 Stage 2: Self-record One-Week Energy Activity

In the second stage, the first author used autoethnography to record one week's electricity-based energy activities (seven continuous days of October 2024) in the household and calculate electricity consumption based on home appliances' power consumption as the baseline dataset for the next steps. The first author lived alone in a 22 m$^2$ studio. For seven continuous days, every energy activity was recorded in real-time from morning wake-up to bedtime, with each appliance usage and its duration. Energy consumption was calculated based on the first author's owned appliances' power consumption and duration of usage. We noticed that the amounts of energy consumption might not be accurate precisely. The first author also recorded emotions and internal dialogue at the time of usage, if the energy activity triggered some thoughts. Emotions and internal dialogue could be crucial in decision-making, as they might influence how individuals perceive energy use, reflect on consumption patterns, and make choices about adjusting their behavior.

## 6 Stage 3: Temporal Interface Design

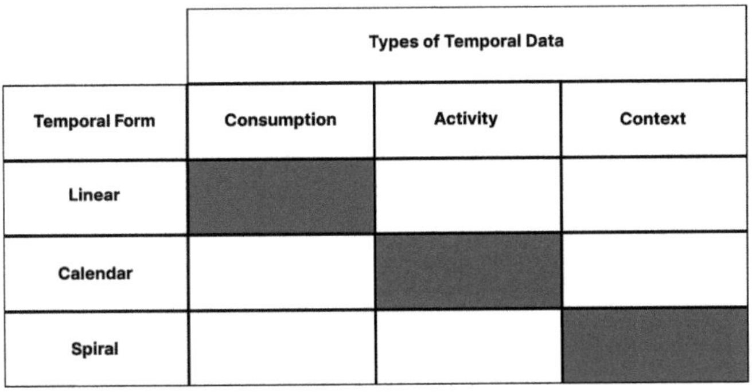

| Temporal Form | Types of Temporal Data | | |
|---|---|---|---|
| | Consumption | Activity | Context |
| Linear | ■ | | |
| Calendar | | ■ | |
| Spiral | | | ■ |

**Fig. 2.** Elements of Temporal Interface

Building on the "Time Machine" analogy, we define that **Temporal Representation** is the presentation of temporal data in the temporal form. Based on this, we define **Temporal Interface** for DTs as user interfaces that emphasize time-based changes as a core aspect of interaction, providing an integrated view of the past (historical data), the present (live monitoring), and the future (predicting possible outcomes). Temporal interfaces integrate dynamic elements that evolve, respond, or shift over time, enabling users to engage with and experience these changes interactively.

Building on existing representational forms, we developed three distinct temporal interfaces: linear interface, calendar interface, and spiral interface. The three formats were initially selected due to their prior use in visualizing time in both everyday contexts and HCI research. By embodying the time machine analogy and its design considerations, specific design choices for the interfaces are:

- Linear Interface: This reflects the linear flow of time from past to future, supporting progression tracking and comparisons, aligning with the design principle of "Presenting Information Across Time" and "Connecting Data Across Timeframes".
- Calendar Interface: This provides a structured view aligning with familiar calendar use in daily life. It supports the principle of "Scheduling and Time Management".
- Spiral Interface: The spiral shows recurring patterns within a linear timeline, enabling both progression and repetitive events (e.g., daily routines or seasonal trends) to be visualized. Spiral provides other design possibilities for visualizing energy patterns.

In addition, each interface focused on a specific type of temporal data: the amount of energy consumption, domestic activity, and context, respectively, see Fig. 2. As mentioned in Theoretical Background, context includes internal context and external context. The internal energy context refers to self-recorded energy activity data, including feelings and internal dialogue triggered by energy activities. The external energy context refers to time, activity (e.g., cooking), consumption (kWh), appliances (e.g., washing machine), and price. The interfaces took the form of interactive digital displays and were presented on laptops with clicking interactions for participant testing purposes.

## 6.1 Interface 1: Linear Energy Consumption

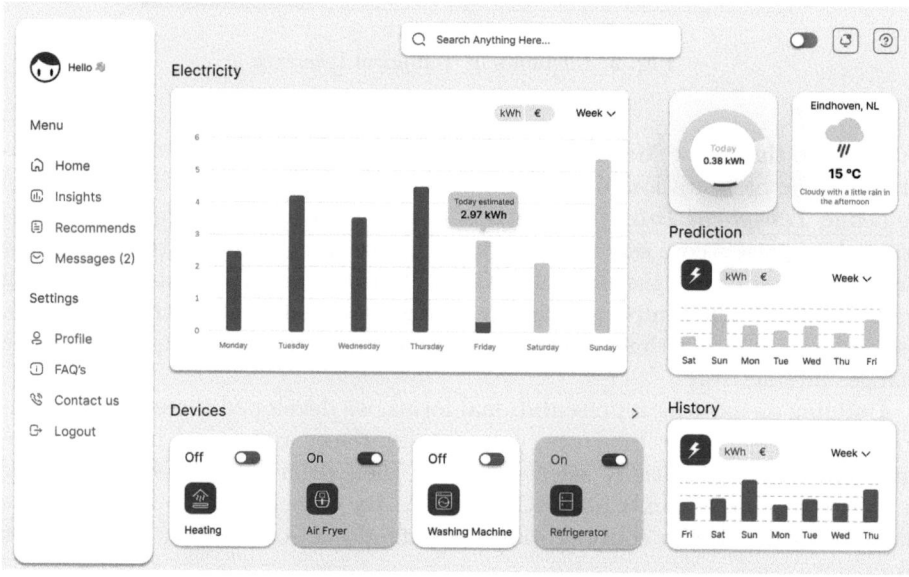

**Fig. 3.** Interface 1: Linear Energy Consumption

In this interface, we adopt a linear representation of time series data. This interface resembles existing energy dashboards, with the addition of predictive capability.

As shown in Fig. 3, the main histogram in the middle of the interface presents time series energy consumption data from Monday to Sunday. The histogram is divided into three time phases, past (Monday to Thursday), present (Friday), and future (Saturday and Sunday). Context, in the form of weather data, is also presented. The devices section at the bottom of the interface presents the status of specific appliances. In addition to energy consumption in kWh, energy can also be viewed as monetary cost.

## 6.2 Interface 2: Calendar Energy Activity

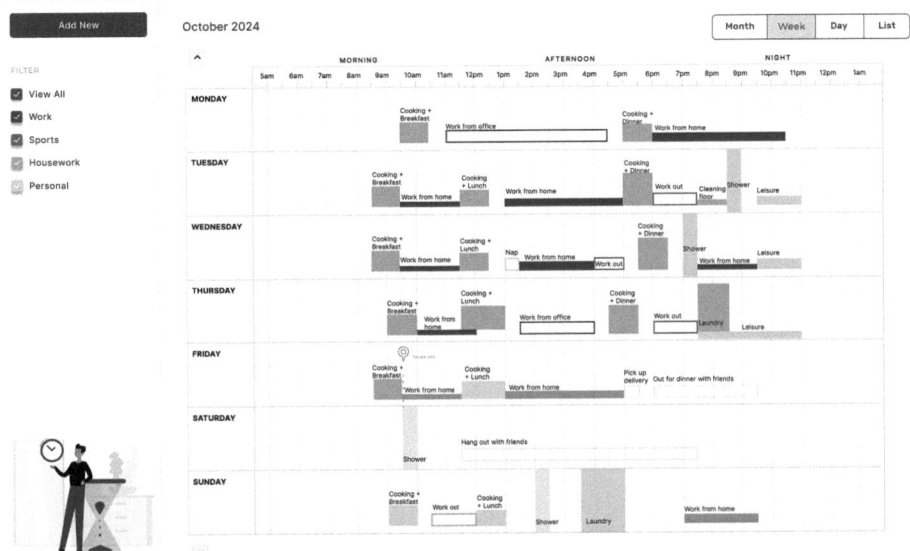

**Fig. 4.** Interface 2: Calendar Energy Activity

As shown in Fig. 4, Calendar Energy Activity presents energy activities using a calendar layout. This interface is similar to Mennicken et al. [22,23] *Casalendar* interface that aims to integrate calendar tools into smart homes, using the temporal nature of routines to enhance interaction with home automation systems. Our calendar interface presents all energy activities from Monday to Sunday showing past activities (Monday to Thursday), present activities (Friday), and future predicted and scheduled activities (Saturday and Sunday). The solid blocks represent energy activities at home. The empty blocks represent out of home activities. The total area of the block indicates the amount of energy consumed. Different colors indicate different categories in the schedule.

## 6.3 Interface 3: Spiral Energy Context

The spiral design presents context about energy consumption in a spiral histogram. It allows for cyclical comparisons while maintaining a continuous timeline along the spiral [15]. The spiral layout and interactive elements resemble Mirlacher et al. [24] *Black Hole* interface and Schrammel et al. [30] *FOREWatch* interface, discussed above. The context presented in our interface was collected during Stage 2 of the research and includes any information that defines or describes the situation such as environment, user, devices, location, time, user's goals, tasks, work context, communication, and emotional and physical states [1,16]. Different colors on the spiral represent different levels of energy consumption. Past energy consumption is presented as solid dots, future (predicted) energy consumption are empty dots. When clicked, detailed context is displayed, as seen in Fig. 5. The spiral is organized around a 24-hour clock-face to assist users in identifying patterns of energy use.

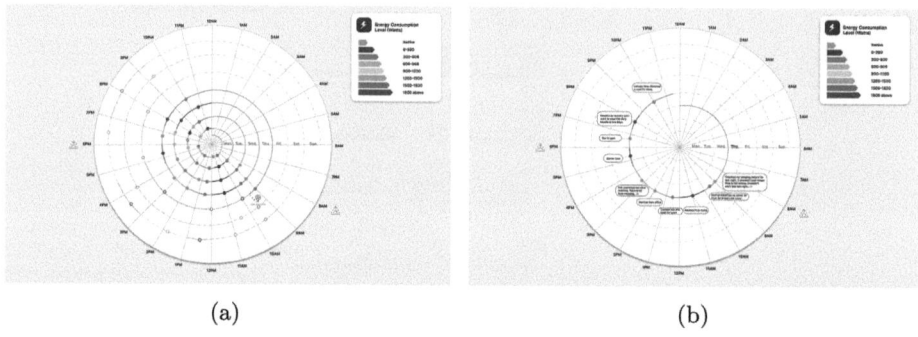

(a)                          (b)

**Fig. 5.** Interface 3: Spiral Energy Context

## 7 Stage 4: Evaluation of User's Understanding of the Three Interfaces

The three interfaces were evaluated using a mixed-methods approach, within-participants study setting in order to identify users' preferences and understanding of temporal information in domestic energy scenario. The three design options enabled an exploration of individual preferences and interactions with representations of time. The aim was not to identify the best or most effective design, rather it was to understand how different modes of representing time relate to people's understanding of temporal data in the context of energy usage.

### 7.1 Participants

Eighteen participants were recruited from the university and authors' network. Eighteen participants (9 male and 9 female) all have a master's degree. Their ages ranged between 26 and 41 years (M = 30.06 years, SD = 4.67 years). Participants' residence were based in the Netherlands (N=14), Spain(N=1), Germany(N=1), Denmark(N=1), Sweden(N=1). The participants' household sizes range from one to three members, with 8 participants living alone, 7 participants living in a two-person household, and 3 participants living in a three-person household.

## 7.2 Study Procedure

We obtained ethical approval from the university's Ethical Review Board. All participants and data were anonymized. All participants signed informed consent forms. Data collected was securely stored and used only for research purposes. To minimize order effects, we employed a counterbalanced order where participants were randomly assigned different sequences of conditions. Participants interacted and explored all three interfaces.

To collect in-depth feedback on participants' understanding of the three temporal interfaces, we used semi-structured interviews combined with a self-developed questionnaire that asked participants to answer statements on a 7-point Likert Scale. The short version of the User Experience Questionnaire was administered after each interface was discussed [31].

Questions of interviews and questionnaires focused on three aspects: part one was to understand energy information in the representations of kWh, energy activities, and context. Part two was to understand temporal representations in linear, calendar, and spiral ways. Part three was to understand people's future expectations for predictive energy use.

## 7.3 Data Analysis

Data were gathered based on pre-structured interview sections, Energy Information, Temporal Representation, and Future Expectations. For qualitative analysis of interview data, we conducted a thematic analysis [2] following an inductive approach to identify emerging patterns in participants' responses based on each section. Within each section, responses were reviewed, and sub-themes were identified based on recurring ideas and perspectives. We used Nvivo 15 software for coding. The first author developed the initial codes and themes, which were then reviewed by the co-authors, who provided feedback on data interpretation and theme organization, offering new perspectives and narratives.

For quantitative data from 7-point Likert Scale questionnaires, we analyzed users' attitudes toward the interfaces by aggregating data based on three sections: Energy Information, Temporal Representation, and Future Expectation. The data analysis process was conducted in the following steps: 1) Correlation Analysis (Pearson's r). We first performed Pearson correlation analysis on Q1-Q4 (Energy Information), Q5-Q8 (Temporal Representation), and Q9-Q10 (Future Expectation) to assess the linear relationship among variables within each dimension. A high correlation ($r \geq 0.5$) suggests that these items measure a similar latent construct and can be aggregated; 2) Reliability Analysis (Cronbach's Alpha). To further validate internal consistency, we computed Cronbach's Alpha coefficients for each dimension. A reliability score of $\alpha \geq 0.7$ is considered acceptable. This analysis indicated that all dimensions had $\alpha > 0.8$, demonstrating satisfactory internal consistency for data aggregation; 3) Data Aggregation. After confirming correlation and reliability, we calculated the mean scores of Q1-Q4, Q5-Q8, and Q9-Q10 for each participant, representing: Energy Information, Temporal Representation, and Future Expectation. This aggregation method simplifies the dataset while preserving meaningful insights; 4) Boxplot Analysis. We generated boxplots to visualize distributions of ratings and assess differences in user perceptions towards three interfaces.

## 8 Findings

### 8.1 Qualitative Results

Different types of energy information, consumption, activity, and context, may shape how users perceive energy consumption in various ways. Consumption such as kWh offers precise data but might feel abstract, while activity-based information could make energy use more tangible and relatable by linking it to daily tasks. Contextual information might provide a broader understanding of energy usage but require more effort to understand.

**Linear Energy Consumption is Effective and Straightforward.** Most participants stated that the linear representation of temporal form is a conventional way that is easy to understand and aligns with their intuition. Some participants also indicated that presenting predictions of energy consumption in a linear form could help them plan energy activities and take timely actions by providing a clear view of expected usage over time. This forward-looking approach might help them to foresee periods of high consumption, adjust their actions proactively, and align their energy use with cost-saving or sustainability goals.

The most commonly mentioned benefit by participants was that the linear representation is highly effective for making straightforward comparisons, as it clearly displays trends and patterns over time. Displaying past and future energy usage as metered amounts helps users to identify patterns in their energy consumption over time and assess the impact of their behaviors. By understanding these trends, they may make more informed decisions to optimize energy usage and reduce waste.

**Linear Energy Consumption Lacks Deeper Insights and is not Effective for Reflection.** Although kWh is widely used in daily life when referring to energy consumption, some participants mentioned that they don't have a clear idea about kWh. Only three participants mentioned that they are clear about the definition of kWh, and even when the definition is clear, it is not necessarily helpful, with one of them stated thatparticipant stating: *"I know it is the kind of standard way to measure electricity, but for me it's not very meaningful."(P11)*.

Some participants questioned its usefulness, claiming it lacked depth and didn't offer actionable insights. While kWh is useful for visualizing energy consumption data, it might not guide users toward understanding the causes of their energy consumption or suggest specific actions to reduce consumption.

**Calendar Helps Plan Future Energy Activity.** Ten participants mentioned the temporal representation of the calendar is a familiar form, which helps them see the connection between activities and energy consumption. This familiarity allows users to intuitively track energy usage in the context of their daily schedules, making it easier to understand how their actions impact consumption. Additionally, the calendar form provides a structured view, helping participants visualize how specific routines or events contribute to overall energy usage.

Participants' understanding of energy activities includes types of activities, amount of energy consumption, activity time, duration of energy usage, appliance usage, energy cost, location, types of energy usage, and people's routine. Some participants indicated that the representation of energy activities is clear and easy to understand with less effort: *"The calendar one made me realize how easy it could be to connect energy usage with an activity."(P18)*.

Many participants found the calendar-based activity representation helpful for planning future energy use. They noted that by scheduling tasks in the calendar, they could estimate their expected energy consumption and reduce unnecessary energy activities. Additionally, participants suggested that the system could offer recommendations for combining tasks or optimizing their actions to improve energy efficiency.

**Calendar Energy Activity is not Comparable.** Some participants noted that the representation of energy activities is not precise enough to compare the energy consumption of activities. As a result, they found it difficult to tell the total number of each day. They found it difficult to get an accurate overview of daily energy consumption and to identify patterns across multiple days.

**Spiral Energy Context is Helpful for Reflection of Energy Actions.** One participant mentioned that energy context could refer to the detailed contents of 5W1H: *"So I think (energy context) basically is 5W and 1H: when, where, who, what, why, and then how. Like when is this energy used? Where does the energy take place? Who are using the energy? What is the amount of energy usage and how is the energy being used as time goes by?"(P10)*. The context provided a deeper understanding of energy usage by linking consumption patterns to specific events, activities, or emotions. Some participants emphasized the role of emotions and internal dialogue in their perception of energy consumption. One participant noted that energy use is not always judged solely by efficiency or cost but also by the emotional value it brings: *"If I do this thing, even though it has lots of energy consumption, but my emotional mood is very high, so I think this energy consumption may be worth it."(P01)*. This suggests that energy decisions would be influenced not just by objective factors like usage data but also by personal satisfaction and emotional well-being. Also, two participants indicated that presenting this context helps better recognize opportunities for improvement and adapt energy-saving strategies to their specific needs: *"It can help me save energy by comparative context."(P04)*.

Additionally, participants appreciated the detailed context presented in the spiral interface: *"This one (spiral context) gives a detailed way of energy use per hour. You can just be aware of the energy consumption per day."(P10).* These detailed insights may help users in reflecting on their habits and making more informed decisions to optimize their energy use.

**Spiral Energy Context Helps Identify Energy Patterns.** Two participants mentioned that it is a continuous data type that is convenient to know the context about the energy from the past to the future. They highlighted that the spiral form offers a unique perspective by displaying patterns across cycles, such as daily or weekly usage: *"When I initially saw this, it is a very surprising way. So it's not my intuitive way. But when I just got used to it, it made sense. Once you understand what is going on, I think it's actually very convenient. Also it's kind of continuous instead of discrete days."(P18).*

Many participants indicated that the spiral representation allows them to compare activities happening at the same time on different days, making it easier to observe differences and similarities in energy usage across periods. This spiral form could be useful for identifying patterns and trends in energy consumption that might otherwise go unnoticed.

Participants commented that different colors represent various energy levels, making it easier to understand energy patterns: *"Having the color of the energy consumption of different activities is very easy to understand. So it's intuitive. I can know these things I have lots of energy consumption."(P01).*

Overall, this representation helps to connect recurring activities to energy consumption in a visually cohesive way.

**Spiral Energy Context Needs More Effort to Understand.** Several participants stated that the temporal representation of spiral is not a straightforward way to understand energy usage. It required more efforts to follow and understand the energy information. One participant mentioned that while his intuition about time is cyclical, the spiral form here was counterintuitive to use: *"I would say it can fit how I think about time. But visually, it's kind of very demanding and it's counterintuitive in a sense that I don't encounter this kind of visualizations before...And it very much depends on the context and kind of unit of information I'm dealing with, whether I'm picking more cyclical or linear terms."(P11).*

**Future Expectations of Predictive Energy Usage.** Participants expressed interest in understanding the reasons behind high energy consumption. They preferred a larger time scale to gain a clearer view of energy usage patterns. They also highlighted the importance of linking energy usage data to specific activities or events, which could provide more context and enhance their understanding.

Participants also claimed that reflecting on past consumption would enable them to adjust their actions and make cost-saving decisions for the future: *"If I have a set budget for a month and I know that there's a prediction towards the future...If the system is telling me it predicts that I will consume more electricity on Thursday, then I could take certain decisions to be more mindful."(P09).*

## 8.2 Quantitative Results

Data from the Likert Scale based questionnaires was not normally distributed. We thus used Kruskal-Wallis tests to assess significant differences among the three interfaces. Although the Kruskal-Wallis test did not reveal statistically significant differences among the three interface designs ($p > 0.05$), descriptive analysis suggests that the Linear Energy Consumption interface had a slightly higher mean score in Energy Information (M = 5.17, SD = 1.39) compared to Calendar (M = 4.89, SD = 1.56) and Spiral (M = 4.41, SD = 1.71). We interpret that this might indicate a tendency for users to perceive kWh as easier to understand. Alternatively, the difference may be due to the familiarity participants felt towards this form of representation.

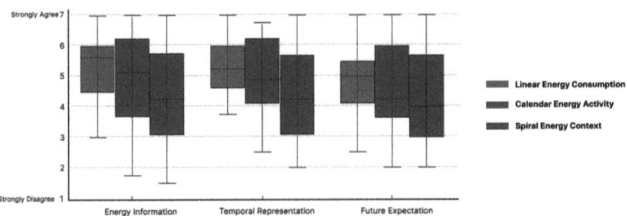

**Fig. 6.** User's Understanding of Three Interfaces in Energy Information, Temporal Representation, and Future Expectation.

Figure 6 illustrates the distribution of user ratings for the three different interface designs across three evaluation dimensions: Energy Information, Temporal Representation, and Future Expectation. The Linear Energy Consumption interface receives higher median ratings across all three dimensions, suggesting that users found it easier to understand energy-related data. The ratings for the Calendar Energy Activity are relatively evenly distributed, indicating that calendar may represent a design approach that sits between traditional and innovative styles, neither as conventional as the kWh one nor as complex as the spiral one. The Spiral Energy Context interface has the lowest median ratings in all dimensions, with a wider spread, suggesting that users may have found it more challenging to interpret energy data and form future expectations.

Figure 7 presents the UEQ-S [31] results for user experience across the three interfaces, evaluated in three dimensions: Pragmatic Quality, Hedonic Quality, and Overall Experience. The Linear Energy Consumption interface has the highest rating in Pragmatic Quality (1.25), indicating that users found it the most

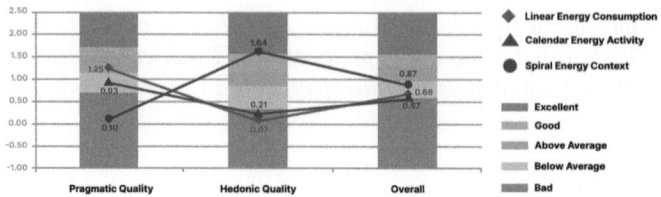

**Fig. 7.** Perceived user experience assessed with the UEQ-short [31]. The bar chart displays the mean values for pragmatic quality (left), hedonic quality (middle), and overall UX score (right) for each mode. The bar colors correspond to the UX scale, ranging from excellent (light green) to poor (orange). (Color figure online)

effective and functional in supporting their understanding. However, its Hedonic Quality (0.07) is the lowest among the three, suggesting that while it is practical, it is not particularly engaging or enjoyable to use. The ratings of the Calendar Energy Activity interface are similar to the linear one, with a slightly lower pragmatic quality score and a slightly higher hedonic quality. The Spiral Energy Context interface exhibits an opposite trend compared to the Linear Energy Consumption and Calendar Energy Activity interfaces. It has the highest Hedonic Quality score (1.64), indicating that users found it more engaging and visually appealing, but it scores the lowest in Pragmatic Quality (0.10), suggesting that users found it more difficult to interpret.

## 9 Discussion

This paper has explored temporal representations through three distinct types of temporal forms of interfaces (linear, calendar, and spiral) with three distinct types of temporal data (consumption, activity, and context). The study provides insights into how different temporal forms and data types may effect how users interpret and engage with energy consumption data that is based on DTs. Based on user feedback, we identify actionable design recommendations for developing temporal interfaces of DTs in the domestic energy engagement context:

1. **Adapt Data Representation to User Needs and Intentions.** Each type of temporal data shapes user understanding by focusing on different aspects of energy use, meeting various levels of detail and user needs.
   (a) **Consumption.** Displaying the amount of energy consumed as kWh provides precise data. While kWh was abstract for users unfamiliar with energy metrics, the metered approach to energy did allow for goal setting and comparisons of energy usage over time. However, without additional information such as activity or context, kWh alone may not effectively drive behavior change.
   (b) **Activity.** Energy activities focus on the specific actions or behaviors that drive energy usage, such as cooking, washing clothes, or heating. This representation is helpful for users to relate energy use to their daily routines,

making it easier to identify and adjust high-consumption behaviors. While this approach is intuitive and relatable, it lacks precise numerical data, making it less effective for users focused on precise monitoring or trend analysis.
(c) **Context.** Energy Context is the comprehensive set of conditions and factors that influence energy consumption externally and internally, including environmental conditions (e.g., time, occupancy, temperature), user emotional states, and system-generated insights (e.g., automation triggers or predictive analytics). Such information could support a more accurate and meaningful interpretation of energy data. Contextual information allows users to understand the causes behind their energy patterns, which might prompt reflection and behavior change. However, this type of data might overwhelm users if not well-organized and prioritized, making it harder to focus on actionable insights.
2. **Choose Temporal Forms that Match User Expectations.** Different types of temporal forms will effect how users perceive and understand energy consumption by shaping clarity, familiarity, and the ability to identify patterns and trends. Designers should align interface structure with user expectations and data characteristics:
   (a) **Linear.** A linear timeline is straightforward and familiar to many users, making it effective for displaying trends and changes over time. Users could easily track energy consumption as it progresses, which is particularly useful for identifying increases or decreases in usage. However, linear forms may struggle to represent repeating patterns, such as daily or seasonal cycles, without additional annotations. This limits users' ability to connect energy usage with cyclical behaviors, such as morning routines or winter heating.
   (b) **Calendar.** Calendar form resonates well with users because it aligns with familiar schedules. By presenting energy data within a structured grid of days or weeks, calendars could make it easier to correlate energy consumption with specific events or routines. This representation could support understanding within short-to-medium (daily and weekly) time frames but may be less effective for displaying long-term (monthly, seasonally, and yearly) trends.
   (c) **Spiral.** The spiral form uniquely combines linear progression with cyclical patterns, offering a holistic view of energy usage over time. Each loop of the spiral can represent a specific cycle, allowing users to compare similar points in different cycles easily. This is particularly helpful for identifying repetitive patterns, such as peak energy usage during specific hours or seasons. However, the spiral forms might be less intuitive and visually demanding for some users, especially if users are unfamiliar with such layouts. The complexity of this representation may require additional explanation or training to be fully understood.
3. **Consider Other Combinations of Temporal Representations.** While this study paired three forms of temporal representation with three types of

data, as shown in Fig. 2, these pairings could have had various other combinations. Such combinations present a broad range of possibilities for adapting energy interfaces to diverse user needs. For instance: a **linear** timeline with **contextual** information might help users see how external factors affect their energy use over time; a **calendar**-based energy interface that shows daily **consumption** in kWh or cost, may allow users to spot fluctuations, identify peak usage (e.g., on weekends due to cooking or laundry), and adjust habits accordingly; a **spiral**-based interface that visualizes recurring energy **activities** may highlight cyclical patterns and enabling users to comprehend and compare how their repeated actions effect energy consumption over time. More advanced interfaces may combine multiple types of data and multiple forms of representation to better address specific user needs.

The "Time Machine" analogy is proposed as a conceptual tool for designing temporal interfaces of DTs. Mental-modeling DTs as a "Time Machine" could clarify how DTs support the navigation of historical data and future predictions. This understanding may prove particularly valuable when DTs are applied outside of engineering and technological fields and need to interact with non-professionals. In the case of domestic environments, designing with the "Time Machine" analogy promotes an understanding of past usage patterns and future needs and may drive improvements in efficiency, sustainability, and occupant satisfaction.

When designing new temporal interfaces, it is important to consider user familiarity and the learning curve. One participant (P11) noted that although cyclical form aligns with how he perceives time, unfamiliar visualizations can feel counterintuitive and visually demanding. DTs can play a key role in cyclical analysis by dynamically mapping recurring patterns, such as daily routines or seasonal trends, making them more interpretable. Designers should match visualization types to the nature of the data: cyclical formats for repetitive patterns and linear timelines for trends and progression. Providing adaptable or hybrid visualizations by DTs would allow users to switch between representations and improve comprehension.

Smart energy technologies should empower residents with a contextual understanding of how their daily activities influence their actual energy consumption [4]. A context-aware DT has the potential to provide real-time insights that relate energy use to specific actions, environmental conditions, and user habits. By dynamically adapting to users' routines and contextual changes, a context-aware DT could offer personalized feedback, making energy data more relevant and actionable. This approach not only enhances user engagement but also supports informed decision-making, ultimately leading to more sustainable and efficient energy consumption.

### 9.1 Limitations and Future Work

Our study has several limitations. 1) This study designs only three forms of temporal interfaces and assigns these interfaces three types of data. As Fig. 2

suggests, additional combinations and design possibilities could be explored in further research. 2) The data sample of this study is relatively small (N = 18), which has reduced the statistical power to detect significant differences in the interfaces tested. As such, the quantitative data primarily assists to support and explain the qualitative findings. The goal of this study is to provide in-depth qualitative insights into user understanding of temporal representations rather than achieving statistical generalization. Future research could involve larger samples for validation. 3) Our conceptual prototypes could efficiently explore early-stage design concepts and gather valuable user insights before real implementation, but the lack of real-world implementation with a DT limits the validation of user understanding and user experience. We acknowledge the need for future studies involving functional prototypes integrated with DTs to validate the effectiveness of the proposed interfaces in real-world domestic energy usage settings. 4) We acknowledge that demographic factors, such as cultural and economic background and lifestyle, may influence users' understanding of temporal interfaces as well as how users consume energy. In our qualitative study, we did not explicitly take these factors into account in the setup and analysis of the study.

The next step of this research will explore how temporal representations in DT interfaces can support users in balancing their own actions with system automation. This involves examining how users interpret and respond to DT-generated insights over time, ensuring that the interface provides contextualized energy information in a way that aligns with user needs. By focusing on temporal representation and contextual understanding, the future study aims to refine context-aware DT temporal interfaces to enhance user engagement, support informed decision-making, and improve adaptability.

## 10 Conclusion

This paper explores how different temporal forms (linear, calendar, and spiral) and energy data types (consumption, activities, and context) influence users' understanding of energy usage. We developed a conceptual tool, the "Time Machine" analogy, for inquiring into how DTs may be interacted with and how their interfaces might be conceived. Represented through the "Time Machine" analogy, three types of temporal interfaces for DTs of domestic energy usage were designed. Our findings suggest that each temporal form serves different needs: linear timelines effectively highlight trends, calendars provide familiarity by linking energy use to daily routines, and spiral forms emphasize cyclical patterns but may require more efforts to interpret. Similarly, different data types shape different user comprehension: consumption such as kWh values provide precise but abstract measurements, activity-based representations make energy use relatable, and context offers a holistic understanding of energy consumption. By combining adaptable temporal representations with different ways of presenting energy data, interfaces could make it easier for users to track, reflect on, and improve their energy usage based on their individual needs and habits.

This paper provides a step toward greater clarity for designers and researchers on how to make temporal interfaces of DTs more understandable for non-expert users.

**Acknowledgments.** This research is conducted under the REDI Program, a project that has received funding from the European Union's Horizon 2020 research and innovation program under the Marie Skłodowska-Curie grant agreement No. 101034328. The authors sincerely appreciate the contributions of all participants in this study.

# References

1. Alexopoulos, K., Makris, S., Xanthakis, V., Sipsas, K., Chryssolouris, G.: A concept for context-aware computing in manufacturing: the white goods case. Int. J. Comput. Integr. Manuf. **29**(8), 839–849 (2016). https://doi.org/10.1080/0951192X.2015.1130257
2. Braun, V., Clarke, V.: Using thematic analysis in psychology. Qual. Res. Psychol. **3**(2), 77–101 (2006). https://doi.org/10.1191/1478088706qp063oa
3. Cross, N.: Designerly Ways of Knowing, vol. 3 (2006). https://doi.org/10.1007/1-84628-301-9
4. De Koning, P., Kuijer, L., Frens, J.: A sensory autoethnography of energy practices in the home: an exploration of combining smart meter data with situated accounts of what energy is for. In: Extended Abstracts of the 2023 CHI Conference on Human Factors in Computing Systems, CHI EA 2023, p. 1 7. Association for Computing Machinery, New York (2023). https://doi.org/10.1145/3544549.3585710
5. Dorst, K., Royakkers, L.: The design analogy: a model for moral problem solving. Des. Stud. **27**(6), 633–656 (2006). https://doi.org/10.1016/j.destud.2006.05.002
6. Fraisse, P.: Perception and estimation of time. Ann. Rev. Psychol. **35**, 1–36 (1984). https://doi.org/10.1146/annurev.ps.35.020184.000245
7. Funk, M., Chen, L.L., Yang, S.W., Chen, Y.K.: Addressing the need to capture scenarios, intentions and preferences: interactive intentional programming in the smart home. Int. J. Des. **12**(1), 53–66 (2018)
8. Gentner, D., Holyoak, K.J.: Reasoning and learning by analogy: introduction. Am. Psychol. **52**(1), 32–34 (1997). https://doi.org/10.1037/0003-066X.52.1.32
9. Gibson, J.J.: Events are perceivable but time is not. In: Fraser, J.T., Lawrence, N. (eds.) The Study of Time II, pp. 295–301. Springer, Heidelberg (1975). https://doi.org/10.1007/978-3-642-50121-0_22
10. Gold, R., Waters, C., York, D.: Leveraging Advanced Metering Infrastructure to Save Energy (2020). https://www.aceee.org/research-report/u2001
11. Hartmann, D., Herz, M., Wever, U.: Model order reduction a key technology for digital twins. In: Keiper, W., Milde, A., Volkwein, S. (eds.) Reduced-Order Modeling (ROM) for Simulation and Optimization, pp. 167–179. Springer, Cham (2018). https://doi.org/10.1007/978-3-319-75319-5_8
12. Sharp, H., Preece, J., Rogers, Y.: Interaction Design: Beyond Human-Computer Interaction, 5th edn. Wiley, Indianapolis (2019)
13. Hribernik, K., Cabri, G., Mandreoli, F., Mentzas, G.: Autonomous, context-aware, adaptive digital twins-state of the art and roadmap. Comput. Ind. **133**, 103508 (2021). https://doi.org/10.1016/j.compind.2021.103508

14. Kjeldskov, J., Skov, M.B., Paay, J., Lund, D., Madsen, T., Nielsen, M.: Facilitating flexible electricity use in the home with eco-feedback and eco-forecasting. In: Proceedings of the Annual Meeting of the Australian Special Interest Group for Computer Human Interaction, OzCHI 2015, pp. 388–396. Association for Computing Machinery, New York (2015). https://doi.org/10.1145/2838739.2838755
15. Koch, M., Weiskopf, D., Kurzhals, K.: A spiral into the mind: gaze spiral visualization for mobile eye tracking. Proc. ACM Comput. Graph. Interact. Tech. **5**(2) (2022). https://doi.org/10.1145/3530795
16. Lee, A.N., Martinez Lastra, J.L.: Enhancement of industrial monitoring systems by utilizing context awareness. In: 2013 IEEE International Multi-Disciplinary Conference on Cognitive Methods in Situation Awareness and Decision Support (CogSIMA), pp. 277–284 (2013). https://doi.org/10.1109/CogSIMA.2013.6523858. https://ieeexplore.ieee.org/document/6523858
17. Lee, H., Yoo, S., Kim, Y.W.: An energy management framework for smart factory based on context-awareness. In: 2016 18th International Conference on Advanced Communication Technology (ICACT), p. 1 (2016). https://doi.org/10.1109/ICACT.2016.7423519. https://ieeexplore.ieee.org/document/7423519
18. Liu, Z., Meyendorf, N., Mrad, N.: The role of data fusion in predictive maintenance using digital twin. AIP Conf. Proc. **1949**(1), 020023 (2018). https://doi.org/10.1063/1.5031520
19. Lu, Q., et al.: Developing a digital twin at building and city levels: case study of west Cambridge campus. J. Manag. Eng. **36**(3), 05020004 (2020). https://doi.org/10.1061/(ASCE)ME.1943-5479.0000763
20. Lucke, D., Constantinescu, C., Westkämper, E.: Smart factory - a step towards the next generation of manufacturing. In: Mitsuishi, M., Ueda, K., Kimura, F. (eds.) Manufacturing Systems and Technologies for the New Frontier, pp. 115–118. Springer, London (2008). https://doi.org/10.1007/978-1-84800-267-8_23
21. Marcello, F., Chouquir, A.Y., Atzori, L., Pilloni, V.: Digital twin framework for personalized building management in ambient assisted living. In: 2024 IEEE 10th World Forum on Internet of Things (WF-IoT), pp. 730–735 (2024). https://doi.org/10.1109/WF-IoT62078.2024.10811267. https://ieeexplore.ieee.org/abstract/document/10811267
22. Mennicken, S., Hofer, J., Dey, A., Huang, E.M.: Casalendar: a temporal interface for automated homes. In: CHI 2014 Extended Abstracts on Human Factors in Computing Systems, CHI EA 2014, pp. 2161–2166. Association for Computing Machinery, New York (2014). https://doi.org/10.1145/2559206.2581321
23. Mennicken, S., Kim, D., Huang, E.M.: Integrating the smart home into the digital calendar. In: Proceedings of the 2016 CHI Conference on Human Factors in Computing Systems, CHI 2016, pp. 5958–5969. Association for Computing Machinery, New York (2016). https://doi.org/10.1145/2858036.2858168
24. Mirlacher, T., et al.: Interactive simplicity for ITV: minimizing keys for navigating content. In: Proceedings of the 8th European Conference on Interactive TV and Video, EuroITV 2010, pp. 137–140. Association for Computing Machinery, New York (2010). https://doi.org/10.1145/1809777.1809806
25. Mohammadi, N., Taylor, J.E.: Smart city digital twins. In: 2017 IEEE Symposium Series on Computational Intelligence (SSCI), pp. 1–5 (2017). https://doi.org/10.1109/SSCI.2017.8285439. https://ieeexplore.ieee.org/document/8285439
26. Nilsson, A., Wester, M., Lazarevic, D., Brandt, N.: Smart homes, home energy management systems and real-time feedback: lessons for influencing household energy consumption from a swedish field study. Energy Build. **179**, 15–25 (2018). https://doi.org/10.1016/j.enbuild.2018.08.026

27. Paredes-Valverde, M.A., Alor-Hernández, G., García-Alcaráz, J.L., Salas-Zárate, M.D.P., Colombo-Mendoza, L.O., Sánchez-Cervantes, J.L.: Intellihome: an internet of things-based system for electrical energy saving in smart home environment. Comput. Intell. **36**(1), 203–224 (2020). https://doi.org/10.1111/coin.12252
28. Pierce, J., Paulos, E.: The local energy indicator: designing for wind and solar energy systems in the home. In: Proceedings of the Designing Interactive Systems Conference, DIS 2012, pp. 631–634. Association for Computing Machinery, New York (2012). https://doi.org/10.1145/2317956.2318050
29. Rosen, R., von Wichert, G., Lo, G., Bettenhausen, K.D.: About the importance of autonomy and digital twins for the future of manufacturing. IFAC-PapersOnLine **48**(3), 567–572 (2015). https://doi.org/10.1016/j.ifacol.2015.06.141
30. Schrammel, J., Gerdenitsch, C., Weiss, A., Kluckner, P.M., Tscheligi, M.: FOREwatch – the clock that tells you when to use: persuading users to align their energy consumption with green power availability. In: Keyson, D.V., et al. (eds.) AmI 2011. LNCS, vol. 7040, pp. 157–166. Springer, Heidelberg (2011). https://doi.org/10.1007/978-3-642-25167-2_19
31. Schrepp, M., Hinderks, A., Thomaschewski, J.: Design and evaluation of a short version of the user experience questionnaire (UEQ-S). Int. J. Interact. Multimedia Artif. Intell. **4**(6), 103 (2017). https://doi.org/10.9781/ijimai.2017.09.001
32. Semeraro, C., Lezoche, M., Panetto, H., Dassisti, M.: Digital twin paradigm: a systematic literature review. Comput. Ind. **130**, 103469 (2021). https://doi.org/10.1016/j.compind.2021.103469
33. Sharma, A., Kosasih, E., Zhang, J., Brintrup, A., Calinescu, A.: Digital twins: state of the art theory and practice, challenges, and open research questions. J. Ind. Inf. Integ. 100383 (2022). https://doi.org/10.1016/j.jii.2022.100383
34. Strengers, Y.: Smart energy in everyday life: are you designing for resource man? Interactions **21**(4), 24–31 (2014). https://doi.org/10.1145/2621931
35. Suchman, L.: Human-Machine Reconfigurations: Plans and Situated Actions. Learning in Doing: Social, Cognitive and Computational Perspectives, 2 edn. Cambridge University Press, Cambridge (2006). https://doi.org/10.1017/CBO9780511808418. https://www.cambridge.org/core/books/humanmachine-reconfigurations/9D53E602BA9BB5209271460F92D00EFE
36. Vine, D., Buys, L., Morris, P.: The effectiveness of energy feedback for conservation and peak demand: a literature review. Open J. Energy Effi. **2**(11), 7–15 (2013). https://doi.org/10.4236/ojee.2013.21002
37. Voros, J.: Big history and anticipation. In: Poli, R. (ed.) Handbook of Anticipation, pp. 425–464. Springer, Cham (2019). https://doi.org/10.1007/978-3-319-91554-8_95
38. Yildiz, M., Coşkun, A.: Time perceptions as a material for designing new representations of time. In: Extended Abstracts of the 2020 CHI Conference on Human Factors in Computing Systems, CHI EA 2020, p. 1 7. Association for Computing Machinery, New York (2020). https://doi.org/10.1145/3334480.3382950
39. Zhang, H., Ma, L., Sun, J., Lin, H., Thürer, M.: Digital twin in services and industrial product service systems: review and analysis. Procedia CIRP **83**, 57–60 (2019). https://doi.org/10.1016/j.procir.2019.02.131

# Exploring the Potential of Interacting with a Virtual Dog in a Virtual Forest for Well-Being: A Study with Informal Caregivers of People with Dementia

Beatriz Peres[1,2(✉)], Lilian Motti[3], Genesis Nobrega[1,2], Jana Janković[4], Diogo Manuel Gouveia[1], and Pedro Campos[1,2,5]

[1] University of Madeira, Funchal, Portugal
beajardim21@gmail.com
[2] Interactive Technologies Institute, LARSYS, Funchal, Portugal
[3] Department Computer Science and Information Systems, University of Limerick, Limerick, Ireland
[4] University of Maribor, Maribor, Slovenia
[5] WoW Systems, Funchal, Portugal

**Abstract.** Previous studies designing Virtual Reality (VR) suggest that interaction with virtual pets can increase users' sense of presence, which consequently could lead to technological interventions for well-being and mental health. However, further studies are needed to assess and understand the effects of VR on users' emotional states. In this study, informal caregivers of People with Dementia or related conditions used VR to navigate in a virtual forest (a Virtual Natural Environment - VNE) and interact with a virtual dog (petting vs. throwing a bone). Through a mixed-methods approach, we found increased energy and decreased tension when participants interacted with the virtual dog. Feelings of joy, companionship, and security were reported by participants after the interaction with the virtual dog in VR. Participants expressed interest in incorporating virtual dog interaction in VR into their daily routines to help them to cope with stressful situations.

**Keywords:** Dementia informal caregivers · Emotional States · Sense of Presence · Virtual Pet · Virtual Natural Environment · VNE

## 1 Introduction

There is an increasing interest in designing technologies that can improve user's well-being, in particular eliciting positive changes and mediating personal experiences [7]. However, research points out two areas that require further studies: the need of empirical evidence on how immersive, interactive experiences can affect positively users' emotional state, and how to employ design elements and interaction most effectively to that end. An innovative approach is the use of Virtual Reality (VR) such as using a Virtual Natural Environment (VNE) which have shown potential in promoting emotional states of general population. We hypothesize that VR could be applicable in the context of informal caregivers of people with Dementia to improve their emotional states.

In this context, VR offers a promising alternative by providing immersive-based experiences that can positively impact emotional states, simulating the benefits of real natural environments [1,4], while meeting users' need for an indoor and safe solution. In addition, there is evidence in the literature that interaction with virtual companions, such a virtual pet, can increase users' Sense of Presence, therefore helping users to diverge their attention from the real context and take a moment to recenter themselves when recovering or before facing stressful situations [13]. In particular, virtual dog companions can decrease stress levels in users [8].

People with Dementia remains an underexplored area of research. Informal caregivers provide continuous support for individuals with dementia [2], often struggling to balance their needs with those of their loved ones [6]. The research calls for the development of systems that not only support patients but also caregivers, addressing the burdens that often hinder their health and well-being. Technologies could help users who are seeking solutions beyond counseling, social support, and medication. VR using VNE and animal-assisted interventions could help alleviate some of the emotional strain informal caregivers face, promoting a quick recovery in their emotional state. By integrating these technologies into the caregiving context, we hope to indirectly support those who are being cared for, such as their family members.

Our research question is: How might interaction with a virtual dog in a virtual forest affect the emotional state of users in an VR system? To address this question, we compared a virtual forest with and without the presence of an interactive virtual dog, and two types of interaction when the virtual dog is presented (petting or throwing a bone). The main contribution of the present study is to demonstrate the impact of a virtual dog within an VR system simulating a nature-based environment, assessing their effects on the emotional state of users, with a particular focus on its potential to improve the well-being of caregivers of people with Dementia.

## 2 Materials and Methods

### 2.1 Sample

This study involved 14 informal caregivers living with people with Dementia family members that include Alzheimer Disease and Related Dementias, predominantly female (11) with an average age of 54 years (SD = 14). On average, they had been caregivers for 11 years (SD = 11), primarily caring for parents, except for one who cared for a friend. Alzheimer's was the most commonly identified dementia type (six participants), followed by Vascular Dementia (three participants), with an average age of 78 years (SD = 16). Three participants had pets at home, predominantly dogs, followed by cats, birds, and fish. The other eleven participants reported reasons such as time or space constraints for not having pets, although they still expressed a fondness for animals, especially dogs. One participant mentioned avoiding larger dog breeds due to other concerns. All participants had previous experience with VR, but none had prior experience with non-immersive activities like Wii Fit, Frisbee, or Sports Resort. This study was approved by the Research Ethics Committee of the University of the first author, as part of a series of similar studies conducted by the first author.

## 2.2 Design Research

**Virtual Natural Environment.** A virtual forest was implemented as opposed to different natural landscapes (e.g. beach or grassland) because of previous studies mentioning benefits of environments with green space [14], independently of the type of forest [5]. We have chosen vegetation assets similar to the geographical location of the participants. The virtual forest contains conifer trees, bloomed bushes, ambient sounds with birdsong and wind animation. It was created using Unity 2022.3.19f1 with the Universal Render Pipeline (URP). To create this environment we used an asset selection from the Unity asset store, available for free[1] To enhance the visual fidelity of the environment, we leveraged the textures from Unity Terrain - URP Demo Scene asset[2]. Finally, we employed post-processing techniques for lighting and added a skybox sourced from the Unity asset store[3]. Figure 1 displays the described environment.

**Virtual Dog.** The reason for incorporating a virtual animal into a virtual forest stemmed from a previous study from Peres et al. [10], where caregivers of people with Dementia were invited to brainstorm companion preferences while experiencing VNE, and their findings suggest virtual animals as one of the three types of companionship (virtual animals, physical human companionship and virtual human companionship). We implemented a dog companion, specifically a Corgi breed model bought from CGTrader[4]. This model features low-polygon rendering with pre-made animations programmed to simulate natural dog behavior.

Two types of interaction with the virtual dog were implemented and are evaluated in the present study. A petting feature initiated when the user approximated the virtual dog and approached it using the controller. In addition to the visual representation of virtual hands in the virtual forest and reaction from the virtual dog, this interaction also started motion controller vibrations. For

---

[1] https://assetstore.unity.com/packages/3d/vegetation/trees/conifers-botd-142076, https://assetstore.unity.com/packages/3d/environments/rocks-and-vegetation-pack-urp-243519.
[2] https://assetstore.unity.com/packages/3d/environments/unity-terrain-urp-demo-scene-213197.
[3] https://assetstore.unity.com/packages/2d/textures-materials/sky/allsky-free-10-sky-skybox-set-146014.
[4] https://www.cgtrader.com/3d-models/animals/mammal/dog-corgi-cf759e07-1a28-4264-a5eb-2d1d26f3e038.

the other task, we introduced a fetching feature. Users initiated the interaction with the virtual dog by grasping a bone object using the VR device controller's grip button. The dog then retrieves the thrown bone, displaying playful animation and excited barking sounds to encourage further engagement. Petting and playing fetch interactions are portrayed in Fig. 1.

**Fig. 1.** (i) Forest environment, (ii) Petting interaction and (iii) Playing fetch interaction (left to right)

### 2.3 Data Collection

Before the study, participants were asked questions about their sociodemographic profile and attitudes towards natural environments and pets, followed by Activation Deactivation Adjective Check List (AD ACL) [3] and the Self-Assessment Manikin (SAM) [12]. The sociodemographic questions covered the caregiver's age, gender, duration of informal care provision, reasons for becoming caregivers, type of dementia their care recipient has, the age of their care recipient, and their relationship with them. We continued the preliminary questionnaire asking whether caregivers have pets, their affinity for pets, their preference for natural environments, and their favorite natural settings. Between the three tasks, AD ACL and SAM scales were used to gauge the emotional state of participants, particularly focusing on arousal (calm to excited) and valence (unpleasant to pleasant feelings). At the end of the study, the Comfort from Companion Animals Scale (CCAS) [15] was used to measure the level of emotional comfort participants derived from interaction with the virtual dog. Then, participants were asked to reflect on their experience and satisfaction through the following questions: How did you feel after interacting with the animal in the forest? Did you prefer a particular activity with the dog? If so, which ones and why? What were your thoughts about interacting with the animal while in the forest? How did you feel after being alone in the forest without the animal? Did you prefer one approach over the other (forest alone or forest with the dog), or did you appreciate both? If so, why? Would you consider incorporating the practice of interacting with a virtual dog in a virtual forest into your daily routine?

## 2.4 Study Design and Tasks

The study took place at the University lab, and the equipment used Oculus Quest 2 VR headsets and controllers. Participants were asked to stand during the three tasks of the study, and each task was explained to them. The study comprised three tasks (counter- balanced): Forest task (Forest without the dog): participants observed the forest for 5 min by rotating their body and head. Petting task (Forest and petting the dog): participants used the controller to interact with the virtual dog. Virtual hands became visible on the VR field-of-view, representing the motion of the user's controllers. Playing fetch task (Forest and playing fetch with the dog: participants interacted a bone-shaped object to play fetch with the dog.

Each task lasted 5 min, a duration supported by research [11], indicating the emergence of positive psychological changes occur when spending this duration of time with any animal, irrespective of whether it is their pet or not [9]. The entire study, including pre and post assessment, last a maximum of 45 min.

## 2.5 Data Analysis

Within our mixed-method approach, quantitative data were collected concurrently with qualitative measures and examined to provide a deeper insight into the quantitative findings. Quantitative data were analyzed in SPSS Statistics 26, where we employed the Friedman test, followed by a post hoc Wilcoxon pairwise test on all combinations. To adjust for multiple comparisons, we divided the initial significance value (0.05) by the total number of tests (six), resulting in a new p-value of 0.008 for the Wilcoxon test.

Qualitative data were analyzed from participants' responses to the open-ended questions after the tasks. For a Thematic Analysis, two researchers employed open coding to develop a codebook after extracting excerpts for analysis. Subsequently, they revisited the data to contextualize the codes accurately in alignment with participant experiences. The identified codes were then organized into themes, refined, and supplemented with relevant excerpts to construct a cohesive narrative.

## 3 Results

### 3.1 Quantitative Data

Statistical analyses revealed significant differences in emotional states among participants: Valence ($X^2(3) = 26.7$, $p \leq 0.001$), arousal ($X^2(3) = 30.7$, $p \leq 0.001$), energy ($X^2(3) = 20.3$, $p \leq 0.001$), tension ($X^2(3) = 17.1$, $p = 0.001$), and calmness ($X^2(3) = 18.8$, $p \leq 0.001$) differed significantly, except for tiredness ($X^2(3) = 7.2$, $p \geq 0.05$). Post-hoc analysis using Wilcoxon's test adjusted the significance level to $p = 0.008$.

Valence significantly increased between baseline and forest and between baseline and playing fetch activity ($p = 0.001$, $r = 0.85$, $p = 0.001$, $r = 0.85$) respectively. Arousal significantly decreased between baseline and forest and between baseline and petting the dog activity and baseline and playing fetch activity ($p = 0.003$, $r = 0.80$, $p = 0.002$, $r = 0.83$, $p = 0.002$, $r = 0.83$) respectively. Energy significantly increased between baseline and petting the dog activity and between baseline and playing fetch activity ($p = 0.002$, $r = 0.82$, $p = 0.005$, $r = 0.75$). Tension significantly decreased between baseline and petting the dog activity and between baseline and playing fetch activity ($p = 0.007$, $r = 0.72$, $p = 0.007$, $r = 0.77$). Calmness significantly increased between baseline and forest, and baseline and petting the dog activity ($p = 0.005$, $r = 0.75$, $p = 0.005$, $r = 0.75$).

Responses to the CCAS show that the virtual animal provided a pleasant activity (Median = Completely agree) and that they enjoyed observing the pet (Median = Completely agree) and derived comfort from interacting with it (Median = Completely agree). Moreover, the virtual dog provided companionship to the caregivers (Median = Agree), fostering moments of playfulness and laughter (Median = Completely agree), giving them something to care for (Median = Completely agree) and something to love (Median = Agree). Also, participants felt loved (Median = Agree), needed (Median = Agree), and trusted (Median = Agree) by the virtual dog.

### 3.2 Qualitative Data

The scope of this analysis is to outline the effects of virtual forest and virtual dog on participants emotional status.

**Virtual Forest Versus Virtual Dog.** Most participants (71%) reported that the virtual forest brought them peace and a sense of connection with nature. While some (29%) were curious about specific forest details like flowers and rocks, the majority (71%) focused more on the virtual animal than on the forest itself.

Interacting with the virtual dog made participants feel cheerful and accompanied ("An intimate activity between the two of us, enjoying nature, the two of us were alone but giving each other company"- P4) Preferences for interacting with the dog varied, with 57% enjoying the dynamic activity of throwing a bone, while 43% found comfort in petting the dog. Companionship was a strong theme, mentioned by 79% of participants ("Because we keep each other company, we play, we have fun because only watching the forest I stay lonely"- P4).

Additionally, 37% felt the virtual dog reduced loneliness and brought security ("With the interaction with the dog, I felt less loneliness in the calm forest environment. The dog brought company and a comforting presence while I was watching the virtual forest environment."- P6)

In general, the virtual dog provided companionship, comfort, and reduced loneliness within the tranquil virtual nature environment.

**Potential of VR for Well-Being of Informal Caregivers of People with Dementia.** Most of the participants (71%) mentioned that the virtual animal could bring benefits to their daily routine by reducing caregiving pressures, offering a refuge, and bringing peace. Many felt that incorporating a virtual dog in VR would relieve caregiving stress, providing companionship, tranquility, and security (e.g. "Having an approach like this at home would be very advantageous"- P12). They appreciated the virtual dog's calming presence and its ability to offer companionship and distraction (e.g. "I liked it because the dog conveys tranquility, calm, security and company that a caregiver needs"- P8), Most participants (71%) also found the virtual dog therapeutic, helping them forget about their caregiving responsibilities for a moment, and expressed they enjoyed the novelty of the interaction (e.g."Because I had something to distract me from my thoughts"- P9). Some participants (43%) expressed their love for animals and compared the interaction with a real dog (e.g. "I did not feel as happy as when I was with a dog because I love animals"- P1).

Despite initial hesitation from two participants due to unfamiliarity with dogs, they ultimately enjoyed the interaction (e.g. "I found it fun because it is a fun activity to interact with the dog, although at first, I was afraid, but that was because I am not used now to dealing with dogs"- P8). However, some participants (29%) would prefer real animals, finding virtual interactions less meaningful and potentially monotonous (e.g. "There is no comparison to the experience of interacting with real animals"- P1).

## 4 Discussion

This study aimed to explore the impact of a virtual dog within a virtual forest, focusing on its potential to improve the emotional state of caregivers. Results showed significant changes in valence, arousal, energy, tension, and calmness indicated the influence of interacting with a virtual dog in a virtual forest on participants' emotional states.

Interacting with the virtual dog produced additional positive emotional responses, characterized by increased energy and decreased tension. Participants reported a sense of companionship, joy, and feeling loved and trusted. We believe that the interaction with the virtual dog may result in an increased sense of Presence, although it as explicitly expressed by only one participant. This finding is in line with results reported in the literature [13] where having a high interaction (a cooperative task) and a realistic behavior (dogs reacts to the subject) led to improvements in mood demonstrating that greater emotional engagement with virtual animals leads to better emotional outcomes.

When asked about their preferred type of interaction with the virtual dog, participants showed a slight preference for the throwing the bone task compared to petting. While we do not have enough data to discuss this difference in preferences, we can argue that these interactive tasks contributed significantly to participants' emotional experiences, reinforcing the idea that interaction is a key factor in promoting an immersive experience leading to positive emotional outcomes. Qualitative results in our study detail the emotional effects more apparent in participants such as reported feelings of energy, calmness, and reduced tension.

Overall, most participants (71%) found the virtual dog could be beneficial for their well-being and that VR/virtual forest with virtual pets could be incorporated into their caregiving routine.

Considering our design recommendations, future studies should support participants with alternative interactions with a virtual animal. Participants in our study expressed concerns about the potential monotony of daily interactions with the virtual dog, preferring real animals for sustained emotional support.

The limitations of this paper are the following: The scope of this study was limited to basic interactions (petting or fetching) with a virtual dog; however, other interactions including multimodal sensory outputs could impact Sense of Presence, and should be studied (e.g. music). For a long-term evaluation, further research should investigate additional side effects (e.g. motion-sickness) and positive impact in other caregiving contexts. Future studies could incorporate physiological measures such as heart rate [13], to assess subtle changes in users' emotional state. An important question to be addressed is how this technology can be incorporated into the caring routines, without being an additional burden, dealing with time constraints, and not losing focus on caring responsibilities. Another important aspect to consider is the need for VR literacy in order to effectively use this equipment.

## 5 Conclusion

In conclusion, this study shows that interactions with a virtual dog in a virtual forest can promote positive emotions, including joy and companionship, to informal caregivers of people with Dementia. Moreover, these informal caregivers expressed interest in a possible integration of a virtual pet companion and VR into their daily routines, recognizing it as a source of distraction and relief. With this, the integration of VR and virtual forest into caregiving on a daily basis emerges as a possible effective intervention for improving the overall emotional state of informal caregivers of people with Dementia.

**Acknowledgments.** We are grateful to all the participants that were generous with their time for this study. We are also grateful to György Varga for the help designing the VR forest. This research was funded by the Portuguese Recovery and Resilience Program (PRR), IAPMEI/ANI/FCT under Agenda C645022399-00000057 (eGames-Lab). This work was supported by FCT - Fundação para a Ciência e Tecnologia, I.P. by project reference 2020.08848.BD and DOI identifier 10.54499/2020.08848.BD.

# References

1. Alanazi, M.O., et al.: Nature-based virtual reality feasibility and acceptability pilot for caregiver respite. Curr. Oncol. **30**, 5995–6005 (2023). https://api.semanticscholar.org/CorpusID:259565008
2. Allen, A.P., et al.: Informal caregiving for dementia patients: the contribution of patient characteristics and behaviours to caregiver burden. Age Ageing **49**(1), 52–56 (2019). https://doi.org/10.1093/ageing/afz128
3. Bradley, M.M., Lang, P.J.: Measuring emotion: the self-assessment manikin and the semantic differential. J. Behav. Ther. Exp. Psychiatry **25**(1), 49–59 (1994). https://doi.org/10.1016/0005-7916(94)90063-9. https://www.sciencedirect.com/science/article/pii/0005791694900639
4. Chan, S.H.M., Qiu, L., Esposito, G., Mai, K.P., Tam, K.-P., Cui, J.: Nature in virtual reality improves mood and reduces stress: evidence from young adults and senior citizens. Virtual Reality 1–16 (2021). https://doi.org/10.1007/s10055-021-00604-4
5. Clark, H., Vanclay, J., Brymer, E.: Forest features and mental health and well-being: a scoping review. J. Environ. Psychol. **89**, 102040 (2023). https://doi.org/10.1016/j.jenvp.2023.102040. https://www.sciencedirect.com/science/article/pii/S0272494423000889
6. Hajek, A., Kretzler, B., König, H.H.: Informal caregiving, loneliness and social isolation: a systematic review. Int. J. Environ. Res. Public Health **18**(22) (2021)
7. Kitson, A., Prpa, M., Riecke, B.E.: Immersive interactive technologies for positive change: a scoping review and design considerations. Front. Psychol. **9** (2018). https://doi.org/10.3389/fpsyg.2018.01354. https://www.frontiersin.org/journals/psychology/articles/10.3389/fpsyg.2018.01354
8. Na, H., Park, S., Dong, S.Y.: Mixed reality-based interaction between human and virtual cat for mental stress management. Sensors **22**(3) (2022)
9. Pendry, P., Kuzara, S., Gee, N.: Characteristics of student–dog interaction during a meet-and-greet activity in a university-based animal visitation program. Anthrozoös **33**, 53–69 (2020). https://doi.org/10.1080/08927936.2020.1694311
10. Peres, B., Lopes, D.S., Jorge, J., Campos, P.F.: Co-designing companions in virtual natural environments for enhanced well-being: insights from dementia informal caregivers. In: Adjunct Proceedings of the 2024 Nordic Conference on Human-Computer Interaction. NordiCHI 2024 Adjunct. Association for Computing Machinery, New York (2024). https://doi.org/10.1145/3677045.3685415
11. Suppakittpaisarn, P., et al.: Durations of virtual exposure to built and natural landscapes impact self-reported stress recovery: evidence from three countries. Landscape Ecol. Eng. **19**, 3 (2022). https://doi.org/10.1007/s11355-022-00523-9
12. Thayer, R.E.: Activation-deactivation adjective check list: current overview and structural analysis. Psychol. Rep. **58**(2), 607–614 (1986). https://doi.org/10.2466/pr0.1986.58.2.607
13. Wanali, W.A.A., Dresel, M., Jochems, N.: Human-animal interaction in immersive virtual reality: the role of social presence and positive effects. In: Proceedings of Mensch Und Computer 2024, MuC 2024, pp. 342–359. Association for Computing Machinery, New York (2024). https://doi.org/10.1145/3670653.3670661

14. Yao, W., Zhang, X., Gong, Q.: The effect of exposure to the natural environment on stress reduction: a meta-analysis. Urban Forestry Urban Green. **57**, 126932 (2021). https://doi.org/10.1016/j.ufug.2020.126932. https://www.sciencedirect.com/science/article/pii/S1618866720307494
15. Zasloff, L.: Measuring attachment to companion animals: a dog is not a cat is not a bird. Appl. Anim. Behav. Sci. **47**, 43–48 (1996). https://doi.org/10.1016/0168-1591(95)01009-2

# Human-Centered Design of Digital Twins: The Case of Green Smart Homes

Barbara Rita Barricelli, Daniela Fogli, and Davide Guizzardi[✉]

Department of Information Engineering, University of Brescia, Brescia, Italy
{barbara.barricelli,daniela.fogli,davide.guizzardi}@unibs.it

**Abstract.** This paper presents the interaction design, prototyping, and evaluation of a digital twin for green smart homes. The proposed system aims to enhance energy efficiency, occupant comfort, and environmental awareness by integrating sustainable design principles with advanced digital technologies, like the Internet of Things and Artificial Intelligence functionalities. The paper aims to demonstrate that a human-centered approach to designing digital twins can satisfy most of the users' expectations and requirements for living in and interacting with green smart homes.

**Keywords:** Digital Twin · Smart Home · Sustainability · Human-Centered Artificial Intelligence

## 1 Introduction

Sustainable consumption and climate action are two of the most important United Nations Sustainable Development Goals (SDGs)[1]. A recent report by the European Union (EU) highlights that around 40% of the energy consumed in the EU is used in buildings, and one-third of Greenhouse Gas (GHG) emissions come from buildings [13]. Worldwide, global primary energy consumption is continuing to grow every year, as well as GHG emissions [12], while electricity demand is expected to rise at a faster rate through 2026, especially in emerging and developing economies [24]. Electricity consumption of buildings accounts for a significant portion of the world's energy consumption [25]. To promote sustainable energy consumption and persuade households to behave sustainably, several digital solutions have been proposed in the literature, like eco-feedback technologies [15, 29], environmental games [3], persuasive technologies that help users manage energy tariffs [1], and conversational agents for environmental sustainability [18]. Another approach to sustainable energy consumption in residential buildings is developing *green* smart homes. A smart home is a home environment endowed with ambient intelligence and automatic control, which allows the home to respond to the behavior of its occupants and provide them with several facilities to enhance comfort, convenience, security, and entertainment [11]. A smart home is regarded as green whenever it helps reduce energy consumption either

---

[1] https://sdgs.un.org/goals.

automatically [2] or with the informed intervention of its inhabitants [16,19]. To develop green smart homes, several proposals leverage digital twins (DTs), which combine Internet of Things (IoT) technologies with machine learning to predict energy consumption and enable efficient management of home appliances (e.g., [2,7,32]). However, user-DT interaction in green smart homes is often overlooked in the literature. DT design and development are usually focused on the efficiency and efficacy of machine learning algorithms (e.g., [14,23]), while the interaction design process and the evaluation of the DT interface with real users are not usually reported in the literature proposals [5]. A further issue is balancing between automation and interactivity [1]: while implementing autonomous systems that accommodate users' habits and preferences is very challenging, it has also been observed that a fully automated system might lead to low user engagement [27]. Users should play an active role by not only triggering automatic behaviors through their commands or movements but also by actively defining automations that tailor the smart home behaviors to their needs and preferences. End-user creation of automations is currently ensured by commercial technologies, like domotic dashboards or virtual assistants (e.g., Amazon Alexa, Google Home, and Apple Siri), but stems from a long history of research in the End-User Development (EUD) domain [4] applied to the smart home [8,17,30]. The involvement of users in smart home management is becoming more and more important for reducing residential energy consumption and environmental impact [1,10,19].

This paper presents the human-centered design of a DT for green smart homes, which pays attention to the interaction with the DT, to ensure that users acquire more awareness about energy consumption through proper data visualization and energy consumption simulations. Suggestions about the sustainability of user-created automations (i.e., trigger-action rules involving home appliances [30]) and direct activation of appliances are also important features of the proposed DT. The DT is a web-based application that exploits Home Assistant[2] to gather energy consumption data from home appliances and applies deep learning to such data for energy consumption prediction and simulation. These algorithms are described in our previous papers [20,21], while here we focus on the interaction design process and the evaluation of the system usability and user experience. Similarly, despite acknowledging the security and privacy risks associated with the collection of smart home data, as reported in [9,26,31], this work does not delve deeper into how to cope with these issues. To limit potential exposure, we applied encryption to secure locally stored data and restricted access to only specific local devices, offering a basic layer of protection.

## 2 Interaction Design of the Digital Twin

Unlike what the literature commonly proposes for DT interaction design, a human-centered approach was adopted, starting with user research, followed by ideation, and ending with the development of a complete interactive prototype.

---

[2] https://www.home-assistant.io/.

User research was performed by administering an online questionnaire to an audience of potential end users of the DT, in order to investigate the attitudes toward home automation technologies and their potential to enhance sustainable behavior. The questionnaire included questions about general and demographic data, opinions on environmental sustainability and green smart homes, questions about whether and how they managed smart devices, their knowledge about home automation, and their potential interest in using an interactive system for controlling a smart home. The questionnaire was completed online by 111 participants (65 male, 45 female, one preferred not to answer), 93% based in Italy, while the remaining were from Hungary, the Netherlands, the United States, Thailand, and Germany. The participants were between 17 and 70 years old ($M = 38.8$, $SD = 12.27$). 63 participants owned smart devices: 9% of them did not know tools for creating automations, 50% knew about the tools but did not use them, while 41% (26 participants) knew and used the tools. The questionnaire presented a further set of questions to the 26 participants who declared to have used smart home automation tools in the past. When asked how often they encountered issues with their tool for automation creation, only 20% reported no problems during the process; unsupported devices, unavailable actions, and conditions that did not align with their desired scenarios are the main obstacles that participants faced during the process. Another challenge users encounter is the difficulty in understanding how to interact with such tools, indicating that their user interfaces may lack intuitiveness or suffer from discoverability issues. The questionnaire highlighted that the primary issue in dealing with home automations is that conflicts may arise when multiple inhabitants cohabitate in the smart home environment. When asked to answer questions about environmental sustainability and green smart homes, the participants showed a nearly unanimous opinion: 37.8% were very concerned, 53.2% indicated concern, and the remaining 9% were neutral or unconcerned. Also, when asked to express their potential interest in an interactive system that provides daily energy consumption data, 43.2% of the participants manifested a high level of interest and 41.4% a medium level of interest. 80% of participants also declared a high or medium level of interest in a system recommending optimal activation times for their smart appliances to reduce energy costs. A further question explored participants' experiences with issues related to excessive energy consumption, such as circuit breaker tripping: 51% of participants reported electricity interruptions. The survey concluded with an open-ended question, allowing participants to freely express their desired features for a green smart home. The respondents asked for a system that lets them choose the energy source of the house (grid, battery, or solar panels) according to their needs. Moreover, they would like to receive suggestions for saving money and minimizing energy consumption, and alerts for excessive consumption. Many users expressed the desire for detailed insights into their daily consumption patterns and tools to analyze each appliance to identify the most demanding devices.

Starting from the data gathered with the questionnaire, we defined three personas – Martina, Anna, and Luca. The construction process of the personas followed an inductive approach, first analyzing the data that emerged from the surveys, then looking for patterns, and finally synthesizing the outcomes into user archetypes. Martina is a 31-year-old graphic designer deeply committed to reducing her carbon footprint. She lives in a small urban apartment and always looks for innovative ways to live more sustainably. She is looking for a smart home application that can help her monitor and control energy usage and optimize her control over home appliances. She wants to track energy consumption and receive personalized tips on reducing it further. Anna is a 38-year-old mother of two children, living with her family in a suburban home. She is highly interested in saving money on household expenses, particularly energy costs associated with running appliances. Having two children, she frequently uses the washing machine and other appliances, leading to significant energy consumption and expenses. Anna's primary goal is to manage appliance usage effectively, ensuring it does not lead to frequent circuit breaker tripping and reducing the cost of household operations as much as possible. Luca is a 56-year-old father and husband who takes pride in managing his household efficiently. He requires a smart home system that synchronizes automations among family members to minimize disruptions and prevent possible conflicts. He needs flexible tools to facilitate coordination within the household. Luca proactively seeks to resolve conflicts between automations and appliance usage to maintain family harmony.

What emerged with the user research and the definition of personas led to the creation of scenarios and storyboards to ideate possible interactions with the system (an example of a storyboard is shown in Fig. 1). These informed the definition of requirements for the DT, whose interface needs to offer:

- Real-time, dynamic representation of the physical space, including information about the current energy consumption of the house and of devices and automations that are active at a given time.
- A profile management tool for the users to access and manage their personal information.
- Dashboards and analytics to visualize and get insights on the home's energy consumption, resource utilization, and automation impacts.
- visualization of the automations created in the system to check and change their status, obtain information about automations scheduled for the current day, and receive suggestions about automations that allow energy saving.
- Explanations that justify the suggestions provided by the DT based on prediction and simulation capabilities based on machine learning algorithms.
- A configuration tool of the DT according to the characteristics of the house, the smart devices available in the home, and the provider's energy plan.

Considering the above requirements, we iteratively worked on the navigation map, paper-based sketches, and digital mock-ups until the creation of a complete interactive prototype to be used as the base for system implementation.

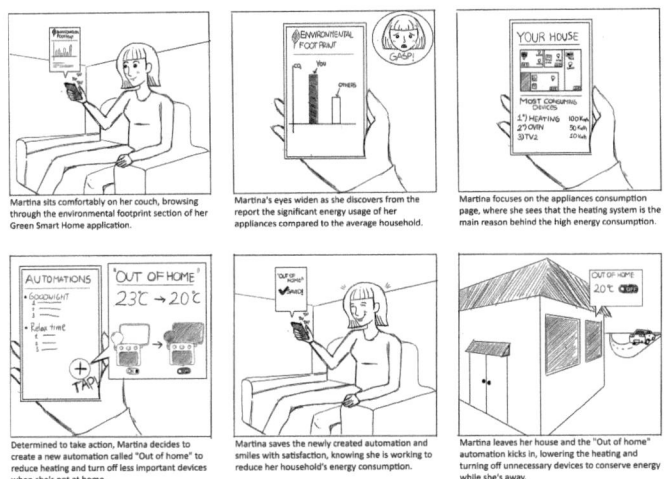

**Fig. 1.** Example of a storyboard produced during the design of the DT.

## 3 The DT Application at Work

The DT for green smart homes has been developed as a responsive web-based application suitable for PCs, tablets, and smartphones. The backend of the application is responsible for the communication with Home Assistant to gather device states and consumption values, and to process this data to offer the intelligent features of the DT, such as consumption predictions and 'what-if' simulations of user-created automations. The users can access the web application using their email address and password. After the login, if no prior configuration of the smart home can be found, the system will redirect the user to the Initial Configuration page, composed of three steps. Firstly, the user needs to upload the planimetry of their house. Then, the user can access the second step, in which they are asked to configure their smart devices. The configuration of a device requires the user to select it from a list and drag it to their real-life location on the map. In the third step, the user can specify on-peak and off-peak hours, entering the energy plan established by their provider.

The home page is presented in Fig. 2. On the left, the map of the smart home is displayed, where each circle, representing a smart appliance, can be clicked to access the device control panel. At the bottom of the map, information about the current overall power demand and the number of active devices is shown. On the right of the map, there are two blocks: the ecological footprint block (on top) and the device list block (on the bottom). The former is a component that helps users assess their environmental impact. It computes the total mass of $CO_2$-equivalent (e$CO_2$) emissions generated in the previous month and compares it to the average emissions of an Italian household. To enhance comprehension,

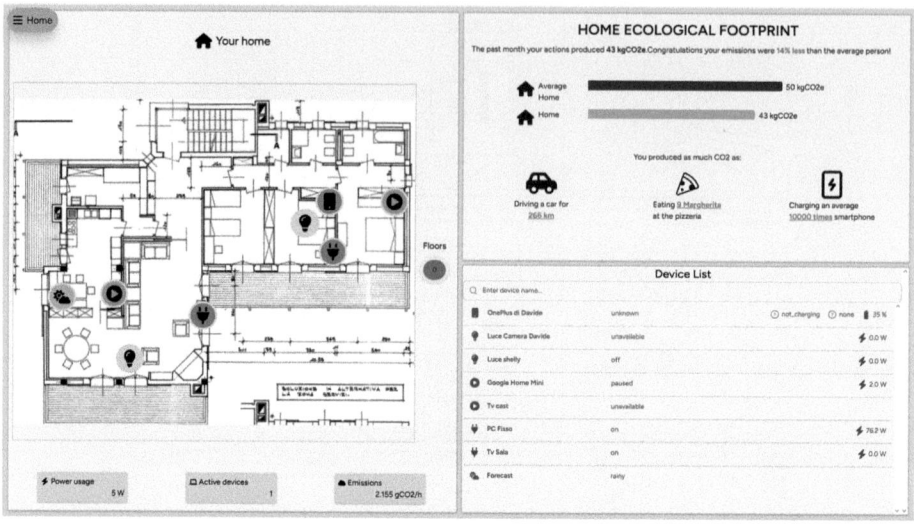

**Fig. 2.** Interface of the Home page

the footprint is also translated into relatable metrics, such as the distance a car would travel or the number of full phone charges the emissions would equate to. The device list block displays a table with information about all the available devices. Each appliance is associated with its current state and current energy demand. By clicking the "Home" green button in the top left corner of the screen, the user can open a drawer containing links to the other pages of the DT.

The Consumption page provides valuable insights into the smart home's energy usage patterns, using a representation that presents three different tabs. The "Total Energy Consumption" tab (see Fig. 3) allows users to visualize energy consumption for either the entire house or a specific device within a selected time range. In the "Consumption comparison" tab, users can compare the energy consumption of two different days or months side-by-side. The "Predicted consumption" tab presents a forecast of the energy consumption for the next hours of the day, given the energy consumption of the past days. For this purpose, a Long Short-Term Memory (LSTM)-based deep learning model [22] was trained on energy consumption data collected from the home of one of this work's authors, from August 2024 to January 2025. Each row of the dataset was composed of a timestamp and the overall house consumption value (in Wh). Prior to training, the raw consumption data were enriched with contextual information, such as the day of the week and the hour of the day, to help the model better capture recurring patterns. The model architecture consists of an LSTM layer, a dropout layer to mitigate overfitting, and a dense output layer serving as the classification head. To identify which combination of hyperparameters would produce the best results, a grid search scheme was employed using Mean Absolute Error (MAE) as the evaluation metric due to its robustness with scaled data. The best model uses 24 past records, including contextual data, to predict 12 future energy consumption values. It achieved an MAE of 30.248 Wh on the test set.

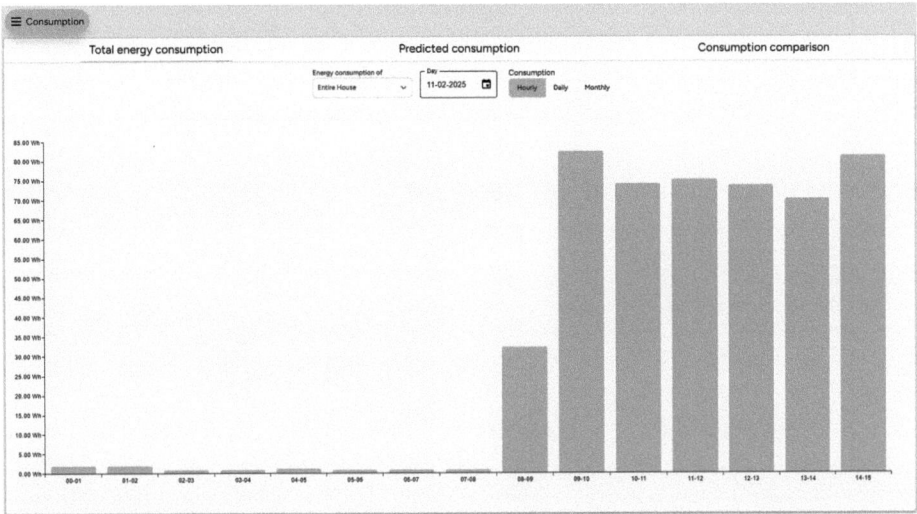

**Fig. 3.** The Consumption page shows the total consumption graph.

The Automation page is presented in Fig. 4. On the left, a list of all the smart home automations is provided. By clicking on one of them, a card with automation details appears on the right. An automation consists of three elements: triggers, which define the events that initiate the automation; an optional set of conditions, which add constraints that must be met for the automation to proceed; and a set of actions, which specify what should happen when the automation is executed. Additionally, the card will report a set of green suggestions, which provide alternative scheduling that optimizes the power consumption of the house. To identify better scheduling, the backend of the DT calculates the original cost of an automation, given its current activation time and the energy plan configuration, and explores alternative start times. The exploration follows a heuristic approach, where time slots are sorted based on (1) their energy cost and (2) their proximity to the original automation time, and are then evaluated sequentially. If a better start time is found, an additional function evaluates potential conflicts with already existing automations. Conflict detection is performed using a matrix that models the status of each device across the week based on the planned automation schedule. It is produced by estimating the expected duration and power demand of each automation action, using historical data. When simulating a new activation time, the system updates this matrix by marking the relevant devices with the desired state and recording the corresponding energy usage; this enables the detection of any overlapping activations and excessive energy demand. Suggestions are displayed only if the alternative scheduling reduces costs without introducing unacceptable conflicts.

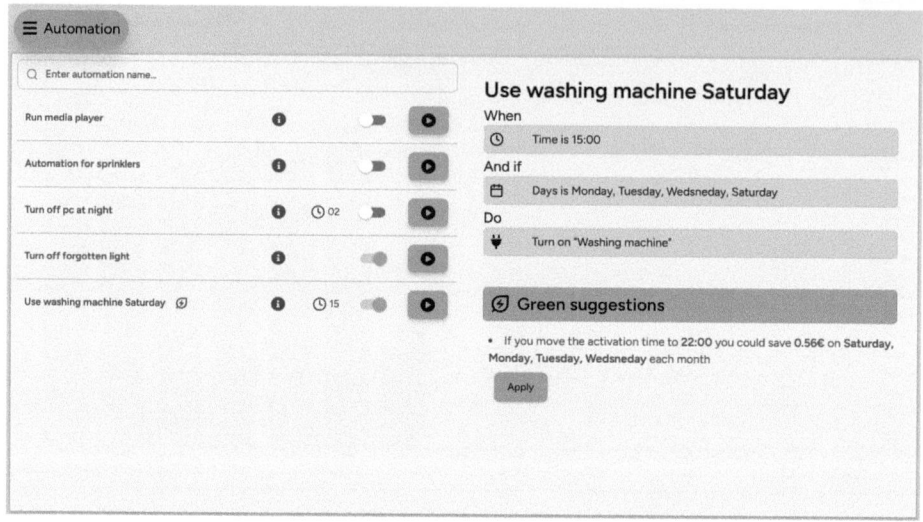

**Fig. 4.** Interface of the Automation page

## 4 Usability and User Experience Evaluation

### 4.1 Method

A user study involving 11 participants (4 females) has been carried out to evaluate the system usability and user experience. The majority of participants (60%) were between 25 and 30 years old, while two participants were between 30 and 35 years old, and another two were between 60 and 65 years old. Over 70% of participants owned at least one smart device at home; however, just over half of them had used a dedicated app to manage these devices. Regarding energy consumption monitoring, only two participants reported using a specific app provided by their energy company.

Users were provided with a pre-configured DT already having a planimetry of the smart home and several months of consumption data. The device list encompassed both real devices, which could be controlled through the application, and dummy ones, for which data have been generated mainly to show plausible consumption graphs. Given this setting, the prediction feature was not included in the system usability and user experience evaluation to prevent misleading the users: the prediction of the model would have been very inaccurate, as the removal of dummy devices' real-time consumption data would have led to a scenario not suitable for the prediction feature.

Each participant was asked to complete 9 tasks related to the interaction with the various page components, and, at the end, to fill in three questionnaires: SUS (System Usability Scale) and CSUQ (Computer System Usability Questionnaire) for measuring usability, and UEQ (User Experience Questionnaire) for assessing user experience. Finally, six open-ended questions were posed to the participants to gather their opinions about the DT, to let them report any issues, suggest improvements, and express their overall satisfaction.

### 4.2 Results

All participants except one completed the 9 tasks. One user could not complete task 1, likely due to a sense of initial disorientation caused by the numerous elements in the first tested page (the user profile).

The SUS results of the DT were positive, with a mean of 82 and a median of 87.5. However, two scores (55 and 63) were below 68, which is considered the threshold for acceptable usability [3]. The participants who assigned these lower scores reported some perceived complexity in using the system. The results of the CSUQ questionnaire on a 5-point scale were positive across all categories, with both the mean and median exceeding 4: SYSUSE (System Usefulness) Mean 4.10 Median 4.22; INFOQUAL (Information Quality) Mean and Median 4.14, INTERQUAL (Interface Quality) Mean 4.18 Median 4.33, and OVERALL (Overall System Evaluation) Mean 4.13 Median 4.26. As to UEQ results, *Efficiency* and *Novelty* were the aspects that reached the highest results (i.e., *Good*), 1.52 and 1.14, respectively. The other aspects were all *Above Average*: *Attractiveness* 1.48, *Perspicuity* 1.61, *Dependability* 1.41, and *Stimulation* 1.25.

Finally, the open-ended questions allowed us to collect some interesting users' feedback. Most users expressed a positive opinion about the overall experience using the application, finding it clear and easy to navigate. One participant particularly appreciated the sub-section organization, considering it intuitive and well-structured. The majority of users did not encounter major difficulties while completing the tasks. However, some specific issues were reported: one user had trouble entering multiple time slots in the energy plan configuration, and another user struggled with date selection in the calendar. When asked about the aspects they found least satisfying, almost all participants did not report issues; only one user found the home map feature impractical, preferring an organization with separate sub-sections for different rooms. As to the capability of the tool to monitor household energy consumption, all participants positively evaluated the application. When asked about any additional features the application should have, participants provided various suggestions: a summary page displaying key performance indicators; integration of heating information and resource consumption data (e.g., water and gas); the implementation of a chatbot capable of explaining consumption data and providing personalized advice. The answers to the question about how the application could be improved provided two interface-related suggestions: keeping the side menu fixed to improve navigation and using larger buttons to simplify interaction.

## 5 Conclusion

This paper has illustrated the application of a human-centered approach to designing a digital twin for green smart homes. Contrary to the existing literature on DTs for buildings, where the focus is on IoT technology management, 3D modeling of buildings, and AI algorithms for predictive and prescriptive data analysis, we conceived the DT starting from households' characteristics, needs, and knowledge about technology and energy issues. Therefore, the focus of this paper is on the interaction design of the DT, even though we also implemented real data management and algorithms for consumption prediction and 'what-if' simulation of automations, to estimate energy consumption and prevent possible issues, like circuit breaker tripping, due to the activation of too many appliances at the same time. The design and implementation of these algorithms in the backend have been, however, *a consequence* of user research, design ideation, and iterative prototype development rather than a starting point that could have yielded biasing the user interface. The results obtained with this approach are very encouraging since almost all participants in the user study appreciated interacting with the system. Most of their suggestions for improving the DT interface have already been applied, and we are almost ready for further evaluation. In summary, a human-centered approach was shown to be adequate to satisfy most of the user expectations about smart homes like those identified in [28]. An in-the-wild evaluation of the DT is planned as future work, leveraging the installation of smart devices and the digital twin in a few sample homes. The integration of a chatbot for automation creation and issue explanation is also under development; a first version of this chatbot has been described in [6].

**Acknowledgments.** This work has been supported by the Italian MUR PRIN 2022 PNRR Project P2022YR9B7, End-User Development of Automations for Explainable Green Smart Homes, funded by European Union - NextGenerationEU.

**Disclosure of Interests.** The authors have no competing interests to declare that are relevant to the content of this article.

## References

1. Alan, A.T., Costanza, E., Ramchurn, S.D., Fischer, J., Rodden, T., Jennings, N.R.: Tariff agent: interacting with a future smart energy system at home. ACM Trans. Comput.-Hum. Interact. **23**(4) (2016). https://doi.org/10.1145/2943770
2. Arsecularatne, B., Rodrigo, N., Chang, R.: Digital twins for reducing energy consumption in buildings: a review. Sustainability **16**(21) (2024). https://doi.org/10.3390/su16219275
3. Bang, M., Torstensson, C., Katzeff, C.: The PowerHhouse: a persuasive computer game designed to raise awareness of domestic energy consumption. In: IJsselsteijn, W.A., de Kort, Y.A.W., Midden, C., Eggen, B., van den Hoven, E. (eds.) PERSUASIVE 2006. LNCS, vol. 3962, pp. 123–132. Springer, Heidelberg (2006). https://doi.org/10.1007/11755494_18

4. Barricelli, B.R., Cassano, F., Fogli, D., Piccinno, A.: End-user development, end-user programming and end-user software engineering: a systematic mapping study. J. Syst. Softw. **149**, 101–137 (2019). https://doi.org/10.1016/j.jss.2018.11.041
5. Barricelli, B.R., Fogli, D.: Digital twins in human-computer interaction: a systematic review. Int. J. Hum.-Comput. Interact. **40**(2), 79–97 (2024). https://doi.org/10.1080/10447318.2022.2118189
6. Barricelli, B.R., et al.: An EUD approach to creating feasible and energy-saving automations for smart homes. In: Santoro, C., Schmidt, A., Matera, M., Bellucci, A. (eds.) IS-EUD 2025. LNCS, vol. 15713, pp. 3–21. Springer, Cham (2025). https://doi.org/10.1007/978-3-031-95452-8_1
7. Bortolini, R., Rodrigues, R., Alavi, H., Vecchia, L.F.D., Forcada, N.: Digital twins' applications for building energy efficiency: a review. Energies **15**(19) (2022). https://doi.org/10.3390/en15197002
8. Caivano, D., Fogli, D., Lanzilotti, R., Piccinno, A., Cassano, F.: Supporting end users to control their smart home: design implications from a literature review and an empirical investigation. J. Syst. Softw. **144**, 295–313 (2018). https://doi.org/10.1016/j.jss.2018.06.035
9. Chiang, Y.-H., Hsiao, H.-C., Yu, C.-M., Kim, T.H.-J.: On the privacy risks of compromised trigger-action platforms. In: Chen, L., Li, N., Liang, K., Schneider, S. (eds.) ESORICS 2020. LNCS, vol. 12309, pp. 251–271. Springer, Cham (2020). https://doi.org/10.1007/978-3-030-59013-0_13
10. Cotti, L., Guizzardi, D., Barricelli, B.R., Fogli, D.: Enabling end-user development in smart homes: a machine learning-powered digital twin for energy efficient management. Future Internet **16**(6) (2024). https://doi.org/10.3390/fi16060208
11. De Silva, L.C., Morikawa, C., Petra, I.M.: State of the art of smart homes. Eng. Appl. Artif. Intell. **25**(7), 1313–1321 (2012). https://doi.org/10.1016/j.engappai.2012.05.002
12. Energy Institute: Statistical review of world energy 2024 (2024). https://www.energyinst.org/statistical-review. Accessed 11 Feb 2025
13. European Union: Energy performance of buildings directive (2024). https://energy.ec.europa.eu/topics/energyefficiency/energy-efficient-buildings/energy-performance-buildings-directive_en. Accessed 11 Feb 2025
14. Fathy, Y., Jaber, M., Nadeem, Z.: Digital twin-driven decision making and planning for energy consumption. J. Sensor Actuator Netw. **10**(2) (2021). https://doi.org/10.3390/jsan10020037
15. Froehlich, J., Findlater, L., Landay, J.: The design of eco-feedback technology. In: Proceedings of the SIGCHI Conference on Human Factors in Computing Systems, CHI 2010, pp. 1999–2008. Association for Computing Machinery, New York (2010). https://doi.org/10.1145/1753326.1753629
16. Gallo, S., Mattioli, A., Paterno, F., Barricelli, B.R., Fogli, D., Guizzardi, D.: An architecture for green smart homes controlled by end users. In: Proceedings of the 2024 International Conference on Advanced Visual Interfaces, AVI 2024. Association for Computing Machinery, New York (2024). https://doi.org/10.1145/3656650.3656710
17. Ghiani, G., Manca, M., Paternò, F., Santoro, C.: Personalization of context-dependent applications through trigger-action rules. ACM Trans. Comput.-Hum. Interact. **24**(2) (2017). https://doi.org/10.1145/3057861
18. Giudici, M., Crovari, P., Garzotto, F.: Candy: a framework to design conversational agents for domestic sustainability. In: Proceedings of the 4th Conference on Conversational User Interfaces, CUI 2022. Association for Computing Machinery, New York (2022). https://doi.org/10.1145/3543829.3544515

19. Giudici, M., Padalino, L., Paolino, G., Paratici, I., Pascu, A.I., Garzotto, F.: Designing home automation routines using an LLM-based chatbot. Designs **8**(3) (2024). https://doi.org/10.3390/designs8030043
20. Guizzardi, D., Barricelli, B.R., Fogli, D.: Enhancing sustainability in smart home management with automation simulations and green suggestions. In: Companion Proceedings of the 30th International Conference on Intelligent User Interfaces, IUI 2025 Companion, pp. 35–38. Association for Computing Machinery, New York (2025). https://doi.org/10.1145/3708557.3716345
21. Guizzardi, D., Barricelli, B.R., Fogli, D.: A user-in-the-loop digital twin for energy consumption prediction in smart homes. In: Workshops at the International Conference on Intelligent User Interfaces (IUI) 2025, pp. 1–8. CEUR Workshop Proceedings, Aachen, Germany (2025)
22. Hochreiter, S., Schmidhuber, J.: Long short-term memory. Neural Comput. **9**(8), 1735–1780 (1997). https://doi.org/10.1162/neco.1997.9.8.1735
23. Huang, J., Koroteev, D.D., Rynkovskaya, M.: Machine learning-based demand response in PV-based smart home considering energy management in digital twin. Sol. Energy **252**, 8–19 (2023). https://doi.org/10.1016/j.solener.2023.01.044
24. IEA: Electricity 2024 - analysis and forecast to 2026 (2024). https://www.iea.org/reports/electricity-2024. Accessed 11 Feb 2025
25. IEA: World energy outlook 2024 (2024). https://www.iea.org/reports/world-energy-outlook-2024. Accessed 11 Feb 2025
26. Luo, Y., Cheng, L., Hu, H., Peng, G., Yao, D.: Context-rich privacy leakage analysis through inferring apps in smart home IoT. IEEE Internet Things J. **8**(4), 2736–2750 (2021). https://doi.org/10.1109/JIOT.2020.3019812
27. Prost, S., Mattheiss, E., Tscheligi, M.: From awareness to empowerment: Using design fiction to explore paths towards a sustainable energy future. In: Proceedings of the 18th ACM Conference on Computer Supported Cooperative Work & Social Computing, CSCW 2015, pp. 1649–1658. Association for Computing Machinery, New York (2015). https://doi.org/10.1145/2675133.2675281
28. Reisinger, M.R., Prost, S., Schrammel, J., Fröhlich, P.: User requirements for the design of smart homes: dimensions and goals. J. Ambient. Intell. Humaniz. Comput. **14**(12), 15761–15780 (2023). https://doi.org/10.1007/S12652-021-03651-6
29. Strengers, Y.A.: Designing eco-feedback systems for everyday life. In: Proceedings of the SIGCHI Conference on Human Factors in Computing Systems, CHI 2011, pp. 2135–2144. Association for Computing Machinery, New York (2011). https://doi.org/10.1145/1978942.1979252
30. Ur, B., McManus, E., Pak Yong Ho, M., Littman, M.L.: Practical trigger-action programming in the smart home. In: Proceedings of the SIGCHI Conference on Human Factors in Computing Systems, CHI 2014, pp. 803–812. ACM, New York (2014). https://doi.org/10.1145/2556288.2557420
31. Xu, R., Zeng, Q., Zhu, L., Chi, H., Du, X., Guizani, M.: Privacy leakage in smart homes and its mitigation: IFTTT as a case study. IEEE Access **7**, 63457–63471 (2019). https://doi.org/10.1109/ACCESS.2019.2911202
32. Yang, B., Lv, Z., Wang, F.: Digital twins for intelligent green buildings. Buildings **12**(6), 856 (2022). https://doi.org/10.3390/buildings12060856

# Making Predictions Tangible: Using Data Physicalization to Explore Expectations Around Health Predictions

Yinchu Li[1,2](✉), Carine Lallemand[1], and Regina Bernhaupt[1]

[1] Eindhoven University of Technology, Het Eeuwsel 53, 5612 AZ Eindhoven, The Netherlands
{y.li1,c.e.lallemand,r.bernhaupt}@tue.nl
[2] RMIT University, 124 La Trobe Street, Melbourne, VIC 3000, Australia

**Abstract.** As predictive technologies like Digital Twin become increasingly applied in healthcare, much focus has been given to improving accuracy, explainability, and trust in health predictions. However, little is known about how people expect to engage with predictions in meaningful ways. In this paper, we explore how people imagine interacting with their health predictions through the physicalization they constructed. We conducted three workshops with 18 design students, using fictional weekly allergy risk predictions and multisensory materials to elicit the embodied, contextual, and creative representations of predicted health risks. Our analysis of the physicalizations revealed that participants envisioned predictions not merely as data points but as embodied and contextual experiences. We identified five sensory mapping strategies and six design themes that illustrate how people engage with predictions. Drawing from these findings, we reflect on design implications to support agency, adaptability, and personally meaningful interactions. We contribute an empirical understanding of users' interpretations and engagements with health predictions, offering inspiration for expanding the interaction design space of future predictive health technologies.

**Keywords:** Health Predictions · Data Physicalization · Workshop · Interaction Design · Digital Twin

## 1 Introduction and Background

Predictive technologies are widely embedded in our everyday life, from weather forecasts, traffic congestion prediction, to potential health risks. In healthcare, technologies like risk calculators [1] and Digital Twins [3,7] are increasingly used to forecast health conditions, such as blood glucose trends [4] and allergy flare-ups [7]. These technologies not only support early disease detection and decision-making for clinicians but also help individuals anticipate health risks and take proactive actions.

However, in practice, users often struggle to make sense of predictive results, not only due to the complexity of numerical scores, charts, and graphs, but because these results may lack explanation, transparency, and relevance to people's daily lives [16,17]. To address these, many studies have focused on enhancing the accuracy of predictions (e.g., integrate more factors into predictive models [17]), clarifying how predictions are generated (e.g., explainable AI [15,16]), and designing better ways to communicate uncertainty (e.g., visualizations like icon arrays or dotplots [5,6,9]). Yet, accuracy and explainability alone do not guarantee users' trust in predictions. People may lose trust after a single mistake in the prediction [12] and require a sense of agency over the predictions [14]. Besides, previous studies in domains like diabetes and mental health have shown that users react differently depending on how predictions are presented (e.g., visual, textual or hybrid [15]) and framed, which can affect their motivation, behavior and anxiety [4,11,12]. These findings point to the need to understand how people expect to interact with predictions.

In response, we explored people's imaginations and expectations to interact with predictive health information through constructive data physicalization workshops. Constructive data physicalization, where participants represent data through physical artifacts [13], offers an opportunity to elicit people's mental models and values in their creation. Previous research has shown that encoding data in a physical form can foster reflection, sense-making, and personal connection to abstract information [2,10,13]. In our workshops, participants were encouraged to physicalize the fictional respiratory allergy risk predicted from a personal Digital Twin [7], by using a variety of sensory materials (visual, sound, touch, smell, taste). A personal Digital Twin in this context refers to a data-driven model that constantly integrates physiological and environmental inputs to make predictions for individual's health [3]. Rather than evaluating how accurately the predictions are mapped into physical forms, we used it as a lens to elicit interaction expectations and embodied or material metaphors beyond numerical data points.

This paper aims to provide design insights into technologies that communicate health predictions by offering two contributions. First, it presents empirical insights into how people use sensory modalities and metaphors to materialize predictive health information, revealing five sensory mapping strategies and six design themes. Second, it outlines the design implications derived from these themes for future interaction design with health predictions.

## 2 Method

### 2.1 Participants

We recruited 18 participants between 21 and 32 years old ($M = 26.67$, $SD = 3.01$; eleven self-identified as men, six as women, and one as self-described). All participants were students with a background in industrial design, recruited through the university network. They had prior experience participating in co-design activities. None had food-related allergies or restrictions related to any materials given in the workshop. The study was approved by the University Ethical Review Board, and informed consent forms were obtained before the workshop.

## 2.2 Procedure

The 90-min workshops were conducted in an indoor space with three tables and a display. Participants completed a consent form and a brief demographic questionnaire. The workshop followed four phases:(1) Introduction (10 min): We introduced the concept of constructive data physicalization—representing data with tangible materials—and framed the study around fictional respiratory allergy risk predictions generated by a personal Digital Twin [7]. (2) Material Engagement (5 min): Participants explored a variety of sensory materials (e.g., essential oils, foam balls, yarns, marshmallows) to spark ideas for multisensory representation. (3) Two Activities (2 × 20 min): Each pair constructed physicalizations based on the scenarios and datasets. The second iteration used updated predictions, while participants could either build on the previous one or redesign a new one. (4) Self-Interview and Discussion (2 × 10 min + 10 min): After each activity, each pair completed a self-interview and at the end a group discussion was held to share and reflect on the designs. Participants audio-recorded their making process and video-recorded their self-interviews.

## 2.3 Materials

**Crafting Materials.** Building on material selections from previous physicalization workshops [8,10], we provided a range of materials that afford multisensory engagement (Table 1) to support the creative process. The open space around the tables was also included as the work area. Participants were explicitly encouraged to use five senses as a way to surface possible metaphors and embodied associations around prediction, expanding how predictions could be experienced beyond conventional visual or verbal forms. An image of the crafting materials is included in the Appendix Fig. 2.

**Scenario Cards.** Each activity was supported by a scenario card inspired by Huron et al. [8]. In activity 1, participants were required to interpret a 1-week respiratory allergy prediction from a Digital Twin and build a (partly) interactive physicalization. In activity 2, they were given an additional week of predictions and expected to build on their first design or create a new artifact to convey these continuous predictions. The full sets of scenario cards can be found in the Appendix Fig. 3.

**Printed Fictional Datasets.** For each activity, we provided an A4 sheet including four visualizations of allergy predictions: (a) daily risk index table, (b) home air quality table, (c) top-3 pollen count line chart, and (d) indoor/outdoor schedule calendar. These formats draw on common pollen-risk and home-IoT visualizations research on Digital Twin allergy [7], as well as Lallemand and Oomen's

**Table 1.** List of Materials Categorized by the Main Sense they Support

| Category | Materials |
| --- | --- |
| Sight | Multicolor pencils, multicolor A4 papers, multicolor crepe papers, post-its |
| Touch | Playdoh, multicolor yarns, multicolor twist sticks, baking paper, toilet paper, felt balls, foam balls (5 sizes) |
| Sound | Aluminum foil, plastic bags, rubber bands, plastic cups (2 sizes), paper cups, chewing gum containers (3 types: paper box, plastic container, metal container) |
| Taste | Lemon juice, water, wasabi, ketchup, candy (2 types: Haribo sour spaghetti, Haribo Duo's fruity), marshmallows, chewing gum (3 types: strawberry, eucalyptus, mint) |
| Smell | Cooling balm, Sichuan pepper, cardamom powder, dried coriander, chili powder, coffee powder, tea (5 types: rooibos, fruit, lemon, green, chamomile), essential oils (6 types: lavender, pepper mint, lemongrass, eucalyptus, sweet orange, tea tree) |
| Building Tools | Pins, paper clips, rulers, tapes, glue, scissors, tea bags, cotton pads, paper plates, wooden blocks, wooden spoons, wooden sticks, coffee stirrer, hand sanitizer |

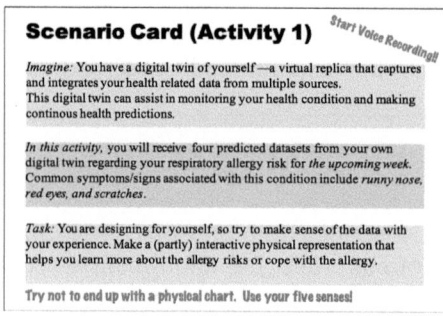
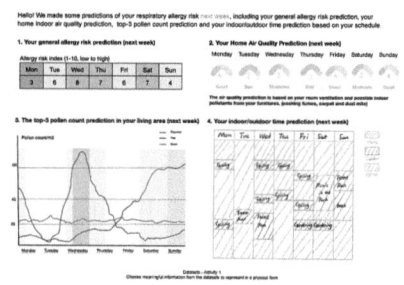

(a) Scenario in Activity 1  (b) Datasets in Activity 1

**Fig. 1.** Example scenario card and datasets, see Appendix Fig. 3 and Fig. 4 for the full contents

approach [10]. In Activity 2, all prediction values were updated to indicate the next week's predictions. See full datasets in the Appendix Fig. 4.

**Printed Self-interview Card.** After each activity, each pair completed a 10-min video-recorded interview, immediately guided by a self-interview card. They explained their physicalization and reflected on their process, without being affected by other groups' creations and interpretations. As the results are not analyzed deeply at this stage, the interview prompts are included in the Appendix Fig. 5 for reference.

## 3 Results

18 physicalizations were produced by 9 paired groups during the workshops. At this stage, we analyzed the sensory modalities and materials participants used in their physicalizations, along with the verbal explanations from self-interview. We mapped their sensory usage to the physicalization and extracted design themes from their explanations through thematic analysis. The pictures, mapping and explanations for each physicalization are presented in the Appendix Table 2. We refer to each group as GX (e.g., G2, G3).

### 3.1 Sensory and Material Mappings to Predictions

Most of the groups produced a single physicalization incorporating multiple sensory interactions. Three groups created several physicalizations to communicate different predictions. We analyze which senses and materials were used and why, with details in the Appendix Table 2.

**Sight as the Dominant Usage.** Every group used visual encoding, including color, shape, size, amount, length, distance, angles, blank space, or spatial layout, to communicate predictions. Moreover, the brightness of the color in G2's example indicates the selected day, while an inconsistent object was used to bring attention to the abnormal activity, which shows people's need to notice critical information at a glance.

**Smell as Embodied Sensation.** Almost every physicalization used some olfactory interaction, not as mere decoration but as an active data channel for "sniffing" future risks. Lemongrass, lavender as "safe" scents (G5), coffee as a "moderate" level of risk (G6), eucalyptus (G9), garlic and chili powder (G6) as "warning" scents. By choosing scents that felt intuitively "good" or "bad", the participants showed that they expected the predictions to be personal and resonate with their own feelings. Several groups mapped the predicted risk level to the scent intensity (e.g., G5's foam balls diffused a stronger lemongrass scent for higher indoor air quality risks), while others connected distinct smells to different predictions (e.g., G3 used lavender for a general allergy index and eucalyptus on marshmallows for indoor risks). Some groups mixed food powders on cotton pads to indicate specific pollen types, such as dried coriander for "grass" pollen, tea tree oil for "tree" pollen, and lemon grass oil for "ragweed" pollen (G2). Beyond direct encoding, scent was also layered atop other modalities (e.g., G1 added essential oils to playdough to emphasize the predictions), or used peripherally to attract people's attention to details (e.g., G7 added spices on top of foam and felt balls).

**Touch for Temporal Engagement.** Participants used tactile interactions to "grasp" predicted risks, including rubbing, lifting, and sliding elements to bring tomorrows' predictions to the present. G2 created two water bags for users to feel predicted pollen particles through tactile feedback while squeezing, while G3's pull-string mechanism allowed users to lift the cord up and down to scroll over hourly predictions. G4 and G5 leveraged contrasting textures (firm foam balls versus soft felt balls) to distinguish different pollen types, so that touching distinct surfaces indicated respective allergens. Meanwhile, G9 introduced a textured string whose spikes grew sharper for higher risks and denser for predictions further in the future, allowing users to sense both the severity and the temporal distance of predictions at once. Similarly, G7 used the tension of the string to mark predicted risks, but it is described as a temporal interaction because users can easily read the tension visually.

**Taste as Surprise and Hidden Insight.** Mapping predictions to flavors makes it a private ritual that uncovers "hidden" truths about users' upcoming week. G1 invited people to understand "the hidden risks" in the coming days with the "surprise taste of candy" from the marshmallow barbecue sticks. To ensure people can still revisit the predictions, a package containing several marshmallow barbecue sticks with the same flavor distributions was planned to be given weekly. Similarly, G9 integrated prediction into the morning ritual of coffee: a spicy blend of chili and Sichuan pepper marked days of high predicted risks, cardamom-infused beans signified moderate, and a naturally sweet, fruity roast indicated low. By choosing flavors that resonated emotionally, participants made the process of revealing predictions playful and personal.

**Sound for Ambient Cues.** By translating predictions into everyday noises, participants imagined predictions as ambient cues of recommendations. G6 used crinkling paper to mimic rustling leaves ("not go outdoors"), while the sound of air through marshmallow-filled tea bags resembled an air conditioner's hum ("indoor is safe"). A gentle jingle of lemon-juice-topped cups evoked familiar domestic sounds such as dish washing, strengthening the "indoor" recommendation. G9 wanted to communicate the predicted pollen types with a "symphony" representing three pollens, which were represented through the cups containing crepe papers, wooden blocks and aluminum foil balls respectively.

## 3.2 Design Themes: How People Physicalize Predictions

As our second activity asked participants to physicalize not only next week's predictions but also the week after, we examined how they extended their initial 7-day timelines (activity 1) into a continuous stream of predictions. In activity 1, almost every group created a simple weekly view, either by labeling each day (M, T, W...) or by repeating a set of elements seven times. Only two groups (G2, G7) created a default daily view of the predictions. In activity 2, we found six design themes emerged to physicalize predictions.

**Theme 1: Scale up predictions with consistency.** G4 regarded it as an additional weekly prediction, explaining that another seven plates of items would represent daily predictions for the week after next. G8 also planned to show a seven-day prediction but emphasized the importance of consistency and reusable elements in the design, so they created a seven-day view of the same set of environments, each with different amount of coffee powder around as predicted risks. G5 and G6 chose to use other modalities for data in the different week.

**Theme 2: Expand predictions through spatial variations.** G5 added spatial qualities to their initial weekly prediction chain and turned it into a shape-changing object for people to display at home. G6 experimented with various materials to make sounds for two types of prediction in the week after next week as a comparison of using color and smell for predictions in their first construction.

**Theme 3: Enable destruction and reflection of predictions.** G1 designed the edible marshmallow strings to be delivered as a package with several same ones inside every week, aiming to allow reflection, destruction of data, and observing whether the data have been consumed or noticed by others. The actual taste was also intentionally hidden behind the plain marshmallows, which was described as a "secret".

**Theme 4: Shift from numbers to impacts.** With more predictions made for the distant future, G2 chose to show its impact on future activities using a spinning wheel of time and red cups as indicators for some affected activities. While, G3 added a dynamic mechanism of time to their design, allowing people to see the changing impacts throughout the day for different days, which we interpret as their way of capturing the dynamic nature of predictions.

**Theme 5: Support shared predictions among family.** The continuous prediction of pollen counts in the environment reminded G7 to care about the access to family members' health predictions and how the environmental predictions should be noticed by every member at home. Therefore, they added smell as a peripheral way to interact with and allow access to different family members' health risks, turning it into a household ritual.

**Theme 6: Present predictions with uncertainty.** Lastly, G9 considered the uncertainty of further predictions, so they crafted a confidence interval of the predictions and an abstract tactile representation of future predictions. The further the prediction, the denser the representation became.

## 4 Discussion

### 4.1 Design Implications

Our study offers possible design directions for future predictive health technologies by exploring how interactions with predictions can be reimagined through embodied, contextual, and multisensory representations. While the findings are shaped by our guided and speculative workshop setting, which encouraged participants to move beyond visual and numerical forms, they reveal underexplored interaction metaphors and sensory strategies for design.

In our workshops, participants used sensory and material strategies to represent ambiguity of prediction. Tactile fuzziness conveyed uncertainty, fading density suggested future distance, and olfactory intensity expressed urgency for awareness. Although these mappings were encouraged by the multisensory materials we provided, they illustrated how embodied representations can represent predictive ambiguity in subtle and intuitive ways. It resonates with previous work which used quantile dotplots to facilitate the understanding of uncertainty [9] and extends it to ambient and haptic modalities and metaphors. Less commonly used modalities, such as smell and taste, also emerged, such as lavender for safety, chili for danger, or a surprise coffee sip marked a personal reveal moment. While we do not claim these as preferred channels, their speculative use suggests how people relate to predictions through embodied metaphors, which were also seen in previous sensory interactions [2,10]. These metaphors suggest that predictive technologies could also support affective interpretations and personal sense-making, beyond traditional numerical forms, aligning with previous work on explainable AI which calls for representations tailored to users' cognitive and affective needs [15,16].

Many physicalizations also reflected the expectations of agency in how predictions are accessed and shared. For example, edible predictions point to the need for people's agency to protect predicted personal insights, allowing explorations of hidden insights, and interaction rituals for daily "reveals", which could be used in design to promote engagements. One participant used ambient scent to share predictions within family without exposing sensitive details. It raises the question on how predictions should balance the sharing with privacy, retaining users' control over details.

Finally, participants experimented with different time presentations of predictions, such as sliding mechanisms, spatial layouts, or abstract representations of far future. These designs suggest supporting flexible zooming across time and shifting between detail to overview in predictions, thereby expanding the possibilities beyond fixed linear timeline-based health interfaces.

Overall, rather than proposing specific design solutions, we treat these physicalizations as design probes that reflect underexplored interaction possibilities, such as ambiguity, ritual, agency, and flexible timelines, for the future design of predictive health technologies.

### 4.2 Limitations

This study has several limitations. First, we explored health predictions only through the lens of predicted allergy risks, which may not represent other types of prediction, such as those related to behavior change or lifestyle. As a result, the metaphors and embodied values in the physicalization are inevitably affected by how people perceive "risk". Secondly, while fictional datasets and scenarios in a controlled setting ensures the comparability among users, participants might generate richer, more personally resonant designs if they had worked with their own health data or in a longitudinal field study. Third, although we provided a wide range of materials covering multiple senses to spark imagination, these materials were not intended to be a validated design toolkit. Additionally, our participants were design students with co-design experience, which distinguishes them from the general population. Their familiarity with creative design approaches likely encouraged more expressive and speculative outputs, which may not reflect how lay users would approach predictive health information and offer generalizable insights. Finally, this study did not address the potential pitfalls of predictive technologies, so our findings do not capture how people might react to incorrect, conflicting, or failed predictions. Prior work suggests that even a single inaccurate prediction can undermine user trust or trigger algorithm aversion [12], which requires further explorations on how people expect predictive technology or system to acknowledge and communicate such aspects.

## 5 Conclusion and Future Work

This study represents an initial step toward understanding how to design interaction with health predictions generated by Digital Twins, with implications that may extend to other predictive health technologies. Through physicalization workshops, we explored how participants make sense of and materialize health predictions. Our reflections on sensory mappings and design themes reveal possible implications to support agency, adaptability, and meaningful engagement with predictions, while treating multisensory creations as a lens to understand user expectations. Future work could build on these insights by involving broader participant groups (e.g., end users and experienced designers) and engaging with real-world health data to deepen understanding of how predictions are interpreted and expected in everyday life. As predictive technologies become more pervasive, questions of privacy, ethics, and interpersonal boundaries will require further design attention, especially in domestic or shared environments.

**Acknowledgment.** This research has been conducted under the REDI Program, a project that has received funding from the European Union's Horizon 2020 research and innovation program under the Marie Sklodowska-Curie grant agreement No. 101034328. We additionally used ChatGPT to help with minor text refinements and improvements to the manuscript, ensuring clarity and coherence while maintaining full authorship control over the content.

# Appendix

**Fig. 2.** An overview of the crafting materials used in the workshops

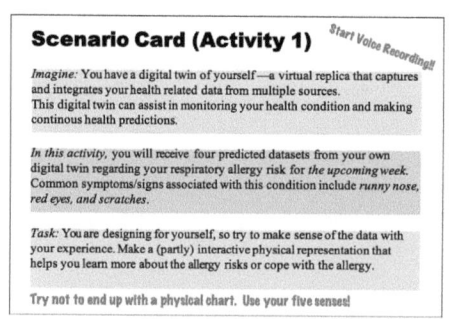

(a) Scenario in Activity 1    (b) Scenario in Activity 2

**Fig. 3.** Scenario Cards

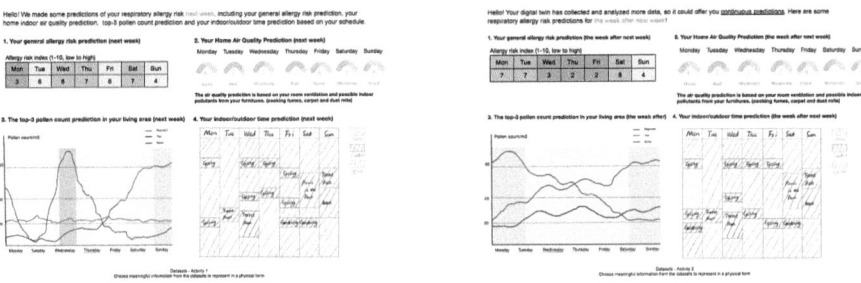

(a) Datasets in Activity 1  (b) Datasets in Activity 2

**Fig. 4.** Fictional Datasets

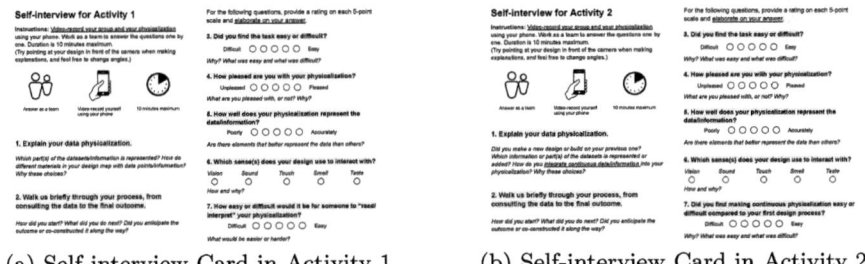

(a) Self-interview Card in Activity 1  (b) Self-interview Card in Activity 2

**Fig. 5.** Self Interview Cards

**Table 2.** Data Physicalization Outcomes and Data Mapping

| Group | Physicalization Top: activity 1 Bottom: activity 2 | Data Mapping | Senses for Interaction |
|---|---|---|---|
| G1 |  | Playdoh with different colors and heights represent the general allergic risks index during the week. The same information is emphasized by the smell of different spices and essential oils on top of the playdoh. Time is written as the capital letter on the paper. The spatial line is created with twist stick and some threads to indicate the trend of the general allergic risk. | Sight, Smell |

(*continued*)

**Table 2.** (*continued*)

| Group | Physicalization Top: activity 1 Bottom: activity 2 | Data Mapping | Senses for Interaction |
|---|---|---|---|
| | | Candy bundles or pocket candies matched colors with their first physicalization. To ensure that people can still revisit their data after tasting it, they envision people will get a box or a bundle of same candies for every day. The wooden marshmallow stick is their final physicalization. The flavored candies were inserted into the marshmallow to indicate risk levels on days of the week. The way in which the candies were hidden from the surface is how they embody the hidden allergic risks. People are considered to receive several strings of wooden sticks with same flavor distributions every week. | Sight, (Touch), (Smell), Taste |
| G2 | | The color of the water bags differentiates indoor (yellow) and outdoor (green) information. The particle amount in the water bag indicates air quality indoors and pollen amount outdoors. The size and number of balls represent three top pollens, which can be observed visually or by touch. The hour of the day is marked by a number on the ruler. The brightness of the water bags suggests whether to go outside or stay home. Three different smells link to the top pollen risks: dried coriander for grass pollen, tea tree oil for tree pollen, and lemongrass for ragweed pollen. | Sight, Touch, Smell |
| | | Red cups highlight schedule changes, with red indicating minor changes and paper cups indicating major changes. Schedules and activities are shown on a small purple triangle with pink papers representing different days. Rotating it changes the daily view, like a casino wheel, with more resistance indicating approaching a highlighted time. Color, smell, brightness, and tactile cues remain consistent. | Sight, Touch, Smell |

(*continued*)

**Table 2.** (*continued*)

| Group | Physicalization Top: activity 1 Bottom: activity 2 | Data Mapping | Senses for Interaction |
|---|---|---|---|
| G3 | | Each double-marshmallow string indicates a day in a week. Only Monday and Tuesday are represented to show the idea here. The space in-between marshmallows are the daily timeline. The amount and color of string around the marshmallow represents different types of pollen counts daily. Lavender smell is chosen to indicate the general allergy risk index while eucalyptus as indication for indoor air quality. The smell intensity of the lavender from the marshmallow links to the general allergy risk index, the stronger the higher risks. A stronger eucalyptus smell indicates a higher indoor air quality. | Sight, Smell |
| | | They built on the previous design by giving some adjustability of the string to dynamically represent time. Each string can have its length change dynamically according to the time of the day and leads to the height change of two marshmallows, which indicates the air quality predictions at different times of a day. If both are high, it means very good air quality. Both are down means bad. The daily general allergy risk is indicated by the intensity of the lavender smell of the string. The amount of tea leaves inside the bag attached to the marshmallow indicates the indoor air quality (the higher the number, the worse). The color and texture of twist sticks indicates pollen type, and rotations indicate pollen amounts, linking to everyday pollen allergy risk outdoor. | Sight, (Touch), Smell |

(*continued*)

**Table 2.** (*continued*)

| Group | Physicalization Top: activity 1 Bottom: activity 2 | Data Mapping | Senses for Interaction |
|---|---|---|---|
| G4 | | It shows Monday and Tuesday by the twist sticks. The capital letter's color and the type and intensity of the smell mean the general allergy risk of the day. The things inside the plates are outdoor predictions, including the type of balls indicating the type of pollen and the amount as the pollen count. The barbecue string indicates suggestions for activities on that day. The unclear prediction for the working place is shown with a single-colored playdoh, while the occupied area on the cube indicates the allergy risk of doing certain activities. Things inside the cup indicate indoor predictions; the more, the worse. | Sight, Touch, Smell |
| | | More plates will show up to match the continuous data input. They created a detailed version of the previous one for Monday, Tuesday, Wednesday, and Friday. The amount and color of crepe paper straps are added as a more obvious general indication of allergy risk. | Sight, Touch, Smell |
| G5 | | The white balls are given different essential oil smells to indicate indoor air quality (e.g., lemon grass for 7, lavender for 2). The balls together compose the weekly prediction chain with angles between the balls that indicate the general prediction of allergy risk (e.g., 30 degrees for 3). In the red cup there is a representation of three types of pollen using ketchup, chili pieces and coriander to create different textures of the foam balls. | Sight, (Touch), Smell |

(*continued*)

**Table 2.** (*continued*)

| Group | Physicalization<br>Top: activity 1<br>Bottom: activity 2 | Data Mapping | Senses for Interaction |
|---|---|---|---|
|  |  | The spatial dimension is added to the chain, making it a 3D shape-changing structure. The first weekly prediction is shown on the front structure, and balls after indicate the prediction of the week after next week. The color of the threads between the balls of the next week and the following week indicates changes in home air quality. Blue means it will be better than the previous week and orange means worse. If there is no change, the same ball is used to connect the others. | Sight, (Touch), Smell |
| G6 |  | The color and size of the playdoh on top refers to the general allergy risk. The different smells in marshmallows also indicate the general risk of allergies (lavender for good, garlic for bad, and coffee for moderate). The little balls on the playdoh show the amount of pollen. Indoor and outdoor time are represented using the colors of the twist sticks on top. The number and lengths of the twist sticks show the length of time spent outdoors or indoors. The time at home is represented by fluffy white twist sticks. In the office it is spiky dark blue and in the outdoors it is light blue. | Sight, Touch, Smell |
|  |  | They added how to make choices to stay home or go outside for the week after the week using sound. The louder the sound, the less is suggested. Marshmallows inside tea bags indicate home air quality, mimicking the sound of a ventilation system when blown. Listening to the sound of lemon juice made while shaking cups is iterated from blowing marshmallows in the bags as an easier way to represent home air quality. The louder the sound, the less it suggested we should stay home. Using paper inside the plastic bag to create sounds like leaves outside to indicate the outdoor pollen allergy risks. The louder the sound, the less we were suggested to go outside. | Sight, Sound, Smell |

(*continued*)

**Table 2.** (*continued*)

| Group | Physicalization Top: activity 1 Bottom: activity 2 | Data Mapping | Senses for Interaction |
|---|---|---|---|
| G7 | | The color of the paper indicates outdoor (pink) and indoor (blue). The lemon juice bottle together with the blue yarn ball works as a personal avatar. The daily view can change by spinning the black essential oil bottle. The flow of the red line indicates the daily schedule of going outside and moving inside. The tension of the red line can be changed by the shape of the surface to indicate the risk level during different scheduled activities. The white objects with three different sizes on top of the pink paper indicate the types of pollen. The distance to the line indicates the relevance or impact of the outdoor activity, and its tension can react to the outdoor activity that people touched on the red line. | Sight |
| | | More colorful yarn balls were added to indicate family member's prediction at home. The group linked the smell of three balls to the predictions of the top 3 pollen counts, e.g., coriander smell for grass pollen, tea tree oil smell for tree pollen, and rooibos tea smell for ragweed pollen. The mixed smell is considered an invitation for people to come closer and take a closer look at the data. | Sight, Smell |
| G8 | | Different playdoh shapes indicate risky activity or environment people may encounter on that day of a week, e.g., sofa->indoor, computer->office, water with sand/umbrella->beach, tree->forest. The amount of coffee powder indicates pollen or indoor pollution. If the scheduled activities on that day do not pose allergy risks, it is indicated with water and a green tick (top left). | Sight, Smell |

(*continued*)

Table 2. (*continued*)

| Group | Physicalization Top: activity 1 Bottom: activity 2 | Data Mapping | Senses for Interaction |
|---|---|---|---|
| G9 | | The group tried to make some consistent, adaptive and reusable creations for every day. In this new set of physicalization, every day, there is a representation of each environment with or without coffee powder around. The strongness of the smell and the amount of coffee powder indicate the level of risk in that environment. | Sight, Smell |
| | | The color of the candy bridge represents the home air quality prediction every day in the week. Every day, the taste of the coffee attached to the bridge changes according to the general prediction of allergy risk. Low risk is fruity sweet coffee, moderate with cardamom spice, high is coffee with cumin, chili and pepper. The colorful playdoh string is a representation of daily activity and how risky people may experience. When people touch the playdoh string, mixed sounds from three red cups can be produced to indicate three types of pollen. The little cup with colorful threads uses the smell in different parts of the thread to indicate the risk level during the day (lavender low risk, eucalyptus quite risky). | Sight, Sound; Sight, Smell; Taste |
| | | The group added one more textured string for coming risk predictions. The spikier, the higher the risk, and the further the prediction, the more density people can feel. Another orange playdoh with changing width was created to indicate the confidence interval of the predictions. | Sight, Sound; Sight, Smell; Taste; Sight, Touch; |

# References

1. Abujarad, F., et al.: Building a digital health risk calculator for older women with early-stage breast cancer. In: Soares, M.M., Rosenzweig, E., Marcus, A. (eds.) HCII 2021. LNCS, vol. 12780, pp. 389–402. Springer, Cham (2021). https://doi.org/10.1007/978-3-030-78224-5_27
2. Brombacher, H., Nikolov, V., Vos, S., Houben, S.: Scent as a sensory modality for data physicalisation for office well-being. In: Extended Abstracts of the 2023 CHI Conference on Human Factors in Computing Systems, CHI EA 2023, pp. 1–8. Association for Computing Machinery, New York (2023). https://doi.org/10.1145/3544549.3585866
3. De Maeyer, C., Markopoulos, P.: Are digital twins becoming our personal (predictive) advisors? In: Gao, Q., Zhou, J. (eds.) HCII 2020. LNCS, vol. 12208, pp. 250–268. Springer, Cham (2020). https://doi.org/10.1007/978-3-030-50249-2_19
4. Desai, P.M., Mitchell, E.G., Hwang, M.L., Levine, M.E., Albers, D.J., Mamykina, L.: Personal health oracle: explorations of personalized predictions in diabetes self-management. In: Proceedings of the 2019 CHI Conference on Human Factors in Computing Systems, Glasgow Scotland UK, pp. 1–13. ACM (2019). https://doi.org/10.1145/3290605.3300600
5. Dolan, J.G., Iadarola, S.: Risk communication formats for low probability events: an exploratory study of patient preferences. BMC Med. Inform. Decis. Mak. **8**(1), 14 (2008). https://doi.org/10.1186/1472-6947-8-14
6. Garcia-Retamero, R., Okan, Y., Cokely, E.T.: Using visual aids to improve communication of risks about health: a review. Sci. World J. **2012**(1), 562637 (2012). https://doi.org/10.1100/2012/562637
7. Gholizadeh HamlAbadi, K., Vahdati, M., Saghiri, A.M., Gholizadeh, K.: Chapter 16 - Digital twins for allergies. In: El Saddik, A. (ed.) Digital Twin for Healthcare, pp. 325–346. Academic Press (2023). https://doi.org/10.1016/B978-0-32-399163-6.00021-4
8. Huron, S., Gourlet, P., Hinrichs, U., Hogan, T., Jansen, Y.: Let's get physical: promoting data physicalization in workshop formats. In: Proceedings of the 2017 Conference on Designing Interactive Systems, DIS 2017, pp. 1409–1422. Association for Computing Machinery, New York (2017). https://doi.org/10.1145/3064663.3064798
9. Kay, M., Kola, T., Hullman, J.R., Munson, S.A.: When (ish) is my bus?: user-centered visualizations of uncertainty in everyday, mobile predictive systems. In: Proceedings of the 2016 CHI Conference on Human Factors in Computing Systems, San Jose, California USA, pp. 5092–5103. ACM (2016). https://doi.org/10.1145/2858036.2858558
10. Lallemand, C., Oomen, M.: The candy workshop: supporting rich sensory modalities in constructive data physicalization. In: Extended Abstracts of the 2022 CHI Conference on Human Factors in Computing Systems, CHI EA 2022, pp. 1–7. Association for Computing Machinery, New York (2022). https://doi.org/10.1145/3491101.3519648
11. Miyake, A., Takahashi, M., Hashimoto, R., Nakatani, M.: StepUp forecast: predicting future to promote walking. In: Proceedings of the 23rd International Conference on Mobile Human-Computer Interaction, MobileHCI 2021, pp. 1–12. Association for Computing Machinery, New York (2021). https://doi.org/10.1145/3447526.3472020

12. Pichon, A., Blumberg, J.R., Mamykina, L., Elhadad, N.: The voice of endo: leveraging speech for an intelligent system that can forecast illness flare-ups. In: Proceedings of the 2025 CHI Conference on Human Factors in Computing Systems, CHI 2025, pp. 1–15. Association for Computing Machinery, New York (2025). https://doi.org/10.1145/3706598.3714040
13. Sauvé, K., Houben, S.: From data to physical artifact: challenges and opportunities in designing physical data artifacts for everyday life. Interactions **29**(2), 40–45 (2022). https://doi.org/10.1145/3511670
14. Schwartz, J.M., et al.: Factors influencing clinician trust in predictive clinical decision support systems for in-hospital deterioration: qualitative descriptive study. JMIR Hum. Factors **9**(2), e33960 (2022). https://doi.org/10.2196/33960
15. Szymanski, M., Millecamp, M., Verbert, K.: Visual, textual or hybrid: the effect of user expertise on different explanations. In: Proceedings of the 26th International Conference on Intelligent User Interfaces, IUI 2021, pp. 109–119. Association for Computing Machinery, New York (2021). https://doi.org/10.1145/3397481.3450662
16. Szymanski, M., Vanden Abeele, V., Verbert, K.: Designing and evaluating explanations for a predictive health dashboard: a user-centred case study. In: Extended Abstracts of the CHI Conference on Human Factors in Computing Systems, CHI EA 2024, pp. 1–8. Association for Computing Machinery, New York (2024). https://doi.org/10.1145/3613905.3637140
17. Tateyama, N., Yokomura, R., Ban, Y., Warisawa, S., Fukui, R.: Planning the future in a longer perspective: effects of a one-week forecast of mental health. Proc. ACM Interact. Mob. Wearable Ubiquitous Technol. **8**(1), 18:1–18:20 (2024). https://doi.org/10.1145/3643538

# Nail pHolish: Sensing Hand-Fluid Interactions Through Biocosmetic Interfaces

Shuyi Sun, Dana Mayfield, Yuan-Hao Ku, Jinho Yon, and Katia Vega(✉)

University of California, Davis, CA 95618, USA
kvega@ucdavis.edu

**Abstract.** This paper introduces Nail pHolish: a colorimetric biosensor nail polish that changes colors when chemical reactions are detected in hand-fluid interactions. Fingernails are in direct contact with a variety of fluids from both the body and the environment, making them an ideal medium for non-invasive monitoring. Nail polish is used as a substrate for biosensors due to its broad range of colors, durability on fingernails, high visibility, and simple reapplication. This work implements a nail polish formulation and mobile app. The formulation is skin-safe and employs anthocyanins with similar colors to those of traditional nail polish. It is showcased in a series of designs featuring conventional nail art. The app converts color readouts from a portable spectrophotometer to pH levels. Technical evaluations conducted on fake nails show the responsiveness and reversibility of color change at four different pH values. We performed durability tests for over 72 h on 20 fingernails from human subjects. We conducted expert interviews with five nail artists on the practical application of Nail pHolish, and a user study with 10 participants in a dental erosion scenario. This work shows the potential of colorimetric biosensor cosmetics to monitor various bodily fluids such as saliva, sweat, and vaginal secretions, as well as exposures to external fluids such as beverages, rainwater, and swimming environments, offering a new interface for health and environmental monitoring.

**Keywords:** colorimetric · biosensors · nail polish · pH sensor · anthocyanin · fingernails · biocosmetic interface

## 1 Introduction

Colorimetric biosensors detect chemical reactions with analytes like pH, glucose, and lead to produce visible color changes, enabling non-invasive biosensing. Common examples include glucose test strips and pregnancy tests. Unlike

---

S. Sun and D. Mayfield—Both authors contributed equally to this research.

---

**Supplementary Information** The online version contains supplementary material available at https://doi.org/10.1007/978-3-032-05002-1_29.

© IFIP International Federation for Information Processing 2026
Published by Springer Nature Switzerland AG 2026
C. Ardito et al. (Eds.): INTERACT 2025, LNCS 16535, pp. 540–561, 2026.
https://doi.org/10.1007/978-3-032-05002-1_29

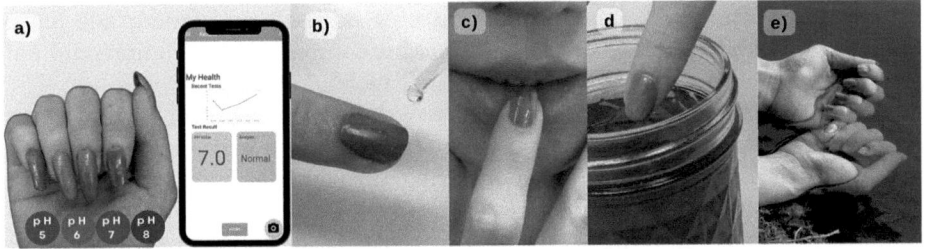

**Fig. 1.** Nail pHolish. a) Color change across four pH levels, and app readout. b) Nail polish displaying visible color transition. Interaction demonstrated with saliva (c), beverage fluids (d), and environmental liquids (e).

traditional wearable sensors, these biosensors do not require power, displays, or heavy hardware. HCI research has explored various color-changing skin interfaces including environmental eyeshadows [26], heat-sensitive hair [9], environmental patches [38], biosensor toothbrushes [22], and temporary tattoos [25,46]. Prior work has also investigated different colorimetric biosensor form factors. Dermal Abyss [52] is a permanent tattoo that reacts to interstitial fluid changes, detecting pH, sodium, and glucose variations. BioCosMe [49] introduces a pH-sensitive lipstick that interacts with saliva to track changes. EarthTones [24] demonstrates eyeshadow that detects environmental hazards. Unlike existing systems, Nail pHolish functions as a hand-fluid interface, enabling biosensing through a nail polish that can interact with multiple bodily fluids and environmental substances (Fig. 1).

Fingernails serve as an ideal platform for hands-fluids interaction with these biosensors due to their frequent exposure to various fluids, including sweat, saliva, tears, genital secretions, food and beverages, cleaning agents, and environmental chemicals. Additionally, it offers users control over when interactions occur, as fingernails can be placed on different bodily fluids or immersed in substances on demand, unlike tattoos or makeup that depend on the passive release of bodily fluids in a specific bodily area. Another difference is that fingernails are an accessible and highly visible area where users can easily notice color changes directly. Inspired by research on pressed-based nail stickers and biosensors [6,28], we propose the use of nail polish as a practical substrate for biosensors because it is durable, widely used, and easy to reapply. Its broad range of colors allows colorimetric responses to blend seamlessly into conventional usage, maintaining both functionality and self-expression.

Color detection in current HCI biosensor wearables usually occurs in controlled laboratories setups such as managed analyte conditions, desktop-attached spectrophotometers [55], or within controlled lighting boxes [46]. In contrast, we used a portable spectrophotometer and a custom app to evaluate Nail pHolish under real-world lighting conditions found in nail artist studios, tested using common beverages and user saliva, and across diverse nail shapes and sizes from actual users. Many of these sensors do not consider safety concerns about skin contact or ingestion [50]. Our formulation uses skin-safe and food-grade materials, allowing for multi-day wear. Additionally, comparisons to commercial nail polishes were informed by feedback from nail technicians.

In this paper, we position Nail pHolish to extend the concept of **Biocosmetic Interfaces** [49]. Biocosmetic Interfaces merge cosmetics with biotechnology to enable health and environmental monitoring through the body's surface. This approach transforms everyday cosmetic products into dynamic displays of biochemical reactions, allowing us to explore typically seamless biodata in fluids. The main contributions of the work are as follows:

(1) **Advancing Biocosmetic Interfaces via hand-fluid interactions.** A nail polish biosensor as a novel form factor for detecting chemical changes in body and environmental fluids. A DIY, skin-safe, food-grade formulation is comparable to commercial nail products.

(2) **The system and technical evaluations.** A mobile app and spectrophotometer for biosensor detection, technically validated the color responsiveness, reversibility, and 72-hour durability on users' fingernails.

(3) **From Lab to Salon.** Insights from lab-to-salon translation through interviews with five professional nail technicians. Design examples showing integration of biosensors into common nail art for seamless health monitoring.

(4) **User-driven scenario.** A dental erosion use case with 10 participants, evaluating wearability, social acceptance and perceived value in daily life.

## 2 Related Works

Nail polish has a rich history, starting in ancient China, where it was initially worn by rulers and high society as a symbol of wealth and power [48]. Traditionally they have an static color, however, modern nail polishes featured nail polishes that change color under different temperatures or UV exposure [8], and artistic explorations on extreme long nails with pH sensitivity [31]. Moreover, changes in nail color and appearance can already be an indicator of health conditions such as trauma, anemia, dietary deficiencies, heart or kidney disease, fungal infections, oxygen levels, or even poisoning.

Figure 2 compares various on-skin interfaces with colorimetric biosensors in HCI, focusing on their use of different fluids and colorimetric sensing techniques on their user studies. Nail pHolish is the only one interacting with multiple fluids. While not creating their own a spectrophotometer (SPM) is more common in similar studies, Nail pHolish uses a portable version with a customized mobile application for supporting portability, data accuracy and real-world applications. The Dermal Abyss project developed a permanent tattoo that interacts with interstitial fluids to measure pH, sodium, and glucose levels [52]. Similarly, BioCosme introduced a pH-sensitive lipstick [49] and BraceIO developed biosensors to dental braces ligatures [51] that change color in response to saliva. The EarthTones project explored using eyeshadows to detect hazardous analytes in the environment [24]. Bioweave, Organic Primitives, HoloChemie and Ecopatches created temporal tattoo patches and on-skin biosensors for sweat analysis [22,46,55].

| Project | Bodily and External Fluids | | | | | Color Detection Technique | | | |
| --- | --- | --- | --- | --- | --- | --- | --- | --- | --- |
| | Saliva | Tear | Sweat | Interstitial | External | Phone Cam | Lab-graded | Custom SPM | Portable |
| Nail pHolish (this work) | ✓ | ✓ | ✓ | ✗ | ✓ | ✗ | ✗ | ✗ | ✓ |
| Dermal Abyss [52] | ✗ | ✗ | ✗ | ✓ | ✗ | ✗ | ✗ | ✗ | ✗ |
| HoloChemie [46] | ✗ | ✗ | ✓ | ✗ | ✓ | ✗ | ✗ | ✓ | ✗ |
| SweatSkin [32] | ✗ | ✗ | ✓ | ✗ | ✗ | ✗ | ✗ | ✗ | ✗ |
| Organic Primitives [21] | ✗ | ✗ | ✗ | ✗ | ✓ | ✗ | ✗ | ✗ | ✗ |
| EcoPatches [39] | ✗ | ✗ | ✗ | ✗ | ✓ | ✓ | ✗ | ✗ | ✗ |
| BioWeave [55] | ✗ | ✗ | ✓ | ✗ | ✗ | ✗ | ✓ | ✗ | ✗ |
| BioCosMe [49] | ✓ | ✗ | ✗ | ✗ | ✗ | ✓ | ✗ | ✗ | ✗ |
| BracelO [51] | ✓ | ✗ | ✗ | ✗ | ✗ | ✓ | ✗ | ✗ | ✓ |

**Fig. 2.** Comparison of related works for on-skin colorimetric biosensors in HCI

Biochemical information can be accessed through various form factors. While transdermal sensors like microneedle patches [17] and permanent tattoos [52] are effective, they can be invasive and cause tissue damage. Non-invasive alternatives include sweat-monitoring patches [10], temporary tattoos [14,19,39], jewelry [50,54], and fabric-based sensors [44,55]. Anthocyanins were selected for this project as pH biosensors due to their well-documented properties [3], food-grade safety (derived from red cabbage), dual function as a pigment, and effectiveness in measuring liquid pH. The natural pH of nails is around 5 [41], while skin pH ranges from 5.4 to 5.9. Although nails can tolerate brief exposure to acids and bases, high-pH soaps may cause dehydration, irritation, and bacterial imbalances [41]. In swimming pools, pH below 6.8 can lead to harmful by-products that pose health risks if ingested [16]. Saliva pH varies with oral health conditions such as gingivitis or periodontitis, offering insights into metabolic, hormonal, and immunological states [1]. It can also reflect stress levels [7] and diabetes [47].

Spectrophotometry, alongside naked-eye detection, is commonly used for accurate colorimetric analysis [13], but lab-grade devices are expensive and require skilled operators, limiting their use outside of labs [33]. Mobile apps with computer vision provide low-cost, portable alternatives [36], though many need additional sensors or attachments for accuracy [5], and DIY devices are generally limited to educational use [12], and not for scientifically significant data that requires reproducibility and accuracy [32,43]. To overcome these, portable, high-quality spectrophotometers have been developed [32], with commercial devices successfully used for color analysis [35]. We use the Nix portable spectrophotometer to ensure accurate color detection as input for the Nail pHolish App.

## 3 Implementation

### 3.1 Design Concept

Nail pHolish merges cosmetics with functional biosensing, providing an interface on fingernails to display molecular changes from fluid interactions. Figure 3 shows the usage process that includes the nail pHolish application, fluids on fingernail trigger a chemical reaction in the biosensor as a color change, a device for detecting color and an app for visualizations and converting data to analyte level. The design criteria includes several considerations to ensure the effectiveness, safety, and aesthetic integration of the colorimetric biosensor with nail polish.

**Color Alignment:** The biosensor matches popular nail polish hues using anthocyanins (pink to purple) for seamless integration [48].

**Skin-Safe:** Nail pHolish uses non-toxic, vegan, water-based ingredients, free of harsh chemicals and animal products.

**Texture and Formulation:** Ensures smooth application, full pigment integration, standard drying time, and a glossy finish.

**Integration with Nail Art:** Traditional techniques conceal biosensor color changes with discreet buffer application.

**Durability:** Designed to withstand water, chemicals, and abrasion while maintaining functionality.

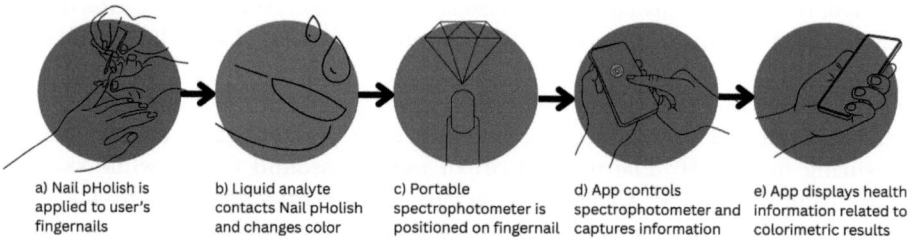

a) Nail pHolish is applied to user's fingernails

b) Liquid analyte contacts Nail pHolish and changes color

c) Portable spectrophotometer is positioned on fingernail

d) App controls spectrophotometer and captures information

e) App displays health information related to colorimetric results

**Fig. 3.** Diagram illustration showing Nail pHolish's usage process

### 3.2 Fabrication Process

Traditional lacquer nail polishes dry with a sealed surface that repels moisture. Since this project requires direct interaction between the anthocyanin biosensor and liquid biomarkers, we used a water-based formula that allows the pigment to dissolve into the solution, making the biosensor more accessible and breathable. This enables liquid biomarkers on the nail's surface to interact with the biosensor, triggering a visible color change. Depending on the biomarker's pH, the nail polish displays a spectrum of colors ranging from pink to green.

Fabrication begins with measuring 0.1 g of non-nano titanium dioxide, 0.2 g of red cabbage powder, and 3 g of water-based nail polish base. The titanium dioxide is finely ground and blended with a commercial water-based nail polish base containing water, styrene/acrylates copolymer, polyacrylic acid, propylene glycol, phenoxyethanol, and caprylyl glycol. Red cabbage powder is then finely ground and added to the mixture, which is blended for five minutes at room temperature. The final mixture is transferred to an empty nail polish bottle

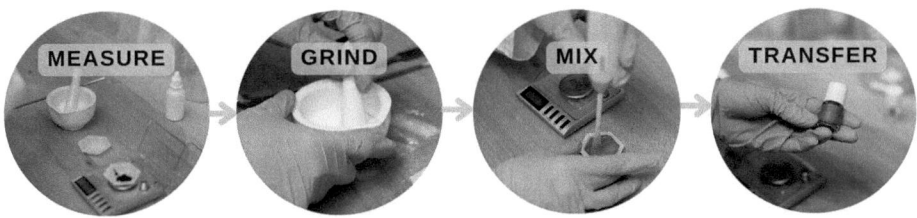

**Fig. 4.** Nail pHolish fabrication process

using a syringe and sealed to prevent drying. Figure 4 illustrates the fabrication process.

Non-nano titanium dioxide was chosen as a white pigment to create an opaque base, preventing variations in users' nail bed tones from affecting color results. Red cabbage powder serves as the biosensor, while water is the primary solvent. Styrene/acrylates copolymer and polyacrylic acid act as film-forming agents, ensuring flexibility and adhesion. Propylene glycol and caprylyl glycol function as humectants and conditioners, maintaining fluidity, while phenoxyethanol acts as a preservative.

To test the biosensor's color response, pH solutions were applied to the nail via sponge. An acidic solution (pH 4) was made by mixing $H_2kO_4P$ with deionized water, while an alkaline solution (pH 8.5) was created using $HK_2O_4P$. These were then used to prepare solutions with pH values of 5, 5.5, 6, 6.5, 7, 7.5, and 8, chosen based on the human body's safe pH range and the biosensor's detection capabilities.

### 3.3 Conventional Nail Art and Bionsensing

We designed a set of nail art samples to demonstrate the versatility and functionality of Nail pHolish when integrated with conventional nail art techniques (Fig. 5). We focused on three key aspects of designing with Nail pHolish:

**Blending Biosensing into Nail Art:** The biosensor can be visually blended using traditional nail art methods such as French tips with variable area coverage (a-c), ombre application over standard polish (d), stamping (e), free-hand designs (f,g) and combining with common nail polis (h,i). This approach supports discreet health monitoring without compromising aesthetic appeal.

**Applying Buffers as Nail Art:** Buffer solutions can be intentionally used as part of the design. For example, drawing dots with a nail brush (j) create visual patterns that also activate the sensor. These buffer applications correspond to different testing procedures, adding an artistic layer to the sensor's function.

**Embellishments for Preserving Biosensor Lifespan:** To control exposure, embellishments like crystals (k) and stickers (l) were applied and later removed, enabling targeted buffer testing. A top coat seals the biosensor to preserve its color response and performance over time.

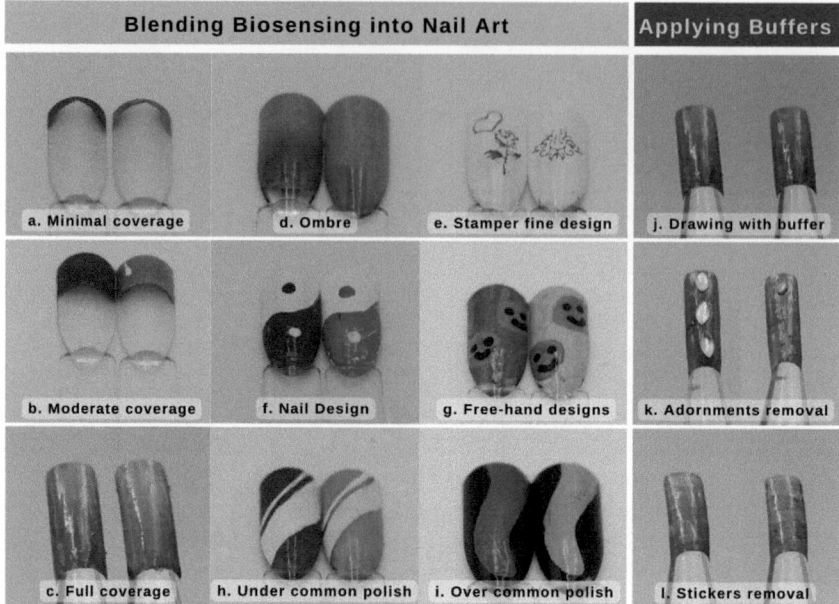

**Fig. 5.** Samples showing how Nail pHolish enables concealed pH sensing through nail art and buffer-based interaction.

### 3.4 pH-Level Detection System

A mobile application was developed to detect the pH levels of Nail pHolish using a spectrophotometer (Nix Spectro 2[1]). A spectrophotometer measures color by shining light on a sample and analyzing the reflected or transmitted light and provides color data for various materials like liquids, plastics, and fabrics. The application processes the RGB values captured from the nail surface with the applied Nail pHolish to estimate pH levels based on colorimetric changes. This approach balances accessibility and functionality, leveraging RGB values to process colorimetric changes in the applied Nail pHolish. The system targets pH values of 5, 6, 7, and 8, offering an efficient and user-friendly solution for pH detection. The application features an intuitive user interface that enables easy calibration and visualization of results, as shown in Fig. 6.

We chose the spectrophotometer for its superior accuracy compared to alternatives like smartphone cameras, which are more susceptible to environmental factors such as lighting conditions, shadows, and glare. Variations in camera hardware, such as sensor quality and white balance settings, further contribute to inconsistent color measurements. Additionally, human skin tone significantly affects the perceived color in images, as light absorption and reflection vary across different tones, altering the captured colorimetric data. These challenges

---

[1] https://www.nixsensor.com/nix-spectro-2/.

were highlighted in previous research [49], where significant accuracy reductions in smartphone-based sensing were observed under diverse conditions.

The pH estimation is achieved by analyzing the RGB values captured by the spectrophotometer. We used the Nix SDK spectrophotometer to receive the color data to our application. The application calculates the Euclidean distance between the captured RGB values and predefined target values. These target values were derived from average measurements obtained during technical evaluations. For evaluation purposes, the technical tests performed three readouts for each pH level and each fingernail. The application is open-source to promote replicability[2].

To increase flexibility, the application allows users to input custom RGB values for biosensor detection (Fig. 6c). This feature accommodates to change to a different range of pH level colors or can be adapted for other biosensors. Users can create libraries of swatches associated with different biosensors, facilitating the measurement and assessment of various colorimetric responses. The system also supports dynamic recalibration, enabling users to adjust target values for diverse applications and scenarios.

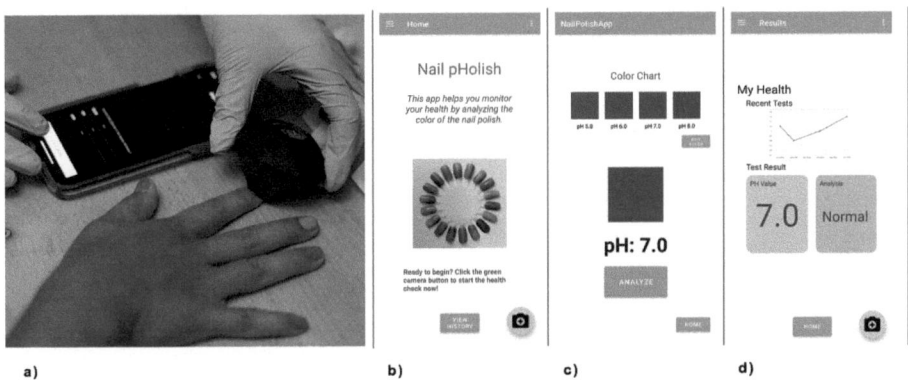

**Fig. 6.** Mobile application: a) Positioning the SPM; b) Camera button sends readout from SPM; c) Data captured is shown on the Estimation page (purple-blue hue corresponds to pH 7.0); d) Health analysis page with graphs and recommendations. (Color figure online)

## 4 Technical Evaluations

The technical evaluations involve color-change responsiveness to 8 different pH solutions, reversibility tests to assess the re-usability of the biosensor evaluated on different concentration solutions, the performance of the system on different human fingernail's sizes and shapes, and the durability of Nail pHolish over 72 h on 4 subjects.

---
[2] https://github.com/InteractiveOrganismsLab/Nail-pHolish.

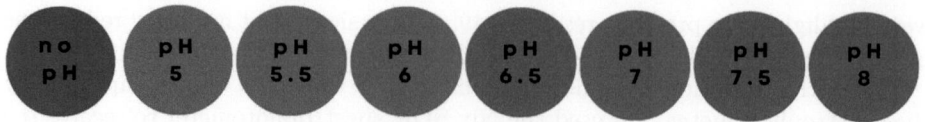

**Fig. 7.** Color changes on swatches on Nail pHolish App. (Color figure online)

### 4.1 Color-Change Responsiveness

We evaluated Nail pHolish on various swatches to observe the color changes across a pH range. Figure 7 illustrates the transition in color. We prepared a range of pH solutions 5, 5.5, 6, 6.5, 7, 7.5, and 8. These pH values were chosen as they are well within the range that is safe for human contact [7] and thus likely to be the pH range of various biomarkers [42] that the nails would be used to measure in the field.

Eight plastic nail swatches, same as those used by nail technicians, were prepared by applying one coat of Nail pHolish and allowed to dry for two hours at room temperature. One swatch was used as a control displaying the nail polish without any addition of pH solution. Solutions of pH 5, 5.5, 6, 6.5, 7, 7.5, and 8 were applied to the remaining seven swatches respectively. A thin application of solutions was applied to the swatches using a soft nail sponge such as those used in nail salons to create gradient techniques.

Application of pH solutions resulted in noticeable color changes ranging from fuschia to blue-green related to their pH levels (Fig. 7). Once dried, the swatches maintained the color change indefinitely. We analyzed the material's reflectance spectra across pH levels, revealing distinct spectral shifts corresponding to visible color changes. The original purple, with minimal reflectance at 500550 nm. Spectra for other pH levels showed increased reflectance in this range at other pH levels. Variations in reflectance between 600650 nm further contributed to the color transitions, demonstrating the material's effectiveness in visually indicating pH changes to be translated to a data input.

### 4.2 Reversibility

A reversibility test was performed to test the capability of the nail polish biosensor to return to its original color after undergoing color changes. The test was performed on a single plastic nail shaped swatch. One coat of Nail pHolish was applied to the swatch and allowed to dry for two hours before testing. To perform the color changes, a nail technician's sponge was dipped into pH solution and dabbed onto the nail swatch. Separate sponges were used for each pH value. Successive pH solutions were applied to the swatch, allowing to dry between applications. First, pH 5, 6, 7, and 8 at 100 mmol were applied to the swatch respectively. Next, reversibility was tested by applying pH 8, 7, 6, and 5 at 500 mmol respectively. Images of the swatch were captured at each color change. The results are shown in Fig. 8.

When the pH solutions at 100 mmol were applied, the swatch changed from purple to blue. Reapplying the 500 mmol solutions in reverse returned the swatch to purple, but in a slightly paler hue than the original. This suggests that while the biosensor maintains its ability to change colors multiple times, some of the biosensor is lost with each application. Although the same color families can be achieved, they become slightly less concentrated and more pastel with each use, never fully returning to the original nail polish color before pH exposure.

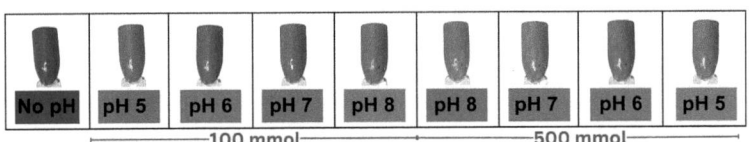

**Fig. 8.** Reversibility test with Nail pHolish app.

## 5 Evaluation on Human Fingernails

### 5.1 Colorimetric Response on Fingernails

To assess the performance of our biosensor on human fingernails, we conducted tests with four participants. Each participant applied the nail polish biosensor, dried it, and then exposed the coated nails to solutions with varying pH levels. We took three measurements for each pH solution using the spectrophotometer, covering four different pH values. In total, we collected 48 data points.

The results, depicting color changes across pH levels, are illustrated in Fig. 9. The color value results are further analyzed; Fig. 9.b and 9.c show the RGB and CIE data across the pH range. These results were utilized to develop the algorithm implemented in our software for converting spectrophotometer readings into estimated pH values.

### 5.2 Evaluating Durability and Usability Across a 72-Hour Period

The durability of the Nail pHolish was assessed through a series of practical tests conducted with four participants (researchers from the project), including three females and one male. The biosensor nail polish was applied to all fingernails on the left hand of each participant, selected for its nondominant use. Each participant used the nail polish for 72 h, a duration chosen as water-based nail polishes on the market have a similar lifespan on nails. After that duration, the participants tested the nail polish, on their nails, with the Nail pHolish system, using pH 5 solution. The results read accurately still after 72 h wear.

Participants engaged in daily activities, including showering, hand washing, cooking, crafting, experiencing a minor cut, and using cleaning products, providing a comprehensive evaluation of the biosensor's performance. To maintain

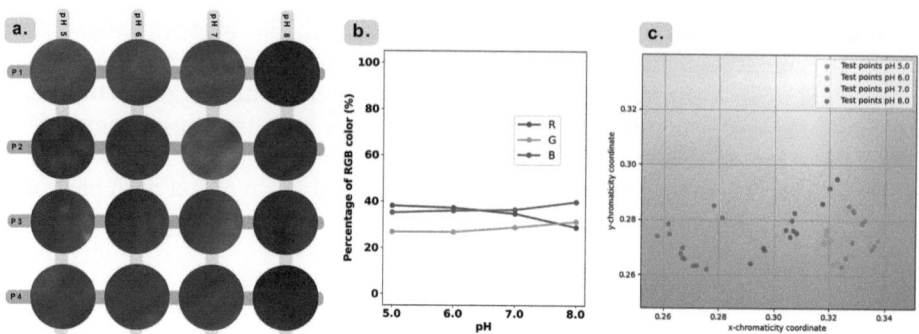

**Fig. 9.** Colorimetric response: a) Color changes on human nails for four distinct pH levels. b) Percentage of RGB for each pH level. c) CIE chromaticity map. (Color figure online)

consistency, they photographed their nails daily at the same time, reducing variability from lighting or camera settings. After three days, they applied a low pH solution (vinegar) to test if the biosensor retained its sensitivity and color-changing properties. Figure 10 shows the log and responsiveness of Nail pHolish.

Durability tests confirmed the biosensor's reliability over extended use. Nail pHolish exhibited durability similar to other water-based biosensors, which typically peel after two to three days. By the last day, participants observed a slightly slower color response, though it still produced accurate results within seconds.

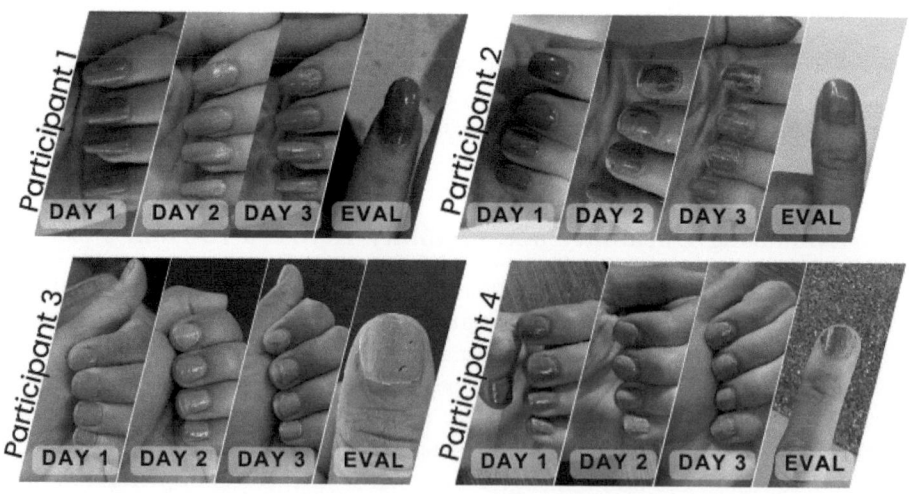

**Fig. 10.** In-the-wild durability test for 72 h with four participants.

## 6 Evaluation

We conducted two sets of user studies to assess Nail pHolish's feasibility and contextual relevance. The first involved expert interviews with five nail technicians, exploring practical integration and product comparisons. The second was a user-driven study with 10 participants focused on dental erosion, assessing wearability, usability, and health-related interpretation of pH changes.

### 6.1 User Study 1: Experts Interviews with Nail Technicians

Our research included expert interviews with professional nail technicians to assess the feasibility and potential applications of Nail pHolish. We also evaluated app performance under various lighting conditions at participants' locations during demonstrations. These interviews offered valuable professional insights into the technology's practicality and future directions.

**Participants and Protocol.** We engaged five English speaking nail technicians (three female, two male), aged 18 to 70, with experience ranging from 3–5 years to 10+ years in nail care, in one-hour sessions at their nail studios. Each participant received a $50 Amazon gift card in appreciation for their time and insights.

Participants observed demonstrations of the biosensor nail polish on fake nails, including its color-changing response to different pH levels and the app for displaying results. They were then shown over 20 nail art designs on fake nail swatches, illustrating the polish's versatility in their practice. This allowed them to provide feedback on additional techniques for showcasing color changes. Participants completed a post-questionnaire and participated in a semi-structured interview, sharing their experiences and professional opinions. All questions were rated on a Likert scale from 1 (Strongly disagree) to 7 (Strongly agree) (Fig. 11).

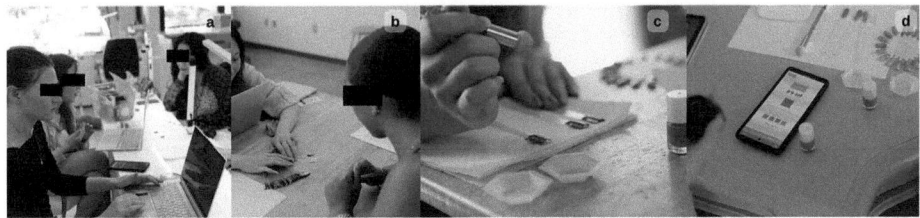

**Fig. 11.** Expert Interviews with Nail Technicians: interviews and setup (a, b), Nail pHolish demo on artificial nails (c), and evaluating app on their studios (d).

**Findings.** Our analysis of the feedback yielded the following themes:

*Usability of the Biosensor Nail Polish:* Four out of five technicians rated the application process as "Very Easy" (STD: 0.89). A few technicians noted liking the texture and consistency. One technician noted, "It's perfect (for applying) the way it is." while another suggested that the formula could be less viscous for easier application. One technician enthusiastically stated, "I like how much creative freedom this product could have and how many designs she could do." These indicate that the biosensor nail polish is user-friendly, requiring minimal training or adjustment for use.

*Similarity to Commercial Products:* Four technicians rated the similarity of the biosensor nail polish to conventional products as 7, with one rating it as 5. This suggests that the biosensor nail polish closely resembles standard nail products in both appearance and texture. One technician even said that "this (Nail pHolish) is better than some brands of nail polishes."

*Color Change Visibility:* All participants found the color change to be clear to visualize (Mean: 6.2, STD: 0.84), demonstrating that the biosensor effectively indicates pH level changes. They also noted that the color change clearly showcases the biosensor's capabilities.

*Aesthetics:* In regards to aesthetics, all technicians rated positively (5 to 7). The colors aligned with seasonal trends, particularly for spring and summer. One technician noted that "these (Nail pHolish) colors were often requested in Spring and Summer." One technician described the colors as "very beautiful" and said, "I see customers request those colors all times of the year." While health monitoring was seen as a unique selling point, there were concerns about the declining popularity of color-changing polishes, especially "mood" (temperature) changing types. Two participants noted, "The customers who like color change would love it; the people who do not will not."

*App Usage:* All participants found the app's data visualization clear and helpful, rating their understanding of pH levels and data display as 7. Four participants reported that they understood pH levels through the app. This suggests the app effectively aids in interpreting pH data.

*Overall Impression:* The biosensor nail polish received highly positive feedback (Mean: 6.8, STD: 0.45), with all participants rating it favorably. One called it a "game changer" for the nail industry, while another highlighted its innovative nature, saying, "It's exciting to see new technology in the nail industry." These strong impressions show Nail pHolish's first impressions in nail care experts.

### 6.2 User Study 2: User-Driven Scenario on Dental Erosion

A second user study demonstrated how the system can monitor specific health and environmental biomarkers, focusing on pH and dental erosion. We chose Dental Erosion as the user-driven scenario to exemplify how Nail pHolish system can be used in a real-world scenario. Participants interacted with the pH of common beverages and their saliva, using the system to support accessible health monitoring while raising awareness of their dental habits.

Tooth erosion, resulting from enamel demineralization without bacterial involvement, is increasingly common due to acidic foods and beverages [21,30]. Erosive potential is determined by pH and buffering properties, including titratable acidity and calcium content. Beverages with pH below 4.0 soften tooth

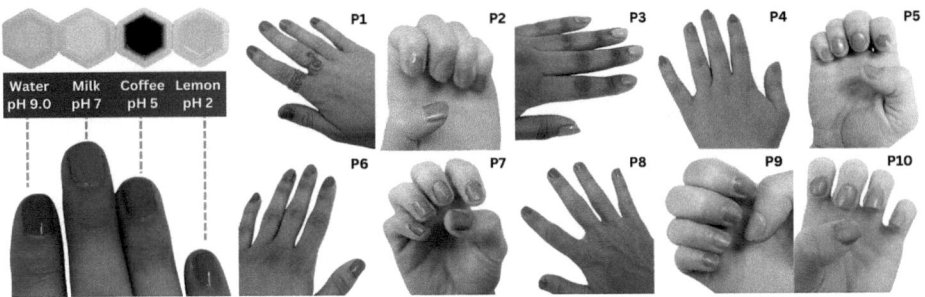

**Fig. 12.** Testing the pH of four beverages with Nail pHolish app, and results on participants fingernails.

surfaces and create an environment conducive to bacterial growth, increasing vulnerability to further damage.

**Aparatus.** Another app was created by adapting the Nail pHolish app to this scenario. The app pairs with the spectrophotometer, allows the capture of beverage and saliva pH readouts, and provides logs and visualizations. It is open-source to promote replicability[3]. Participants used the fabricated Nail pHolish on their fingernails. Several beverages of varying pH were used as buffers to represent different pH levels: alkaline water (pH 9), whole milk (pH7), black coffee (pH 5), and unsweetened lemon juice (pH 2). These were chosen due to their relevance in dental health research on acidic exposure [30]. Our system's pH measurements were compared with a lab-graded pH meter, and the results (Fig. 12) showed distinct color changes in the nail polish for each beverage.

**Participants and Protocol.** Ten particpants were recruited through personal networks. They self-identified as five women, three men, one non-binary, and one transmasculine individual, aged 20 to 27. All had previous experience wearing nail polish. Each participant received a $15 Amazon gift card after the study.

**(1) System introduction and demonstration (10 mins).** Participants completed a pre-questionnaire and received an overview of the study, including its purpose, an introduction to colorimetric biosensors and wearable technology for health monitoring. To demonstrate Nail pHolish, they observed a palette of pre-made Nail pHolish designs, and learned how to use the app to sense the pH levels using the spectrophotometer and observed the visualizations.

**(2) Application and interaction (15 mins).** Participants were invited to apply Nail pHolish on their own hands. The liquids (lemon juice, coffee, milk, alkaline water, and saliva) were lightly daubed onto the nails using a nail technician's sponge and allowed to dry. Participants then observed the color changes on

---

[3] https://github.com/InteractiveOrganismsLab/Nail-pHolish-Dental.

their own nails and explored the spectrophotometer and app system to sense and record color changes of each fingernail. Users were given time to navigate through the pages of the app, looking at graphs, comparing how beverage pH might affect their saliva pH, and learning how pH plays a role in dental erosion.

**(3) Feedback collection (20–25 mins).** Participants completed a post-questionnaire and a semi-structured interview on polish usability, comfort, visual response, and their interpretation of health-related color changes. All questions are rated on a Likert scale from 1 (Strongly disagree) to 7 (Strongly agree) (Fig. 13).

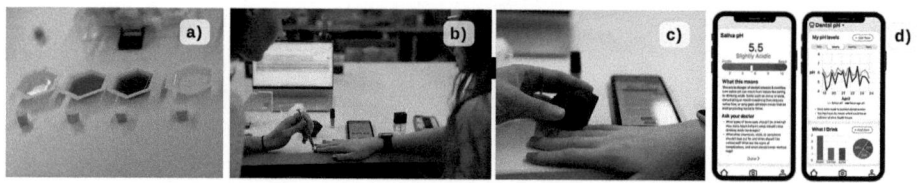

**Fig. 13.** Dental Erosion User Study: a) Beverages to be tested, b) Testing beverages on user's hands, c) Demonstrating the SPM in tandem with the app, d) Two visualizations: oral pH reading with health indications (left) and health tracking graphs (right).

## Findings

*Hand-Fluid Interaction with Nail pHolish:* All ten participants expressed surprise and delight at witnessing visible color changes (M: 5.88, STD: 0.56). All participants said that the color changes were obvious in relation to the acidity of the beverages (M: 6.38, STD: 1.06). Nine out of ten said that they would be excited to wear the color changing Nail pHolish in public and used words such as, "fun," "exciting," and interactive." One person said that they prefer nail polish that does not change color to not interfere with their outfit selection.

*Color Analysis Using the App:* All ten users found that the app displayed a pH reading that matched the pH of the fluids. The majority of users felt the color change was easy to notice (M: 5.88, STD: 0.64) and that the color changes made sense in relation to the acidity of the beverages (M: 6.38, STD: 1.06). One user had applied Nail pHolish too thin at first, but received accurate readings upon a slightly thicker reapplication. Most said that the color changes felt appropriate for public or social settings (M: 6.63, STD: 0.74). They all showed excitement when testing their saliva pHs with nine participants demonstrating saliva pH of 6 and one with saliva pH of 7.

*Health and Habit Analysis Using the App:* Prior to the study, nine out of ten participants were unaware that beverage pH could cause dental erosion. One participant had heard of this but was unsure of the impact. This participant reported drinking water between beverages to neutralize oral pH, the remaining nine did not. After using the Nail pHolish system, all participants reported increased awareness of beverage and food pH. Six stated it would change their drinking habits, three felt reassured about their preference for water, one said it would not change their beverage choices but would reduce frequency, and one remained willing to take the risk without changing habits. Participants reported that the app helped them better understand the pH of their saliva (M: 6.50, STD: 0.76), the pH of common beverages (M: 6.63, STD: 0.52), and made them reflect on how acidic beverages might affect their health (M: 5.75, STD: 1.91).

*Privacy and Social Acceptance:* Visibility of color changes on a wearable product could raise privacy concerns for wearers, so we asked participants how they felt about visibly displaying health indicators, whether they feared judgment or privacy issues, and how they expected onlookers to react. Surprisingly, all ten participants reported no privacy concerns, believing the color changes would not reveal sensitive health information to others. They agreed that if the technology became common for testing various conditions, privacy would be maintained because onlookers would not know the specific condition being tested. Participants were generally comfortable with visible health indicators (M: 6.13, STD: 1.13). Nine expected onlookers to respond with interest, curiosity, and excitement rather than judgment or malice. One participant anticipated potential judgment if others knew the purpose but stated they, "...would not feel any obligation to explain what it was for." Additionally, eight participants were happy to show off the color, seeing it as a way to raise awareness about wearable health testing, and one believed it could even, "inspire others to care about their dental health."

## 7  Potential Applications for Nail pHolish

Figure 14 illustrates potential applications that interact with a variety of fluids.

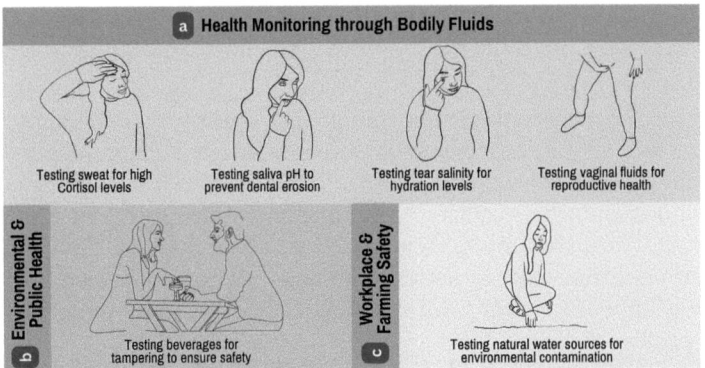

**Fig. 14.** Applications when interacting a) with body fluids: sweat, saliva, tears, vaginal fluids, b) with external fluids for environmental and public health applications such as drugs in beverages, and c) when exposed to substances on workforce such as farmers.

(a) **Health Monitoring Through Bodily Fluids.** Nail pHolish offers a non-invasive method to detect biomarkers in various fluids: saliva for oral health and hydration [4,49,51], tears for hydration and electrolyte balance [40], sweat for metabolic conditions and electrolyte imbalances [50,54], and vaginal fluids for reproductive health, detecting infections like bacterial vaginosis or yeast infections [34]. Additionally, cortisol-sensing nail polish could monitor stress levels through saliva or sweat, supporting mental health tracking [18,29,37].

(b) **Environmental and Public Health Applications.** Nail pHolish can detect chemicals like contaminants and nutrients in external fluids. For instance, it can identify drug residues in beverages for safety [11,16], monitor pH and chlorine levels in swimming pools, crucial for outdoor areas exposed to rain or inconsistent maintenance [45], and signal pollutants or acidity changes in rain or lake water, supporting environmental safety efforts like acid rain detection [23].

(c) **Workplace and Farming Safety.** In the food industry, Nail pHolish can detect spoilage and contamination, supporting hygiene protocols [15,27]. Medically, it may serve as a visual hygiene indicator for tracking sterilized devices. In dermatology or cosmetics, it offers real-time feedback on nail or skin pH during product testing. For farmers, it can detect pesticide residues on skin, preventing dermatitis or other conditions [2,20], and assess soil pH or residue content, promoting sustainable farming and environmental monitoring [2,53].

## 8 Discussion and Future Works

**Multiple Biosensors in Multiple Fingernails.** Nail pHolish effectively demonstrated color changes in response to pH using anthocyanin for safety, practicality, and visual appeal. While currently focused on pH, expanding to detect different analytes through each fingernail could broaden its applications. For instance, wearing in each fingernail a nail polish with chloride, nitrate, and lead biosensors can be use as traditional water quality test strips. This would involve developing new formulations and assessing chemical interactions with various fluids.

**From Lab to Salon Evaluations.** Nail practitioners provided valuable insights on materials, nail art, and customer preferences, making them ideal participants for evaluating the biosensor nail polish. Their feedback validated compatibility with salon standards, praising ease of application, resemblance to conventional products, intuitive app design, and clear color changes. Practitioners supported salon adoption, suggesting competitive pricing, expanded color options, and potential appeal for nail-health patients, health-conscious individuals, and healthcare professionals.

**Longevity.** Integrating biosensors into nail art presents durability and maintenance challenges. Common water-based polish is softer and less durable than conventional options, while traditional polishes can block with biosensor functionality, which must remain exposed. We proposed some alternatives for prolonging the lifespan and responsiveness such as using protective coatings, as well as techniques like adornment removal to maintain sensor functionality.

**Privacy.** Past biocosmetic interfaces research showed that users didn't have strong privacy concerns on having their pH level potentially exposed to others through cosmetics [49]. Participants reported no privacy concerns about visibly displaying health indicators with color-changing nail polish, believing that onlookers would not recognize the specific condition being tested. Most saw it as an opportunity to raise awareness about wearable health testing, with one noting it could even, "inspire others to care about their dental health."

**Portable Spectrophotometer for Wearables.** Given that the contributions of the paper do not rely on the development of spectrophotometers but in the implementation of our formulation and own app, we opted for a commercial spectrophotometer for its portability, connectivity and accuracy in diverse conditions [12]. Next steps could involve developing a customized spectrophotometer designed to match the curvature of fingernails and to detect the fine lines of nail art designs. Alternatively, computer vision and machine learning could be used; however, the accuracy of app for biosensing is still under development.

## 9 Conclusion

This research introduced Nail pHolish, a nail polish with anthocyanins that merges biosensing technology with traditional nail art for detecting chemical changes in hand-fluid interactions. We present the fabrication process of a biosensor nail polish that is skin-safe, aligns with conventional color preferences, and with a similar composition to existing products. Various nail art designs and the integration of buffer solutions showcased the biosensor's versatility to align with current nail care solutions. A mobile application connects with a portable spectrophotometer to translate color changes into precise pH measurements. Our formulation and software are open-source to be customized for different biosensor and applications, proving its adaptability to other projects.

Evaluations in humans' fingernails showcased nail pHolish color sensitivity, durability, and a dental erosion use case. Interviews with five nail technicians provided insights into the practical application of the biosensor in salon settings, affirming its feasibility and identifying areas for improvement. A 10-participant user study focused on dental erosion discussed the hand-fluids interactive possibilities, usability of the system, and social acceptability of Nail pHolish.

Nail pHolish build on the concept of Biocosmetic Interfaces which merge everyday cosmetics with biotechnology for health monitoring. Nail pHolish not only enable access to seamless health data on bodily, but also provides an alternative for sensing environmental fluids. This work transforms nail polish into dynamic displays of biochemical reactions on fingernails to be detected and analyzed by an app. This work bridges scientific research into HCI, opening new avenues for health and environmental monitoring with interactive devices.

**Acknowledgments.** This work was supported by the National Science Foundation under Grant No 2146461, and UC Davis Academic Senate. We thank Yulia Yu for initial support in fabrication, and the participants for their feedback.

# References

1. Baliga, S., Muglikar, S., Kale, R.: Salivary pH: a diagnostic biomarker. J. Indian Soc. Periodontol. **17**(4), 461–465 (2013). https://doi.org/10.4103/0972-124X.118317
2. Balkrishna, A., et al.: Biosensors for detection of pesticide residue, mycotoxins and heavy metals in fruits and vegetables: a concise review. Microchem. J. **205**, 111292 (2024). https://doi.org/10.1016/j.microc.2024.111292
3. Bhatia, D., Paul, S., Acharjee, T., Ramachairy, S.S.: Biosensors and their widespread impact on human health. Sensors Int. **5**, 100257 (2024). https://doi.org/10.1016/j.sintl.2023.100257
4. de Castro, L.F., de Freitas, S.V., Duarte, L.C., de Souza, J.A.C., Paixão, T.R.L.C., Coltro, W.K.T.: Salivary diagnostics on paper microfluidic devices and their use as wearable sensors for glucose monitoring. Anal. Bioanal. Chem. **411**(19), 4919–4928 (2019). https://doi.org/10.1007/s00216-019-01788-0
5. Chen, Y., et al.: A smartphone colorimetric reader integrated with an ambient light sensor and a 3D printed attachment for on-site detection of zearalenone. Anal. Bioanal. Chem. **409**, 6567–6574 (2017)
6. Choe, A., Yeom, J., Shanker, R., Kim, M.P., Kang, S., Ko, H.: Stretchable and wearable colorimetric patches based on thermoresponsive plasmonic microgels embedded in a hydrogel film. NPG Asia Materials **10**(9), 912–922 (2018)
7. Cohen, M., Khalaila, R.: Saliva pH as a biomarker of exam stress and a predictor of exam performance. J. Psychosom. Res. **77**(5), 420–425 (2014). https://doi.org/10.1016/j.jpsychores.2014.07.003
8. Colors, C.: Shop Thermal Nail Polish - Color Change Nail Polish - Cirque Colors. https://www.cirquecolors.com/collections/thermal. Accessed 12 Sept 2024
9. Dierk, C., Sterman, S., Nicholas, M.J.P., Paulos, E.: Häiriö: Human hair as interactive material. In: Proceedings of the Twelfth International Conference on Tangible, Embedded, and Embodied Interaction, pp. 148–157 (2018)
10. Gao, N., Cai, Z., Chang, G., He, Y.: Non-invasive and wearable glucose biosensor based on gel electrolyte for detection of human sweat. J. Mater. Sci. **58**(2), 890–901 (2023). https://doi.org/10.1007/s10853-022-08095-7
11. Granica, M., Tymecki, L.: Analytical aspects of smart (phone) fluorometric measurements. Talanta **197**, 319–325 (2019). https://doi.org/10.1016/j.talanta.2019.01.032. zSCC: 0000018
12. Grasse, E., Torcasio, M., Smith, A.: Teaching UV–vis spectroscopy with a 3D-printable smartphone spectrophotometer. J. Chem. Educ. **93** (2015). https://doi.org/10.1021/acs.jchemed.5b00654
13. Gu, Y., et al.: A real-time detection method of hg2+ in drinking water via portable biosensor: using a smartphone as a low-cost micro-spectrometer to read the colorimetric signals. Biosensors **12**(11) (2022)
14. Guinovart, T., Bandodkar, A.J., Windmiller, J.R., Andrade, F.J., Wang, J.: A potentiometric tattoo sensor for monitoring ammonium in sweat. Analyst **138**(22), 7031 (2013). https://doi.org/10.1039/c3an01672b

15. Guo, Y., et al.: A colorimetric biosensor with infrared sterilization based on CUSE nanoparticles for the detection of e. coli o157:h7 in food samples. Microbiol. Spectrum **12**(8), e03978–23 (2024)
16. Hansen, K.M., Albrechtsen, H.J., Andersen, H.R.: Optimal PH in chlorinated swimming pools-balancing formation of by-products. J. Water Health **11**(3), 465–472 (2013)
17. He, R., et al.: a colorimetric dermal tattoo biosensor fabricated by microneedle patch for multiplexed detection of health-related biomarkers. Adv. Sci. **8**(24), 2103030 (2021)
18. Hellhammer, D.H., Wüst, S., Kudielka, B.M.: Salivary cortisol as a biomarker in stress research. Psychoneuroendocrinology **34**(2), 163–171 (2009). https://doi.org/10.1016/j.psyneuen.2008.10.026
19. Bandodkar, J., et al.: Tattoo-based potentiometric ion-selective sensors for epidermal pH monitoring. Analyst **138**(1), 123–128 (2013). https://doi.org/10.1039/C2AN36422K
20. Jain, U.: Emerging vistas on pesticides detection based on electrochemical biosensors – an update. Food Chem. **371**, 131126 (2022)
21. Johansson, A.K., Lingström, P., Imfeld, T., Birkhed, D.: Influence of drinking method on tooth-surface PH in relation to dental erosion. Eur. J. Oral Sci. **112**(6), 484–489 (2004)
22. Kan, V., et al.: Organic primitives: Synthesis and design of PH-reactive materials using molecular i/o for sensing, actuation, and interaction. In: Proceedings of the 2017 CHI Conference on Human Factors in Computing Systems. CHI '17, New York, NY, USA, pp. 989–1000. Association for Computing Machinery (2017). https://doi.org/10.1145/3025453.3025952
23. Kan, V., et al.: Organic primitives: synthesis and design of PH-reactive materials using molecular i/o for sensing, actuation, and interaction. In: Proceedings of the 2017 CHI Conference on Human Factors in Computing Systems. CHI '17, New York, NY, USA, pp. 989–1000. Association for Computing Machinery (2017). https://doi.org/10.1145/3025453.3025952
24. Kao, C.H.L., Nguyen, B., Roseway, A., Dickey, M.: Earthtones: chemical sensing powders to detect and display environmental hazards through color variation. In: Proceedings of the 2017 CHI Conference Extended Abstracts on Human Factors in Computing Systems. CHI EA '17, New York, NY, USA, pp. 872–883. Association for Computing Machinery (2017). https://doi.org/10.1145/3027063.3052754
25. Kao, H.L., Johns, P., Roseway, A., Czerwinski, M.: Tattio: fabrication of aesthetic and functional temporary tattoos. In: Extended Abstracts on Human Factors in Computing Systems, pp. 3699–3702 (2016)
26. Kao, H.L., Mohan, M., Schmandt, C., Paradiso, J.A., Vega, K.: Chromoskin: towards interactive cosmetics using thermochromic pigments. In: Proceedings of the 2016 CHI Conference Extended Abstracts on Human Factors in Computing Systems, pp. 3703–3706 (2016)
27. Kim, D., Cao, Y., Mariappan, D., Bono, M.S., Jr., Hart, A.J., Marelli, B.: A microneedle technology for sampling and sensing bacteria in the food supply chain. Adv. Func. Mater. **31**(1), 2005370 (2021). https://doi.org/10.1002/adfm.202005370
28. Kim, J., Cho, T.N., Valdés-Ramírez, G., Wang, J.: A wearable fingernail chemical sensing platform: PH sensing at your fingertips. Talanta **150**, 622–628 (2016)
29. Kinnamon, D., Ghanta, R., Lin, K.C., Muthukumar, S., Prasad, S.: Portable biosensor for monitoring cortisol in low-volume perspired human sweat. Scientific Reports **7** (2017). https://doi.org/10.1038/s41598-017-13684-7

30. Kitchens, M., Owens, B.: Effect of carbonated beverages, coffee, sports and high energy drinks, and bottled water on the in vitro erosion characteristics of dental enamel. J. Clin. Pediatr. Dent. **31**(3), 153–159 (2007)
31. Lab, H.B.: Xtreme long PH sensing nail
32. Laganovska, K., et al.: Portable low-cost open-source wireless spectrophotometer for fast and reliable measurements. HardwareX **7**, e00108 (2020). https://doi.org/10.1016/j.ohx.2020.e00108
33. Li, B., et al.: A self-designed versatile and portable sensing device based on smart phone for colorimetric detection. Anal. Bioanal. Chem. **413**(2), 533–541 (2020). https://doi.org/10.1007/s00216-020-03024-6
34. Lin, Y.P., Chen, W.C., Cheng, C.M., Shen, C.J.: Vaginal PH value for clinical diagnosis and treatment of common vaginitis. Diagnostics **11**, 1996 (2021). https://doi.org/10.3390/diagnostics11111996
35. Luka, G., Nowak, E., Kawchuk, J., Hoorfar, M., Najjaran, H.: Portable device for the detection of colorimetric assays. Roy. Soci. Open Sci. **4**, 171025 (2017). https://doi.org/10.1098/rsos.171025
36. Luka, G., Nowak, E., Toyata, Q., Tasnim, N., Najjaran, H., Hoorfar, M.: Portable on-chip colorimetric biosensing platform integrated with a smartphone for label/PCR-free detection of cryptosporidium RNA. Sci. Rep. **11** (2021). https://doi.org/10.1038/s41598-021-02580-w
37. Madhu, S., et al.: Review–towards wearable sensor platforms for the electrochemical detection of cortisol. J. Electrochem. Soc. **167**, 067508 (2020). https://doi.org/10.1149/1945-7111/ab7e24
38. Mariakakis, A., et al.: Ecopatches: maker-friendly chemical-based UV sensing. In: Proceedings of the 2020 ACM Designing Interactive Systems Conference. DIS '20, New York, NY, USA, pp. 1983–1994. Association for Computing Machinery (2020). https://doi.org/10.1145/3357236.3395424
39. Mariakakis, A., et al.: Ecopatches: maker-friendly chemical-based uv sensing. In: Conference on Designing Interactive Systems, pp. 1983–1994 (2020)
40. Miller, I., Schlosser, S., Palazzolo, L., Veronesi, M.C., Eberini, I., Gianazza, E.: Some more about dogs: proteomics of neglected biological fluids. J. Proteomics **218** (2020). https://doi.org/10.1016/j.jprot.2020.103724
41. Murdan, S., Milcovich, G., Goriparthi, G.: An assessment of the human nail plate PH. Skin Pharmacol. Physiol. **24**(4), 175–181 (2011)
42. Narasimhan, A., Jain, H., Muniandy, K., Chinnappan, R., Mani, N.K.: Bio-analysis of saliva using paper devices and colorimetric assays. J. Anal. Testing (2023). https://doi.org/10.1007/s41664-023-00282-y
43. Niakan, S., Safi, M., Younespour, S., Khoshtarkib, S.: Comparative analysis of smartphone colorimeter apps and spectrophotometry for measuring forehead skin color in maxillofacial prosthesis fabrication. J. Prosthodontics (2024)
44. Promphet, N., et al.: Non-invasive textile based colorimetric sensor for the simultaneous detection of sweat PH and lactate. Talanta **192**, 424–430 (2019)
45. Rapacewicz, R., Kudlek, E., Brukało, K.: Rainwater and stormwater quality in terms of its potential use in swimming pool installations. Desalin. Water Treat. **321**, 100918 (2025). https://doi.org/10.1016/j.dwt.2024.100918
46. Roy, S., Chowdhury, M.U.S., Noim, J.O., Pandey, R., Nittala, A.S.: Holochemie - sustainable fabrication of soft biochemical holographic devices for ubiquitous sensing. In: Proceedings of the 37th Annual ACM Symposium on User Interface Software and Technology. UIST '24, New York, NY, USA. Association for Computing Machinery (2024). https://doi.org/10.1145/3654777.3676448

47. Seethalakshmi, C., Reddy, R.J., Asifa, N., Prabhu, S.: Correlation of salivary PH, incidence of dental caries and periodontal status in diabetes mellitus patients. J. clin. Diagnostic Res. JCDR **10**(3) (2016)
48. Sun, C., Adhikari, K., Koppel, K.: An exploratory study of the factors that may affect female consumers' buying decision of nail polishes. Cosmetics **2** (2015)
49. Sun, S., et al.: Biocosme: lip-based cosmetics with colorimetric biosensors for salivary analysis using deep learning. In: Proceedings of the 2024 ACM International Symposium on Wearable Computers. ISWC '24 (2024). https://doi.org/10.1145/3675095.3676610
50. Sun, S., Ruiz, A., Pirmoradi, S., Vega, K.: Biosparks: jewelry as electrochemical sweat biosensors with modular, repurposing and interchangeable approaches. In: Adjunct Proceedings of the 2023 ACM International Joint Conference on Pervasive and Ubiquitous Computing & the 2023 ACM International Symposium on Wearable Computing, pp. 315–320. ACM (2023)
51. Vasquez, E.S.L., Yetisen, A.K., Vega, K.: BraceIO: biosensing through hydrogel dental ligatures. In: Proceedings of the 2020 ACM International Symposium on Wearable Computers, Online, pp. 87–89 (2020)
52. Vega, K., et al.: The dermal abyss: interfacing with the skin by tattooing biosensors. In: Proceedings of the 2017 ACM International Symposium on Wearable Computers, pp. 138–145. ACM (2017). https://doi.org/10.1145/3123021.3123039
53. Wang, X., Luo, Y., Huang, K., Cheng, N.: Biosensor for agriculture and food safety: recent advances and future perspectives. Adv. Agrochem **1**(1), 3–6 (2022). https://doi.org/10.1016/j.aac.2022.08.002
54. Young-Ng, M., Chen, G., Kiyama, D., Giannicola, A.S., Şeker, E., Vega, K.: Sweatcessory: a wearable necklace for sensing biological data in sweat. In: Adjunct Proceedings of the 2022 ACM International Joint Conference on Pervasive and Ubiquitous Computing and the 2022 ACM International Symposium on Wearable Computers, pp. 141–143. UbiComp/ISWC '22 Adjunct, Association for Computing Machinery, New York, NY, USA (Apr 2022). https://doi.org/10.1145/3544793.3560342
55. Zhu, J., El Nesr, N., Simon, C., Rettenmaier, N., Beiler, K., Kao, C.H.L.: BioWeave: weaving thread-based sweat-sensing on-skin interfaces. In: Proceedings of the 36th Annual ACM Symposium on User Interface Software and Technology, pp. 1–11. ACM (2023)

# Human-AI Interaction

# A Feature Mapping on GenAI Tools from the Perspective of HCI

Rafael A. Pereira(✉) and Natasha M. C. Valentim

Department of Computer Science, Federal University of Parana, Curitiba, Brazil
rafaelpontoandrade@gmail.com, natasha_costa16@yahoo.com.br

**Abstract.** This paper presents a feature mapping-based evaluation of generative artificial intelligence (GenAI) tools from a Human-Computer Interaction (HCI) perspective. This mapping aims to explore and compare how GenAI tools support interaction, usability, and user-centered features. This is relevant because GenAI systems become increasingly integrated into creative, educational, and productivity contexts. For this mapping, we chose the tools developed and provided by the company responsible for the base model, as cited in the AI Index Report 2025 and with high popularity in 2024, according to the AI Tools portal. We analyzed 15 publicly available GenAI platforms, using a multidimensional framework that considers interaction styles, interface types, and functional aspects such as transparency, collaboration, user support, adaptability, and technical accessibility. The results reveal strong convergence in interface design, with 100% of tools adopting graphical interfaces and 93% supporting touch. However, advanced features such as multimodal integration, response customization, real-time feedback, and collaborative editing are unevenly distributed across platforms. Only 67% of tools support actual multimodal interaction, and just one tool offers real-time collaborative editing. In addition, transparency about data usage and the presence of explanations or citations in outputs remains limited. This mapping details the maturity of GenAI tools regarding interaction design and highlights areas where HCI principles remain underutilized. The findings support future research and development focused on enhancing user experience, inclusiveness, and contextual adaptability in emerging GenAI systems.

**Keywords:** Features Mapping · GenAI · HCI · User-centered

## 1 Introduction

Generative Artificial Intelligence (GenAI) has emerged as a transformative technology in the contemporary technological landscape, with tools capable of generating content in various formats such as text, image, audio, and video. The AI Index 2025 Annual Report [13] highlights this accelerated growth, noting that private investment in generative AI reached USD 33.9 billion globally in 2024, representing an 18.7% increase compared to the previous year. The report also indicates that 78% of organizations reported using AI in 2024, a significant rise from 55% the year before.

Recent research by McKinsey and Company [5] indicates that 71% of organizations already use GenAI regularly in at least one business function, with emphasis on text, image, and code generation. This growing and multimodal use reinforces the importance of methodologies that consider not only technical performance but also interactive practices and real-world usage contexts. In the GenAI context, generative models do not merely respond to prompts they act as co-creators and mediators, demanding new taxonomies and metrics to assess the quality and effectiveness of the interaction.

In this context, the advent of generative AI-based systems introduces new possibilities and challenges related to HCI and user experience (UX). Shi et al. [14] observed that aspects related to interaction and user experience remain underexplored compared to the volume of studies focusing on technical aspects of these tools, such as model training specifics, technology, training cost, and performance.

In this light, this paper proposes a Feature Mapping of publicly available GenAI tools, based on functional and technical characteristics of these tools, such as user support, technical accessibility, input and output types, personalization, and adaptability. Feature mapping is a comparative analysis methodology used to systematically identify, catalog, and compare the functionalities and attributes of a set of products or systems. Unlike a traditional benchmark, which focuses on measuring and comparing quantitative performance metrics (such as speed, accuracy, or resource consumption), the main objective of feature mapping is not to classify systems as "better" or "worse" but rather to provide a structured overview of the existing landscape [15]. In this paper, the mapping is used as a structured quantitative methodology, enabling a systematic and detailed analysis of various publicly accessible GenAI tools. This analysis focus on human-computer interaction dimensions, such as considers functional, technical, and usability aspects, providing a detailed view of the interaction models adopted, the levels of control offered, the adaptability of the tools, and their implications for the user experience. These findings can assist designers, developers, and researchers identify recurring patterns and gaps in the interactive design of GenAI systems, contributing to more grounded evaluations and user-centered improvements.

This paper is organized as follows: Sect. 2 presents the related work. Section 3 outlines the methodology used to carry out the mapping. Section 4 presents the results. Section 5 addresses the discussion. Finally, Sect. 6 provides conclusions and future work.

## 2 Related Works

Recent research reveals significant progress in evaluating GenAI tools from the Human-Computer Interaction (HCI) perspective. Studies have explored topics ranging from interaction taxonomies to performance benchmarks, emphasizing the importance of considering aspects such as usability, user experience, and human-centered design.

For example, Shi et al. [14] proposed a taxonomy to categorize HCI-GenAI by analyzing 291 papers published between 2013 and 2024. The study classifies interactions based on user control, feedback type, level of engagement, and application domain, contributing a broad overview of how these interactions have been conceived. However, the authors do not conduct direct comparisons between public tools or address practical characteristics such as accessibility, support, personalization, or technical architecture.

In another study, Yetistiren et al. [17] conducted an empirical comparison of GitHub Copilot, Amazon CodeWhisperer, and ChatGPT in terms of code quality, using the HumanEval benchmark. ChatGPT achieved the highest performance (65.2% accuracy), followed by Copilot (46.3%) and CodeWhisperer (31.1%). Despite its technical focus, the study provides a replicable quantitative benchmark useful for broader analyses of the practical effectiveness of GenAI tools. Catchpoint [3] conducted a technical evaluation of GenAI tools such as ChatGPT, Google Gemini, Watsonx.ai, and H2O.ai, considering metrics like response time and authentication. Although technically focused, the study complements user experience benchmarks by highlighting relevant performance differences between platforms. In contrast to the technical approaches of Catchpoint [3] and Yetiştiren et al. [17], Borović et al. [6] conducted a comparative study on the applicability of GenAI tools in educational contexts, evaluating them based on criteria including accuracy, empathy, and response speed.

While technical benchmarks offer performance metrics, other research adopts deep user-centered evaluation methodologies, though often with a narrower scope. For example, Calisto et al. [8] investigated how personalizing the communication tone of an AI agent (assertive vs. non-assertive) impacts the performance and receptiveness of clinicians with different experience levels. Through a detailed study with 52 clinicians, the research offers a deep empirical evaluation of a specific facet of interaction but does not provide a broad view of the features available across a diverse set of GenAI tools. In a complementary manner, Li et al. [12] employed a qualitative methodology, through interviews with User Experience Design (UXD) professionals, to capture the complexity of the subjective experience, including perceptions, fears, and expectations about the impact of GenAI on creative practice. While fundamental for understanding human dimensions, this type of study does not focus on a systematic mapping of the tools' interactive capabilities. The very design of a system with a strong HCI foundation, as detailed by Calisto in his thesis [7], demonstrates the complexity of a User-Centered Design (UCD) process, which involves iterative prototyping, interviews, and observations to develop a single robust application—an unfeasible approach for a broad comparative analysis of multiple existing platforms.

Finally, complementing these perspectives, the AI Index Report 2025 [13], coordinated by Stanford HAI, represents a large-scale benchmarking initiative that tracks the evolution of GenAI with a technical, economic, and geographic focus. The report analyzes generative models based on metrics such as technical performance, inference cost, energy efficiency, and regulatory impacts. Notably, it states that 90% of notable models released in 2024 were produced by industry, while open-source models reduced their performance gap to just 1.7% compared to closed-source models. In terms of adoption, GenAI usage in business functions increased from 33% in 2023 to 71% in 2024, indicating rapid integration into corporate contexts. Although the report does not focus directly on user experience or HCI, it provides valuable contextual insights into the technical and institutional ecosystem in which these tools are embedded.

The literature, therefore, reveals a spectrum of approaches: on one end, large-scale technical benchmarks that often overlook HCI aspects; on the other, deep qualitative and usability studies that, while human-centered, focus on a single aspect of interaction or a specific user group. Despite the advances described, there remains a gap for a comprehensive analysis that bridges these approaches by providing a structured, comparative overview of the interactive features available across a wide range of tools. This work aims to fill that gap by proposing a structured feature mapping centered on HCI. The goal is not to conduct in-depth usability tests, but rather to systematically catalog and compare the features that reflect the complexity of real-world use, offering an overview that can guide future, more specific evaluations and user-centered improvements.

## 3 Methodology

The benchmark was carried out in three stages: (1) Planning; (2) Execution; and (3) Analysis.

In stage (1) Planning, strategies were defined to achieve the objectives of the feature mapping and to determine which characteristics would be analyzed in the tools. The adopted strategies included: i) the selection of which GenAI tools were evaluated; and ii) the definition of which comparison characteristics were analyzed. For i) the selection of tools, two criteria were used: The first criterion was the presence of generation models in the data presented by the AI Index Report 2025 [13], which indicates high relevance. The second criterion was the popularity of the tools in 2024, according to the AI Tools portal [4], which evaluated solutions based on access volume, engagement, and user reviews. This approach enabled the integration of both the technical perspective and real-world usage. Only tools developed and provided by the company responsible for the base model were included to define the scope. This restriction aimed to avoid redundancies caused by the proliferation of third-party applications based on identical underlying models, which could compromise the objectivity of the analysis.

For ii) the definition of comparison characteristics, seven evaluation perspectives inspired by HCI foundations were listed, namely: 1) Registration, Access and Commercial Resources Registration barriers were analyzed based on the Technology Acceptance Model (TAM), which emphasizes perceived usefulness and ease of use as key drivers of technology adoption [10]. Additionally, this category evaluates the subscription model, commercial API availability, among others. 2) Interaction considers the types proposed by Hornbæk and Oulasvirta [11] (dialogue, transmission, tool use, optimal behavior, embodied action, experience, and control), as well as interface styles described by Uzegbu [16] (graphical interfaces, touch, command line, voice, natural interfaces, and multimodal interfaces). 3) Functionalities and technical features evaluates issues such as available platforms, supported languages, among others. 4) Input/output types assesses the accepted input types and export possibilities. 5) User Support, Personalization and Adaptation related to Nielsen's heuristics [1], which include help and documentation as essential elements for reducing the learning curve and supporting usage in unfamiliar tasks. In parallel, personalization evaluates the tool's ability to recall previous interactions, which is related to transactional memory, essential for maintaining coherent dialogues in conversational systems [9]. 6) Transparency and trustworthiness aligned with the FATE (Fairness, Accountability, Transparency, Ethics) framework proposed by Microsoft Research [2] to assess the sociotechnical impacts of AI systems. Finally, 7) Collaboration analyzes cooperative usage features such as shared viewing and editing.

In stage (2) Execution, the evaluation of each tool was conducted by the first author, who acted as the primary evaluator. This process involved systematic manual testing of the functionalities and analysis of the official documentation, with the results being rigorously recorded in the standardized checklist defined in the planning stage. To mitigate the bias of a single evaluator and ensure consistency in the application of the criteria, the second author acted as a reviewer in a peer-review process. After the primary author's evaluation of each tool, the results were submitted for review by the second author. This review consisted of validating the findings, questioning interpretations, and ensuring that the application of the criteria was aligned with the definitions established in the planning phase. Ambiguities or disagreements were resolved through discussion and joint re-evaluation of the feature in question until a consensus was reached.

Finally, in stage (3) Analysis, the consolidated and validated data from the checklist were used to perform the comparative analysis among the tools. The results were then structured to identify patterns, highlight the most and least common features, and extract the insights presented in this study. This two-step process of evaluation and review was implemented to reinforce the rigor, objectivity, and reproducibility of the feature mapping.

## 4 Results

The Feature Mapping was conducted based on 15 GenAI tools, all in their publicly available versions for use in Brazil. Table 1 presents the tools included in this study. In this Table, the tools were numbered from 1 to 15.

Regarding registration, access, and commercial resources, 40% of the tools (2) Gemini, (4) ChatGPT, (5) Grok, (12) Pi, (8) Le Chat, (14) Meta AI allow some level of use without requiring user registration. However, this access is typically limited in terms of functionality. The remaining 60% of the tools require mandatory registration for any use.

**Table 1.** Generative AI Tools Analyzed

| (1) Character AI | (2) Gemini | (3) Midjourney | (4) ChatGPT | (5) Grok |
|---|---|---|---|---|
| (6) Stable Assistant | (7) Claude | (8) Le Chat | (9) RunwayML | (10) DeepSeek |
| (11) Leonardo AI | (12) Pi | (13) ElevenLabs | (14) Meta AI | (15) Wordtune |

Regarding user restrictions, 93% of the tools explicitly impose age limitations, generally requiring users to be at least 18 or 13 years old with parental consent. Only one tool (15) Wordtune does not specify its age policy. Regarding access models, one tool (3) Midjourney, does not offer a free version or trial period. Conversely, 13% of the tools, (14) Meta AI and (12) Pi, are free for personal use. Expanding the analysis to commercial features, 87% of the tools provide APIs for integration with third-party systems, except Midjourney and Character AI, which do not offer an official public API. This approach of providing facilitated initial access points to a dominant 'freemium' business model, which aims to reduce the barrier to entry and encourage user experimentation, aligning with principles of technology adoption.

Based on this theoretical framework [11], each tool was classified according to its predominant interaction concept(s), considering its intended use and the

**Table 2.** AI Tools Analyzed

| AI | Interaction Concept(s) and Explanation |
|---|---|
| c.ai | **Dialogue, Experience.** Focus on natural and engaging conversations with virtual characters to foster emotional bonds and immersive experiences |
| | **Dialogue, Transmission, Tool use.** Multimodal interaction (text, image, audio) as a creative and consulting tool, with real-time responses. |
| | **Tool use, Control, Experience.** Image creation through prompts, iterative refinement of results, and aesthetic and creative experience. |
| | **Dialogue, Transmission.** Fluid conversation, answering questions, explanations, and supporting various tasks in natural language. |
| | **Dialogue, Transmission.** Conversational chatbot with real-time information access and an informal tone, prioritizing fast and up-to-date responses. |
| S. | **Tool use, Control.** Tool for creating and editing images, videos, audio, and 3D, focusing on creative manipulation and user adjustments |
| | **Dialogue, Transmission.** Natural language conversation, text summarization, decision support, with a focus on safety and ethics. |
| | **Dialogue, Transmission.** Conversational assistant with web access, fast responses, and document analysis, combining dialogue and information delivery. |
| | **Tool use, Control.** Platform for creating and editing videos and images, with collaborative features and iterative adjustments. |
| | **Dialogue, Transmission, Control.** Generative AI for content and code, showing step-by-step reasoning, allowing response tracking and refinement. |
| | **Tool use, Control.** Versatile platform for creating AI solutions, integrating with other services, creative manipulation, and personalized adjustments. |
| Pi | **Dialogue, Experience.** Personal assistant with a strong emphasis on empathy, emotional support, and a humanized conversational experience. |
| | **Tool use, Control.** Personalized synthetic voice generation, with detailed vocal attribute adjustments, focusing on creative audio manipulation. |
| O | **Dialogue, Transmission.** Virtual assistant integrated with social platforms, natural language interaction, and fast, personalized responses. |
| | **Tool use, Control.** Assisted writing tool that suggests real-time improvements and allows text and tone adjustments. |

type of user engagement it promotes. Table 2 presents the classification of the analyzed GenAI tools based on each tool's use case and the interaction style it fosters. An analysis of Table 2 reveals a bifurcation in interaction models: conversational tools like Gemini and Claude prioritize 'Dialogue', while creative tools like Midjourney and Leonardo AI focus on 'Tool use' and 'Control', showing how the tool's purpose dictates its interactive paradigm.

Based on the interface styles described by Uzegbu [16], 100% of the analyzed tools offer graphical user interfaces (GUIs), while approximately 93% also support touch interaction, usually through mobile applications. The ubiquity of GUIs and touch support demonstrates a market convergence towards user-friendly paradigms, prioritizing accessibility for a broad audience over niche interfaces. Multimodality, understood here as the dynamic integration of different modes of interaction (text, image, audio, and voice) within a continuous interaction flow [15] is present in about 67% of the tools, such as (2) Gemini, (4) ChatGPT, (7) Claude, (5) Grok, (8) Le Chat, (9) RunwayML, (6) Stable Assistant, Pi, ElevenLabs, and Meta AI. Users can switch freely between modalities in these platforms while maintaining the interaction context. Voice user interface (VUI) support appears in 53% of the platforms. In summary, most solutions already incorporate integrated multimodal experiences, while one-third still limit users to segmented interactions, highlighting that full multimodality remains a competitive differentiator in the GenAI ecosystem.

Regarding technical functionalities, all analyzed tools are available via web browser, and 93% also offer mobile versions, either through native apps or responsive interfaces, and only tool (6) Stable Assistant is available exclusively on the web. Only two tools ((4) ChatGPT and (7) Claude) provide dedicated desktop versions (Windows/macOS). Regarding language support, about 46% of the tools offer multilingual interfaces, including Character AI, Gemini, Grok, Le Chat, Meta AI, ChatGPT, and Claude, while the remaining operate in English. For interaction, only 20% do not offer multi-language tools such as Stable Assistant, Wordtune, and Midjourney. Concerning access to real-time information, approximately 47% of the tools ((3) Midjourney, (2) Gemini, (5) Grok, (8) Le Chat, (10) DeepSeek, (14) Meta AI, (4) ChatGPT, (7) Claude) are integrated with web search engines, enhancing their ability to provide up-to-date and context-aware responses. This division in access to real-time information represents a critical functional differentiator, separating the tools into 'closed-world' models and dynamic interfaces to current knowledge, which has direct implications for their suitability for fact-based tasks.

The input and output modalities analysis reveals a diverse and expanding set of interaction capabilities among GenAI tools. While text is the dominant modality, many platforms already integrate multimodal capabilities. Table 3 visually details this flow of modalities. The diagram illustrates how text input functions as a universal gateway that branches out to generate various outputs, such as text and images, while more specialized inputs like video and documents are supported by a smaller subset of platforms.

**Table 3.** Input and output modalities

| AI | Input(s) | Output(s) |
|---|---|---|
| c.ai | Text, Audio | Text, Audio |
| | Text, Image, Audio, Video, Document | Text, Image, Audio, Video |
| | Text, Image | Image |
| | Text, Image, Audio, Video, Document | Text, Image, Audio, Vídeo, Document |
| | Text, Image, Audio, Document | Text, Image, Audio, Document |
| S. | Text, Image | Image, Audio, Vídeo |
| | Text, Image, Audio, Document | Text, Image, Document |
| | Text, Image, Document | Text, Image, Document |
| R | Text, Image, Audio | Image, Audio, Vídeo |
| | Text, Image, Document | Text, Document |
| | Text, Image | Image, Vídeo |
| Pi | Text, Audio | Text, Audio |
| | Text, Audio | Text, Audio, Vídeo |
| O | Text | Text, Image |
| | Text | Text |

Regarding user support, 100% of the tools offer some tutorial or documentation. About 80% allow users to customize the response style or tone. Additionally, 73% provide real-time feedback options, such as thumbs-up or similar mechanisms for evaluating responses. Tools that do not offer this feature include: (1) Character AI, (6) Stable Assistant, (12) Pi, and (13) ElevenLabs.

Collaboration features are still limited among GenAI tools. About 12 out of 15 tools (80%) offer shared viewing of generated content, including (1) Character AI, (2) Gemini, (3) Midjourney, (4) ChatGPT, (5) Grok, (6) Stable Assistant, (7) Claude, (8) Le Chat, (9) RunwayML, (11) Leonardo AI, (13) ElevenLabs, and (14) Meta AI. In terms of real-time editing, only one tool (7%), ChatGPT, supports full or partial collaborative editing features.

Although collaborative interaction demonstrably enhances productivity, creativity, and learning outcomes, current GenAI platforms primarily focus on individual use cases, revealing a significant gap for UX innovation in mediating human collaboration, not just human-machine interaction.

## 5 Discussion

The results of this mapping reveal a rapidly evolving GenAI tool ecosystem, with emerging patterns of interaction and functionality, as well as significant gaps in areas like collaboration and advanced personalization. While most tools already offer intuitive graphical interfaces and support for multimodal input, only 7%

enable full collaborative editing features, indicating a potential area for future development.

This comparative analysis highlights that, despite the substantial technical progress documented by the AI Index Report 2025 [1], the user experience dimension in GenAI tools still presents unexplored opportunities. As noted by Amershi et al. [17], user-centered design for AI systems requires special consideration of users' needs in real-world contexts, suggesting that GenAI tool developers need to go beyond merely implementing technical capabilities to create truly effective and satisfying interaction experiences. The findings of this mapping provide a structured foundation to guide future improvements in the interaction design of GenAI systems, prioritizing not only technical performance but also the quality of the human-computer experience.

The mapping identified significant gaps, most notably the lack of real-time collaboration, as only 7% of tools offer collaborative editing, distancing them from modern cooperative work practices. Furthermore, the analysis revealed limited transparency in data usage and source citation, reflecting the "black-box" nature of many models. To address these issues, future HCI research should focus on mitigating risks such as biases and "hallucinations." This includes developing methods to audit for data bias, designing hybrid systems that ground generative outputs in verifiable knowledge bases, and exploring interaction models that empower users as active "curators" of the AI's knowledge, thus fostering more trustworthy and genuinely collaborative systems.

## 6 Conclusion and Future Works

The Feature Mapping developed in this study contributes to a structured understanding of the current landscape of generative AI tools from a Human-Computer Interaction perspective. By systematically comparing 15 publicly available platforms, the analysis identified common design approaches, such as the widespread use of graphical interfaces and the growing presence of multimodal interaction, as well as notable gaps, including limited collaborative editing features and inconsistent transparency regarding data usage. In accordance with ethical HCI practices, this evaluation focused strictly on publicly available functionalities and documentation. This approach ensured that no personal or sensitive data from researchers or third parties was used, input, or collected.

This work provides an empirical basis for future evaluations by mapping the presence of usability-related features across tools, such as help documentation, response customization, and memory of past interactions. It also shows that aspects like adaptability, transparency, and user support are unevenly distributed, even among technically advanced platforms.

Future research can expand this mapping by including a broader range of tools and applying the criteria to specific domains. Additionally, empirical studies with users are needed to assess how these features impact interaction quality in practice. Developing specific protocols for evaluating user experience and usability in GenAI contexts could also help standardize assessments and support more user-centered design processes. Furthermore, expanding this exploration beyond standalone conversational agents to include GenAI tools embedded within existing applications (writing assistants, creative tools, IDEs) would offer a more complete view of how GenAI is reshaping user interfaces across various domains.

# References

1. 10 Usability Heuristics for User Interface Design — nngroup.com. https://www.nngroup.com/articles/ten-usability-heuristics/. [Accessed 19 May 2025]
2. FATE: Fairness, Accountability, Transparency & Ethics in AI - Microsoft Research — microsoft.com. https://www.microsoft.com/en-us/research/theme/fate/. [Accessed 19 May 2025]
3. Gen AI Tool Performance Benchmark 2024 — catchpoint.com. https://www.catchpoint.com/learn/gen-ai-benchmark. [Accessed 19 May 2025]
4. Most Popular AI Tools: Top 100 Rankings, Year 2024 — aitools.xyz. https://aitools.xyz/popular-ai-tools/2024/. [Accessed 19 May 2025]
5. The state of AI: How organizations are rewiring to capture value — mckinsey.com. https://www.mckinsey.com/capabilities/quantumblack/our-insights/the-state-of-ai 19 May 2025]
6. Borović, F., Aleksić-Maslać, K., Vranešić, P.: Comparative analysis of generative AI tools in enhancing educational engagement. In: 2024 47th MIPRO ICT and Electronics Convention (MIPRO),pp. 514–519 (2024)
7. Calisto, F.M.: Medical Imaging Multimodality Breast Cancer Diagnosis User Interface. Ph.D. Thesis (2017). https://doi.org/10.13140/RG.2.2.15187.02084
8. Calisto, F.M., et al.: Assertiveness-based agent communication for a personalized medicine on medical imaging diagnosis. In: Proceedings of the 2023 CHI Conference on Human Factors in Computing Systems. CHI '23, Association for Computing Machinery, New York, NY, USA (2023). https://doi.org/10.1145/3544548.3580682
9. Carston, R.: Herbert h. clark, using language. cambridge: Cambridge university Press, 1996. pp. xi+ 432. J. Ling. **35**(1), 167–222 (1999)
10. Davis, F.D., et al.: Technology acceptance model: tam. Al-Suqri, MN, Al-Aufi, AS: Info. Seeking Behav. Technol. Adopt. **205**(219), 5 (1989)
11. Hornbæk, K., Oulasvirta, A.: What is interaction? In: Proceedings of the 2017 CHI Conference on Human Factors in Computing Systems, pp. 5040–5052. CHI '17, Association for Computing Machinery, New York, NY, USA (2017). https://doi.org/10.1145/3025453.3025765
12. Li, J., Cao, H., Lin, L., Hou, Y., Zhu, R., El Ali, A.: User experience design professionals' perceptions of generative artificial intelligence. In: Proceedings of the 2024 CHI Conference on Human Factors in Computing Systems. CHI '24, Association for Computing Machinery, New York, NY, USA (2024). https://doi.org/10.1145/3613904.3642114
13. Maslej, N., et al.: Artificial intelligence index report 2025 (2025)
14. Shi, J., Jain, R., Doh, H., Suzuki, R., Ramani, K.: An HCI-centric survey and taxonomy of human-generative-AI interactions. arXiv preprint arXiv:2310.07127 (2023)
15. Sofian, H., Yunus, N.A.M., Ahmad, R.: Systematic mapping: artificial intelligence techniques in software engineering. IEEE Access **10**, 51021–51040 (2022). https://doi.org/10.1109/ACCESS.2022.3174115

16. Uzegbu, C.: Interaction in HCI: Principles, types, and examples - LogRocket Blog — blog.logrocket.com. https://blog.logrocket.com/ux-design/interaction-hci-principles-types-examples/, [Accessed 19 May 2025]
17. Yetistiren, B., Özsoy, I., Ayerdem, M., Tüzün, E.: Evaluating the code quality of AI-assisted code generation tools: an empirical study on Github Copilot, Amazon Codewhisperer, and Chatgpt. arxiv preprint arxiv: 2304.10778. 2023. arXiv preprint arXiv:2304.10778 (2023)

# Eliciting Multimodal Approaches for Machine Learning–Assisted Photobook Creation

Sara-Jane Bittner[1]([✉]), Michael Barz[1,2], and Daniel Sonntag[1,2]

[1] German Research Center for Artificial Intelligence (DFKI), Kaiserslautern, Germany
{sara-jane.bittner,michael.barz,daniel.sonntag}@dfki.de
[2] University of Oldenburg, Oldenburg, Germany

**Abstract.** Machine learning (ML) is increasingly applied in various end-user applications. To provide successful human-AI collaboration, co-creation for Interactive Machine Learning (IML) has become a growing topic, iteratively fusing the human creative view with the algorithmic strength to diverge ideas. Interactive photobook creation represents an ideal use case to investigate ML co-creation as it covers a range of typical ML tasks, like image retrieval, caption generation and layout generation. However, existing solutions do not exploit the benefits of introducing multimodal interaction to co-creation. We propose common operations for IML tasks related to interactive photobook creation and conduct an elicitation study (N = 14) investigating which (combination of) modalities could well support these tasks. An open-ended questionnaire revealed how users imagine an ideal IML environment, focusing on device setup, key factors, and the utility of specific features. Our findings show that 1) enabling a wide variety of modalities allows for most intuitiinteractions, 2) Informing users about uncommon modalities opens up suitable modality choices, that are otherwise missed, and 3) Multimodal interactions represent a high consensus, when chosen by the users.

**Keywords:** multimodal interaction · elicitation · machine learning · IML · user study · co-creation · interaction design

## 1 Introduction

Machine learning (ML) is increasingly applied in a wide range of fields [12]. While ML models perform well in a range of applications, imperfect performance leads to users being unsatisfied and feeling reluctant to adapt the new technologies [17]. To match the model's performance the users' needs, it is crucial to enable a collaboration between the human view and the ML model. One promising approach is represented by interactive machine learning (IML), which has become a growing topic in the literature [30]: User input is used to retrain the model and improve the performance in following iterations [18]. In a further effort of fusing the human's point of view and algorithmic solutions, Artificial Intelligence

(AI) co-creation was introduced into research. Human-in-the-loop feedback is utilized in the collaborative human-AI process, in which the iterative creation of a human-centred artifact is set as an goal. Co-creation combines the strengths of humans - to act creatively and guide the process - with strengths of the ML - to explore possibilities and generate diverse artefacts [35,49].

A key aspect of IML and co-creation is the interaction with the system. While most solutions for IML present mouse and keyboard interaction [54], Multimodal-Multisensor-Interfaces (MMI) enable intuitive and novel ways for the user to participate in the co-creation process. Research explores a wide range of modalities for user interactions such as speech, touch, gesture, and eye tracking [40,50]. Including these interaction techniques can improve user experience and foster more dynamic, tailored feedback to the model, which then potentially improves model performance [24,32,58]. The selected modalities are especially important in IML co-creation as it influences the feedback characteristics, which directly impact the re-training of the model and the user experience.

One domain that represents a suitable testbed for co-creation and IML is photobook creation as it incorporates a set of complex ML tasks like image retrieval and selection, caption generation and designing of layout [44,47]. While some studies already address individual tasks for ML-assisted photobook creation [2,23,33], they do not explore it in the context of a co-creation framework. Additionally, current solutions do not exploit the novel and intuitive possibilities of multimodal approaches. This reveals a gap in research for comprehensive multimodal interaction for IML-supported photobook co-creation.

Our paper investigates how humans use multimodal interaction intuitively in the context of ML-supported co-creation. For this, we apply the use case of interactive photobook creation as it covers a range of IML tasks. We hypothesize that further advances in IML will not only be based on technological factors, but that interactions with IML systems will benefit from the implementation of multimodal approaches in regards of model performance and user experience. After investigating the literature on IML co-creation and multimodal approaches, we conducted an elicitation study. In this study, participants have two rounds to go through a list of common operations (so-called referents) for interactive photobook creation and propose interactions. The proposed interactions are used to identify suitable modalities and combinations of such. In the first round, participants suggest modalities intuitively based on their experience. In the second round, they are primed with a common list of technologies in Human-Computer Interaction (HCI). Additionally, a questionnaire about ideal ML-assisted photobook creation is conducted, focusing on device setup and key factors. Based on this, our work covers the following contributions:

- Proposing a set of common operations in IML for tasks in photobook co-creation such as image-, caption- and layout-related tasks.
- Investigating users's perception of the commonly used modalities in HCI and explore what modalities users find suitable for which IML co-creation task.
- Investigating the users' thoughts about an ideal ML-assisted co-creation focusing on device setup and key factors.

## 2 Related Work

The following section covers ML and the use of human-in-the-loop feedback for interactive human-AI collaboration. Additionally, literature on multimodal approaches and the positive effect on intelligent user interfaces is presented. Then, photobook co-creation is introduced as an use case that combines different ML-supported tasks. Finally, elicitation studies are explained as a method to investigate intuitive interaction and human perception towards modalities.

### 2.1 Machine Learning

In recent years, the application of ML has increased in various fields such as material sciences, or data analysis [12]. Although ML models are widely used, they are black boxes that offer limited transparency to users. Furthermore, they often demonstrate imperfections and inconsistencies in performance, which can lead to user dissatisfaction and reluctance to adapt these technologies [17]. To improve on these imperfections, it is essential to combine the algorithmic performance with the human point of view. One promising approach is IML: Compared to traditional ML approaches, which do not allow for user intervention, IML enables model updates in response to user input [1]. User interaction with the model is often handled through the integration of human-in-the-loop feedback, which was shown to enhance the model performance [30, 43], adapt models to a specific domain [51], or tailor it to specific user preferences and needs [60]. By empowering users to influence the model's behaviour through experimentation, IML facilitates an intuitive and dynamic approach to model refinement [1, 16].

This human-in-the-loop feedback is often given through traditional mouse and keyboard interactions [54]. For example, a study increased the accessibility of text generation and segmentation proposals for videos by creating automatic generations that could be adjusted with mouse selection [60]. Based on the growing importance of IML, it is relevant to investigate effective interactions to interact with the user and collect feedback for the model effectively.

With recent advances focusing on generative AI, the field of IML has been extended to focus on the collaborative process of humans and AI. While traditional research in IML centres on optimising models through iterative user feedback, newer advances investigate co-creation as a process to generate new, user-tailored artefacts. Within this process, humans and AI are positioned as equal partners in a dynamic and interactive process: Humans contribute intuition, guidance, and flexibility, while AI assists by exploring possibilities, generating diverse artefacts, and supporting iterative development; this collaboration empowers users to actively steer the creative process, leveraging AI to achieve outcomes that surpass what either could accomplish alone [35, 42, 49, 57].

### 2.2 Multimodal-Multisensor Interfaces

IML can be combined with MMI to enable intuitive and novel interaction approaches. MMI utilize various human senses and behavioral cues—such as speech, mid-air gestures, touch, controller and gaze—to enhance the interaction between user and system [40,50]. In the context of developing multimodal interaction design for ML-supported systems, the concept of Intelligent User Interfaces (IUI) was introduced [34]. They define IUI as "human-machine interfaces that aim to improve the efficiency, effectiveness, and naturalness of human-machine interaction by representing, reasoning, and acting on models of the user, domain, task, discourse, and media." A combination of HCI and advances in technology in a synergistic manner will lead to benefits for users. With that, it aligns with Jameson et al.'s metaphor of a *binocular view* [27]: It introduces the design of interactions and intelligent algorithms as a single design problem, in which both aspects should be considered simultaneously for successful development.

By incorporating multiple input modalities, MMI can improve flexibility [58], boost user satisfaction, and enhance task efficiency during model interaction [22], compared to traditional mouse-and-keyboard interactions. For example, multimodal interactions - like eye tracking gestures, and natural language - increase time efficiency and are effective for user satisfaction [22]. The impact of the selected modalities on the interaction is especially important in IML co-creation as it can influence the feedback characteristics, which directly impacts the retraining of the model and the user experience.

Researchers have investigated the effect of a range of MMI, including speech, eye tracking, controller, touch and mid-air gestures: *Speech-based interfaces* show two main benefits: Users experience a lower barrier to express their intent [3], and enable flexible, natural language interactions [13]. For example, integrating a multimodal approach in which users could specify and perform semantic image search tasks can enhance image retrieval [4]. The user provides natural language queries as well as positive and negative examples, and based on them, fitting images are retrieved. *Eye tracking* enables the user to engage with elements based on their gaze with hands-free, intuitive interactions [15,25]. Through that, assumptions about the intention and ongoing actions can be made. This can be important to indicate relevant context information for spoken feedback as humans fixate on an object just before they include a speech command [21]. The use of *gestures* represents an intuitive way to interact with a system [59]. It was applied in a range of applications as an interaction modality and can improve the user experience [24,32,36]. *Controllers* pose a similar function to gestures and can be used for navigation, interaction, and to provide context. Integrating multimodal, natural interaction methods into IML and co-creation processes has the potential to enhance the engagement, adaptability and flexibility of human-AI partnerships. However, IML remains largely confined to 2D interfaces and conventional input methods such as mouse and keyboard [54]. We are not aware of studies that investigate which modalities or combinations of such could be effective and are intuitive for human-in-the-loop co-creation with ML systems.

## 2.3 UseCase: Photobook Creation

The domain of photobook creation presents an opportunity to apply co-creation and IML due to its incorporation of complex ML tasks like image retrieval and selection, caption generation and designing of layout [44,47,48]. Although individual ML tasks have been investigated—such as image selection techniques [33], user-specific caption generation with iterative feedback [2], and multimodal interactions for person identification [23]—there's a lack of research within a co-creation framework. Existing solutions like PICANOVA[1], photobook.ai[2], and Journi[3] focus on automating the process towards a final product, but they lack the iterative and flexible nature of co-creation and are constrained by their commercial ties [8,19,29]. Additionally, most available solutions apply traditional mouse-and-keyboard interactions, not utilizing the indicated benefits of multimodal interaction for co-creation. This reveals a gap in research for comprehensive multimodal human-AI collaboration for IML-supported photobook co-creation. MMI can be utilized in various ways for co-creation tasks. For instance, combining speech and eye tracking could be used to indicate the objective of user reference for a caption-feedback: the user has an image in which their dog *Paula* is sitting in front of a lake. The system displays the caption *A dog sitting in front of a lake*, missing the context information of the dog's name. Then the user could fixate the dog and explain *This is my dog Paula*, which can then be processed and corrected by the system. Adapting to the specific user's context is especially relevant in photobook creation as important information can vary between users and the motivation of the photobook significantly [5].

### 2.4 Elicitation Studies

Elicitation studies have gained popularity for the design of natural interfaces and new symbol sets for the use of such [56]. They represent a method of participatory design in which the user group is actively involved in the design process to create a system that fits the user needs better [7,46]. In regards to elicitation, the immediate use of a system can be improved by increasing the guessability of the input that the system requires to execute a certain operation [24,55]. Early studies mainly focused on gesture elicitation [55,56]. However, newer advances tend to investigate multimodal interaction [24,36]. For example, Morris [36] investigated the use of gestures and speech for interacting with a web browser on a TV. The study highlighted how users would be open to using their TV for web browsing, and that multimodal synonyms should be implemented so that the user can decide which modality they would like to use for the interaction. Further, a study by Herbig et al. investigated the interaction of post-editing machine translation systems with 5 modalities ranging from mouse and keyboard to eye tracking and a combination of these [24].

To execute an elicitation, the participant gets a list of referents, which are common operations in the given system. For example, a referent for editing a caption could entail: *"Caption Location: The caption is to general. You want the caption to contain the specific place."* For each referent, the participant proposes one or several actions containing how they would achieve these referents [20].

---

[1] www.picanova.com.
[2] https://photobook.ai/.
[3] https://www.journiapp.com.

An elicitation study often contains two rounds: 2) An unbiased elicitation - in which the referents are iterated through without any additional information. 2) A biased follow-up, in which participants receive a list of modalities. That way, awareness is created for technologies that might be uncommon in the daily life of participants, and which they hence might overlook in the task. For each modality, an explanation is provided, and an example is given of how the modality could be used in an application. For example, speech is connected to voice assistance, and touch is connected to smartphone usage.

The participants are introduced to two rules before proposing actions: 1) The participants' suggestions are always acceptable - This rule enables intuitive and unlimited proposals [56] and 2) The system will recognize the participants' proposals correctly without any technical errors - This rule leads participants away from technical thinking to not let them be limited by current technical capabilities [38]. Further, potential biases need to be considered: The legacy bias describes that the user's previous experience with technology has an impact on their proposed actions [36]: Technologies that participants are more familiar with are proposed in higher number and are perceived more positively. In comparison, technologies that participants are less familiar with, could be missed, as participants potentially do not recall them as an option during proposals. Approaches to limit this bias include proposing in groups (*partners*), or proposing several actions (*production*) for one referent. Additionally, as applied in the biased elicitation *priming* the participant by introducing a set of technologies before the elicitation, can open up the participant's mind to unfamiliar technologies [36].

Different formalization strategies are applied for elicitation studies which differ in the amount of proposals per referent: For elicitations that only allow for one proposal per referent, the *agreement rate* - which indicates the consensus between participants - and *co-agreement rate* - which indicates how much agreement two referents share- are applied [36]. In our study, participants are encouraged to propose multiple interactions, aligning with the production strategy [24, 36]. Therefore, we apply the *max-consensus*, which represents the percentage of participants proposing the most popular proposal, and the *consensus-distinct-ratio*, which represents the percentage of distinct interactions for a given referent, when this interaction reached a threshold.

## 3 User Study on Interactive Photobook Co-Creation

We conducted a user study to investigate the users' perception on different modalities in co-creation and to explore which multimodal approaches might be effective for photobook editing in a human-AI collaboration. We aim to derive implications for multimodal interaction with ML systems, including ML tasks such as image selection, caption generation and layout design. An ethical approval was submitted and approved at the *DFKI Ethics Committee*. Participants were recruited through distributed flyers at photobook creation booths, or online through a mailing list. Participants were a minimum of 18 years old and had experience creating at least one photobook with a web or desktop service.

## 3.1 Study Plan

The following section introduces the study plan. For this, the participants, as well as the procedure with corresponding methods and measures, are introduced.

**Participants.** In total, 14 user participated in our user study, who were between 22 and 67 years old ($M=33$, $Std=9.60$). Nine participants are female (64%) and five participants are male (36%). They have created a minimum of one and a maximum of ten photobooks ($M=2.67$, $Std.=2.56$). The participants reported how familiar they are with 1) devices and 2) modalities in five categories: *Never, less than once per month, between once a week and once a month, a few times per week, almost every day*. First, the modalities included gestures, speech, eye tracking, controller, and touch. Participants are most familiar with touch, which was used by 13 out of 14 participants daily. The participants are least familiar with gestures and eye tracking. For each 10 of the participants reported to have *never used it*. Speech and controller were used in a medium range with some participants *never* or *rarely* using them and some participants using them *between once a week and once a month*. Second, the devices included computers, virtual reality (VR), situated screens and mobile handhelds such as tablets or smartphones. The participants were most familiar with the computer and handheld devices, with 13 of 14 participants that use them daily. However, participants were mainly unfamiliar with VR environments and situated screens: Seven out of 14 participants have *never* used VR and 13 out of 14 participants have *never* used a situated screen. Lastly, their self-assessed experience in creating photobooks averaged $M=3.5$ ($Std.=0.50$) on a scale from 1 (unexperienced) to 5 (very experienced), indicating they assume that they are quite experienced. In general, they assessed the creation of a photobook to be a rather easy task ($M=2.28$, $Std.=0.88$, 1 = very easy, 5 = very hard).

**Procedure.** First, participants filled out a consent form and received a briefing with the study context. Then, the study plan consisted of three steps: 1) An initial questionnaire consisting of questions about their prior photobook experience. 2) The elicitation task, which can be split into an unbiased and a biased elicitation. 3) A final questionnaire, that focuses on ideal photobook creation.

*1) Initial Questionnaire.* First, a questionnaire that covers the user's experience with photobook editing is filled out. It features pain and gain points, and motivation for photobook creation. Additionally, demographic data is gathered.

*2) Elicitation.* Similar to [24], we conducted a study with an unbiased and biased elicitation. Aligning with previous studies, we provided a non-interactive prototype, which is held simple to not limit the interaction space of the participants [24]. We used FIGMA to provide a low-fidelity version, which displayed a general photobook view (see Fig. 1). In the beginning participants were informed to extend the shown prototype by their own expectations of the system. Participants were able to express these during the proposals.

First, the participants are introduced to the concept of multimodal photobook creation. Corresponding to the common guidelines for elicitation studies, the participants were briefed that "their proposed interactions will be recognized and executed as they intended perfectly" and that they should "not propose mouse and keyboard interactions". While, traditional interaction with mouse and keyboard, might be efficient, our paper aims to explore AI co-creation in a novel interaction space, considering different modalities and combinations aligning with previous work [24,36]. After this, participants will go through a list of 14 referents, and will propose several actions for each. The referents represent common operations that are relevant for the process of photobook creation [20].

To derive referents, the process of photobook creation was analysed using four photobook services. Based on this, 14 common operations were defined. For each referent, a description was presented to the participant to ensure understanding, which can be seen in Table 1. The referents focus on three common ML tasks: Selection of images, creation of captions, and adjustment of the layout. The referents were adapted to the use case of ML co-creation, with the majority of referents posing the potential for AI collaboration. Referents one to five cover image-related tasks. For example, referent *4) image search* covers the retrieval of images based on the processing and with that gained understanding of the image space. Further, referents six to eleven cover caption-related tasks, and, referents 12–13 refer to layout-related tasks. In the context of ML co-creation, a majority of the referents focus on users changing the current photobook version via feedback to the system. In the study they are ordered based on a balanced Latin square. The participants are encouraged to propose more than on action per referent. This addresses the legacy bias, in which participants tend to propose interactions that they are familiar with [6,37].

After the unbiased elicitation, the second round represents a biased elicitation: Participants are introduced to a list of six modalities and their descriptions: Mouse and keyboard (MK), touch (T), mid-air gestures (G), speech (S), eye tracking (E) and controllers (C). Also, combinations of modalities were listed as combinations of the letters, such as *SE* for speech and eye tracking (See Table 4). With that, we introduce a priming strategy into the biased elicitation. This opens up the proposals to modalities that participants have not considered intuitively during the prior round of proposals [24]. To not limit the possible interaction space and enable participants to propose interactions intuitively, we decided to include a wide range of modalities, including modalities that are considered for more passive interaction such as eye-tracking [40]. For each modality, a description and an example video was shown, depicting how the modality can be used. A correct understanding of the modalities is crucial for an elicitation study. Previous approaches utilized mainly textual descriptions, in which the functionality of modalities might be hard to grasp [24]. Videos show the use in an interaction context, leading to a better understanding. If possible, the video corresponded to the use of the modality in daily life. For example, speech was connected to voice assistance and touch to smartphone usage. To make sure that participants had sufficient understanding of each modality, they were asked to propose an interaction per modality for an example referent. After this, participants went through the list of referents a second time, updating their proposals.

**Table 1.** Referents (*Ref*) of the elicitation study.

| Nr | Referent | Description |
|---|---|---|
| 1 | insert image | Add a picture at a specific location. |
| 2 | image selection | The system shows you an overview of images and you want to select some for the photobook |
| 3 | image alternatives | You want to get image alternatives to replace the current image. |
| 4 | image search | You want to replace the current image with another image. You know which picture you are looking for. |
| 5 | similar images | There is a better version of the current image (better crop, image definition). You want to replace the current image with it. |
| 6 | caption alternative | You want to display alternative captions and select one |
| 7 | caption style | The caption is too objective. You want a funnier caption. |
| 8 | caption context | The caption is too general. You want it to contain more contextual information. |
| 9 | caption location | The caption is too general. You want the caption to contain the specific place. |
| 10 | caption person | The caption is too general. You want it to contain a specific person that is in the image. |
| 11 | caption correction | The statement in the caption is incorrect. You would like to correct it. (*Example:* "A farm is surrounded by water" rather than "A castle is surrounded by water") |
| 12 | move elements | You want to move elements to another position on the page. |
| 13 | change image size | You want to change the size of an image. |
| 14 | change font size | You want to change the size of the caption. |

*3) Ideal Multimodal Photobook Creation* Finally, a second questionnaire is conducted to investigate how participants would picture multimodal photobook creation ideally. Hereby, they were asked how they imagined interactive photobook creation in different settings such as virtual reality (VR), situated screens, mobile applications and web or desktop applications. Further, they were asked how such a design would look, how they would rate the utility of features and components, and how they imagined interacting with them. As an analysis method for the questionnaire, a *reflexive thematic analysis* (RTA) was conducted. Braun and Clarke's analysis was first published in 2006 and has been widely validated to be a suitable method of qualitatively analysing data sets [9,10]. It was chosen based on the importance of reflexivity in qualitative studies. An *RTA* consists of 6 steps that are executed incrementally (See appendix 7). Lastly, participants were asked to rate how often they use the proposed modalities.

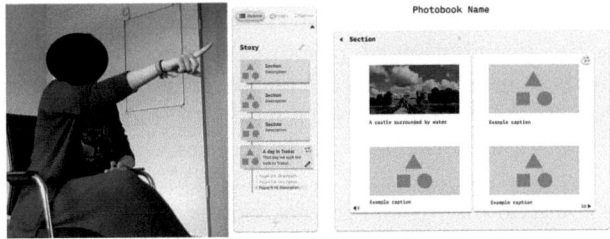

**Fig. 1.** Overview of the elicitation study displayed with re-enacted participant left and screenshot of the photobook mock up right.

## 3.2 Results

The results of our user study are presented below. 1) A overview of the proposed modalities that were utilized by participants is presented. 2) More detailed insights per proposed modality are given, focusing on the use of certain ML-supported tasks and in comparison of the unbiased and biased elicitation. 3) Insights into different setups for ML co-creation and highlighted key factors that were derived from the questionnaire are reported. Concerning data saturation, 14 participants suffices the amount to draw conclusions: 1) Regarding the elicitation task, a literature review reports 38% of elicitation studies to include in between 10 to 20 participants [53]. Thus, 14 participants, align with previous approaches and allow to draw conclusions about the proposed interactions [24]. This aligns with the assessment of the semi-structured interview as in the analysis new themes stopped emerging in responses.

**Elicitation.** In the unbiased elicitation, participants suggested a total of 172 common proposals. After the priming strategy was applied in the biased elicitation, that number increased by 39.5% to 240 common proposals. For both elicitation tasks, the most proposed modality was speech (unbiased:86, biased:91), followed by touch (unbiased:56, biased:71) and a combination of speech and touch (unbiased:20, biased:40). Also, during the biased elicitation, participants proposed gesture (17), speech combined with gesture (15) and eye tracking (6). For the unbiased elicitation, speech and touch seem to be similarly popular for image-related tasks, while speech seems to be preferred for caption-related tasks, and touch for layout tasks. After applying the priming strategy in the biased elicitation, not only speech was considered for caption-related tasks but also the combination of speech with 1) touch or 2) mid-air gestures. In general, after priming mid-air gestures show the highest increase of proposed interactions.

In the unbiased elicitation, 13.7% of proposals are multimodal, with the biased elicitation showing a small increase to 14.6%. While this is considerably higher than for Morris's [37] study (3.1%), it only reaches less than half of the amount of multimodal proposal compared to Herbig et al.'s [24] study (33.0%), who investigated multimodal approaches for post-editing in machine translation.

For each referent, the max-consensus ratio - the peak - and the consensus-distinct ratio - the distribution of proposals - were measured. Two different granularities for these measures were calculated: The ratios 1) overall modalities (All $C_m$, $C_d$), and 2) individually for each modality (modality $C_m$, $C_d$). In later, the ratios give indications of the different interactions proposed for one modality. For example, verbally commanding to add images via number ( *"Add image 1."*) versus verbally commanding to add images via description ( *"Add images with a sunset"*). For this study, only modalities that got $\geq 3$ proposals were included. The results can be seen for the unbiased elicitation in Tables 2 and 5 and for the biased elicitation in Tables 3 and 6. Tables 5 and 6 display extended results and can be found in the appendix. Regarding different modalities, *speech* shows the highest *max-consensus* and *consensus-distinct ratio* for caption-related and image-related tasks. For both unbiased and biased elicitation, referents with the overall highest ratio were the caption-related referents *caption alternatives*, changing *caption style* and *caption correction*, followed by the image-related referent *similar images*. However, after priming, speech was additionally proposed in combination with touch or mid-air gestures. For layout-related tasks, *touch* showed the highest measures for both rounds of elicitation.

**Table 2.** Unbiased Elicitation: Proposals per referent (Ref). Number of proposals (total and distinct), the percentage of multimodal proposals (MM%), and modalities suggested $\geq 3$ times

| Nr | Referent | Number (tot/dist) | MM% (tot/dist) | Common Proposals |
|---|---|---|---|---|
| 1 | insert image | 18/5 | 5.5/20 | T(8),S(4),ST(3) |
| 2 | image selection | 17/5 | 5.8/20 | T(9),S(4) |
| 3 | image alternatives | 14/4 | 0/0 | S(8),T(4) |
| 4 | image search | 18/8 | 22.2/50 | S(10) |
| 5 | similar images | 16/5 | 6.25/20 | S(9) |
| 6 | captions alternative | 17/7 | 17.6/42.8 | S(6),ST(4) |
| 7 | caption style | 14/4 | 14.2/50 | T(8),S(3) |
| 8 | caption context | 17/5 | 17.6/60 | S(11),ST(3) |
| 9 | caption location | 16/5 | 18.8/60 | S(9),ST(3) |
| 10 | caption person | 17/5 | 23.5/80 | S(9),ST(4) |
| 11 | caption correction | 15/6 | 26.7/66.7 | S(8),ST(3) |
| 12 | move elements | 16/5 | 6.2/20 | T(9),S(3) |
| 13 | change image size | 15/6 | 13.3/33.3 | T(9) |
| 14 | change font size | 14/5 | 14.3/40 | T(9) |

*Speech.* Participants showed a high experience with speech compared to other modalities, with 14.3% using it daily, 21.4% multiple times per week, and 28.6%

**Table 3.** Biased Elicitation: Proposals per referent (Ref). Number of proposals (total and distinct), the percentage of multimodal proposals (MM%), modalities suggested ≥ 3 times.

| Nr | Referent | Number (tot/dist) | MM% (tot/dist) | Common Proposals |
|---|---|---|---|---|
| 1 | insert image | 26/6 | 7.7/33.3 | T(11),S(4),ST(4),E(3) |
| 2 | image selection | 21/5 | 47.6/20 | T(11),S(4),G(3) |
| 3 | image alternatives | 19/6 | 5.3/16.7 | S(9),T(5) |
| 4 | image search | 21/7 | 14.2/42.9 | S(11),ST(4) |
| 5 | similar images | 20/5 | 5/20 | S(9),T(5),ST(3) |
| 6 | captions alternative | 24/6 | 12.5/50 | S(6),ST(6),SG(4),T(4),E(3) |
| 7 | caption style | 19/4 | 10.5/50 | S(8),T(4),ST(5) |
| 8 | caption context | 19/5 | 15.7/60 | S(11),ST(4) |
| 9 | caption location | 19/5 | 15.7/60 | S(9),ST(4),SG(4) |
| 10 | caption person | 21/5 | 19.0/80 | S(9),ST(5),SG(4) |
| 11 | caption correction | 21/6 | 19.0/67 | S(11),ST(4),SG(3) |
| 12 | move elements | 25/6 | 8/33 | T(11),G(6),S(3) |
| 13 | change image size | 22/7 | 13.6/42.9 | T(10),G(6) |
| 14 | change font size | 19/5 | 10.5/40 | T(10),G(5) |

at least once a month. In both rounds of elicitation, Speech was proposed for all referents other than the layout-related referents *13) change image size* and *14) change font size*. Speech was proposed in combination with a command and a specification. Two different strategies for co-creation can be distinguished: 1) Relying on the system's "intelligence" - the changes are left to the system choice. This includes requesting a new image with the specification of processed image data (P1: *"Show me similar images"* or prompting the system to consider metadata (P6: *"Please include the location in the caption"*). 2) Specifying the exact changes that the system should make. This includes specifying a description of an image (P4: *"Find me the picture of the beach with an ice cream"*) or commanding an edit of the new caption (*P12 "Insert: Maria in front of Trakai Castle"*)

For both rounds, the *max-consensus ratio* and *consensus-distinct ratio* are rather high. Regarding caption- and image-related tasks, the *consensus-consensus ratio* for the unbiased rounds showed slightly higher values with 75% for all but one referent. Compared to that, the biased elicitation indicates a little lower consensus over all referents featuring only speech (63.7% to 100%), which indicates that most people would use speech in a similar way. The *consensus-distinct ratio* for image- and caption-related tasks range from 0.33 to 1.00, indicating that while a few people deviate, the majority often choose similar speech interactions.

*Touch.* Participants were most familiar with using touch, with 100% reporting to use it daily. It represents the modality with the second-highest number of proposals in the unbiased and biased elicitation. It was mostly proposed for image- and layout-related tasks. For caption-related tasks, touch was only considered for referent *7) caption style*. The pointing touch-gesture was proposed most: Shortly pointing on an element indicates selection, while longer pointing initiated further interaction with a sub-menu. Also, a pointing touch-gesture was commonly used for drag and drop. Specifically for changing the size of elements for the layout tasks, two strategies were used: Pinching the index finger and thumb together and diagonally moving them apart or closing together, or selecting the corner of an element and dragging it to another size. Specifically, for font size, some people used touch to change the numerical value of the font size, as it is common in word editors. Most unity is shown for the referent *5) similar images* where all participants proposed to touch longer on an image to receive similar suggestions.

For both rounds, the *max-consensus ratio* is medium to high. Regarding image- and layout-related tasks, the unbiased rounds showed slightly lower values(50% to 87.5%) compared to the biased round (50% to 90.1%). This indicated a medium consensus of proposed touch interactions between the participants. The consensus-distinct ratio for the image-related tasks ranges widely for the unbiased (0.00 to 0.66) and biased elicitation(0.00 to 1.00), which indicates that participants used a wide variety of touch interactions. In comparison, the consensus-distinct ratio for the layout-related tasks ranges from 0.50 to 0.75 for both rounds of elicitation, indicating that while a few people deviate in proposed touch interactions, there is a fair overlap of similar intuitive interactions.

*Speech and Touch.* Participants were quite familiar with speech and touch as individual modalities (see the results of speech 3.2 and touch 3.2). For the unbiased elicitation, the combination of speech and touch (ST) was mainly used for caption-related (excluding referent *7) caption style*) and once for image-related tasks with referent *1 insert image*. However, in the biased elicitation the number of proposals for image-related tasks including ST increased. This combination was mostly proposed by participants who have suggested speech-only interactions in the unbiased elicitation. For both elicitations, the participants used mainly two approaches for ST interactions: 1) Pointing at the element and then specifying the aimed action with a command (P2:*Selecting an image to interact with a pointing touch-gesture + "That is the Castle XY"*)or switching the order (P3: *"Where is this castle?"+ pointing touch-gesture on the castle.*

For both rounds, the *max-consensus ratio* is medium to high. For the unbiased elicitation, the ratio for caption-related tasks reaches mainly 66.7% to 100%, while the values for the biased elicitation show slightly less consensus with 50% to 100%. Both results indicate that a fairly high number of participants use the combination ST in a similar way. Further, the consensus-distinct ratio shows a wide variety for unbiased (0.33 to 1.00) and biased elicitation (0.25 to 1.00), which indicates a higher variety in multimodal ST interactions.

*Mid-air Gesture.* Participants were not familiar with using mid-air gestures, with 71.4% reporting to have never used it and 28.6% using it less than once per month. Thus, they did not represent a common proposal in the unbiased elicitation. However, proposals increased after applying the priming strategy in the biased elicitation, especially for layout-related tasks. The proposed mid-air gesture interactions are similar to the proposed touch interactions with the pointing gesture or drag and drop to move elements. Also, changing the size of elements remained similar with a pinched index finger and thumb and moving them diagonally apart or dragging the corner of elements. Longer pointing decreased in proposals, as short pointing was commonly used to select elements and initiate further interaction. Mid-air input was reported to be less strenuous as P9 indicated: "Then I can simply sit here, without needing to go the screen").

The max-consensus ratio for layout tasks ranges from 50% to 83.3%, showing a slightly lower consensus than the touch interactions. The consensus-distinct ratio for these tasks ranges from 0.25 to 0.50, showing that a wider variety of mid-air interactions is proposed compared to touch interactions (0.50 to 0.75).

*Speech and Mid-Air Gesture.* Participants were not familiar with mid-air gestures (see mid-air gesture 3.2), but reported high familiarity with speech interactions (see speech 3.2). The combination of speech and gesture (SG) was only proposed in the biased elicitation and resembled the use of ST, with most proposals targeting caption-related tasks. The combination was mostly proposed as an addition by participants who already used ST as a multimodal combination in the unbiased elicitation. The approaches of participants show high similarity to the proposed ST interactions with initiating a verbal command that is then specified via mid-air gesture (P1: *"Add the word castle here instead of farm"* + *pointing mid-air-gesture on the castle*).

The max-consensus ratio for caption-related tasks reaches 50% to 100%, showing slightly higher consensus compared to touch interactions. The same tendency is shown in the slightly higher consensus-distinct ratio, which reaches from 0.50 to 1.00, showing that a majority uses mid-air gestures in a similar way.

*Eye Tracking.* Participants were not familiar with using eye tracking, with 71.4% reporting to have never used it and 28.6% using it less than once per month. Eye tracking was only proposed as a common modality in the biased elicitation for the two referents: *1) Insert image* and *6) caption alternative*.

For both referents, the max-consensus ratio is 66.7%, and the consensus-distinct ratio is 0.50, indicating that a majority would use eye-tracking in a similar way. Most participants suggested focusing on elements to initiate further interaction, get alternatives or select elements.

## 3.3 Ideal Multimodal Photobook Creation

In a questionnaire, we collected how participants imagined an human-AI collaboration. The analysis covers 1) different setups, and 2) how an ideal version of interactive photobook creation would look like.

*Setup and Environment.* Regarding the setup for an interactive photobook co-creation, participants showed a positive tendency towards situated screens, with 12 participants (85.7%) being in favor of them. They highlighted that the larger display helps to *have a good overview* (P12) and creates an *interactive experience* (P2,P7). Only one participant expressed that they would prefer another option *such as a tablet* (P5) for feasibility. Further, a VR setup showed split opinions: Nine participants (64%) showed enthusiasm to *turn[...] the creation of a photobook into an experience* (P2) and described it as *exciting* (P5,P6,P7,P11) and *fun* (P2,P6,P7). In comparison, five participants are sceptical, expressing that it *doesn't seem to make much sense [...]* to use a 3D environment (P10) or that it is *cumbersome* (P9). Regarding more common setups, a web setup was mostly seen positively by all participants, describing it as a *good* P(5) or even the *easiest* P(10) solution. This aligns with the high level of familiarity that participants recorded in the initial questionnaire. Two participants were more critical, focusing on the advantages of other setups such as *VR* (P4). The mobile application was least preferred, with nine participants (64%) expressing to reject this option. Participants highlighted the *small display* (P2,P4,P5, P6,P7,P8,P9,P10,P11) which leads to *clutter* and a *lack of clarity* (P2,P5,P8,P11).

*Co-Creation Process.* Three different themes were identified for the participants ideal photobook creation: The process should 1) be interactive and multimodal, 2) alternate between automatic and co-creation, and 3) adapt to user preferences.

For the first theme, nine participants (64.3%) expressed that they would like an *interactive tool* (P5) that feels *intuitive* (P3,P6) to use. Further, they would like to use a *combination* of modalities (P4,P4,P5). Most participants highlighted speech as the base and combined it with another modality such as touch, mid-air gestures and eye tracking (P2,P3,P4,P10,P13). They highlighted that the system should support multiple combinations of modalities to be used *easily* and *most intuitively* (P13). However, three participants showed hesitation towards speech and expressed to feel *uncomfortable using it when other people are around* (P14).

Regarding the second theme, eight (57.1%) participants expressed that they would prefer an interaction pattern in which parts are automatically created for them, which they can then adapt in a co-creation process. For example, P7 states *I think it would be quite good if the AI could do a lot of the work for you [...], so that you only have to make minor adjustments* aligning with P8 who describes the process as follows: *I import my photos. A few design questions are asked. Then, a photo book is automatically created that can be customized afterwards.* However, while some automation is preferred, interactive adaptation of the content by the user remains important. P6 states: *Not everything should be done for me, as I also enjoy designing.* While users enjoy needing less effort in engaging with the photobook system, they like to be part of the creation process.

Lastly, five participants (35.7%) expressed that the system should *learn[...] [their] preferences regarding the layout* (P1) and learn *[their] style* P(13). This links to the wish for photobooks to be created more automatically in the previous theme. Users want to *feel understood* (P14) by the system to reduce the effort and *reach [their] goal* faster (P13).

## 4 Discussion

We conducted an elicitation study to explore the user's perception of commonly used modalities in HCI and to investigate which modalities users find most suitable for ML-supported co-creation. Additionally, we investigated how users imagine an ideal IML environment.

Three themes emerged for an ideal ML-assisted co-creation: The process should 1) be interactive and multimodal - to foster an intuitive experience -, 2) alternate between automatic and co-creation - highlighting the need to reduce the workload of the process while maintaining personalization - 3) adapt to user preferences. Aligning with the preference for MMI in theme one, users highlighted situated screens as a suitable setup due its comprehensive overview and enhanced interactivity. Conversely, handheld devices were viewed as least ideal due to their small screen, which resulted in a lack of clarity.

In general, two approaches for human-AI collaboration could be identified throughout the elicitation: Participants either 1) trusted the system's *intelligence* to realize their request, or 2) specified the exact changes the system should realize. Less experience with AI corresponded with less trust into the system to realize their requests. This difference in trust of participants can be linked to two opposing biases in human-AI interaction that are discussed in the literature: While some users experience automation bias - over-reliance in the capabilities of the AI - other users are prone to algorithmic aversions - distrust into the AIs capabilities [45,52]. To enable a successful interaction, it is necessary to establish a correct-as-possible understanding of the capabilities and limits of the AI system for the user. This can be supported by explanations of the model behavior or additional data in the co-creation process [14,52]. Future work should thus investigate the impact of XAI methods and additional data on the users understanding of the AI system and their behavior in the co-creation process.

Regarding suitability for ML-assisted co-creation, our findings revealed that speech (S) and touch (T), or a combination of speech and touch (ST), support these tasks best. While the priming in the biased elicitation led to more proposals of uncommon modalities (like mid-air gestures (G)), the most proposed modalities remained the ones that participants were most familiar with [37].

Caption-related tasks were most supported by speech (S) and only showed a low number of proposals for touch (T). This low consideration could be based on the perceived difficulty of transferring language into touch data. Captions represent textual data which is closer to speech and, thus, might be easier for users to verbalize. In comparison, touch (T) or mid-air gestures (G) were mainly applied for layout- and image-related tasks. This could be based on the characteristic of touch to perform actions intuitively with direct manipulation. Transferring spatial information into a verbal expression might be more challenging for the user. This close transfer to spatial data led to layout-related tasks being best supported by touch (T) or mid-air gesture (G) interactions [61]. For image-related tasks, a wide range of modalities is suggested, allowing users to interact intuitively based on their prior experiences. However, the wide range of proposals might point towards problems in finding common modalities.

Further, multimodal suggestions were made in the form of a combination of speech-touch (ST) or speech-gestures (SG), as common for selection tasks [39],. However, the number of multimodal proposals remained low throughout the elicitation (unbiased:13.4%; biased 14.6%). This contradicts the questionnaire results, which reveal a preference for MMI with theme 1) *The process should be interactive and multimodal.* This finding aligns with indications that providing a multimodal system does not necessarily lead to multimodal interaction [39]. However, the preference for MMI could be due to the high max-consensus and consensus-distinct ratio for the combination of speech and touch (ST). A majority of people would use the combination of speech and touch (ST) in a similar manner when correcting captions, which makes it a suitable modality for ML co-creation. Multimodality was mainly proposed in combination with speech. It specified a verbal command with another modality like touch (T) or mid-air gestures (G). Pointing to an element enables precise corrections, leading to feedback iterations that are faster and contain more information.

Further, it is noticeable that while mid-air gestures (G) were not proposed intuitively in the unbiased elicitation, primed participants proposed mid-air gestures (G), or a combination of speech-gestures (SG) as an alternative to touch (T) or speech and touch (ST) proposals. While enabling multimodal interaction offers higher flexibility, this is only applicable if users are able to make good modality choices [40]. The low experience with gesture interfaces - as indicated in the questionnaire - could prevent the users from making this modality choice, even though it is considered a suitable option when the user is primed. Thus, implementing strategies to help users make better modality choices could help integrate modalities that could be suitable, but are not familiar to the users. One way to address this is the ASPECT and ARCADE Model [26]. ARCADE summarizes six strategies to help people make better modality choices: For example, *A* in ARCADE stands for *Access Information and Experience* and refers to the use of textual, auditive or graphical introductory tutorials. It should be investigated how introducing uncommon modalities with these strategies impacts the user's ability to make good modality choices. Additionally, most users that proposed the multimodal combination speech-touch (ST) in the unbiased round already, proposed the combination speech-gesture (SG) in the biased round. This could indicate that participants who are intuitively prone to use multimodal interactions are also more likely to explore less familiar multimodal interactions.

Eye tracking was only sparsely proposed for two referents in the biased elicitation. The low number of proposals could be tied back to the unfamiliarity of the users with the modality - with 71.4% reporting to never have used it before. Modalities, such as speech and touch, are familiar active modalities that are used consciously, while gaze represents a modality for which users are not used to form active interactions. Based on the foreground-background theory, interactions within a system should combine passive and active interaction [11,40]. Future research should explore how to combine passive gaze interaction and the modalities that were derived in this work within a foreground-background interaction system. Lastly, it stands out that interactions with controllers were not proposed during the elicitation study. This can be tied to the low amount of experience that participants showed as 42.9% never used controller before.

*Implications.* Based on the evaluation, we derived the following implications: 1) Enabling a wide variety of modalities allows for the most intuitive interactions. 2) Informing users about uncommon modalities opens up suitable modality choices, which are otherwise missed. 3) Multimodal interactions represent a high consensus when chosen by the users. 4) Automation and user-adaptation should be balanced in the creation process.

*Limitations and Future Work.* This paper investigates what modalities users find suitable for which IML task. However, the study was based on elicited proposals. Thus, all findings should be verified on a working prototype in future work. That way, it would be possible to completely compare the techniques, including potential technical limitations [24]. Further, this work indicates how to design interaction for co-creation processes, in which, one relevant aspect is the imperfect performance that the system can display towards the user. This mismatch of system results and user expectations can lead to 1) decreased user trust in the system [31,41], and 2) adapted user behaviour [40]. For example, an error-prone multimodal system can lead to a shift in the co-timing of user signals to clarify their behaviour to the system (e.g., hypertiming) [40]. Thus, future work should investigate the impact of imperfect performance in co-creation processes on trust and user behaviour, as well as explore strategies to handle model ambiguity in human-AI collaboration. One possible strategy is the use of Explainable Artificial Intelligence (XAI) to give insight into the model behaviour [28].

## 5 Conclusion

Our paper explored user's perceptions on modalities in HCI in the context of co-creation for ML tasks. Photobook creation was applied as a use case as it includes a variety if ML tasks like image-, caption-, and layout-related tasks. We suggested a list of 14 common operations for ML tasks and conducted an elicitation study with 14 participants. Additionally, through a questionnaire, we investigated how users imagine an ideal ML co-creation environment. Our findings indicate that 1) interaction and multimodality, 2) balance between automation and co-creation, and 3) adaptation to user preferences, represent relevant themes for co-creation. Even though multimodal proposals remained sparse in the elicitation, the participant's proposals of speech combined with touch or mid-air gestures showed high consensus between participants, matching the highlighted preference of MMI. The modalities speech and touch - either individually or combined, effectively support various tasks in ML co-creation. Caption-related tasks are best handled by speech, layout-related tasks are most effectively managed through touch or mid-air gestures, and image-related tasks, are supported by a variety of modalities. Thus, providing a system that covers multiple modalities enables users to interact intuitively based on their prior experiences. Finally, introducing uncommon modalities - such as mid-air gestures - to the user can open up suitable modality choices, that are otherwise missed.

**Acknowledgments.** This work was funded by the German Federal Ministry of Education and Research (BMBF) under grant numbers 01IW23002 (No-IDLE) and 01IW24006 (NoIDLEChatGPT), as well as by the Endowed Chair of Applied AI at the University of Oldenburg.

# A Appendix

## A.1 Briefing of Study Context

You would like to create a travel photo book from your last trip. To do this, you use a new system for creating a photo book digitally. The system is supported by AI and gives you the freedom to choose how you want to interact with it. All technologies are possible and whatever you have in mind - the photo book creation system will understand you and execute your input as intended. A photo book is created from your input. The study is a prototype that simulates the functionalities you will use. The prototype is kept simple by intention to give you an idea of the user interface but enable you to include own ideas and creativity.

## A.2 Priming Strategy List of Modalities

The following table displays the list of five modalities with corresponding descriptions which were shown to participants in a step of the priming strategy for the user study. After reading the content of this table participants first watched videos for each referent in which the interaction with the modality was shown. Then they were asked to propose interactions for an example referent to ensure that the participants understood the modality sufficiently.

**Table 4.** List of modalities and corresponding explanations for the priming strategy

| Modality | Description |
|---|---|
| Speech | The system will pick up your speech and understand your intended action. The system will then implement your command. |
| Eye Tracking | The system can monitor what you are looking at. For one, the system knows what you are referring to on the screen (photobook page, images, captions, chapter overview etc.). For another, it can interpret intended eye movements such as blinks or focusing on an element of the photobook. |
| Controller | The system will pick up where the controller is pointing at and you can interact with the systems by actions such as click, circle, drag or keep pressed, shake and more. |
| Mid-Air Gestures | The system will pick up your mid-air hand movements and understand your intended action. The system will then implement your command. |
| Touch | The system will pick up your hand movements on the screen and understand your intended action. The system will then implement your command. |

## A.3 Questionnaire

The following table displays the questions of the final questionnaire (Table 7). It contains 13 questions, divided into six categories: Current digital photobook creation, ideal photobook creation, ideal photobook creation setup, familiarity with modalities, experience with photobook creation and additional questions. It consists of open-ended questions and 5-point Likert scales (Fig. 2).

| Final Questionnaire – Ideal Interactive Photobook Creation | |
|---|---|
| **Question** | **Type** |
| *Current digital photobook creation* | |
| 1. What functionalities are you using now in digital photobook creation? | Open-ended question |
| 2. What did you like about creating a digital photobook? | |
| 3. What did you dislike about creating a digital photobook? | |
| 4. Based on your experience with the creation of digital photo books, what functions are you missing? | |
| *Ideal photobook creation* | |
| 5. Describe an ideal AI-assisted photobook creation. | Open-ended question |
| *Ideal photobook creation setup* | |
| 6. What do you think about creating a photobook on a situated screen (similar to the test scenario)? | Open-ended question |
| 7. What do you think about creating a photobook in virtual reality? | |
| 8. What do you think about creating a photobook in a mobile app? | |
| 9. What do you think about creating a photobook in a web/desktop app? | |
| *Familiarity with modalities* | |
| 10. How often do you use the following technologies? *(never, less than once per month, between once a week and once a month, a few times a week, almost every day)* <br> a. Computer/Laptop <br> b. Virtual Reality (VR) <br> c. Gesture Recognition <br> d. Speech Input <br> e. Gaze-Tracking <br> f. Controller (VR, Xbox, PlayStation, Wii) | 5-point Likert scale |
| *Experience with photobook creation* | |
| 11. On a scale of 1 to 5, how would you rate your experience with digital photobook creation? *(1 = very inexperienced, 5 = very experienced)* | 5-point Likert scale |
| 12. On a scale of 1 to 5, how complicated did you find creating digital photo books? *(1 = very simple, 5 = very complicated)* | |
| *In addition* | |
| 13. Is there anything you would like to add? | Open-ended question |

**Fig. 2.** Content of the final questionnaire including questions about ideal photobook creation

## A.4 Results

**Table 5. Unbiased Elicitation:** Proposals per referent (Ref) in the unbiased elicitation study - Extension. The max-consensus (Cm) and consensus-distinct (Cd, threshold = 2) ratios for all and the modalities suggested ≥ 3 times (S=Speech, T=Touch, XY=combination of X and Y, e.g. ST for speech and touch).

| Nr | Referent | All | | S | | T | | ST | |
|----|----------|-----|-----|-----|-----|-----|-----|-----|-----|
| | | $C_m$ | $C_d$ | $C_m$ | $C_d$ | $C_m$ | $C_d$ | $C_m$ | $C_d$ |
| 1 | insert image | 57.1 | 0.80 | 75 | 0.50 | 87.5 | 0.00 | 66.7 | 0.50 |
| 2 | image selection | 64.3 | 0.60 | 75 | 0.33 | 55.6 | 0.66 | - | - |
| 3 | image alternatives | 57.1 | 0.50 | 87.5 | 0.50 | 50 | 0.33 | - | - |
| 4 | image search | 71.4 | 0.12 | 80 | 1.00 | - | - | - | - |
| 5 | similar images | 64.3 | 0.80 | 88.9 | 0.66 | - | - | - | - |
| 6 | captions alternative | 42.9 | 0.57 | 100 | 1.00 | - | - | 100 | 1.00 |
| 7 | caption style | 57.1 | 0.75 | 100 | 1.00 | 66.6 | 1.00 | - | - |
| 8 | caption context | 78.6 | 0.4 | 63.6 | 0.75 | - | - | 66.7 | 0.50 |
| 9 | caption location | 64.3 | 0.6 | 88.9 | 1.00 | - | - | 66.7 | 0.50 |
| 10 | caption person | 64.3 | 0.6 | 88.9 | 0.50 | - | - | 75.0 | 0.33 |
| 11 | caption correction | 57.1 | 0.33 | 100 | 1.00 | - | - | 66.7 | 0.50 |
| 12 | move elements | 64.3 | 0.60 | 66.7 | 0.50 | 87.5 | 0.50 | - | - |
| 13 | change image size | 64.2 | 0.33 | - | - | 55.6 | 0.66 | - | - |
| 14 | change font size | 44.4 | 0.75 | - | - | 44.4 | 0.75 | - | - |

**Table 6. Biased Elicitation:** Proposals per referent (Ref) in the biased elicitation study - Extension. The max-consensus (Cm) and consensus-distinct (Cd, threshold = 2) ratios for all and the modalities suggested ≥ 3 times (S=Speech, T=Touch, G=Gesture, E=Eye, C= Controller, XY=combination of X and Y, e.g. ST for speech and touch).

| Nr | Referent | All | | S | | T | | G | | ST | | E | | SG | |
|----|----------|-----|-----|-----|-----|-----|-----|-----|-----|-----|-----|-----|-----|-----|-----|
| | | $C_m$ | $C_d$ | $C_m$ | $C_d$ | $C_m$ | $C_d$ | $C_m$ | $C_d$ | $C_m$ | $C_d$ | $C_m$ | $C_d$ | $C_m$ | $C_d$ |
| 1 | insert image | 78.6 | 1.0 | 75 | 0.50 | 81.8 | 0.0 | - | - | 75 | 0.50 | 66 | 0.5 | - | - |
| 2 | image selection | 78.6 | 0.80 | 75 | 0.33 | 54.5 | 0.66 | 66.7 | 0.33 | - | - | - | - | - | - |
| 3 | image alternatives | 64.3 | 0.5 | 77.8 | 1 | 60 | 0.33 | - | - | - | - | - | - | - | - |
| 4 | image search | 78.6 | 0.29 | 81.8 | 1 | - | - | - | - | 50 | 0.25 | - | - | - | - |
| 5 | similar images | 64.3 | 0.80 | 88.9 | 0.67 | 60 | 1 | - | - | 66.7 | 0.5 | - | - | - | - |
| 6 | captions alternative | 42.9 | 0.83 | 100 | 1.0 | 50 | 1.00 | - | - | 100 | 1 | 66.7 | 0.5 | 100 | 1.00 |
| 7 | caption style | 57.1 | 1 | 100 | 1 | 75 | 1 | - | - | 80 | 0.5 | - | - | - | - |
| 8 | caption context | 78.6 | 0.60 | 63.6 | 0.75 | - | - | - | - | 75 | 0.5 | - | - | - | - |
| 9 | caption location | 64.3 | 0.60 | 88.9 | 1.0 | - | - | - | - | 50 | 0 | - | - | 75 | 0.50 |
| 10 | caption person | 64.3 | 0.80 | 88.9 | 0.5 | - | - | - | - | 60 | 0.25 | - | - | 75 | 0.50 |
| 11 | caption correction | 78.6 | 0.50 | 100 | 1.00 | - | - | - | - | 50 | 0.3 | - | - | 66.7 | 0.5 |
| 12 | move elements | 78.6 | 0.83 | 66.7 | 0.5 | 90.1 | 0.50 | 50 | 0.25 | - | - | - | - | - | - |
| 13 | change image size | 71.4 | 0.42 | - | - | 60 | 0.67 | 83.3 | 0.50 | - | - | - | - | - | - |
| 14 | change font size | 71.4 | 0.0 | - | - | 50 | 0.75 | 80 | 0.5 | - | - | - | - | - | - |

## A.5 Analysis

**Table 7.** The 6 stages of the Reflexive Thematic Analysis by Braun et al.(2019) [10]

| Stage | Explanation |
|---|---|
| Familiarize | The researcher familiarize themselves with the data set. The questionnaire answers are read through several times. Additionally, notes are taken. |
| Coding | The data set is coded throughout several iterations to break the data into manageable content. |
| Generate Initial Themes | Patterns are explored through the re-grouping of codes. These form potential themes. |
| Reviewing and Developing Themes | The initial themes are checked if they hold the true meaning of the data set and then are further developed. This can include the splitting or fusion of themes. |
| Refining, Defining, and, Naming Themes | Themes are named. Moreover, the scope and concept of the themes are defined. |
| Producing the Report | The story of the data set is presented. This involved the themes, the definition of the themes, and examples of the data set as well as their interpretation. |

# References

1. Amershi, S., Cakmak, M., Knox, W.B., Kulesza, T.: Power to the people: the role of humans in interactive machine learning. AI Mag. **35**(4), 105–120 (2014). https://doi.org/10.1609/aimag.v35i4.2513, https://ojs.aaai.org/aimagazine/index.php/aimagazine/article/view/2513, number: 4
2. Anagnostopoulou, A., Hartmann, M., Sonntag, D.: Putting humans in the image captioning loop. arXiv preprint arXiv:2306.03476 (2023)
3. Aurisano, J., et al.: Show me data": observational study of a conversational interface in visual data exploration. In: IEEE VIS, vol. 15, p. 1 (2015)
4. Barnaby, C., Chen, Q., Wang, C., Dillig, I.: Photoscout: synthesis-powered multimodal image search. In: Proceedings of the CHI Conference on Human Factors in Computing Systems, pp. 1–15 (2024)
5. Barz, M., Sonntag, D.: Automatic visual attention detection for mobile eye tracking using pre-trained computer vision models and human gaze. Sensors **21**(12), 4143 (2021)
6. Beşevli, C., Buruk, O.T., Erkaya, M., Özcan, O.: Investigating the effects of legacy bias: user elicited gestures from the end users perspective. In: Proceedings of the 2018 ACM Conference Companion Publication on Designing Interactive Systems, pp. 277–281 (2018)
7. Bossen, C., Dindler, C., Iversen, O.S.: Evaluation in participatory design: a literature survey. In: Proceedings of the 14th Participatory Design Conference: Full papers-Volume 1, pp. 151–160 (2016)
8. Bown, O., Brown, A.R.: Interaction design for metacreative systems. New Direct. Third Wave Hum. Comput. Interact. Vol. 1 Technol. **1**, 67–87 (2018)
9. Braun, V., Clarke, V.: Thematic analysis. American Psychological Association (2012)

10. Braun, V., Clarke, V.: Reflecting on reflexive thematic analysis. Qualit. Res. Sport Exerc. Health **11**(4), 589–597 (2019)
11. Buxton, B.: Integrating the periphery & context: a new model of telematics. In: Graphics Interface, pp. 239–239. Canadian Information Processing Society (1995)
12. Choudhary, K., et al.: Recent advances and applications of deep learning methods in materials science. NPJ Comput. Mater. **8**(1), 59 (2022)
13. Cox, K., Grinter, R.E., Hibino, S.L., Jagadeesan, L.J., Mantilla, D.: A multi-modal natural language interface to an information visualization environment. Int. J. Speech Technol. **4**, 297–314 (2001)
14. De-Arteaga, M., Fogliato, R., Chouldechova, A.: A case for humans-in-the-loop: decisions in the presence of erroneous algorithmic scores. In: Proceedings of the 2020 CHI Conference on Human Factors in Computing Systems, pp. 1–12 (2020)
15. Duchowski, A.T.: Gaze-based interaction: a 30 year retrospective. Comput. Graph. **73**, 59–69 (2018). https://doi.org/10.1016/j.cag.2018.04.002, https://www.sciencedirect.com/science/article/pii/S0097849318300487
16. Dudley, J.J., Kristensson, P.O.: A review of user interface design for interactive machine learning. ACM Trans. Int. Intell. Syst. **8**(2), 1–37 (2018). https://doi.org/10.1145/3185517
17. Dzindolet, M.T., Peterson, S.A., Pomranky, R.A., Pierce, L.G., Beck, H.P.: The role of trust in automation reliance. Int. J. Hum Comput Stud. **58**(6), 697–718 (2003)
18. Fails, J.A., Olsen Jr, D.R.: Interactive machine learning. In: Proceedings of the 8th International Conference on Intelligent User Interfaces, pp. 39–45 (2003)
19. Gmeiner, F., Holstein, K., Martelaro, N.: Team learning as a lens for designing human-AI co-creative systems (2022). https://doi.org/10.48550/arXiv.2207.02996, https://arxiv.org/abs/2207.02996
20. Good, M.D., Whiteside, J.A., Wixon, D.R., Jones, S.J.: Building a user-derived interface. Commun. ACM **27**(10), 1032–1043 (1984)
21. Griffin, Z.M., Bock, K.: What the eyes say about speaking. Psychol. Sci. **11**(4), 274–279 (2000)
22. He, Z., Li, S., Song, Y., Cai, Z.: Towards building condition-based cross-modality intention-aware human-ai cooperation under vr environment. In: Proceedings of the CHI Conference on Human Factors in Computing Systems, pp. 1–13 (2024)
23. Henze, N., Boll, S.: Who's that girl? handheld augmented reality for printed photo books. In: Human-Computer Interaction–INTERACT 2011: 13th IFIP TC 13 International Conference, Lisbon, Portugal, September 5-9, 2011, Proceedings, Part III 13, pp. 134–151. Springer (2011)
24. Herbig, N., Pal, S., Van Genabith, J., Krüger, A.: Multi-modal approaches for post-editing machine translation. In: Proceedings of the 2019 CHI Conference on Human Factors in Computing Systems, pp. 1–11. ACM, Glasgow Scotland Uk (2019). https://doi.org/10.1145/3290605.3300461, https://dl.acm.org/doi/10.1145/3290605.3300461
25. Jacob, R.J.K.: What you look at is what you get: eye movement-based interaction techniques. In: Proceedings of the SIGCHI Conference on Human Factors in Computing Systems. pp. 11–18. CHI '90, Association for Computing Machinery, New York, NY, USA (1990). https://doi.org/10.1145/97243.97246, https://dl.acm.org/doi/10.1145/97243.97246
26. Jameson, A., Berendt, B., Gabrielli, S., Cena, F., Gena, C., Vernero, F., Reinecke, K., et al.: Choice architecture for human-computer interaction. Found. Trends® Hum. Comput. Interact. **7**(1–2), 1–235 (2014)

27. Jameson, A.D., Spaulding, A., Yorke-Smith, N.: Introduction to the special issue on "usable AI". AI Mag. **30**(4), 11–11 (2009)
28. Kadir, M.A., Mosavi, A., Sonntag, D.: Evaluation metrics for XAI: a review, taxonomy, and practical applications. In: 2023 IEEE 27th International Conference on Intelligent Engineering Systems (INES), pp. 000111–000124. IEEE (2023). https://ieeexplore.ieee.org/abstract/document/10297629/?casa_token=XOX77E8HqXoAAAAA:Yk_l1fc1QX3Ir-ehABucnIhxh-zYwd9Qyfj2ioLWs8m54WiiXC7gjBeN19N6kw8Lv4zGypr3-A
29. Kantosalo, A., Ravikumar, P.T., Grace, K., Takala, T.: Modalities, styles and strategies: an interaction framework for human-computer co-creativity. In: ICCC, pp. 57–64. International Conference on Computational Creativity, Online (2020)
30. Kath, H., Gouvêa, T.S., Sonntag, D.: A human-in-the-loop tool for annotating passive acoustic monitoring datasets. In: IJCAI, pp. 7140–7144 (2023)
31. Kocielnik, R., Amershi, S., Bennett, P.N.: Will you accept an imperfect AI? Exploring designs for adjusting end-user expectations of AI systems. In: Proceedings of the 2019 CHI Conference on Human Factors in Computing Systems, pp. 1–14 (2019)
32. Luo, Y., Yu, J., Liang, M., Wan, Y., Zhu, K., Santosa, S.S.: Emotion embodied: unveiling the expressive potential of single-hand gestures. In: Proceedings of the CHI Conference on Human Factors in Computing Systems, pp. 1–17 (2024)
33. Maszuhn, M., Abdenebaoui, L., Boll, S.: A user-centered approach for recognizing convenience images in personal photo collections. In: 2021 International Conference on Content-Based Multimedia Indexing (CBMI), pp. 1–4. IEEE (2021)
34. Maybury, M., Wahlster, W.: Readings in intelligent user interfaces. Morgan Kaufmann (1998)
35. McGuire, J., De Cremer, D., Van de Cruys, T.: Establishing the importance of co-creation and self-efficacy in creative collaboration with artificial intelligence. Sci. Rep. **14**(1), 18525 (2024). https://doi.org/10.1038/s41598-024-69423-2, https://www.nature.com/articles/s41598-024-69423-2, publisher: Nature Publishing Group
36. Morris, M.R.: Web on the wall: insights from a multimodal interaction elicitation study. In: Proceedings of the 2012 ACM International Conference on Interactive Tabletops and Surfaces, pp. 95–104. ACM, Cambridge Massachusetts USA (2012). https://doi.org/10.1145/2396636.2396651, https://dl.acm.org/doi/10.1145/2396636.2396651
37. Morris, M.R., Danielescu, A., Drucker, S., Fisher, D., Lee, B., schraefel, m.c., Wobbrock, J.O.: Reducing legacy bias in gesture elicitation studies. Interactions **21**(3), 40–45 (2014). https://doi.org/10.1145/2591689
38. Nielsen, M., Storring, M., Moeslund, T.B., Granum, E.: A procedure for developing intuitive and ergonomic gesture interfaces for man-machine interaction. Aalborg, Denmark (2003)
39. Oviatt, S.: Ten myths of multimodal interaction. Commun. ACM **42**(11), 74–81 (1999)
40. Oviatt, S., Schuller, B., Cohen, P.R., Sonntag, D., Potamianos, G., Krüger, A. (eds.): The Handbook of Multimodal-Multisensor Interfaces: Foundations, User Modeling, and Common Modality Combinations - Volume 1, vol. 14. Association for Computing Machinery and Morgan & Claypool (2017). https://doi.org/10.1145/3015783
41. Papenmeier, A., Kern, D., Englebienne, G., Seifert, C.: It's complicated: the relationship between user trust, model accuracy and explanations in AI. ACM Trans. Comput. Hum. Interact. (TOCHI) **29**(4), 1–33 (2022)

42. Rezwana, J., Maher, M.L.: Designing creative AI partners with COFI: a framework for modeling interaction in human-AI co-creative systems. ACM Trans. Comput. Hum. Interact. **30**(5), 1–28 (2023). https://doi.org/10.1145/3519026
43. van Rijn, P., Mertes, S., Janowski, K., Weitz, K., Jacoby, N., André, E.: Giving robots a voice: human-in-the-loop voice creation and open-ended labeling. In: Proceedings of the CHI Conference on Human Factors in Computing Systems, pp. 1–34 (2024)
44. Sandhaus, P., Thieme, S., Boll, S.: Processes of photo book production. Multimedia Syst. **14**, 351–357 (2008)
45. Schecter, A., Bogert, E., Lauharatanahirun, N.: Algorithmic appreciation or aversion? The moderating effects of uncertainty on algorithmic decision making. In: Extended Abstracts of the 2023 CHI Conference on Human Factors in Computing Systems, pp. 1–8 (2023)
46. Schuler, D., Namioka, A.: Participatory Design: Principles and Practices. CRC Press (Mar 1993), google-Books-ID: pWOEk6Sk4YkC
47. Sonntag, D., Barz, M., Gouvêa, T.: A look under the hood of the interactive deep learning enterprise (no-idle) (2024). https://arxiv.org/abs/2406.19054
48. Sonntag, D., Gouvea, T., Barz, M., Anagnostopoulou, A., Liang, S., Bittner, S.J., Scheurer, F.: The Interactive Deep Learning Enterprise (No-IDLE) meets ChatGPT. Tech. rep, German Research Center for AI (2024)
49. Talamo, M.: The Digital Revolution and the Art of Co-creation. In: Arbizzani, E., et al. (eds.) Technological Imagination in the Green and Digital Transition, pp. 27–35. Springer International Publishing, Cham (2023). https://doi.org/10.1007/978-3-031-29515-7_4
50. Turk, M.: Multimodal interaction: a review. Pattern Recogn. Lett. **36**, 189–195 (2014)
51. Tusfiqur, H.M., et al.: DRG-Net: interactive joint learning of multi-lesion segmentation and classification for diabetic retinopathy grading. arXiv preprint arXiv:2212.14615 (2022)
52. Vasconcelos, H., Jörke, M., Grunde-McLaughlin, M., Gerstenberg, T., Bernstein, M.S., Krishna, R.: Explanations can reduce overreliance on AI systems during decision-making. Proc. ACM Hum. Comput. Interact. **7**(CSCW1), 1–38 (2023)
53. Villarreal-Narvaez, S., Vanderdonckt, J., Vatavu, R.D., Wobbrock, J.O.: A systematic review of gesture elicitation studies: What can we learn from 216 studies? .In: Proceedings of the 2020 ACM Designing Interactive Systems Conference, pp. 855–872 (2020)
54. Wang, Z., Huang, Y., Song, D., Ma, L., Zhang, T.: Promptcharm: text-to-image generation through multi-modal prompting and refinement. In: Proceedings of the CHI Conference on Human Factors in Computing Systems, pp. 1–21 (2024)
55. Wobbrock, J.O., Aung, H.H., Rothrock, B., Myers, B.A.: Maximizing the guessability of symbolic input. In: CHI '05 Extended Abstracts on Human Factors in Computing Systems, pp. 1869–1872. CHI EA '05, Association for Computing Machinery, New York, NY, USA (2005). https://doi.org/10.1145/1056808.1057043
56. Wobbrock, J.O., Morris, M.R., Wilson, A.D.: User-defined gestures for surface computing. In: Proceedings of the SIGCHI Conference on Human Factors in Computing Systems, pp. 1083–1092. CHI '09, Association for Computing Machinery, New York, NY, USA (2009). https://doi.org/10.1145/1518701.1518866
57. Wu, Z., Ji, D., Yu, K., Zeng, X., Wu, D., Shidujaman, M.: AI Creativity and the Human-AI Co-creation Model. In: Kurosu, M. (ed.) Human-Computer Interaction. Theory, Methods and Tools. pp. 171–190. Springer International Publishing, Cham (2021). https://doi.org/10.1007/978-3-030-78462-1_13

58. Yang, J., et al.: Reactgenie: a development framework for complex multimodal interactions using large language models. In: Proceedings of the CHI Conference on Human Factors in Computing Systems, pp. 1–23 (2024)
59. Yasen, M., Jusoh, S.: A systematic review on hand gesture recognition techniques, challenges and applications. PeerJ Comput. Sci. **5**, e218 (2019)
60. Yuksel, B.F., et al.: Increasing video accessibility for visually impaired users with human-in-the-loop machine learning. In: Extended abstracts of the 2020 CHI Conference on Human Factors in Computing Systems, pp. 1–9 (2020)
61. Zhou, X., Williams, A.S., Ortega, F.R.: Eliciting multimodal gesture+ speech interactions in a multi-object augmented reality environment. In: Proceedings of the 28th ACM Symposium on Virtual Reality Software and Technology, pp. 1–10 (2022)

# Interaction Trace Analysis to Identify AI Competencies: Preliminary Results from a Pilot Project

Daniela Marques[1,2](✉) and Marcelo Morandini[1]

[1] University of São Paulo, São Paulo, Brazil
{mdaniela,m.morandini}@usp.br
[2] Federal Institute of São Paulo, São Paulo, Brazil
marquesdaniela@ifsp.edu.br

**Abstract.** Artificial Intelligence (AI), particularly generative AI (GenAI) tools like ChatGPT, has gained significant visibility in education due to its ability to simulate natural language interactions. While AI offers opportunities to enhance learning - such as personalized tutoring, research assistance, and code debugging - it also presents risks, including over-reliance, the spread of misinformation, and reduced development of critical thinking. To ensure ethical and effective use, students must develop AI literacy, which involves understanding how AI systems work, recognizing their limitations, and critically evaluating their outcomes. While existing researches rely on self-assessment questionnaires to identify AI competencies, this approach can be subject to bias and lacks insights into actual user behavior. To address this limitation, this research explores an alternative method by analyzing student interaction traces with ChatGPT, combined with self-assessment data, to identify AI competencies in an educational context. Interaction traces are defined as the entire history of interactions between students and the AI tool during the execution of a task. This paper presents the results of a pilot study involving undergraduate students in computer science-related courses. The analysis highlights discrepancies between self-perceived and demonstrated competencies, emphasizing the need for more practical assessment strategies. The results suggest that an understanding of AI competencies can be made more comprehensive if there is another form of assessment besides a self-assessment questionnaire, thus allowing students to improve themselves and become critical citizens in the use of AI.

**Keywords:** Generative AI · AI Literacy · Interaction trace

## 1 Introduction

Artificial Intelligence (AI) has been applied in various areas of everyday life. Since the release of ChatGPT in 2022, generative AI (GenAI) has gained widespread attention, especially due to its ability to simulate natural language interactions with humans, significantly contributing to the democratization of access to this technology.

In the educational context, AI has been used by teachers, students, school administrators, and education managers in several ways. From the students' perspective, it serves as a tool for answering questions, offering personalized tutoring, assisting in research, supporting academic writing, solving exercises, debugging and understanding code, and even correcting grammar [11].

AI holds the potential to profoundly transform pedagogical practices, influencing what is taught, how it is taught, and to whom it is taught [18]. Unlike other technologies used in the teaching-learning process, AI provides access to vast amounts of data, which students can apply to a wide range of academic activities. However, this potential is accompanied by important challenges. The often superficial responses generated by language models may lead users—particularly those with less experience—to trust inaccurate or decontextualized information [1]. Furthermore, the excessive use of large language models can hinder the development of essential learning skills, such as critical thinking and the ability to apply knowledge in different contexts [6].

Taking that into consideration, it is essential that students develop competencies to understand how AI works in order to use it effectively and ethically. This includes recognizing its limitations, identifying potential biases, and adopting a critical approach to the information produced by such systems [12,18].

In the literature, given the various AI competency models proposed [2,10,14,16], the approach to identify competencies uses self-assessment questionnaires [4,8,9,13]. This approach, although relevant, has limitations, such as susceptibility to bias, which highlights the need to explore complementary methods [8,18].

In view of the above, this paper presents part of a study on GenAI competencies in the educational context, aimed at evaluating the interaction traces to determine their AI competencies. An interaction trace is defined as the entire history of interaction between student and AI; in this article, ChatGPT was used as the GenAI tool. The objective of this paper is to present the results obtained in the application of the pilot project to identify AI competencies according to the analysis of the data collected through a self-assessment made by the students and the interaction traces sent by the participants.

## 2 Theoretical Background

### 2.1 Generative Artificial Intelligence

AI has been evolving over the past decade, but GenAI, and specifically the arrival of ChatGPT in 2022, has launched an unprecedented wave of AI innovation and adoption.

Unlike traditional AI models, which focus on analyzing or classifying existing data, GenAI refers to deep learning models that can create original content including conversations, stories, images, videos, and music in response to a user prompt or request [3,15]. GenAI works on the basis of large language models (LLMs), which are trained on vast data sets to learn patterns and relationships between words, images, or other types of information.

In educational settings, GenAI tools like ChatGPT offer advantages such as increased productivity and student engagement, but also present challenges, including plagiarism, ethical concerns, limited critical evaluation of responses, and potential negative effects on critical thinking. Socioeconomic factors may further exacerbate educational inequalities [1,5–7].

## 2.2 AI Literacy

AI literacy can be defined as "a set of competencies that enables individuals to critically evaluate AI technologies; communicate and collaborate effectively with AI; and use AI as a tool online, at home, and in the workplace" [10]. There is a growing need to promote critical digital literacies in educational contexts—not only to ensure technical proficiency in the use of technologies, but also to foster reflective experiences regarding the content accessed and produced in digital networks [17].

AI competency framework for students identifies four essential aspects of competence that students should develop to interact effectively and ethically with AI. These are: (1) a human-centered mindset, which emphasizes the importance of keeping human values at the core of AI development and use; (2) an ethics of AI, which equips students to critically reflect on and address ethical implications associated with AI technologies; (3) AI techniques and applications, which involve understanding how AI works and how it can be used across different contexts; and (4) an AI system design, which encourages students not only to use existing AI tools but also to actively engage in creating and developing their own AI solutions [18].

## 3 Method

This section describes the survey procedure, data collection instruments, analysis methods, and limitations of a study that aims to evaluate the interaction of GenAI in the educational context by observing students' competencies in using AI. This research was submitted to Plataforma Brasil under number 85896325.8.0000.5390 and approved by the Research Ethics Committee of the Schools of Arts, Sciences, and Humanities of the University of São Paulo.

A qualitative analysis was employed to examine both the self-assessment instruments completed by the students and the manual analysis conducted by the researchers on the interactions trace. The interaction trace analysis was done because the way to interact with ChatGPT is through prompts.

Participants were undergraduate students from fields such as System Analysis, Computer Science, and related courses, with varying levels of familiarity with AI tools. Before the experiment, an initial questionnaire was administered to collect demographic information and assess participants' prior experience levels.

The experiment was based on the ordering of a vector, a concept usually addressed in the first semesters of Computer Science courses. The answer to the exercise was analyzed specifically in ChatGPT, and the result was unsatisfactory. This implies that the student needs to adopt a critical stance in relation to the result in order to generate a correct answer.

### 3.1 Procedure

**Step 1: Survey Distribution Strategy.** In the initial phase of the study, the survey was distributed online to specific groups of students. The selection of these groups was based on the desired participant profile, allowing for a controlled first round of responses. The purpose of this preliminary distribution was to assess the clarity of the questions, the usability of the form, and to obtain feedback from the target audience before expanding the data collection to a wider population.

**Step 2: Experiment Execution.** Participants were instructed to use a GenAI tool (ChatGPT) to solve a coding exercise. During the process, they performed the following activities: (1) Completed a pre-experiment survey; (2) Used ChatGPT to solve the assigned coding task; and, (3) Submitted their interaction trace with ChatGPT for analysis. Figure 1 illustrates the project architecture, with the aforementioned steps indicated by their corresponding numbers in the diagram.

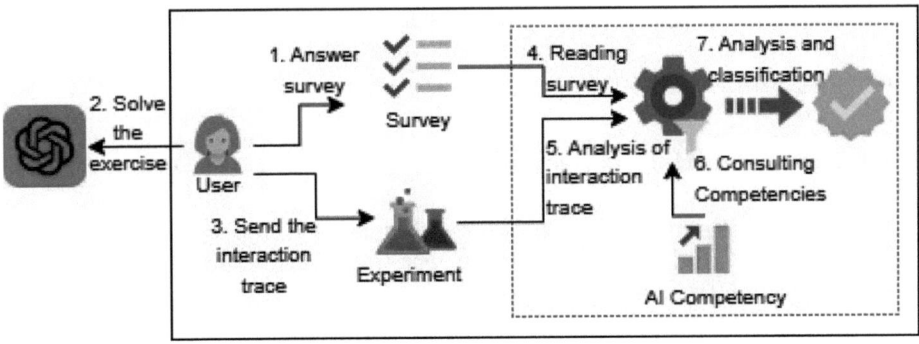

**Fig. 1.** Project architecture. Source: Author.

**Step 3: Data Collection Instruments.** During data collection, the surveys (number 4 in Fig. 1), the user's interaction with ChatGPT (number 5 in Fig. 1), and the classification of competencies (represented by number 6 in Fig. 1) were analyzed for the purpose of competency analysis and classification. Two surveys were applied: (1) a pre-experiment survey, which included general questions about the participants' profiles and a technical self-assessment; and (2) a post-experiment survey, composed of 20 questions related to AI competencies, using a Likert scale ranging from 1 (strongly disagree) to 5 (strongly agree). At this stage of the research, only the qualitative analysis is presented; classification will be carried out at a later time.

## 4 Experiment

The experiment was available for 10 d, between March 1 and March 10. The survey was answered by 15 participants, all students from the computer field. Despite 15 participants, 3 responses were canceled because the interaction trace was not sent for analysis.

### 4.1 Data Analysis

The interaction traces were analyzed qualitatively to identify patterns of engagement with the GenAI tool and cross-reference these findings with the closed-ended responses from the pre-experiment questionnaire. The results can show whether the personal analysis made by the students is equivalent to the knowledge applied when using the tool.

### 4.2 Limitations

As this is a pilot project, the main limitations are related to the sample size, the short duration of the experiment, and the potential influence of previous experiences with similar tools.

## 5 Analysis and Discussion

Of the twelve students whose responses were analyzed, ten were male and two were female. Regarding age, ten students were between 18 and 27 years old, and two were between 28 and 37 years old.

Regarding the academic programs, nine students were enrolled in the Systems Analysis and Development course, two in Computer Science, and one in Information Systems. Participants included students from both public and private institutions. Only one respondent was in the first semester of their program, while six were in the third semester, and five were in more advanced stages: one in the fifth, two in the sixth, and two in the eighth semester. It is important to note that the pilot was conducted in March, at the beginning of the academic semester. Despite the online dissemination, all participants were from the South and Southeast regions of Brazil.

Regarding experience with AI usage, five students reported having taken some type of AI course, although the duration and nature of the courses were not specified. Only one student stated that they did not use AI to help with schoolwork. Most students (11) mentioned ChatGPT as their main AI tool, followed by Gemini and Copilot, GrokAI, and finally DeepSeek and BlackBox. The majority of respondents use AI tools for understanding concepts or code, grammar correction, code debugging, solving exercises, and conducting general research.

During the manual analysis of the interaction traces, it was observed that most students simply copied the exercise prompt into ChatGPT and accepted the generated response as correct, without performing any further validation. Seven participants specified at least the desired programming language in their prompts. One participant explicitly mentioned being a student and requested assistance in solving a coding task. Besides these cases, three other exceptions were identified.

The first survey respondent questioned the result presented by the tool and then asked ChatGPT to evaluate the code based on the modifications he had made. The second respondent elaborated a more detailed prompt, indicating his role as a student solving a programming exercise. Despite the more careful formulation, he also accepted the response as correct without questioning it. The third respondent requested specific commands from the tool and, based on that, proposed his own solution, using ChatGPT only as targeted support for more specific technical aspects.

Given the lack of evidence in the interaction traces regarding how students validated the generated code, a follow-up email was sent requesting clarification about this process. Three responses were received: (1) "I didn't do any analysis"; (2) "I did a superficial analysis of the response"; and (3) "I used an online IDE to run tests".

When correlating the responses with the students' current semester, it was observed that the three students who demonstrated more effective use of ChatGPT were enrolled in the fifth, sixth, and eighth semesters. These students also reported having advanced programming knowledge, including familiarity with design patterns, an understanding of different software architectures, the ability to optimize code, and assess system security. Regarding their knowledge of AI, two reported having an intermediate level - indicating an understanding of algorithms and a conscious use of AI agents, including verifying the information provided - while one reported advanced knowledge, expressing an understanding of the strengths and weaknesses of using AI agents, as well as the ability to craft prompts that enhance the performance of these tools.

The students from the first and third semesters, as well as one student from the sixth semester, consider their programming knowledge to be basic (able to use assignment commands, logical and comparison operators, conditional control structures, and loops) or intermediate (using data structures such as lists, arrays, object-oriented concepts, SQL, Git). Regarding their knowledge of AI, some reported having no knowledge, while others had basic knowledge (understanding the limitations of AI but not the algorithms behind it), intermediate knowledge, and advanced knowledge.

## 5.1 Human-Centred Mindset Aspect

Based on the students' perception of their AI knowledge and the analysis of the interaction traces, it was possible to observe, in relation to the human-centred mindset aspect, whether participants recognize that AI systems are developed by humans and that the decisions made by their creators directly influence their functioning. It was also investigated whether students understand that, by using AI, they remain legally responsible for the decisions made and that the use of these technologies requires social responsibility and critical thinking.

The majority of students reported not adopting a critical approach when receiving responses from AI, nor conducting any prior analysis before using them. This behavior was confirmed by the analysis of the interaction traces, highlighting a consistency between the participants' stated perception and their actual practice. On the other hand, the two students who reported the importance of critical analysis and affirmed adopting this approach were precisely those who demonstrated a more in-depth interaction with ChatGPT.

## 5.2 Ethics Aspect

Regarding ethics and the responsible use of AI, aspects related to the students' concern about using AI agents that do not cause harm to humans and that preserve data privacy were analyzed. Also considered were their ability to identify potential gender, ethnic, or cultural biases in the responses provided, the care taken to avoid using sensitive or confidential data, and the practice of verifying references provided by the agents to respect copyright.

Ten students stated that they were concerned about the presence of gender, ethnic, or cultural prejudices in the responses generated by AI agents. As for the other aspects analyzed - such as data privacy, the use of sensitive information, and reference verification - five respondents either disagreed or adopted a neutral stance. Once again, the exception was the two students who demonstrated a more careful and efficient use of ChatGPT, as they expressed concern about all the ethical aspects considered.

## 5.3 AI Techniques and Applications Aspect

The aspect related to AI techniques and applications was analyzed based on competencies aimed at verifying the mastery of fundamental concepts in the field and the understanding of AI usage in different contexts.

All participants demonstrated an understanding that the responses provided by GenAI tools are produced based on data. However, four students revealed that they were unaware of the existence of different AI algorithms and specific tools for various application contexts.

Furthermore, regarding basic concepts, it was observed that most respondents do not understand that GenAI produces new content in response to queries, unlike traditional search engines such as Google. Another relevant finding from the questionnaire was that only six students stated that they were able to reinterpret or reuse the information obtained from AI in other ways; on the other hand, eight reported being able to apply the content generated in practical situations. Although nine respondents indicated that they contextualize their questions and direct the desired output from the AI, the interaction traces analyzed confirmed these competencies in practice for only two respondents.

## 6 Conclusion and Future Work

These results are part of a research project aimed at identifying AI competencies through interaction traces. The pilot project was conducted to validate the entire process to be carried out on a large volume of data. The article highlights how students interact with GenAI to solve problems.

The results indicate that, although many students demonstrate an understanding of basic GenAI concepts, a significant portion of the sample lacks critical engagement with the responses provided. The research showed that most respondents accept the tool's answers without verification or contextual reflection. The analysis also revealed that students with advanced programming knowledge, enrolled in the fifth, sixth, or eighth semesters, and with a better understanding of AI concepts and functionality, used ChatGPT more efficiently.

However, a general lack of awareness regarding the ethical implications and diversity of AI systems was observed. These results highlight the urgent need to promote AI literacy in education - not only to enhance students' technical skills but also to foster a human-centered and ethically responsible mindset. As the presence of AI in academic contexts becomes increasingly common, educational institutions must ensure that students are not only users but also critical evaluators and responsible agents in the digital landscape.

The interaction traces analyzed were important to verify how students use the tool and to compare this interaction with their self-assessment. Based on the results obtained, it was noted that there is a need to modify the proposed activity. In addition to the activity, students will have to show or indicate how they ensure that the response provided by the AI is correct.

As future work, these interactions analyzed alongside the self-assessment will indicate a level of knowledge in AI. This level will allow the student to receive training to improve their AI knowledge and, thus, use the tools efficiently, not only in the educational context but also in their daily life.

## References

1. Anderson, N., McGowan, A., Galway, L., Hanna, P., Collins, M., Cutting, D.: Implementing generative AI and large language models in education. In: 2023 7th International Symposium on Innovative Approaches in Smart Technologies (ISAS), pp. 1–6 (2023). https://doi.org/10.1109/ISAS60782.2023.10391517
2. Annapureddy, R., Fornaroli, A., Gatica-Perez, D.: Generative AI literacy: twelve defining competencies. Digit. Gov.: Res. Pract. (2024). https://doi.org/10.1145/3685680, just Accepted

3. AWS: O que é ia generativa? (2025). https://aws.amazon.com/pt/what-is/generative-ai/. Accessed 25 Oct 2023
4. Carolus, A., Koch, M.J., Straka, S., Latoschik, M.E., Wienrich, C.: Mails - meta AI literacy scale: development and testing of an AI literacy questionnaire based on well-founded competency models and psychological change- and meta-competencies. Comput. Hum. Behav. Artif. Hum. **1**(2), 100014 (2023). https://doi.org/10.1016/j.chbah.2023.100014, https://www.sciencedirect.com/science/article/pii/S2949882123000142
5. Chan, M.M., Amado-Salvatierra, H.R., Hernandez-Rizzardini, R., De La Roca, M.: The potential role of AI-based chatbots in engineering education. experiences from a teaching perspective. In: 2023 IEEE Frontiers in Education Conference (FIE), pp. 1–5 (2023). https://doi.org/10.1109/FIE58773.2023.10343296
6. Elsayed, S.: Towards mitigating ChatGPT's negative impact on education: optimizing question design through bloom's taxonomy. In: 2023 IEEE Region 10 Symposium (TENSYMP), pp. 1–6 (2023). https://doi.org/10.1109/TENSYMP55890.2023.10223662
7. Flores-Vivar, J.M., García-Peñalvo, F.J.: Reflections on the ethics, potential, and challenges of artificial intelligence in the framework of quality education (SDG4). Comunicar **31**(74) (2023). https://api.semanticscholar.org/CorpusID:252586795
8. Hornberger, M., Bewersdorff, A., Nerdel, C.: What do university students know about artificial intelligence? Development and validation of an ai literacy test. Comput. Educ. Artif. Intell. **5**, 100165 (2023). https://doi.org/10.1016/j.caeai.2023.100165, https://www.sciencedirect.com/science/article/pii/S2666920X23000449
9. Laupichler, M.C., Aster, A., Haverkamp, N., Raupach, T.: Development of the "scale for the assessment of non-experts' AI literacy" – an exploratory factor analysis. Comput. Hum. Behav. Rep. **12**, 100338 (2023). https://doi.org/10.1016/j.chbr.2023.100338, https://www.sciencedirect.com/science/article/pii/S2451958823000714
10. Long, D., Magerko, B.: What is AI literacy? Competencies and design considerations. In: Proceedings of the 2020 CHI Conference on Human Factors in Computing Systems, pp. 1–16. CHI '20, Association for Computing Machinery, New York, NY, USA (2020). https://doi.org/10.1145/3313831.3376727
11. Marques, D., Morandini, M.: Uso do ChatGPT no contexto educacional: uma revisão sistemática da literatura. In: 2024 Anais do XXXV Simpósio Brasileiro de Informática na Educação (SBIE), pp. 1784–1795 (2024). https://doi.org/10.5753/sbie.2024
12. Prather, J., et al.: The robots are here: navigating the generative AI revolution in computing education. In: Proceedings of the 2023 Working Group Reports on Innovation and Technology in Computer Science Education, pp. 108–159. ITiCSE-WGR '23, Association for Computing Machinery, New York, NY, USA (2023). https://doi.org/10.1145/3623762.3633499
13. Sanusi, I.T., Olaleye, S.A., Oyelere, S.S., Dixon, R.A.: Investigating learners' competencies for artificial intelligence education in an African k-12 setting. Comput. Educ. Open **3**, 100083 (2022). https://doi.org/10.1016/j.caeo.2022.100083, https://www.sciencedirect.com/science/article/pii/S2666557322000118
14. Stolpe, K., Hallström, J.: Artificial intelligence literacy for technology education. Comput. Educ.Open **6**, 100159 (2024). https://doi.org/10.1016/j.caeo.2024.100159, https://www.sciencedirect.com/science/article/pii/S2666557324000016
15. Stryker, C., Kavlakoglu, E.: What is AI? (2025). https://www.ibm.com/think/topics/artificial-intelligence. Accessed 25 Oct 2023

16. Tenório, K., Romeike, R.: Ai competencies for non-computer science students in undergraduate education: towards a competency framework. In: Proceedings of the 23rd Koli Calling International Conference on Computing Education Research. Koli Calling '23, Association for Computing Machinery, New York, NY, USA (2024). https://doi.org/10.1145/3631802.3631829
17. TREVISAN, D., Maciel, C., SOUZA, T.: O lugar da crÍtica na mobilizaÇÃo de letramentos digitais. Revista de Educação do Vale do Arinos - RELVA **9**, 110–133 (2022). https://doi.org/10.30681/relva.v9i2.6023
18. UNESCO: AI competency framework for students. UNESCO (2024). https://doi.org/10.54675/JKJB9835, https://unesdoc.unesco.org/ark:/48223/pf0000391105

# The Challenge of Understanding Explanations for User Trust in AI: Insights From an Online Experiment About Job Matching

Glenda Hannibal(✉) and Christine Bauer

Department of Artificial Intelligence and Human Interfaces,
University of Salzburg, Salzburg, Austria
{glenda.hannibal,christine.bauer}@plus.ac.at

**Abstract.** Artificial Intelligence (AI) is widely used in recruitment with Job Recommender Systems (JRS) being designed for job matching. However, poor matches can significantly impact individuals' livelihoods, business profits, and organizational productivity. Thus, it is critical to study whether users trust JRS and their outputs, especially after receiving explanations for job matches. In a between-subjects, mixed-methods online experiment, we study whether varying explanations of trust violations embedded in a job match influence user trust in the mock-up JRS algorithm JobMatcher. We found that such explanations had limited effect on trust in the JobMatcher algorithm or understanding of the job match. We discuss the findings about the complexity of explanations concerning trust, the problematic role of high or low agency perception of AI for trust measures, and the need to address the moral dimension of trust.

**Keywords:** Job Recommender Systems · Job Matching · Online Experiment · User Trust · Explanations · Understanding · Agency Perception

## 1 Introduction

Artificial Intelligence (AI) has become integral to many websites and online services, aiming to help people with their everyday activities (e.g., working, studying, traveling, searching, dating, and shopping). In particular, AI algorithms that provide recommendations have gained momentum because they successfully deliver personalized solutions that meet individuals' needs. Drawing on research from various fields (e.g., Machine Learning, Data Mining, Information Retrieval, and Human-Computer Interaction (HCI)), Recommender Systems (RSs) help mitigating choice complexity and overload [9,28] by suggesting personalized products and services across markets (e.g., e-commerce, recruitment, entertainment, banking, and social media) [59]. With this, RSs are effective tools to support users in finding items of interest. Despite the widespread development and use of RSs, trust remains a major challenge because many rely on black-box AI models to provide recommendations.

While extensive empirical research has studied trust in AI [19], trust in RSs specifically [7,26], and efforts into trust formalization [29], findings are still inconclusive with ongoing questions about how trust is influenced by individual and contextual factors [19]. Recently, a focus on explaining AI and their outputs has been considered promising in fostering user understanding and trust [16]. To this end, Explainable AI (XAI) offers methods and techniques that provide users with oversight and control over black-box AI models [15]. XAI models provide users additional information about the complex AI model and its output, which enables them to (better) understand them [25]. Moreover, Human-AI Interaction (HAI) research studies how such explanations can support users' understanding to establish, maintain, and repair trust [52,71]. In RSs research specifically, explanations are also considered means to increase trust (e.g., [38,55]). To engage with these discussions, we explore whether or not explanations support user trust in AI, focusing on a RS for job matching. Considering the enormous and growing labor market [13], it is timely and highly relevant to explore their interconnection in this context from the user's perspective. Human Resource (HR) departments and recruitment agencies increasingly rely on recruiting platforms (e.g., LinkedIn, Indeed, CareerBuilder) to match labor-market supply and demand. By now, RSs are being developed and used for *job recruitment* specifically [17] because a considerable amount of job-related information is posted daily online by job seekers and job providers. Recommending jobs that meet the needs of both the job seeker and the job provider is challenging [44]. Unlike lower risk RSs domains (e.g., entertainment, tourism, e-commerce), user trust in Job Recommender Systems (JRSs) carries higher stakes. Mismatches can have a serious psychological impact on job seekers and lead to productivity or profit losses for job providers [31]. Given the central role of work in people's lives, explaining the success or failure of a JRS is important for both parties to better understand the match outcome.

Although the importance of trust in a JRS and the need for explanations in cases of failure are increasingly recognized, little research has examined whether or not explanations support user trust in the context of job matching. To address this gap, we conducted an online experiment using varying explanations of trust violations embedded in a job match to explore the research questions:

**RQ 1**: Do people trust in a JRS that recommends a job match?
**RQ 2**: Do people understand why a JRS recommends the job match?

In this paper, we present the results of our online experiment investigating user trust in a JRS during a job matching task, focusing on how understanding and explanations influence trust. Our study contributes to future research on explanations for user trust in AI in three ways. By (1) emphasizing the importance of the moral dimension of trust, although it is hard to measure, (2) highlighting the complexity of explanations, and (3) stressing the problematic role of agency perception for trust measures in HAI. Based on our findings, we advise AI developers—especially those working in JRSs—to develop more knowledge about the relationship between explanations and user trust because this relationship is more complex than often assumed (e.g., [38,55]). Moreover, the explanations must also enhance users' understanding to positively impact their trust in AI outputs.

After this short introduction, the structure of the paper is as follows. Section 2 provides an overview of related work regarding JRSs, trust in AI, and XAI that guided our study. Presenting the study design in Sect. 3, we detail the online experimental setup, used measures, study procedure, and participant recruitment. In Sect. 4, we provide the results of the quantitative and qualitative data analysis. We present, in Sect. 5, a broader discussion of our work and reflect on the practical implications of our study results. Section 6 lays out what we consider limitations of our online experiment. We summarize the main points and conclude the paper in Sect. 7.

## 2 Related Work

We situate our work within the research areas of HCI and AI around the topics of JRSs, trust in AI, and XAI.

### 2.1 Recommender Systems for Recruitment

There is an extensive body of literature on research and development into e-recruitment RSs and JRSs [17,75], and various system architectures have been proposed [75]. Compared to traditional RSs focused on unilateral item-to-user interactions, JRSs must support bidirectional engagement between job seekers and job providers [44]. Consequently, the automatic computation and optimization of recommendations is more complex [51]. Many conventional JRSs use algorithms that automatically extract keywords from job descriptions (e.g., job title, role, salary, location, skill requirements, and responsibilities) and resumes (e.g., name, gender, age, location, education, experience, skills, and interests) [4]. Although JRS research has advanced, most systems still rely on extracting features from textual data. To keep our online experiment realistic, our mock-up JRS is inspired by this textual feature extraction approach.

### 2.2 Trust in Recommender Systems

Literature on trust in RSs is sizable—with a focus on technical challenges [60]. However, the user perspective on whether to trust a RS is underexplored, although increasingly addressed in work on trustworthy RSs [67]. To compensate for failures and mitigate biases in RSs, which people can experience as trust violations, research has emphasized making RSs more robust, fair, secure, transparent, and explainable [18]. This has led to an increasing interest in human trust in RSs. For example, Harman et al. [26] studied how the dynamic adaptation to social needs influences human trust in a RS. Liao et al. [41] found that users trust RSs more when given rich social information about the preferences and tastes of other people. Considering JRSs, Laumer et al. [40] explored the influence of trust on the intention of their use. Lacroux and Martin-Lacroux [39] identified a discrepancy between recruiters' low trust in algorithmic resume recommendations and their reliance on them, despite their inconsistent performance. While

RSs research has studied trust from multiple angles, user trust in JRSs remains underresearched. Our study aims to fill this gap by focusing specifically on the user perspective in job matching.

## 2.3 Explainable Recommendations

There is a considerable amount of literature on explainable recommendations, which Zhang and Chen [73] surveyed comprehensively. While recommendation accuracy has improved, explaining recommendations to users has become more challenging [74]. Explainable RSs generate explanations alongside recommendations using various model explainability techniques. Several explainability techniques have been proposed in the XAI literature. Popular XAI techniques— such as Local Interpretable Model-agnostic Explanations (LIME) [58], SHapley Additive exPlanations (SHAP) [42], and counterfactual reasoning—have been adopted to the RSs context (e.g., [47,56,70]). User studies investigating explanations for trust are central to RSs research [48]. For instance, Kunkle et al. [38] investigated how human or automatically generated explanations impact human trust in a RS. In the JRSs context, Ogunniye et al. [49] studied how recommendation explanations influenced human perceptions of fairness, transparency, and trustworthiness of e-recruitment systems. Despite growing insights into the importance of explainable recommendations in shaping user perceptions of a RSs, few user studies specifically focused on them in the JRSs context. Our work addresses this gap by investigating how users perceive a job match explanation inspired by LIME.

# 3 Study Design

To address the complexity of explanations and user trust in a JRS, we used a mixed-methods study design for our online experiment, combining quantitative and qualitative methods. Our study was grounded in the theoretical assumption of default trust, which asserts that people ordinarily trust each other and only pay attention to trust when it is questioned or broken [6,45]. We integrated this assumption into our study design by (1) introducing trust violations before measuring trust and (2) using a control group for comparison rather than using a baseline trust measure.

## 3.1 Setup

To study whether or not explanations support user trust in a JRS, we used a job recruitment scenario in our online experiment. In this scenario, our mock-up JRS algorithm JobMatcher would compute the best job match score considering two job seekers' profiles and six job posting descriptions. The work by Appadoo et al. [3] inspired the basic structure and presentation of our mock-up JobMatcher algorithm (Fig. 2). At this first stage, we inquired about people's understanding of the job match and their reasoning. Thereafter, our mock-up XAI algorithm would compute and present the explanation for the match score. Its design was inspired by current research on feature-based XAI methods. In particular, we adopted the visualization style of explanations generated with the LIME [58] technique because it uses word highlights for textual data for the interpretation representation [63]. This aligns well with the common approach of keyword matching used by JRSs [23]. However, since LIME does not automatically generate a user understandable explanation, we added a user-friendly version using natural language (i.e., "The JobSeeker MH was recommended the JobPosting 03 because the feature importance of X, Y, Z, and Q were the most significant for the match.") in addition to the regular textual highlights (Fig. 1).

### 3.2 Conditions

Research into the effect of trust violations in HAI has shown that such interventions help study both the performative and moral dimensions of trust [62]. Drawing on the work by Rezaei et al. [57], we designed a between-subjects online experiment with three conditions: performance or moral trust violation, and a control with no trust violation (Fig. 1). The conditions and control were constructed as follows: *No Trust Violation.* In the control condition, the job match explanation was framed as correct and unbiased. The JobMatcher algorithm based its job match prediction on sound reasoning and would thus be perceived as an appropriate tool for the job-matching task. As such, the explanation for the job match was delivered in a neutral tone to avoid the experience of any trust violation. *Performance Trust Violation.* This condition presented the job match explanation as incorrect but unbiased. The JobMatcher algorithm was portrayed as flawed because it would include lower-ranked keywords for the job match prediction. This clearly indicated a performance trust violation, suggesting poor performance and would thus be considered an unreliable tool for the job-matching task. *Moral Trust Violation.* For this condition, the explanation was framed as correct but biased. The explanation would reveal that the JobMatcher algorithm exhibited a gender and age bias. This constituted a moral trust violation because it did something morally wrong and would thus be considered a potentially harmful tool.

### 3.3 Measures

We measured participants' attitudes towards AI using the four-item version of the *AI Attitude Scale* (AIAS-4) developed by Grassini [21]. It uses a 10-point scale to measure how the public perceive AI technology as they rate their belief about the impact of AI on their life (i.e., "I believe that AI will improve my life"), careers (i.e., "I believe that AI will improve my work"), future usage (i.e., "I think I will use AI technology in the future"), and humanity overall (i.e., "I think AI technology is positive for humanity"). With a *single-item question* (i.e., "I understand why the job profile MH and the job posting 3852 were matched"), we measured how the participants would assess their understanding of the job match recommendation provided by the mock-up JobMatcher algorithm. Using a 5-point scale, if the participants rated their understanding on 4

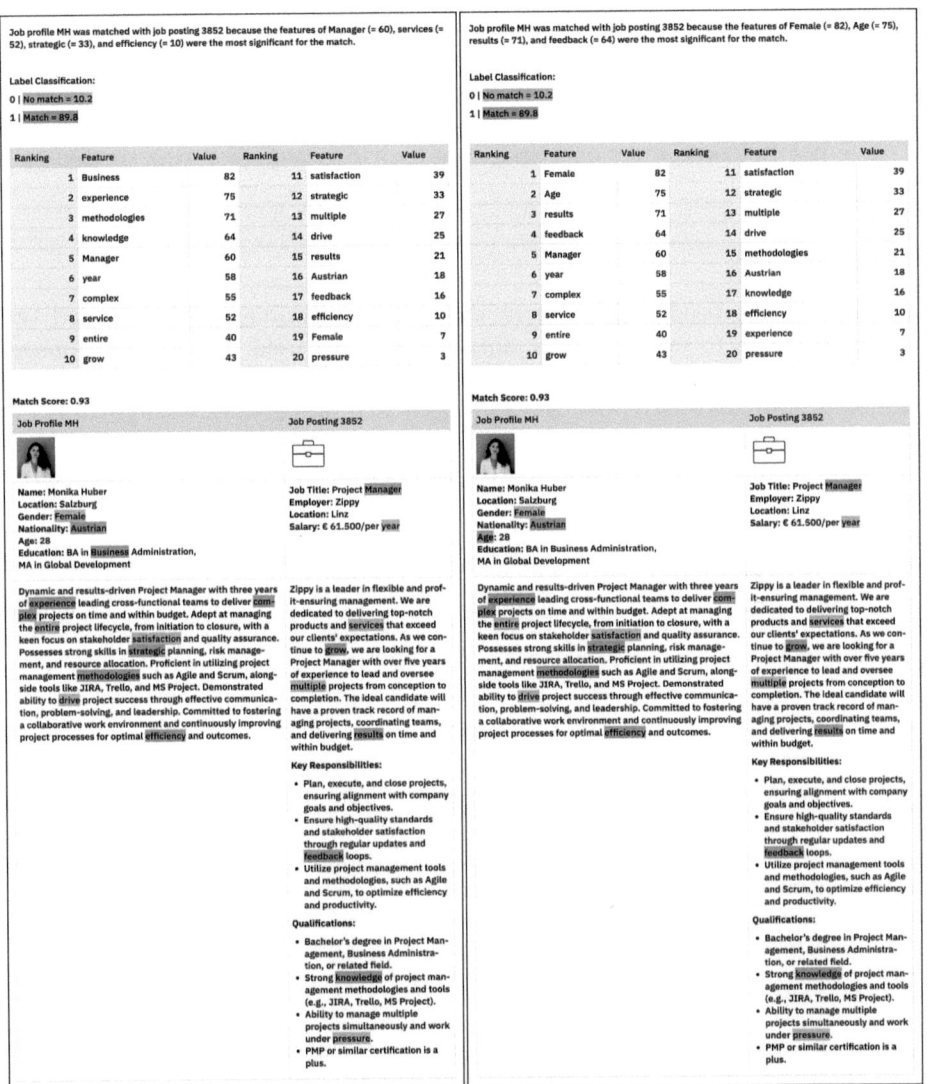

**Fig. 1.** Overview of how the XAI algorithm explained to the participants the different trust violations embedded into the job match. Left: Performance trust violation (incorrect). Right: Moral trust violation (biased).

or 5, they were required to answer an open-ended question about their comprehension of the job match recommendation. Numerous questionnaires have been developed to measure trust specifically in HAI and Human-Robot Interaction (HRI) [1,66]. We decided to use the updated version of the *Multidimensional Measure of Trust* (MDMTv2) developed by Ullman and Malle [43,64,65] because it captures both the performance-based and moral-based dimension of trust. The MDMTv2 scale comprises the five subscales *reliable*, *competent*, *ethial*, *transparant*, and *benevolent*. Each subscale consists of four items, which are calculated as the average of its item scores. Items are rated on an 8-point discrete rating scale from 0 (Not at all) to 7 (Very). To avoid forcing responses, a "does not fit" option for each item was provided and they was treated as a missing value.

### 3.4 Materials

LimeSurvey was used to implement our online experiment. We included two attention checks to ensure higher data quality. We used AI-generated images and text for the experimental probes to make them realistic without the use of real job profiles and data postings. This approach provided us with greater control over the conditions and addressed our concerns about the ethical and data protection regulations. As explained by Boldi et al. [8], job seekers worry about their privacy when using job-matching systems that lack transparency regarding data collection and handling, which can eventually lead to distrust. Therefore, the use of any real job profile and job posting information retrieved from any e-recruitment services (e.g., LinkedIn, Indeed, CareerBuilder) without consent is not only adding to these kinds of worries, but it is also in conflict with good scientific practice. The images were downloaded from the royalty-free AI stock photo library Lummi using the search terms "business [woman/man]". We used ChatGPT v.4o for text generation using different prompts for the job seeker profiles (i.e., "Write a short job seeker profile text as a person with [project manager/customer service] experience and skill set") and job posting descriptions ("Write a short job posting description offering a [project manager/research assistant/school teacher/sales/IT quality assurance/HR consultant] position"). We edited all generated texts to shorten them and ensure a natural reading flow.

### 3.5 Procedure

Participants were presented with a welcome page outlining the overall research aim and the institution responsible for the study. They were then shown a consent form detailing their rights as participants and what it involved to participate in the online experiment. Participants who did not consent were automatically redirected to the end page, whereas those consenting proceeded with the experiment. Participants first completed a short questionnaire about their attitudes towards AI (i.e., AIAS-4). Next, the JobMatcher algorithm used in the experiment was introduced, and participants were given the option to view additional details (Fig. 2). Afterward, the job matching task was explained, followed by a presentation of the respective job seeker profiles and job posting descriptions. After considering the extensive information, they were told that the JobMatcher algorithm would compute the best job match when they continued the experiment. The participants were then asked to imagine themselves in the recruiter role to rate their understanding of the specific job match using the single-item scale, with a follow-up question for those who rated their understanding highly.

Understanding Explanations for User Trust in AI    619

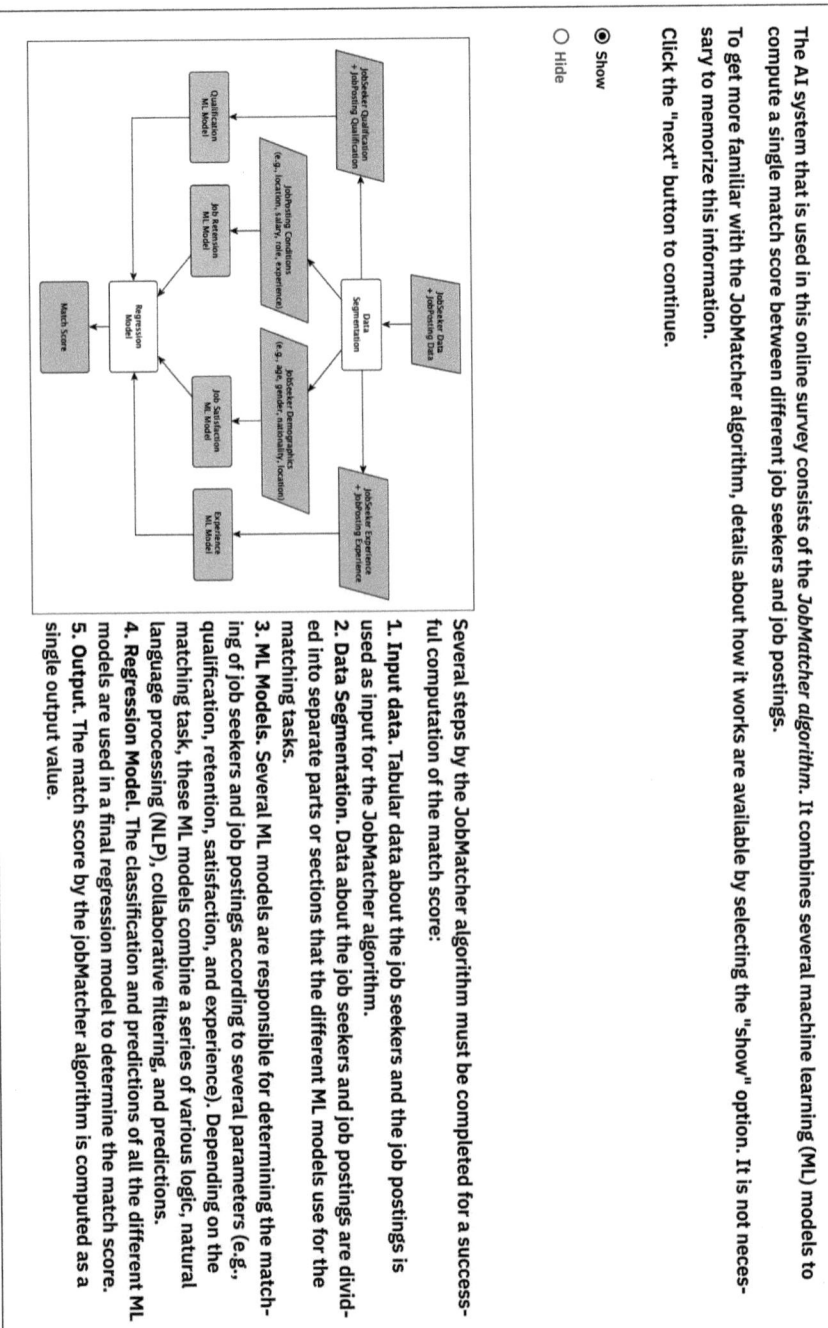

The AI system that is used in this online survey consists of the *JobMatcher algorithm*. It combines several machine learning (ML) models to compute a single match score between different job seekers and job postings.

To get more familiar with the JobMatcher algorithm, details about how it works are available by selecting the "show" option. It is not necessary to memorize this information.

Click the "next" button to continue.

◉ Show
○ Hide

Several steps by the JobMatcher algorithm must be completed for a successful computation of the match score:

**1. Input data.** Tabular data about the job seekers and the job postings is used as input for the JobMatcher algorithm.
**2. Data Segmentation.** Data about the job seekers and job postings are divided into separate parts or sections that the different ML models use for the matching tasks.
**3. ML Models.** Several ML models are responsible for determining the matching of job seekers and job postings according to several parameters (e.g., qualification, retention, satisfaction, and experience). Depending on the matching task, these ML models combine a series of various logic, natural language processing (NLP), collaborative filtering, and predictions.
**4. Regression Model.** The classification and predictions of all the different ML models are used in a final regression model to determine the match score.
**5. Output.** The match score by the jobMatcher algorithm is computed as a single output value.

**Fig. 2.** Presentation of the mock-up JobMatcher algorithm as shown to participants who opted to view details during the survey.

Then, the XAI algorithm used to explain the computed job match was introduced. Participants were randomly assigned to one of the study conditions or control group and shown the corresponding explanation (Fig. 1). They could optionally leave one or more comments about the explanation. Upon continuing, they completed a questionnaire assessing their trust in the JobMatcher algorithm (i.e., MDMTv2) based on the job-matching task and match explanation. Finally, participants reported demographic information (i.e., age, nationality, gender, employment status, area of profession) and indicated whether they develop or use AI in their current profession.

### 3.6 Pilot

We conducted a small pilot for our online experiment to get feedback on the study design and any potential technical issues. The participants ($N = 10$) were recruited through personal correspondence and had experience with AI research. We asked them to review the whole setup and provide feedback on any aspects that were unclear or needed improvement. We received their feedback via email, and it included grammar checks, sentence formulation issues, mobile display issues, uncertainty about perspective-taking, image size or quality, information or instruction redundancies, terminology use, and rephrasing suggestions. Moreover, the feedback suggested that the explanations of the trust violations embedded in the job match were perceived by the participants as intended. This indicates that the study condition scenarios were meaningful to them. For example, a pilot participant allocated to the explanation of the moral trust violation clearly noticed the gender bias ("[...] that particular example seems quite sexist: she was chosen because she's female.").

### 3.7 Recruitment

We recruited participants through the crowdsourcing platform *Prolific*, which is widely used for human-subject research studies and recognized for providing high data quality [14]. Since our goal was to explore whether or not varying explanations of trust violations embedded in the job match influence trust ratings in general, we chose to sample participants from a broad pool of non-expert users (i.e., potential JRSs users) as domain expertise in recruiting was not required to investigate trust. Each participant received 2.25 GBP for participating in the online experiment, which took place in October and November 2024. Although formal ethical approval for user studies with non-vulnerable participants is not a requirement at the University of Salzburg, we adhered to ethical principles of good scientific practice and ensured compliance with the necessary General Data Protection Regulation (GDPR) regulations throughout the online experiment.

## 4 Results

Considering our mixed-methods online experiment, we present below the results from our quantitative and qualitative data analysis.

## 4.1 Descriptive Analysis

We recruited 251 participant, of whom 7 were excluded due to poor quality (i.e., identical ratings for all items on the AIAS-4 and MDMTv2 scales, or only the latter). Hence, the final sample consists of $N = 244$ valid surveys across the different study conditions (i.e., control group = 94, performance trust violation = 75, and moral trust violation = 75).

**Sample.** The mean age of the participants was 37.5 years ($SD = 13.9, min = 18, max = 75$). 56.1% ($n = 137$) identified as female, 42.2% ($n = 103$) as male, and 1.6% ($n = 4$) as non-binary. Regarding the job status at the time when they took part in our online experiment, 44.3% ($n = 108$) were full-time employed, 15.6% ($n = 38$) part-time employed, 9.0% ($n = 22$) unemployed and looking for work (i.e., active job seekers), 1.6% ($n = 4$) unemployed and not looking for work, 2.5% ($n = 6$) unemployed due to disability or illness, 9.4% ($n = 23$) self-employed, 4.9% ($n = 12$) retired, 10.2% ($n = 25$) students, and 2.5% ($n = 6$) chose the option for self-description (i.e., other). 36.9% ($n = 90$) of the participants indicated that their current profession involves the development or use of AI, while 63.1% ($n = 154$) reported that this was not the case. This suggests that at least some participants are familiar with AI tools.

Overall, the participants represented our target group well. We expected the higher mean age because we targeted the part of the population connected to the job market in some capacity, and there was only a slight majority of female participants. Almost half of the participants worked full-time, and the majority stated that their work did not involve developing or using AI.

**Observations.** Considering the 10-point AIAS-4 scale ($[0, 9]$), we observed that our sample scored relatively high in general ($M = 5.7, SD = 2.161$), suggesting a slight bias toward a positive attitude toward AI. This tendency might be attributed to the recruitment method, which required participants to opt-in based on the study description, potentially favoring those already interested in AI. Moreover, current media coverage and hype about AI might also have contributed to this positive bias in the sample.

Given the 8-point discrete MDMTv2 scale ($[0, 7]$), participants' ratings on *PerformanceTrust* were relatively high ($M = 4.8, SD = 1.505$), indicating that the trust violation we used for the study condition of violating performance trust had moderate effectiveness. In contrast, the ratings for *MoralTrust* were relatively low ($M = 3.7, SD = 1.785$), indicating that the study condition with the moral trust violation was more effective. We also observed that participants scored very high ($M = 3.0, SD = 0.918$) on the 5-point *Understanding* scale ($[0, 4]$), suggesting that they felt confident about their understanding of the reasons for the job match in our study scenario.

**Scale Reliability.** We calculated Cronbach's $\alpha$ to assess the internal consistency of the AIAS-4 and MDMTv2 scales. The reliability analysis for the

AIAS-4 scale yielded a value of $\alpha = 0.92$, indicating excellent reliability. The MDMTv2 scale and its subscales (*reliable, competent, ethical, transparent,* and *benevolent*) demonstrate strong to excellent internal consistency ($\alpha = 0.96, 95\%\ CI[0.95, .097]$). While the *transparent* subscale's reliability is slightly lower and varied only minimally when removing items ([0.71, 0.79]), this moderate reliability still falls within acceptable ranges.

The total item correlations for the whole scale ranged from 0.45 to 0.86, confirming that all items contributed significantly to the scale's internal consistency. Performing trust ($\alpha_{reliable} = 0.84$ and $\alpha_{competent} = 0.87$) and moral trust ($\alpha_{benevolent} = 0.91, \alpha_{ethical} = 0.81, \alpha_{transparent} = 0.78$) show differences in reliability, with moral trust being more consistently measured. However, we observe that the subscales of moral trust exhibit a substantial number of missing values (i.e., "does not fit"): 35 missing values for the *benevolent* subscale, 6 for the *transparent* subscale, and 6 for the *ethical* subscale. In contrast, the *reliable* and *competent* subscales do not show any missing values.

## 4.2 Quantitative Analysis

As the study is exploratory, we included several categorical and numerical predictors, for which linear regression is an appropriate analytical choice. To this end, we conducted a backward stepwise linear regression separately for the outcome variables $Y_{PerformanceTrust}$ and $Y_{MoralTrust}$. The goal of the stepwise linear regression was to identify possible predictors from the following candidate variables: *Understanding, Gender, Age, StudyCondition,* and *StudyCondition:Understanding*. At each step, variables were dropped based on $p$-values, and the Akaike Information Criterion (AIC) was used to limit the total number of variables in the final model.

For the outcome variable $Y_{PerformanceTrust}$, the regression model could be reduced to the four predictor variables *StudyCondition, Understanding, Age,* and *StudyCondition:Understanding* (Table 1). *Understanding* was a significant predictor ($\beta = 0.357, SE = 0.154, p = .022$), which indicates a positive relationship between higher levels of *Understanding* and $Y_{PerformanceTrust}$. Additionally, the interaction between *StudyCondition*(Moral) and *Understanding* was significant ($\beta = -0.588, SE = 0.254, p = .021$). This result suggests that the effect of *Understanding* varied depending on the *StudyCondition*. The overall model was statistically significant ($R^2 = 0.053,$ Adjusted $R^2 = 0.029, F(6, 237) = 2.192, p < .05$), indicating that the four predictors collectively explain a significant portion of the variance in $Y_{PerformanceTrust}$.

For the outcome variable $Y_{MoralTrust}$, the regression model could be reduced to the two predictor variables *Gender* and *Age* (Table 2). *Age* was a significant negative predictor of $Y_{MoralTrust}$ ($\beta = -0.024, SE = 0.008, p = .003$). This result suggests that with increasing *Age*, the levels of $Y_{MoralTrust}$ tend to decrease. This model was statistically significant ($R^2 = 0.062,$ Adjusted $R^2 = 0.051, F(3, 238) = 5.278, p < .001$) too, indicating that the two predictors explain a significant portion of the variance in $Y_{MoralTrust}$.

**Table 1.** Regression results of the final model for PerformanceTrust.

|  | β (SE) | 95% CI | p-value |  |
|---|---|---|---|---|
| (Intercept) | 4.231 (0.537) | [3.173, 5.290] | <0.001 | *** |
| StudyCondition(Moral) | 1.415 (0.790) | [−0.140, 2.971] | 0.074 | |
| StudyCondition(Performance) | 0.331 (0.802) | [−1.250, 1.912] | 0.680 | |
| Understanding | 0.357 (0.154) | [0.053, 0.661] | 0.022 | * |
| Age | −0.010 (0.007) | [−0.024, 0.003] | 0.143 | |
| StudyCondition(Moral): Understanding | −0.588 (0.254) | [−1.089, −0.088] | 0.021 | * |
| StudyCondition(Performance): Understanding | −0.109 (0.253) | [−0.607, 0.388] | 0.665 | |

*$p < .05$, **$p < .01$, ***$p < .001$; $Number\ of\ observations = 244$

**Table 2.** Regression results of the final model for MoralTrust.

|  | β (SE) | 95% CI | p-value |  |
|---|---|---|---|---|
| (Intercept) | 4.568 (0.343) | [3.892, 5.245] | <0.001 | *** |
| Gender(Male) | 0.351 (0.229) | [−0.099, 0.802] | 0.125 | |
| Gender(Non-Binary) | −1.740 (0.885) | [−3.482, 0.003] | 0.050 | |
| Age | −0.024 (0.008) | [−0.040, −0.008] | 0.003 | ** |

*$p < .05$, **$p < .01$, ***$p < .001$; $Number\ of\ observations = 242$

In simpler terms, our regression analysis indicates that four factors (i.e., *StudyCondition*, *Understanding*, *Age*, and the interaction of *StudyCondition* and *Understanding*) are relevant for *PerformanceTrust*. However, these factors only explain about 3% of the variation. For *MoralTrust*, instead, only *Gender* and *Age* were significant predictors, explaining about 5% of the variation. These results suggest that the two models captured only a small part of the overall picture, suggesting other important factors might be at play.

For instance, using Kendall's $\tau$, we observed a strong and significant correlation between *PerformanceTrust* and *MoralTrust* ($\tau = 0.520, p < 0.001$). This observation is expected since both are trust dimensions on the MDMTv2 scale. Additionally, we observed a moderate but significant correlation between AIAS-4 and *PerformanceTrust* ($\tau = 0.247, p < 0.001$), which suggests that people's attitude toward AI might influence *PerformanceTrust*, but possibly not *MoralTrust*. However, given that our sample scored high on the AIAS-4 scale ($M = 5.7, SD = 2.161$), this result should be interpreted with caution and warrants further investigation in a follow-up study.

Although our residual analysis showed minor deviations from normality, this result does not compromise the models' reliability considering our sample size ($N = 244$). Multicollinearity was not an issue ($GVIF \approx 1$) for all predictors. However, we detected heteroscedasticity in the PerformanceTrust model ($p = 0.02$), suggesting some variability in the residual spread. Though a larger sample may provide further insights, these results still support the validity of our regression model for predictive purposes.

In addition, we conducted a two-way MANOVA, and in line with our regression analysis, we used PerformanceTrust and MoralTrust as outcome variables, while *StudyCondition* and *Understanding* were used as categorical factors. We found that the interaction effect was not significant ($p = 0.239$), which aligns with the regression results, suggesting differing predictors in the two trust dimensions.

### 4.3 Content Analysis

Given the inconclusive results of our statistical analysis, we used content analysis of the open-ended questions for contextualization. Specifically, we conducted two content analyses of the responses by the participants regarding (i) their high self-rated understanding of the job match and (ii) their comments about the job match explanation. We used a deductive approach to the content analysis because the coding scheme development relied on theoretically informed expectations about the collected data [54]. However, we also allowed for categories to be added inductively if unexpected but important codes needed to be integrated into the initial coding scheme [2,36]. We used several procedural steps for the content analysis. Keeping in mind the aim of the study, each team member independently skim-read all the participant's responses and noted their initial impressions (i.e., familiarization with the data). Afterward, the team members decided upon the coding scheme for the first round of coding, which was then discussed and refined through several iterations (i.e., schematic coding of the data). With the implemented refinements and cross-checking of the coding by each team member, the final version of the scheme was fixed (i.e., verifying the final coding scheme).

**Reasoning About Job Match Understanding.** The final coding scheme contained a total code count of $N = 551$ distributed over the codes *job seeker qualifications*, *rationalization*, *evaluation*, *comparing*, *perspective taking*, *Job-Matcher capabilities*, and *keyword match* (Table 3).

We found that the participants would mainly provide reasons relating to the task carried out by the JobMatcher algorithm. Although the participants mainly highlighted commonalities in the provided information, we also noticed two tendencies to point out discrepancies. One was related to the differences in the working experience either required or listed (e.g., "[...] the advert is requiring at least 5 years experience, but the applicant only has 3." P09). Another was related to the difference in the location where the job seeker was living and the place where the job was offered (e.g., "The candidate lives in Salzburg, but the job offer is in Linz." P262). We also found that people would often state a positive or negative judgment about the job match and mainly consider whether it was satisfactory or not (e.g., "It is a successful match." P161). Other times, whether they would agree to the job match or not (e.g., "I thought it was a great match." P173). In this sense, participants seemed to consider whether the job match was good or bad relative to their expectations of the JobMatcher algorithm's performance.

As expected, we saw that participants would also regularly mention the skills or experience of the job seeker, as they would stress the noted job seeker's competencies (e.g., "She had knowledge of the project management methodologies required" P184) or qualifications (e.g., "The candidate is very well educated." P59). Other participants understood the job match relative to the various abilities (e.g., "The algorithm demonstrated a strong understanding of both the technical competencies and soft skills needed for the role, ensuring a good fit." P226) or accomplishments (e.g., "The JobMatcher algorithm [sic!] was able to utilize vocabulary to hone in on the most relevant and suitable candidate for the job." P170) they would ascribe to the underlying algorithm.

Interestingly, some participants would base their understanding of the job match on the kind of justification (e.g., "a younger candidate would be more flexible that someone [sic!] with more experience that is set in their ways." P52) or validation (e.g., "They would bring a complimentary thinking to their projects" P104) they could provide. We saw that the participants would sometimes explain their understanding of the job match by considering any favorable outcomes from the perspective of either the job seeker (e.g., "The job is relevant to the seeker both education wise and experience wise." P120) or job provider (e.g., "Her software experience is what Zippy is looking for" P17). Some participants mentioned the keyword matching method by the JobMatcher algorithm. Some participants focused on the fact that the keywords they spotted were also singled out by the JobMatcher algorithm (e.g., "The algorithm correctly identified these key words." P240). Others were more skeptical about using this keyword-matching method for recruitment (e.g., "While it was effective in terms of keyword matching, the overall job-matching process lacked thoroughness." P110).

**Commenting Job Match Explanation.** The final coding scheme consisted of the codes *study condition, alternative, evaluation, understanding, reaction,* and *AI recruitment* with a total of $N = 168$ code counts (Table 4).

Overall, there were few comments related to the intended aspects of the trust violation that the participants were assigned. Several of them commented on the moral condition (e.g., "i don't believe that age and gender should be a consideration" P69), which indicated that they noticed the specific trust violation they were exposed to. Participants could also identify the weak performance of the JobMatcher algorithm given the explanation provided for the performance study condition (e.g., "some highlighted words don't [sic!] seem applicable to the cause (i.e. Entire)" P51). We noticed, however, that some participants commented on aspects that were not pertinent to their study condition but on aspects that would have applied to another. While we intended that the control group would not experience a trust violation because the job match was both correct and

**Table 3.** Coding scheme for participant's responses about their job match understanding.

| Code | Description | Example |
|---|---|---|
| Comparing ($n = 164$) | Stressing overlaps between the job profile and job posting information. | "[...] the candidate met many qualities outlined in the job description." (P81) |
| Evaluation ($n = 117$) | Expressing positive or negative judgment about the job match. | "i believe this is an excellent match, [...]" (P196) |
| Job Seeker Qualifications ($n = 109$) | Mentioning skills or experiences of the job seeker. | "MH has the relevant qualification and skills that is required for the job" (P54) |
| Rationalization ($n = 57$) | Relying on further assumptions or inferences. | "Her abilities and attitude show she can grow with the company" (P83) |
| JobMatcher capabilities ($n = 47$) | Focusing on the capabilities or achievements of the algorithm behind the job match. | "The JobMatcher algorithm did a very good job at selecting a candidate." (P81) |
| Perspective Taking ($n = 44$) | Considering the benefit or wishes of either the job seeker or job caller. | "Her experience matched closely to what the company was looking for." (P212) |
| Keyword Match ($n = 13$) | Mentioning keyword matching usage. | "The applicant's resume consists of keywords that appear in the job posting." (P38) |

unbiased, it seems that the participant pointed out a problem of sexism in the interpretation of a word-matching aspect as morally concerning.

With interest in how helpful the explanations were, we found that while some participants commented on their agreement with the match of the job seeker (e.g., "I feel she is a good match" P147), others would comment on their disagreement with how the JobMatcher algorithm arrived at the exact job match (e.g., "I also do not agree with the other matching terms like 'feedback'? or 'knowledge' being used as the matching terms." P138). Participants would also often express how well they understood the explanation for the job match after the XAI algorithm provided it. While most of these comments referred to the lack of understanding or confusion by the participants (e.g., "I don't really understand this information without studying it in mor [sic!] detail." P61), other comments would instead underline or confirm their understanding (e.g., "seems to pick out keywords used rather than abilities" P141).

Common comments also reflected the reactions that the additional information sparked, which was unexpected. Whereof most were negative, emotionally-loaded reactions (e.g., "I am slightly horrified how a CV needs to be a buzzword match and not a personal (human) exposition." P159). Some comments referred to more positive emotional reactions such as surprise (e.g., "I'm surprised about how what it has weighted" P142). Some participants also articulated how unimpressed they were with the prospect of AI being part of the recruitment process despite also noticing the potential benefits (e.g., "In my opinion word matching in interview processes is a poor way to search for candidates but I suppose is useful in narrowing down a few potential applicants." P247). A more critical attitude towards AI recruitment was also expressed by some participants (e.g., "I can see how this is a way of matching but It might have problems." P78).

**Table 4.** Coding scheme for participant's comments about the job match explanation.

| Code | Description | Example |
|---|---|---|
| Evaluation ($n = 48$) | Providing a judgment about the job match given the explanation. | "Seems like a strong candidate to take forward." (P210) |
| Understanding ($n = 47$) | Expression of confusion or lack of understanding of the explanation. | "It's not very clear to me to be honest" (P227) |
| Reaction ($n = 28$) | Expressing strong (emotionally loaded) reactions to the explanation. | "It's interesting to see how it works but bit disappointing" (P251) |
| Study Conditions ($n = 16$) | Mentioning aspects aligned with the assigned study condition. | "That is bizarre. I don't see how her gender or her age have anything to do with her ranking well." (P173) |
| Alternative ($n = 16$) | Having reactions or mentioning aspects misaligned with the assigned study condition. | N/A |
| AI Recruitment ($n = 13$) | Opinions or views in general about using AI for the task of job matching. | "do not feel that matching words to score is accetable [sic!]" (P152) |

## 5 Discussion

In this following discussion, we highlight two points that, in our view, contribute to current and future work on user trust in AI considering the context of JRSs. We will also discuss the practical implications of our findings.

### 5.1 The Complexity of Explanations

According to Wardatzky et al. [69], it is difficult to determine how explanations acquire their effect because individual characteristics also need to be considered. Even though we need further studies to reach more conclusive results, we wonder if they hint at demographic factors as important contributors because the small portion of the variation in the performance and the moral trust dimension was caused partly by age and, for the latter, also gender. In that case, we agree with current research in human-centered XAI stating that the information gained from explanations does not single-handedly provide much value. Instead, this information must also be considered in connection with the prior beliefs or needs of people to which they are targeted [34]. This is especially true when different user groups might find themselves underrepresented or discriminated against when AI is being used. These issues are currently discussed in literature about algorithmic bias, fairness, and potential societal impacts of JRSs [37,72].

Since employment is important to people's livelihood and financial security, unfair loss of job opportunities due to algorithmic bias in recruitment platforms can be devastating to the mental and physical well-being of users and even impact their fundamental sense of dignity and meaning [11]. Consequently, various intervention methods have been proposed in the JRSs literature to counterbalance unfair ranking of job seekers considering both individual and group fairness. However, it has been shown by Rus et al. [61] that the most effective interventions (i.e., LFR, iFair) were also the least explainable. As such, even if developers strive to mitigate algorithmic bias, trust violations by a JRS without helpful explanations for understanding the unfairness will significantly affect the perceived fairness of AI-based decisions. Yet, as noted by Wang et al. [68], explanations of unfairness in RSs is a topic currently underexplored.

Considering recent discussions among philosophers about the relation between explanations and understanding [22], it is important to differentiate between explanations that only provide information (i.e., transparency) and those that go a step further to provide information for argumentive or justification purposes (i.e., reasons). As Páez [50] pointed out in his analysis of XAI, trust cannot be reduced to mere epistemic factors of predictive reliance or explanations after the fact. The various contextual factors, he argues, that relate to the person using the system (e.g., vulnerability experience, specific interests, set goals, available resources, or risk aversion tendencies) influence how the information provided with the explanation will contribute (or will not) to the perception of trust. Considering the study results, we deliberate whether there might not only be a need to gaze into the reasons why people believe they understand the job match recommendation but also to what extent these beliefs are susceptive or resistant to good or bad explanations disclosed with the additional information (i.e., or manipulation of a correct/incorrect and biased/unbiased explanation). As Hernandez-Bocanegra et al. [27] already noticed with their user study, it seems that a favorable type of argumentative explanation for transparency by a RS does not necessarily imply that people understand the reason behind the recommendation. Consequently, we stress that any investigation into the relation between explanations and trust in AI must also consider how people understand their interconnection to form trust.

## 5.2 Perceived Agency and Trust Measures

Given the continuous lack of clarity about the concrete relation between explanations and user trust in AI, it is important to further inspect the applicability of current trust measures across different types of interfaces. This concern has already been raised in the HRI research community because the interface designs of robots can vary considerably (e.g., [10,12,33]). Moreover, this may pose further problems when applied to more diverging contexts and application domains.

The extensive philosophical literature on trust stresses the importance of conceptually distinguishing between trust and mere reliance [20]. While it is widely accepted that trust entails reliance, it was Baier's [6] influential work that brought the salient social and ethical interrelations became essential to discussions about trust. Unlike other human-AI trust scales that focus on reliance or compliance for the measure [66], the MDMTv2 scale incorporates the moral dimension for operationalizing trust in balance with performance-based aspects. As we observed in our study, using this trust scale originally developed for HRI research may be less applicable in the context of JRSs. The notable number of missing values on items measuring moral trust suggests that several participants might have been confused or uncertain about how to respond when ascribing more socially and ethically loaded words to the JobMatcher algorithm. In line with the discussion about the trust scale robustness by Chita-Tegmark et al. [12], the frequent choice for the N/A option (i.e., "does not fit" on MDMTv2) indicates that the participants hesitated to anthropomorphize the mock-up Job-Matcher algorithm. In this sense, measuring the moral dimension of trust using the MDMTv2 scale requires a (relatively) high agency ascription (i.e., anthropomorphism), which is likely lower in the context of JRSs. This result demonstrates the importance of perceived agency as a factor when studying trust across different AI application domains. Hence, we stress that trust measures in the context of RSs require careful calibration with to people' perceived level of agency to ensure that the moral dimension of trust is more consistently rated.

With the current development and adoption of large language models (LLMs) and conversational RSs, the perceived agency of a JRS might increase or change over time. For now, it is still a matter of exploration whether the design choice of a more human-like interface for a JRS will convey higher agency perception, as has been the case with robots. Moreover, there might be nuances to user trust in a JRSs that are explored better when considering their unique features and capabilities. A tailored trust measure for this specific AI application domain might thus be required.

### 5.3 Practical Implications

Overall, our study results align with previous research, suggesting that there is no definite evidence that explanations support user trust in AI [53] or in RSs more specifically [38]. In our online experiment, the explanations of the respective trust violations did not influence participants' trust in the JobMatcher algorithm. Similarly, the explanations did not seem to affect participants' understanding of the job match recommendation. We found that the high self-assessment by the participants about their understanding of the job match recommendation mainly related to matching the job profile with the job description (i.e., comparing code) and their judgment of how well it was carried out (i.e., evaluation code). Both aspects align with the performance dimension of trust. Considering the comments by the participants regarding the different explanations of trust violations, we found that the information provided would either challenge or confirm their comprehension (i.e., understanding code). This suggests that the explanation had both positive and negative effects.

Although these results are inconclusive, it might be important for AI developers to consider in which way explanations are limited in supporting user trust in JRSs. As pointed out by Keil [32], it is challenging to assess when explanations have been successful in achieving understanding because the criteria for success are often unclear. To support user trust in JRSs, explanations must be closely linked to understanding—through methods of inquiry that are meaningful to people. In this context, providing unsolicited explanations as trust violations might be necessary, but insufficient. Our findings suggest that the explanations did not always help the participants recognize incorrect or biased job matching, hence not enhancing their understanding. A promising path forward—already explored in the field of HRI [24]—involves user-driven information-seeking approaches to explanations. We advise AI developers to look beyond the direct connection between explanations and trust. It is equally important to design explanations that encourage users to engage analytically and critically with AI outputs, rather than presenting explanations merely as competency-related features of AI.

## 6 Limitations

There are several limitations to our online experiment, which need consideration. We used text-based explanations of the trust violations inspired by the LIME technique with added user-friendly natural language formulations. It should be noted that alternative explanations types (e.g., dialog-, audio-, or graphic-based explanations) are worth investigating, and that results from such usages could lead to more insight into how users trust in AI in the particular context of JRSs.

We found that the MDMTv2 trust measure is less effective when used in the application domain of JRSs. Thus, additional trust measures from the literature on trust in automation (e.g., [30,35,46]) can be considered for future work because the concepts used to describe trust in this context might better aligned with the low agency perception of a JRS.

Relying only on one crowdsourcing platform for the recruitment of participants can be a limitation to the ecological validity, and it might be good to explore whether experiments on other platforms (e.g., *MTurk, CloudResearch, Qualtrics, and SONA*) would yield similar results.

We did not, in our first exploratory study, consider domain expertise in recruitment a relevant factor since the main focus was on the impact of explanations on the trust ratings by potential JRSs users. However, in future work, it might be interesting to compare results with participants having domain expertise (i.e., HR professionals and recruiters) because they might be more critical of the job recommender system or its output, resulting in lower trust ratings overall. As such, a more careful study design considering domain knowledge might be needed to see a similar effect.

We cannot exclude the possibility that confounding factors might have affected our measure of user trust in the JRS because prior research on user trust in AI has shown that many factors come into play (e.g., prior experience with AI, perceived risk, educational level, and personality traits [5]). Careful control of confounding factors will be needed in future work as this kind of investigation might also help contextualize our quantitative data analysis.

The effect sizes and variance estimates required for a power analysis were unavailable to us in advance because the relationships between the concepts we explored have not yet been systematically investigated in previous research. To guide future studies, we conducted a post-hoc power analysis, which showed that for MoralTrust, our sample size ($n = 244$) exceeded the minimum required sample size of 183 participants determined by our analysis ($f^2 = 0.054, \beta = 0.09$). For PerformanceTrust, the analysis suggests that a larger samples ($n = 405$) may yield more robust insights ($f^2 = 0.030, \beta = 0.20$).

## 7 Conclusion

With our online experiment, we investigated whether or not explanations of trust violations embedded in the job match support user trust in AI in the specific context of a JRS. We found that neither people's self-assessed understanding of the job match recommendation nor the different explanations of the trust violation substantially contributed to people's trust in the JobMatcher algorithm. Still, our results suggest that it is essential to take into account the complexity of explanations aiming to foster user trust and to distinguish the performance-based and moral-based dimensions of trust as seemingly different factors come into play. We also discussed that the increasingly used MDMTv2 trust measure is highly domain sensitive as it might be less apt at capturing the moral dimension of trust in cases of low agency attribution typical of the JRSs context. We encourage the research communities working on user trust in JRSs, and more broadly AI, to continue exploring the interconnection between explanations and trust. With our online experiment, and more research into this direction in the future, we believe that these insights will help ensure that explanations for users' trust in JRSs are more attuned to their understanding. As such, HAI researchers and AI developers will be better equipped to advance JRSs that are more user-centered.

**Acknowledgments.** We thank Georg Zimmermann, Arne Bathke and Eleonora Carrozzo for their valuable advice regarding the statistical data analysis. We also thank Manfred Tscheligi and Florian Beck for their support during the rebuttal and shepherding process. A thank also to all the anonymous reviewers who helped us significancy improve the presentation of our work. This publication was supported by the "Excellence in Digital Sciences and Interdisciplinary Technologies" (EXDIGIT) project, funded by Land Salzburg under grant number 20204-WISS/263/6-6022.

# References

1. Alsaid, A., Li, M., Chiou, E.K., Lee, J.D.: Measuring trust: a text analysis approach to compare, contrast, and select trust questionnaires. Front. Psychol. **14** (2023). https://doi.org/10.3389/fpsyg.2023.1192020
2. Anandarajan, M., Hill, C., Nolan, T., Anandarajan, M., Hill, C., Nolan, T.: The fundamentals of content analysis. In: Practical Text Analytics: Maximizing the Value of Text Data, pp. 15–25. Springer (2019). https://doi.org/10.1007/978-3-319-95663-3_2
3. Appadoo, K., Soonnoo, M., Mungloo-Dilmohamud, Z.: JobFit: Job recommendation using machine learning and recommendation engine. In: 2020 IEEE Asia-Pacific Conference on Computer Science and Data Engineering, p. 9411584. CSDE '20, IEEE (2020). https://doi.org/10.1109/CSDE50874.2020.9411584
4. Audeh, B., Sutter, M., Largeron, C.: Comparative study of unsupervised keyword extraction methods for job recommendation in an industrial environment. In: International Conference on Research Challenges in Information Science, pp. 551–558. Springer (2023). https://doi.org/10.1007/978-3-031-33080-3_37
5. Bach, T.A., Khan, A., Hallock, H., Beltrão, G., Sousa, S.: A systematic literature review of user trust in AI-enabled systems: an HCI perspective. Int. J. Hum. Comput. Int. **40**(5), 1251–1266 (2024). https://doi.org/10.1080/10447318.2022.2138826
6. Baier, A.: Trust and antitrust. Ethics **96**(2), 231–260 (1986). https://doi.org/10.1086/292745
7. Berkovsky, S., Taib, R., Conway, D.: How to recommend? User trust factors in movie recommender systems. In: Proceedings of the 22nd International Conference on Intelligent User Interfaces, pp. 287–300. IUI '17, ACM, New York, NY, USA (2017). https://doi.org/10.1145/3025171.3025209
8. Boldi, A., Silacci, A., Rapp, A., Caon, M.: Designing for transparency: a web job board for e-recruitment to explore job seekers' privacy behaviours. Behav. Info. Technol. (2024). https://doi.org/10.1080/0144929X.2024.2427111
9. Bollen, D., Knijnenburg, B.P., Willemsen, M.C., Graus, M.: Understanding choice overload in recommender systems. In: Proceedings of the Fourth ACM Conference on Recommender Systems, pp. 63–70. RecSys '10, ACM, New York, NY, USA (2010). https://doi.org/10.1145/1864708.1864724
10. Campagna, G., Rehm, M.: A systematic review of trust assessments in human-robot interaction. ACM Trans. Hum. Rob. Int. **14**(2) (2025). https://doi.org/10.1145/3706123
11. Chan, G.K.: AI employment decision-making: integrating the equal opportunity merit principle and explainable AI. AI Soc. **39**(3), 1027–1038 (2024). https://doi.org/10.1007/s00146-022-01532-w
12. Chita-Tegmark, M., Law, T., Rabb, N., Scheutz, M.: Can you trust your trust measure?. In: Proceedings of the 2021 ACM/IEEE International Conference on Human-Robot Interaction, pp. 92–100. HRI '21, ACM, New York, NY, USA (2021). https://doi.org/10.1145/3434073.3444677
13. Di Battista, A., et al.: Future of Jobs Report 2025 (2025). Accessed 18 Jan 2025. https://reports.weforum.org/docs/WEF_Future_of_Jobs_Report_2025.pdf
14. Douglas, B.D., Ewell, P.J., Brauer, M.: Data quality in online human-subjects research: Comparisons between MTurk, Prolific, CloudResearch, Qualtrics, and SONA. PLoS ONE **18**(3), e0279720 (2023). https://doi.org/10.1371/journal.pone.0279720

15. Dwivedi, R., et al.: Explainable AI (XAI): Core ideas, techniques, and solutions. ACM Comput. Surv. **55**(9) (2023). https://doi.org/10.1145/3561048
16. Ferrario, A., Loi, M.: How explainability contributes to trust in AI. In: Proceedings of the 2022 ACM Conference on Fairness, Accountability, and Transparency, pp. 1457–1466. FAccT '22, ACM, New York, NY, USA (2022). https://doi.org/10.1145/3531146.3533202
17. Freire, M.N., de Castro, L.N.: e-Recruitment recommender systems: a systematic review. Knowl. Inf. Syst. **63**(1), 1–20 (2020). https://doi.org/10.1007/s10115-020-01522-8
18. Ge, Y., et al.: A survey on trustworthy recommender systems. ACM Trans. Recomm. Syst. **3**(2) (2024). https://doi.org/10.1145/3652891
19. Glikson, E., Woolley, A.W.: Human trust in artificial intelligence: review of empirical research. Acad. Manag. Ann. **14**(2), 627–660 (2020). https://doi.org/10.5465/annals.2018.0057
20. Goldberg, S.C.: Trust and reliance 1. The Routledge Handbook of Trust and Philosophy, pp. 97–108 (2020). https://doi.org/10.4324/9781315542294-8
21. Grassini, S.: Development and validation of the AI attitude scale (AIAS-4): a brief measure of general attitude toward artificial intelligence. Front. Psychol. **14**, 1191628 (2023). https://doi.org/10.3389/fpsyg.2023.1191628
22. Grimm, S.R., Baumberger, C., Ammon, S.: Explaining Understanding: New Perspectives from Epistemology and Philosophy of Science. Routledge, New York, NY, USA (2016). https://doi.org/10.4324/9781315686110
23. Gugnani, A., Misra, H.: Implicit skills extraction using document embedding and its use in job recommendation. Proc. AAAI Conf. Artif. Intell. **34**(08), 13286–13293 (2020). https://doi.org/10.1609/aaai.v34i08.7038
24. Hannibal, G., Lindner, F.: Towards a questions-centered approach to explainable human-robot interaction. In: Social Robots in Social Institutions, vol. 366, pp. 406–415. IOS Press (2023). https://doi.org/10.3233/FAIA220641
25. Haque, A.B., Islam, A.N., Mikalef, P.: Explainable artificial intelligence (XAI) from a user perspective: a synthesis of prior literature and problematizing avenues for future research. Technol. Forecast. Soc. Chang. **186**, 122120 (2023). https://doi.org/10.1016/j.techfore.2022.122120
26. Harman, J.L., O'Donovan, J., Abdelzaher, T., Gonzalez, C.: Dynamics of human trust in recommender systems. In: Proceedings of the 8th ACM Conference on Recommender Systems, pp. 305–308. RecSys '14, ACM, New York, NY, USA (2014). https://doi.org/10.1145/2645710.2645761
27. Hernandez-Bocanegra, D.C., Donkers, T., Ziegler, J.: Effects of argumentative explanation types on the perception of review-based recommendations. In: Adjunct Publication of the 28th ACM Conference on User Modeling, Adaptation and Personalization, pp. 219–225. UMAP '20, ACM, New York, NY, USA (2020). https://doi.org/10.1145/3386392.3399302
28. Iyengar, S.S., Lepper, M.R.: When choice is demotivating: can one desire too much of a good thing? J. Pers. Soc. Psychol. **79**(6), 995–1006 (2000). https://doi.org/10.1037/0022-3514.79.6.995
29. Jacovi, A., Marasović, A., Miller, T., Goldberg, Y.: Formalizing trust in artificial intelligence: prerequisites, causes and goals of human trust in AI. In: Proceedings of the 2021 ACM Conference on Fairness, Accountability, and Transparency, pp. 624–635. FAccT '21, ACM, New York, NY, USA (2021). https://doi.org/10.1145/3442188.3445923

30. Jian, J.Y., Bisantz, A.M., Drury, C.G.: Foundations for an empirically determined scale of trust in automated systems. Int. J. Cogn. Ergon. **4**(1), 53–71 (2000). https://doi.org/10.1207/S15327566IJCE0401_04
31. Kalleberg, A.L.: The mismatched worker: when people don't fit their jobs. Acad. Manag. Perspect. **22**(1), 24–40 (2008). https://doi.org/10.5465/AMP.2008.31217510
32. Keil, F.C.: Explanation and understanding. Annu. Rev. Psychol. **57**(1), 227–254 (2006). https://doi.org/10.1146/annurev.psych.57.102904.190100
33. Kessler, T.T., Larios, C., Walker, T., Yerdon, V., Hancock, P.: A comparison of trust measures in human–robot interaction scenarios. In: Proceedings of the AHFE 2016 International Conference on Human Factors in Robots and Unmanned Systems, pp. 353–364. Springer (2017). https://doi.org/10.1007/978-3-319-41959-6_29
34. Kim, J., Maathuis, H., Sent, D.: Human-centered evaluation of explainable AI applications: a systematic review. Front. Artif. Intell. **7**, 1456486 (2024). https://doi.org/10.3389/frai.2024.1456486
35. Körber, M.: Theoretical considerations and development of a questionnaire to measure trust in automation. In: Proceedings of the 20th Congress of the International Ergonomics Association, pp. 13–30. IEA '18, Springer (2019). https://doi.org/10.1007/978-3-319-96074-6_2
36. Krippendorff, K.: Content analysis: An introduction to its methodology. Sage Publications, 4th Edn. (2019). https://doi.org/10.4135/9781071878781
37. Kumar, D., Grosz, T., Rekabsaz, N., Greif, E., Schedl, M.: Fairness of recommender systems in the recruitment domain: an analysis from technical and legal perspectives. Front. Big Data **6**, 1245198 (2023). https://doi.org/10.3389/fdata.2023.1245198
38. Kunkel, J., Donkers, T., Michael, L., Barbu, C.M., Ziegler, J.: Let me explain: impact of personal and impersonal explanations on trust in recommender systems. In: Proceedings of the 2019 CHI Conference on Human Factors in Computing Systems. CHI '19, ACM, New York, NY, USA (2019). https://doi.org/10.1145/3290605.3300717
39. Lacroux, A., Martin-Lacroux, C.: Should I trust the artificial intelligence to recruit? Recruiters' perceptions and behavior when faced with algorithm-based recommendation systems during resume screening. Front. Psychol. **13**, 895997 (2022). https://doi.org/10.3389/fpsyg.2022.895997
40. Laumer, S., Gubler, F., Maier, C., Weitzel, T.: Job seekers' acceptance of job recommender systems: results of an empirical study. In: Proceedings of the 51st Hawaii International Conference on System Sciences. HICSS '18 (2018). https://doi.org/10.24251/HICSS.2018.491
41. Liao, M., Sundar, S.S., B. Walther, J.: User trust in recommendation systems: a comparison of content-based, collaborative and demographic filtering. In: Proceedings of the 2022 CHI Conference on Human Factors in Computing Systems. CHI '22, ACM, New York, NY, USA (2022). https://doi.org/10.1145/3491102.3501936
42. Lundberg, S.M., Lee, S.I.: A unified approach to interpreting model predictions. In: Proceedings of the 31st International Conference on Neural Information Processing Systems, pp. 4768–4777. NIPS'17 (2017). https://doi.org/10.5555/3295222.3295230
43. Malle, B.F., Ullman, D.: A multidimensional conception and measure of human-robot trust. In: Nam, C.S., Lyons, J.B. (eds.) Trust in Human-Robot Interaction, pp. 3–25. Elsevier (2021). https://doi.org/10.1016/B978-0-12-819472-0.00001-0

44. Mashayekhi, Y., Li, N., Kang, B., Lijffijt, J., De Bie, T.: A challenge-based survey of e-recruitment recommendation systems. ACM Comput. Surv. **56**(10), 252 (2024). https://doi.org/10.1145/3659942
45. Mollering, G.: Trust: Reason, Routine. Reflexivity. Elsevier, Amsterdam, The Netherlands (2006)
46. Muir, B.M., Moray, N.: Trust in automation. Part II. Experimental studies of trust and human intervention in a process control simulation. Ergonomics **39**(3), 429–460 (1996). https://doi.org/10.1080/00140139608964474
47. Nóbrega, C., Marinho, L.: Towards explaining recommendations through local surrogate models. In: Proceedings of the 34th ACM/SIGAPP Symposium on Applied Computing, pp. 1671–1678. SAC '19, ACM, New York, NY, USA (2019). https://doi.org/10.1145/3297280.3297443
48. Nunes, I., Jannach, D.: A systematic review and taxonomy of explanations in decision support and recommender systems. User Model. User-Adap. Inter. (1), 393–444 (2017). https://doi.org/10.1007/s11257-017-9195-0
49. Ogunniye, G., Legastelois, B., Rovatsos, M., Dowthwaite, L., Portillo, V., Vallejos, E.P., Zhao, J., Jirotka, M.: Understanding user perceptions of trustworthiness in e-recruitment systems. IEEE Internet Comput. **25**(6), 23–32 (2021). https://doi.org/10.1109/MIC.2021.3115670
50. Páez, A.: The pragmatic turn in explainable artificial intelligence (XAI). Mind. Mach. **29**(3), 441–459 (2019). https://doi.org/10.1007/s11023-019-09502-w
51. Palomares, I., Porcel, C., Pizzato, L., Guy, I., Herrera-Viedma, E.: Reciprocal recommender systems: analysis of state-of-art literature, challenges and opportunities towards social recommendation. Information Fusion **69**, 103–127 (2021). https://doi.org/10.1016/j.inffus.2020.12.001
52. Papagni, G., de Pagter, J., Zafari, S., Filzmoser, M., Koeszegi, S.T.: Artificial agents' explainability to support trust: considerations on timing and context. AI Soc. **38**(2), 947–960 (2023). https://doi.org/10.1007/s00146-022-01462-7
53. Papenmeier, A., Kern, D., Englebienne, G., Seifert, C.: It's complicated: the relationship between user trust, model accuracy and explanations in AI. ACM Trans. Comput. Hum. Int.**29**(4) (2022). https://doi.org/10.1145/3495013
54. Potter, W.J., Levine-Donnerstein, D.: Rethinking validity and reliability in content analysis. J. Appl. Commun. Res. **27**(3), 258–284 (1999). https://doi.org/10.1080/00909889909365539
55. Pu, P., Chen, L.: Trust-inspiring explanation interfaces for recommender systems. Knowl.-Based Syst. **20**(6), 542–556 (2007). https://doi.org/10.1016/j.knosys.2007.04.004
56. Ranjbar, N., Momtazi, S., Homayoonpour, M.: Explaining recommendation system using counterfactual textual explanations. Mach. Learn. **113**(4), 1989–2012 (2024). https://doi.org/10.1007/s10994-023-06390-1
57. Rezaei Khavas, Z., Kotturu, M.R., Ahmadzadeh, S.R., Robinette, P.: Do humans trust robots that violate moral trust? ACM Trans. Hum. Rob. Int. **13**(2), 25 (2024). https://doi.org/10.1145/3651992
58. Ribeiro, M.T., Singh, S., Guestrin, C.: "Why should I trust you?" Explaining the predictions of any classifier. In: Proceedings of the 22nd ACM SIGKDD International Conference on Knowledge Discovery and Data Mining, pp. 1135–1144. KDD '16, ACM, New York, NY, USA (2016). https://doi.org/10.1145/2939672.2939778
59. Ricci, F., Rokach, L., Shapira, B.: Recommender systems: Techniques, applications, and challenges. In: Recommender Systems Handbook, pp. 1–35. Springer US, New York, NY, USA, 3rd edn. (2022). https://doi.org/10.1007/978-1-0716-2197-4_1

60. Roy, F., Hasan, M.: Comparative analysis of different trust metrics of user-user trust-based recommendation system. Comput. Sci. **23** (2022). https://doi.org/10.7494/csci.2022.23.3.4227
61. Rus, C., Yates, A., de Rijke, M.: A study of pre-processing fairness intervention methods for ranking people. In: Proceedings of the 46th European Conference on Information Retrieval, pp. 336–350. ECIR '24, Springer (2024). https://doi.org/10.1007/978-3-031-56066-8_26
62. Schelble, B..G., et al.: Towards ethical AI: empirically investigating dimensions of AI ethics, trust repair, and performance in human-AI teaming. Hum. Factors **66**(4), 1037–1055 (2024). https://doi.org/10.1177/00187208221116952
63. Sokol, K., Flach, P.: Interpretable representations in explainable AI: from theory to practice. Data Min. Knowl. Disc. **38**(5), 3102–3140 (2024). https://doi.org/10.1007/s10618-024-01010-5
64. Ullman, D.: Developing a multi-dimensional model and measure of human-robot trust. PhD dissertation, Brown University, Providence, RI, USA (2021)
65. Ullman, D., Malle, B.F.: Measuring gains and losses in human-robot trust: evidence for differentiable components of trust. In: 2019 14th ACM/IEEE International Conference on Human-Robot Interaction, pp. 618–619. HRI '19, IEEE (2019). https://doi.org/10.1109/HRI.2019.8673154
66. Vereschak, O., Bailly, G., Caramiaux, B.: How to evaluate trust in AI-assisted decision making? A survey of empirical methodologies. Proc. ACM Hum. Comput. Int. **5**(CSCW2) (2021). https://doi.org/10.1145/3476068
67. Wang, S., Zhang, X., Wang, Y., Ricci, F.: Trustworthy recommender systems. ACM Trans. Intell. Syst. Technol. **15**(4), 84 (2024). https://doi.org/10.1145/3627826
68. Wang, Y., Ma, W., Zhang, M., Liu, Y., Ma, S.: A survey on the fairness of recommender systems. ACM Trans. Info. Syst. **41**(3), 52 (2023). https://doi.org/10.1145/3547333
69. Wardatzky, K., Inel, O., Rossetto, L., Bernstein, A.: Whom do explanations serve? A systematic literature survey of user characteristics in explainable recommender systems evaluation. ACM Trans. Recom. Syst. **3**(4), 49 (2024). https://doi.org/10.1145/3716394
70. Yin, F., Fu, R., Feng, X., Xing, T., Ji, M.: An interpretable neural network TV program recommendation based on SHAP. Int. J. Mach. Learn. Cybern. **14**(10), 3561–3574 (2023). https://doi.org/10.1007/s13042-023-01850-5
71. Zafari, S., de Pagter, J., Papagni, G., Rosenstein, A., Filzmoser, M., Koeszegi, S.T.: Trust development and explainability: a longitudinal study with a personalized assistive system. Multi. Technol. Int. **8**(3), 20 (2024). https://doi.org/10.3390/mti8030020
72. Zhang, S., Kuhn, P.: Understanding algorithmic bias in job recommender systems: an audit study approach. Am. Econ. Assoc. **12** (2022)
73. Zhang, Y., Chen, X.: Explainable recommendation: a survey and new perspectives. Found. Trends® Info. Retr. **14**(1) (2020). https://doi.org/10.1561/1500000066
74. Zhang, Y., Lai, G., Zhang, M., Zhang, Y., Liu, Y., Ma, S.: Explicit factor models for explainable recommendation based on phrase-level sentiment analysis. In: Proceedings of the 37th International ACM SIGIR Conference on Research & Development in Information Retrieval, pp. 83–92. SIGIR '14, ACM, New York, NY, USA (2014). https://doi.org/10.1145/2600428.2609579
75. Zou, Z., Huspi, S.H., Nuar, A.N.A.: A review on job recommendation system. J. Adv. Res. Appl. Sci. Eng. Technol. **41**(2), 113–124 (2024). https://doi.org/10.37934/araset.41.2.113124

# Correction to: Before It Falls: Supporting Drone Fleet Management Through Battery Visualizations

Maria-Theresa Bahodi, Nathan Lau, Niels van Berkel, Kasper Andreas Rømer Grøntved, Mikael B. Skov, and Timothy Merritt

**Correction to:
Chapter 19 in: C. Ardito et al. (Eds.):** *Human-Computer Interaction – INTERACT 2025,* **LNCS 16109, https://doi.org/10.1007/978-3-032-05002-1_19**

In the original version of this chapter, the affiliation of the third author were wrong. This has been corrected. Correctly it should read as: "Human Centered Computing, Department of Computer Science, Aalborg University, Aalborg, Denmark.

---

The updated version of this chapter can be found at
https://doi.org/10.1007/978-3-032-05002-1_19

© IFIP International Federation for Information Processing 2026
Published by Springer Nature Switzerland AG 2026
C. Ardito et al. (Eds.): INTERACT 2025, LNCS 16109, p. C1, 2026.
https://doi.org/10.1007/978-3-032-05002-1_34

# Author Index

**A**

Abdelnour-Nocera, José Luis 399
Ahmad, Muneeb I. 135
Aljuneidi, Saja 87
Allen, Carly Grace 300
Amorim, Clara 399
Andarini, Lidwina 25
Andreasen, Troels 289

**B**

Bahodi, Maria-Theresa 347
Bakala, Ewelina 430
Baranauskas, M. Cecilia C. 177
Barricelli, Barbara Rita 509
Barz, Michael 576
Bauer, Christine 612
Bernhaupt, Regina 309, 477, 521
Bezerra, Francisco Wesley Gomes 243
Bittner, Sara-Jane 576
Bøen, Karen Eide 289
Boll, Susanne 87

**C**

Cabezas, Daniel 399
Campos, Pedro 499
Caon, Maurizio 332
Carvalho Pereira, Vinícius 243
Cherubini, Mauro 332
Cmentowski, Sebastian 309
Conte, Tayna 410

**D**

da Silva, Deógenes P. Junior 177, 269
da Silva Macedo Alves, Letícia 452
Dalvi, Girish 167
de Souza, Joana Gabriela Ribeiro 452
Dhamelia, Malay 167
Doneddu, Daniele 135

**F**

Fennessy, Liam 477
Filho, Mauro 157
Fogli, Daniela 509
Frens, Joep 45

**G**

Gouveia, Diogo Manuel 499
Grøntved, Kasper Andreas Rømer 347
Guerino, Guilherme 410
Guerra, Jonas Lopes 269
Guizzardi, Davide 509

**H**

Hacioglu, Naile 109
Häkkilä, Jonna 226
Hannibal, Glenda 612
Heuten, Wilko 87
Hobye, Mads 289
Hourcade, Juan Pablo 430
Hu, Jun 45, 309

**I**

Inal, Yavuz 300
Ishii, Ryo 25
Ishii, Yoko 25

**J**

Janković, Jana 499

**K**

Khanshan, Alireza 71
Kim, Nakyung 109
Knudsen, Lise Aagaard 289
Ku, Yuan-Hao 540

**L**

Lallemand, Carine 521
Lau, Nathan 347
Lee, Hyowon 109

© IFIP International Federation for Information Processing 2026
Published by Springer Nature Switzerland AG 2026
C. Ardito et al. (Eds.): INTERACT 2025, LNCS 16109, pp. 637–638, 2026.
https://doi.org/10.1007/978-3-032-05002-1

Leva, Maria Chiara 109
Li, Yinchu 521
Logan, Jade 135
Lou, Yunyin 309
Lourenço Silva, Gonçalo 157

## M
Macdonald, Shaun 203
Maciel, Cristiano 243
Markopoulos, Panos 71
Marques, Daniela 602
Martinie, Célia 371
Masthoff, Judith 3
Matos, Diogo 157
Matsuo, Kazuya 25
Mayfield, Dana 540
McLafferty, Kevin 135
Menezes, Krissia M. L. 269
Merritt, Timothy 347
Micallef, Nicholas 135
Mitchell, Scott 477
Mor, Enric 399
Morandini, Marcelo 602
Motti, Lilian 499

## N
Nobrega, Genesis 499

## O
Otsuka, Atsushi 25

## P
Paananen, Siiri 226
Pacheco, Marcos Vinícius Caldeira 452
Palanque, Philippe 371
Pereira, Rafael A. 565
Pereira, Roberto 269
Peres, Beatriz 499
Pimenta, Josiane Rosa de Oliveira Gaia 177
Pinheiro, Tânia Saraiva de Melo 243
Prates, Raquel O. 452

## R
Ranten, Maja Fagerberg 289
Rocha, Ana Patrícia 157
Rodriguez-Hernando, Daniel 371

## S
Saleh, Mennatallah 203
Santos, Inês 157
Silacci, Alessandro 332
Silva, Deivid 410
Silva, Samuel 157
Silvestre, Tiago 157
Skov, Mikael B. 347
Sonntag, Daniel 576
Steere, Sandra 371
Sturm, Christian 203
Sun, Shuyi 540
Sveen, Tanja 300

## T
Teixeira, António 157
Tejera, Gonzalo 430

## V
Valentim, Natasha M. C. 410, 565
van Berkel, Niels 347
van Essen, Harm 477
Van Gorp, Pieter 71
van Kasteren, Anouk 3
Vaughan, Laurene 477
Vega, Katia 540
Veneroso, Lucas Xavier 452
Vidal, Nuno 157
Virkkula, Minna 226
Visser, Hannah 3
Volden, Frode 300

## W
Wolters, Maria 87
Wu, Tzu-Hui 309

## Y
Ye, Xinhui 45
Yon, Jinho 540

## Z
Zheng, Yaxin 477

MIX
Papier aus verantwortungsvollen Quellen
Paper from responsible sources
FSC® C105338

If you have any concerns about our products,
you can contact us on
**ProductSafety@springernature.com**

In case Publisher is established outside the EU,
the EU authorized representative is:
**Springer Nature Customer Service Center GmbH
Europaplatz 3, 69115 Heidelberg, Germany**

Printed by Libri Plureos GmbH
in Hamburg, Germany